INTERNATIONAL LAW

SECOND EDITION

INTERNATIONAL LAW

Classic and Contemporary Readings

EDITED BY

Charlotte Ku and Paul F. Diehl

LYNNE
RIENNER
PUBLISHERS

BOULDER
LONDON

Published in the United States of America in 2003 by
Lynne Rienner Publishers, Inc.
1800 30th Street, Boulder, Colorado 80301
www.rienner.com

and in the United Kingdom by
Lynne Rienner Publishers, Inc.
3 Henrietta Street, Covent Garden, London WC2E 8LU

Library of Congress Cataloging-in-Publication Data
International law : classic and contemporary readings /
   Charlotte Ku and Paul F. Diehl, editors. — 2nd ed.
      p.   cm.
   Includes bibliographical references and index.
   ISBN 1-58826-132-8 (alk. paper)
   1. International law. I. Ku, Charlotte, 1950–   II. Diehl, Paul F. (Paul Francis)

KZ1242.I583   2003
341—dc21   2003043238

British Cataloguing in Publication Data
A Cataloguing in Publication record for this book
is available from the British Library.

Printed and bound in the United States of America

         The paper used in this publication meets the requirements
   ∞   of the American National Standard for Permanence of
         Paper for Printed Library Materials Z39.48-1992.

   5 4 3 2 1

CONTENTS

International Legal Structures

PART 2 INTERNATIONAL LAW AS NORMATIVE SYSTEM

To Regulate the Use of Force

For the Protection of Individual Rights

For the Protection of the Environment

Managing the Commons

PART 3 THE FUTURE OF INTERNATIONAL LAW

1

International Law as Operating and Normative Systems: An Overview

CHARLOTTE KU AND PAUL F. DIEHL

THE END OF THE COLD WAR IN 1989 HERALDED THE ADVENT OF A NEW international order including a renewed emphasis and concern with international law. The U.S. president at the time, George H. W. Bush, and others identified international relations "governed by the rule of law" as the defining feature of the emerging world order. Yet acts of genocide in Bosnia and Rwanda, together with the failure of the United Nations (UN) to meet renewed expectations, have left us with a world in which rules and norms are not always clearly defined or carefully observed.

In this collection, we consider international law from a fresh perspective, seeking to move beyond esoteric descriptions of the law prevalent in scholarly legal treatments, by examining international law's influence on political behavior, something largely ignored in standard analyses of international relations. There are several unique features of this effort. First, this book is perhaps the only collection that focuses on the politics of international law and does so by covering the main topics of the subject (e.g., sources, participants, courts, dispute settlement, jurisdiction, and sovereignty). Second, it is contemporary, reflecting the major changes in international relations after the Cold War and covering emerging topics in the subject such as human rights and the environment. Third, it attempts to draw a bridge between the purely legal and purely political considerations of public international law. Finally, this book offers a new organizational scheme for considering international law, drawing the distinction between elements of international law that function as an operating system for international relations (e.g., courts, jurisdiction, etc.) and those that present a normative system that seeks to direct behavior in the international system (e.g., human rights, environmental prescriptions).

We begin by addressing the most basic of questions: What is international law? We then move to develop our conception of international law as a dual system for regulating interactions, both generally and within specific areas.

1

What Is International Law?

The basic question that we ask here—What is international law?—is straightforward enough, and it seems simple enough to answer. After all, we have a general image of what the *law* is, and the meaning of the word *international* seems self-evident. Yet when we put the two words together, we find ourselves faced with other questions that stem from our understanding of their meanings. In Western democracies, the word *law* immediately conjures up images of legislatures, police, and courts that create law, enforce it, and punish those who violate it. *International* brings up images not only of the United Nations but also of wide-ranging global differences—economic, cultural, and political. How can these two images come together? How can one imagine a structured and developed legal system functioning in a political environment that is diffuse, disparate, unregulated, and conventionally described as anarchic?

The basic question What is international law? embodies several other questions that need to be answered in order to understand what we are examining: (1) What does international law do? (2) How does it work? (3) Is it effective in what it does? And ultimately (4) What can we expect from it?

The first three questions necessarily deal with the diffusion and lack of regulation that exist in a political system consisting of multiple sovereign actors. As the principal possessors of coercive means in international relations, states seem to have their own exclusive recourse to the resolution of disputes. How can states be restrained? What can possibly modify their behavior? Yet behavior is restrained, and anarchy is not always the dominant mode of international politics. States also do not have a monopoly on international intercourse. International organizations, nongovernmental organizations (NGOs), multinational corporations, and even private individuals have come to play an increasing role in international relations, and accordingly international legal rules have evolved to engage these new actors.

This leads to the last of the four questions: If international law is a factor in state behavior, then what can we expect it to do? First, we expect it to facilitate and to support the daily business of international relations and politics. It does so principally by allocating decisionmaking power within the international system, thereby providing an alternative to unregulated competition. The structure and process of international law prevent the pursuit of multiple national or private interests from dissolving into anarchy. It also allows for the coexistence of multiple political units and their interaction. It provides a framework for the international system to *operate* effectively. Second, international law advances particular values—the regulation of the use of force, the protection of individual rights, and the management of the commons are prominent examples of such values. In this area, international law promotes the creation of a *normative* consensus on international behavior.

The Dual Character of International Law

International law provides both an operating system and a normative system for international relations. Conceptualizing international law as an operating system considers, in a broad sense, how it sets the general procedures and institutions for the conduct of international relations. As an operating system, international law provides the framework for establishing rules and norms, outlines the parameters of interaction, and provides the procedures and forums for resolving disputes among those taking part in these interactions. In contrast, international law as a normative system provides direction for international relations by identifying the substantive values and goals to be pursued. If the operating system designates the "structures" (in a loose sense) that help channel international politics, then the normative element gives form to the aspirations and values of the participants of the system. As a normative system, law is a product of the structures and processes that make up the operating system. The operating system is based on state consensus as expressed through widespread practice over time; the normative system must build a base of support for each if its undertakings. As an operating system, international law functions much as a constitution does in a domestic legal system by setting out the consensus of its constituent actors (states) on distribution of authority, responsibilities in governing, and the units that will carry out specific functions. We chose the word *operating* as one would conceive of a computer's operating system. It is the basic platform upon which a system will operate. When a computer's operating system (e.g., Microsoft Windows) functions to allow the use of specific word-processing programs, spreadsheets, and communications software, there is little direct consideration given to that system by the user. Similarly, the operating system of international law provides the signals and commands that make multiple functions and modes possible and when functioning often requires little conscious effort. As a normative system, international law takes on a principally legislative character by mandating particular values and directing specific changes in state behavior.

Below we outline our conceptions of the operating and normative systems and discuss their similarities and differences with related conceptions. We also briefly identify some trends in the evolution of the two systems. Integrated into these analyses are descriptions of the remaining chapters in the collection.

The Operating System

The dual character of international law results from its Westphalian legacy in which law functions between, rather than above, states and in which the state carries out the legislative, judicial, and executive functions that in domestic legal systems are frequently assigned by constitutions to separate institutions. Constitutions also provide legal capacity by allocating power and by recognizing rights and duties. Constitutions further condition the environment in which power is to be used and rights and duties to be exercised. Robert Dahl identified a number of such items that constitutions generally specify, including several of which international law also specifies: competent decisions, accountability, and ensuring stability, to name a few.[1]

In order for the operating system to maintain vibrancy and resiliency, and to assure the stability necessary for orderly behavior, it must provide for a dynamic normative system that facilitates the competition of values, views, and actors. It does so by applying the constitutional functions as described above when including new actors, new issues, new structures, and new norms. Who, for example, are the authorized decisionmakers in international law? Whose actions can bind not only the parties involved but also others? How do we know that an authoritative decision has taken place? When does the resolution of a conflict or a dispute give rise to new law? These are the questions that the operating system answers. Note, in particular, that the operating system may be associated with formal structures, but not all operating system elements are institutional. For example, the Vienna Convention on Treaties entails no institutional mechanisms, but it does specify various operational rules about treaties and therefore the parameters of lawmaking.

The operating system has a number of dimensions or components that are typically covered in international law textbooks but largely unconnected to one another. Some of the primary components include:

1. Sources of Law: These include the system rules for defining the process through which law is formed, the criteria for determining when legal obligations exist, and which actors are bound (or not) by that law. This element of the operating system also specifies a hierarchy of different legal sources. For example, the operating system defines whether UN resolutions are legally binding (generally not) and what role they play in the legal process (possible evidence of customary law).

2. Actors: This dimension includes determining which actors are eligible to have rights and obligations under the law. The operating system also determines how and the degree to which those actors might exercise those rights internationally. For example, individuals and multinational corporations may enjoy certain international legal protections, but those rights might be asserted in international forums only by their home states.

3. Jurisdiction: These rules define the rights of actors and institutions to deal with legal problems and violations. An important element is defining what problems or situations will be handled through national legal systems as opposed to international forums. For example, the 1985 Convention

on Torture allows states to prosecute perpetrators in their custody, regardless of the location of the offense and the nationality of the perpetrator or victim, affirming the principle of universal jurisdiction.

4. Courts or Institutions: These elements create forums and accompanying rules under which international legal disputes might be heard or decisions enforced. Thus, for example, the Statute of the International Court of Justice provides for the creation of the institution, sets general rules of decisionmaking, identifies the processes and scope under which cases are heard, specifies the composition of the court, and details decisionmaking procedures (to name a few).

Our conception of an operating system clearly overlaps with some prior formulations but is different in some fundamental ways. Regime theory[2] refers to decisionmaking procedures as practices for making and implementing collective choice, similar to "regulative norms,"[3] that lessen transaction costs of collective action. Although these may be encompassed by the international law operating system, our conception of the latter is broader. The operating system is not necessarily issue-specific but may deal equally well (or poorly) with multiple issues—note that the International Court of Justice may adjudicate disputes involving airspace as well as war crimes. Regime decisionmaking procedures are also thought to reflect norms, rules, and principles without much independent standing.

H.L.A. Hart developed the notion of "secondary rules" to refer to the ways in which primary rules might be "conclusively ascertained, introduced, eliminated, varied, and the fact of their violation conclusively determined."[4] This comports in many ways with our conception of an international legal operating system. Yet Hart views secondary rules (his choice of the term *secondary* is illuminating) as "parasitic" to the primary ones. This suggests that secondary rules follow in time the development of primary rules, especially in primitive legal systems (which international law is sometimes compared to). Furthermore, secondary rules are believed to service normative ones, solving the problems of uncertainty, stasis, and inefficiency inherently found with normative rules.

Our conception of an international legal operating system is somewhat different. For us, the operating system is usually independent of any single norm or regime and, therefore, is greater than the sum of any parts derived from individual norms and regimes. The operating system in many cases, past its origin point, may precede the development of parts of the normative system rather than merely reacting to it. In this conception, the operating system is not a mere servant to the normative system, but the former can actually shape the development of the latter. For example, established rules on jurisdiction may restrict the development of new normative rules on what kinds of behaviors might be labeled as international crimes. Neither is the operating system as reflective of the normative system as Hart implies it is. The operating system may develop some of its configurations autonomously from specific norms, thereby serving political as well as legal needs (e.g., the creation of an international organization that also performs monitoring functions). In the relatively anarchic world of international relations, we argue that this is more likely than in the domestic legal systems on which Hart primarily based his analysis.

Indeed, this may explain why, in many cases, the operating system for international law is far more developed than its normative counterpart; for example, we have extensive rules and agreements on treaties but relatively few dealing with the use of force. Furthermore, the operating system has a greater stickiness than might be implied in Hart's formulations. The operating system may be more resistant to change and not always responsive to alterations in the normative system or the primary rules. This is not merely a matter of moving from a primitive legal system to a more advanced one (as Hart would argue) but rather considering how adaptive the two systems are to each other. Finally, our formulation sees effective norm development as dependent on the operating system or the structural dimension. A failure to understand this dependence may stall or obstruct a norm's effectiveness. Again, the metaphor of a computer's operating system may be useful, as the failure of the operating system to support adequately a software application will slow down or render inoperable features of that application for the user.

The evolution of the operating system in all of the areas enumerated above has been toward expansion—in the number of actors, in the forms of decisionmaking, and in the forums and modes of implementation. Although international law remains principally a body of rules and practices to regulate state behavior in the conduct of interstate relations, much of international law now also regulates the conduct of governments and the behavior of individuals within states and may address issues that require ongoing transnational cooperation. Human rights law is an example of the normative system regulating behavior within states. Such human rights law, however, may configure elements of the operating system in that the human rights granted may convey legal personality to individuals, thereby rendering them capable of holding or exercising legal rights. Activities such as the follow-up conferences to the Helsinki Accords or the periodic meetings of the parties to the Framework Convention on Climate Change are specific examples of the operating system designed to give such norms effect.

Because international law lacks the institutional trappings and hierarchical character of domestic law, its organizing principles and how they work are important to identify. These are the elements of the operating system. First, one must know where to find international law. Because the international legal system has no single legislative body, it is sometimes difficult knowing where to start. One begins with state behavior and examines the sources of international law to interpret state behavior and to identify when such behavior takes on an obligatory character. The sources of international law further provide guidance on how to find the substance of international law by highlighting key moments in the lawmaking process. Sources help us to locate the products of the lawmaking process by identifying its form. For example, international agreements are generally to be found in written texts. Law created by custom, however, will require locating patterns of state behavior over time and assessing whether this behavior is compelled by any sense of legal obligation. In Chapter 2, the first selection in our collection, Anthony Arend provides a methodology for identifying the existence and extent of an international legal rule. Among his points are that even the obvious, such as a formal treaty, does not necessarily indicate the presence of a legal obligation. Central to his argument for the presence of rules are two conditions: authority (whether decisionmakers perceive the rule to be authoritative or not) and control (whether the rule is reflected in state practice or not). In the absence of these, international law cannot be said to exist.

There has been an expansion in the forms of law. This has led to thinking about law as a continuum "ranging from the traditional international legal forms to soft law instruments."[5] This continuum includes resolutions of the UN General Assembly, standards of private organizations such as the International Standards Organization, as well as codes of conduct developed in international organizations. An example is the adoption of a code of conduct on the distribution and use of pesticides by the Food and Agriculture Organization in 1985. The concept of a continuum is useful because these modes are likely not to operate in isolation but rather interact with and build on each other. Chapter 3, the second selection in Part 1 of this book, contrasts hard and soft international law. States may choose one form of law over the other, and Kenneth Abbott and Duncan Snidal explore some of the rationales for this; for example, hard law provides for more credible commitments than softer legal instruments. The two scholars thus reveal that international law is not inherently weak or strong or necessarily precise or imprecise. Rather, the configuration of law in the international system comes from explicit choice, and, whatever the form, advantages and disadvantages are attendant to it.

This is the case even within more traditional forms of making international law in which customary practice and conventions work in tandem to regulate state behavior. The law applicable to the continental shelf is an example of this, as customary practice became codified in a subsequent convention. Traditional conceptions of international law sources have focused on custom and treaty-making between states. Framed in this way, traditional custom may be seen in steep decline relative to the international community of states' preference for more formal arrangements. In Chapter

4, Anthea Roberts challenges that notion by reconceptualizing the bases of customary behavior. She contends that even though traditional views of custom emphasized consistent state practice over time, we now analyze key statements of leaders and decisionmakers rather than state action. Thus, the balance of modern custom has shifted away from state practice and more toward the perception of a legal obligation *(opinio juris)* by those partaking in international relations activities. Such a conception provides for more numerous instances of customary law and lessens its decline in importance vis-à-vis formal international agreements. Beyond their increase in numbers, treaties have also undergone a metamorphosis in recent decades. Among the most significant changes has been the process of treaty formulation. As Jose Alvarez illustrates in detail in Chapter 5, the last selection in Part 1, the prevalence of states negotiating bilateral treaties has been replaced with multilateral negotiating forums, often under the auspices of international organizations and involving significant input from NGOs and various other private actors that comprise part of civil society.

A second element of the international law operating system includes the participants or actors in the process who create the law and are the subjects of its precepts. This is central because international law is a system that relies largely on self-regulation by the system's units. The number of participants will affect the character of the political process of creating law by determining the number of interests that need to be taken into account, the available resources, and the modes of implementation. The substance of international law will reflect the participants' interests and capacities in the international system. Issues of how, where, and with what effect the law is implemented depend on the economic, political, and other circumstances of participants.

In part because of the expansion in the forms of international law, participants in the international legal process today include more than 190 states and governments, international institutions created by states, and elements of the private sector—multinational corporations and financial institutions, networks of individuals, and NGOs. Not all participants carry the same level of authority in the legal process, but they are recognized either in fact or in practice as playing a role in identifying and promoting particular values.[6] The partnership struck between NGOs and the government of Canada to promote a convention to ban the use of antipersonnel landmines is an example of the collaboration that various actors have undertaken in the international legal process, thereby giving new actors a role in the lawmaking and the subsequent implementation process.

It is in the steady increase in both the number and type of participants in the international legal process that we see some of the most tangible changes in international law. This increase is a critical change, because who is included and who is allowed a voice in the process both affects how the law operates and determines the content of the law. This is amply demonstrated in the intricate political and doctrinal interplay that today serves as the basis for international protection of the environment and the management of the commons.

The increase in participants began with the end of the Thirty Years' War in 1648 and the acceptance of participation by Protestant princes within the same system as Catholic princes in Europe. The next increase resulted from the empire-building activities of the European powers, which brought non-European states into the international legal process. Most recently, the move has been to include individuals and NGOs, including multinational corporations, into the process. Each addition of participants increases the complexity of the lawmaking process. At the same time, many of the issues in international law today require multiple layers of cooperative and coordinated activity crossing public and private sectors for effective regulation and implementation. Complexity, therefore, cannot be avoided and, indeed, may now be required for the effective operation of international law.

Despite this trend toward adding new participants, states remain key to the creation and operation of international law. But how do states become part of the international legal process and under what terms? In Chapter 6, Oscar Schachter describes the interaction between law and politics as reflected in the practice on state succession, which determines each new state's initial legal obligations. This is an especially important concern in the post–Cold War era with the breakup of states in Eastern Europe and other possible changes on the horizon on various continents. Schachter reviews past practice on state succession and reflects on the emerging law in this area; this will become critical as the need increases to sort out the status of various obligations as states continue to implode or separate.

If the addition of states and governments to the system is not a routine matter, the difficulty of adding a different category of participant should be apparent. This is particularly so in the area of individuals, when according them legal status might result in individuals challenging the authority of states. This is also the heart of the issue in Patrick Thornberry's analysis (see Chapter 7) of the rights that groups (especially ethnic groups) might have under international law, including whether special rights to form their own state exist or whether special international protections might be accorded their treatment by the dominant group within states. The developing rights of groups are one of the most sensitive areas for international law as it tries to reconcile potentially inconsistent values. The inconsistency stems from the dilemma most states face in balancing the goal of national unity with a tolerance of ethnic heterogeneity. Yet the issue of how to recognize the existence of various groups within a common set of borders without compromising the ability of the state to govern its population is emerging as one of the keenest problems of the post–Cold War world.

As the network of international economic activity expands, transnational enterprises are growing in importance as international participants. As Donna Arzt and Igor Lukashuk note in Chapter 8, many of these are more powerful than all but the largest states, yet they mostly lack their own international legal personality. And this is unlikely to change as long as substantial portions of the international community oppose such a status. There has been a major shift, however, since the middle of the twentieth century with individuals undertaking more active rather than passive interactions with international law. And it appears that this trend is only beginning.

A third element of the international law operating system is the process under which law is implemented and actors comply (or fail to do so) with international law. Although the number of international agreements has increased and the requirements are more elaborated, surprisingly little is known about what induces compliance with international obligations. The absence of an international police force and other traditional coercive mechanisms for compliance add to the puzzle of why states obey international law (and, in fact, we know they do so most of the time). Beth Simmons (Chapter 9) reviews different explanations for state compliance. These include those based on realpolitik formulations, those based on rationalist ideas, and those that emphasize more normative and less utilitarian considerations. In various ways, she finds each of these lacking in understanding the puzzle.

Another aspect of creating an effective international law operating system is determining how remedies for wrongful acts or grievances will work. This requires an understanding of what the wrongful act or grievance is, who the aggrieved party is, who might be responsible for the act, and the applicable law for the situation. The applicable law will then determine the relevant forum or procedure for examining the grievance and will identify available remedies. Among the most critical of those operating rules concern jurisdiction: Which states are allowed to use their own national courts to prosecute individuals for which crimes? Perhaps the most controversial jurisdiction principle has been universal jurisdiction, which allows any state the right to try the accused, provided they have that person in custody. This principle was central in Spanish attempts to try General Augusto Pinochet for actions he took in Chile, as well as aborted attempts to prosecute Israeli prime minister Ariel Sharon in Belgium for acts committed in Lebanon. The Princeton Project (Chapter 10) has developed a set of guidelines, presented here, for how universal jurisdiction should be applied. This commentary on new principles for universal jurisdiction reveals the various disputes and competing interests that arise in constructing such operating system rules.

The forums and modes for implementation have also expanded. International law has developed vigorously beyond the concept of *dedoublement fonctionnel,* whereby national officials were deemed to function also as international officials in carrying out their duties.[7] With no separate institutions available to implement international law, this was a reasonable approach. Although international law still relies on domestic legal and political structures for implementation, the international community has also created new international institutions and recognized transnational legal processes that have over time become recognized forums in which to engage in decisionmaking, interpretation, and recently even the prosecution of individuals on the basis of violations of international law.[8] Not only do representatives of states continue to meet to make law; they also meet routinely in international settings to ensure its implementation and compliance (e.g., meetings of UN organs or the Conference on Security and Cooperation in Europe follow-up meetings after the Helsinki Accords in 1975).

Two developments are particularly noteworthy. One is the emerging systematic understanding of how international norms or rules of behavior are actually being given effect and implemented through domestic legal systems. The other is the creation of international courts adding to the institutional underpinnings of international law. Both developments are additions to the capacity of the international legal system to meet its objectives.

The first development is evidenced by studies on transnational law, transnational legal process, and transnational networks. In his classic *Transnational Law,* Philip Jessup coined this term in order to capture the "complex interrelated world community which may be described as beginning with the individual and reaching up to the so-called 'family of nations' or 'society of states.'"[9] Honju Koh puts a contemporary gloss on this by describing a

> transnational legal process . . . whereby an international law rule is interpreted through the interaction of transnational actors in a variety of law declaring fora, then internalized into a nation's domestic legal system. Through this three-part process of interaction, interpretation, and internalization, international legal rules become integrated into national law and assume the status of internally binding domestic legal obligations.[10]

Anne-Marie Slaughter adds a political-science dimension to her contribution by recognizing a diffusion of state power and functions that makes possible the emergence of transnational networks of government regulators and administrators who can set standards and effectively make law.[11]

On the international level, the most notable operating system development is the creation of international courts to interpret and to implement the law. Standing permanent courts with impartial judges and a published jurisprudence are important building blocks in any legal system as means for not only settling disputes but also interpreting and elaborating existing law. When the decisions made are published, state behavior can be modified by setting a range of acceptable conduct and interpretation in particular areas. One of the most significant developments in building international legal institutions was the establishment of the International Court of Justice, a permanent tribunal with judges elected to serve in their individual capacities to settle disputes between states. Nevertheless, the nearly ninety years of the operation of the Permanent Court of International Justice and its successor (the International Court of Justice) demonstrate that the existence of a standing court has replaced neither the use of force nor other nonjudicial methods to resolve international disputes.

Since the early 1990s, however, there has been an explosion of new international legal institutions and the increased use of extant courts. Jonathan Charney explores these trends, most notably the shift from ad hoc to permanent tribunals, in Chapter 11. He considers broadly the implications for the coherence of the international legal system that follows from the growth of institutions. Following Charney's contribution, we include examinations of two of the most prominent and controversial new judicial mechanisms: the World Trade Organization (WTO) dispute resolution process and the International Criminal Court (ICC).

A key element of the General Agreement on Tariffs and Trade, the landmark economic treaty concluded in April 1994, was the establishment of a WTO that has legal authority to monitor and adjudicate trade disputes between states. Steven Croley and John Jackson (Chapter 12) provide a review of those procedures and analyze the role of the WTO vis-à-vis the responsibilities left to national governments. The story of the institutionalization of the WTO's dispute settlement mechanism illustrates the great care that international procedures and organizations must take in order to gain acceptance and to earn credibility in the international system. Mahnoush Arsanjani (Chapter 13) provides a descriptive overview of the ICC, a very different kind of forum than the WTO mechanisms. The ICC is one of the few international courts in which individuals, rather than states, may be parties to the proceedings. Arsanjani traces the history of some of the key provisions of the ICC statute, and it becomes clear that many of the provisions reflect the necessity of finding a middle ground between the ideals of punishing international crimes and the realities of diplomatic compromise between states with different political and cultural agendas.

Overall, the operating system provides the framework within which international law is created and implemented, and it defines the roles of different actors and also provides mechanisms for the protection of rights and the settlement of disputes. The materials presented in Part 1 demonstrate that even though key elements of the operating system are settled, they do not remain static. Pressures for change are ongoing and will succeed when changes are required to keep the operating system appropriate and effective in supporting contemporary international politics. The elements of the operating system must continuously pass a test of functionality: if they fail to perform, the elements will be replaced by others that serve the broad and general interest of allocating power and of ensuring reasonable order in the conduct of international relations. Competing demands and interests among the operating elements help to identify areas in which adjustments are needed so that when the political circumstances dictate change, international law is ready to respond.

The Normative System

We choose the word *normative* to describe the directive aspects of international law because this area of law functions to create norms out of particular values or policies. Using a different set of analogies, we could imagine normative processes as quasilegislative in character by mandating particular values and directing specific changes in state and other actors' behaviors. Use of the terms *norm* and *norms* abound in the study of international relations, and it is not always clear what meaning is conveyed by a particular construction. In the regimes literature, norms and principles (e.g., orthodox versus embedded liberalism in trade) are broader philosophies of how states and other actors should behave.[12] Although they tend to be issue-specific (e.g., trade, human rights), regime norms are not generally defined at the micro level (e.g., precise changes in rules governing certain human rights violations). In this sense, they are similar to what Michael Barnett refers to as "constitutive norms."[13] Our conception of norms in one sense is narrower and more precise. We focus only on normative elements that have a legally binding character, analogous to the idea of rules in the regime literature. Because we are interested in the international legal system, we are not concerned with acts of "comity," which might be appropriate subjects for a broader inquiry of international norms. In another sense, we have a deeper conception for norms that goes beyond broad general principles to include specific elements about behavior. That is, our normative system is concerned with particular prescriptions and proscriptions, such as limitations on child labor.

Our conception of a normative system is similar to what Hart defines as primary rules that impose duties on actors to perform or abstain from actions.[14] But there is an important difference: Hart sees primary rules as the basic building blocks of a legal system, logically and naturally coming before the development of what we define as the operating system components. For Hart, a primitive legal system can be one with developed rules but without substantial structures to interpret or enforce those rules. We see a more developed international legal system in which norms may exist without specific reference to the operating system yet cannot function without using the operating system's mechanisms. Nevertheless, the normative system may remain somewhat autonomous from the operating system and may even lag behind in its development.

In defining the normative system, the participants in the international legal process engage in a political and legislative exercise that defines the substance and scope of the law. Normative change may occur slowly with evolution of customary practices, a traditional source of international law. Yet in recent historical periods, normative change has been precipitated by new treaties (e.g., the Nuclear Non-Proliferation Treaty) or by a series of actions by international organizations (e.g., the activities of the first team of UN weapons inspectors in Iraq).[15] Nevertheless, the establishment of international legal norms still is less precise and structured than in domestic legal systems where formal deliberative bodies enact legislation.

In contrast to the general terms associated with topics of the operating system (e.g., jurisdiction or actors), the topics of the normative system are issue-specific, and many components of the system refer to subtopics within issue areas (e.g., the status of women within the broader topic area of human rights). Many of these issues have long been on the agenda of international law. Proscriptions on the use of military force have their roots in natural law and early Christian teachings on just war. Many normative rules concerning the law of the sea (e.g., seizure of commercial vessels during wartime) also have long pedigrees in customary practice. Yet recent trends in the evolution of the normative system represent expansions in its scope and depth. Some current issue areas of international legal concern, most notably with respect to human rights and the environment, have developed almost exclusively during the latter half of the twentieth century. Furthermore, within issue areas, legal norms have sought to regulate a wider range of behaviors; for example, international law on the environment has evolved beyond simple concerns of riparian states to include concerns with ozone depletion, water pollution, and other problems.

The range of agreement on the normative content in particular issue areas varies and is not necessarily a function of the length of time that the issue has been on the international legal agenda. For example, in the area of the use of force, the United Nations Charter prohibits its use other than in self-defense. Yet empirically, the use of force in international relations has not been eliminated. Nevertheless, efforts to regulate its use have changed state behavior at least in its initial use and in the response of others to its use. Despite the legal standards and the institutional structures to support these standards, debates continue on the appropriate levels of force and on the appropriate responses to situations that may require stepping over the principle of nonintervention in the internal affairs of states. In the area of human rights, the normative content of human rights is unsettled.[16] The United States, for example, promotes items included in the Covenant on Political and Civil Rights but eschews involvement with the Covenant on Economic and Social Rights. The place of democracy in the panoply of rights is not automatically accepted. Debates surrounding the universal versus culture-based character of human rights are another indication that the normative content of international human rights law is still under development.

In summary, the normative system of international law defines the acceptable standards for behavior in the international system. These are issue-specific prescriptions and proscriptions, with some variation in the consensus surrounding them among the international community of states. The normative system of international law has undergone explosive growth, in scope and specificity, over the past half-century or so, although it remains underdeveloped relative to its domestic counterparts.[17]

The effectiveness of the normative system, however, depends largely on the operating system—the mechanisms and processes that are designed to ensure orderly compliance with norms, and these will change if problems signal a need for change. The normative system may facilitate compliance in isolation from the operating system by "compliance pull."[18] Compliance pull is induced through legitimacy, which is powered by the quality of the rule and/or the rulemaking institution. Still, "primary rules, if they lack adherence to a system of validating secondary rules, are mere *ad hoc* reciprocal arrangements."[19] Compliance pull may exist under such circumstances, but it will be considerably weaker than if secondary rules (related to the operating system) are present. Note that we are speaking of more than compliance concerns in dealing with norms. Regime theory has typically assumed that it is the desire to improve the efficiency of interstate interactions (e.g., reduce transaction costs) that drives the adoption of normative rules. Our view is that states adopt normative rules in order largely to promote shared values in the international system. Rule adoption and institution creation (largely operating system changes) may be helpful in implementation and in reducing transaction costs, but they are not a necessary element or purpose of normative change.

Prominent activity in the normative system of international law has been in the regulation of the use of force, the protection of human rights, the protection of the environment, and the management of the commons. In each of the four normative areas we have selected, the political bases of international law can be seen as states struggle to ensure the goals of peace, justice, and prosperity while not fully negating the rights accorded to them under national sovereignty. We find that many of these areas require the balancing or reconciling of inconsistencies as international law searches for generally applicable standards against a background of economic disparity and historic exploitation that stemmed from political and technological weakness.

The oldest segment of the international normative system concerns the use of force. Paradoxically, at the same time it is the most developed and also the least restrictive on state behavior. Anthony Arend and Robert Beck (Chapter 14) provide a historical perspective and analyze whether the legal paradigm has shifted from one based on self-help to a more restrictive principle. More than a shift in norms, however, has been the shift, especially following the September 11 terrorist attacks, in the forms of threats to international peace and security. Civil wars have become more common since the end of the Cold War. Yet terrorist attacks provide the greater challenge for international legal prescriptions given that such attacks are generally precipitated by individuals or groups (not states) and do not take traditional military forms. Accordingly, most international legal provisions for dealing with aggression seem to fit poorly with this form of conflict. In Chapter 15, M. Cherif Bassiouni reviews the current legal provisions for dealing with terrorism, revealing a broader set of laws than might be first evident, but still indicating an underdeveloped normative system in this area.

The piercing of the shell of state sovereignty is perhaps most dramatic in the area of human rights, where states no longer have full reign over actions within their borders. Dinah Shelton (Chapter 16) considers how globalization has affected attempts to protect human rights through international law. Recent developments throughout the world, including failed states, economic deregulation, privatization, and trade liberalization across borders—components of what has come to be known as *globalization*—have led to the emergence of powerful nonstate actors who have resources sometimes greater than those of many states. She considers four different approaches for promoting human rights in a globalized society: (1) emphasizing state responsibility for the actions of nonstate actors; (2) imposing international legal obligations directly on nonstate actors, including international institutions, multilateral enterprises, and individuals; (3) encouraging private regulation through corporate codes of conduct, product labeling, and other consumer or corporate actions; and (4) involving nonstate actors directly in the activities of international organizations to promote and protect human rights.

The protection of human rights involves more than setting standards that states and other actors must meet. International law also conditions the actions of states and international organizations that wish to redress violations of human rights law. Traditional notions of state sovereignty limited the ability of others to intervene directly in the affairs of states, at least without the permission of that host state. Yet there has been a slow erosion of support for this concept of so-called hard-shell sovereignty. One key idea is that states or collectivities of states may have the right to intervene in other countries in order to respond to humanitarian emergencies. Ralph Zacklin (Chapter 17) looks at the case of NATO intervention in Kosovo. He looks at the international law surrounding that intervention and ultimately provides a series of principles around which a legal norm of humanitarian intervention might form.

Environmental protection is relatively new on the international legal agenda. Yet since the 1980s, states have increasingly regulated their own behavior by signing agreements establishing strict environmental standards and controls. The Rio summit of 1992 is only a recent example of how prominent the environmental issue has become in international relations. In Chapter 18, A. Dan Tarlock makes a strong case for the necessity of integrating domestic and international legal regimes with respect to the environment. Specifically, environmental protection is unlikely to be successful unless both regimes are coordinated. Yet one of the acts that international policymakers must perform is to balance concerns with environmental protection against those of national economic development. Accordingly, the concept of sustainable development was devised. A working committee of the International Law Association (Chapter 19) documents how this concept has become embedded in international environmental law, and this chapter specifies some of the key legal principles (e.g., the common heritage of mankind) consistent with it. Catherine Tinker (Chapter 20) adds a post-Rio overview in the area of protection of biological diversity. The environmental area challenges international law to address changing situations that render regulation through specific legal standards and obligations difficult. This has moved lawmaking into creating frameworks for cooperation and coordination in addition to creating specific legal obligations.

Closely related to international environmental efforts are normative constraints designed to preserve the benefits and riches of the global commons for all. Global commons law has generally developed in accordance with technological development and need; thus, the law of the sea is the oldest segment of law in this issue area, but even there issues such as seabed mining have appeared only recently. In Chapter 21, Christopher Joyner and Elizabeth Martell look at the third UN Law of the Sea Conference for insights on how the law of the sea has developed and to derive lessons for international law as it turns to other parts of the global commons. Likely to be one of the next major areas of concern is outer space. David Tan (Chapter 22) provides a summary of current international law on space as well as some proposals for how that law might further develop.

In Chapter 23, the concluding chapter of this book, John King Gamble and Charlotte Ku take a look into the future. These contributors contend that technological changes will drive the kind of challenges that face international law in the future as well as the processes designed to deal with them. Using a few recent examples (such as efforts to ban landmines), they conclude that NGOs are likely to take a more central role in the formulation and implementation of new international laws in the so-called information age. This conclusion is drawn because of the plethora of information that needs to be factored into addressing many of today's regulatory needs, and also because of the roles public and private actors increasingly need to play together in their resolution.

To address new challenges effectively will require adjustments to the operating system. Like much else in contemporary life, international law will be expected to make more complicated adjustments more rapidly and more frequently than at any other period of its development. This makes the study of this subject a richly rewarding exercise. It makes the practice of international law a daunting, but richly creative, exercise as new legal ground is broken to address changing circumstances. It further affirms the symbiotic relationship between the operating system and the normative system in which the capacity to sustain the operating system will increasingly depend on how well the international community can address its normative concerns.

Notes

1. Robert Dahl, *On Democracy* (New Haven, CT: Yale University Press, 1998).
2. Stephen Krasner, "Structural Causes and Regime Consequences: Regimes as Intervening Variables," in *International Regimes*, edited by Stephen Krasner (Ithaca, NY: Cornell University Press, 1982), pp. 1–2.
3. Michael Barnett, "The United Nations and Global Security: The Norm Is Mightier than the Sword," *Ethics and International Affairs* 9 (1995): 37–54.
4. H.L.A. Hart, *The Concept of Law*, 2nd ed. (Oxford, UK: Clarendon, 1994), p. 94.
5. Christine Chinkin, "The Challenge of Soft Law: Development and Change in International Law," *International and Comparative Law Quarterly* 38 (1989): 850–866; see also Prosper Weil, "Toward Relative Normativity in International Law," *American Journal of International Law* 77 (1983): 413–442.
6. Rosalyn Higgins, *Problems and Process: International Law and How We Use It* (Oxford, UK: Clarendon, 1994).
7. Georges Scelle, *Precis de deoit des gens: principes et systematique* (Paris: Librarie du Recueil Sirey, 1932).
8. See Charlotte Ku and Christopher Borgen, "American Lawyers and International Competence," *Dickson Law Review* 18(3) (2000).
9. Philip C. Jessup, *Transnational Law* (New Haven, CT: Yale University Press, 1956), p. 1.
10. Koh, Honju, "Transnational Legal Process," *Nebraska Law Review* 75 (1996): 181.
11. Slaughter, Anne-Marie, "The Real New World Order," *Foreign Affairs* 76 (1997): 103.
12. Krasner, "Structural Causes and Regime Consequences."

13. Barnett, "The United Nations and Global Security."

14. Hart, *The Concept of Law*.

15. We do, of course, recognize that even with the trend toward treaties as the primary source of new international law, many treaties in recent decades have largely codified existing customary practice (e.g., significant portions of the Law of the Sea Conventions).

16. See, for example, Louis Henkin and John Lawrence Hargrove, *Human Rights: An Agenda for the Next Century* (Washington, DC: American Society of International Law, 1994).

17. See Christian Wiktor, *Multilateral Treaty Calendar, 1648-1995* (Dordrecht, Netherlands: Martinus Nijhoff, 1998), which contains 6,000 treaties.

18. Thomas M. Franck, *The Power of Legitimacy Among Nations* (New York: Oxford University Press, 1990).

19. Ibid., p. 184.

PART 1.1

International Law
as Operating System:
Sources of International Law

2

A Methodology for Determining an International Legal Rule

ANTHONY CLARK AREND

WHILE THERE IS GENERAL AGREEMENT ABOUT THE PRIMARY MEANS THAT states use to develop these rules, it is not always easy to determine when states have truly expressed their consent. Indeed, one of the most difficult and time-consuming tasks for contemporary scholars and government officials is to determine when a rule of international law exists. . . . Customary international law has always been quite elusive. When is there sufficient state practice? And when is there sufficient *opinio juris*? Similarly, general principles of law can be quite difficult to identify—especially since there is no common understanding of precisely what a general principle is. How do we know when the principle is truly "general"?

For treaty provisions, it would appear at first to be much easier to determine whether a legal rule existed. . . . Ideally, one would simply find the treaty provision and determine if a particular state were a party. If that state were a party, it would be bound by the provision. But, I would submit, it is not even that easy with treaties for at least two reasons. First, it can often be very difficult to determine the exact nature of the obligation contained in a particular treaty. Many significant legal debates have centered around the precise meaning of a treaty. During the 1980s, for example, there was a great controversy both within, and outside of, the Reagan administration about whether the development of a space-based ballistic missile defense system was prohibited under the Anti-Ballistic Missile Treaty. The applicable provisions of the treaty were sufficiently ambiguous to permit arguments on both sides of the question. And this is, of course, but one example. Very few treaties are without such ambiguities. Second, as

I will argue below, the existence of formal treaty provision—even if it is unambiguous—does not *necessarily* mean that there is a legal obligation. While the existence of treaty provision does, I believe, constitute a prima facie case for the existence of a legal rule, it is not dispositive. This is a rather controversial position, but one that reflects the dynamic nature of international law. . . .

Existing Methodologies

When natural law dominated international jurisprudence the method most often employed by those seeking to determine if a rule of international law existed is what might be called "deductive."[1] The great scholastic writers, such as Francisco Suarez and Francisco Victoria, deduced particular legal rules from basic natural law propositions. In their examinations of the laws of warfare, for example, these writers drew on Hebrew and Christian Scripture, theological treatises, classical philosophy and even mythology, to establish certain truths that could then be translated into specific rules for the conduct of war.[2]

With the emergence of the modem state system in the seventeenth century, scholars began to move away from a primarily deductive approach. As states came to be regarded as the creators of international legal rules, writers began to introduce "inductive" methods into their scholarship. While "some of the early positivists still vacillated between the traditional [deductive] approach and the newly-discovered truth that international law was the sum total of the rules actually considered law by the subjects of international law,"[3] positivism as it developed became essentially inductive. Positivists, in their quest to find rules of international law, looked at the "raw data,"[4] at state practice. From this practice they would then induce the legal rules. A positivist scholar would, for example, engage in an exhaustive examination of state behavior relating to jurisdictional claims to the sea, before concluding that a particular jurisdictional zone was established under international law.

Throughout the twentieth century, this positivist inductive approach has predominated. Scholars, ranging from Georg Schwarzenberger to Lassa Oppenheim to C. Wilfred Jenks to Prosper Weil, have used some version of the positivist method to provide their assessment of the rules of international law. Nonetheless, since the mid-century, a slightly different method has played an important role in international legal scholarship. Beginning in the 1950s with monumental works by Myres McDougal and Harold Lasswell of Yale, the New Haven School has gained many adherents. Such distinguished scholars as Myres McDougal, W. Michael Reisman, John Norton Moore, Richard Falk, Florentino Feliciano, and Rosalyn

Higgins have written extensively using the methodology of the New Haven School. The New Haven approach draws on many of the insights of positivism, but, as will be discussed below, uses new concepts and some deductive methods in the process of determining rules of international law.

While there are perhaps as many different international legal methodologies as there are scholars, this section will explore traditional positivism and the New Haven school as examples of two of the most prominent of the current methodologies. It will lay out the basic contours of these two approaches and provide a critique of them. This examination will then set the stage for the explication of a new methodology.

Traditional Positivism

As noted above, traditional positivism teaches that international law is created through state practice. Accordingly, an inductive method is used to determine the nature of legal rules. In setting forth his inductive approach, Professor Schwarzenberger explains that this approach places "emphasis on the working hypothesis—historical research and the near-universality of Article 38 of the Statute of the World Court tend to transform it into a certainty—of the exclusive character of the three law-creating processes in international law: consensual understandings in the widest sense, international customary law, and the general principles of law recognised by civilized nations."[5] Under positivism, the scholar discovers rules of law by determining what states have consented to through these sources. As Professors McDougal, Lasswell, and Reisman have explained, in a positivist world, "the jurist is regarded as neither authorized nor qualified seriously to consider the social context in which rules are generated or the sociopolitical consequences which rules, in turn, engender in specific instances of application."[6] In other words, the positivist scholar is not to examine the context or to consider broader goals or purposes of the international political system in determining specific rules. He or she is not to impose a particular teleology on the law-finding task. The law is what states have created. If on a particular issue there is no rule of international law, the scholar is not to fill the "gap" by reference to these other goals. As Professor Kelsen notes, "if there is no norm of conventional or customary international law imposing upon the state (or other subject of international law) the obligation to behave in a certain way, the subject is under international law legally free to behave as it pleases."[7]

How does this approach translate into a concrete method for dealing with the three basic sources of international law? With respect to treaties, positivists typically assert legal rules can be found by consulting provisions of treaties that have entered into force. Among these scholars, there seems to be a great deal of sanctity accorded to the written text. The treaty is the law. Although even positivist writers may assert that "immoral treaties"[8] are not valid, they generally express great skepticism about treaties being superseded or altered by anything other than another treaty. Hans Kelsen, for example, has grave reservations about the entire concept of *rebus sic stantibus*—the notion that treaties can be terminated when a "fundamental change of circumstances" takes place.[9] He explains "that it is the function of the law in general and treaties in particular to stabilize the legal relations between states in the stream of changing circumstances."[10] "If circumstances did not change," he continues, "the binding force conferred upon treaties by the law would be almost superfluous."[11] Moreover, "the relatively few cases in which states have referred to essential change of circumstances to justify their noncompliance with treaty obligations may be interpreted simply as violations of international law rather than evidence of the *clausula rebus sic stantibus*."[12] "As a matter of fact," Kelsen concludes, "no international tribunal has, until now [1952], unreservedly confirmed the existence of this rule *[rebus sic stantibus]*."[13]

More recently, another contemporary positivism Professor Prosper Weil, has expressed concerns about the concept of *jus cogens*—the notion that there are certain "preemptory" rules of international law and that treaties cannot be concluded that violate these rules. The theory of *jus cogens* works something like this: If, for example, a *jus cogens* existed that prohibited states from engaging in slave trade, they could not by treaty consent to undertake that behavior; such treaty would be void and thus without legal effect. For Professor Weil, the concept of *jus cogens* creates difficulties for the basic positivist notion of the equality of all rules— whatever their source. He explains that "one can scarcely overemphasize the uncertainties inflicted on the international normative system by the fragmentation of normativity that the theories of *jus cogens* and international crimes have brought in their wake.[14] How does one determine whether a rule is a *jus cogens* or merely ordinary rule of international law?[15] Moreover, if distinctions be drawn between regular legal rules and superrules, what is to prevent even more specific normative gradations?[16] "A normativity subject to unlimited gradation is," in his opinion, "one doomed to flabbiness, one that in the end will be reduced to a convenient term art, covering a great variety of realities difficult to grasp."[17] Like Kelsen, Weil is very skeptical about doctrines that would interfere with the basic proposition that states can establish whatever law they wish through treaties.

To a positivist scholar, therefore, one bit of "raw evidence" of legal rules is a treaty. It is a primary way in which states consent. If a treaty exists on a particular issue and a state is a party to a treaty, that written document almost certainly establishes legal rules binding the state.

With customary international law, positivists have developed extremely involved methods for finding consent in the vicissitudes of state practice. Consistent with a general understanding of the sources of international law . . . positivists contend that both the "objective" and the "subjective" elements of custom must be present in order for there to be a rule of customary international law. First, there must be physical practice. States must engage in some activity. They must arrest fishing vessels; or they must refrain from arresting fishing vessels. They must grant immunity from criminal jurisdiction; or they must refuse to grant immunity from jurisdiction. This is the objective element. It is what states do in practice. Second, there must be *opinio juris*. The practice in which the states engage must be regarded as law. This is the subjective element.

To determine the existence of these two elements, positivists consult a wide array of data. Indeed, any international law textbook or casebook contains a recitation of the kinds of evidence scholars of positivism and other persuasions would muster to determine the existence of a rule of custom. Such a listing, as observed in the previous chapter, could include statements by government officials, actions and decisions taken by government officials, domestic legislation, activities of diplomatic personnel, behavior of military commanders, decisions of domestic courts, and the like. But how does the observer evaluate this data? How does one measure practice and *opinio juris*? Professor Weil, noting that "it is not always easy to draw the frontier between the prelegal and the legal,"[18] cites Justice Stuart's famous comment about pornography—"I know it when I see it." Explains Weil: "This celebrated formula of a Justice of the United States Supreme Court aptly illustrated this difficulty."[19]

Positivists typically provide a variety of guidelines to assist the observer in evaluating the status of putative legal rules. They generally begin with the assertion that there must be a long, well-established, nearly universal practice of states. Sir Hersch Lauterpacht, himself not a strict positivist,[20] expresses this point nonetheless. As he notes, "international custom signifies constant and uniform practice followed by States as a matter of obligation."[21] Similarly, Kelsen explains that "custom is a usual or habitual course of action, a long-established practice; in international relations, a long-established practice of states."[22] Hence, a scholar operating under the traditional approach would first attempt to find a practice that was consistent. Day after day, year after year, states would have to engage in the practice. They would, for example, have to consistently refrain from shooting prisoners of war, or from denying foreign vessels transit through international straits. Second, the scholar would determine that the practice was nearly universal. Most positivists would assert that not all states need participate or acquiesce in a practice, but there should be near uniformity.

These positivist guidelines are, of course, still quite vague. As Lauterpacht notes, "constancy and uniformity of practice are a matter of degree."[23] "There is," Lauterpacht explains, "no rule of thumb which renders it possible to predict with any degree of assurance what amount of precedent will cause an international tribunal to assume in any given case that the degree of accumulation of precedent qualifies as custom."[24]

Finally, traditional positivists seem to have some difficulties with the third formal source of international law—general principles of law. It is remarkable that in his 1952 treatise, entitled *Principles of International Law,* Professor Kelsen does not even discuss general principles as a source of international law. In his chapter on "The Creation (Sources) of International Law," Kelsen declares that "the two principal methods of creating international law are custom and treaties."[25] He then devotes two long sections in the text to each of those methods, but only discusses "general principles" in a passing comment about the International Court of Justice.[26] Later, he contends that "it is doubtful whether such principles common to the legal orders of the civilized nations exist at all."[27] He further notes that "Article 38, paragraph 1 [of the Statute of the International Court of Justice], expressly stipulates that the function of the Court is 'to decide in accordance with international law.'"[28] "Hence," he continues, "it might be argued that 'the general principles of law' are applicable only if they are part of international law, and that means part of the law referred to in clauses (a) [conventions] and (b) [custom] of Article 38."[29] If this is the case, "clause (c) [general principles] is superfluous."[30] In short, for general principles to be part of international law, these principles must have been enacted through either treaties or custom. They do not, under Kelsen's positivism, seem to be an independent source of legal rules.

Other positivists are not as ardent in their rejection of general principles. While they do not generally acknowledge any notion of general principles that involves concepts of higher law, such as those of equity and humanity, some positivists accept the notion that common principles of municipal law may be a source of international law. Professor Schwarzenberger, for example, supports this understanding of general principles. He approvingly cites a test for determining the existence of such principles developed by H. C. Gutteridge: "If any real meaning is to be given to the words 'general' or 'universal' and the like, the correct test would seem to be that an international judge before taking over a principle from private law must satisfy himself that it is recognised in substance by all the main systems of law and that in applying it he will not be doing violence to the fundamental concepts of any of those systems."[31] In other words, for a rule to be regarded as a general principle, a survey of the world's major legal systems must take place. If the principle is found in civil law systems, common law systems, and all other different legal systems that may exist, the principle can be applied to interstate cases.

Traditional Positivism: A Critique

Traditional positivism has much to commend itself as a useful methodology for determining legal rules. It recognizes the anarchic nature of the international system and accepts states as the creators of international legal rules. It draws a fairly clear distinction between legal rules and moral rules. While not denying the existence of moral rules, positivist scholars, unlike natural law writers, refrain from conflating the two types of rules. There are, however, a number of difficulties with the traditional positivist approach.

First, positivism tends to place too much emphasis on the absolute sanctity of treaties. While undoubtedly treaties create law among states, the international law-creating process remains dynamic. As noted earlier, I believe the existence of a treaty is prima facie evidence of a rule of law. But states can choose to alter legal rules established by treaty through customary practice. A concrete example can serve to illustrate this point. Article 2(4) of the United Nations Charter prohibits "the threat or use of force against the territorial integrity or political independence of any state or in any other manner inconsistent with the Purposes of the United Nations."[32] This provision has not been formally changed by amendment; nor has any state formally invoked the doctrine of *rebus sic stantibus* as provided for in the Vienna Convention on the Law of Treaties. Nonetheless, as Professor Robert Beck and I have argued elsewhere,[33] through customary practice, states have effectively withdrawn their consent from this provision. In their practice, states do not refrain from such uses of force, and they no longer truly accept the provision as law. Many positivists would assert that the mere existence of the U.N. Charter provision is sufficient to demonstrate that Article 2(4) is reflective of a legal rule. The Charter is, after all, still in force as a multilateral treaty.[34] This claim, I believe, denies the right of states to withdraw their consent through custom and thus denies the dynamic nature of international law.

Second, positivism tends to underrate the role of general principles of law. In particular, positivists do not generally acknowledge the notion of general principles about the nature of international law. These principles, as noted in the previous chapter, undergird the international legal system. They are still created by consent because they form the shared a priori assumptions of states—the primary international actors. Most positivists acknowledge principles such as *pacta sunt servanda,* but they tend to think of these principles as something other than consent-created general principles.

Third, the positivist methodology for determining the existence of legal rules is rather vague. As noted above, many positivists recognize how difficult it is using this methodology to verify the existence of a legal rule. The notion that the observer would "know it when he or she saw it" is not particularly easy to operationalize. Perhaps this will always remain a major stumbling block in the development of a methodology for determining legal rules. But perhaps it may be possible to formulate more specific guidelines that will provide greater assistance to scholars, officials, and others seeking to find rules of international law.

The New Haven Approach

In the post–World War II era, the major challenge to positivism in international legal theory has come from the McDougal-Lasswell school of jurisprudence. Despite arguments by some that this method has become passé,[35] a substantial number of legal scholars throughout the world have been greatly influenced by the theories of Myres McDougal, Harold Lasswell, and their students.[36] In their writings those of the New Haven School have provided a new definition of law and have elaborated a very detailed methodology for use in determining the law. While it would be impossible to do justice to this approach in a few pages, the following material will attempt to set out the most basic contours of this approach.

As noted earlier, adherents of the New Haven School define law not as a set of rules but as a particular kind of social process. To be specific they define law as the process of "authoritative decision." According to this approach the world can be understood in terms of a series of overlapping social processes. At the broadest level is what McDougal and Lasswell call the "world social process."[37] The world social process is a process of interaction consisting of human beings "acting individually in their own behalf and in concert with others with whom they share symbols of common identity and ways of life of varying degrees of elaboration."[38] The purpose of this process is "the maximization of values within the limits of capability."[39] "A value," they explain, "is a preferred event."[40] It is, thus, whatever individuals desire. Since a complete list of all conceivable values is impossible, McDougal and Lasswell believe that most values can be understood as falling into one or more of the following categories: health, safety, comfort (well-being), affection, respect, skill, enlightenment, rectitude, wealth, and power.[41] In other words, human beings seek a variety of values that aim at achieving skill or power or affection and so on. Operating within this broad social process is yet another process—what McDougal and company refer to as the "world power process."[42] The world power process is the process by which certain values are actually realized in the world. In other words, this is the process that determines specific "outcomes"—what really happens, who gets what. From this process come decisions that control behavior—whether or not those decisions are perceived to be legitimate or not. For example, during the period of Western colonization, the world power process led to the Western states gaining control over much of the developing world. It was the Western states who had the resources—military might, economic wealth, etc. As a consequence, as these states interacted with less resourceful political units in the system, these Western states were able to realize their values.

Finally, within the world power process is the legal process. This process McDougal and Lasswell define as "the making of authoritative and controlling decisions."[43] With this phrase, they introduce the two most critical concepts for understanding law under their framework: authority and control. They define "authority" as "the structure of expectation concerning who, with what qualifications and mode of selection, is competent to make which decisions by what criteria and what procedures."[44] Professor John Norton Moore explains this a bit more clearly. In a 1968 law review article entitled "Prolegomenon to the Jurisprudence of Myres McDougal and Harold Lasswell," he explains that authority "is used to signify community expectations about how decisions should be made and about which established community decision-makers should make them."[45] As a consequence, "decisions made in conformance with community expectations about proper decision and proper decision-makers, as distinguished from decisions based on mere naked power, are said to be authoritative."[46]

In essence, a decision is authoritative if "the members of the community" perceive the decision to be made in a legitimate manner, irrespective of whether it actually controls behavior. A few examples may illustrate. If the Congress of the United States passes a tax bill and the president signs the bill, that act is generally perceived to be authoritative by the citizens of the United States. People believe that Congress and the president had the authority to undertake this action. Similarly, if a treaty concerning the prohibition on torture is concluded and ratified by a number of states but ignored by most of them, the procedure is regarded as authoritative, even if the treaty did not control behavior.

As can be seen, the concept of authority seems to be similar to the traditional notion of *opinio juris*. There do, however, seem to be distinctions. One will be noted here; the other will be discussed later in this section. In a typical positivist approach, when scholars ask if a rule has *opinio juris*, they are asking if that rule is perceived to be law. In the New Haven approach, scholars seem to ask something else. The McDougalian scholars want to know if the *process* whereby a decision is made is perceived to be legitimate. They ask if the decision was made by legitimate decision makers through a legitimate process. If the decision was so made, then it has authority. Herein lies the distinction. As noted earlier, positivists contend that law consists of *rules*. Accordingly, they are first and foremost concerned about whether the *rule* itself is perceived to be law. Generally speaking, of course, a rule that is produced through a legitimate process will be perceived to be legitimate. But it is certainly possible that a rule could emerge through a less than legitimate process that, over time, would nonetheless come to be perceived to be the law.[47] Similarly, it is possible that a rule could be produced through a legitimate process but come to be perceived to no longer be the law. Positivists are not primarily interested in the legitimacy of the process—although that would certainly provide important data—but rather in the legitimacy of the result. The other element of the legal process according to the New Haven approach, "control" is defined as "an effective voice in decision, whether authorized or not." A decision is controlling if it determines an actual outcome, irrespective of whether or not it was perceived to be authoritative. So, to take the previous example, if individuals pay the amount of tax prescribed in legislation, that action by Congress and the president was controlling. If, however, the legislation is widely ignored by the populace, it is not controlling, even though it may have been authoritative. In the international arena, there are a plethora of controlling events that are not authoritative. When China suppressed the Tiananmen Square demonstration or the United States invaded Panama, these acts were ultimately controlling, yet many perceived them to be made through an illegitimate process—not authoritative.[48]

Using these two concepts, the members of the New Haven School can thus define law: "The conjunction of common expectations concerning authority with a high degree of corroboration in actual operation is what we understand by law."[49] Hence, the process that produces decisions that are both authoritative and controlling is the legal process. McDougal, Lasswell, and Reisman explain that "an authoritative and controlling decision can be contrasted with decisions involving only effective power ("naked power") or mere barren authority ("pretended power").[50] They then proceed to give examples of these two extremes. They see "naked power in action when a strong empire coerces a weak neighboring polity, and nothing happens [i.e., the international community as a whole does not respond]."[51] "Pretended power" they find in a situation "when a superseded monarch vainly claims acceptance as the legitimate head of the body-politic from which he has been expelled."[52]

With this understanding of law as the conjunction of authority and control, McDougal and colleagues can explain their method for determining the existence of international law. In order to examine this method, it is necessary to explore their answers to four specific questions. First, whose expectations of authority are to be sought? Second, how does an observer "measure" authority and control? Third, how much authority and control are necessary for "law" to exist? Fourth, are there factors other than authority and control that are involved in the law-determining process?

As noted earlier, authority in the New Haven formulation is somewhat different from *opinio juris*. In addition to the difference noted above, there is at least one more distinction. For positivists, it is the perceptions of *states* that is used to determine *opinio juris*. For those of the New Haven School, the perceptions of authority come from a broader group. McDougal, Lasswell, and Reisman explain that "authority will be sought, not in some mysterious or transempirical source of 'obligation' or 'validity,' but rather, empirically, in the perspectives, the genius expectations, of the people who constitute a given community about the requirements for lawful decision in that community."[53] It is the expectations of "the people" of the "community" that are used to determine whether something is authoritative, not those of "the state." Elsewhere, the authors explain that "in the optimum public order which we recommend, the expectations of all *individuals equally* comprise authority."[54] But recognizing that in contemporary "public order systems, full universality and democracy are rarely achieved," they assume that "the expectations and demands of the effective elites of a polity may be the dominant element of authority in a particular community."[55] In other words, given the current status of developments in the global system, it is too early to examine the expectations of *all* human beings. At present, therefore, a scholar seeking to explore perceptions of authority should look at the expectations of "effective elites." But who are these effective elites? Are these the decision-making elites that are empowered by the people of states to act on their behalf? Or is this a broader category of elites? Is this a category that might include leaders of intergovernmental and nongovernmental organizations, scholars, members of the intelligentsia?

Given the general orientation of the New Haven approach, it would seem that they seek to find authority not just in expectations of decision-making elites of states, but in a broader group of elites.[56] Anthony D'Amato argues that the New Haven scholars "seem to view authoritative so broadly as to encompass just about any decision made by an international decisionmaker."[57] I believe, especially given the desire of the New Haven scholars for inclusivity, that they would examine an even larger group of elites than Professor D'Amato suggests, not just "international decisionmakers." As such, the group whose perceptions of authority are used in assessing law is much larger than the group sought by positivists in determining *opinio juris*.

In light of this larger group, how does a New Haven scholar "measure" authority and control? What does he or she examine to determine the existence of authority and control and, therefore, law? In an essay entitled "The Identification and Appraisal of Diverse Systems of Public Order,"[58] McDougal and Lasswell preliminarily spell out the process of gathering information on the nature of a public order system.

In the process, scholars would of necessity determine expectations of authority and control. This process is described briefly in a section called "What the Scholar Does in Gathering and Processing Data." In a nutshell, they prescribe three "operations" in which the scholar should engage to get the appropriate information. In "Operation 1," the researcher is to "establish the provisional identity of a public order system within a community context by means of an inventory of explicit legal formulae."[59] What this means in the international context is that the scholar should examine treaties, resolutions, and other formal indices of authority and control. It is important to note, however, that with respect to authority, these formal items are not dispositive. As McDougal, Lasswell, and Reisman explain elsewhere, "there can . . . be no automatic assumption of identity between formal and actual controlling institutional structures and expectations of authority."[60] Operation 2 moves the scholar a bit further. In that undertaking, the scholar is urged to "add accuracy and detail to the inventory obtained by Operation 1 by describing the frequency with which each prescription found in the legal formulae is invoked or purportedly applied in controversies."[61] In other words, the scholar will examine how often the formal expressions of authority are really controlling. Finally, Operation 3 calls on the scholar to "analyze all other sources for the purpose of making a fuller identification of the systems of public order provisionally revealed by the preceding operations."[62] The scholar should "describe the legal process in the context of the decision process as a whole, and of the social process within the entire community."[63] "Most of the scholarly effort at this phase," they explain, "is devoted to obtaining data by methods that are not conventional to traditionally trained legal scholars."[64]

The procedure they have in mind can be reinforced by examining some comments that McDougal, Lasswell, and Reisman make in another article that discusses authority. "Genuine expectations of authority," they explain, "are discerned by contextual examination of past decision as well as by the utilization of all the techniques of the social sciences for assessing the current subjectivities of individuals."[65] Hence, McDougal and colleagues seem to suggest that the scholar needs to do two additional things. First, he or she needs to examine the responses of individuals to various cases in which a normative question arises ("contextual examination of past decision"). For example, to determine whether it were legal for a state to engage in forcible intervention abroad to rescue its nationals, a scholar would examine how "members of the community" responded when such intervention took place. What were their perceptions of the legitimacy (i.e., the authority) of such intervention? Second, McDougal and company suggest that other social science methods ("all the techniques of the social sciences") should be used to assess perceptions of authority. These techniques could, presumably, run the gamut from content analysis of official documents to actual surveying and interviewing the "members of the community."

If this is the case, then the third question logically follows. We can measure authority and control using recognized methods, but how much authority and control is necessary for something to be called "law"? What threshold must be achieved for "law" to exist? Like the traditional positivists, the New Haven scholars are well aware of the difficulty of finding this threshold. Moreover, they seem to suggest that the amount of these two elements necessary for law will vary depending upon the case. For example, McDougal, Lasswell, and Reisman note that "the precise degree of effectiveness or 'control' required for 'law'—whether in national or international arenas—cannot . . . be stated absolutely; it is a function of context and will vary."[66] Professor Moore seems to reflect this contextual approach when he notes that "whether or not one postulates any particular combination of authority and control as the most useful definition of law for a particular purpose, the observer of the legal system must be concerned with patterns of authority and patterns of control."[67] In "The Identification and Appraisal of Diverse Systems of Public Order," McDougal and Lasswell note, almost in passing, that "as a matter of definition it will often be clarifying for the scholar to specify the minimum level of frequency of invocation and purported application that he requires before accepting a particular pattern of authority and control as "law."[68] In essence, the New Haven School avoids setting any standard authority-control threshold; it will vary from case to case, and perhaps even from scholar to scholar.

From the preceding analysis, the New Haven method for determining the existence of international law would appear to be reasonably clear. If the scholar identifies the expectations of authority in conjunction with a certain amount of control, there is law. But much of the New Haven literature suggests that there are other factors that the scholar may use in the determination of law. In "Some Basic Theoretical Concepts about International Law: A Policy Oriented Framework," Professor McDougal explains that "international law" is "the process of authoritative decision *insofar as it approximates a public order of human dignity.*"[69] Here the author is suggesting that law is not purely authority and control, but rather authority and control if they promote the goal of "human dignity." In effect, the New Haven scholars seem to assume that there is an international community[70] that has the promotion of human dignity as its highest goal. Accordingly, legal scholars are to find the law in the authoritative and controlling decisions that promote that goal. As Professor Friedrich Kratochwil notes, this signals a "teleological orientation to law."[71] Kratochwil explains that "law in this conception is no longer susceptible to a clear statement in rules or precedents, but consists in an agglomeration of shifting and interacting standards, policies, and preferences of the various decision-makers."[72] As a consequence, "the legal character of a decision has to be ascertained by means of an appraisal which includes the description of past trends, factors affecting the decision, projection of future trends, and evaluations of policy alternatives in terms of the overarching goal of human dignity."[73] Under this logic, therefore, an international legal rule exists not merely when there is a sufficient degree of authority and control, but only when the putative rule is directed toward the promotion of human dignity.

This idea that is present in some of the New Haven literature greatly complicates the more straightforward authority-control approach.

A Critique of the New Haven Approach

Almost since the New Haven approach was developed, other scholars have provided many extensive critiques. The purpose here is not to dissect what Kratochwil has called "McDougal's exceedingly complex 'theory' about law."[74] Instead, this section will attempt to provide a basic critique of the primary elements of the New Haven method for determining law.[75]

One of the most useful contributions of the New Haven approach is the introduction of the concepts of authority and control. These two concepts, as will be discussed below, can serve as excellent tools for ascertaining both the objective and subjective element of international law. But there are a number of difficulties with these concepts as the New Haven scholars develop them.

First, as noted above, McDougal and associates seem to seek expectations of authority not only in the decision-making elites of states, but also in a much larger group, the members of the international community. This raises many problems. How does a scholar determine who belongs to this group? Ideally, the New Haven scholars submit, it is to consist of all individuals in the world. But at present, it is the "effective elite." Who are these people? Moreover, the claim that the expectations of authority of individuals of this broader group should be sought seems to reject a fundamental proposition in the current international system: states make the law. It is thus the expectations of the decision-making elites in *states* that should be sought. Perhaps at some future point the international system will become so differentiated that other actors will play an unmediated role in the law-creating process, but that is not yet the case.

Second, as has been noted above, McDougal and company view authority as expectations concerning the method through which a decision was produced. This clearly reflects these scholars' understanding of law not as a body of rules but as a process. Yet, if one does regard law as a body of rules, a body of rules produced through a process, but a body of rules nonetheless, that scholar is going to be most concerned about whether a putative legal rule is perceived to be law now—irrespective of whether the process was legitimate. While ideally, as observed above, a rule that is produced through a legitimate method would itself be perceived to be legitimate, this is not always the case. As a consequence, I believe that the authoritativeness of the *rule* is still the indicator of the subjective element of a rule of international law.

Third, the contradictory ways in which the New Haven scholars define law presents not only logical difficulties but also proposes a definition of law that clearly is not law. If law were the conjunction of authority and control alone, scholars would have a reasonably clear criterion. But, as noted above, the New Haven scholars also suggest that law may be authority and control insofar as they promote human dignity. There are many problems here. What is human dignity? At one point, McDougal and Lasswell define human dignity. "The essential meaning of human dignity as we understand it can be succinctly stated,"[76] they say. Human dignity, they continue, "refers to a social process in which values are widely and not narrowly shared, and in which private choice, rather than coercion, is emphasized as the predominate modality of power."[77] But what does this mean? And why postulate human dignity as the "overarching goal"? McDougal and colleagues seem to recognize that there is no absolute philosophical necessity in positing human dignity as the goal of the international community, but seem to do so because it is, so they allege, recognized universally. "All systems," they contend, "proclaim the dignity of the human individual and the ideal of a worldwide public order in which this ideal is authoritatively pursued and effectively approximated."[78] Do all systems truly accept human dignity as a goal? Is it possible to reach any kind of international consensus on the meaning of this term? Does "human dignity" mean the same to decision-making elites in the United States as it does to those in Iran, China, or Nigeria?

The New Haven School's focus on human dignity—while commendable from a moral perspective—introduces into the law-determining process an extremely subjective element. As Professor Kratochwil notes, this aspect of the New Haven method reintroduces a "natural law" conception.[79] Kratochwil argues that "even if we agree that human dignity is of overarching importance, it is rather questionable whether such a teleological conception of human actions can provide us with standards sufficiently precise to come to a consensus as to what is to count as law."[80] Moreover, I do not believe we can agree. In the diverse international system, there is, at present, no one conception of human dignity that the decision-making elites have affirmed.

A Proposed Methodology

In light of the preceding examination of traditional positivism and the New Haven approach, this section will set forth the basic contours of a new method for determining rules of international law. This method will draw on the insights of both positivism and the New Haven School while attempting to avoid the pitfalls of these approaches. Accordingly this section will do two things. First, it will lay out the fundamental assumptions that animate this proposal. Second, it will explain the essence of the proposal itself.

Fundamental Assumptions

Throughout the course of this book, I have expressed several basic assumptions about the nature of the international system in general and the international legal system in particular. At risk of repetition, I would like to note these assumptions here. It is, I believe, extremely important to make very clear the foundation upon which this methodology is constructed. First, I assume that the international system is an "anarchic" system. This, of course, means that the system is anarchic in the formal sense.[81] There is no centralized legislative, executive, or judicial body. The system is not anarchic in the literal sense of the word; it is not completely without governance or law. Second, I assume that states are the primary actors in the international system. While I recognize a plethora of nonstate actors—and indeed an ever increasing role for these actors—states remain the major players. Third, I assume that states are essentially unitary actors. Notwithstanding the complicated internal workings within states, I believe that for purposes of understanding international legal rules and their creation, states can be discussed as unitary actors. Fourth, I assume that in this decentralized international system, states are sovereign. While there is a great deal of debate within the academic community about the precise meaning of "sovereignty," the term is employed as noted in the previous chapter. Sovereignty means that all states are juridically equal; accordingly, they can be bound by law only through their consent. In the absence of a law to which states have consented, they are therefore legally allowed to do as they choose. Fifth, I assume that states consent to the creation of international law in three basic ways: treaties, custom, and general principles. "General principles" I take to mean the two consent-based definitions provided earlier: general principles of law found in the domestic legal systems of states and general principles about the nature of the international legal system.

The Proposed Methodology

The basic authority-control test. In light of these assumptions about the international system and international legal rules, the best test for determining the existence of a rule of international law is what might be called the "authority control" test.[82] Drawing on the language developed by the New Haven School, a putative rule of international law can be regarded as "law" if it possesses authority and control. First, the decision-making elites in states must perceive the rule to be authoritative; they must perceive it to be law. There must be *opinio juris*. Second, the rule must be controlling. It must be reflected in the actual practice of states.

This approach uses the language and basic concepts of the New Haven School, but there are three important differences. First, as noted above, the

New Haven approach uses perceptions of the "members of the international community" to determine the existence of authority. I believe this phrase is too vague to put into practice. Moreover, at present, international law is created by states. As a consequence, it is the decision-making elites in states that participate in the law-creating process. Accordingly, it is the perceptions of these individuals—those involved in the day-to-day policy making and policy implementation of states—whose perceptions of authority matter. Second, the concept of authority in New Haven parlance relates to perceptions that the process by which the "decision" is rendered is authoritative. As explained earlier, I believe that the critical subjective element is whether the putative *rule* itself is seen to be the law—not whether the process is perceived to be legitimate.

Accordingly, in keeping with a basic assumption of positivism, I will use the concept of authority to describe the authoritativeness of the rule. In other words, authority, as employed here, is a synonym for *opinio juris*. Third, the New Haven scholars suggest that there can also be a teleological element to the determination of a rule of law. International law becomes something that is authoritative and controlling insofar as it promotes human dignity. While I personally believe that human dignity should be a goal of the international system, I do not believe that it should be used in the process of determining *legal* as distinct from *moral* rules. Law is created by states. If they choose to enshrine human dignity in legal rules, that is commendable. But the task of the legal scholar must not be to impose his or her definition of morality onto the legal system, but rather to identify those rules that states have in fact created.[83] Indeed, it is only in refusing to conflate morality with legality that the moral deficiencies of the law can be identified.

How does this approach work in practice? Under the authority-control test, if a scholar or decision maker is called on to determine the existence of a rule of international law, he or she would ask two questions: Is it authoritative? And is it controlling? Irrespective of the particular source of international law—custom, treaty, or general principle—the same fundamental test can be applied.

The application of this approach to putative rules of customary international law is fairly clear. Asking if a rule is authoritative and controlling is essentially the same as asking if there is *opinio juris* and if there is state practice. If, for example, someone were to suggest that it was a rule of customary international law that public warships passing each other on the high seas must display a particular light configuration, the investigation would be very straightforward. First, a scholar would engage in the empirical examination. He or she would observe such vessels passing and determine if they did, in practice, display the appropriate light configuration. Second, the scholar would then determine if the decision-making elites in states believe that this practice is required by law—if they believe that this practice is authoritative. If the scholar determined that there was a practice and that the practice was, in fact, perceived by these elites to be authoritative, then it could be concluded that there was a rule of customary international law requiring that naval vessels display this particular light configuration when passing each other.

Applying this approach to international conventions may seem a bit more difficult. Traditional positivists would claim that in most circumstances the very existence of a treaty would indicate that there was a rule of international law.[84] But, as noted earlier, if a treaty or a particular provision of a treaty is neither authoritative nor controlling, states no longer consent to that rule. One way to view this is to argue that under the doctrine of *rebus sic stantibus* the treaty or provision is no longer law because there has been a fundamental change of circumstances. If states no longer believe the rule is authoritative and if it is not controlling, there seems to have been a very fundamental change in circumstances. Some scholars, however, might object to this argument. Under the Vienna Convention on the Law of Treaties, they would argue, there is a formal procedure for invoking the doctrine of "fundamental change of circumstances." Unless this formal procedure is followed, the treaty is still the "law."[85] If, however, one were to argue that *rebus sic stantibus* is regarded as a general principle about the nature of international law, it would lie at the very heart of the consent process. A fundamental a priori assumption of states, it could be contended, is that they are not bound by treaty provisions if a fundamental change occurs. Accordingly, notwithstanding the formal requirements in the Vienna Convention, if a treaty is lacking in authority and control, it is not law. But a scholar need not take recourse to the controversial doctrine of *rebus sic stantibus*.[86]

A second—and more appropriate—way to approach the application of the authority-control test to treaties would be to make the following argument. When a treaty is concluded and enters into force, there is a *presumption* that authority and control exist. In formulating and ratifying the agreement, states are expressing a belief in the authoritativeness of the treaty and pledging to carry out the provisions of the treaty in their practice. If, however, as time passes, the treaty as a whole, or a particular provision of the treaty, loses authority and control, the putative rule contained in the treaty or the provision no longer reflects the willingness of states to restrict their behavior in a given way. Once states are no longer willing to restrict their behavior, as sovereigns, they are legally free to do as they choose. If, for example, a treaty provided that all states were required to guarantee to their citizens paid vacations, once that treaty entered into force, it would create the presumption that there was a legal obligation to grant paid holidays. But if most states did not grant such holidays and statements of decision-making elites and other manifestations indicated that there were low perceptions of authority with respect to the putative rule, it would seem that states were no longer willing to be bound by this restriction, and, accordingly, it would no longer be considered a *legal* rule.

It should, of course, be noted that in making this argument, I am not suggesting that a *single* violation or even *several* violations by states are in and of themselves sufficient to remove the legal obligation contained in a treaty provision. For example, when Iranian authorities consented to the holding of American diplomats hostage in 1979, that act constituted a violation of the Vienna Convention on Diplomatic Relations. The Iranian action *did not* alter the provision of the Convention dealing with diplomatic immunity. The Iranian act was illegal. Only if there were substantial indication that a treaty provision generally lacked authority and was generally not controlling of behavior, could one conclude that the provision was no longer law.

In short, it seems clear that treaties are susceptible to the authority-control test. In order for consent to remain the basis for the creation of international law, states must be able to alter treaty provisions through new authoritative practice. As a consequence, while a treaty creates a presumption of the existence of a legal rule, unless that treaty or the provision in question is still authoritative and controlling, it is not the law. States have effectively withdrawn their consent.

Finally, this test could also be applied to general principles of law. For general principles of law found in the domestic legal systems of states, a scholar would undertake this two-prong test. If, for example, estoppel is submitted to be a general principle in this sense, the scholar would first attempt to determine if the principle were controlling. Do the municipal legal systems in the world use estoppel in domestic cases? Then, the scholar would ask if these legal systems regard this principle as authoritative—do they perceive it to be law. If estoppel is found to have both these qualities, it can be said to be a rule of law.

Measuring authority and control. While the general nature of the authority-control test can be set out in a fairly straightforward fashion, a more difficult question is how to measure authority and control. In other words, what elements would a scholar consult to be able to determine if a putative rule possessed authority and control? Over the years, legal scholars have suggested a wide variety of methods for determining the necessary components of a rule of international law. What follows is one attempt to operationalize the authority-control test. Clearly, this is not the only way of fleshing out the authority-control test. But it is, I hope, a useful method.

Authority. A putative rule is authoritative when the decision-making elites in states perceive the rule to be authoritative. What indicators can a scholar use to determine if this perception exists? There are, no doubt, a variety of factors that would help an observer determine the extent to which a putative rule is perceived to be authoritative. A rough indication of the authoritativeness of a rule can be gained from asking the following questions.

1. Are there manifestations of authority? And if so, how many? Here the scholar is asking if there are clear representations that the decision-making elites in states perceive the putative rule to be authoritative. In asking this question, the scholar should look for both *formal* and *informal* manifestations of authority. Examples of such formal manifestations would include treaties, United Nations Security Council resolutions, domestic laws, executive orders, and domestic judicial decisions. These kinds of items all have a certain solemnity that would reflect an official indication that a particular rule is perceived to be authoritative.

This type of manifestation can be illustrated in operation in the following example. Suppose, for instance, one submitted that it were a rule of international law that diplomats should not be arrested. A scholar might first look at existing treaties[87]—both bilateral and multilateral. Are there provisions in these treaties that prohibit the arresting of diplomats? If there are, that would indicate certain perceptions of authority. Are there Security Council resolutions that affirm the inviolability of diplomats? During the Gulf War, for example, the Security Council adopted numerous resolutions upholding various principles of international law. Even though these dealt with a very specific case, the resolutions represented nonetheless formal reaffirmation of the principles involved.

But while it is convenient to have formal manifestations of authority, often they are not present. This does not necessarily mean that perceptions of authority are low. There may be other indicators of authority, including public statements by leaders and spokespersons for states, speeches in parliaments, negotiating documents, diplomatic notes, letters or memoranda. A scholar should consult these indicators of authority as well as the more formal manifestations.

2. How universal are the manifestations of authority? Virtually all scholars would agree that in order for a rule of general international law to exist—one that is globally valid—there has to be nearly universal acceptance of the authoritative nature of the rule. In other words, the greater the number of states that accept the rule as authoritative, the higher the overall authoritativeness of the rule. This acceptance can be identified by finding positive manifestations coming from a particular state or by noting acquiescence on the part of a state when other states assert the authoritativeness of the rule. While it is certainly possible that a rule of international law can exist on a less-than-universal basis,[88] for a rule to be proclaimed general international law, there must be exceptionally "wide-spread"[89] perceptions of authority.

In addition, as the International Court of Justice noted in the *North Sea Continental Shelf* cases, for there to be a rule of customary international law, there must be the participation of those "states whose interests are specially affected."[90] In the case in question, the Court was discussing the procedure for the delimitation of the continental shelves for states that are adjacent. As a consequence, the states "whose interests are specially affected" would be those in similar situations—in this case, those adjacent states with continental shelves. What the Court was saying was that it would be impossible for a rule of customary international law relating to the delimitation of continental shelves to develop, unless those states that had a direct stake in the rule had participated. In a broader context, this principle suggests that for any global rule of international law to exist, the participation or acquiescence of certain states—those whose interests are specially affected—is virtually mandatory. It would thus follow logically that in any assessment of authority, special weight should be given to the views of these states. An example may serve to illustrate. Let us suppose some states claim it is a rule of international law that states launching spacecraft have to file copies of the flight plan with the Secretary-General of the United Nations. If 188 states have expressed strong indications that the rule is authoritative, but the United States and Russia—traditionally two of the major actors in space travel—do not believe that the putative rule is required by law, the authority accorded to that would-be rule is exceedingly low.

3. How significant are the manifestations of authority? Not only is it critical that there be many manifestations of authority coming from nearly all members of the international community, these manifestations of authority must also be *significant*.[91] If a lower-level State Department official sends a cable claiming that a particular behavior reflects the law, that is a manifestation of authority. But if the president of the United States issues an Executive Order contending that this behavior is the law, that is a more significant manifestation of authority. Needless to say, the more significant the manifestations of authority, the greater the overall authority of the putative legal rule.

Another factor that affects significance relates to the frequency of both formal and informal manifestations of authority. The more frequent the manifestations, the easier it is to conclude that the putative rule is authoritative. If, for example, states issue memoranda on a monthly basis that support a particular rule relating to transit passage, an observer would be more secure in pronouncing the rule to be authoritative than a case where such memoranda came infrequently. Accordingly, the scholar should factor in frequency when making judgments about the significance of the manifestations.

4. Are there contrary manifestations of authority? A final question that can be used to examine the authority of a particular rule relates to what might be called "contrary manifestations" of authority. It is possible that there may be many indications that a particular rule is authoritative and, at the same time, various manifestations that a rule is not authoritative. For example, there may be numerous formal and other manifestations of authority supporting the existence of a rule prohibiting the use of force to collect contract debts of nationals abroad.[92] But even as states are proclaiming the authoritativeness of this rule, they may be sending other signals that it is permissible to use force for this purpose. Hence, there may be treaties and presidential statements declaring that it is illegal to use force to resolve these debts *and* memoranda and other presidential speeches that express a belief that is it is permissible to use force to recover contract debts. If this were the case, these contrary examples would detract, and perhaps cancel out, the positive examples of authority. Because states frequently send mixed signals of this kind, it is important that the scholar be certain to look for such contrary manifestations of authority.

Control. In order for a would-be legal rule to be a genuine rule of international law, it must have authority *and* control. Not only must the decision-making elites perceive the rule to be law, but also the rule must be reflected in state practice. The rule must be controlling of state behavior. But how can a scholar measure control? What indicators exist to enable an observer to determine if a rule is, in fact, reflected in practice? As with authority, I believe that there are several questions that a scholar or practitioner can ask that will provide a rough indication of the control enjoyed by a putative legal rule.

1. Are there violations of the rule? If so, how many? The most basic question that the scholar should ask relates to violations of the putative rule. If there are frequent and widespread violations of a particular "rule," it is very difficult to conclude that the rule is truly controlling of state behavior. If a rule purports to prohibit the arresting of diplomats, but an examination of state practice indicates that diplomats are frequently arrested, the rule is not really controlling. Conversely, if there are no violations of a particular rule, then the rule is controlling; it is reflected in practice.

2. How universal are the violations of the rule? If one state violates a particular rule with great frequency, the rule may still have a large degree of control provided the violations are not widespread throughout the international community. The scholar must, therefore, inquire about the universality of violations. How many different states in the international system violate the rule? And, most important, the scholar must ask if the states "whose interests are specially affected" by the rule comply. If these states do not follow the rule, this behavior would indicate that the control of that rule was very low.

3. How serious are the violations of the rule? A final criterion that can be used to evaluate the control of a would-be rule is the seriousness of the violation.[93] If one U.S. marine stationed at Guantanamo Base shoots, without being provoked, at Cuban nationals walking outside the base, that is a violation of a rule of law. But this single action should not count the same as a concerted action by the entire contingent of American forces at the base to attack civilians outside the base.

Conclusion

This methodology set offers, I believe, several advantages. First, it is firmly based on the notion that international legal rules are created through the consent of states. The authority-control test allows the investigator to gage both the degree to which states have accepted the legitimacy of the putative rule and have put it into practice. As such, the test avoids the teleological element present in the New Haven approach. Second, the methodology provides a guide that scholars and others can use to provide a rough numerical valuation of authority and control. At present, scholars have no explicit way of weighing authority and control. Accordingly, scholarly analysis reflects a scholar's "feeling" that a particular rule has a certain amount of authority or control. . . .

Notes

1. See Georg Schwarzenberger, *The Inductive Approach to International Law* 9–13 (1965).
2. Speaking of natural law writers in general, Professor Schwarzenberger observes that their treatises contained "quotations from the Bible, Church Fathers, classical writers, mythology, history, and State practice." Id. at 11.
3. Id. at 13.
4. Schwarzenberger speaks of the "raw material of international law." Georg Schwarzenberger, *The Inductive Approach to International Law,* at 33.
5. Id. at 5. Professors McDougal, Lasswell, and Reisman explain that positivism, or what they call "analyticalism," focuses principally upon the strict application of a variety of rules emanating from fixed authoritative sources and holds that the appropriate function of jurisprudence, even at its loftiest levels, is the syntactic clarification of the interrelations of such rules." Myres S. McDougal, Harold D. Lasswell & W. Michael Reisman, Theories about International Law: Prologue to a Configurative Jurisprudence, reprinted in Myres S. McDougal & W. Michael Reisman, *International Law Essays* 43, 92 (1981).
6. McDougal, Lasswell & Reisman, Theories about International Law, at 92.
7. Hans Kelsen, *Principles of International Law* 305 (1952).
8. Id. at 342.
9. It is interesting to note that in the 1969 Vienna Convention of the Law of Treaties, the term *rebus sic stantibus* is not used. Instead, that convention refers

only to a "fundamental change of circumstances." Vienna Convention on the Law of Treaties, art. 62.

10. Hans Kelsen, *Principles of International Law,* at 359.

11. Id.

12. Id. at 360.

13. Id.

14. Prosper Weill, Towards Relative Normativity?, at 430.

15. Id. at 425.

16. Id. at 427.

17. Id.

18. Id. at 417.

19. Id.

20. See his comments in one Hersch Lauterpacht, *Collected Papers* 56–58 (1970), where he expresses his reservations about positivism.

21. Id. at 61.

22. Hans Kelsen, *Principles of International Law,* at 307. Kelsen, of course, recognizes that "the frequency of conduct, the fact that certain actions or abstentions have repeatedly been performed during a certain period of time, is only one element of the law-creating fact called custom." Id. *Opinio juris* is the "second element." Id.

23. Hersch Lauterpacht, *Collected Papers,* at 61.

24. Id.

25. Hans Kelsen, *Principles of International Law,* at 304.

26. Id. at 305–307.

27. Id. at 395.

28. Id. at 394.

29. Id.

30. Id.

31. H. C. Gutteridge, 21 *British Yearbook of International Law* 5 (1944), cited in Georg Schwarzenberger, *The Inductive Approach to International Law,* at 36–37.

32. U.N. Charter, art. 2, para. 4 (1945).

33. This is the thesis of Anthony Clark Arend & Robert J. Beck, *International Law and the Use of Force: Beyond the Charter Paradigm* (1993).

34. This is the claim made by Professor Edward Gordon. For example, Gordon explains that "The rule embodied in Article 2 (4) is not just a freestanding rule of customary law; it is also a formal treaty obligation. States may withdraw their consent to be bound by treaty obligations, but may not simply walk away from them." Edward Gordon, Article 2 (4) in Historical Context, 10 *Yale J. Int'l* 271, 275 (1985). Gordon argues: "The existence of an operational code [which I take to mean 'state practice'] different from the formal commitment may be cause for withdrawing state consent, but it does not supplant the process for withdrawing consent called for by the treaty or treaty law generally." Id.

35. See Graham C. Lilly, Law Schools without Lawyers: Winds of Change in Legal Education, 81 *Va. L. Rev.* 1451 (1995) ("The 'policy-science' of Myres McDougal and Harold Lasswell, once in the limelight, is now a distant memory.").

36. This is a point often made by Professor William V. O'Brien.

37. Myres S. McDougal & Harold D. Lasswell, The Identification and Appraisal of Diverse Systems of Public Order, reprinted in *International Law Essays,* at 15, 20.

38. Id. at 20.

39. Id.

40. Id.

41. Id.

42. Id. at 21–22.

43. Id. at 22.

44. Id.

45. John Norton Moore, Prolegomenon to the *Jurisprudence* of Myres McDougal and Harold Lasswell, 54 *VA L. Rev.* 662, 666 (1968).

46. Id.

47. John Norton Moore makes a similar argument.

48. Myres S. McDougal & Harold D. Lasswell, The Identification and Appraisal of Diverse Systems of Public Order, at 22.

49. Id.

50. Myres S. McDougal, Harold D. Lasswell & W. Michael Reisman, The World Constitutive Process of Authoritative Decision, reprinted in *International Law Essays,* at 191, 192.

51. Id.

52. Id.

53. Myres S. McDougal, Harold D. Lasswell & W. Michael Reisman, Theories about International Law, at 56.

54. Myres S. McDougal, Harold D. Lasswell & W. Michael Reisman, The World Constitutive Process of Authoritative Decision, reprinted in *International Law Essays,* at 191 (emphasis added).

55. Id.

56. This argument has been made elsewhere. Anthony Clark Arend & Robert J. Beck, *International Law and the Use of Force,* at 206–207.

57. Anthony D'Amato, *International Law: Process and Prospect* 11–12 (1987).

58. Myres S. McDougal & Harold D. Lasswell, The Identification and Appraisal of Diverse Systems of Public Order, at 38.

59. Id.

60. Myres S. McDougal, Harold D. Lasswell & W. Michael Reisman, The World Constitutive Process of Authoritative Decision, at 191.

61. Myres S. McDougal & Harold D. Lasswell, The Identification and Appraisal of Diverse Systems of Public Order, at 39.

62. Id.

63. Id.

64. Id.

65. Myres S. McDougal, Harold D. Lasswell & W. Michael Reisman, The World Constitutive Process of Authoritative Decision, at 191. Id.

66. Id. at 192

67. John Norton Moore, Prolegomenon to the *Jurisprudence,* at 666.

68. Myres S. McDougal & Harold D. Lasswell, The Identification and Appraisal of Diverse Systems of Public Order, at 39.

69. Myres S. McDougal, Some Basic Theoretical Concepts about International Law: A Policy Oriented Framework, in two Richard A. Falk & Saul Mendlovitz, eds., *The Strategy of World Order: International Law* 129 (1966) (emphasis added).

70. Professor Trimble notes this aspect of the New Haven approach. Phillip R. Trimble, International Law, World Order, and Critical Legal Studies, 42 *Stan. L. Rev* 811, 815–818 (1990).

71. Friedrich V. Kratochwil, *Rules, Norms, and Decisions* 1995 (1989).

72. Id.

73. Id.

74. Id. at 196–197.

75. This section draws upon the critiques of the new Haven School found in Friedrich V. Kratochwil *Rules, Norms, and Decisions,* at 193–200, and Philip R. Trimble, International Law, World Order, and Critical Legal Studies.

76. Myres S. McDougal & Harold D. Lasswell, The Identification and Appraisal of Diverse Systems of Public Order, at 24.

77. Id.

78. Id. at 19.

79. Friedrich V. Kratochwil, *Rules, Norms, and Decisions,* at 197.

80. Id.

81. See Robert J. Lieber, *No Common Power* (3rd ed. 1995).

82. This approach has been applied in some of our previous work. See Anthony Clark Arend & Robert J. Beck, *International Law and the Use of Force,* at 9–10; Anthony Clark Arend, International Law and the Recourse to Force 27 *Stan J. Int'l L.* 1 (1990).

83. In the *South West Africa* case, the International Court of Justice made the same point:

> Throughout this case it has been suggested, directly and indirectly, that humanitarian considerations are sufficient in themselves to generate legal rights and obligations, and that the Court can and should proceed accordingly. The Court does not think so. It is a court of law, and can take account of moral principles only in so far as these are given sufficient expression in legal forms.

South West Africa Case, 1966 I.C.J. 6, 34. See also Anthony A. D'Amato, *The Concept of Custom in International Law* 77 (1971) for a discussion of this point.

84. Interestingly enough, Hans Morgenthau Raises this criticism of positivism. Hans Morgenthau, Positivism, Functionalism, and International Law, 34 *Am. J. Int'l L.* 260–84 (1940).

85. I am grateful to Professor Don Piper of the University of Maryland who presented this critique of this argument.

86. Previously, I have made the argument that *rebus sic stantibus* is such a general principle of international law. After reflection, I am less inclined to believe this. Even though scholars such as Hedley Bull have argued in favor of this concept as a constitutive principle of the international legal system, the efforts by the international community in recent years to greatly limit the application of this doctrine indicate that it probably does not have this status. Michael Akehurst, for example, has noted the degree to which this doctrine was previously regarded. He explains that "in previous centuries writers tried to explain this rule by saying that every treaty contained an implied term that it should remain in force only as long as circumstances remained the same (*rebus sic stantibus*) as at the time of conclusion." Michael Akehurst, *A Modern Introduction to International Law* 140 (6th ed. 1992). But, Akehurst continues, "such an explanation must be rejected, because it is based on a fiction, and because it exaggerates the scope of the rule." Id. "In modern times," Akehurst explains, "it is agreed that the rule applies only in the most exceptional circumstances; otherwise it could be used as an excuse to evade all sorts of inconvenient treaty obligations." Id.

87. In this case, it should be noted, treaties are being used as one indicator of authority. This is similar to the way in which treaties were cited by the United States Supreme Court in the *Paqueta Habana* case. In that case, the Court was attempting to determine the legal rule dealing with the seizure of fishing vessels that was binding

on the United States and Spain. Since there was no bilateral or multilateral treaty on this issue to which Spain and the United States were parties, the Court had to establish if there were a rule of customary international law. In an effort to make that determination, one thing the Court cited was various other bilateral and multilateral treaties in an effort to evince practice. Similarly, I am suggesting that treaties can be used as examples of formal manifestations of authority in the determination of a rule of general international law. If a scholar is trying to determine the law for a particular state or group of states, a treaty to which those states are party is, as noted earlier, a prima facie indicator of the rule between those states. Nonetheless, the authority and control of that rule should also be tested as explained above.

88. The International Court of Justice upheld the concept of less-than-universal international law in the *Asylum* case. *Asylum Case* (Columbia v. Peru), 1950 *I.C.J.* 266.

89. In the *North Sea Continental Shelf* cases, the International Court of Justice refers to the need for "widespread" practice. *North Sea Continental Shelf Cases* (Fed. Reep. Ger. V. Den.), 1969 *I.C.J.* 3, at para. 73.

90. *North Sea Continental Shelf Cases*, 1969 *I.C.J.* 3, at para. 74.

91. I am most grateful to an anonymous reviewer for bringing this factor to my attention. I draw here upon his or her comments on an earlier draft of this book.

92. I was inspired by Professor Martha Finnemore to use this example.

93. This factor was also raised by an anonymous review of an earlier draft of this work.

3

Hard and Soft Law
in International Governance

KENNETH W. ABBOTT AND DUNCAN SNIDAL

CONTEMPORARY INTERNATIONAL RELATIONS ARE LEGALIZED TO AN IMPRES-
sive extent, yet international legalization displays great variety. A few international institutions and issue-areas approach the theoretical ideal of hard
legalization, but most international law is "soft" in distinctive ways. Here
we explore the reasons for the widespread legalization of international governance and for this great variety in the degrees and forms of legalization.[1]
We argue that international actors choose to order their relations through
international law and design treaties and other legal arrangements to solve
specific substantive and political problems. We further argue that international actors choose softer forms of legalized governance when those
forms offer superior institutional solutions. We analyze the benefits and
costs of different types of legalization and suggest hypotheses regarding the
circumstances that lead actors to select specific forms. . . .

We begin by examining the advantages of hard legalization. The term
hard law as used in this special issue refers to legally binding obligations
that are precise (or can be made precise through adjudication or the issuance
of detailed regulations) and that delegate authority for interpreting and
implementing the law. Although hard law is not the typical international
legal arrangement, a close look at this institutional form provides a baseline
for understanding the benefits and costs of all types of legalization. By using
hard law to order their relations, international actors reduce transactions
costs, strengthen the credibility of their commitments, expand their available
political strategies, and resolve problems of incomplete contracting. Doing

---

Excerpt from Kenneth W. Abbott and Duncan Snidal, "Hard and Soft Law in International Governance," *International Organization* 54:3 (summer 2000), pp.
421–456. Copyright 2000 by the IO Foundation and the Massachusetts Institute of
Technology.

so, however, also entails significant costs: hard law restricts actors' behavior and even their sovereignty.

While we emphasize the benefits and costs of legalization from a rational perspective focused on interests, law simultaneously engages normative considerations. In addition to requiring commitment to a background set of legal norms[2]—including engagement in established legal processes and discourse—legalization provides actors with a means to instantiate normative values. Legalization has effect through normative standards and processes as well as self-interested calculation, and both interests and values are constraints on the success of law. We consider law as both "contract" and "covenant" to capture these distinct but not incompatible characteristics. Indeed, we reject vigorously the insistence of many international relations specialists that one type of understanding is antithetical to the other.

The realm of "soft law" begins once legal arrangements are weakened along one or more of the dimensions of obligation, precision, and delegation. This softening can occur in varying degrees along each dimension and in different combinations across dimensions. We use the shorthand term soft law to distinguish this broad class of deviation from hard law—and, at the other extreme, from purely political arrangements in which legalization is largely absent. But bear in mind that soft law comes in many varieties; the choice between hard law and soft law is not a binary one.

Soft law has been widely criticized and even dismissed as a factor in international affairs. Realists, of course, focus on the absence of an independent judiciary with supporting enforcement powers to conclude that all international law is soft—and therefore only window dressing. But some international lawyers dismiss soft international law from a more normative perspective. Prosper Weil, for example argues that increasing use of soft law "might destabilize the whole international normative system and turn it into an instrument that can no longer serve its purpose."[3] Others justify soft law only as an interim step toward harder and therefore more satisfactory legislation. The implication is that soft law—law that "falls short" on one or more of the three dimensions of legislation—is a failure.

We argue, in contrast, that international actors often deliberately choose softer forms of legalization as a superior institutional arrangement. To be sure, soft law is sometimes designed as a way station to harder legalization, but often it is preferable on its own terms. Soft law offers many of the advantages of hard law, avoids some of the costs of hard law, and has certain independent advantages of its own.[4] Importantly because one or more of the elements of legalization can be relaxed, softer legalization is often easier to achieve than hard legalization. This is especially true when the actors are states that are jealous of their autonomy and when the issue at hand challenges state sovereignty. Soft legalization also provides certain benefits not available under hard legalization. It offers more effective ways to deal with uncertainty, especially when it initiates processes that allow actors to learn about the impact of agreements over time.[5] In addition, soft law facilitates compromise, and thus mutually beneficial cooperation, between actors with different interests and values, different time horizons and discount rates, and different degrees of power.

The specific forms of soft law chosen reflect the particular problems actors are trying to solve. While our analysis focuses on softness in general, different forms of softness may be more acceptable or more efficacious in different circumstances. We suggest a number of variables—including transaction costs, uncertainty, implications for national sovereignty, divergence of preferences, and power differentials—that influence which forms of soft law, which combinations of obligation, precision, and delegation, are likely to be selected in specific circumstances. . . .

We employ a range of examples, to illustrate the wide variety of international legal arrangements. Although these examples do not provide a true empirical test of our arguments, they do provide evidence for their plausibility. To characterize our examples economically along the hard law/soft law continuum, we use the notation [O,P,D]. The elements of each triplet refer to the level of obligation, precision, and delegation, respectively. Variations along each dimension are indicated by capital letters for high levels (for example, O), small letters for moderate levels (for example, o), and dashes for low levels (-). Thus [O,P,D] indicates an arrangement that is highly legalized on all three dimensions and therefore constitutes "hard law"; [o,P,-] indicates an issue that has a moderate level of legal obligation coupled with high precision but very limited delegation; and [O,-,-] indicates an issue with high legal obligation but very low precision and very limited delegation. Although this tripartite categorization remains somewhat coarse, it suggests the continuous gradations of hardness and softness that are blurred when the hard law/soft law distinction is incorrectly taken as binary.

Rationales for Hard Law

Credible Commitments

The difficulty states have in credibly committing themselves to future behavior is widely viewed as a characteristic feature of international "anarchy" and an impediment to welfare-enhancing cooperation. In contracting theory, credible commitments are crucial when one party to an agreement must carry out its side of the bargain before other parties are required to perform, or more generally when some parties must make relation-specific investments in reliance on future performance by others. . . .[6]

Other assurance issues appear when one begins to disaggregate the state. For one thing, relation-specific investments can be political as well as material: a government offering economic or political concessions in return for human rights pledges, for example, would suffer domestic political costs if the other party reneged; it would therefore demand credible assurances. The government making those pledges might also wish to enhance credibility for internal purposes; to bind its successors in office or other branches of government, or to strengthen its citizens' incentives to adjust their practices and attitudes. . . .

In domestic societies, legal commitments are credible because aggrieved parties can enforce them, with the power of the state if necessary. Even "hard" international law falls short of this standard: international regimes do not even attempt to establish legal obligations centrally enforceable against states.[7] Yet it is erroneous to conclude that the "formal legal status" of international agreements is therefore meaningless. Legalization is one of the principal methods by which states can increase the credibility of their commitments.[8]

One way legalization enhances credibility is by constraining self-serving auto-interpretation. Precision of individual commitments, coherence between individual commitments and broader legal principles, and accepted modes of legal discourse and argument all help limit such opportunistic behavior. Granting interpretive authority to courts or other legal institutions further constrains auto-interpretation.[9] Another way legalization enhances credibility is by increasing the costs of reneging. Regime scholars argue that agreements are strengthened when they are linked to a broader regime: violating an agreement that is part of a regime entails disproportionate costs, because the reputational costs of reneging apply throughout the regime. Legal commitments benefit from similar effects, but they involve international law as a whole in addition to any specific regime.

When a commitment is cast as hard law, the reputational effects of a violation can be generalized to all agreements subject to international law, that is, to most international agreements.[10] There are few alternatives to legalization when states wish to identify undertakings as reliable commitments. Alternatives like bonding and escrow are much more costly. In addition, international law provides the very foundations of statehood: principles of sovereignty, recognition, territorial competence, nonintervention, and so on. Violations weaken the international legal system and are self-defeating, at least over time.

More concretely, legalization enhances (albeit modestly) the capacity for enforcement. First, hard legal commitments, $[O,P,D]$ or $[O,p,D]$, are interpreted and applied by arbitral or judicial institutions, like those associated with the European Union (EU), the European human rights regime or the World Trade Organization (WTO). (Softer commitments may be invoked in political institutions.) Because legal review allows allegations and defenses to be tested under accepted standards and procedures, it increases reputational costs if a violation is found. The EU may currently be experiencing such aggravated costs as a result of the repeated negative legal rulings by WTO dispute settlement bodies in litigation over European restrictions on imports of hormone-treated beef (for which the EU was unable to demonstrate a legitimate scientific justification) and bananas.

Second, the law of state responsibility fixes consequences for legal violations. In particular, like some legalized regimes (such as the WTO), it authorizes proportional "countermeasures" where other remedies are unavailable. This legitimizes retaliation and clarifies its intent, reducing the costs and risks of self-help. Third, even international law can draw on some forms of centralized enforcement, through institutions like the UN Security Council and the international financial institutions.

Other interest-based costs of legal violations arise because international legal commitments often become part of domestic law. As John K. Setear points out, for example, Congress has provided that violations of the Whaling Convention and the Convention on International Trade in Endangered Species (CITES) constitute violations of U.S. law, carrying criminal penalties.[11] Ellen L. Lutz and Kathryn Sikkink further describe how international rules condemning torture and other atrocities have been characterized as customary international law and applied by U.S. courts.[12] When international commitments are incorporated into domestic law, the level of delegation associated with them rises dramatically (though it evokes weaker concern for national sovereignty): the commitments can now be applied by well-established systems of courts and administrative agencies; private actors can often initiate legal proceedings; and lawyers have incentives to invoke the rules. When supranational bodies like the European Court of Justice (ECJ) have also been granted legal authority, they can nurture "partnerships" with their domestic counterparts, strengthening both institutions.[13]

Domesticated commitments can more easily be enforced against private persons and their assets. A striking example is the litigation against General Pinochet, which was initiated by a Spanish magistrate enforcing international conventions banning torture and other atrocities that had become part of Spanish law. Although the British House of Lords ruled that Pinochet could not be held responsible for most of the charges against him, it did hold him answerable for acts committed after the torture convention had been incorporated into British law.

Legal commitments mobilize legally oriented interest and advocacy groups, such as the organized bar, and legitimize their participation in domestic decision making. They also expand the role of legal bureaucracies within foreign offices and other government agencies. Finally, so long as domestic actors understand legal agreements to be serious undertakings, they will modify their plans and actions in reliance on such commitments, increasing the audience costs of violations.

Legalization also increases the costs of violation through normative channels. Violation of a legal commitment entails reputational costs—again generalizable to all legal commitments—that reflect distaste for breaking the law. International law reinforces this effect through its strong emphasis on compliance (*pacta sum servanda* and the principle of good faith).[14] To the extent that states (or certain states) see themselves as members of an international society structured by international law, reputational effects may be even broader.[15] Law observance is even more highly valued in most domestic societies; efforts to justify international violations thus create cognitive dissonance and increase domestic audience costs.

Legal obligations are widely perceived as having particular legitimacy. In Thomas Franck's words, legitimacy creates an independent "compliance pull."[16] Individuals, government agencies, and other organizations internalize rules so that the advantages and disadvantages of compliance need not be recalculated each time they are invoked. Franck argues that the legitimacy of rules varies according to certain substantive qualities—determinacy and coherence, among other properties—and the procedures by which they were approved. Legal rules are often strong on these dimensions: relatively precise, internally consistent, and adopted through formalized and often elaborate procedures.

Legalization entails a specific form of discourse, requiring justification and persuasion in terms of applicable rules and pertinent facts, and emphasizing factors such as text, precedents, analogies, and practice. Legal discourse largely disqualifies arguments based solely on interests and preferences. The nature of this discourse affords legal professionals a prominent role. When authority is delegated to adjudicative institutions, proceedings can be highly formalized, Even without strong delegation, however, this discourse imposes some constraint on state action: governments will incur reputational costs within the legal community, and often beyond, if they act without a defensible position or without reasonable efforts to justify their conduct in legal terms.

Certain hypotheses regarding the independent variables that lead states to use hard law can be distilled from this analysis. First, states should use hard legal commitments as assurance devices when the benefits of cooperation are great but the potential for opportunism and its costs are high. These conditions are most likely in "contracts," such as trade or investment agreements, that include reciprocal commitments and nonsimultaneous performance. But they may also appear in "covenants"—such as environmental or labor agreements—when violations would impose significant externalities on others. Opportunism is less significant in coordination situations, where agreements are largely self-enforcing.[17] Indeed, international coordination standards are often voluntary, [-,P,d], and are created through institutions in which private actors have a significant role. Opportunism, and thus international legalization, is also less significant in settings where national actions have few external effects.[18]

Second, states should use hard legalization to increase the credibility of commitments when noncompliance is difficult to detect, as in most arms control situations. Legal arrangements often include centralized or decentralized monitoring provisions as an aspect of delegation. Even apart from these, however, legal commitments compensate in part for the reduced likelihood of detection by increasing the costs of detected violations.

Third, states should find hard law of special value when forming "clubs" of sincerely committed states, like the EU and NATO. Here legalization functions as an *ex ante* sorting device: because hard legal commitments impose greater costs on violators, a willingness to make them identifies one as having a low propensity to defect. Conversely, hard legalization is less significant in looser groupings like the Asia-Pacific Economic Cooperation forum (APEC), described by Miles Kahler that are not pursuing deep cooperation and thus do not require *ex ante* evidence of a sincere commitment from members.[19]

Fourth, looking within the state, executive officials should look to hard international law to commit other domestic agencies (especially legislatures) or political groups when those officials are able to make international agreements with little interference or control, and when their preferences differ significantly from those of competing power centers. In this perspective, domestic politics and constitutional law are significant explanatory variables.

Finally, as a secondary hypothesis, legal commitments should be more credible when made by states with particular characteristics. Externally, participation in other international legal regimes should enhance credibility: it exposes states to greater reputational costs and makes them more vulnerable to countermeasures. Internally, strong domestic legal institutions and traditions should enhance credibility. Many of the special costs of violating legal commitments stem from these characteristics.

Reducing Transactions Costs

On balance, at least, hard legalization reduces the transactions costs of subsequent interactions.[20] Two types of interactions are especially relevant: one is the "managerial" process of applying and elaborating agreed rules; the other is the more adversarial process of enforcing commitments. The role of international regimes in reducing transactions costs—especially the costs of negotiating supplementary agreements—has been extensively analyzed.[21] That literature has not, however, distinguished legalization from other institutional forms.[22]

Consider the need to "manage" the application and evolution of agreements. With virtually all agreements, even those that are quite precise, provisions must be interpreted, applied to specific fact situations, and elaborated to resolve ambiguities and address new and related issues. Delegation to courts and other legal institutions is one important way states address these problems; we discuss delegation later in connection with incomplete contracts. Even where delegation is weak—for example, [O,p,d] or [O,p,-]—legalization facilitates interpretation, application, and elaboration by setting relatively clear bounds on dispute resolution and negotiation. Substantively, legalization implies that proposals for resolving disputes and for new or expanded rules must be integrated with existing norms. They should be compatible with settled rules if possible, so that bargains need not be reopened. In any case they should be compatible with the basic principles of the relevant regime, so that legal coherence is maintained.

Procedurally, hard law constrains the techniques of dispute settlement and negotiation when delegation is relatively low, legalization implies that most disputes and questions of interpretation should be addressed through specialized procedures, operated primarily by legal professionals using professional modes of discourse. Even when directly negotiated solutions are permitted, the existence of legal institutions means that states will bargain "in the shadow" of anticipated legal decisions. When legal rules are in effect, moreover, unauthorized coercive behavior is generally seen as illegitimate. It is no coincidence that legalization in the WTO was explicitly tied to a requirement that member states resolve their trade disputes through the new dispute settlement procedures, not through unilateral determinations and responses—a provision aimed directly at the coercive tactics of the United States under Section 301. Even hard international law is not foolproof, of course; the principles discussed here may be ignored in practice, especially by powerful states. Nonetheless, on the whole legalization remains an effective device for organizing ongoing interactions.

Consider next the need to "enforce" commitments. The previous section examined how legalization helps states increase the credibility of their own commitments. But legalization is also significant from the perspective of the states (and other actors) that have worked to obtain commitments from others, often in the face of strong resistance. We refer to such parties as "demandeurs." Whenever there are incentives for noncompliance with international commitments, demandeurs will seek ways to forestall or respond to violations by others.

As discussed earlier, hard legalization offers a rich assortment of international and domestic institutions and procedures and normative and reputational arguments for actors in this position. Compared to alternatives like frequent renegotiation, persuasion, or coercion, it materially reduces the costs of enforcement. Other things being equal, assuming in particular that the substance of an agreement is acceptable, demandeurs should prefer hard legalization, especially in the form [O,P,D].[23] Of course, other things being equal, states that resist agreement or desire greater flexibility should resist hard legalization, or at least strive for [O,p,D] commitments, for these very reasons. The compromises and tradeoffs that result are discussed in the following section.

Many of the hypotheses in the previous subsection can be reformulated from the demandeur's perspective. Demandeurs should seek hard legalization (1) when the likelihood of opportunism and its costs are high, and noncompliance is difficult to detect; (2) when they wish to limit participation to those strongly committed to an agreement; and (3) when executive officials in other states have preferences compatible with those of the demandeurs, but other elites within those states have divergent preferences. Finally, demandeurs should place greatest reliance on commitments by states that participate actively in legal regimes and have strong legal institutions, professions, and traditions.

Modifying Political Strategies

As proponents of legal process theory make clear, hard legalization allows states (and other actors) to pursue different political strategies as they work to extend and enforce (or to weaken or escape) international agreements.[24] Indeed, those strategies are often unavoidable. Both demandeurs and resisters may be as concerned with these tactical attributes as with the strategic issues of credibility and enforceability.

As defined in this issue, hard law includes specialized legal institutions. Regimes of the form [O,P,D] and [O,p,D] include judicial or arbitral organs that offer the specialized procedures and techniques for addressing disputes, questions of interpretation, and instances of noncompliance. Nonjudicial institutions, as in [O,p,d] regimes, are often authorized to interpret governing instruments, issue regulations or recommendations, draft proposed conventions, and the like. . . .

Hard legal commitments are sometimes incorporated directly into the internal law of participating states; even more frequently international agreements require states to enact implementing legislation, and sometimes to establish particular implementing institutions. Domestic litigation then becomes part of the international toolkit. There may, however, be jurisdictional obstacles to litigation by state claimants. In those situations, states must engage in the subtle process of identifying, encouraging, and supporting private litigants who will advance their interests.[25] Recent scholarship analyzes the strategies that supranational judges pursue to encourage actions by private litigants and national courts that will strengthen international law.[26] National governments presumably follow parallel strategies.

We hypothesize broadly that states will be more likely to seek hard legalization when the political strategies it offers are advantageous to them. Mundane issues such as the availability of resources and trained personnel can be quite significant; the United States and other advanced industrial nations with large legal staffs should be more amenable to legalization than countries with few trained specialists. States should also favor hard legalization when they can be confident that agreements will track their preferences, for legal procedures will allow them to implement those preferences efficiently and at low political cost. This suggests that powerful states have a significant and often overlooked stake in hard legalization. And states that seek to minimize political conflict in relations with other states or in particular issue-areas should favor hard legalization, for it sublimates such conflict into legal argument.

Handling Problems of Incomplete Contracting

States sometimes attempt to write detailed agreements to constrain auto-interpretation, reduce transactions costs, and increase enforceability. But though precision has great value, it also has several problems. It may be wasteful, forcing states to plan for highly unlikely events; it may be counterproductive, introducing opaque and inconsistent provisions; it may lead to undesirable rigidity; and it may prevent agreement altogether.

In any case, writing complete contracts is extremely difficult.[27] The principal-agent literature demonstrates that asymmetric information typically makes it impossible to write an optimal contract if the agent is risk-averse. Yet even this literature assumes that one could in principle write a contract complete with respect to all possible future states of the world. In fact, given bounded rationality and the pervasive uncertainty in which states operate, they can never construct agreements that anticipate every contingency. This problem invites opportunistic behavior and discourages both relation-specific investments and value-enhancing agreements.

Delegation is often the best way to deal with incomplete contracting problems. Regimes of the form [O,p,D] are clearly designed with this purpose in mind: they utilize administrative and judicial institutions to interpret and extend broad legal principles. The Treaty of Rome, for example, authorizes the ECJ and the European Community's legislative institutions to elaborate and apply general principles of competition law, such as "concerted practices" and "distortion of competition," through individual cases and general regulations. Even [O,P,D] regimes grant significant powers to administrative organs and judicial or arbitral bodies. Although many provisions of the European Convention on Human Rights, for example, are quite detailed, the European Court of Human Rights must still apply general standards—such as "inhuman and degrading treatment" and "respect for . . . private and family life"—in situations that could not have been anticipated when the convention was drafted.

Softer regimes often include nonjudicial procedures for filling out incomplete contracts, though these normally require state consent. Hard legal regimes, in contrast, grant greater independence to judicial or arbitral bodies but require them to follow agreed upon principles and to act only on specific disputes and requests. This combination of attributes, along with the background rules and expectations of international law, simultaneously constrains and legitimates delegated authority. One can hypothesize that states will grant such authority when the anticipated gains from cooperation are large and there is reasonable consensus on general principles, but specific applications are difficult to anticipate.

The Advantages of Soft Legalization

Hard law facilitates international interactions in the many ways already discussed, but it has significant costs and limitations. In this section, we explore how softer forms of legalization provide alternative and often more desirable means to manage many interactions by providing some of the benefits of hard law at lower cost. We emphasize both rationalist concerns, such as contracting costs, and the special role soft legal rules and institutions play in promoting learning and normative processes.

Contracting Costs

A major advantage of softer forms of legalization is their lower contracting costs. Hard legalization reduces the post-agreement costs of managing and enforcing commitments, but adoption of a highly legalized agreement entails significant contracting costs.[28] Any agreement entails some negotiating costs—coming together, learning about the issue, bargaining, and so forth—especially when issues are unfamiliar or complex. But these costs are greater for legalized agreements. States normally exercise special care in negotiating and drafting legal agreements, since the costs of violation are higher. Legal specialists must be consulted; bureaucratic reviews are often lengthy. Different legal traditions across states complicate the exercise.

Approval and ratification processes, typically involving legislative authorization, are more complex than for purely political agreements. . . .

The costs of hard legalization are magnified by the circumstances of international politics. States, jealous of their sovereign autonomy, are reluctant to limit it through legalized commitments. Security concerns intensify the distributional issues that accompany any agreement, especially ones of greater magnitude or involving greater uncertainty. Negotiations are often multilateral. The scope of bargaining is often not clearly delimited, since the issues themselves are ill defined (for example, is free trade in magazines an economic issue or a cultural one?). Finally, the thinness of the international institutional context (including the low prevailing level of legalization) does little to lower the costs of agreement.

Soft legalization mitigates these costs as well. For example, states can dampen security and distributional concerns by opting for escape clauses, [o,P,d]; imprecise commitments, [O,p,d]; or "political" forms of delegation that allow them to maintain future control if adverse circumstances arise, [O,p, -]. These institutional devices protect state sovereignty and reduce the costs and risks of agreement while providing some of the advantages of legalization. Furthermore, soft legalization offers states an opportunity to learn about the consequences of their agreement. In many cases such learning processes will lower the perceived costs of subsequent moves to harder legalization.

The international nuclear regime illustrates these advantages.[29] Although fundamental nonproliferation obligations are set out in the Nuclear Non-Proliferation Treaty and other legally binding agreements, [O,P,d], many sensitive issues—such as the protection of nuclear materials—are regulated predominantly through recommendations from the International Atomic Energy Agency (IAEA), [-,P,d]. Recommendations deal with technical matters, such as inventory control and transportation, at a level of detail that would be intractable in treaty negotiations. They also address issues of domestic policy, such as the organization of national regulatory agencies and the supervision of private actors, that states might regard as too sensitive for treaty regulation. When a high level of consensus forms around an IAEA recommendation, member states may incorporate its provisions into a binding treaty—as occurred with rules on the management of spent nuclear fuel and radioactive waste—but even these treaties must usually be supplemented by recommendations on technical issues. . . .

In sum, we argue that states face tradeoffs in choosing levels of legalization. Hard agreements reduce the costs of operating within a legal framework—by strengthening commitments, reducing transactions costs, and the like—but they are hard to reach. Soft agreements cannot yield all these benefits, but they lower the costs of achieving (some) legalization in the first place. Choices along this continuum of tradeoffs determine the "hardness" of legalization, both initially and over time.

In general, we hypothesize that softer forms of legalization will be more attractive to states as contracting costs increase. This proposition should be true both for relatively mechanical costs—such as those created by large numbers of actors and rigorous national ratification procedures—and for more intensely political costs like those prevailing in negotiations with potentially strong distributional effects. In the remainder of this section, we explore the hard law/soft law tradeoff in terms of several key independent variables, each of which increases the costs of international agreement. These variables include sovereignty costs, uncertainty, divergence among national preferences, differences in time horizons and discount rates, and power differentials among major actors.

Sovereignty Costs

The nature of sovereignty costs. Accepting a binding legal obligation, especially when it entails delegating authority to a supranational body, is costly to states. The costs involved can range from simple differences in outcome on particular issues, to authority over decision making in an issue-area, to more fundamental encroachments on state sovereignty. While we recognize that the concept of "sovereignty" is broad and highly contested,[30] we use "sovereignty costs" as a covering term for all three categories of costs to emphasize the high stakes states often face in accepting international agreements. The potential for inferior outcomes, loss of authority, and diminution of sovereignty makes states reluctant to accept hard legalization—especially when it includes significant levels of delegation.

Sovereignty costs are relatively low when states simply make international legal commitments that limit their behavior in particular circumstances. States typically accept these costs in order to achieve better collective outcomes. . . . Such agreements are undoubtedly exercises of legal sovereignty. Nevertheless, even they may limit the ability of states to regulate their borders (for example, by requiring them to allow goods, capital, or people to pass freely) and to implement important domestic policies (as when free trade impinges on labor, safety, or environmental regulations), thus encroaching on other aspects of sovereignty.

Greater sovereignty costs emerge when states accept external authority over significant decisions. International agreements may implicitly or explicitly insert international actors (who are neither elected nor otherwise subject to domestic scrutiny) into national decision procedures. These arrangements may limit the ability of states to govern whole classes of issues—such as social subsidies or industrial policy—or require states to change domestic laws or governance structures. Nevertheless, the impact of such arrangements is tempered by states' ability to withdraw from international agreements—although processes of enmeshment may make it increasingly costly for them to do so.

Sovereignty costs are at their highest when international arrangements impinge on the relations between a state and its citizens or territory, the traditional hallmarks of (Westphalian) sovereignty. Of course, ordinary restrictions on domestic policies can have such effects in contemporary welfare states, but these are heightened and generalized when, for example, an international human rights regime circumscribes a state's ability to regulate its citizens. Similarly, the United States has correctly been concerned that an International Criminal Court might claim jurisdiction over U.S. soldiers participating in international peacekeeping activities or other foreign endeavors. Agreements such as the Law of the Sea Convention both redefine national territory (for example, by delineating jurisdiction over a territorial sea, exclusive economic zone, and continental shelf) and limit the capacity of states to restrict its use (for example, by establishing rights of innocent passage). Here, too, individual states retain the capacity to withdraw, but doing so may actually diminish their (legal) sovereignty, risking loss of recognition as members in good standing of the international community.

Legalization can lead to further, often unanticipated sovereignty costs over time. Even if rules are written precisely to narrow their range, or softened by including escape clauses or limiting delegation, states cannot anticipate or limit all of the possible effects.

Delegation provides the greatest source of unanticipated sovereignty costs. As Charles Lindblom points out, a grant of "authority always becomes to a degree uncontrollable."[31] Even nonjudicial organizations like the IMF or World Bank exert their independence in ways that go beyond the initial intentions or anticipations of the contracting states.[32]

The delegation of legal authority to independent domestic courts and agencies can create similar unexpected consequences. However, states generally feel they have ultimate control over domestic courts—they appoint the judges and control the justice departments that bring criminal actions—and so they find, in general, that domestic delegation has lower sovereignty costs.

Even the most powerful states recognize that legalization will circumscribe their autonomy. U.S. opposition to autonomous international institutions, whether the Enterprise in the Law of the Sea Convention, the International Criminal Court, or the UN more generally, reflects the special concern that delegation raises.[33] Even in NAFTA, where its political influence is paramount, the United States resisted delegating authority to supranational dispute settlement bodies for interstate disputes; only the Chapter 19 procedure for reviewing antidumping and countervailing duty ruling creates significant delegated authority. Congress also explicitly provided that the agreement would not be self-executing in domestic law, limiting delegation to national courts. More recently, concern that highly legalized

WTO dispute settlement institutions might expand the meaning of the Uruguay Round agreements led Congress to provide for an early review of the costs and benefits of WTO membership, including the results of legal proceedings, tied to a fast-track procedure for withdrawal from the organization. Conversely, the willingness of the United States and other countries to subscribe to more constrained institutions indicates that their benefits outweigh their sovereignty costs—at least up to a point.

The notion of sovereignty costs is more complicated when competing domestic and transnational interests affect the development of international legalization. Certain domestic groups may perceive negative sovereignty costs from international agreements that provide them with more favorable outcomes than national policy. Examples include free-trade coalitions that prefer their states' trade policies to be bound by WTO rulings rather than open to the vagaries of individual legislatures, and environmental groups that believe they can gain more from an international accord than from domestic politics. For similar reasons, although a government that anticipates staying in power may be reluctant to limit its control over an issue, a government less certain of its longevity may seek to bind its successors through international legal commitments.[34] We discuss such domestic variations in the following section.

Sovereignty costs may also be negative for external reasons, as where participation in international arrangements enhances a state's international and domestic position.[35] Key aspects of sovereignty have been codified in a variety of legal instruments, including the 1933 Montevideo Convention on the Rights and Duties of States, Article 2 of the UN Charter, and the UN General Assembly Declaration on Principles of International Law Concerning Friendly Relations Among States. Regional legal arrangements like the Organization of American States (OAS) provide much-needed support for state sovereignty. Chapter IV of the OAS Charter promotes the independence and sovereign equality of member states regardless of power differentials and protects internal sovereignty through principles of nonintervention.

Although negative sovereignty costs are an important exception, positive sovereignty costs are the more standard (and more difficult) case for international legalization. Hard legalization—especially the classic legal model with centralized judicial institutions capable of amplifying the terms of agreements in the course of resolving disputes—imposes high sovereignty costs. Thus states face tradeoffs between the benefits and sovereignty costs of different forms of legalization.

States can limit sovereignty costs through arrangements that are nonbinding or imprecise or do not delegate extensive powers. Most often, states protect themselves by adopting less precise rules and weaker legal institutions, as in the Council of Europe's framework Convention for the Protection of National Minorities, [O,p,d]. They frequently provide that member states must adhere to a special treaty protocol before a court or quasi-judicial body can assert jurisdiction over them, as in the inter-American human rights system, or that all parties to a particular dispute must consent before the case can be litigated. Still weaker forms of delegation—such the consultation arrangements characteristic of arms control agreements, [O,P,-]—limit sovereignty costs even more, coupling legal obligations with political mechanisms of control and defense. Thus soft legalization offers a variety of means—none of them perfect—by which states can limit sovereignty costs. . . .

Soft law provides a means to lessen sovereignty costs by expanding the range of available institutional arrangements along a more extensive and finely differentiated tradeoff curve. How states evaluate these trade-offs—and thus determine their preferences for different forms of legalization—depends on their own characteristics and the circumstances of particular issue-areas.

Sovereignty costs and issue type. Viewing constraints on national autonomy and sovereignty as costs that vary across issues, we hypothesize that states will prefer different forms of legalization in different issue-areas. At one extreme, sovereign costs are especially high in areas related to national security. Adversaries are extremely sensitive to unanticipated risks of agreement for the standard reasons advanced by realists, including relative gains. Even allies facing common external threats are reluctant to surrender autonomy over their security affairs. Therefore it is unsurprising that even in NATO, the most institutionalized alliance ever, delegation is moderate, [O,p,d], or that security arrangements have lagged behind other institutional developments in the EU. Similarly, bilateral arms control agreements like SALT can be very precise in specifying missile numbers and types and are unquestionably binding but are only minimally institutionalized, [O,P,-].

Political economy issues display a wide range of sovereignty costs and hence of legalization. At one extreme lie technical matters on which state interests are closely aligned, such as international transportation or food standards. Here sovereignty costs are low and the incidence of legalized agreements is correspondingly high. One even sees a significant level of delegation—including to organizations in which private actors play major roles, such as the International Organization for Standardization (ISO)—where sovereignty costs are low and technical complexity makes it hard to adapt agreements rapidly without some coordinating authority. Political economy issues like investment policy, money laundering, and security-related export controls, however, remain sensitive and have not been legalized to nearly the same extent. Similarly, tax policy, which lies at the core of all state functions but increasingly requires international coordination, is characterized by many bilateral treaties but displays little overall institutionalization.

Trade issues range between these extremes—sovereignty costs are significant but are frequently outweighed by the perceived benefits of legalized agreements. This is due partly to lesser conflicts of interest among states and partly to strong domestic support from beneficiaries of legalization. Consequently, even on a given issue, sovereignty costs can vary across states and over time. For example, the sovereignty costs of agricultural agreements are typically greater for less-developed states where the sector is larger and politically central; they have gradually decreased in OECD countries along with the relative importance of agriculture.

Finally, the most highly institutionalized arrangements, such as the EU, occur where there is a strong commitment to reducing sovereignty, or where a long process of legalized cooperation has led to institutionalization even against state resistance. The history of trade institutionalization is again instructive. In many respects, the WTO today is a stronger institution than the proposed International Trade Organization. Continued success in expanding trade under GATT changed domestic political balances and lowered the costs of further legalization. Moreover, states "learned" that harder legalization (such as a stronger dispute settlement mechanism) can produce greater benefits; they may also have been reassured regarding the dangers of enmeshment. Nevertheless, vigorous continuing disputes over the future of the WTO reflect states' continued wariness of sacrificing autonomy.

Uncertainty

Many international issues are new and complex. The underlying problems may not be well understood, so states cannot anticipate all possible consequences of a legalized arrangement. One way to deal with such problems is to delegate authority to a central party (for example, a court or international organization) to implement, interpret, and adapt the agreement as circumstances unfold. This approach avoids the costs of having no agreement, or of having to (re)negotiate continuously, but it typically entails unacceptably high sovereignty costs. Soft legalization provides a number of more attractive alternatives for dealing with uncertainty.

First, states can reduce the precision of their commitments: [O,p,d]. Of course, if they do not know the relevant contingencies, they cannot achieve the precision of hard law even if they wish to do so, except as to better-understood aspects of the problem. Thus an arms control agreement can precisely control known technologies and can even limit research into technologies whose results can reasonably be anticipated (such as testing antiballistic missile systems). But it cannot govern technologies whose military impact cannot be foreseen. And blanket limitations on all research with potential military implications would unacceptably impair the development of beneficial civilian technologies.

But uncertainty makes precision less desirable as well as less attainable. The classic distinction between risk and uncertainty is significant here. When risk is the central concern—that is, when actors cannot predict the outcome of an agreement but know the probability distribution of possible outcomes, conditional on agreement terms—precise agreements offer a way to manage and optimize risk-sharing.[36] But when circumstances are fundamentally uncertain—that is, when even the range for distribution of possible outcomes is unknown—a more precise agreement may not be desirable. In particular, if actors are "ambiguity-averse,"[37] they will prefer to leave agreements imprecise rather than face the possibility of being caught in unfavorable commitments. Unfamiliar environmental conditions like global warming provide good illustrations: because the nature, the severity, even the very existence of these threats—as well as the costs of responding to them—are highly uncertain, the imprecise commitments found in environmental "framework" agreements may be the optimal response.

A second way to deal with uncertainty is through arrangements that are precise but not legally binding, such as Agenda 21, the Forest Principles, and other hortatory instruments adopted at the 1992 Rio Conference on Environment and Development [-,P,-]. These allow states to see the impact of rules in practice and to gain their benefits, while retaining flexibility to avoid any unpleasant surprises the rules might hold. Sometimes precision is actually used to limit the binding character of obligations, as with carefully drawn exceptions or escape clauses. These also protect the parties in case the agreement turns out to have hidden costs or unforeseen contingencies, so that states are not locked into commitments they regret.

Third, although strong delegation can aggravate the uncertainty of agreements, moderate delegation—typically involving political and administrative bodies where states retain significant control—provides another way to manage uncertainty. UN specialized agencies and other international organizations, [-,p,d], play restricted administrative roles across a wide variety of issues, and a small number of (mainly financial) organizations have more significant autonomy.[38] These organizations have the capacity to provide information (and thus reduce uncertainty) and some capacity to modify and adapt rules or to initiate standards.[39] In general, however, even this level of delegation appears only in areas with low sovereignty costs, such as technical coordination. More fundamental elaboration of arrangements is typically accomplished through direct political processes. Thus arms control agreements are precise and binding but limit delegation to forums that promote political bargaining, not independent third-party decision making, [O,P,-].

Viewed dynamically, these forms of soft legalization offer strategies for individual and collective learning.[40] Consider the case where states are legally bound but in an imprecise way, as under the original Vienna Ozone

Convention, [O,p,-]. These obligations offer flexibility and protection for states to work out problems over time through negotiations shaped by normative guidelines, rather than constrained by precise rules. Hortatory rules, for example, [-,p,d], similarly provide general standards against which behavior can be assessed and support learning processes that reduce uncertainty over time. Some emerging arrangements on the rights of women and children fit this model. Agreements that are precise but nonbinding, like the Helsinki Final Act, [-,P,d], often include institutional devices such as conferences and review sessions where states can potentially deepen their commitments as they resolve uncertainties about the issue.

Indeed, moderate delegation—including international organizations that provide support for decentralized bargaining, expertise, and capacities for collecting information—may be more appropriate than adjudicative procedures (domestic or international) for adapting rules as circumstances are better understood. Examples include the numerous international agencies that recommend (often in conjunction with private actors) international standards on a range of issues, including technology, transportation, and health. Although not binding, their recommendations provide precise and compelling coordination points to which states and private actors usually adhere. In other cases, consultative committees or formal international organizations may be empowered to make rules more precise as learning occurs. Effective institutions of this sort require a certain autonomy that states may be reluctant to grant over truly important issues. . . .

In this section we have argued that soft legalization provides a rational adaptation to uncertainty. It allows states to capture the "easy" gains they can recognize with incomplete knowledge, without allowing differences or uncertainties about the situation to impede completion of the bargain. Soft legalization further provides a framework within which states can adapt their arrangement as circumstances change and can pursue "harder" gains through further negotiation. Soft law avoids the sovereignty costs associated with centralized adjudication or other strong delegation and is less costly than repeated renegotiation in light of new information.

Our discussion also suggests hypotheses as to when different forms of legalization are most likely to be used. Consider the four possible high/low combinations of uncertainty and sovereignty costs, two of the major independent variables in analysis. Where both variables are low, states will be inclined toward hard legal arrangements to efficiently manage their interactions, [O,P,D]. When sovereignty costs are high and uncertainty is low, states will be reluctant to delegate but will remain open to precise and/or binding arrangements, [O,P,-]. Conversely, if sovereignty costs are low and uncertainty is high, states will be willing to accept binding obligation and at least moderate delegation but will resist precise rules, [O,p,d]. Finally, when both uncertainty and sovereignty costs are high, legalization will focus on the statement of flexible or hortatory obligations that are neither precise nor highly institutionalized, [o,p,-] or [-,p,-]. In all these cases, legalization provides a framework with which states can work to resolve their uncertainty, making harder legalization more attractive.

Soft Law as a Tool of Compromise

Compromise at a point in time. Soft law can ease bargaining problems among states even as it opens up opportunities for achieving mutually preferred compromises. Negotiating a hard, highly elaborated agreement among heterogeneous states is a costly and protracted process. It is often more practical to negotiate a softer agreement that establishes general goals but with less precision and perhaps with limited delegation.

Soft legalization allows states to adapt their commitments to their particular situations rather than trying to accommodate divergent national circumstances within a single text. This provides for flexibility in implementation, helping states deal with the domestic political and economic consequences of an agreement and thus increasing the efficiency with which it is carried out. Accordingly, soft law should be attractive in proportion to the degree of divergence among the preferences and capacities of states, a condition that increases almost automatically as one moves from bilateral through regional to multilateral negotiations.

Flexibility is especially important when uncertainty or one sticky problem threatens to upset a larger "package deal." Rather than hold up the overall agreement, states can incorporate hortatory or imprecise provisions to deal with the difficult issues, allowing them to proceed with the rest of the bargain. The labor and environmental side agreements to NAFTA are suggestive on this point.

Softness also accommodates states with different degrees of readiness for legalization. Those whose institutions, laws, and personnel permit them to carry out hard commitments can enter agreements of that kind; those whose weaknesses in these areas prevent them from implementing hard legal commitments can accept softer forms of agreement, perhaps through exceptions, reservations, or phase-in periods. Many treaties make such special provisions for developing countries, transitional economies, and other categories of states. States may prefer such an arrangement to either a softer agreement among all or a harder agreement with limited membership. Over time, if the soft arrangements are successful and without adverse consequences, the initially reluctant states may accept harder legalization. . . .

Advantages of flexibility do not come without cost. Soft law compromises make it hard to determine whether a state is living up to its commitments and therefore create opportunities to shirk. They also weaken the ability of government to undo the agreement. Again, states face a tradeoff between the advantages of flexibility in achieving agreement and its disadvantages in ensuring performance.

States can design different elements of an agreement with different combinations of hardness to fine-tune this tradeoff on different issues. Alternative forms of delegation can be used to limit the tendencies to shirk. In some cases, international reporting requirements may be sufficient to determine whether states are meeting their commitments. Elsewhere, requirements for domestic implementation, including domestic legalization, may empower private actors like firms or NGOs to enforce the agreement.

Compromise over time. Because even soft legal agreements commit states to characterize forms of discourse and procedure, soft law provides a way of achieving compromise over time. Consider a patient state (low discount rate) that is seeking a concession but is unwilling to offer enough immediately (for example, in linkage to other issues) to induce an impatient state to offer the concession. The patient state may nevertheless be willing to make a (smaller) current payoff in return for a soft legal agreement that has some prospect of enmeshing the impatient state in a process that will deliver the concession down the road. Insofar as states find it progressively costly to extricate themselves from legal processes, soft law helps remedy the commitment problem that looms large in international relations. . . .

The longer-term consequences of soft law, including processes of learning, do mean that legal agreements have an inevitable life cycle from softer toward harder legalization. Hard law is probably more likely to evolve from soft law than from (utopian) plans to create hard law full-blown. But this does not imply that all soft legalization is a way station to hard(er) legalization, or that hard legalization is the optimal form. The contracting difficulties noted earlier may never be resolved in some issue-areas; here, the attainable soft legalization will be superior to hard law that cannot be achieved. In these cases, continuing movement toward greater legalization is neither inevitable nor necessarily desirable. . . .

States may learn from experience that even soft forms of legalization can have powerful effects over time. As states internalize this lesson, they will be more alert to the possibilities of enmeshment and evolutionary growth in other negotiations. It would not be surprising, for example, if the Helsinki experience were still informing China's position on (even soft) human rights commitments. Impatient states may be forced to accept soft legalization in order to obtain current payoffs, but they may demand a higher price.

Compromise between the weak and the strong. Soft legalization facilitates compromise between weak and powerful states. The traditional legal view is that law operates as a shield for the weak, whereas the traditional international relations view is that law acts as an instrument of the powerful. These seemingly contradictory views can be reconciled by understanding how (soft) law helps both types of states achieve their differing goals.

Whatever their views on soft law, traditional legal scholars generally agree that legalization aids weak states. Weil, a severe critic of soft law, writes that "it is [hard] law with its rigor that comes between the weak and the mighty to protect and deliver."[41] Michael Reisman, more favorable toward soft law, agrees that law advantages the weak.[42] These views echo analyses of constitutionalism as a movement to create a government of laws, not of men (or states), in order to constrain the powerful.[43] At the international level, rules ranging from general principles of nonintervention to agreements like the Nuclear Non-Proliferation Treaty can be seen as bounding the struggle for power.

For just these reasons, small and dependent states often seek hard legalization. To the extent it is effective, hard law offers protection and reduces uncertainty by demarcating the likely behavior of powerful states. Lutz and Sikkink argue that Latin American states have long seen international law as providing them with exactly this type of protection from the United States.[44] Since they have less direct control over their own fates, small states also incur lower sovereignty costs from hard legalization. Indeed hard law may entail negative sovereignty costs, enhancing international standing and offering at least formal equality. Widespread African support for postcolonial boundaries, which make little sense on ethnic, political, or economic grounds, provides a striking illustration of the value of legal arrangements to weak states.

In contrast, many international relations scholars (and some critical legal scholars) hold the more skeptical view that international law is wholly beholden to international power. Powerful states have greater control over international outcomes, are less in need of protection, and face higher sovereignty costs. They have less need for legalization and more reason to resist it, even though their adherence is crucial to its success.

For these reasons, realists see international law largely as epiphenomenal, merely reflecting the distribution of power. Institutionalists also treat power (for example, hegemony and/or a capacity for decentralized retaliation) as a primary source of order and rules in the international system. Unlike realists, however, they argue that institutions have real effects, resulting in a disjuncture between the distribution of power and benefits in the system.

These perspectives can to some extent be reconciled by understanding legalization, especially soft legalization, as furthering the goals of both classes of states. Most importantly, legally binding and relatively precise rules allow strong and weak states to regularize their asymmetric relations.

Because the continual, overt exercise of power is costly, powerful states gain by embodying their advantage in settled rules. Because weaker states are at a constant disadvantage in bargaining, they benefit from the certainty and credibility of legalized commitments. The result is not unlike an insurance contract, where a weaker party gladly pays a premium to a stronger one in return for the latter bearing, or in this case reducing, certain risks. In addition, both sides benefit by reducing the transactions costs of continual bargaining.

Of course, stronger states have disproportionate influence over the substance of agreed upon rules. But even the most powerful states cannot simply dictate the outcome of every negotiation because of the high costs of coercion. Instead, strong states must typically make the substantive content of legalized arrangements (just) attractive enough to encourage broad participation at an acceptable cost. Reduced bargaining costs normally provide ample room for such concessions.

Powerful states are most concerned with delegation, the major source of unanticipated costs. As a result, forms of legalization that involve limited delegation, for example [O,p,-] or [O,p,d], provide the crucial basis for cooperation between the weak and the strong. Lower levels of delegation prevent unexpected intrusions into the sovereign preserves of powerful countries while allowing them significant influence over decision making. Delegation to administrative bodies rather than judicial organs allows powerful states to retain control over ongoing issue management. The structure and decision-making rules of those bodies, including formal voting procedures, provide further means of balancing members' interests.

Soft legalization provides other important grounds for cooperation as well. We described earlier how legalization helps states solve commitment problems. This point becomes relevant when powerful states want small states to take actions that would leave them vulnerable. Powerful states can induce cooperation in such cases by agreeing to operate within a framework of legally binding rules and procedures, credibly constraining themselves from opportunistic behavior; with low levels of delegation, though, they can maintain predominant influence over decision making. For example, the United States ran its Gulf War operation through the UN Security Council, [O,p,d], even though doing so was burdensome, because this helped it to mobilize valuable support from weaker states, including bases in Saudi Arabia and financing from Japan. Involving the Security Council also allowed the supporting states to monitor and influence the scope of U.S. activities, notwithstanding the U.S. veto.

Finally, even without an external commitment problem, governments of weak states may find it domestically costly to be perceived as following the dictates of a powerful state. Organizing international arrangements in a legalized way, and delegating without unduly interfering with the outcomes desired by the powerful state. We have elsewhere described the role of formal international organization as vehicles for this type of "laundering. . . ."[45]

The Nuclear Non-Proliferation Treaty reflected an explicit bargain: weaker states accepted the existing nuclear oligopoly: powerful states agree to pursue weapons restraints and technology transfer. Obligation was high, though limited by escape clauses and the twenty-five-year renegotiation clause. Precision was high in limiting the transfer of military technology, but lower with regards to commercial technology transfers. Delegation to the IAEA has been largely controlled by the major powers (who monopolize the necessary expertise).

An understanding of soft legalization helps reconcile the seemingly contradictory views of the effect of law. Viewed as a process, legalization is a form of political bargaining where powerful states are advantaged. However, the efficiency gains of legalization for the powerful—cynically, providing an efficient means to extract benefits from the weak—depend on their offering the weak sufficiently satisfactory terms to induce their participation. Viewed as an outcome, legalization appears less political, since even powerful states must accept the constraints of legal principles and discourses to take advantage of legalized arrangements. Yet powerful states have the greatest influence on the substantive legal rules, and the institutions associated with (soft) international legalization are frequently constructed to ensure them a leading voice.

Conclusion

We have analyzed the spectrum of international legalization from soft informal agreements through intermediate blends of obligation, precision, and delegation to hard legal arrangements. Although even hard international law does not approach stereotypical conceptions of law based on advanced domestic legal systems, international legalization nevertheless represents a distinctive form of institutionalization. Ultimately, we can only understand the inclination of actors to cast their relations in legal form, and the variety of ways in which they do so, in terms of the value those institutional forms provide for them. Put plainly, international legalization is a diverse phenomenon because it helps a diverse universe of states and other actors resolve diverse problems.

Legalization reflects a series of tradeoffs. States are typically torn between the benefits of hard legalization—for example, mitigating commitment and incomplete contracting problems—and the sovereignty costs it entails. For their part, private actors generally seek hard legal arrangements that reflect their particular interests and values, but these demands often conflict with those of the other private actors or of governments. In settings like these, soft legalization helps balance competing considerations, offering techniques for compromise among states, among private actors, and between states and private actors. In addition, soft law helps actors handle the exigencies of uncertainty and accommodate power differentials.

Notes

1. We have profited from the insights in Keohane, Moravcsik, and Slaughter 1997, which was prepared in connection with this project.

2. The international legal system has developed over several centuries. International law includes secondary norms prescribing how primary rules are to be made, interpreted, and applied, as well as institutions through which both kinds of rules are implemented. The background legal system shapes many international interactions—indeed, it helps define the very notion of an international actor.

3. Weil, 1983, 423.

4. For a related discussion of the benefits and costs of informal agreements, see Lipson 1991.

5. We draw on Koremenos's insightful work on how states structure treaties to enable mutual learning. Koremenos 1999.

6. Williamson 1989.

7. Keohane 1984, 88–89.

8. A more extreme way to address commitment problems, analogous to the merger of firms in business relationships that raise assurance problems, is to integrate separate sovereignties into a single political unit, such as a federal state. Integration can be partial as well as complete, as the EU illustrates. Even full integration, though, cannot solve commitment and other contracting problems among the many political, economic, and other interests within and across societies.

9. Deconstructionists, of course, would contest these statements. In practice, however, even observers of this bent see law as constraining interpretation. Koskenniemi 1999.

10. Keohane observes that states can reduce the force of reputational effects by distinguishing the circumstances of a violation from those surrounding other agreements. Keohane 1995. In the nineteenth century, the United States sought in this way to distinguish its treaties with "savage" Indian Tribes, which it frequently violated, from agreements with European countries. The effort devoted to making this distinction, however, suggests that reputational effects would otherwise have spread across all legal agreements.

11. Setear 1999.

12. Lutz and Sikkink 2000.

13. See Burley and Mattli 1993; and Helfer and Slaughter 1997.

14. The rule of *pacta sunt servanda* is to some extent weakened by exceptions and defenses, notably the broad change-of-circumstances defense known as *rebus sic stantibus*. Yet these doctrines introduce needed flexibility; when they are found inapplicable, the normative force of the basic rule is enhanced.

15. See Wight 1977; Bull 1977; Hurrell 1993; and Buzan 1993.

16. Franck 1990.

17. Coordination agreements may not be self-enforcing when the benefits of moving the group to a new equilibrium are high. In these situations, especially when the gains to certain parties are large enough to make sure attempts feasible, hard law may be useful as an assurance device.

18. Abbott and Snidal 1998.

19. Kahler 1988.

20. As discussed later, the costs of reaching a fully legalized agreement are often relatively high, leading actors to adopt softer forms of legalization.

21. Keohane 1984.

22. Compare Abbott & Snidal 1998.

23. We consider later the specific forms of legalization preferred by powerful and weak states.

24. Koh 1997.

25. This reverses the process associated with more traditional institutions like the Iran-U.S. Claims Tribunal where private actors encourage governments to initiate proceedings and provide support and encouragement to government litigators.

26. See Burley and Mattli 1993; Helfer and Slaughter 1997; Alter 1998b; Garrett, Kelemen, and Schulz 1998; and Mattli and Slaughter 1998b.

27. Incomplete contracting problems arise when any agreement is negotiated under conditions of incomplete or asymmetric information, risk, and uncertainty. For a recent overview, see Hart 1995.

28. The regimes literature does not always distinguish between the costs of transacting within regimes and the costs of creating regimes. In early work, regimes are seen as the legacy of hegemony, so that their creation is not directly addressed.

29. Kellman 1998.

30. Krasner offers four meanings or categories of sovereignty: domestic sovereignty (the organization of authority and control within the state), interdependence sovereignty (the ability to control flows across borders), international legal sovereignty (establishing the status of a political entity in the international system), and Westphalian sovereignty (preventing external actors from influencing or determining domestic authority structures). Krasner 1999. These categories overlap and do not covary in any necessary pattern.

Krasner argues that sovereignty has never been immutable, although legal sovereignty has tended to be more respected than Westphalian or other types of sovereignty. Indeed, some legal purists see sovereignty as a fundamental and inviolable legal concept relating to state supremacy in making and withdrawing from international treaties. But recent legal theorists argue that such a view is untenable given ongoing developments in international legalization; they conclude that "it is time to slowly ease the term out of polite language in international relations, surely in law." See Henkin et al. 1999, 19. We skirt these conceptual debates, focusing instead on the fact that states often perceive international legalization as infringing on their sovereignty, broadly construed.

31. Lindblom 1977, 24.

32. Abbott and Snidal 1998.

33. Shapiro takes the extreme view that such developments are an inevitable part of the development of any legal system. Shapiro 1981. Our view is that the advantages of legalization exert a powerful pull in this direction but that sovereignty costs provide significant resistance; we should expect a mixed level and international legalization according to the characteristics of issues and states, at least in the foreseeable future.

34. Colombatto and Macey offer a related view in arguing that governmental agencies seek international legalization in order to protect their administrative positions at a cost to domestic groups. Colombatto and Macy 1996.

35. In Krasner's terminology, these constitute international legal and Westphalian sovereignty, respectively.

36. See Knight 1921; and Ellsberg 1963.

37. Ambiguity aversion means that actors prefer known outcomes (including the status quo) to unknown ones. When actors know the possible outcomes but do not know which of two alternative probability distributions governs them, Ellsberg characterizes ambiguity aversion as assuming that an act leads to the minimum possible expected outcome. Ellsberg 1963. In this case, agents prefer incomplete to complete contracts even at zero contracting costs. See Mukerji 1998.

38. Abbott and Snidal 1998.

39. Gold 1983.

40. For a rational approach to learning, see Morrow 1994; and Koremenos 1999. For a more constructivist approach, see Finnemore 1996. Our view is that both learning as acquiring information and learning as changing preferences or identity are relevant (and compatible) aspects of legalization.

41. Weil 1983, 442.

42. Reisman 1988, 377.

43. Lindblom 1977.

44. Lutz and Sikkink 2000.

45. Abbott and Snidal 1998.

Bibliography

Abbott, Kenneth W., and Duncan Snidal. 1998. Why States Use Formal International Organizations. *Journal of Conflict Resolution* 42 (1): 3–32.

Alter, Karen J. 1998b. Who Are the Masters of the Treaty? European Governments and the European Court of Justice. *International Organization* 52 (1):121–47.

——— 2000. International Standards and International Governance. Unpublished manuscript, University of Chicago, Chicago, Illinois.

Bull, Hedley. 1977. *The Anarchical Society: A Study of Order in World Politics.* New York: Columbia University Press.

Burley, Anne-Marie, and Walter Mattli. 1993. Europe Before the Court: A Political Theory of Legal Integration. *International Organization* 47 (1): 41–76.

Buzan, Barry. 1993. From International System to International Society: Structural Realism and Regime Theory Meet the English School. *International Organization* 47: 327–52.

Colombatto, Enrico, and Jonathan R. Macey. 1996. A Public Choice Model of International Economic Cooperation and the Decline of the Nation State. *Cardozo Law Review* 18: 925–56.

Ellsberg, Daniel. 1963. Risk, Ambiguity, and the Savage Axioms. *Quarterly Journal of Economics* 75 (4): 643–69.

Finnemore, Martha. 1996. *National Interests in International Society.* Ithaca, N.Y.: Cornell University Press.

Franck, Thomas M. 1990. *Power of Legitimacy Among Nations.* New York: Oxford University Press.

Garret, Geoffrey, R. Daniel Kelemen, and Heiner Schulz. 1998. The European Court of Justice, National Governments, and Legal Integration in the European Union. *International Organization* 52 (1): 149–76.

Gold, Joseph. 1983. Strengthening the Soft International Law of Exchange Arrangements. *American Journal of International Law* 77: 443–89.

Hart, Oliver. 1995. *Firms, Contracts, and Financial Structure.* Oxford: Oxford University Press.

Helfer, Laurence, and Anne-Marie Slaughter. 1997. Toward a Theory of Effective Supranational Adjudication. *Yale Law Journal* 107 (2): 273–391.
Henkin, Louis, Gerald L. Neuman, Diane F. Orentlicher, and David W. Leebron. 1999. *Human Rights.* New York: Foundation Press.
Hurrell, Andrew. 1993. International Society and the Study of Regimes: A Reflective Approach. In *Regime Theory and International Relations,* edited by Volker Rittberger, 49–72. Oxford: Oxford University Press.
Kahler, Miles. 1988. Organizing the Pacific. In *Pacific-Asian Economic Policies and Regional Interdependence,* edited by Robert A. Scalapino, Seizaburo Sato, Jusuf Wanandi, and Sung-joo Han, 329–50. Berkeley: Institute of Asian Studies.
Kellman, Barry. 1998. Protection of Nuclear Materials. Paper prepared for meeting of American Society of Law Project on Compliance with Soft Law, 8–10 October, Baltimore, Md.
Keohane, Robert O. 1984. *After Hegemony: Cooperation and Discord in the World Political Economy.* Princeton, N.J.: Princeton University Press.
———. 1995. Contested Commitments and Commitment Pathways: United States Foreign Policy, 1783–1989. Paper presented at annual meeting of International Studies Association, 21–25 February, Chicago.
Keohane, Robert O., Andrew Moravcsik, and Anne-Marie Slaughter. 1997. Toward a Theory of Legalization. Paper presented at the Conference on International Law and Domestic Politics, 4–7 June, St. Helena, Calif.
Knight, Frank H. 1921. *Risk, Uncertainty, and Profit.* Boston: Houghton Mifflin.
Koh, Harold Hongju. 1997. Why Do Nations Obey International Law? *Yale Law Journal* 106: 2598–2659.
Koremenos, Barbara. 1999. On the Duration and Renegotiation of International Agreements. Ph.D. diss., University of Chicago.
Koskenniemi, Martti. 1999. Letters to the Editors of the Symposium (Symposium on Method in International Law). *American Journal of International Law* 93: 351–61.
Krasner, Stephen D. 1999. *Sovereignty: Organized Hypocrisy.* Princeton, N.J.: Princeton University Press.
Lindblom, Charles E. 1977. *Politics and Markets: The World's Political-Economic Systems.* New York: Basic Books.
Lipson, Charles. 1991. Why Are Some International Agreements Informal? *International Organization* 45 (4): 495–538.
Lutz, Ellen L, and Kathryn Sikkink. 2000. International Human Rights Law and Practice in Latin America. *International Organization* 54 (3): 633–659.
Mattli, Walter, and Anne-Marie Slaughter. 1998b. Revisiting the European Court of Justice. *International Organization* 52 (1): 177–209.
Morrow, James D. 1994. Modeling the Forms of International Cooperation: Distribution Versus Information. *International Organization.* 48 (3): 387–423.
Mukerji, Sujoy. 1998. Ambiguity Aversion and the Incompleteness of Contractual Form. *American Economic Review* 88 (5): 1207–31.
Reisman, W. Michael. 1988. Remarks. *Proceedings of the 82nd Annual Meeting of the American Society of International Law* 22: 373–377.
Setear, Johm K. 1999. Whaling and Legalization. Unpublished manuscript, University of Virginia, Charlottesville, Virginia.
Shapiro, Martin. 1981. *Courts: A Comparative and Political Analysis.* Chicago: University of Chicago Press.

Weil, Prosper. 1983. Towards Relative Normativity in International Law? *American Journal of International Law* 77: 413–42.

Wight, Martin. 1977. *Systems of States*. Leicester: Leicester University Press.

Williamson, Oliver. 1989. Transaction Cost Economics. In *Handbook of Industrial Organization*, edited by R. Schmalensee and R.D. Willig, 135–182. Amsterdam: North Holland.

4

Traditional and Modern Approaches to Customary International Law: A Reconciliation

Anthea Elizabeth Roberts

The Problem of Traditional and Modern Custom

The demise of custom as a source of international law has been widely forecasted.[1] This is because both the nature and the relative importance of custom's constituent elements are contentious. At the same time, custom has become an increasingly significant source of law in important areas such as human rights obligations.[2] Codification conventions, academic commentary, and the case law of the International Court of Justice (the Court) have also contributed to a contemporary resurrection of custom.[3] These developments have resulted in two apparently opposing approaches, which I term "traditional custom" and "modern custom." The renaissance of custom requires the articulation of a coherent theory that can accommodate its classic foundations and contemporary developments. This article seeks to provide an enriched theoretical account of custom that incorporates both the traditional and the modern approaches rather than advocating one approach over the other.

The Statute of the International Court of justice describes custom as "evidence of a general practice accepted as law."[4] Custom is generally considered to have two elements: state practice and *opinio juris*.[5] State practice refers to general and consistent practice by states, while *opinio juris* means that the practice is followed out of a belief of legal obligation.[6] This distinction is problematic because it is difficult to determine what states believe as opposed to what they say. Whether treaties and declarations constitute state practice or *opinio juris* is also controversial. For the sake of clarity, this article adopts Anthony D'Amato's distinction between action

81

(state practice) and statements *(opinio juris)*.[7] Thus, actions can form custom only if accompanied by an articulation of the legality of the action.[8] *Opinio juris* concerns statements of belief rather than actual beliefs.[9] Further, treaties and declarations represent *opinio juris* because they are statements about the legality of action, rather than examples of that action. As will be demonstrated below, traditional custom and modern custom are generally assumed to be alternatives because the former emphasizes state practice, whereas the latter emphasizes *opinio juris*.[10]

What I have termed traditional custom results from general and consistent practice followed by states from a sense of legal obligation.[11] It focuses primarily on state practice in the form of interstate interaction and acquiescence. *Opinio juris* is a secondary consideration invoked to distinguish between legal and nonlegal obligations.[12] Traditional custom is evolutionary[13] and is identified through an inductive process in which a general custom is derived from specific instances of state practice.[14] This approach is evident in *S.S. Lotus,*[15] where the Permanent Court of International Justice inferred a general custom about objective territorial jurisdiction over ships on the high seas from previous instances of state action and acquiescence.[16]

By contrast, modern custom is derived by a *deductive* process that begins with general statements of rules rather than particular instances of practice.[17] This approach emphasizes *opinio juris* rather than state practice because it relies primarily on statements rather than actions.[18] Modern custom can develop quickly because it is deduced from multilateral treaties and declarations by international fora such as the General Assembly, which can declare existing customs, crystallize emerging customs, and generate new customs.[19] Whether these texts become custom depends on factors such as whether they are phrased in declaratory terms, supported by a widespread and representative body of states, and confirmed by state practice.[20] A good example of the deductive approach is the Merits decision in *Military and Paramilitary Activities in and Against Nicaragua*.[21] The Court paid lip service to the traditional test for custom but derived customs of non-use of force and nonintervention from statements such as General Assembly resolutions.[22] The Court did not make a serious inquiry into state practice, holding that it was sufficient for conduct to be generally consistent with statements of rules, provided that instances of inconsistent practice had been treated as breaches of the rule concerned rather than as generating a new rule.[23]

The tests and justifications for traditional and modern custom appear to differ because the former develops slowly through state practice, while the latter can arise rapidly based on *opinio juris*.[24] This difference has spurred considerable discussion over two related issues. First, the legitimacy of traditional and modern custom has been debated at length.[25] David Fidler characterizes the various approaches to this issue as the dinosaur, dynamo, and dangerous perspectives.[26] The dinosaur approach focuses on traditional custom and argues that massive changes in the international system have rendered it an anachronism. For example, Jonathan Charney claims that the increasing number and diversity of states, as well as the emergence of global problems that are addressed in international fora, makes traditional custom an inappropriate means for developing law.[27] The dynamo perspective concentrates on modern custom and embraces it as a progressive source of law that can respond to moral issues and global challenges. For example, Theodor Meron, Richard Lillich, and Lori Bruun argue that modern custom based on declarations by international fora provides an important source of law for human rights obligations.[28] Finally, the dangerous perspective views modern custom as a departure from the traditional approach that has created an opportunity for legal and political abuse. Thus, Michael Reisman characterizes the increased dependence on custom as a "great leap backwards" designed to serve the interests of powerful states.[29] Similarly, Arthur Weisburd holds that modern custom often lacks the legitimacy of state consent because it is formed despite little, or conflicting, state practice.[30]

Second, the divergence between traditional and modern custom has been criticized as undermining the integrity of custom as a source of law. Patrick Kelly argues that custom is an indeterminate and malleable source of law, simply a "matter of taste."[31] According to D'Amato, the modern approach trashes the theoretical foundations of custom by inverting the traditional priority of state practice over *opinio juris*.[32] Sir Robert Jennings insists that "most of what we perversely persist in calling customary international law is not only *not* customary law: it does not even faintly resemble a customary law."[33] The phrases "modern," "new,"[34] "contemporary,"[35] and "instant"[36] custom appear inherently contradictory and obscure the real basis for forming this law. Hilary Charlesworth contends that modern custom can be rationalized only by dispensing with the traditional rhetoric of custom.[37] Bruno Simma and Philip Alston argue that the modern approach has created an "identity crisis"[38] for custom and would be better understood as a general principle of international law.[39] Likewise, Charney, Daniel Bodansky, and Hiram Chodosh conclude that modern custom is really a new species of universal declaratory law because it is based on authoritative statements about practice rather than observable regularities of behavior.[40]

Both the legitimacy and the integrity of traditional and modern custom have received considerable attention and polarized positions are evident. However, few commentators have transcended these debates by attempting to provide an overall theory of custom. Frederic Kirgis rationalizes the divergence in custom by analyzing the requirements of state practice and *opinio juris* on a sliding scale.[41] At one end, highly consistent state practice can establish a customary rule without requiring *opinio juris*. However, as the frequency and consistency of state practice decline, a stronger showing of *opinio juris* will be required. Kirgis argues that the exact trade-off between state practice and *opinio juris* will depend on the importance of the activity in question and the reasonableness of the rule involved.[42] Simma and Alston claim that this approach reinterprets the concept of custom so as to produce the "right" answers.[43] However, John Tasioulas argues that the sliding scale can be rationalized on the basis of Ronald Dworkin's interpretive theory of law, which balances a description of what the law has been with normative considerations about what the law should be. This perspective shows why the Court may be less exacting in requiring state practice and *opinio juris* in cases that deal with important moral issues.

This article builds on the work of Kirgis and Tasioulas and offers a defense of custom by seeking to reconcile the traditional and modern approaches. The second part analyzes the competing values of descriptive accuracy and normative appeal that are used to justify international law. These values characterize traditional and modern custom, respectively, because of their inductive and deductive methodologies and facilitative and moral content. The third part examines custom on a sliding scale and rejects this interpretive approach because it does not accurately describe the process of finding custom and would create customs that are apologies for power or utopian and unachievable.[44] The fourth part presents an alternative vision of Dworkin's interpretive theory of law applied to custom, which incorporates the justifications of descriptive accuracy and normative appeal and seeks to balance them in a Rawlsian reflective equilibrium.[45] The fifth part outlines the advantages of the reflective interpretive approach over the sliding-scale methodology. Rearticulating the theoretical foundations of custom in this more principled and flexible fashion will provide international actors with a coherent theory for applying custom. It will also help to justify the traditional and modern approaches to custom as two aspects of a single source of law, rather than characterize one approach as illegitimate and the choice between them as undermining the integrity of custom.

The Descriptive and Normative Approaches to Custom

Descriptive Accuracy and Normative Appeal

The values of descriptive accuracy and normative appeal provide important, and sometimes competing, justifications for international law. Descriptive accuracy (which focuses on what the practice has been) is valuable in justifying the content of international law because laws should correspond to reality.[46] Laws must bear some relation to practice if they are to regulate conduct effectively, because laws that set unrealistic standards are likely to be disobeyed and ultimately forgotten. This consideration particularly applies to decentralized systems of law, such as international law, where traditional enforcement mechanisms are unavailable or underdeveloped.[47] Descriptive accuracy is also essential to predictive power[48] because a theory that accurately describes practice enables more reliable predictions of future state behavior.[49]

The alternative justification for international law provided by normative appeal (which focuses on what the practice *ought to be*) involves procedural and substantive aspects. First, procedural normativity requires that the process for forming laws be transparent, so that states are aware of the real basis for forming customs and can regulate their actions accordingly.[50] It also entails an opportunity for states to participate in law formation and have their positions considered.[51] Legal rules are more likely to engender respect in a decentralized system, possibly even when the outcome is less favorable, if they result from a process perceived as legitimate.[52] Second, substantive normativity requires that laws be coherent and that their content be morally good or at least neutral, depending on their subject matter. Claims about "morality" are contentious because it remains unclear whether morality is objective or culturally relative. By morality, I am referring to commonly held subjective values about actions that are right and wrong, which a representative majority of states has recognized in treaties and declarations.[53]

Facilitative and Moral Customs

The best balance between the justifications of descriptive accuracy and normative appeal depends on the facilitative or moral content of the custom involved. International laws are ranged on a spectrum between facilitative and moral rules.[54] At one extreme, there are completely facilitative rules, which promote coexistence and cooperation but do not deal with substantive moral issues (such as that ships must pass on the left). Next come primarily facilitative rules that regulate interaction but also give rise to some moral considerations (such as the fair distribution of resources in a continental shelf). Moving to the middle, one finds rules that involve important facilitative and moral considerations (such as environmental rules). Toward the other extreme, the laws are primarily moral rather than facilitative (such as some human rights obligations) and peremptory rules that prohibit actions whether or not they affect coexistence and cooperation (such as *jus cogens* laws prohibiting genocide). While it is possible for a law to facilitate interaction between states and also have a strong moral content (such as the prohibition on the use of force), laws often tend more toward one or the other end of the spectrum.

Facilitative customs are more descriptive than normative because they turn a *description of actual practice* into a prescriptive requirement for future action.[55] Moral customs are more normative than descriptive because they prescribe future action based on *normative evaluations of ideal practice*. Traditional customs primarily facilitate coexistence and cooperation between sovereign states without having a peremptory moral character; for example, the law on diplomatic immunity.[56] State practice is dominant in establishing traditional facilitative customs because these rules turn empirical descriptions of past practice into prescriptive requirements for future practice.[57] However, international law has expanded since 1945 to include many moral issues such as human rights,[58] the use of force,[59] and environmental protection.[60] Louis Henkin characterizes this development as a move from state values to human values, and from a liberal state system to a welfare system.[61] State practice is less important in forming modern customs because these customs prescribe ideal standards of conduct rather than describe existing practice.[62] For example, the customary prohibition on torture expresses a moral abhorrence of torture rather than an accurate description of state practice.[63]

The moral content of modern custom explains the strong tendency to discount the importance of contrary state practice in the modern approach. Irregularities in description can undermine a descriptive law, but a normative law may be broken and remain a law because it is not premised on descriptive accuracy. For example, *jus cogens* norms prohibit fundamentally immoral conduct and cannot be undermined by treaty arrangement or inconsistent state practice.[64] Since the subject matter of modern customs is not morally neutral, the international community is not willing to accept any norm established by state practice.[65] Modern custom involves an almost teleological approach, whereby some examples of state practice are used to justify a chosen norm, rather than deriving norms from state practice. As noted above, this approach was evident in the *Nicaragua* case, where the Court held it sufficient for the conduct of states to be generally consistent with statements of rules, provided that contrary state practice had generally been "treated as breaches of that rule, not as indications of the recognition of a new rule."[66] Thus, the importance of descriptive accuracy varies according to the facilitative or moral content of the rule involved. . . .

The relative importance of substantive and procedural normativity links to criticisms of modern custom as creating quasi legislation on the basis of declarations and treaties.[67] Declarations of international fora are formally nonbinding, while states can determine whether, and to what extent, they wish to be bound by treaties.[68] By contrast, custom is generally binding except for the limited and contentious persistent objector rule.[69] Transforming declarations and treaties into custom changes their nature because customs can bind non-parties to treaties and declarations[70] and are not affected by reservations[71] or denunciation.[72] Thus, Prosper Weil argues that the requirements of treaties have "not been frontally assaulted but cunningly outflanked."[73] However, the emphasis on community consensus over individual state consent in modern custom reflects the priority of substantive normativity over procedural normativity in important moral issues. Modern custom evinces a desire to create general international laws that can bind all states on important moral issues.[74] According to Kirgis, "The alternative would be an international legal order containing ominous silences—where treaty commitments cannot be found—concerning the ways in which states impose their wills on other states or on individuals."[75] The international community discounts the importance of dissenting states and contrary state practice because it is not prepared to recognize exceptions to the maintenance of certain fundamental values. Recognizing exceptions to such rules would "shock the conscience of mankind"[76] and be contrary to "elementary considerations of humanity."[77] The substantive normativity of modern custom can therefore be used to justify a reduced focus on procedural normativity and descriptive accuracy.

The importance of descriptive accuracy and normative appeal, and procedural and substantive normativity, varies according to the facilitative and moral content of traditional and modern custom. The reduced focus on state practice in the modern approach is explained by its use to create generally binding laws on important moral issues.

Apology and Utopia

Descriptive accuracy and normative appeal provide important bases for justifying international law. While facilitative and moral rules respectively tend more toward descriptive accuracy and normative appeal, neither value is sufficient to justify all international laws. According to Koskenniemi, international law mediates between the competing tendencies of apology (description) and utopia (normativity).

> A law which would lack distance from State behaviour, will or interest would amount to a non-normative apology, a mere sociological description. A law which would base itself on principles which are unrelated to State behaviour, will or interest would seem utopian, incapable of demonstrating its own content in any reliable way.[78]

The conflicting values of description and normativity, and their respective risks of being an apology for power or utopian and unachievable, represent the fundamental tension in legal argument.[79] Theorists oscillate between these two extremes and each position remains open to challenge from the opposite perspective.[80] Thus, international legal argument is always dynamic. David Kennedy argues that "[e]ither international law has been too far from politics and must move closer to become effective, or it has become dangerously intermingled with politics and must assert its autonomy to remain potent."[81] The dynamic between description and normativity represents the "deep doctrinal schizophrenia" of law[82] or a "disciplinary hamster wheel" from which theorists appear unable to escape.[83]

While the justifications for traditional and modern custom mainly align with descriptive accuracy and normative appeal, neither approach is completely descriptive or normative because both recognize the importance of state practice and *opinio juris* to varying degrees. However, as the two approaches to custom tend toward opposite ends of the theoretical spectrum, the strongest criticisms of each come from the counterstandpoint. Traditional custom embodies the value of descriptive accuracy but the risk of apologism, so that one of the main criticisms of traditional custom is that it lacks democratic legitimacy (a normative criticism). By contrast, modern custom is normatively appealing but risks creating utopian rules, so it is criticized for producing norms that are divorced from reality (a descriptive criticism). The critiques of traditional and modern custom rest on this basis.

The advantages and disadvantages of traditional and modern custom are "dynamic" because criticisms of traditional custom tend to correspond to advantages of modern custom and vice versa. An improvement in normative appeal will often correspond to a decline in descriptive accuracy, while an enhancement of descriptive accuracy will often result in a deterioration of normative appeal. Whereas some rules are descriptively accurate and normatively appealing, the two justifications often have a relationship of inverse proportionality. For example, relying on declarations by international fora is potentially more democratic than relying on the actions of powerful states (a normative improvement in modern custom)—but since these declarations are supported by a majority of states rather than a predominance of power, they are less likely to be enforced in practice (a descriptive deterioration from traditional custom).[84] Similarly, the relationship between procedural and substantive normativity is also dynamic. For example, one could bind all states on important moral issues (a substantive normative advantage), but doing so would bind some states without their consent (a procedural normative problem).[85] Thus, the values of description and normativity represent the fundamental tension in legal argument[86] and both approaches remain open to challenge from the opposite perspective.[87] As seen, international law reveals a dynamic tension between descriptive accuracy and normative appeal. Traditional custom has descriptive strengths but lacks democratic legitimacy, while modern custom deals with substantive moral issues but produces laws that do not reflect reality. This tension leads to the issue of whether the two approaches can be reconciled in a single interpretive theory.

Custom on an Interpretive Sliding Scale

The divergence between the traditional and modern approaches to custom has been criticized as making custom indeterminate and malleable.[88] This part analyzes one attempt at reconciling them by applying Dworkin's interpretive theory of law to custom on a sliding scale.

Law as Interpretation: Dworkin

Dworkin argues that legal decisions aim at reformulating past decisions and practice in the most coherent and morally attractive way, consistent with the facts of legal history. Dworkin outlines three steps in the interpretive process: preinterpretation, interpretation, and post-interpretation.[89] In the preinterpretive stage, the rules and facts that form the practice to be interpreted are identified. The term *preinterpretation* is somewhat misleading because the collection of data is theory dependent.[90] Consequently, this stage requires a high degree of consensus to provide a common focus for interpretation.[91]

In the interpretive stage, the interpreter formulates a general explanation for the main elements of the practice. This explanation is called the "dimension of fit" and it imposes a rough threshold requirement that accepts an interpretation as eligible only if the raw data of legal practice adequately support it.[92] There can be three outcomes at this stage: no eligible interpretations, if every possible interpretation is inconsistent with the bulk of raw material available; easy cases, when there is only one eligible interpretation; and hard cases, where a range of eligible interpretations result because the tests are unsettled or the practice conflicting.

Postinterpretation only becomes relevant in hard cases, where interpreters must choose the best eligible interpretation according to the "dimension of substance."[93] The best interpretation is the one that makes the practice appear in the best light, judged according to the substantive aspirations of the legal system. This criterion involves consideration of moral and political ideals, as well as higher-order convictions about how these ideals should be prioritized when they conflict.[94]

The interpretive stage is backward looking and descriptive, while the postinterpretive stage is forward looking and normative. Dworkin's interpretive theory of law combines a descriptive historical investigation about what the law has been (*fit*) with a normative moral inquiry about what it should be (substance).[95] According to Dworkin: "propositions of law are not simply descriptive of legal history in a straightforward way, nor are they simply evaluative in some way divorced from legal history. They are interpretive of legal history, which combines elements of both description and evaluation but is different from both."[96]

What, however, is the relationship between fit and substance? Dworkin originally proposed a lexical ordering between them,[97] but in *Law's Empire* he revised the relationship. Fit provides a rough threshold criterion.[98] Interpretations need not fit every aspect of the existing practice, but they must fit enough for the interpreter to be "interpreting that practice, not inventing a new one."[99] On the other hand, if there are multiple eligible interpretations, then fit and substance must be balanced against each other.[100] Thus, any inadequacies of fit will count against an interpretation at the substantive stage because "an interpretation is *pro tanto* more satisfactory if it shows less damage to integrity than its rival."[101] Similarly, "defects of fit may be compensated . . . if the principles of that interpretation are particularly attractive."[102] The interpreter must therefore balance the relative strengths of fit and substance in different interpretations to determine the best interpretation. Dworkin likens this process to multiple authors writing consecutive chapters in a chain novel. Each author must contribute a chapter that provides sufficient continuity with the earlier chapters (fit) and develops the book in the best way (substance).[103] However, Dworkin details no method for weighing fit and substance other than the metaphor *balance*.[104] Hence, anyone using Dworkin's interpretive theory must correctly identify fit and substance and develop a working theory about how to balance them.

Custom on a Sliding Scale: Kirgis and Tasioulas

The international legal system is decentralized, resulting in multiple interpreters of custom. The existence and content of custom is usually determined by states and academics, though the Court remains the ultimate arbiter in some cases.[105] These interpreters are meant to determine customs on the basis of state practice and *opinio juris*.[106] However, the traditional and modern forms of custom both appear to emphasize one element at the expense of the other. Kirgis argues that the two approaches can be understood by viewing state practice and *opinio juris* as interchangeable along a sliding scale:[107]

> On the sliding scale, very frequent, consistent state practice establishes a customary rule without much (or any) affirmative showing of an opinio juris, so long as it is not negated by evidence of non-normative intent. As the frequency and consistency of the practice decline in any series of cases, a stronger showing of an opinio juris is required. At the other end of the scale, a clearly demonstrated opinio juris establishes a customary rule without much (or any) affirmative showing [of state practice].[108]

Yet when will a custom be formed on the basis only of state practice or *opinio juris,* instead of requiring both elements? According to Kirgis, the answer depends on the importance of the activity in question and the reasonableness of the rule involved. If an activity is not very destructive, then the Court will be more exacting in requiring both state practice and *opinio juris* to form a custom. By contrast, Kirgis states, "[t]he more destabilizing or morally distasteful the activity—for example, the offensive use of force or the deprivation of fundamental human rights—the more readily international decision makers will substitute one element for the other, provided that the asserted restrictive rule seems reasonable."[109]

Custom as a Reflective Interpretive Concept

Dworkin's interpretive theory of law incorporates the values of fit (description) and substance (normativity) but does not provide a mechanism for balancing them. Analyzing custom on a sliding scale is flawed because it misconceives the nature of fit and substance and risks creating customs that are apologies for power or utopian and unachievable. This part presents an alternative vision of Dworkin's interpretive theory as applied to custom, which re-conceptualizes the nature of fit and substance and balances them in a Rawlsian reflective equilibrium. . . .

Balancing Fit and Substance: A Reflective Methodology

Applying Dworkin's interpretive theory to custom is useful because it incorporates description (fit) and normativity (substance) into a single approach. If there are multiple eligible interpretations, the best interpretation is the one that most *coherently* explains the dimensions of fit and substance.[110] Coherence, which Dworkin calls *integrity,* is an important value in international law.[111] Interpretations should aim for coherence by mediating between fit and substance in the same way as Rawls mediates between intuitions and moral principles in ethical theories.[112] Instead of prioritizing one value above the other, Rawls advocates revising our interpretation of practice and principles, back and forth, until we have done everything possible to render our interpretation coherent and justified from both ends.[113] Rawls calls this a "reflective equilibrium. . . ."[114]

While custom and moral theories involve very different considerations, a Rawlsian reflective approach can be used more generally to reconcile the inductive and deductive methodologies that are common to both.[115] The dimension of fit and the theory of moral intuitionism are both inductive because they seek to infer a general rule from particular instances of practice. The dimension of substance is similar to moral principles because both deduce norms about practice from abstract statements of principles. Instead of prioritizing one value above the other, we should revise our interpretation of practice and principles until the two approaches are coherent and justified from both ends in a reflective equilibrium. While Dworkin argues that the best interpretation is objectively determinable,[116] I believe that subjectivity is inherent in interpreting raw data. However, the reflective process provides some guidelines for reconciling practice and principles rather than allowing one element to override the other. It also explains why the best interpretation of practice and principles will change over time in light of new data or theories.

Practical Application of the Reflective Interpretive Concept

A reflective equilibrium requires revising our *interpretations of practice* (fit) *and principles* (substance) to find the most coherent explanation of both dimensions in the case of multiple eligible interpretations. This section explores how the reflective interpretive approach applies to two practical problems in custom, first, by applying it to the spectrum of facilitative and modern customs, and second, by using it to explain the fluid nature of custom. This analysis demonstrates that the reflective interpretive approach is dynamic, varying over time and according to the nature of the custom involved.

The best balance between fit and substance will depend on the relative strength of the practice and principles in the custom involved. This is because the best interpretation of a custom usually leans toward the stronger element (practice or principles) as providing the greatest consistency with both elements. Traditional facilitative customs will result in a more descriptive equilibrium because they do not involve strong issues of principle. By contrast, modern customs with a strong moral content require a more normative equilibrium because they involve important issues of principle. Other customs, such as environmental protection, may involve strong normative and descriptive considerations, requiring a more even balance of fit and substance. Thus, traditional and modern customs exist on a facilitative-moral spectrum, which explains the asymmetrical application of fit and substance to them. . . .

The Fluid Nature of Custom

Customs can generally change and harden over time because custom is a fluid source of law. The content of custom is not fixed; it can develop and change in light of new circumstances. The formation and modification of custom is an uncertain process because international law lacks an authoritative guide as to the amount, duration, frequency, and repetition of state practice required to develop or change a custom.[117] Using Hart's terminology, custom would be a primitive source of law because it lacks clear rules of change. Instead, custom develops through a "slow process of growth, whereby courses of conduct once thought optional become first habitual or usual, and then obligatory, and the converse process of decay, when deviations, once severely dealt with, are first tolerated and then pass unnoticed."[118]

One reason for the difficulty of identifying the formation and change of custom is the radical decentralization of the international system. States are both legislators and subjects of international law, which explains why D'Amato argues that every breach of a customary law contains the seed for a new legality.[119] In one sense, the action is a breach because the state is judged as a subject of international law; in another sense, the action is a seed for a new law because the state acts as a legislator of international law.[120] However, whether a custom develops or changes depends not only on the actions of some states but also on the reactions of other states. This is because states are also both legislators and enforcers of international law. Thus, a breach will effectively repeal or modify an existing custom only if other states emulate the breach or acquiesce in its legality.[121]

The reflective interpretive approach is useful in explaining the fluid nature of custom. Just as customs can develop and change in light of new circumstances, so a reflective equilibrium is not stable because the best explanation of practice and principles must be reevaluated in light of new state practice, *opinio juris,* and moral considerations.[122] The best balance between practice and principles must be regularly reassessed. Consequently, conflicting data should never be discounted as irrelevant because they may significantly affect future interpretations. What is now an exception to, or a breach of, an accepted rule may later become integral to the explanation of a new general rule. According to D'Amato:

> When a state violates an existing rule of customary international law, it undoubtedly is "guilty" of an illegal act, but the illegal act itself becomes a disconfirmatory instance of the underlying rule. The next state will find it somewhat easier to disobey the rule, until eventually a new line of conduct will replace the original rule by a now rule.[123]

The number of disconfirmatory acts that are required before the breach of an old rule will constitute the basis for a new rule depends on the extent of previous practice and the importance of the moral principles involved. Moral customs, and in particular *jus cogens* norms, are unlikely to be undermined by contrary practice. Furthermore, well-established customs will demonstrate relative resistance to change because new state practice or *opinio juris* must be weighed against a wealth of previous contrary practice.[124] However, a custom can change quickly in the face of very strong state practice or *opinio juris,* particularly if the rule was uncertain or still developing.[125] Recent practice may also carry proportionately greater weight than past practice in determining the present or future state of custom. Customs can develop or change in light of the recognition of new moral considerations in international law. For example, the customary prohibition against genocide stemmed from the recognition of human rights as a substantive aim of international law after World War II. Likewise, currently nonbinding aspirations may harden into legally binding custom in the future. For example, D'Amato and Sudhir Chopra have argued that whales may have an emerging right to life under customary international law.[126] Thus, the content of custom can change in view of new practice and principles in international law.

The fluidity of custom is demonstrated by the debate over whether NATO's intervention in Kosovo has formed the basis for an emerging customary right to unilateral humanitarian intervention. In the *Nicaragua* case, the Court found a general customary prohibition on intervention in other states but held that "[r]eliance by a State on a novel right or an unprecedented exception to the principle might, if shared in principle by other States, tend towards a modification of customary international law."[127] Whether states have successfully created an exception to the general custom of nonintervention will depend in part on whether they "justified their conduct by reference to a new right of intervention or a new exception to the principle of its prohibition."[128] It will also depend on whether the action provokes protest by other states or is emulated or met with acquiescence. However, if a state prima facie breaches a custom but "defends its conduct by appealing to exceptions or justification contained within the rule itself, then whether or not the State's conduct is in fact justifiable on that basis, the significance of that attitude is to confirm rather than to weaken the rule."[129]

Most commentators have concluded that NATO's intervention in Kosovo was illegal under existing international law.[130] For example, Charney finds it indisputable that NATO's intervention violated the United Nations Charter and international law.[131] However, the precedential status of the intervention is more contentious. Simma argues that NATO's intervention should not become a precedent because of the exceptional factual circumstances in Kosovo, the insistence by participating states such as France and Germany that the intervention did not form a precedent, and the detrimental impact of allowing an isolated breach of collective security to become a general rule for unilateral action.[132] By contrast, Antonio Cassese argues that NATO's action may support an emerging custom allowing the use of forcible countermeasures to impede a state from committing large-scale atrocities within its own territory, in circumstances where the Security Council is incapable of responding to the crisis.[133] I submit that these conflicting arguments can he understood by employing a reflective interpretive approach.

To determine eligible interpretations of fit, one must primarily consider the state practice respecting unilateral humanitarian intervention. Opponents of the norm focus on the lack of explicit authorization of NATO's action by the Security Council and the likelihood that China or Russia would have vetoed any resolution supporting intervention. The intervention also provoked significant protests by China, India, Namibia, Belarus, and the Russian Federation,[134] which undermines its ability to form a custom. Prominent members of NATO, including France and Germany, insisted that the intervention did not constitute a precedent for a general right to unilateral humanitarian intervention.[135] In pleadings for the case brought by the Federal Republic of Yugoslavia against ten NATO members in 1999, only Belgium expressly mentioned humanitarian intervention as a possible legal justification for action.[136] Thus, the intervening states did not attempt to justify their intervention on the basis of a new exception to the general prohibition on intervention.[137]

States have also repeatedly abstained from invoking the right of humanitarian intervention where there were grounds for doing so, including India's intervention in East Pakistan in 1971, Vietnam's invasion of Kampuchea in 1978, and Tanzania's intervention in Uganda in 1979.[138] These states justified their interventions on other grounds, such as self-defense, which suggests that they did not believe that unilateral humanitarian intervention was accepted in international law.[139] However, states will generally resort to factual or legal exceptions rather than openly admit they have breached a law, even if they wish to change it.[140] The absence of intervention in potentially analogous situations involving, for example, the Kurds in Turkey, the Chechens in Russia, and the Tibetans in China may also suggest that states did not believe that unilateral humanitarian intervention was permitted under international law.

By contrast, proponents of an emerging norm argue that NATO had authority to act because the Security Council had defined the situation in Kosovo as a "threat to peace and security in the region."[141] The lack of condemnation of NATO's intervention by the Security Council and most other states also indicates a general acquiescence in its legality. For example, a draft resolution condemning NATO's use of force was rejected by a vote of 12 to 3 in the Security Council,[142] and no state requested an immediate meeting of the General Assembly to condemn the intervention. Precedents can also be found for humanitarian intervention without explicit authorization by the Security Council, such as the action by the United States, France, and Great Britain in Iraq in 1991. Moreover, the interventions in Iraq and Kosovo provide more modern, and thus potentially more weighty, precedents than the counterexamples from the 1970s. Contrary examples of states seeking Security Council approval before intervening in other situations could represent a politically prudent course of action, rather than a necessary element of legality. Further, the failure of states to intervene in previous humanitarian crises represents discretionary nonaction, rather than obligatory negative practice or acquiescence, because a custom allowing intervention is a permissive right rather than an obligatory duty.[143]

The range of eligible interpretations brings the dimension of substance into play to help determine the best interpretation in light of the substantive aims of international law. Unilateral humanitarian intervention involves the conflicting substantive considerations of state sovereignty (which would support a duty of nonintervention) and humanitarian aims (which would support a right to intervention). Prohibitions on intervention and the use of force appear to be peremptory norms of international law.[144] Some humanitarian considerations, such as the prohibition on genocide, have also achieved *jus cogens* status.[145] The dimension of substance must include consideration of how the substantive aims of international law should be prioritized when they conflict. While state sovereignty has traditionally been accorded primary importance in international law, arguably the international community is increasingly recognizing exceptions to this principle in extreme humanitarian crises.[146] Thus, which principle will prevail when the two conflict depends on the extremity of the humanitarian crisis in question.

The dimension of substance also requires consideration of the procedural normativity of unilateral intervention. Critics of unilateral intervention argue that it is open to abuse and likely to result in selective and self-interested action.[147] Proponents argue that selective application is inherent in the concept of rights rather than duties, that selective intervention may be better than no intervention, and that it is unrealistic to expect states to intervene only when they are completely disinterested.[148] Some of the objections may also be met by clearly identifying the conditions for intervention so as to provide safeguards against abuse, rather than creating a blanket prohibition on intervention. Further, the alternatives to unilateral intervention, which are no intervention and collective intervention,[149] should be taken into account. Collective intervention, approved by the Security Council, is arguably less partisan and less open to abuse than unilateral intervention. However, the legitimacy of the Security Council itself is questionable because it comprises only fifteen states and the five permanent members all have the power of veto. Thus, collective action may not enjoy the advantages of procedural normativity. Collective action may also not be possible even in the face of extreme violations of human rights such as genocide. In such cases, unilateral intervention may be justified on the basis that the importance of the substantive moral issues involved outweighs deficiencies in procedural normativity.[150]

In applying the reflective equilibrium, we need to consider which explanation most coherently explains the competing conceptions of practice and principles outlined above. There are two eligible interpretations of custom, one prohibiting unilateral humanitarian intervention and one permitting it. Since the first interpretation more adequately explains the raw data of practice to date, the second interpretation would only be preferred if supported by a strong dimension of substance. Substantively, the principles of state sovereignty and nonintervention generally prevail, except in cases of extreme human rights violations such as genocide. From a procedural perspective, collective intervention is usually preferable to unilateral intervention, though the latter may be justified if the Security Council is paralyzed by the veto power. Thus, the dimension of substance provides equivocal support for both interpretations, which varies according to the circumstances of the case. The present state of practice and principles probably leads to the conclusion that unilateral humanitarian intervention is not currently recognized as an exception to the principle of nonintervention. However, a narrow right to unilateral humanitarian intervention may be emerging in exceptional circumstances where there are gross violations of human rights, peaceful avenues for settling the dispute have been exhausted, the veto power has rendered the Security Council incapable of taking coercive action, the action is undertaken by a group of states with the support (or at least the nonopposition) of the majority of states, and the armed force is used exclusively to stop the violations.[151] Whether this emerging norm is transformed into a binding custom will depend on future developments in the practice and principles of international law. Thus, the reflective interpretive approach can be used to demonstrate the fluid nature of custom as a source of law.

The Advantages of a Reflective Interpretive Approach

The contemporary interest in custom as a source of international law poses a challenge to articulate a coherent theory of custom. This is a difficult exercise because the traditional and modern approaches to custom appear to be opposed, with traditional custom emphasizing state practice and modern custom emphasizing *opinio juris*. The divergence between the descriptive and normative approaches of traditional and modern custom causes problems because the tests and justifications for traditional custom do not apply to modern custom and vice versa. Instead of advocating the rival merits and legitimacy of either approach, this article has sought to build an enriched theoretical account of custom that analyzes the competing justifications for traditional and modern custom and accommodates both approaches in a consistent interpretive theory.

This reconciliation provides a methodology for assessing asserted customs. After gathering evidence of state practice and *opinio juris,* one must apply the threshold criterion of fit to determine if there are any eligible interpretations that adequately explain the raw data of practice. Fit provides continuity and descriptive accuracy, so that state practice will assume primary importance at this stage. However, state practice is open to interpretation and should include intrastate action and inaction, not just interstate interaction and acquiescence. Some articulation of legality is needed to differentiate between legal custom and social practice. If there is no eligible interpretation, then there is no custom. If there is one eligible interpretation, then the custom is clear. If there are multiple eligible interpretations, then one must weigh the dimensions of fit and substance to determine the best interpretation.

Strong statements of *opinio juris* become relevant at this third stage because they represent normative considerations about what the law should be. The best interpretation is the one that most *coherently* explains fit and substance, which varies according to the facilitative or moral content of the custom involved. Primarily facilitative customs do not involve strong substantive considerations and thus will be determined principally by fit. Primarily moral customs give rise to strong procedural and substantive normative considerations, which must be balanced against deficiencies in fit. Custom is also a fluid source of law, which causes the point of equilibrium to vary over time in light of new state practice, *opinio juris,* and moral considerations. Consequently, the reflective interpretive approach results in a more sophisticated understanding of fit and substance and constitutes a more nuanced method for reconciling them than the sliding scale in various ways.

First, the reflective interpretive approach recognizes that the role of the dimension of fit is to provide descriptive accuracy. Questions of fit and descriptive accuracy are both backward looking because they focus on whether a custom is supported by past practice. Tasioulas claims that strong statements of *opinio juris* can form the basis of eligible interpretations at the dimension of fit. Similarly, Michael Akehurst has argued that state practice should include paper practice in the form of statements, declarations, and resolutions.[152] I have demonstrated that this approach is not feasible because statements often fuse *lex lata* and *lex ferenda* and thus lack descriptive accuracy. However, one can still form eligible interpretations of traditional and modern custom by considering the open-textured nature of practice. State practice should also include consideration of intrastate action (not just interstate interaction), obligations being observed (not just obligations being breached), and reasons for a lack of protest over breaches (other than acquiescence in the legality of those breaches). These forms of practice reflect the changing subject matter of international law to include intrastate issues and are descriptively accurate because they focus on action and inaction.

Second, I have outlined a dimension of substance that embodies both substantive and procedural normativity. Kirgis refers to strong moral issues but does not provide a theory for determining them. Tasioulas deliberately limits his discussion of the substantive aims of international law to coexistence and cooperation. By contrast, my approach provides a more expansive understanding of the substantive aims of international law, which includes recognized moral aims (such as the protection of human rights) that do not necessarily affect coexistence and cooperation. Substantive aims are frequently criticized as being subjective value judgments that serve as a vehicle for normative chauvinism. For this reason, I have defined moral issues as commonly held subjective values about right and wrong that have been adopted by a representative majority of states in treaties and declarations. This approach has several advantages. Focusing on commonly held, or intersubjective, values avoids the need to consider whether moral values can be objectively determined and it explains why these values can change over time. It also denotes an agreed set of values rather than requiring interpreters to determine what they believe the substantive aims of international law should be. It builds the concept of procedural normativity into the dimension of substance because these values have been accepted by a majority of states, which helps prevent accusations of Western ideological bias. Finally, while these statements may include *lex lata* and *lex ferenda,* the dimension of fit already provides a threshold test to determine if a custom is adequately supported by practice.

Third, I have suggested a more nuanced approach to balancing fit and substance than the crude sliding scale. Finding traditional custom on the strength of state practice and fit alone allows it to become an apology for state power.[153] Similarly, deducing modern custom purely from *opinio juris* and substance can create utopian laws that cannot regulate reality. Thus, the sliding scale can allow one element completely to outweigh the other. While a reflective equilibrium will lean toward the stronger value, it avoids extremes of apology and utopia. The strength of fit and state practice in traditional customs must still be balanced against their substantive deficiencies, such as a lack of procedural normativity. Similarly, modern customs must be supported by state practice because they must pass the threshold of it and deficiencies in their fit may still outweigh their moral content.[154] A lower standard of practice may be tolerated for customs with a strong moral content because violations of ideal standards are expected.[155] However, while occasional breaches may not nullify their legal character, massive, grave, and persistent violations will.[156] The only exceptions are *jus cogens* norms, which by definition cannot be undermined by contrary practice unless that practice creates another rule of *jus cogens.*[157]

Fourth, Kirgis and Tasioulas argue that the more morally distasteful an activity, the more readily the Court will substitute *opinio juris* for state practice and vice versa. However, I have explained that substantive considerations apply asymmetrically to traditional and modern customs because of their facilitative and moral content. This reasoning results in a better explanation of when, and on what basis, traditional and modern customs will be formed. It also means that, to the extent that the reflective equilibrium can still be criticized for apology and utopia, these criticisms are less compelling because they apply to facilitative and moral customs, respectively. Criticizing a facilitative custom for being an exercise of power is not problematic because it does not concern substantive moral issues. Instead, these customs are akin to domestic traffic rules. If developing states wish to challenge a traditional custom, they can enact declarations in international fora, as they did on whether there should he an international minimum standard of compensation for expropriation[158] or a national treatment standard.[159] Similarly, modern customs that set up ideal standards about moral issues are expected to be somewhat utopian. Meron argues that the international community is willing to accept gradual or partial compliance as fulfilling the requirements for forming moral customs.[160] Alasdair MacIntyre argues that the charge of utopianism is made by "the deliberately shortsighted who congratulate themselves upon the limits of their vision."[161] While hard law that is always enforced may be preferable to soft law, the choice in areas such as human rights is often between soft law and no law.[162] Giving these aspirations some legal force may be preferable to giving them no legal status, because they can be enforced in extreme situations such as apartheid in South Africa[163] and their legal status may harden over time.[164]

Finally, the reflective equilibrium can be used to explain the fluid nature of customary international law. The sliding scale assumes that state practice and *opinio juris* are fixed and irreconcilable quantities that must be traded off against each other to form eligible interpretations of custom. However, I have demonstrated that state practice is open textured and capable of being interpreted in various ways. For example, contrary state practice can be analyzed as a breach of an old rule or as the seed of a new rule. Finding the best interpretation of practice and principles requires one to determine the most coherent explanation of state practice and *opinio juris,* rather than simply giving preference to one and discounting the other. For this reason, conflicting state practice should never he discounted as irrelevant to interpretation, because it may contain the seed for a new custom. It also clarifies how customs change over time in light of new state practice, *opinio juris,* and moral considerations.

The reflective interpretive approach rearticulates the theoretical foundations of custom in a more principled and flexible fashion. Instead of debating the relative merits and legitimacy of traditional and modern custom, this interpretive theory seeks to justify and reconcile the two approaches and, in so doing, offers a coherent theory of custom that helps to defend its integrity as a source of international law.

Notes

1. *E.g.*, N. C. H. Dunhar, *The Myth of Customary International Law*, 1983 Austl. Y.B. Int'l. L. J. Patrick Kelly, *The Twilight of Customary International Law*, 40 Va. J. Int'l L. 449 (2000).

2. Theodor Meron, Human Rights and Humanitarian Norms as Customary Law (1989) [hereinafter Human Rights and Humanitarian Norms as Customary Law].

3. Eduardo Jimenez de Arechaga, *Custom*, in Change and Stability in International Law-Making 1, 2973 (Antonio Cassese & Joseph H. H. Weiler eds., 1988) [hereinafter Change and Stability]; W. Michael Reisman, *The Cult of Custom in the Late 20th Century*, 17 CAL. W. Int'l. L. J. 133 (1987).

4. International Court of Justice Statute Art. 38(1) (h) [hereinafter ICI Statute].

5. North Sea Continental Shelf (FRG/Den.; FRG/Neth.), 1969 ICJ Rep. 3, 44 (Feb. 20).

6. Restatement (Third) of the Foreign Relations Law of the United States sec. 102(2) (1987) [hereinafter Restatement]; Ian Brownlie, Principles of Public International Law 497il (5th ed. 1998); Michael Byers, Custom, Power, and the Power of 130 (1999) [hereinafter Custom, Power, and the Power of Rules].

7. Anthony D'Amato, The Concept of Custom in International Law at 89–90,160 [hereinafter The Concept of Custom].

8. D'Amato, The Concept of Custom at 74–75.

9. D'Amato at 35–39; Michael Akehurst, *Custom as a Source of International Law* (1974–75) at 36–37.

10. *E.g.*, Ted Stein, Remarks [on customs and treaties], in Change and Stability at 12,13.

11. North Sea Continental Shelf, 1969 ICJ Rep. at 44. . . .

12. North Sea Continental Shelf, 1969 ICI Rep. at 44; Right of Passage over Indian Territory (Port. v. India), Merits, 1960 ICJ REP. 6, 42–43 (Apr. 12); Asylum (Colom./Peru), 1950 ICJ Rep. 266, 276–77 (Nov. 20); S.S. "Lotus" (Fr. v. Turk.), 1927 PCIJ (Ser. A) No. 10, at 28 (Sept. 7).

13. The Paquete Habana, 175 U.S. 677, 686 (1900). . . .

14. Delimitation of the Maritime Boundary in the Gulf of Maine Area (Can. v. U.S.), 1984 ICJ Rep. 246, 299 (Oct. 12). . . .

15. S.S. "Lotus," 1927 PCIJ (ser. A) No. 10, at 18, 29; *see also* Nottebohm (Liech. v. Goat.), Second Phase, 1955 ICJ Rep. 4, 22 (Apr. 6); S.S. Wimbledon, 1923 PCIJ (ser. A) No. 1, at 25 (Aug. 17).

16. Hiram Chodosh, *Neither Treaty nor Custom. The Emergence of Declarative International Law*, 26 Tex. Int'l. L. J. 87, 102 n.70 (1991).

17. Bruno Simma & Philip Alston, *The Sources of Human Rights Law: Custom, Jus Cogens, and General Principles*, 1988–89 Austl. YB. Int'l. L. 82 [hereinafter The Sources of Human Rights Law].

18. Bin Cheng, *United Nations Resolutions on Outer Space: "Instant" International Customary Law?* 5 Indiana J. Int'l. L. 23 (1965), reprinted in International Law: Teaching and Practice 237 (Bin Cheng ed., 1982).

19. North Sea Continental Shelf, 1969 ICJ Rep. at 44; Eduardo Jimenez de Arechaga, Remarks [on general principles and General Assembly resolutions], in Change & Stability at 48.

20. Akehurst, *Custom as a Source* at 6977; Jonathan I. Charney, *Universal International Law*, 87 AJIL 529, 544–45 (1993).

21. Military and Paramilitary Activities in and Against Nicaragua (Nicar. v. U.S.), Merits, 1986 ICJ Rep. 14 (June 27) [hereinafter *Nicaragua*]; see also Western Sahara, Advisory Opinion, 1975 ICJ Rep. 12, 30–37 (Oct. 16); Legal Consequences for States of the Continued Presence of South Africa in Namibia (South West Africa) Not withstanding Security Council Resolution 276 (1970), Advisory Opinion, 1971 ICJ Rep. 16, 31–32 (June21) [hereinafter Namibia Advisory Opinion].

22. *E.g.,* Declaration on Principles of International Law Concerning Friendly Relations and Co-operation Among States in Accordance with the Charter of the United Nations, GA Res. 2625, UN GAOR, 25th Sess., Supp. No. 28, at 121, UN Doc. A/8028 (1970); Conference on Security and Co-operation in Europe, Final Act, Aug. 1, 1975, 73 Dept St. Bull. 323 (1975), reprinted in 14 ILM 1292 (1975) [hereinafter Helsinki Accord].

23. *Nicaragua,* 1986 ICJ Rep. at 98, para. 186.

24. Georges Abi-Saab, Remarks [on custom and treaties], in Change and Stability at 9; Louis Henkin, *Human Rights and State "Sovereignty,"* 25 GA .J. Int'l. L. 37 (1995/96) [hereinafter *Human Rights and State "Sovereignty"*]; Simma & Alston, *Twilight of Customary International Law* at 90; Ted Stein, *The Approach of a Different Drummer. The Principle of the Persistent Objector in International Law,* 26 Harv. Int'l. L. J. 457, 457 (1985) [hereinafter *The Approach of a Different Drummer*].

25. Consider, for example, the strong and conflicting responses to the *Nicaragua* case. Symposium, *Appraisals of the ICJ's Decision: Nicaragua.* United States *(Merits),* 81 AJIL 77 (1987).

26. David Fidler, *Challenging the Classical Concept of Custom,* 1996 Ger. Y. B. Int'l L. 198, 216–31 [hereinafter *Challenging the Classical Concept of Custom*].

27. Charney, *Universal International Law* at 543.

28. Meron, Human Rights and Humanitarian Norms; Lori Bruun, *Beyond the 1948 Convention—Emerging Principles of Genocide in Customary International Law,* 17 MD. J. Int'l. L. & Trade 193, 2169717 (1993) [hereinafter *Beyond the 1948 Convention*]; Richard B. Lillich, *The Growing Importance of Customary International Human Rights Law,* 25 GA. J. Int'l. & Comp. L. 1, 8 (1995/96) [hereinafter *The Growing Importance of Customary International Human Rights Law*].

29. Reisman, *The Cult of Custom* at 135.

30. Arthur A. Weisburd, *Customary International Law: The Problem of Treaties,* 21 Vand. J. Transnational L. 1 (1988) [hereinafter Weisburd, *Customary IL*].

31. Kelly, *The Twilight of Customary International Law* at 451.

32. Anthony A. D'Amato, *Trashing Customary International Law,* 81 AJIL 101 (1987).

33. Robert Y. Jennings, *The Identification of International Law,* in International Law Teaching at 3, 5.

34. Curtis A. Bradley & Jack L. Goldsmith, *Customary International Law as Federal Common Law: A Critique of the Modern Position,* 110 Harv. L. Rev. 815, 838 (1997); Kelly, *The Twilight of International Law* at 454 n.20, 484.

35. Stein, *Remarks [on customs and treaties]* in Change and Stability at 12.

36. Bin Cheng, in International Law at 249.

37. Hilary C. M. Charlesworth, *Customary International Law and the* Nicaragua *Case,* 1984–87 Austl. YB. Int'l. L. [hereinafter *Customary International Law and the* Nicaragua *Case*].

38. Simma & Alston, *The Sources of Human Rights Law* at 88, 96.

39. 1d. at 102–06.

40. Daniel Bodansky, *Customary (and Not So Customary) International Environmental Law,* 3 IND.J. Global Legal Stud. 105, 116–19 (1995) [hereinafter *Customary (and Not So Customary) International Environmental Law*].

41. Frederic L. Kirgis Jr., *Custom on a Sliding Scale*, 81 AJIL 146 (1987) [hereinafter *Custom on a Sliding Scale*]; John Tasioulas, *In Defense of Relative Normativity: Communitarian Values and the* Nicaragua *Case*, 16 Oxford J. Legal Stud. 85 (1996) [hereinafter *In Defense of Relative Normativity*].

42. Kirgis, *Custom on a Sliding Scale* at 149.

43. Simma & Alston, *The Sources of Human Rights Law* at 83.

44. For an explanation of the phrases "apology for power" and "utopian and unachievable," see Martti Koskenniemi, From Apology to Utopia: The Structure of International Legal Argument 2 (1989).

45. Ronald Dworkin, Law's Empire (1986); John Rawls, A Theory of Justice 20 (1972).

46. Bin Cheng, *Custom: The Future of General State Practice in a Divided World*, in The Structure and Process of International Law: Essays in Legal Philosophy, Doctrine, and Theory 513, 539 (Ronald St. J. Macdonald & Douglas M. Johnston eds., 1983).

47. Bodansky, *Customary (and not so Customary) International Environmental Law* at 116–19.

48. Jerome Frank, *Law and the Modern Mind*, in Lloyd's Introduction to Jurisprudence (Michael Freeman ed., 6th ed. 1994); Oliver Wendell Holmes, *The Path of Law*, 10 Harv. L. Rev. 457, 457 (1896–97); Karl Llewellyn, *Some Realism About Realism*, 44 Harv. L. Rev. 1222 (1931).

49. Simma & Alston, *The Sources of Human Rights* at 89.

50. Bin Cheng, *Custom: The Future of General State Practice in a Divided World* at 539; Charlesworth, *Customary International Law and the* Nicaragua *Case* at 27.

51. Thomas R. Tyler, Why People Obey the Law 170–73 (1990). . . .

52. Tyler, Why People Obey the Law at 163, 170–73, 175–78; Thomas M. Franck, *Legitimacy in the International System*, 82 AJIL 705. . . .

53. These values are intersubjective, i.e., values commonly held by a group of subjects, in this case states. Jan Narveson, *Inter-subjective*, in The Oxford Companion to Philosophy (Ted Honderich ed., 1995) [hereinafter Oxford Companion].

54. H. L. A. Hart, The Concept of Law at 225.

55. Hans Kelsen, Principles of International Law 307–08, 418 (1952).

56. Kelly, *The Twilight of Customary Law*, at 479–80.

57. Simma & Alston, *The Sources of Human Rights Law*, at 89.

58. Bruun, *Beyond the 1948 Convention* at 2169717; Lillich, *The Growing Importance of Customary International Human Rights Law* at 8.

59. *E.g.*, *Nicaragua*, 1986 ICJ Rep. 14.

60. Bodansky, *Customary (and Not So Customary) International Environmental Law*.

61. Henkin, *Human Rights and State "Sovereignty"* at 34–35.

62. Schacter, *supra* note 15, at 11; Fernando R. Teson, Humanitarian Intervention: An Inquiry Into Law and Morality 14 (1988); Theodor Meron, *On a Hierarchy of International Human Rights*, 80 AJIL 1, 199720 (1986); Oscar Schachter, *Entangled Treaty and Custom*, in International Law at a Time of Perplexity 717, 733–34 (Yoram Dinstein ed., 1989).

63. Restatement, sec. 102.

64. Vienna Convention on the Law of Treaties, *opened for signature* May 23, 1969, Art. 53, 1155 UNTS 331; *see also* Restatement, sec. 102; David Harris, Cases and Materials on International Law 42, 835 (5th ed. 1998); H. W. A. Thirlway, International Customary Law and Codification 110 (1972); Charlesworth, *Customary International Law and the* Nicaragua *Case* at 4; H.W.A. Thirlway, International Customary Law and Codification (1989); Antonio Cassese, International Law in a Divided World 179 (1989).

65. Schachter, International Law in Theory and Practice (1995) at 11; see also Schachter, *Entangled Treaty and Custom,* in International Law at a Time of Perplexity (Yoram Dinstein ed., 1989), at 733–34 [hereinafter *Entangled Treaty and Custom*].

66. *Nicaragua,* 1986 ICJ REP, at 98, para. 186.

67. Henkin, *Human Rights and State "Sovereignty"* at 37; Fred L. Morrison, *Legal Issues in the* Nicaragua *Opinion,* 8] AJIL 160, 162 (1987).

68. Vienna Convention on the Law of Treaties, Art. 26; Schachter, *Entangled Treaty and Custom* at 727–28.

69. According to the persistent objector rule, states that have persistently objected during the emergence of a custom are not bound by it. Gerald Fitzmaurice, *The General Principles of International Law Considered from the Standpoint of the Rules of Law,* 92 Recueil Des Cours 1, 49–50 (1957); Stein, *The Approach of a Different Drummer* at 457. However, the International Court of Justice has endorsed the persistent objector rule only twice, and arguably in *obiter dicta.* Fisheries case (UK v. Nor.), 1951 ICJ Rep. 16, 131 (Dec. 18); Asylum (Colom./Peru), 1950 ICJ Rep. 266, 2779778 (Nov. 20); *see also* Nuclear Tests (Austl. v. Fr.), 1974 ICJ Rep. 253, 286–93 (Dec. 20) (Gross, J., sep. op.). Further, a state cannot be a persistent objector to *jus cogens* rules and theorists have generally concluded that the practical application of the rule is limited. Byers, Custom, Power, and the Power of Rules at 181; Anthony A. D'Amato, The Concept of Custom in International Law (1971) at 187–99, 233–63 [hereinafter The Concept of Custom in International Law]; Jonathan I. Charney, *The Persistent Objector Rule and the Development of Customary International Law,* 1986 Brit, YB. Int'l. L. 1, 11–16.

70. It may also discourage states from voting for aspirational instruments. Thomas M. Franck, *Some Observations on the ICJs Procedural and Substantive Innovations,* 81 AJIL 116, 119 (1987).

71. *Nicaragua,* 1986 ICJ Rep. at 113–14, paras. 217–18; Meron, Human Rights and Humanitarian Norms as Customary Law at 6–7, 27; Pierre Imbert, *Reservations and Human Rights Conventions,* 6 Hum. Rts. Rev. 28 (1981); Schachter, *Entangled Treaty and Custom* at 727–28.

72. Vienna Convention on the Law of Treaties, art. 43.

73. Prosper Weil, *Towards Relative Normativity in International Law?* 77 AJIL 413, 438 (1983).

74. Cassese, International Law in a Divided World at 31, 110, 398; Charlesworth, *Customary International Law and the* Nicaragua *Case* at 1973; Tasioulas, *In Defense of Relative Normativity* at 116–17.

75. Kirgis, *Custom on a Sliding Scale* at 148.

76. Reservations to the Convention on the Prevention and Punishment of the Crime of Genocide, Advisory Opinion, 1951 ICJ Rep. 15, 23 (May 28).

77. Corfu Channel case (UK v. Alb.), Merits, 1949 ICJ Rep. 4, 22 (Apr. 9).

78. Koskenniemi, From Apology to Utopia at 2.

79. Byers, Custom, Power, and the Power of Rules at 49.

80. Koskenniemi, From Apology to Utopia at 42.

81. David Kennedy, *When Renewal Repeals: Thinking Against the Box,* 32 N.Y.U. J. Int'l. L. & Pol. 335, 355 (2000) [hereinafter *When Renewal Repeals*].

82. Dworkin, Law's Empire at 271.

83. Kennedy, *When Renewal Repeals* at 407.

84. Mohammed Medjaoui, Toward a New International Economic Order (1929) at 141–44 [hereinafter Toward a New International Economic Order].

85. Fidler, *Challenging the Classical Concept of Custom* at 220–22, 224–25.

86. Byers, Custom, Power and the Power of Rules at 49.

87. Koskenniemi, From Apology to Utopia at 42.

88. Kelly, *The Twilight of Customary International Law* at 451.

89. Dworkin, Law's Empire at 66.

90. Id.

91. Id. at 65–66.

92. Id. at 255.

93. Id. at 256.

94. Id.

95. Ronald Dworkin, *Law and Morals, Natural Law,* and *Legal Positivism,* in Oxford Companion, at 473, 473–74, 606, 606–07, and 476,476–77, respectively; Ronald Dworkin, *Law as Interpretation,* 60 Tex. L. Rev. 527, 528 (1982) [hereinafter Dworkin, *Interpretation*].

96. Dworkin, *Interpretation* at 528.

97. Ronald Dworkin, Taking Rights Seriously 340–41 (3d ed. 1981); Ronald Dworkin, *Is There Really No Right Answer in Hard Cases?* in A Matter of Principle 143 (1985).

98. Dworkin, Law's Empire at 255–57.

99. Id. at 66.

100. John Finnis, *On Reason and Authority* in Law's Empire, 6 Law & Phil. 357, 373–74 (1987) [hereinafter *On Reason and Authority*].

101. Dworkin, Law's Empire at 246–47.

102. Id. at 257.

103. Id. at 228–32.

104. Finnis, *On Reason and Authority* at 374.

105. Bodansky, *Customary (and Not So Customary) International Environmental Law.*

106. ICJ Statute Art. 38(1) (b); North Sea Continental Shelf (FRG/Den.; FRG/Neth.), 1969 ICJ Rep. 3, 44 (Feb. 20).

107. See *Nicaragua,* 1986 ICJ Rep. 14; Namibia Advisory Opinion, 1971 ICJ Rep. 16; Corfu Channel case (UK v. Alb.), Merits, 1949 ICJ Rep. 4, 34 (Apr. 9).

108. Kirgin, *Custom on a Sliding Scale* at 149.

109. Id.

110. See also "coherentism" in epistemology. Nicholas Everitt & Alec Fisher, Modern Epistemology 102–07 (1995).

111. Thomas M. Franck, Fairness in International Law and Institutions (1995); Thomas M. Franck, The Power of Legitimacy Among Nations (1990); Franck, *Legitimacy in the International System* at 735–36.

112. Rawls, A Theory of Justice (1972) at 20; John Rawls, *Outline of a Decision Procedure for Ethics,* 60 Phil. Rev. 177 (1951); see also Dworkin, Law's Empire at 66 is.17. I am not arguing that the international system is akin to Rawls's concept of the original position; rather, that his notion of a reflective equilibrium can be used more generally to reconcile inductive and deductive methodologies.

113. Rawls, A Theory of Justice at 21.

114. Id. at 19–20.

115. Rawls, A Theory of Justice at 20 n.7; see also Nelson Goodman, Fact, Fiction, and Forecast 65–68 (4th ed. 1983).

116. Dworkin, Law's Empire at 239–40.

117. Byers, Custom, Power, and the Power of Rules at 156–62; D'Amato, The Concept of Custom at 56–66.

118. Hart, The Concept of Law at 90.

119. D'Amato, The Concept of Custom at 97–98.

120. Weisburd, *Customary IL* at 30–31.

121. North Sea Continental Shelf (FRG/Den.; FRG/Neth.), 1969 ICJ Rep. 3, 44 (Feb. 20); id. at 230–31 (Lachs, J., dissenting); Akehurst, The Concept of Custom at 37; Weisburd, *Customary IL* at 107.

122. Rawls, A Theory of Justice at 20.

123. D'Amato, The Concept of Custom at 97.

124. Byers, Custom, Power, and the Power of Rules at 157–59.

125. Bin Cheng, in International Law at 249.

126. Anthony A. D'Amato & Sudhir K. Chopra, *Whales: Their Emerging Right to Life,* 85 AJIL 21 (1991).

127. *Nicaragua,* 1986 ICJ Rep. at 109, para. 207.

128. Id.

129. Id. at 98, para. 186.

130. *E.g.,* Charney, *supra* note 124, at 834; Louis Henkin, *Kosovo and the Law of Humanitarian Intervention,* 93 AJIL 824, 824–25 (1999).

131. Charney, *Anticipatory Humanitarian Intervention in Kosovo* at 834.

132. Bruno Simma, *NATO, The UN and the Use of Force: Legal Aspects,* 10 Eur. J. Int'l. L. 1 (1999), at <http://www.ejil.org/journal/index.html> (visited Oct. 1, 2001) [hereinafter *NATO, The UN and the Use of Force*].

133. Cassese, Ex iniuria ius oritur: *Are We Moving Towards International Legitimation of Forcible Humanitarian Countermeasures in the World Community?*

134. The draft resolution condemning NATO's use of force, UN Doc. S/I 999/328, was sponsored by Belarus, India, and the Russian Federation and supported by China, Namibia, and the Russian Federation in the Security Council.

135. For example, German Foreign Minister Kinkel stated, "The decision of NATO [on air strikes against the Federal Republic of Yugoslavia] must not become a precedent." Deutscher Bundesug, Plenarprotokoll 13/248, at 23, 129 (Oct. 16, 1998), quoted in Simma, *NATO, the UN and the Use of Force.*

136. Some states focused exclusively on the preliminary issue of jurisdiction; others, including Germany, argued that the intervention represented a justifiable exception to the normal rules. The United States focused on the humanitarian catastrophe, the acute threat to security of neighboring states, the serious violation of humanitarian law, and the resolutions of the Security Council but did not expressly argue for a right to unilateral humanitarian intervention. Oral pleadings (Yugo. v. U.S. et al.), 1999 ICJ Pleadings (Legality of Use of Force), at http://www.icj.cij.org.

137. Charney, *Anticipatory Humanitarian Intervention in Kosovo* at 836–39.

138. C. Gray, *After the Ceasefire: Iraq, the Security Council and the Use of Force,* 1994 Brit. Y.B. Int'l L. 135, 162; Dino Kritsiotis, *Reappraising Policy Objections to Humanitarian Intervention,* 19 Mich. J. Int'l. L. 1005, 1014 (1998).

139. Charney, *Anticipatory Humanitarian Intervention in Kosovo* at 836–37.

140. Cassese, Violence and Law in the Modern Age 35–39; Meron, Human Rights and Humanitarian Norms as Customary at 60; Henkin, How Nations Behave at 70; Charlesworth, *Customary International Law and the* Nicaragua *Case* at 21.

141. SC Res 1203 (Oct. 24, 1998); see also SC Res. 1199 (Sept. 23, 1998); SC Res. 1160 (Mar. 31, 1998).

142. *See* UN Doc. S/1999/328.

143. This distinction is made by D'Amato, The Concept of Custom at 61–63, though not with respect to unilateral humanitarian intervention.

144. Brownlie, Principles of Public International Law at 515; Cassese, International Law in a Divided World at 147.

145. Brownlie, Principles of Public International Law at 515; Shaw, *Genocide in International Law* in International Law in a Time of Perplexity.

146. Kritsiotis, *Reappraising Policy Operations in Humanitarian Intervention* at 1040–46.

147. Christine M. Chinkin, *Kosovo: A "Good" or "Bad" War?* 93 AJIL 841, 847 (1999).

148. Kritsiotis, *Reappraising Policy Operations in Humanitarian Intervention* at 1040–46.

149. Henkin, *Kosovo and the Law of "Humanitarian Intervention"* at 824–25.

150. Ruth Wedgwood, *NATO's Campaign in Yugoslavia,* 93 AJIL 828, 833 (1999).

151. Cassese, Ex iniuria ius oritur; Charney, *Anticipatory Humanitarian Intervention in Kosovo* at 836–39; Wedgwood, *NATO's Campaign in Yugoslavia* at 828.

152. Akehurst, *Custom as a Source of International Law* at 53.

153. Koskenniemi, From Apology to Utopia at 2.

154. Meron, Human Rights and Humanitarian Norms as Customary Law at 44–45.

155. Id. at 44; Schachter, *New Custom: Power,* Opinio Juris *and Contrary Practice* at 539; Schachter, *Entangled Treaty and Custom* at 735.

156. Meron, Human Rights and Humanitarian Norms as Customary Law 58.

157. Vienna Convention on the Law of Treaties, art. 53.

158. Supported by Resolution on Permanent Sovereignty over Natural Resources, GA Res. 1803, UN GAOR, 17th Sess., Supp. No. 17, at 15, UN Doc A/5217 (1962). *See also* Brownlie, Principles of Public International Law at 527–29, 535–38.

159. Supported by Charter of Economic Rights and Duties of States, GA Res. 3281, UN GAOR, 29th Sess., Supp. No. 30, at 50, UN Doc. A/9030 (1974). See also Brownlie, Principles of Public International Law, at 526–27, 538.

160. Meron, Human Rights and Humanitarian Norms as Customary Law 44.

161. Alasdair Macintyre, Three Rival Versions of Moral Enquiry: Encyclopaedia, Genealogy, and Tradition 234 (1990); see also Tasioulas, *In Defense of Relative Normativity* at 127.

162. Condorelli, Remarks [on *lex lata* and *lex ferenda*] at 81; Pellet, *The Normative Dilemma* at 47.

163. D'Amato, The Concept of Custom at 89; Henkin, *Human Rights and State "Sovereignty"* at 39, 42.

164. Chinkin, *The Challenge of Soft Law* at 857–858.

5

The New Treaty Makers

Jose E. Alvarez

The Proliferation of Treaties

. . . There is little doubt that recent decades have witnessed a striking proliferation in treaties, including multilateral agreements of ambitious substantive scope that aspire to universal participation. Since the establishment
of the U.N., treaties have attempted to codify both traditions topics of international law (e.g., the law of the sea, diplomatic and consular relations, the
law of treaties, the law of war, or international humanitarian law) as well as
newer subjects not previously regarded as amenable to or suitable for international regulation (such as trade, intellectual property, investment, and
international criminal law). From 1970 through 1997, the number of international treaties more than tripled.[1] Even that ostensible unilateralist, the
United States, has not been immune from being drawn into this dense treaty
network. In the 1990s the United States concluded 3106 treaties, after 3690
in the 1980s, 3212 in the 1970s, and 2438 in the 1960s.[2] We often suggest
that the primary explanation for international legalization is functionalism. In
other words, states are driven to regulate at the international level by ever-
rising movements of people, goods, and capital across borders, along with
positive and negative externalities emerging from such flows—from the rise
in a common house rights ideal to emerging threats to the global commons.
But we should not lose sight of the fact that the proliferation of treaties is
aided and abetted by the concomitant rise in intergovernmental organizations.[3] The age of global compacts is not incidentally also the age of IOs.

As of 1995, of some 1,500 multilateral treaties in existence, nearly half
were attributable to U.N. system organizations, and the rate of production

Reprinted by permission of the Boston College International and Comparative Law
Review.

of new treaties undertaken within the auspices of international organization appears to be steadily increasing.[4] A substantial number of the approximately 3500 meetings undertaken annually within the U.N. involve some kind of treaty-making activity and that organization alone has been involved in the conclusion of some 300 multilateral agreements.[5] The U.N. and other comparable institutions have helped to create a "gigantic treaty network . . . regulating all major international activities."[6] Some international organizations—such as the U.N. itself, the International Labour Organization (ILO), and the WTO—were intended to be what they have become: virtual treaty machines. Whole areas of modern international law including human rights, would be unimaginable absent treaties chided under IO auspices.[7]

The Role of International Organization

How have IOs changed the realities of treaty making to bring about multilateral regimes that are both decried and praised for eroding sovereignty?

In the 19th century, the fundamental mechanism for multilateral treaty making was the ad hoc conference. Before the advent of multilateral treaty making required the initiative of a state sufficiently aroused about an issue that it was willing to devote scarce diplomatic resources to motivate others and to convene such a conference on its territory. Usually, the initiator state determined which states to invite and the negotiating agenda. Once convened, the success or failure such conferences turned on the acumen and leverage exercised by the government representatives present. In accordance with the principle of sovereign equality, decisions were usually taken on the basis of unanimity. The governments present determined whether there would be subsequent efforts to complete the treaty or, if the treaty concluded, whether there would be any procedures for following the usual case, enforcement was left to reciprocal action by the individual state parties. Except in unusual circumstances, each multilateral treaty negotiation was a freestanding and entirely ad hoc undertaking, with no necessary connection to any other treaty arrangement.

The shortcomings of such conferences are, in retrospect, obvious.[8] Since they were dependent on the willingness of a particular state host, treaty making was haphazard and proposals for negotiations on such compacts usually came long after the need for international regulation had become acute. Even when treaty conferences were convened, there were no guarantees that all states needed to resolve the underlying problem or that would be affected by any proposed solution would be present. Complications could ensue due to the failure either to include all relevant state parties or all interests not being adequately represented by state delegations. Those invited and present at those conferences could not be sure that the full dimensions of an issue, much less related questions that might be of interest only to some states, would be aired—especially if such issues were deemed outside the scope of the host state's agenda or would raise prickly issues for the gracious host. Since preparations for such conferences were typically left to each state that managed to send a delegation, there was no assurance that negotiations would be based on all available technical or factual data or that all states would have equal access to any such information or to applicable legal precedents. Individuals at such negotiations may have met for the first time at the negotiating site and, given the absence of instantaneous communications, were relatively cut-off from their national capitals during the negotiation period. All of these factors led to rigidities in states' negotiating positions. All of them dampened the likelihood of success.[9]

In game theoretic terms, the ad hoc conferences of the 19th century resembled single play prisoners' dilemmas, lacking the benefits that we might achieve with repeated play or long term association, including reductions in transactions costs and uncertainty, and mutual reliance on long term reputation over short-term calculations of interest. There were few sunk costs involved in such forms of treaty making. No international civil servants existed to serve as repositories of knowledge, to transmit information or to propose compromise formulations; without international institutions, there were fewer mechanisms to enable states to pool their resources. There were few established rules of bureaucratic procedure that could be relied upon at the international level to encourage what economists and others have called "path dependencies."[10]

Further, multilateral treaties were, in the 19th century at least, not very multilateral. If a treaty was, despite evident deficiencies, concluded, the state designated as the state of registry was in a position to deny attempts to ratify by governments that it did not wish to associate with, thereby discouraging actual universal participation. Nor was this an entirely academic concern: this was a time, after all, when many states of the world were considered to be beneath the notice of "civilized states." Worse still, in the absence of ongoing mechanisms for follow-up, treaty regimes failed to deepen and could even become obsolete due to changing needs or technology.

The establishment of organizations aspiring to universal or nearly universal membership corrected many of these shortcomings and have made the ad hoc treaty conference unconnected to an established IO a less preferred venue for treaty making. Most multilateral treaty regimes of any depth today are the product of one or more of the following four organizational patterns for treaty making: (1) IO (especially U.N. sponsored) treaty-making conferences; (2) expert treaty-making bodies; (3) "managerial" forms of treaty making; or what some have called institutional mechanisms for "treaty making with strings attached." Each will be briefly described below.

U.N. treaty-making conferences—such as the massive 1998 negotiations at Rome to establish an International Criminal Court (ICC) involving approximately 160 states, 33 intergovernmental organizations, over 200 NGOs, and over 400 journalists on site—usually occur after a canvassing of views, occasionally exhaustive, and often convene with a draft text in hand. Modern treaty making conferences operate on the basis of flexible determinations of consensus rather than rigid unanimity rules. They follow established organizational patterns, such as division between a plenary and more specialized bodies and formal versus informal sessions. They rely as well on reasonably clear rules procedure that avoid the need to reinvent the wheel on such topics the credentials of delegates or rules for submitting proposals or quorums.[11] Often they rely upon familiar groupings of states seen elsewhere in the U.N.—associations that encourage issue linkage package deals. They use IO secretariats to conduct advance preparations (such as circulating detailed questionnaires among participants) to formulate manageable work plans, and to encourage reliance on final standard clauses as with respect to reservations and entry into force. IO staff also serve as legitimating conduits for proposals made by unpopular or isolated states. Members of the international civil service even on occasion assist in drafting compromise language.

The second organizational pattern relies on experts—as with respect to public international law (such as the International Law Commission [ILC]), international economic law (such as the United Nations Commission on International Trade Law [UNCITRAL]), or more specialized topics (such as the International Civil Aviation Organizations delineated), predictable procedures that produce large volumes of information, as with respect to the current practices and opinions of states. Usually working in tandem with U.N. conferences, these institutionalized experts produce drafts that, at their best, achieve technocratic legitimacy because of their source an quality. For example, ILC commentaries and draft provisions for proposed treaties that have yet to be concluded have sometimes been relied upon by states and others as reliable accounts of existing custom.

Managerial forms of treaty making, in areas such as trade, the environment, and human rights, attempt to secure the benefits of institutionalization on an on-going basis and not only when treaties are initially concluded. They establish entities that are authorized to elaborate standards, as well as monitoring bodies charged with enforcement and interpretation, including, in the cases of regional human rights and trade, binding forms of dispute settlement. Thus, environmental framework conventions establish committees of the parties and other working groups for on-going norm elaboration, interpretation, and "soft" enforcement, such as consideration of states reports of implementation. These framework conventions establish "living" treaty regimes without recourse, in the usual case, to formal international organizations with distinct legal personality or substantial secretariats. Whether or not they resort to harder forms of enforcement such as binding dispute settlement, several of these managerial regimes have deepened over time and all offer "the prospect of a virtually continuous legislative enterprise"[12] capable of responding to changes in technology or to the needs of the parties. The success of these modern treaty regimes can no longer be judged the way we judged the 19th century compact—through a snapshot frozen at a single moment in time. The success of these living treaties is now best measured through a modern motion picture, which is able to record their evolutionary development across time. The twelve protocols of the European system of Human Rights, the 1987 Montreal Protocol on Substances that Deplete the Ozone Layer, and the Uruguay Round are all products of managerial regimes and are characteristic of how they function.

Finally, there is treaty making that is constitutionally sanctioned, even mandated, under the charter of a formal full-fledged IO that tries to pressure its members to ratify the treaties produced by the regime. The clearest manifestation of such "treaty making with strings attached" is the ILO. The ILO's Constitution incorporates a highly structured, relatively rigid set of procedures that produce, at predictable intervals, treaty instruments—at last count over 1170 of them. The ILO's Constitution ties "strings" to its instruments, requiring ILO members to bring the conventions to the attention of their legislatures and requiring periodic follow-up reports on implementation. A variety of ILO expert bodies thereafter engage in monitoring and dispute settlement, though not clearly with binding effect. The ILO attempts, with mixed success, something of an end-run around sovereign consent. The reporting and other obligations imposed under the ILO's Charter mobilize shame on behalf of treaty ratification.

Of course, these four organizational patterns for treaty making are not invariably successful. Some organizational venues have delegitimized treaty negotiation efforts. During the bad old days of the New International Economic Order (NIEO), for example, endorsement of an economic treaty by the General Assembly was the kiss of death—at least among western business constituencies. IO bureaucracies like bureaucracies elsewhere, may also prove inefficient or ineffective at encouraging agreement; they may develop their own agendas at the expense of the state principals they ostensibly serve. Ritualized institutional precedents may sometimes limit negotiators' field of vision; path dependencies, such as an infatuation with decisions by "consensus" however cosmetic, may lock negotiations onto the wrong historical path or result in meaningless lowest common denominator solutions. Modern international law is strewn with the wreckage of package deals that fail to secure the rates of ratification expected within a reasonable time—even when these result from the efforts of experts as in the ILO. And there is no guarantee that even when IOs promulgate widely

ratified treaties, what IOs produce are any better at taking care of the underlying problems sought to be solved. As with respect to domestic law, more
law or more treaties is not necessarily a good thing. Quantity should not be
confused with quality.

But, these four organizational patterns have changed the landscape of
treaty making in at least *five* respects that are essential to understanding both
the nature of globalization as well as perceived erosions of sovereignty.

First, IOs have dramatically expanded the diversity of actors involved
in treaty making. The winners have been less powerful governments, NGOs
and other interest groups, the international civil service and experts, including public international law scholars. Due to the use of IOs as venues, it is
now far more likely that even small less powerful states will be able to
make an impact on the types of issues that are subject to treaty negotiations,
as well as with respect to the substance of what is ultimately concluded.
Thanks to such venues less powerful governments are more likely to be
able to secure the benefits of a treaty obligation with powerful states. Without IOs, powerful states would be freer to engage bilaterally or multilaterally only with those states with whom they have an interest in contracting.
IOs, even if only by making the neutral U.N. and not a host state the depository of treaty ratifications, have made modern multilateral treaties more
truly multilateral, thereby democratizing treaty making.

Structural aspects of IOs, including provisions for access to documents
and for observer or other forms of non-voting status, have in addition provided entry points for NGOs' growing participation in various forms of
interstate diplomacy, including treaty making. They permit domestic interest groups, along with relevant domestic government agencies, to direct
their lobbying efforts on those IOs that are the most promising venues for
their concerns. Thus, business groups in the United States whose competitive interests were threatened by the United States' Foreign Corrupt Practices Act sought to multilateralize the regulation of bribery—and thereby
level the playing field—in the forum most likely to reach their main European and Japanese competitors, namely the Organization for Economic
Cooperation and Development (OECD). Similarly, a transnational alliance
of business leaders anxious to secure enforceable intellectual property
rights, dissatisfied with World Intellectual Property Organization's (WIPO)
efforts, were able to frame this issue as a proper matter for the WTO.[13]

In addition, the conception of an international civil service as a breed
apart, distinct from the governments from which these individuals emerge,
has legitimized the participation of IO secretariats in treaty making. The
power of such individuals to become active in treaty making, only sometimes
explicitly conferred—as in a resolution inviting secretariat participation in
the compiling of state views or in drafting an initial negotiating text—has
been generally assumed to be part of a secretariat's "implied powers."

Expert treaty-drafting bodies have opened the door to yet other type of non-state actor: the individual legitimized by their expertise and claim to independence. In other organizations, such as the ILO, the participation of distinct constituencies—namely employers and labor unions—is built into the constitutional structure treaty making. In these respects as well the involvement of IOs treaty making has "democratized" the process. The wider diversity of state and non-state actors helps to explain the wider diversity of treaties concluded in the age of IOs, as well as the variety of pressures that are brought to bear on those governmental representatives who are still, in most respects, at least formally in charge of the initiation of treaty making, as well as formal ratification.

Second, IOs have either multiplied the options for treaty initiators or complicated their lives depending on one's point of view. Today, the initiation of a multilateral treaty negotiation requires, as a key and crucial decision, the matter of organizational venue. Those in on negotiating modern international compacts need to decide just between whether to convene a special ad hoc conference or resort to a standing international organization. They also need to decide which international organization and which organs within them ought to be involved. In recent years, the international community has confronted a number of such choices. Treaty efforts on bribery have involved regional IOs such as the OECD, the European Union, the OAS, and the Council of Europe, as well as international financial organizations and the U.N. General Assembly.[14] Nuclear proliferation issues have involved choices as between the IAEA or the U.N. General Assembly, while foreign investment, initially considered in the OECD (and in regional treaties), may yet be folded into the WTO.

Determining which organization and which sub-organ ought be the venue in which to initiate a treaty process may determine whether the process will involve time-consuming and exhaustive analysis of the current state of the law by general legal experts,[15] more superficial examination of the need for a treaty by those attentive to the political desires of states,[16] or thorough examination of the need for a treaty relegated to technical experts in relatively narrow specialties.[17] Alternatively, treaty initiators may opt for processes that contain elements of all of these, such as the ILO. Organizational venues may also determine whether negotiators will be able to take advantage of credible dispute settlement process[18] or other supervisory procedures, be able to engage in a gradualist strategy that relies initially on soft law and soft enforcement, or be able to secure efficacious regional credibility.[19] The choice of organizational venue may determine whether treaty negotiations will be more or less transparent since distinct IOs have different traditions in this respect. Given this range of choices, the ability to choose among organizational venues implicitly forces treaty initiators to consider matters relating to the substance of the proposed treaty even before formal negotiations begin.

The choice of organizational venue speaks volumes concerning the intent of principal treaty backers. Those who attempt to insert a new issue in a WTO trade round, for example, would appear to be suggesting that the issue has an implicit link to trade, since that is the WTO's domain, and that it is an issue that can be appropriately made the subject of WTO dispute settlement as well as WTO-sanctioned trade retaliation if necessary, since these remedies have, at least since the Uruguay Round, been assumed to be applicable to all or most matters within the WTO. Anticipation that both the linkage to trade and enforcement issues will need to be addressed casts a shadow—a positive and a negative—over the prospect of initiating negotiations within the WTO.[20] While it might be assumed that the prospective binding dispute settlement would tend to discourage adding new issues to the trade regime, it would appear that in at least some cases such organizational realities may enhance the attractiveness of the WTO. Certainly the pressure to link some issues to the trade regime such as labor rights or environmental concerns, stems in part from penance-envy:[21] the perception, accurate or not, that WTO dispute settlement constitutes the most effective enforcement tool available at the global level and that such a potentially effective tool ought to be made applicable to these other concerns. At the same time, IOs develop distinct institutional cultures that may hinder attempts to use them as negotiating venues in some cases. The WTO's tradition of including issues in trade rounds only if these can be the basis of reciprocal concessions, for example, may make it difficult to build into regime treaty commitments less amenable to such trades.[22]

Third, because IOs increase the number of actors involved as well as the options available to treaty makers, they have a third impact; they alter the role of state power. The involvement of IOs may decrease the salience of traditional state power. Unlike in the 19th century, a serious multilateral treaty negotiation today does not require a hegemonic prime mover. Suggestions for such negotiations may be and are made even by the least powerful state representatives to an international organization, as in the U.N. General Assembly or comparable plenary bodies where the formal rules for voting (state/one vote), can secure majority support for proposed treaty making over the opposition of a minority of powerful states. The 1990 action by the General Assembly that ultimately led to the successful conclusion of the Rome Statute for the ICC on July 17, 1998, stemmed from a 1989 initiative by Trinidad and Tobago, for example. Thanks to IOs, smaller or less powerful states are also more likely to find allies in a common cause, thereby permitting some leverage to be asserted even as against powerful states.

The access rights given to NGOs also increase the proportionate power of these purported representatives of international civil society over treaty-making decisions. Intense and successful NGO lobbying efforts on behalf of some treaties—as with respect to land-mines or to establish an individual complaints mechanism for the Convention of the Elimination of Discrimination Against Women (CEDAW)—are the predictable result.[23] The increasing attention given to the power NGOs misses part of the picture if it fails to acknowledge that intergovernmental organizations are often the conduit for the growing clout of NGOs.[24]

The very existence of IOs conditions the traditional use of state power. In theory, governments retain the option of starting treaty negotiations the old-fashioned way, namely through a diplomatic approach to select states and invitations to a special ad hoc conference to conclude a stand-alone treaty. In practice, while such ad hoc conferences continue to be used for some treaty negotiations, many modern multilateral treaty negotiations have been authorized by an IO, such as the U.N. General Assembly, and many of these treaties establish bodies that function much like IOs even after a text is concluded, as in environmental regimes. The reasons are straightforward: most treaty initiators want to secure the advantages of an organizational setting, and even when key players do not, there may be considerable political pressure brought to bear to secure the endorsement of the organizational body whose established competence appears most directly relevant. Today, even a powerful state would find it difficult to attempt a major multilateral treaty-making effort regarding international civil aviation, for example, without at least attempting to involve ICAO or presenting credible reasons why that institution's involvement would be inappropriate. In addition, should the relevant organs of ICAO, including the expert bodies normally involved in such efforts, reject such a proposal, the prospects for a successful negotiation involving a credible number of participants are considerably diminished. Where an IO exists with jurisdiction over a matter that is proposed for treaty making, its mere existence affects the decision of whether, when, and where to initiate such a negotiation.

At the same time, IOs remain vehicles for the assertion of power. The choice among organizational venues is often influenced not to say determined, by the continuing realities of relative power. It was important in the now comparatively innocent 1960s and 1970s when airline hijackings first dominated the headlines, for example, for the primary movers of anti-terrorism conventions, like the United States, to have these negotiations initiated in the relatively efficient confines of ICAO rather than in the U.N. General Assembly. Western preferences have also prevailed with respect to other choices of venue—as respect to the trade regime (over WIPO) for intellectual property; the International Atomic Energy Agency (IAEA) (over the General Assembly) for certain proliferation conventions; and OECD (over the WTO) for the aborted Multilateral Agreement Investment (MAI). Power still matters to modern treaty making but it is often exercised to a distinct end: to favor one organizational forum for negotiations over another.[25]

Even when powerful states prevail in their choice of organizational venue, that choice may constrain them. Particular organizational venues often constrain even the powerful. The United States paid a price for the various anti-terrorism conventions that it successfully and speedily concluded under ICAO auspices some thirty years ago. While the United States would have preferred a comprehensive treaty regime leading to the suppression of the most serious acts of terrorist violence regardless of setting, the ICAO setting for such negotiations, while far preferable to the U.S. standpoint than the General Assembly, compelled a narrower and more piecemeal approach. It virtually ensured criminalization only for acts directly relating to civil aviation, namely violence on board aircraft, the target of aircraft for destruction, aircraft hijacking, and offenses at international airports.[26] In addition, while the United States initially wanted a regime that would permit joint enforcement action such as an international civil aviation boycott against a state that failed to honor its obligations to extradite terrorists, it quickly abandoned this goal when negotiators realized that such a hard sanction was a non-starter in an organization with an ethos that identifies the right to engage in civil aviation as a fundamental sovereign right.[27] Today, in the wake of September 11th, the United States appears to be scrambling back to an organization that it sought to avoid in the 1970s, namely the U.N., since that organization now offers the better prospect for achieving broader anti-terrorism goals, including treaties that fill gaps remaining in the wake of ICAO's efforts.

In addition, since states rightly assume that the choice of organizational forum matters, they expend considerable resources to make sure the right one is chosen. Strenuous and diplomatically costly efforts were necessary to make sure that, for example, foreign investment negotiations were initiated in the OECD, and not the WTO. In that instance, while the United States and many of the other leading exporters of capital would have preferred a regime for foreign investment with global reach, the decision to negotiate the MAI within an organization with a more limited membership was a calculated, ultimately unsuccessful, gamble to forego geographical reach in favor of presumptive depth of obligation.

Fourth, international organizations have vastly increased the amount of information available to treaty initiators. The information supplied by organizational venues may encourage the initiation of treaty making directly, as through proposals made by IOs, or indirectly, by inspiring certain governments to act. Many have contended that the negotiations leading to the 1987 Montreal Protocol would never have been initiated, for example, but for the level of scientific data concerning ozone depletion generated by the various entities established by the preceding Vienna Convention for the Protection of the Ozone Layer.[28] The supply of information may alter not only the decision of whether to initiate treaty making, but how and where to do so. Today, decisions to pursue particular topics in a distinct organizational setting are likely to be taken with full awareness of the prior history of that forum with respect to the topic in question and may reflect an intention to affect the substantive result on many matters—and not merely enforcement method, as in the WTO example above. A decision to attempt to initiate today the subject of foreign investment in the next WTO trade round, for example, would appear tantamount to a decision to give up on certain investment protections. This would certainly be the implication a prospective treaty initiation would take from the WTO's extensive reports on its diverse membership's views on the subject, as well as the organization's prior efforts, as in connection with Trade Related Investment Measures (TRIMs) or the General Agreement on Trade in Services (GATS).[29] Those who, desiring a successful conclusion to such a negotiation, propose adding investment issues to the next WTO Round would presumably be doing so because they want investment guarantees to extend to the WTO's global membership, because even the "lesser" investor rights, and possible duties, would presumably be subject to binding WTO dispute settlement open only to GATT parties (and not directly to investors themselves as under bilateral investment treaties [BITs] and NAFTA's Chapter 11) because the failure of the OECD's prior efforts leaves no other credible organizational option, or because of some other presumed benefit, such as possible trade offs with respect to other issues anticipated within the same trade round. As this suggests, organizational venues and the information they produce considerably enhance the likelihood of "nesting" issues in a broader context so that the "fabric of one provides the foundation of another"[30] as well as with respect to making links between issues that facilitate package deals. It is also important to recognize that information produced by one organizational venue in the course of one treaty negotiation, such as the lengthy negotiations to conclude the U.N. Convention on the Law of the Sea, have had important spillover effects on other negotiations, as with respect to later dealings with respect to environmental accords; such effects are increasingly anticipated, thereby influencing interstate reactions in both the earlier and later sets of negotiations.

A decision to pursue negotiations in a particular organization might also be tantamount to a decision *not* to conclude a full-scale multilateral treaty on the subject but some other kind of instrument. Thus, decisions to initiate discussions in, for example, UNGITRAL, are taken with the full knowledge that, given the practices of that body, this may be tantamount to deciding in favor of either a "model law" that can inspire the harmonization of domestic laws or nonbinding "guidelines" instead of a binding treaty.[31] Certain organizational settings are suited to regulatory or recommendatory action and not the initiation of binding treaty instrument—and prove themselves attractive negotiating sites precisely for that reason. Indeed, we are becoming increasingly aware that IOs are dramatically changing the other primary source of international obligation—custom—as well as treaties. The new treaty makers are also generating new custom that differs markedly from the slow, laborious accumulation of bilateral practices and expressions of *opinio juris* that characterized traditional customary international law.[32]

As this suggests, international organizations may occasionally have an adverse impact on the possibility that particular multilateral negotiations will be initiated. Judging from the large number of multilateral efforts sponsored annually under their auspices, however, it would appear that the existence of permanent organizational venues for such negotiations has generally made states more amenable to multilateral treaty making—or at least made it more likely that a shrewd initiator will be able to find a forum that favors treaty negotiations.

This implies a fifth and final change from 19th century treaty-making efforts: particularly to the extent anticipated treaty negotiations are to take place within established organizational fora and not through the convening of a special ad hoc conference, support for initiating treaty negotiations may emerge much more easily and quickly than in an earlier age when states were required to mobilize and devote substantial diplomatic and other resources for such efforts. Treaty negotiations are, in short, more likely when they can take advantage of organizational venues whose "sunk costs" have already been absorbed by their members. Voting in favor (or, more common, merely refusing to disturb consensus) of a resolution that directs that international civil servants ought to study "topic x" with respect to the "propriety of concluding an international convention" on said topic is often seen as an anodyne or a relatively cost free decision. Even when a state's delegate to the IO in question realizes that such decision is not really cost free and that it may begin a process whose momentum may prove difficult to stop, it is usually less painful politically to join consensus in favor of initiating treaty negotiations than resist. In addition, to the extent organizational venues with a diverse membership tend to expand the potential negotiating agenda and increase the potential for nesting and package deals, these realities increase the numbers of states willing to engage in negotiations or to whom such negotiations are of interest.

Notes

1. Stewart Patrick, *Multilateralism and its Discontents: The Causes and Consequences of U.S. Ambivalence,* in *Multilateralism and U.S. Foreign Policy* 10 (Stewart Patrick & Shepard Forman eds., 2002).

2. *United States Senate, Treaties and Other International Agreements: The Role of the United States Senate—A Study Prepared for the Committee on Foreign*

Relations, S. Doc. No. 106–71, 106th Cong., 2d Sess. 39 (2001). A study of the treaty practices of the United States in the most recent period, after its rise to the status of sole superpower, finds traditional U.S. ambivalence towards adherence to treaties only "slightly more marked" than in prior periods. See Nico Krisch, *Weak as a Constraint, Strong as a Tool. The Place of International Law in U.S. Foreign Policy,* in *Unilateralism and U.S. Foreign Policy* (David Malone & Yuen Foong Khong eds., 2003).

3. At present, there are more than 250 conventional international governmental organizations, roughly another 5200 intergovernmental bodies of various kinds, and over 1500 non-governmental organizations registered with the U.N. See Charlotte Ku, *Global Governance and the Changing Face of International Law,* 2 AUNS Rep. And Papers 5, 24 (2001). While these numbers are impressive, it is important to recognize that international institutions have life cycles and occasionally die. The growth in these institutions "occasionally plateau[s] following periodic organizing burst." Id. at 22 (quoting Shanks, Jacobson, and Kaplan).

4. Paul Szasz, *General Law-Making Processes,* in 35 United Nations Legal Order 59 (Oscar Schachter & Christopher C. Joyner eds., 1995). While, according to one study, there were only eighty-six multilateral treaties concluded in the 100 years between 1751–1850, there were more than 2000 concluded for the twenty-five year period between 1951–1975. Ku, *supra* note 10, at 5. This is not to suggest, however, either that the number of multilateral treaties has been raising in predictable or steady fashion over recent years or that even greater numbers of traditional intergovernmental organizations on the model of the U.N. are being established by such treaties. Neither is true. That study reveals a drop-off in the number of new multilateral treaties being concluded in the 1976–1995 period compared to the period of 1951–1976, along with a decrease in the number of treaties that create conventional intergovernmental organizations in the model of the U.N. Id. at 5–23. That study also indicates that multilateral treaties intended for general participation by all states still constitute a minority of all treaties concluded annually and that the bulk of treaty making remains on a bilateral basis. Id. at 5. But note that the absence of growth in traditional intergovernmental organizations does not signify a withdrawal of commitment from other forms of institutionalization considered here, including the rise in unconventional forms of institutions. For a survey of these in one specified field, see for example, Paul C. Szasz, *The Proliferation of Arms Control Organizations,* in *Proliferation of International Organizations* 135 (N. M. Blokker & H. G. Schermers eds., 2001); see also Philippe Sands & Pierre Klein, *Bowett's Law of International Institutions* 121–28 (5th ed. 2001) (discussing environmental accords).

5. Roy Lee, *Multilateral Treaty-Making and Negotiation Techniques: An Appraisal,* in *Contemporary Problems of International Law: Essays in Honour of Georg Schwarzenberger on His Eightieth Birthday* 157 (Bin Chang & Edward Brown eds., 1998).

6. Id. at 158.

7. See id. at 177–216.

8. See, e.g., Sands & Klein, *supra* note 11, at 1–4. This is not to deny the impact, over the long term, of conferences such as the First Hague Peace Conference in 1899 which, in the views of some, helped to usher in the modern period devoted to building international institutions culminating in the establishment of the League of Nations. See, e.g., Ku, *supra* note 10, at 14–15.

9. See, e.g., Sands & Klein, *supra* note 11, at 3–4.

10. For a survey and critique of path dependency theory, see S. J. Liebowitz & Stephen E. Margolis, *Path Dependence, Lock-in, and History,* 11 J. L. Econ. & Org.

205 (1995). For consideration of the relevance of path dependency to the evolution of the common law, see Oona A. Hathaway, *Path Dependence in the Law: The Course and Pattern of Legal Change in a Common Law System*, 86 Iowa L. Rev. 601, 622–30 (2001).

11. Robbie Sabel, *A Study of the Rules of Procedure for Conferences and Assemblies of International Intergovernmental Organizations* (1997).

12. Gunter Handl, *Environmental Security and Global Change: The Challenge of International Law* in *Environmental Protection and International Law* 199 (W. Lang et al. eds., 1991).

13. See Kenneth W. Abbott, *Rule-Making in the WTO: Lessons from the Case of Bribery and Corruption*, 4 J. Int'l. Econ. L. 275, 282–83 (2001). Abbott goes on to explain that business interests did not pursue their interests in transnational regulation on bribery within the WTO because leveling the playing field against the smaller non-OECD competitors "was not a sufficiently high priority." Id. at 282.

14. Id.

15. Such as the ILC.

16. E.g., in the assemblies of various IOs representing the full membership.

17. Such as in ICAOs Legal Committee.

18. As in the WTO.

19. See, e.g., id. at 289–90 (noting how the U.S.'s strategy with respect to the regulation of bribery was highly congenial to the OECD given that organization's tendency to act through a variety of both hard and soft instruments, as well as reliance on peer review and public pressure rather than litigation).

20. Id.

21. I owe this colorful turn of phrase to Joel Trachtman.

22. See, e.g., Abbott, *supra* note 20, at 286, 291. Abbott contends that the WTO's culture of focusing on market access to the exclusion of more normative dimensions as well as emphasis on hard law rather than softer obligations, made it an unlikely forum for focusing on the normative aspects of the bribery and corruption issue in the ways that the OECD was able to do. Id. at 286–291.

23. For a discussion of the early evolution of an Operational Protocol to CEDAW, and the impact of U.N.-sponsored human rights conferences at Vienna (1993) and Beijing (1995), see Lilly Sharipa-Behrmann, *An Optimal Protocol to CEDAW: A Further Step Towards Strengthening of Women's Human Rights,* in *Liber Amicorum: Professor Ignaz Siedl Honhenveldern in Honour of His 80th Birthday* 683 (Gerhard Hafner et al. eds., 1998). For a critical view of the significant role played by NGOs with respect to the landmines convention, see Kenneth Anderson, *The Ottawa Convention Banning Landmines, the Role of International Non-governmental Organizations and the Idea of International Civil Society,* 11 Eur. J. Int'l. L. 91 (2000).

24. Indeed, some believe that international society has entered a new post-institutional period dominated by international civil society. See, e.g., Ku, *supra* note 10 at 26–34 (noting the larger rise in the numbers of NGOs relative to the more modest increase in the numbers of traditional intergovernmental organizations).

25. Nor, of course, does power cease to be relevant once negotiations begin or a treaty is concluded. As ICAO's anti-terrorism conventions remind us, use of an organizational venue for purposes of negotiation does not ensure that organizational mechanisms will be used for enforcement. Those conventions avoid the use of established ICAO fora, including the methods of dispute settlement within ICAO's constitution (resort to the ICAO Council and to the ICJ). Instead, the extradition and prosecution regime effectively puts the onus of enforcement back on state parties,

thereby giving powerful states, capable of exerting leverage on others, considerable free rein.

26. See Tokyo Convention on Offenses and Certain Other Acts Committed on Board Aircraft, Sept. 14, 1963, 20 U.S.T. 2941, 704 U.N.T.S. 219; Hague Convention for the Suppression of Unlawful Seizures of Aircraft, Dec. 16, 1970, 22 U.S.T. 1641, 860 U.N.T.S. 105; Montreal Convention for the Suppression of Unlawful Acts Against the Safety of Civil Aviation, Sept. 23, 1971, 24 U.S.T. 565; Protocol for the Suppression of Unlawful Acts of Violence at Airports Serving International Civil Aviation, Feb. 24, 1988, ICAO Doc. 9518, 27 I.L.M. 627.

27. See Geoffrey M. Levitt, *Democracies Against Terror* 10–11 (1988) (discussing history of the 1970 Hague Convention for the Suppression of Unlawful Seizure of Aircraft).

28. See, e.g., Robin R. Churchill & Geir Ulfstein, *Autonomous Institutional Arrangements in Multilateral Environmental Agreements: A Little-Noticed Phenomenon in International Law*, 94 AM. J. Int'l. L. 623 (2000). For a more critical view of managerial regimes, see George W. Downs et al., *The Transformative Model of International Regime Design: Triumph of Hope or Experience?* Colum. J. Transnat'l L. 465 (2000).

29. See General Agreement on Trade in Services, Apr. 15, 1974, Marrakesh Agreement Establishing the World Trade Organization, Annex 1B, *Legal Instruments—Results of the Uruguay Round*, 33 I.L.M. 1167 (1994) [hereinafter GATS]; Agreement on Trade Related Investment Measures, Apr. 15, 1994, Marrakesh Agreement Establishing the World Trade Organization, Annex 1A, *Legal Instruments—Results of the Uruguay Round* 33 I.L.M. 81 (1994) [hereinafter TRIMS]; see also *International Trade Law Handbook* 387–531 (Raj Bhala ed., 2001). These Agreements are also available on the WTO web site at http://www.wto.org (last visited Feb. 21, 2002).

30. For a description of nesting, see Duncan Snidal, *The Game Theory of International Politics*, 58 World Pol. 25, 45 (1985).

31. For a recent report of UNCITRAL's efforts, see *Report of the United Nations Commission on International Trade Law on the Works of its Thirty-Second Session*, U.N. GAOR, 54th Sess., Supp. No. 17, U.N. Doc. A/54/17 (1999).

32. New custom may emerge from consciously created norms applicable even with respect to non-parties to a widely ratified convention; it may also result from information generated in plenary organizational fora such as the U.N. General Assembly. See Jonathan I. Charney, *Universal International Law*, 87 AM. J. Int'l. L. 529, 536–42 (1995).

PART 1.2

International Law
as Operating System:
Participants in the
International Legal Process

6

State Succession:
The Once and Future Law

OSCAR SCHACTER

THIS [ARTICLE] RESPONDS TO THE DRAMATIC AND UNFORESEEN DISSOLUTION of states in Eastern Europe—the U.S.S.R., Yugoslavia and Czechoslovakia. It focuses on the legal category of "succession," a somewhat imprecise term that deals with the transmission or extinction of rights and obligations of a state that no longer exists or has lost part of its territory. State succession is one of the oldest subjects of international law. Even Aristotle speculated in his *Politics* on the problem of continuity when "the state is no longer the same."[1] Grotius and the other founding fathers of international law proposed distinctions on grounds of reason and natural justice.[2] State practice, as usual in international law, was largely determined by perceived political interests influenced in some degree by conceptions, analogies and metaphors derived from juristic commentary. Underlying the legal discourse we can discern the human dramas: the break-up of age-old empires and the emergence of new identities, new voices, new frontiers separating peoples or uniting them, deeply affecting their personal lives. These events are not only the stuff of history; they foreshadow the future. We can be quite sure, as we look around us today, that some states will split, others will be absorbed, frontiers will be moved, and new generations will question old alliances and commitments. The problem that concerned Aristotle in the fourth century B.C., of the stability of legal obligation when political identities change, will persist on both the international as well as the domestic level.

[We are reminded] that international law is in motion and that old formulas may not meet current needs. The prevailing legal view in the nineteenth and much of the twentieth century accepted two basic principles relating to succession. One was the critical difference between succession of states and changes in government. The principle of succession was relevant only where one state was replaced by another in the responsibility for the international relations of a territory. The legal problem of succession did not arise when government—that is, internal political regimes—changed, no matter how profound or revolutionary a change. This principle, traced by scholars to Grotius, has been generally accepted by scholars, courts and foreign ministries. It was challenged, as Detlev Vagts points out, by the Soviet regime in its early effort to repudiate obligations of the Czarist government, an effort that did not succeed in changing doctrine or practice. It is evident that in sharply differentiating between "sovereignty" and "government," the law weighs heavily on the side of continuity of obligations when major political changes occur within sovereign states.

This basic differentiation between changes in government and changes in sovereignty is rarely questioned but, as pointed out by Daniel O'Connell (an eminent authority), the distinction "in some instances wears thin to the point of disappearance" and may be "quite arbitrary."[3] In his words, "[t]o permit the solution of complex political and economic problems to depend on this arbitrary cataloguing is to divorce the law from the actualities of international life."[4] Although O'Connell did not abandon the conceptual distinction, his skeptical comment is a reminder that the formal categories (which he attributes to hegelian notions of state "personality") are not as important as considering the practical consequences of political change in particular context. This pragmatic approach suggests that radical transformations of regimes may in some cases result in breaking the continuity of obligations, by applying the principle of *rebus sic stantibus* (or by treaty interpretation) rather than under the doctrine of state succession. [We are] more concerned with the practical consequences of continuity or disruption of sovereign obligations than with the formal structure of succession law. This does not mean that the traditional structure of the law of state succession will be quickly jettisoned, but we can be quite sure that it will change in response to political developments.

The Law of Succession—Then and Now

A few words about the doctrinal history may be appropriate here. In its origin, the law of succession on the international level drew a basic distinction between obligations that were "personal" (as were the sovereigns) and obligations that were "dispositive" because they were linked to the "land" (or "real"). Only the latter survived the extinction of the personality. This personal-dispositive dichotomy seemed to provide a simple solution. Political treaties, treaties of alliances, and at least some debts not linked to territorial benefits ("odious" debts) did not survive. (When the United States took over Cuba in 1898 and when the British annexed South Africa, neither successor paid the debts of the predecessor states.[5]) With regard to treaties, McNair introduced the metaphor of "clean slate" in the following much-quoted passage:

> [N]ewly established States which do not result from a political dismemberment and cannot fairly be said to involve political continuity with any predecessor, start with a clean slate . . . except as regards the purely local or 'real' obligations of the State formerly exercising sovereignty over the territory of the new State.[6]

Local or "real" obligations included, most importantly, the preexisting boundaries whether or not included in a treaty instrument. As Rein Muller-son points out in this symposium, *uti possidetis juris* is now recognized as a customary law principle that establishes continuity of borders. This was noted by the Arbitration Commission of the European Community in regard to the frontiers of the newly recognized states resulting from the break-up of the former Socialist Federated Republic of Yugoslavia.[7]

One effect of the prevailing "personal-real" dichotomy was that delictual responsibility of an extinct state was not transferred to a successor state. Wrongful acts and obligations flowing from such acts were generally treated as "personal" by tribunals in claims cases and by most writers.[8] Some acts of the communist states of Eastern Europe must have involved violations of international law for which those states would have been responsible internationally. The old view that such responsibility should not be transferable to successors is by no means self-evident and persuasive arguments based on general principles of law (including unjust enrichment) can be made to support succession of liability in some situations.[9]

In the 1960's, state succession was placed high on the agenda of international lawyers in many countries as a result of the wave of decolonization and the efforts of the U.N. International Law Commission to codify the law of succession in relation to treaties and, separately, in regard to debts, state property and state archives. In the 1960's and 1970's, this gave rise to considerable controversy centered mainly on the applicability of the clean slate principle to the newly independent states resulting from decolonization. Many members of the International Law Commission and the majority of states concluded that new states should not be bound by agreements made by former colonial rulers. Self-determination was often cited in support of this principle. It was included in the convention on treaty succession proposed by the International Law Commission and adopted by majority of states at the Vienna Plenipotentiary Conference in 1978.[10] That Vienna Convention did not, however, apply the clean slate principle to new states that arose from separation rather than decolonization.[11] Unlike colonies, those new states presumably had a voice in making and accepting the treaty. As Professor Vagts observes, this differentiation was rejected by the Restatement (Third) of the Foreign Relations Law of the United States ("Restatement"), which favored giving all newly independent states freedom to start afresh. The Vienna Convention went a step beyond the clean slate rule by giving the ex-colonial state a right to become a party to a multilateral agreement to which its predecessor state had adhered unless the new state's adherence would radically change the conditions for the operation of the treaty or if the consent of all treaty parties is expressly or impliedly required.[12] Thus, ex-colonial states not only had a right to escape the obligations of the predecessor state in this respect; they also could choose to become a party to a multilateral treaty in many cases irrespective of the consent of other parties. Although the Vienna Convention has not come into force, it has not been without influence. For example, the State Department Legal Adviser expressed the opinion in 1980 that the rules of the Vienna Convention were "generally regarded as declarative of existing customary law by the United States."[13]

Now that decolonization has come to an end, questions still remain whether states that have separated (*i.e.,* seceded) will be able to claim the right to pick and choose (as the Restatement would allow) or whether they would be bound by the principle of the Vienna Convention (but as a customary law rule) that a separated state which was not a colony is presumed to succeed to the treaty obligations and rights of the predecessor state unless this result would be incompatible with the object of the treaty.[14] The experience thus far with respect to the cases of the former Soviet Union and the former Yugoslavia supports a general presumption of continuity. That presumption would not, however, apply to membership in the United Nations or other general international organizations that provide for the election of new members. Nor would the separated states continue to have the rights of the predecessor where this would be contrary to the object of a treaty. A good example of the latter point, brought out in the article by Bunn and Rhinelander, relates to the important Nuclear Non-Proliferation Treaty ("NPT") of 1968, a general multilateral treaty open to all states.[15] Under that treaty, the U.S.S.R. was designated as a nuclear power. After the dissolution, Russia was recognized as the successor in this respect to the former U.S.S.R. However, to recognize some or all of the other republics as successors to the U.S.S.R. with the right to have nuclear weapons would undoubtedly be incompatible with the main objective of the NPT, which was to limit nuclear weapons to the five states that were nuclear powers prior to January 1, 1967. Obviously, a presumption of continuity that would give nuclear rights to the new states could not be acceptable.

The Future Law of Succession

Although state succession has been a subject of great controversy in the last fifty years, [there is] a good indication of the tendencies likely to shape future state practice and legal doctrine.

First, it seems probable that a general presumption of continuity of the obligations of a predecessor state will be accepted for new states that have come into being by secession or by dissolution of existing states. This is in accord with the position of the United States described by Williamson and Osborn in their authoritative article on recent U.S. practice. Most other countries may be expected to follow. Thus it is unlikely that the Restatement's rule of a clean slate for all new states will prevail in practice or theory.[16] We might recall, as James Crawford has pointed out, that "[t]he process of evolution towards a general regime of treaty continuity . . . was, remarkably, completed at the Second Session of the Vienna Conference."[17]

A presumption of continuity does not mean a categorical black-letter rule of succession. It is important to recognize that the particular circumstances may call for non-succession. This would apply to all successions whether of treaty, debt or delictual liability. As noted earlier, the symposium contributors all give examples of the need for exceptions to a continuity presumption. I suggest that the exceptions should not, of course, swallow the rule.

As a matter of policy, the case for presuming continuity makes sense today when the state system is increasingly fluid. Nation-states no longer appear immortal. Many seem likely to split or to be absorbed by others. Autonomous regions are likely to increase, central governments may even disappear for a time (as in Somalia or Cambodia), and mergers and integration will probably occur.

In this predictably pluralist world of kaleidoscopic change, stability in expectations will matter; it becomes more important than would be the case in a more settled period. The responses to the fragmentation of the Eastern European regimes revealed the concerns over the disruption of treaty relations. At the same time, the diversity and the particularities call for avoiding rigidities and for taking account of context in specific cases. Contextual solutions may be facilitated by relying on treaty rules, such as *rebus sic stantibus* or on equitable principles applicable to state debts or liability.

An especially strong case for continuity can be made in respect of multilateral treaties of a so-called "universal" character that are open to all states. Such treaties include the codification conventions like those on the law of treaties and on diplomatic and consular relations. In addition, there is good reason to include in this category other law-making treaties that have been widely accepted, even though they fall in the category of "development" of new law rather than codification of preexisting law. Mullerson supports this view, mentioning especially the U.N. human rights treaties which, while not codificatory, have been adhered to by the majority of states. He notes that Croatia and Slovenia declared themselves to be successor states to the former Yugoslavia in regard to human rights treaties which had been in force for Yugoslavia. While Mullerson is cautious in asserting a legal rule in this connection, I am inclined to predict that most such treaties of a general "legislative" character will be treated in the future as automatically binding on new states on the basis of adherence by their respective predecessor states. Support for this conclusion can even be found in earlier writings of European jurists.[18] The increase in such universal conventions expressing norms adopted at international assemblies by near-unanimity on the part of states from all regions of the world is indicative of a trend that should support succession by new states as a matter of course.

Mullerson also brings a helpful reminder that many treaties create acquired rights on the part of individuals. In this connection he refers to the decision of the Permanent Court of International Justice in the case of the German settlers which declared that acquired rights of individuals do not cease on a change of sovereignty.[19] Mullerson's suggestion that individual human rights should also be treated like acquired property rights entitled to respect in successor states is likely to be a much-cited legal contention on behalf of individuals in new states.

Still another reason to expect that a presumption of continuity will be widely accepted by new states is that it is helpful to the administration of treaties and other international legal relations of new states. International lawyers in the United States probably do not realize how difficult it is for new states to cope with the hundreds, even thousands, of treaties to which their predecessor states were parties. Lacking adequate documentation, severely limited in legally trained personnel and administrative resources, they cannot examine most treaties afresh and pick or choose among them. If these states are not considered presumptive successors to the treaties, they may not become parties because of their own administrative and technical deficiencies. A presumption of continuity would enable them to maintain rights and obligations generally. In the absence of that presumption, they may forego their rights and be heedless of obligations that call for action. For this reason, among others, it makes good sense for states to accept *prima facie* continuity as a basic premise, leaving for adjustment or exceptions when they appear necessary or desirable in a particular case.

In sum, my speculation about the future law of state succession rests on what appear to be the political trends relating to changes and turbulence in the nation-state system. It also gives weight to the practical aspects of administering the complicated effects of transfers of sovereignty and the need to avoid rigidity and doctrinaire solutions.

This approach, as some scholars may note, is far removed from the learned discourse of the renowned international legal authorities who discussed state succession largely in terms of philosophical theories of the state and justice. Enticing as these works may be to students of legal and political philosophy, they offer little guidance to the solution of actual problems. Our hope for a more orderly and equitable adjustment to political change lies in practical wisdom rather than in abstract theory.

Notes

1. Aristotle, The Politica, bk. III, ch. 3 (Stephen Everson ed., Cambridge University Press 1988).

2. Hugo Grotius, De Jure Belli ac Pacis Libri Tres, bk II, ch. IX at 310–19 (Carnegie Endowment trans. 1925 (1646)). For a comprehensive bibliography, see 1 D.P. O'Connell, State Succession in Municipal Law and international Law 543–62 (1967).

3. 1 O'Connell, supra note 2, at vi.

4. Ibid. Cf. Krystyna Marek, Identity and Continuity of State in Public International Law 31 (1954) ("The rule that revolution does not affect State identity and continuity has been fully adhered to in State practice for an impressively long period of time.")

5. See Ernst H. Feilchenfeld, Public Debts and State Succession 287–88, 294–96, 329–33 (1931).

6. Arnold D. McNair, The Law of Treaties 601 (1961).

7. Conference on Yugoslavia Arbitration Commission, Opinion No. 3, Jan. 11, 1992, reprinted in 31 I.L. M. 1499 (1992).

8. See Wladyslaw Czaplinski, Sate Succession and State Responsibility, 1990 Can. Y.B. Int'l L. 339, 353–54.

9. See Michael J. Volkovitsch, Note, Righting Wrongs: Towards a New Theory of State Succession to Responsibility for International Delicts, 92 Colum L. Rev. 2162 (1992).

10. Vienna Convention on Succession of State in Respect of Treaties, art. 16 17 IIL. M. on August 23, 19878, but has not yet received the required number of ratification or accessions to enter into force.

11. Ibid. art.34.

12. Treaty Succession Convention, supra note 10, arts. 17, 18. See 1 Restatement, supra note 5, para 210.

13. 1980 Digest of United States Practice in International Law 1041 n.43 (quoting memorandum of Roberts Owen, U.S. State Department Legal Adviser).

14. Treaty Succession Convention, supra note 10, art. 34.

15. Treaty on the Non-Proliferation of Nuclear Weapons, July 1, 1968, 21 U.S.T. 483, 729 U.N.T.S. 161.

16. 1 Restatement, supra note 5, para 210. Brownlie has supported the principle that all new states should have a clean slate on the basis of their sovereign rights. Ian Brownlie, Principles of Public International Law 668 (4th ed. 1990).

17. James Crawford, The Contribution of Professor D.P. O'Connell to the Discipline of International Law, 1980 Brit. Y.B. Int'L 1. 40.

18. See, for example, Charles De Visscher, Theory and Reality in Public International Law 179 (P.E. Corbett trans., rev. ed. 1968), who wrote that "the growing part played by multilateral treaties in the development of international law should count in favor of transmission rather than disappearance of obligations."

19. Advisory Opinion No. 6, 1923 P.C.I.J. (ser. B) No. 6, at 36.

7

Self-Determination, Minorities, Human Rights: A Review of International Instruments

Patrick Thornberry

Some Preliminary Questions

Self-determination and the rights of minorities are two sides of the same coin. When a colony or subject people accedes to independence in the name of self-determination, political unity and integral statehood will rarely be matched by national unity and ethnic homogeneity.[1] The new State will frequently be dominated by a particular ethnic group in a majority, and there will be ethnic minorities. The consequences for the smaller groups of the transition from Empire to statehood may be severe, inter-ethnic solidarity in the face of a common alien oppressor may be ruptured and replaced by a more intimate, local and knowing oppression. This applies both when the new State is "national" in the sense of having a developed national character at the inception of statehood, and when the new State is born of a territorial concept, and nationality is still to be forged, if necessary by the plundering of small groups to achieve assimilation.[2]

Accession to independence and defence of that independence parade under the banner of self-determination, a concept enshrined in the United Nations Charter, the International Covenants on Human Rights and other international instruments. The legal implications of this concept for minorities are, therefore, a matter of considerable moment. Self-determination is a concept of liberation. Its inscription in legal texts has coincided with an astounding transformation of political geography. States have replaced Empires. The age of colonialism becomes a historical *datum*, even if its long-term effects are profound. But the facts of ethnic diversity and diverg-

This article is reproduced from (1989) 30 I.C.L.Q. 867–869 with permission from the publishers, The British Institute of International and Comparative Law, 17 Russell Square, London WC1B 5DR.

ing political and moral ambitions within States require that questions be asked of self-determination. Does it liberate ethnic groups within States or even concern them? Has the phrase "All peoples have the right of self-determination" in the International Covenants on Human Rights a real function as a principle of human rights? What are "peoples"? Are minorities justified in appropriating self-determination to state their claims and aspirations? Are they wise to do so?

The connection between minorities and self-determination has been discussed in the legal literature, though the volume of writings is limited and minorities are frequently not the main focus of enquiry. Minorities appropriate the vocabulary of self-determination whether governments or scholars approve or not. Conflicts between State and minority demonstrate a quality of endurance. Contemporary State-minority disputes of high topicality include those involving the Basques, Corsicans, Eritreans, Kurds, Sikhs, the protagonists in the civil strife in the Sudan, and the Tamils of Sri Lanka—there are many others. Minorities have utilised the notion of secession, where a group would form its own State. The Biafrans wanted to secede from Nigeria; the Bengalis achieved secession from Pakistan and statehood in Bangladesh. Even if the demands of minorities are not so "extreme," self-determination is part of their vocabulary.

Most recently, indigenous peoples have begun to articulate their grievances through the medium of self-determination. A document of the Four Directions Council "Declares that indigenous populations are 'peoples' within the meaning of the International Covenants of Human Rights . . . "[3] Principles drafted by the World Council of Indigenous Peoples paraphrase international instruments: "1. All indigenous peoples have the right of self-determination. By virtue of that right they may freely determine their political status and freely pursue their economic, social, religious and cultural development"[4] Indigenous groups are mostly within the international law governing minorities, but see themselves as "more than" minorities and entitled to the rights of peoples. This conveys a sentiment that self-determination is not "for" or "about" minorities—a proposition assented to by the governments of many States. Some minorities are nonetheless convinced that self-determination is the only concept that penetrates to the heart of their claims. This implies that the potential of self-determination is not yet exhausted, that it is not "passé."[5]

Towards the United Nations Charter

The United Nations Charter gave expression to a doctrine which had been maturing in international relations certainly since the American and French revolutions. These demonstrated two aspects of self-determination: casting off alien rule, and putting forward the people as the ultimate authority within the State—"external" and "internal" self-determination, respectively. Self-determination and the right of minorities were linked in the legal arrangements accompanying nineteenth-century examples of nations becoming States. The doctrine of the nation-State shaped these arrangements: the ideal State is the State of single nationality. Mazzini's conception of Italy included its ethnic and cultural uniformity, even if this meant denationalising "foreign" populations. Slavs, Greeks and Romanians gave expression to similar views. Political theory stressed the benefits to democracy of ethnic homogeneity.[6] International law reflected a colder view. Statesmen foresaw the disruptive potential of nationalist fervour carried to excess. Legal constraints, usually in treaty form, were deployed to protect ethnic and religious minorities threatened by self-determination.[7]

The reciprocity of self-determination and safeguarding treaty was maintained throughout the nineteenth century. The "pattern" was flawed and betokened the existence of first- and second-class States: those which could be trusted to extend the benefits of democracy to all citizens and those which could not. The powers at the Paris Peace Conference following the First World War organised and expanded the "system" of independence coupled with a minorities guarantee into a determinate form. There was no "universal" arrangement. The powers did not threaten their own empires with self-determination. Nor were they subjected to minorities treaties. President Wilson's exhortations in favour of general acceptance of self-determination and obligations towards minorities were to little avail. While the mandate system inscribed in the Covenant promised ultimate self-government for ex-enemy colonies, minorities were not accorded any special position therein, but were dealt with through treaties and declarations applying to specific groups, under the supervision of the League. States under this regime were obliged to grant to all their inhabitants basic human rights. Special minorities provisions were designed to ensure that nationals belonging to minorities would enjoy the same treatment in law and in fact as other nationals. Autonomy rights were granted to certain groups.

The basic premises of the system was summed up by the Permanent Court of International Justice. It was:

> . . . to secure for certain elements incorporated in a State, the population of which differs from them in race, language or religion, the possibility of living peaceably alongside that population and co-operating amicably with it, while at the same time preserving the characteristics which distinguish them from the majority, and satisfying the ensuing special needs.[9]

But the promises of "peaceful living" and "amicable co-operation" were not realised. Some States treated their minorities badly; some minorities were "disloyal" to their States. Beyond pragmatic reconciliation of States and minorities, the ultimate purposes of the League regime were unclear. Latin American views implied that the regime was a staging post on the way to a complete national unity; the ideal State was a melting-pot of races and cultures, a cauldron of assimilation.[10] The rights of minorities under the League system fell far short of self-determination.

The United Nations Charter

Despite its invocation in the inter-war years, self-determination was not part of positive international law. The "principle" is expressly mentioned in the United Nations Charter, in Articles 1(2) and 55. Article 1(2) places the principle among the purposes of the United Nations. Article 55 provides: "With a view to the creation of conditions of stability and well-being which are necessary for peaceful and friendly relations among nations based on respect for the principle of equal rights and self-determination of peoples, the United Nations shall promote . . . "—there follows a list of important political, social and economic goals. By Article 56, UN members pledge themselves to support the purposes in Article 55.

Notwithstanding initial equivocation, it can now be seen that real obligations were created, if imperfectly expressed, in the Charter. Self-determination in the Charter attaches to "peoples." The meaning of "peoples" occasioned inconclusive discussion at the San Francisco Conference. The terms "State," "nation" and "people" are all used in the Charter. The UN Secretariat examined the terms: "The word 'nation' is broad . . . enough to include colonies, mandates, protectorates and quasi-States as well as States"; and, " . . . 'nations' is used in the sense of all political entities, States and non-States, whereas 'peoples' refers to groups of human beings who may, or may not, comprise States or nations."[11] The broad interpretation provoked a French delegate to say that the Charter appeared to sanction secession. Others disagreed.[12] But the opinions of statesmen at the San Francisco Conference towards minorities were largely negative in character. Despite the high level of interest in human rights, proposals for the protection of minorities were lacking. Claude doubts whether the Charter carries any view of the minorities issue: "The United Nations Charter . . . was drafted without recognition of the minority problem as a significant item on the agenda of international relations."[13] It may be argued, however, that the Charter does have a view: the future of the "problem of minorities" merges into universal human rights. There is no lacuna: when the details of the new system of human rights were expounded, a rule for minorities would emerge. This is some distance from attributing self-determination to minorities.

The references to self-determination in Articles 1(2) and 55 are complemented by Chapters XI and XII on non-self-governing territories, and the international trusteeship system. Bowett states that it is permissible "to regard the entirety of Chapters XI and XII of the . . . Charter as reflections on the basic idea of self-determination."[14] Neither Chapter contains an express reference to self-determination, but the principle is established indirectly. Article 73 in Chapter XI describes the development of self-government in non-self-governing territories as a "sacred trust." Article 76 on the international trusteeship system refers to progressive development in the Trust Territories towards "self-government or independence." A key issue was the distinction between "self-government" and "independence." The colonial powers were unhappy about referring to "independence" in the generally applicable Article 73. In the view of the United States, however,"self-government" did not rule out "independence" in appropriate cases.[15] The Philippines interpreted Article 73 to imply eventual independence for dependent territories.[16]

Chapter XI of the Charter gave a tremendous impetus to the development of self-determination with a real possibility of implementation. Subsequent practice has hardened the meaning of Charter terms, but the result has been unfavourable to minorities. Chapter XI is a declaration on "Non-Self-Governing Territories." The territorial aspect is vital: the Chapter refers to "*territories* whose peoples have not attained a full measure of self-government"; the sacred trust is to promote "the well-being of the inhabitants of these *territories*." A territorial concept of self-determination appears to rule out minorities without a specific territorial base. Further, concentration on territory, in the light of the reality of mixed and inextricable populations, languages and religions, weighs heavily towards taking political demarcations as they stand, and making these the focal point of political change.

The Belgian Thesis

Article 73 of the Charter was utilised by the General Assembly in the promotion of self-determination through the requirement of reports on the progress made by States administering territories towards the objectives set by the Article. The main thrust of the Assembly's effort was in the direction of the colonial empires. The Belgian representatives pointed out that the Charter does not single out "colonialism," but non-self-governing territories. Belgium stated that:

> . . . a number of States were administering within their own frontiers territories which were not governed by the ordinary law; territories with

> well-defined limits, inhabited by homogeneous peoples differing from the
> rest of the population in race, language and culture. These populations
> were disenfranchised; they took no part in national life; they did not enjoy
> self-government in any sense of the word.[17]

It was not clear how such groups were excluded from the terms of Chapter
XI. Groups in respect of which Chapter XI applied would include Indian
tribes of Venezuela, the Nagas of India, indigenous African tribes in
Liberia, Somalis in Ethiopia, tribals of the Philippines, Dyaks of Borneo,
etc. The generality of the Belgian concerns was expressed in the delegate's
remark that: "Similar problems [to colonialism] existed wherever there
were underdeveloped groups."[18] The thesis radicalises self-determination
by insisting that it can apply to indigenous groups and minorities.

The thesis did not prevail. Latin American States and their allies did not
agree that their situation could be assimilated to that of the colonies. The
problems of the indigenous groups were economic rather than colonial.[19] In
the view of Iraq, the Belgian argument was based on "anger at the criticism
directed against conditions in the non-self-governing territories by less
advanced States."[20] One of the authors of the thesis, Dr. Van Langenhove,
effectively admitted to the thesis as a Belgian tactic.

The United Nations built a consensus on self-determination in response
to the Belgian thesis to bring order to the inevitable historical movement of
decolonisation. The delegate of Iraq to the Fourth Committee of the General Assembly offered the opinion that: "In the long run, colonialism must
give way to self-government . . ."[21] The thesis was rejected in favour of the
theory of "salt-water" colonialism, summed up in General Assembly Resolution 1541(XV). Principle IV states that: "Prima facie there is an obligation . . . to transmit information in respect of a territory which is geographically separate and is distinct ethnically and/or culturally from the country
administering it."[22] The coupling of geography and the ethnic factor is
important; without geography, the designation of non-colonial territories as
entitled to self-determination was a possibility, though even with this factor, the definition is not perfect if the intention is to exclude all minority
groups.

The restrictive view of the non-applicability of self-determination to
minority groups is strengthened by a consideration of General Assembly
Resolution 1514—the Colonial declaration—passed on the day before Resolution 1541. The holder of the right of self-determination is, once more,
declared to be the people. The meaning of the term "people" is conditioned
by repeated references to colonialism. Paragraph 6 of the Resolution states
that: "Any attempt aimed at the partial or total disruption of the national
unity and the territorial integrity of a country is incompatible with the
Purposes and Principles of the Charter of the United Nations." The effect is

that colonial boundaries function as the boundaries of the emerging States. Minorities, therefore, may not secede from States—at least, international law gives them no *right* to do so. The logic of the resolution is relatively simple: peoples hold the right of self-determination; a people is the whole people of a territory; a people exercises its right through the achievement of independence.

General Assembly
Resolution 2625(XXV) and Minorities

Resolution 2625(XXV) appears, on one reading, to construct a link between self-determination and minorities.[23] The text deals with the most important principles of international law,[24] each principle to be construed in the light of the others.[25] Three preambular paragraphs of the Declaration refer to self-determination—the third reference reiterates the prohibition on disruption of the national unity and territorial integrity of a country, etc. The principle is set out at some length in the operative part of the Declaration. There is not the same emphasis on colonialism as in Resolution 1514(XV). The preferred modes of implementing self-determination reflect more flexible options set out in Resolution 1541(XV): independence, free association or integration with an independent State, "or the emergence into any other political status freely determined by a people."

Writers have given attention to the penultimate paragraph on self-determination:

> Nothing in the foregoing paragraphs shall be construed as authorising or encouraging any action which would dismember or impair, totally or in part, the territorial integrity or political unity of sovereign and independent States conducting themselves in compliance with the principle of [self-determination] and thus possessed of a government representing the whole people belonging to the territory without distinction as to race, creed or colour.[26]

This is followed by the obligatory clause on territorial integrity.

The reference to representative government has been picked out as innovative by Rosenstock: ". . . a close examination of its text will reward the reader with an affirmation of the applicability of the principle to peoples within existing States and the necessity for governments to represent the governed."[27] Thus, if "peoples within existing States" are treated in a grossly discriminatory fashion by an unrepresentative government, they can claim self-determination and not be defeated by arguments about territorial integrity. The guarantee of integrity is contingent upon the existence of representative government. There are, however, reasons to caution against this kind of claim, and Cassese doubts if the Declaration can be pressed too far.[28] In his view, the paragraph could apply only to a few peoples living under racist regimes. He emphasises the negative wording as forbidding self-determination where there is representative government and in particular where this government is non-racist.

The drafts support the more cautious views. A proposal of the United States made the "internal" aspect of self-determination much clearer:

> The existence of a sovereign and independent State possessing a representative government, effectively functioning as such to all distinct peoples within its territory, is presumed to satisfy the principle of equal rights and, self-determination as regards those peoples.[29]

A text proposed by Czechoslovakia and others made a similar point.[30] The crucial difference between the United States draft and the final version is that, in the former, the key phrase is "all distinct peoples," whereas the final wording is "the whole people." The gaze of the international community is deflected from detailed "internal" scrutiny of most States and the conduct of governments towards the "peoples" within their territories: only pariah States like South Africa, which oppressed its majority on racial grounds, are likely to be affected. Whether one discusses "internal" or "external" self-determination, the point is that "whole" territories or peoples are the focus of rights, rather than ethnic groups, Cassese's analyses of "internal" self-determination should not be taken to fragment the meaning of "people."

The Covenant on Civil and Political Rights

Articles 1 and 27

The juxtaposition of self-determination in Article 1 of the Covenant on Civil and Political Rights and the rights of minorities in Article 27 provides an opportunity to compare closely what international law offers to peoples and minorities, respectively. Neither Article is particularly expansive, but there is an implementation framework, and a reasonable drafting record. Article 1 of both UN Human Rights Covenants commences with "All peoples have the right of self-determination." The other paragraphs refer to economic self-determination (paragraph 2); and to the duty of States parties to the Covenants to promote self-determination (paragraph 3). Article 27, which still stands as the only whole and general statement of the treaty rights of minorities in modern international law provides:

> In those States in which ethnic, religious or linguistic minorities exist, persons belonging to such minorities shall not be denied the right, in community

with the other members of their group, to enjoy their own culture, to profess and practise their own religion, or to use their own language.

Neither Article ventures into further definition. The Special Rapporteur of
the UN Sub-Commission on the Prevention of Discrimination and Protection of Minorities, Professor Capotorti, offered this definition for the purposes of Article 27: a minority is

> a group numerically inferior to the rest of the population of a State, in a
> non-dominant position, whose members—being nationals of the State—
> possess ethnic, religious or linguistic characteristics differing from those
> of the rest of the population and show, if only implicitly, a sense of soli
> darity, directed towards preserving their culture, traditions, religion or
> language.[31]

A similar definition proposed to the Sub-Commission by the Canadian
member in 1985 was forwarded to the UN Human Rights Commission,
which is working on a draft declaration on minority rights.[32] The Capotorti
definition is not part of any UN instrument but it is doubtful if a subsequent
definition would diverge greatly from it. Article 27 and the Capotorti definition may be taken as a basis for comparing self-determination and minority rights in the Covenant.

The right of self-determination in the Covenants is universal. The text
and *travaux* support the view that the Covenants reach beyond the colonial
situation,[33] though there are indications of narrower views.[34] Some interest
in this respect attaches to the declaration made by India on Article 1: " . . .
the Government of the Republic of India declares that the words 'the right
of self-determination' . . . apply only to the peoples under foreign domination and that these words do not apply to sovereign independent States or to
a section of the people or nation—which is the essence of national
integrity." Other States have objected to the declaration, which clearly curtails the scope of the Article. The Netherlands objection reads, in part:
"Any attempt to limit the scope of [the] . . . right or to attach conditions
. . . would undermine the concept of self-determination itself and would
. . . seriously weaken its universally acceptable character."[35] The position
of India has, however, been marked by inconsistency. Its delegate had carlier stated in the General Assembly's Third Committee that, "although there
were good reasons to make special reference to the peoples of non-self-
governing territories, it must be recognised that the field of application of
the principle of self-determination was wider than that."[36] There is little
reason to doubt the view that the Covenants mean what they say: that Article 1 applies to all peoples, and is not confined to colonial territories.

The "broad" view of the applicability of Article 1 is a fundamental
assumption underlying the "General Comment" issued by the Human

Rights Committee: " . . . it imposes specific obligations on States Parties, not only in relation to their own peoples but vis-a-vis all peoples which have not been able to exercise or have been deprived of the possibility of their right to self-determination."[37] This makes it clear that the right is universal, as can be expected in a document of human rights. The promotion of self-determination must be consistent with other provisions of international law: "in particular, States must refrain from interfering in the internal affairs of other States and thereby adversely affecting the exercise of the right." Self-determination in the Covenants includes internal self-determination. The Comment alludes to this: "With regard to paragraph 1 of Article 1, States Parties should describe the constitutional and political processes which in practice allow the exercise of [self-determination]." The Committee complains that many States in their reports "completely ignore Article 1, provide inadequate information in relation to it or confine themselves to a reference to election laws." The comment makes no contribution to the elucidation of any people/minority distinction. The assumption appears to be that minorities are covered by Article 27. The Committee has been unable to formulate a comment on the latter Article.[38]

The tension between "people" and "minority" is apparent at various stages in the drafting. Afghanistan and Saudi Arabia, authors of a draft resolution on self-determination, at one time deleted the term "peoples" from their draft. This was at the suggestion of delegations who feared that the term "might encourage minorities within a State to ask for the right to self-determination."[39] On the other hand, India argued that the problem of minorities should not be raised in the context of self-determination.[40] China declared that the issue "was that of national majorities and not of minorities."[41] The reference to "majorities" reflected the views of many in the debates; it may be taken as an infelicitous expression of the conviction that the right of self-determination is one for whole peoples, and not for sections of them. This view of self-determination dominates the *travaux,* despite occasional hesitations.

Sections of the people—minorities—enjoy more limited rights than the people itself. The Capotorti definition refers to "non-dominant" groups in a State and Article 27 is a statement of rights essential to the defence of minority identity in the face of assimilationist pressures: it encapsulates their "right to an identity" ("dominant" minorities, such as the whites of South Africa, have no need of such rights). There is a qualitative difference between the two categories: the right of self-determination means full rights in the cultural, economic and political spheres. The essence is political control, accompanied by other forms of control. The rights of minorities are enumerated and finite, and do not include political control. Article 27 does not even grant the minority an unequivocal collective right: it is "persons belonging to such minorities" who are accorded rights. The collective aspect of minority rights bedevils the elaboration of a more detailed instrument on minority rights—States are reluctant to concede rights to collectivities which may come to rival the State itself." The opening phrase of the Article, "In those States in which . . . minorities exist . . . ," almost invites States to deny that they exist, and many States have responded to the "invitation." Such denials of the presence of minority groups on State territory should not be allowed to function as an escape for States, most of which are obviously multi-ethnic: the absence of a final definition of minority has not inhibited the Human Rights Committee in its questioning of States on treatment of their minorities.

Finally, Article 27 appears to impose only a duty of toleration on States, a duty of non-interference with the cultural and religious practices of the groups. But it can also be read to impose positive duties upon the State, based on the argument that, in order to function, the Article must go beyond the rule of non-discrimination and equality in law towards equality in fact, so that the continued existence of the minority group is not placed in jeopardy in a situation in which it is inherently the weaker party. Tenuous as these rights are, they are vital for minority groups and represent a minimum from which there should be no derogation.

Positive and Negative Interpretation

In the light of the limitations of Article 27, it appears ambitious to argue for a connection between minorities and self-determination. There are, however, at least two possibilities of "positive" interpretation implying a connection: (a) minorities are peoples within the meaning of Article 1—a view which is not supported by the *travaux;* (b) attribution of rights to whole peoples benefits minorities *indirectly* through "internal" self-determination. There is also a negative possibility: (c) self-determination is best understood as external, and internal self-determination is supererogatory.

In relation to (a), the practice of the Human Rights Committee is equivocal, but may be taken to buttress the view that minorities are not peoples. Questions on individual groups in a State which might imply that they are covered by Article 1 are often "fielded" by that State under Article 27. In the "communication" to the Committee by the Grand Captain of the Mikmaq Tribal Society, the applicant focused on Article 1 rather than Article 27. The communication was rejected at the admissibility stage because the author had "not proven that he is authorised to act as a representative . . . of the Mikmaq tribal society. In addition, the author has failed to advance any pertinent facts supporting his claim that he is personally a victim of any rights contained in the Covenant."[42] The impediments to his claim may have been procedural or substantive: the Committee's statement is not clear. This statement is hardly a basis for broad claims on the applicability of Article 1.

On the other hand, another communication involving Canadian Indians, that of Sandra Lovelace, has produced an unequivocal response from the Committee on the applicability of Article 27.[43] This case demonstrates that Article 27 applies to individuals belonging to Indian groups as members of minorities; the case involved the loss by an Indian woman of the right to live on a reservation following marriage to a non-Indian. The Committee did not, in fact, trouble to discuss the application of the term "minority" to the Indian band to which Sandra Lovelace belonged, but appears to have assumed the correctness of the attribution. The applicability of Article 27 was so clear to the Committee that it considered it unnecessary to examine the case under the other articles of the Covenant. The case contrasts vividly with the uncertainty engendered by the Mikmaq case. Whatever the self-descriptive terms employed by indigenous groups, the text of the Covenant accommodates them better under Article 27 than under Article 1.

If minorities are not the "peoples" of the Covenants, this does not mean that self-determination has no relevance to them. Minorities are protected by international law through such instruments as the Genocide Convention 1948 and the International Convention on the Elimination of all Forms of Racial Discrimination 1966, even though the protection is indirect. Similarly in the present context: the "internal" aspect of self-determination may have some incidence upon ethnic groups, even though the formal subject of a right is the "whole people." Internal self-determination has been much favoured as a concept by Western States, reflecting their notions of democracy. President Wilson's early use of the term depended very much on American constitutional tradition. From a socialist point of view, Lenin wrote that "the recognition of the right of all nations to self-determination implies the maximum of democracy and the minimum of nationalism."[44] For the States of the Third World, concerned with ridding themselves of Western domination, self-determination is externally orientated, and, in so far as it has an internal aspect, this is to do with majority rule (rule of the "whole people") and the avoidance of rule by minorities, especially white minorities. The question is, to what extent may any of these conceptions be taken to govern the Covenants? The comment of the Human Rights Committee is neither optimistic nor very illuminating. States do not find much use for Article 1 "internally." But the Committee's comment also incorporates a view about self-determination "underlying" human rights: "The right of self-determination is of particular importance because its realisation is an essential condition for the effective guarantee and observance of individual human rights." This could be read together with the reference to "political and constitutional processes" to signify that States must organise these processes to support the programme of human rights contained in the Covenants. The application of internal self-determination is to be gauged with reference to human rights, and not to ideologies beyond it. Violations of self-determination are violations of human rights. The "democracy" of the Covenants can be none other than the implementation of their provisions.

Such an interpretation appears to do little more than reiterate existing rights. It does, however, direct attention to the organisation of the State as a whole and how that organisation favours or disfavours human values to the benefit of all within the State, minorities included. It is probably in advance of the opinions of most States parties, which leads to possibility (c): perhaps the truth is that self-determination has little to do with human rights. The implementation of the covenant has not succeeded in showing how self-determination can be effective "internally." Frequently, the questions of the Human Rights Committee are directed to divining the attitude of States to apartheid, Namibia and Palestine, rather than to their own peoples, who should be the primary focus of interest.

Other Instruments

While this article does not attempt to present a full picture of minority rights in international law, it may be noted that minorities are guaranteed a basic "right of existence" through the Genocide Convention.[45] Further, the rule of non-discrimination in the enjoyment of human rights makes constant reference to race, colour, religion and language as impermissible grounds of distinction in human rights. Indigenous groups are given a measure of protection by the International Labour Organization's Convention No. 107 on Indigenous and Tribal populations, as well as being entitled to whatever rights accrue to minorities, since they are mostly minorities in the States they inhabit. The Convention (Article 1(i)) applies to:

> members of tribal or semi-tribal populations in independent countries whose social and economic conditions are at a less advanced stage than . . . other sections of the national community, and whose status is regulated wholly or partially by their own customs or traditions or by special laws or regulations . . . [and members of populations] regarded as indigenous on account of their descent from the populations which inhabited the country... at the time of conquest or colonisation, and which . . . live more in conformity with the . . . institutions of that time than with the institutions of the nation to which they belong.

The preferred term in the Convention, it may be noted, is not "peoples" but "populations": connotations of self-determination are thus avoided. The rights granted to indigenous groups under this Convention encompass the protection of their way of life and range through civil and political rights to recognition of rights to land traditionally occupied, and economic, social and cultural rights.

Unfortunately, the Convention lay heavy stress on "integration" of the populations to the benefit of States rather than the populations as such: it is a Convention on "the protection and integration" of indigenous populations. Indigenous groups see the Convention as little more than a licence for States to assimilate and eradicate them under the guise of humanitarianism and have demanded its revision. In no sense does the Convention incorporate a right of self-determination: Article 2(1) provides that "*Governments* shall have the primary responsibility for developing coordinated and systematic action for the protection of the populations concerned and their progressive integration into the life of their respective countries" (author's emphasis). Provisions for consultation with the indigenous groups are minimal: in the application of the Convention, governments shall, according to Article 5, "seek the collaboration of these populations and their representatives"—seek, but not necessarily find. Revision of the Convention will require less stress on integration and more on the wishes of the populations concerned, though it is doubtful if self-determination by that name will figure on the agenda.[46]

Other instruments maintain the dichotomy between minority rights and self-determination. The Helsinki Final Act is a case in point. Principle VII of the "Declaration on Principles" deals with human rights, and includes the following paragraph:

> The participating States on whose territories national minorities exist will respect the right of persons belonging to such minorities to equality before the law, will afford them the full opportunity for the actual enjoyment of Human Rights and fundamental freedoms and will, in this manner, protect their legitimate interests in this sphere.

This endorsement of minority rights is more limited than Article 27 of the Covenant on Civil and Political Rights. There is the same question of the "existence" of minorities; the different minorities are narrowed down to "national" minorities, implying a limitation of scope; there is no consideration of a "right to identity," only to equality before the law; and the Article describes "interests," which represent a lower logical category than "rights." This contrasts strongly with statements on self-determination in Principle VIII, which includes:

> By virtue of the principle of equal rights and self-determination of peoples, all peoples always have the right, in full freedom, to determine, when and as they wish, their internal and external political status, without external political interference, and to pursue as they wish their political, economic, social and cultural development.

As Cassese points out, the chief innovations here are the bold phrases on internal self-determination and the commitment to a continuing role for the principle of self-determination: peoples *always* have the right of self-determination, and in *full freedom*. He regards as "incontrovertible" the fact that "the Helsinki Declaration, when it discusses the principle of self-determination, extends the right only to groups identifying with sovereign States (for example, Italian, French and Soviet citizens)". The *travaux,* while rather sketchy, support his propositions.[47] Another commentator notes that "States with militant minorities, such as Canada and Yugoslavia, felt the need . . . for a limit to the application . . . [of self-determination] . . . to national minorities in order to avoid any implication that . . . [it] could be used to bring about the dissolution of federated States comprised of peoples of different nationalities or other minorities."[48] Rights of minorities in the Final Act are clearly of a lower order than the rights of peoples.

The African Charter on Human and Peoples' Rights 1981 offers even less to minorities: this is unsurprising, and reflects the view of many African States that the minorities "problem" is essentially European. The "peoples" of the Charter are not defined, but they have important rights. Article 19 reads: "All peoples shall be equal; they shall enjoy the same respect and shall have the same rights. Nothing shall justify the domination of a people by another." Article 20(1) reads: "All peoples shall have the right to existence. They shall have the unquestionable and inalienable right to self-determination." The rights of peoples are buttressed by the duties of individuals, which include the duty to "preserve and strengthen the national independence and the territorial integrity of . . . [their] country."[49] There is no explicit reference to "minorities," though Article 2 and the Preamble refer to discrimination based on "ethnic group," as well as "race, colour . . . language, religion . . . national and social origin." The Charter lays tremendous stress on its "African" character throughout. This includes the African views on self-determination which stress the integrity of the State, even in cases of severe oppression of minorities. There is little to suggest that "peoples" are other than the "whole peoples" of the States, and not ethnic or other groups. This conclusion is strongly supported by discussions at the Nairobi Conference convened by the International Commission of Jurists in December 1985, and is likely to represent the future practice of the African Commission of Human Rights.

Conclusion

Minorities use the vocabulary of self-determination and States deny its relevance to them. International law gives little support to minorities in their endeavours. The right of self-determination is a right of peoples, with strict limits on application. The international system is not immutable, and States are regularly subjected to challenge by minorities, occasionally to the point of dismemberment. It may come to pass that the legal texts will more clearly associate minorities with a right of self-determination, in terms of meaningful approaches to internal self-determination, and in cases of severe mistreatment.[50] On the other hand, existing norms on the rights of minorities are limited and inadequate to the task of ensuring that minorities do not have assimilation or integration forced upon them as a threat to their existence and identity.

Instead of starting from the collective right of self-determination, it may, therefore, be more productive to start from the rules of basic human rights. Minority protection could also be taken to require autonomy in certain instances. Many States accord a high level of self-management to ethnic groups in their constitutional law, though autonomy is not widely perceived as an obligation in general international law. These remarks also apply to indigenous populations—though there is a stronger international movement in their favour than for minorities in general. The International Labour Organisation's Convention on Indigenous and Tribal Populations is on the brink of revision, and the UN Working Group on Indigenous Populations is drafting a set of principles. A key concept in process of elaboration is that of "ethnodevelopment": the development of ethnic groups within the larger society as a compromise between ethnic self-determination and the nation-State.[51]

For both categories, there is need to strengthen implementation procedures, to amplify and specify norms, and to press for just treatment of groups. The humane regime should attempt to convince States that maltreatment of their minorities is a primary cause of internal and international strife. There is need also to bring to fruition the efforts of the United Nations to draft a minorities' instrument, and further to advance work on the rights of indigenous groups.[52] To achieve this would be to build rather than dream the future, starting from what is, rather than what might be.

Notes

1. The present author is compiling "profiles" of 50 States for the UN University which examine their legal arrangements relating to minorities, and include review of population composition. Some results of this Study are reviewed in Minorities and Human Rights Law, Minority Rights Group Report No. 73. (1987).

2. Definitions of assimilation, integration, etc., are essayed in the UN Special Study on Racial Discrimination in the Political, Economic, Social and Cultural Spheres, UN Sales No. 71./ XIV.2.

3. UNDOC E/CN. 4/Sub.2/AC.4/1983/CRP.1, annex.

4. UNDOC E?CN.4/Sub.2/AC.4/1985/WP.5

5. S. Prakash Sinha, "Is Self-Determination Passé?" (1973) 12 Col. J. Trans. L. 260.

6. ". . . . it is in general a necessary condition of free institutions that the boundaries of governments should coincide . . . with those of nationalities." Mill,

"Considerations on Representative Government," in *John Stuart Mill, Three Essays* (1975), pp. 382 and 384. Some of the hierarchical assumptions which may lie under the surface of arguments in favor of assimilation of cultures are well expressed by Mill: "Experience proves, that it is possible for one nationality to merge and be absorbed in another: and when it was originally an inferior and more backward portion of the human race, the absorption is greatly to its advantage,: idem, p. 385.

7. Claude, *National Minorities. An International Problem* (1065); Fouques-Duparc, La Protection des Minorités de Race, de Langue et de Religion (1922); Laponce, *The Protection of Minorities* (1960); Macartney, *National States and National Minorities* (1934).

8. For a list of the States affected by the system, and its results, see De Azcárate, *The League of Nations and National Minorities* (1945), Robinson et al., *Were the Minorities Treaties a Failure?* (1943); Thornberry, "Is There a Phoenix in the Ashes?, *International Law and Minority Rights*· (1980) 15 *Texas Int. L.J.*

9. "In order to attain this object, two things were regarded as particularly necessary . . . The first is to ensure that nationals belonging to racial, religious or linguistic minorities shall be placed in every respect on a footing of perfect equality with the other national of the State. The second is to ensure for the minority . . . suitable means for the preservation of their . . . peculiarities, their traditions and their national characteristics," *Minority Schools in Albania* (1935), *PCIJ Ser.A/B.* No. 64, p. 17.

10. Yepes, "Les Problèmes Fondamentaux du Droit des Gens en Amérique" (1934) 30(I) *Rec. des Cours* 14.

11. UNCIO DOCS, Vol. XVIII, pp. 657–658.

12. UNCIO DOCS, Vol. XVII, P. 142; Cassese, in Buergenthal and Hall (eds.), *Human Rights, International Law and the Helsinki Accord* (1977), pp. 95 et seq.; Russell and Muther, *A History of the United National Charter, The Role of the United States 1940–1945* (1958).

13. Claude, *op. cit. supra* n. 7 st p.113.

14. "Problems of Self-Determination and Political Rights Developing Countries" *Procs A.S.I.L.* (1966), p. 134.

15. Generally, Russell and Muther, *op. cit. supra* n. 12, at pp. 813 et seq.

16. Ibid.

17. Van Langenhove, "Le Problème de la Protection des Populations Aborigenes aux Nations Unites: (1956) 89 Rec. des Cours 3211, and The Question of Aborigines Before the United Nations: The Belgian Thesis (1954); Toussaint, "The Colonial Controversy in the United Nations" (1956) Y.B. World Affairs 177; Bennett, Aboriginal Rights in International Law, Occasional Paper of the Royal Anthropological Institute of Great Britain and Ireland (1978); UNDOC A/Ac. 67/2, p. 3–31.

18. UNDOC A/C.4/SR.419, paras. 14 et seq. The delegate also noted that the indigenous were still recognised as having problems akin to colonialism by the I.L.O.: see infra on I.L.O. convention 107.

19. Delegate of Peru to the Fourth Committee, UNDOC A/C.4/SR.420, para.40.

20. UNDOC A/C.4/SR.257, para.11.

21. UNDOC A/C.4/SR.257, paras. 11 14. The reference of the delegate is to Chap. XI; this need not be taken to rule out a post-colonial future for self-determination as such.

22. GAOR, 15th session, supp. 16. p. 29.

23. Rosenstock, "The Declaration of Principles of International Law, etc.: (1971) 65 *A.J.I.L.* 713.

24. See Arangio-Ruiz, "The Normative Role of the General Assembly of the United Nations and the Declaration of Principles on Friendly Relations" (1972) 137 *Rec. des Cours* 528.

25. The Declaration states: "In their interpretation and application the above principles are interrelated and each principle should be construed in the context of the other principles . . . Nothing in this Declaration shall be construed as prejudicing in any manner the provisions of the Charter or the rights and duties of Member States under the Charter or the rights of peoples under the Charter taking into account the elaboration of these rights in this Declaration: (authors' emphasis). This means that the self-determination principle must fit consistently with such principles as that of non-intervention in the domestic affairs of other States, the principle of the sovereign equality of States, and the principle of the non-use of force. The text of the Declaration contains a number of references to territorial integrity and political independence of States. Under the heading of "The Principle of Sovereign Equality of States," we may note: "(d) The territorial integrity and political independence of the State are inviolable; (e) Each State has the right freely to choose and develop its political, social, economic and cultural systems." These principles clearly impinge on self-determination. The last would be just as appropriate in the context of the paragraphs on self-determination in that it states an important aspect of that concept. It may also, by implication, hint at the effective transformation of the right-holder into the State itself.

26. As in Res. 1514(XV). India expressed satisfaction that Res. 26256(XXV) retained this element, UNDOC A/8018.

27. Rosenstock, *op. cit. supra*. n. 23, at 732.

28. Cassese, in Buergenthal and Hall (eds.), *Human Rights, International Law and the Helsinki Accord* (1977), pp. 88–92.

29. UNDOC A/AC.125/L.32.

30. UNDOC A/AC.125/L. 74.

31. Capotorti, *Study of the Rights of Persons Belonging to Ethnic, Religious and Linguistic Minorities* (1979), Chap. 1.

32. Professor Deschenes defines a minority as a "group of citizens of a State, constituting a numerical minority and in a non-dominant position in that State, endowed with ethnic, religious or linguistic characteristics which differ from those of the majority of the population, having a sense of solidarity with one another, motivated, if only implicitly, by a collective will to survive and whose aim is to achieve equality with the majority in fact and in law," UNDOC E/CN.4/Sub.2/1985/31, p. 30.

33. Art.1(3): "The States Parties to the present Covenant, *including those having responsibility for . . . Non-Self-Governing and Trust territories,* shall promote the realisation of the right of self-determination . . ." (author's emphasis). The post-colonial future of self-determination was matter of relative unconcern to many States, though Western States insisted on a continuing function. Among other States, we may note the forthright statement of Afghanistan that self-determination "will have to be proclaimed even in a world from which colonial territories have vanished," UNDOC A/C.3/SR.644, para. 10.

34. Europe "had reached the ultimate goal where self-determination was concerned; now that European Powers were denying the right of self-determination to Asian and African peoples, there could be no doubt that the question of the inclusion of Article 1 of the Covenants was a *purely colonial issue*" (author's emphasis), UNDOC A/C.3/SR.648, para. 8 (Syria). Many States expressed the view that the colonies would be the first beneficiaries of self-determination. This does not rule out later beneficiaries.

35. UNDOC ST/HR/4/Rev. 4. p. 64.

36. UNDOC A/C.3/SR.399, para. 4.

37. There is a useful collection of these comments by the Human Rights Committee in 9 E.H.R.R. 169. The comment on self-determination was adopted by the Committee on 12 Apr. 1984.

38. The Human Rights Committee, in its report of 1986, stated that the draft of Art. 27 would be suspended pending "information gathering," and promised that particular attention would be devoted to this article in the future, UNDOC A/41/40, para. 412.

39. A/C.3/SR.310, para. 3.

40. A/C.3/SR.399, paras. 5–6.

41. A/C.3/SR.369, para. 13.

42. UNDOC A/39/40 (1984), p. 200, at p. 203; Communication No. 78.1980.

43. UNDOC A/36/40 (1981), p. 166; Communication No. R6/24; Selected Decisions under the Optional Protocol, 2nd-16th Sessions (New York, 1983), pp. 10, 37 and 83, UNDOC CCPR/C/OP/1.

44. *The Right of Nations to Self-Determination* (Eng. ed., Moscow, 1947), p. 45.

45. 78 U.N.T.S. 277. The Convention prohibits a range of grave attacks on the existence of national, ethnic, racial or religious groups, including the killing of their members. Minorities are natural victims of genocide, and any new instrument on minority rights must be concerned, *de minimis,* with securing existence at this basic level.

46. The revision of ILO Convention 107 will, in all probability, adopt the term "peoples" instead of "populations." However, a number of States contributing to the revision process have made it clear that the inclusion of "peoples" should not function as a base for an expanded range of claims by indigenous groups, International Labour Conference, 75th Session 1988, Report VI(2), Partial Revision of the Indigenous and Tribal Populations Convention, 1957 (No. 107), p. 13.

47. For a "reconstruction" of the *travaux,* see Ferraris (ed.), *Report on Negotiation, Helsinki-Geneva-Helsinki 1972–75* (1979).

48. Russell, "The Helsinki Declaration: Brobdingnag or Lilliput?" (1976) 70 A.J.I.L. 242, 269–270.

49. Art. 29.

50. See Kuper, *Genocide, Its Political Use in the Twentieth Century* (1981), and *The Prevention of Genocide* (1985).

51. For the proposed text for the International Labour Conference 1989, see *Report IV(2), Partial Revisions of the Indigenous and Tribunal Populations Conventions 1957, No. 107.*

52. *Editors' Note.* Developments since publication of this article in 1989 include: The Council of Europe Framework Convention for the Protection of National Minorities, done at Strasbourg, February 1, 1995, 1 at 34 I.L.M. 351 (1995); the CSCE Document of the Copenhagen Meeting of the Conference on the Human Dimension, June 19, 1990 at 20 I.L.M. 1305 (1990); and UN General Assembly Resolution 47/135, December 18, 1992 adopting the Declaration on the Rights of Persons Belonging to National or Ethnic, Religious and Linguistic Minorities at 32 I.L.M. 911 (1993).

8

Participants in
International Legal Relations

DONNA E. ARZT AND IGOR I. LUKASHUK

THE CLASSICAL THEORIES OF INTERNATIONAL LAW IN BOTH THE UNITED
States and the former Soviet Union took for granted that states were and
would continue to be the principal subjects of international legal relations.
This traditional "Westphalian" conception[1] is reflected in the systematic
treatises expounding international law in the two countries and in their
respective textbooks used for teaching international law.[2] The conception is
also reflected in the limitation on the contentious jurisdiction of the International Court of Justice, and before it the Permanent Court of International
Justice, to cases in which the parties are states.

The traditional doctrine came under challenge years ago. It has long
been understood that parties other than states can and do exert a great deal
of influence on the international legal system. Gradually at least one category of these other parties came to be accepted as a full participant in international legal relations. By the middle of the twentieth century, international organizations came to be treated as subjects of international law
for most purposes. It is no longer controversial that international organizations enjoy rights and exercise duties under international law and can enter
into treaties with states and with other international organizations.[3]

Areas of controversy remain, nevertheless. Some of these have been
framed in the literature as disputes in which the legal community in the former Soviet Union and the socialist bloc supposedly clung to the traditional
state-centered view, while many U.S. and other Western scholars advocated
a more inclusive perspective. The characterization of the controversy along

U.S.-Soviet lines is undoubtedly too simplistic, however, because there was never a monolithic position on either side.[4] In fact, some in the United States did not differ significantly from the approaches shared by the preponderance of the Soviet legal community, and likewise some Soviet scholars advocated positions that diverged considerably from traditional doctrine.[5] By the end of the 1980s it seemed that the gap, if there had in fact been one, was narrowing. Nevertheless, by the beginning of the 1990s, the question of a hypothetical U.S.-Soviet doctrinal split was overshadowed by new challenges to the international legal system, stemming from the disintegration of the USSR and related developments.

Neither interstate relations nor international law can avoid exposure to the wide range of influences that are today a part of global affairs. Ethnic groups and liberation movements, supranational economic communities and political parties, businesses, social and advocacy organizations, communications networks, and many other entities exert influence not only on relations within their own spheres but also on relations between states. As the international system becomes more democratic, the impact of these non-state actors can be expected to increase. This is not to say that states themselves must necessarily play a diminished role. The growing power of transnational corporations, for example, which was widely noted by many authors during the 1970s,[6] did not at that time lead to a decrease in the regulatory role of states. Indeed, it could be argued that over the same time frame, many states took on expanded regulatory powers, both within national economies and with respect to international transactions.[7] Nonetheless, the democratization of international life and the decentralization of political and economic authority are trends which must be taken into account.

In this chapter, we pose the question: Should there be expansion or stability among the participants in international legal relations? Should state domination continue, or should a trend be encouraged toward greater pluralism or, if you will, "privatization," in the international legal order? Rather than concentrating on the formal problem of what is a "subject" of international law, or who should enjoy "international legal personality," we ask more functional questions: Who should— and who, in effect, already does—enjoy rights and obligations under international law? Who should— and does—actually participate in the process of creating, making claims under, and enforcing international law?[8]

In particular, we focus on two of the currently more controversial participants in international legal relations: individuals and transnational enterprises. While these do not exhaust the areas of debate among and between the different legal schools (we could also have considered, for example, issues concerning federations, supra-national organizations, or dependent peoples with national liberation movements), these two categories have had special significance and are also especially relevant to the current period of transition to a new international legal order.

Individuals

Schools of Thought

The status of the individual is one of the most important yet difficult questions or modern international law. On the one hand, individuals occupy the central position in social life. The ancient Greeks developed the notion that the human being is the measure of all things. People unite in tribes, societies, nations, governments, and states in order to satisfy their spiritual and material needs. The missions of each of these unions is to serve humanity. On the other hand, as history testifies, the abuse of power by societies and states has been a constant occurrence. Government serves as an instrument not only for the defense of human rights but for their violation as well. Accordingly, determining the optimal relations between the rights of society and the rights of individuals is the central problem of any normative system, moral or juridical, national or international.

For most of its history, international law has dealt solely with states, completely ignoring the individual. Not until the end of the nineteenth century did it even begin to address problems such as slavery and injury during wartime. Only with the adoption of the U.N. Charter did it truly begin to be concerned with relations between states and their citizens, calling for "international cooperation . . . in promoting and encouraging respect for human rights and for fundamental freedoms for all without distinction as to race, sex, language or religion."[9] Contemporary international law is now firmly related to the rights of the person, one of which is the right to a social and international order in which human rights and freedoms can be fully realized.[10] Today, the individual is with ever greater frequency an active rather than a passive participant in international affairs, in ever closer contact with international law. From the Universal Declaration of Human Rights (1948) to the Vienna, Copenhagen, and Moscow final documents of the Conference on Security and Cooperation in Europe (1989, 1990, and 1991, respectively),[11] it is recognized that people have the right to contribute actively, either individually or in association with others, in the promotion and protection of their rights and freedoms. Moreover, international human rights norms play a crucial role in evaluating a regime's legitimacy and level of civilization.

Do these developments mean the collapse of the Westphalian conception of the international legal order—the "de-étatization" of international law? It is perhaps too soon for a definitive answer to this question. Two schools of thought can be identified, however, which begin to suggest an answer by addressing the status of the individual in international legal relations. One school, while supporting developments in the field of human rights, firmly believes that only states and international organizations can be subjects of international law. Another school maintains that to the extent that international law now contains norms on the rights of the individual, the latter is increasingly a subject of it. (A third school would consider the individual not as a subject but as a "beneficiary" of international law. This is really but a subsidiary of the first school.)

The first school of thought emphasizes that although international law requires respect for individual freedom and dignity, it is through states that this respect is to be implemented. In this view, in giving effect to the "international cooperation" called for under the U.N. Charter, states accept obligations to accord to the individual various rights, and also to create international procedures for the defense of those rights. Individuals enjoy the fruits of this cooperation. Although customary international law and global public opinion reduce the degree to which states, even by mutual agreement, can introduce limitations on these rights and procedures, states do retain the collective power to change or even to abolish them. Sovereign states still remain the source of the commanding energy of international law—energy without which international law could not function. By virtue of their sovereignty, states create international legal norms, give them obligatory force, and put into effect the mechanisms for their realization. This school sees individuals, at best, as having a derivative legal personality, as their connection with international law is mediated through another governing political-legal institution, the state.

It was through the legal writings of socialist scholars in the pre-Gorbachev era that this first school of thought was most cogently articulated. However, this view is also reflected in many aspects of the official United States approach to international law. It is among Western scholars (including in this group some former Soviets), as opposed to Western governments, that the second school finds its strongest adherents. These scholars believe that international law is departing from a state-centered orientation—that it must be a law created by human beings for human beings. This school rejects the notion that there is anything fixed or immutable in the lack of access of individuals to the International Court of Justice or to world-wide law-making bodies. As one of its advocates has posed the question: "Is the international community still composed of the "governors" only, or are the "governed" allowed to have a say?[12]

The tension between these two schools of thought reflects the crossroads at which international law finds itself today. In what follows in this chapter, traces of this tension will be detectable. We now review prior doctrine concerning individuals in international relations, describe the current practice of individual access to human rights and other international tribunals, and then discuss emerging trends and issues.[13]

Prior Doctrine

In the late eighteenth and early nineteenth centuries, Blackstone and other Western jurists believed that individuals as well as states were bound by international law and were thereby liable for offenses against the law of nations, such as piracy and assault on diplomats. But this view lost its sway during the positivist era of state sovereignty, when the doctrine became entrenched that states alone have rights and duties and can make claims under international law. Publicists such as Oppenheim could then write that "since the Law of Nations is a law between States only and exclusively, States only and exclusively are subjects of the Law of Nations," individuals being only its objects. In the 1920s the Permanent Court of International Justice stated that while international agreements could adopt individual rights and duties enforceable in national courts, they do not create "direct" international rights and obligations for private individuals.[14] It also held that when a dispute between a private person and a state is taken up by the individual's government through diplomatic action or international judicial proceedings, "a State is in reality asserting its own rights—its right to ensure, in the person of its [nationals], respect for the rules of international law.[15]

The Court was reflecting the then-prevailing theory that treaties, at most, might impose the duty on states to incorporate individual rights into their municipal laws and that states, in their discretion, might diplomatically "espouse" the claims of their nationals, but that individual rights existed, at best, as rights of the state. This "espousal process," which has been called "a legal fiction,"[16] requires the national a) to convince its government to espouse the claim, b) to risk politicization of the claim, and c) to depend on its uncertain enforcement. All in all, this is a less than satisfactory posture. The U.S. State Department has long supported the "discretionary espousal" approach, maintaining that U.S. nationals have no automatic right to diplomatic intervention and no right to object to the amount of compensation negotiated on their behalf for injuries inflicted by other states. However, it recognizes that international human rights, at least, apply to individuals against violations by their own governments.

Beginning with the period after World War II, and occasionally even earlier, some Western publicists began to reassert the pre-nineteenth century position that individuals do have rights and duties under international law, even if their capacities "may be different from and less in number and substance than the capacities of states."[17] Thus in Lauterpacht's revision of Oppenheim's treatise, the word "primarily" is inserted in the original, "Since the Law of Nations is . . . a law between States . . . ," and the author acknowledges developments which tend "to extend recognition, by means of international supervision and enforcement, to the elementary rights of at least some sections of the population of the state."[18] These developments include the International Military Tribunal at Nuremberg, treaties articulating standards of humanitarian law, and the human rights conventions of the United Nations system. However, these are all changes brought about by treaty or by an international authority deriving its power from states, thus indicating that if international rules protect or bind individuals, it is still only through the will of states.

Some U.S. courts have recently conferred jurisdiction over individuals for alleged violations of customary international law, regardless of the nationality of the victim,[19] but these are apparently minority positions, both within American and international jurisprudence. In cases involving human rights, such a construction is necessary because other than the Genocide and Torture conventions, and only recently the International Covenant on Civil and Political Rights, the U.S. has not ratified many of the other major human rights treaties.

Until the Gorbachev era, the Soviet view had concurred with the prevailing positivistic conception. "The Soviet science of international law has proved that individuals are under State jurisdiction and are legal persons in relations inside the State. They have no independent legal status and are not capable of the independent accomplishment of international rights and duties. Therefore, they are not international persons.[20] . . . Although these views reflected the traditional doctrine, the USSR had also rejected the traditional rule that a state is responsible under international law for injuries resulting from the taking of property of the national of another state, on the theory that an alien acquires property in and enters the territory of another state subject wholly to local law.

Soviet representatives argued in U.N. forums against the recognition of individuals because it would restrict the sovereignty of states over their own citizens and offer opportunities for interference with the internal affairs of states. F.I. Kozhevnikov, for instance, stated to the International Law Commission in 1953 that "the rights of the individual lay outside the direct scope of international law, and, it was only by virtue of the legal bond which existed between the individual and the State that his right could be protected."[21] Although in 1973 the USSR ratified the International Covenant on Civil and Political Rights—but not until July 1991 the Optional Protocol—it originally opposed the creation of the Human Rights Committee on the grounds that it would violate the U.N. Charter, the principle of national sovereignty, and the rule that individuals are not subjects of international law.

Even before the dissolution of the country, this orthodox Soviet view appears to have changed. Before speculating on the implications of such change, as well as evolving Western views, we will survey the international and regional tribunals in which individuals are held accountable or are able to seek their remedies.

Tribunal Practice

Although no international criminal court or penal tribunal has yet been established on a permanent basis, various humanitarian and other conventions require states to bring to punishment individuals, both officials and private citizens, who have violated the laws of war,[22] engaged in genocide,[23] or committed international terrorist acts.[24] Indeed, since 1815, over three hundred multilateral agreements have been reached which provide for over twenty categories of international crimes.[25] But until 1993 (when a special tribunal was created for crimes committed in the former Yugoslavia) there had been only two ad hoc international tribunals, at Nuremberg and Tokyo, that were created to try individuals for international crimes.

In his opening statement at the Nuremberg Trial of the Major War Criminals, the U.S. Chief Prosecutor, Justice Robert Jackson, declared, "Crimes against international law are committed by men, not by abstract entities, and only by punishing individuals who commit such crimes can the provisions of international law be enforced."[26] This Nuremberg principle of individual responsibility, originally proclaimed in the Charter entered into by the U.S., the USSR, France, and the U.K., has been reaffirmed unanimously by the United Nations and by numerous jurists as forming an authoritative part of contemporary international law. However, Nuremberg alone cannot establish the international legal personality of individuals, for it applied only to individuals acting under color of state law, not individuals acting on a purely private basis, and it did not provide for claims brought by individual victims.

In a limited number of international and regional fora, most predominantly in the area of human rights, individuals may bring claims against states for violations of international obligations; however, in each such forum, jurisdiction over individual claims has been specifically agreed to by the respondent state.[27] Conditions under which the claims are heard are, accordingly, quite restrictive and hardly favorable to individual litigants. Under Resolution 1503 of the U.N. Economic and Social Council, for instance, although a broad range of persons and groups is empowered to communicate directly with the U.N. Sub-Commission on Prevention of Discrimination and Protection of Minorities, petitioners must remain silent about the communication until the Sub-Commission makes a recommendation, and single individuals can assert claims only if their claim is an expression of a "consistent pattern of gross and reliably attested violations of human rights and fundamental freedoms." Given the confidentiality requirements and the fact that states which offer to cooperate can usually avoid public condemnation while continuing to violate human rights, many observers have concluded that this procedure "operates to protect rather than to expose countries responsible for systematic and gross violations of human rights."[28]

Under the Optional Protocol to the International Covenant on Civil and Political Rights, by contrast, individuals can petition the U.N.'s Human Rights Committee concerning just a single violation of the underlying Covenant. However, the claimant must normally be a personally affected victim or a duly appointed, closely connected representative. Over sixty states have ratified or acceded to the Optional Protocol, but that is only about half of all the state parties to the Covenant. A procedure for hearing individual communications is also established by the International Convention on the Elimination of All Forms of Racial Discrimination and by the Torture Convention, but like the International Covenant procedure, such communications will not be received if the state complained about has not consented to the procedure.

Individual claimants are afforded somewhat less obstructed access in the European and Inter-American human rights systems; in fact, many more individual petitions have been adjudicated by the European Commission on Human Rights than by the U.N.'s Human Rights Committee under the Optional Protocol. While the Protocol speaks of "individuals," the European Convention for the Protection of Human Rights and Fundamental Freedoms permits "any person, non-governmental organization or group of individuals" claiming to be victimized by a member state's violation to lodge an application with the European Commission, provided that the respondent state "has declared that it recognizes the competence of the Commission to receive such petitions."[29] This is a narrower standard than the Convention's inter-state procedure, by which "any alleged breach of the provisions of the Convention by another High Contracting Party" may be referred to the Commission.[30] Nevertheless, realizing that "the Convention and its institutions were set up to protect the individual," the European Court of Human Rights has ruled that procedures must "be applied in a manner which serves to make the system of individual applications efficacious."[31] Thus, while the *actio popularis* is excluded, individuals may claim to be victims of a violation occasioned by the mere existence of legislation providing (for instance) for secret surveillance or, in the absence of an actual measure of implementation of a law, if they "run the risk of being directly affected by it."

According to Merrills, the European Court of Human Rights "sees itself as much more than a provider of remedies for isolated complaints. In the interests of the effectiveness of the Convention as a whole it is prepared to use individual applications as an opportunity to make points which it considers need to be made and interprets the concept of 'victim' accordingly."[32] Although individuals cannot institute proceedings directly in the European Court, under a recently revised rule, in cases that have been referred by the Commission or one of the concerned states, the individual "may present his own case" to the Court, either directly or through an advocate.

Individual access in the Inter-American human rights system is similar to the European, in that only states and the Commission can submit cases to the Court. However, an individual can petition the Commission concerning any state that has ratified the American Convention on Human Rights and may be a spouse, relative, friend, or even a person unknown to the aggrieved party. While the Inter-American system is newer than the European and far fewer cases have been adjudicated, its bar on individual standing before the Court has been criticized as weakening the Court's ability to effect fully its mandate to promote the observance of individual rights.

Outside the context of human rights, a small number of fora receive or were envisioned to receive individual claims. Within the U.N. system, individual inhabitants of trust territories have the theoretical right to petition the Trusteeship Council, while employees of the Organization have often attained legal recourse in the Administrative Tribunal. In addition, when it is established, the International Tribunal for the Law of the Sea will be open "to entities other than States Parties" in any case submitted pursuant to "an agreement conferring jurisdiction on the Tribunal which is accepted by all the parties to that case."[33]

By far the longest experience with individual access is in the Court of Justice of the European Communities, to which private persons may, in some limited circumstances, bring claims against the main organs of the EC, though not against Member States or other individuals. (Jurisdiction over some individual suits has been transferred to the EC's new Court of First Instance.) Individual standing in the European Court of Justice has been said to serve the important functions of checking the political power of Community institutions, circumventing possible efforts of the national judiciaries to rob the Court of its powers, and filling the void created by political barriers to Member State challenges, "thus preserving the smooth functioning and goodwill of the economic union."[34] But recognition that individuals are subjects of European Community law has more than a utilitarian purpose. As the Court has stated: "[T]he community constitutes a new legal order of international law for the benefit of which the States have limited their sovereign rights, albeit within limited fields, and the subjects of which comprise not only Member States but also their nationals independently of the legislation of Member States."[35]

Finally, mention should be made of The Iran–United States Tribunal, which is accessible to natural and juridical persons, as well as to the two states. Because most of the non-state litigants are corporations, the

Tribunal is described in the "transnational enterprises" section of this chapter, below.

Emerging Trends and Issues

The preceding review of prior doctrine and tribunal practice reveals that at the present time, individuals have a precarious and uncertain status in international law. To the extent that they have international obligations, those are not enforced in any extant, permanent forum. The procedural right to initiate proceedings before an international body is meager and often rudimentary, limited to forwarding a complaint, without necessarily the opportunity to make a personal appearance. Even worse, the procedural right is granted only by treaty, so that it exists only in regard to selective, discrete matters, and often only in regard to states that have consented to individual claims. These ratifications, moreover, can be withdrawn at the state's discretion. Finally, the concomitant remedy to these procedural rights is often a mild, unenforceable report. The exceptions to this general set of restrictive conditions are further limited by region, respondent, or even time.

Despite these serious limitations, the current status of individuals in international law illustrates some remarkable developments. First, when individuals have an international procedural right, it is granted without regard to nationality. They can thereby complain against their own states or other states, irrespective of whether their own state agrees to represent their claim. Second, although the voluntary relinquishing of some sovereign prerogatives has not been easy, states have come to respect the tribunals which have adjudicated individual claims against them. Third, there is a growing emphasis on codification of individual responsibilities, in addition to rights, as illustrated by the Convention on the Rights of the Child (1989), which imposes on parents as well as states the affirmative duty to act on behalf of their children. These may seem like minor triumphs, but not when measured against what had been, at least until recently, the ostensibly absolute intractability of the Westphalian conception of public international law. Added together, the myriad of discrete tribunal procedures receiving individual claims, along with the influence of non-governmental organizations representing the interests of individuals, constitute a de facto, if not de jure, international personality for individuals. . . .

In the *Reparations* case, the World Court defined an international person as "capable of possessing international rights and duties . . . and [having the] capacity to maintain its rights by bringing international claims."[36] It further stated that in any legal system, the subjects of law are not necessarily identical in nature or extent of their rights, "and their nature depends upon the needs of the community."[37] Although the Court was considering, in 1949, the international personality of an intergovernmental organization, the United Nations, this same test can be applied to individuals today. As already indicated, individuals do already possess international rights and duties, albeit limited in scope. But as with organizations, the rights and duties of individuals need not be identical to that of states. Whether individuals are capable of asserting rights by means of international demands is a function of what states are willing to allow. If not, this part of the I.C.J. definition is tautological: individuals are not capable of asserting international demands, because they are not recognized international subjects. International personality must mean more than merely the availability of a remedy, but how much more, and how much need be independent of the will of states?

An advocate of the traditional school of thought criticized in 1972 those Western jurists who drew "the conclusion that the existing subjects of international law are absolutely free to transform any object into a subject of international law. In order to achieve this, the presence of their wish is [according to them] the only necessary requirement needed."[38] He insisted at that time on two other prerequisites to international recognition: participation in the creation of international norms and the application and implementation of such norms. It was then and continues now to be unrealistic to expect individuals to create international law, although the prospect of a world legislature representing private persons seems less illusory today than only twenty years ago. . . .

The regional rudiments of such a body now exist in the European Parliament, in which members represent transnational political groups such as Socialists, Communists, Greens, and Christian Democrats. A world parliament of individuals might include representatives of transnational groups such as indigenous peoples, women, and scientists.

Individuals will fully be able to apply and to implement international norms only when they are held accountable for them in an international penal tribunal—the creation of which, again, depends on the will of states. This realization turns back to the I.C.J.'s formula that the nature of an international subject's rights "depends upon the needs of the community." Or as one of us articulated it in 1972, "the need . . . for the development of international cooperation based on the generally accepted principles of international law. Such a proposition testifies that international legal personality cannot exist without a social basis. The range of subjects of law, their types, and their nature are determined by social needs.[39]

The most important development of the recent period is that the world community is closer to agreeing on its common social needs. If both East and West (and, perhaps, North and South) can agree that cooperation through peaceful coexistence and the pursuit of common human values is wiser than world-wide class struggle, then surely they can cooperate in the recognition of an expanded legal status for individuals. Sovereign prerogatives are less imperative in a collaborative world than in an antagonistic one. The instrumental benefits of individual personality have already been demonstrated in the European Community, and even antagonists as polarized as the U.S. and Iran have experienced the gains, if not willingly or intentionally.

If states have heretofore been reluctant to grant legal personality to individuals, it was because they feared, quite accurately, that individual claims would be directed at them. But individuals with greater international status would not make demands on states alone. They are likely to direct them increasingly at international organizations. Or as Anthony D'Amato has speculated:

> [I]f the nineteenth century was characterized by State v. State, and the twentieth by Individual v. State, the twenty-first century might see international law becoming addressed to the claims of Individual v. Individual. Transboundary international legal claims involving individuals only, but invoking public international law, might be the direction in which we are headed.[40]

Moreover, if states can collectively recognize that with the end of the Cold War, the greatest threats to world peace now come from drug trafficking and terrorism, torture and genocide, global warming and water contamination—acts committed not only by states but by individuals—then they can agree that an urgent need of the world community is the establishment of a world criminal court, to try individuals as well as states. The arguments to this effect of numerous individuals and organizations in both the United States and the former Soviet Union deserve wider attention.

International legal personality for individuals should not only result in a forum for enforcing international duties. It should also lead to wider ratification of human rights treaties, as well as to liberalization of the standing requirements in the existing tribunals that enforce international rights. As the World Court held in the *Barcelona Traction* case, obligations to the international community as a whole derive in contemporary international law from

> the outlawing of acts of aggression, and of genocide, as also from the principles and rules concerning the basic rights of the human person, including protection from slavery and racial discrimination. . . . In view of the importance of the rights involved, all States can be held to have a legal interest in their protection; they are obligations *erga omnes*.[41]

If all states are deemed injured by breaches of human rights, then surely are all individuals.

We now turn to perhaps an even more controversial topic, the status of transnational enterprises.

Transnational Enterprises

The Status of Transationals

Whether labeled "Transational" or "multinational corporations," "global enterprises" or variations thereof, the entities which we will call "transnational enterprises"[42] generally consist of economic organizations performing manufacturing, financial, technological or similar functions, headquartered in industrialized countries and pursuing business activities abroad, often in developing countries. They frequently operate through affiliates linked by common managerial and financial control, which share information, resources, and responsibilities and pursue integrated policies and strategies. Some are economically more powerful than all but the largest states. . . .

Despite their size and influence, transnational enterprises such as ITT, GM, Toyota, Royal Dutch/Shell, and Unilever have no formal international rights or duties. While they may participate in international proceedings with states, agree that public international law may govern their transactions with states, or otherwise exert influence on national and international policies, transnational enterprises have heretofore been treated within the international legal order as nationals of a given state, lacking their own international legal personality.

Admittedly, transnational enterprises are not totally without legal status in international tribunals. Private business ventures have legal standing in the European Economic Community and the European Coal and Steel Community. The Convention on the Settlement of Investment Disputes Between States and Nationals of Other States provides international methods of settlement for some such disputes. However, a provision in a contract between a transnational and a state stipulating that the governing law is international or general principles of law does not make the contract a treaty. Breach by the state does not normally permit the transnational to seek enforcement in an international forum.

One significant exception to this rule is the Iran-United States Claims Tribunal, established pursuant to the Algiers Declaration in 1981 to resolve claims against Iran by U.S. nationals, primarily corporations, claims against the U.S. by Iranian nationals, including corporations, and interstate claims. Although subject to a wide range of interpretations as to whether its law is private, public, national, "a-national," or international, the Tribunal was established to be a legal process, not a mediation or negotiation. Therefore, its practice regarding non-state litigants is more significant than that of regular commercial arbitration, and it clearly reflects an advance beyond the old "espousal doctrine," described above, in which claims of nationals were resolved intergovernmentally by lump sum settlement.

Although under typical commercial arbitration the capacity to agree to arbitration depends on the parties' own national law, because the Tribunal was created by international agreement, not private contract, it can be argued that the law of the Tribunal is public international law and that the corporate claimants are subjects thereof. Indeed, the Tribunal has rarely relied on national systems of law as the source of controlling rules, a process fundamental to arbitration under the auspices of the International Chamber of Commerce, the rules of the U.N. Commission for International Trade Law (UNCITRAL), and other typical approaches. Instead, it has regularly applied principles derived from the parties contracts, general principles of law, and public international law. Moreover, despite the positions taken by Iran and the U.S., respectively, that non-state claims in the Tribunal are in actuality diplomatically espoused interstate claims or that they are akin to commercial arbitration under the law of the forum state, the Netherlands, the Tribunal itself has uniformly rejected both of these views and has indicated that the claims belong to the private party and not to the state. Not only are awards made directly to corporate and individual litigants and claims captioned in litigants' private names, but the private parties themselves can argue their own claims and decide whether to accept settlement.

Whether or not the Iran-U.S. Claims Tribunal will have a lasting jurisprudential effect will depend on whether in later years it is viewed as a watershed or as merely *sui generis*. The U.N. Claims Commission established as part of the Gulf War ceasefire accepts consolidated claims submitted by governments on behalf of their nationals—pursuant to the traditional "espousal" doctrine—though, in an innovation, the Commission will hear claims by stateless or unrepresented parties, such as Palestinians. Unlike the Iran-U.S. Claims Tribunal, which largely ignored the losses of individual claimants, the U.N. Compensation Commission has put corporate claimants on hold, giving priority to individuals.

As regards transnational enterprises generally, states have almost universally agreed that their status should not be upgraded. Through the 1980s it could be said:

> Socialist countries are politically opposed to them and the majority of developing States are suspicious of their power; both groups would never allow them to play an autonomous role in international affairs. Even Western countries are reluctant to grant them international standing; they prefer to keep them under their control—of course, to the extent that this is possible.[43]

Moreover, the directors of transnationals "appear to agree with many national governments that [transnationals] ought not to participate directly in the international legal system—evidenced by the fact that [they] have not overtly sought broad international legal personality."[44] In the 1990s, the question of what to do about transnational enterprises may emerge as the centerpiece for restructuring the inequities in global economic relations. For no groups—including possibly the transnationals themselves—are happy with their current status. As the United Nations Group of Eminent Persons reported on these enterprises in 1974:

> Home countries are concerned about the undesirable effects that foreign investment by multinational corporations may have on domestic employment and the balance of payments, and about the capacity of such corporations to alter the normal play of competition. Host countries are concerned about the ownership and control of key economic sectors by foreign enterprises, the excessive cost to the domestic economy which their operations entail, the extent to which they may encroach upon political sovereignty and their possible adverse influence on sociocultural values. Labour interests are concerned about the impact of multinational corporations on employment and workers' welfare and on the bargaining strength of trade unions. Consumer interests are concerned about the appropriateness, quality and price of the goods produced by multinational corporations. The multinational corporations themselves are concerned about the possible nationalization or expropriation of their assets without adequate compensation and about restrictive, unclear and frequently changing government policies.[45]

To these concerns a more contemporary report would add the problems of product dumping, destruction of the environment and modification of the climate in the course of states couraged development, and collaboration in the bolstering of unlawful *apartheid* regimes. Just as most states have concurred that transnationals are not subjects of international law, "[a]lmost all nations agree on the desirability, if not the necessity, of some form of international regulation of TNC's."[46] The problem is that they cannot agree on a form. Even if they could, because of the limitations of contemporary jurisprudence, regulation might not be effective.

In the remaining sections of this chapter, we will briefly review the efforts to assert international regulatory control over transnational enterprises. We will then speculate on future directions and discuss some current problems, including two reciprocal questions: how can the international claims of transnationals be presented, and how can international claims be presented against them?

Regulatory Efforts

The earliest regulation of transnationals took the form of bilateral investment, promotion, and protection treaties between "home" (state of incorporation) and "host" (state of operation) countries. Intended to protect foreign investors by dealing, most prominently, with questions of nationalization and compensation, these have traditionally been favored by industrialized states. Developing countries prefer newer forms of regulation by intergovernmental and nongovernmental organizations. Some categories and examples of these include: sectoral strategies by producers' associations, such as the Organization of Petroleum Exporting Countries or the inter-state Union of Banana Exporting Countries; harmonized policies and institutional arrangements at the subregional and regional levels, such as by the European Community, Latin American Free Trade Association and the Andean Common Market; guidelines issued by the inter-regional group of industrialized countries, the Organization for Economic Cooperation and Development; and international efforts within the U.N. system, which have commonly consisted of codes—both specialized ones by the Economic and Social Council (ECOSOC), the U.N. Conference on Trade and Development, the International Labour Organization, the Food and Agriculture Organization and other agencies, and the more general Draft U.N. Code of Conduct on Transnational Corporations, prepared by the Commission and Centre on Transnational Corporations on the recommendation of the Group of Eminent Persons. A common objective of all the codes, supported even by transnationals themselves, is harmonization of what are now unpredictable national laws and regulations through the formulation of internationally accepted models. The Draft U.N. Code of Conduct, lacking a preamble and list of objectives and containing some alternative provisions, is addressed to both transnationals and states. Its provisions include both standards for corporate conduct and principles for the treatment of transnationals by states. A major substantive dispute that is unresolved is the "host-state treatment" conflict. Industrialized countries insist on "national treatment" no less favorable than that given to the host state's domestic corporations. Developing countries support "qualified national treatment" which would allow them to refer to national objectives and priorities rather than international law or "established" development plans, as sought by developed countries.

Socialist countries, at least through the 1980s, believed that transnationals should enjoy a less privileged status than national corporations, denying, for instance, the former the investment incentives granted to the latter. On many issues related to transnationals, socialist states generally supported the position of developing countries, while simultaneously promoting their own ideological positions. The "host state treatment" conflict may be resolved depending on the position taken, and the influence asserted, by the formerly socialist states.

Among other legal issues remaining to be resolved are the relevance of customary international law to the norms established under the Code, questions concerning choice of law and the jurisdiction of national courts, and, most significantly for our purposes, the legal nature of the Code. ECOSOC originally called for a code that is "effective, comprehensive, generally accepted and universally adopted," without reference to its legal status.[47] During the drafting period, developing and socialist countries argue for a mandatory, legally binding code in the form of a treaty, believing that adopting states would then be obliged to observe not only those provisions addressed to them but also to enforce the sections relating to transnational conduct through national legislation and national enforcement machinery. A binding treaty would also entail effective international institutions not only to assess developments under the Code but also to reinforce national action. Industrialized countries and business interests, in contrast, rejected the notion of a binding code, urging instead the adoption of a voluntary code relying on moral suasion and without enforcement mechanisms. Although initially in favor of a binding code, since the Ford Administration the U.S. has supported a voluntary one and has also taken the position that code responsibilities must be balanced between governments and transnationals and must apply to state-owned enterprises as well, regardless of whether they are profitmaking.

From the look of the most recent draft of the Code, it is a typical compromise: more of its provisions apply to transnationals than to states, while the question of whether it applies to public corporations is left unresolved. However, it is expected to turn out to be a voluntary instrument. Nevertheless, merely reaching an agreement to put transnationals on a relatively equal footing with states in the Code has been a major concession of sovereignty by the drafters.

Given the current status of transnational enterprises in international law, both binding and non-binding codes are problematic. Some of these and other enforcement issues are taken up in the next section.

Current Problems and Proposals

Non-binding codes, with their guage and reliance on moral suasion, do not constitute international law, although one author has argued that voluntary codes may become recognized as such as a result of wide endorsement, national practice and intergovernmental monitoring. A possible virtue of voluntary codes is that, paradoxically, drafters may be willing to adopt stronger language and stricter standards in them than in enforceable codes. However, experience with the Sullivan Principles, a voluntary code of fair labor practices for U.S. firms operating in South Africa, indicates that even mild, progressively-structured yet optional standards would fail to meet ECOSOC's "effectiveness" test. After six years in existence, the Sullivan program had only 120 participants out of 400 eligible firms, and only two of the seven companies employing over 5000 workers. Moreover, host states as well as transnationals are legally free to disregard voluntary codes when enacting national laws, thus undermining the harmonization and predictability objectives of the code-drafting process.

Despite the uproar that it would cause in Western circles, a mandatory code would be binding only on states, which along with international organizations are the only entities that can enter into international conventions. Code provisions concerning standards of corporate conduct would then be implemented and enforced on the national level, without a real guarantee of state-to-state uniformity, either substantively or procedurally.

Only if transnationals themselves could become parties to the mandatory codes would all perspectives—industrialized and developing states, plus transnationals and non-corporate, private interests—be assured of protection for what is a mutual interest: equal access to fair tribunals, whether international or national, in which all claims concerning transnational enterprises can be heard.

The current system's failure to provide this kind of access extends beyond the problem of code enforcement to other sorts of legal claims. This is illustrated by the following all too real problem:[48]

> Transnational enterprise ABC, incorporated in the United States and doing business in South American country XYZ, intends to construct oil and gas pipelines and processing plants in a tropical rainforest that is ecologically crucial to the survival of numerous plant and animal species and an indigenous tribal population, as well as the planet as a whole, as recent scientific studies have reported. Country XYZ supports and has approved permits for the construction.

Assuming current law, including the non-existence of a Code of Conduct, either binding or not, in what forum could relief be sought that would prevent this construction? In theory, there are three possibilities, but none is terribly viable. The first is the International Court of Justice, as no other relevant international forum exists. (A complaint which emphasized human rights rather than environmental issues might be presented before the Inter-American Commission on Human Rights, but this would seemingly require a stretch of the American Convention on Human Rights.) In the World Court, only state XYZ could be a respondent (naming the U.S. would be frivolous) and only another state could be a petitioner. Assuming that another state could be persuaded to espouse the ecological interests (an unlikely possibility), despite the probable *erga omnes* character of obligations to protect the environment, no obvious provisions of international law have been violated by XYZ in its approval of a permit for ABC to develop within XYZ. While a second avenue is litigation by the indigenous tribe or by environmentalists against ABC within the national courts of XYZ, it is unlikely that any national laws would prohibit the construction. Moreover, political considerations might make it unlikely that a suit concerning government-supported development would be taken seriously in XYZ's courts.

That essentially leaves litigation in the federal courts of the state of incorporation, the United States, under the Alien Tort Claims Act. Members of the tribe, backed by environmentalists, might sue both transnational ABC and state XYZ. However, claims against XYZ would almost certainly fail under sovereign immunity principles, and, unless bribery or other corruption was alleged, the act of state doctrine. That would leave ABC as a defendant, but it is not apparent that either laws of the U.S. or any international laws, conventional or customary, are applicable. Even if the U.N. Code of Conduct had been adopted as a binding agreement, its environmental provisions are weak and vaguely drafted. Unless transnational corporations are made parties to it, the Code would be binding only on state XYZ, which would have been dismissed from the suit. However, if the Code were binding on transnationals, ABC could be held accountable in U.S. courts (assuming either that the U.S. was a signatory or that it reflected customary international law[49]) or in an international tribunal with jurisdiction over transnationals that might be set up under such a Code system.

Transnationals also suffer from their inability to bring legal claims in their own name. In the *Barcelona Traction* case, involving expropriation of property of a transnational by Spain after the Spanish Civil War, the World Court faced the question whether Belgium could exercise diplomatic protection for shareholders, the overwhelming majority of whom were its nationals, but where the company was incorporated not in Belgium but in Canada. The Court held that only the state of incorporation could espouse the claim. This rule has left transnational enterprises and their shareholders subject to the whims of the "espousal doctrine," meaning the unappealable, unpredictable vagaries of government policy, a predicament shared by individuals. Where the place of incorporation becomes more and more a technicality, unrelated to the locus of corporate management or ownership, this rule is especially unrealistic.

It has already been suggested that an international companies law be created which would grant international charters to transnational enterprises. Such a law would also establish an intergovernmental agency to enforce standards such as share dispersal. In the European Community, a European Company Statute has already been proposed that would permit large corporations to achieve supranational incorporation under a law applicable in all EC jurisdictions. The proposal would obviate the need to harmonize the existing laws in the twelve member states without supplanting national securities and disclosure laws or local administrative and judicial supervision. Throughout the world, as the environmental impact of transnationals becomes more urgent—and more transborder—it should become even clearer that only through international status, supervised by international agencies and international tribunals, can the problems of transnationals be adequately addressed.

The main obstacle is that, so far, almost all relevant parties have opposed international personality for transnational enterprises. While international legal status for individuals is threatening enough to state sovereignty, most states, developing countries in particular, are likely to view such a development as over-empowering the very entities, corporations, that are already overly powerful. Perhaps the present gridlock can be broken by the formerly socialist states, which are in the process of reexamining their own relationships to transnationals, given their need and desire for development, as well as their growing awareness of the fragility of their own environments. . . .

Notes

1. The phrase is derived from the Peace of Westphalia (1648), which ended the Thirty Years War and led to the era of the nation-state. See Falk, *The Interplay of Westphalia and Charter Conceptions of International Legal Order,* in The Future of the International Legal Order 43 (R. Falk & C. Black, eds, 1969.)

2. In the United States, the traditional treatment is followed in, inter alia, Restatement (Third) of the Foreign Relations Law of the United States, para.201-223 (1987) [hereinafter Restatement]; and in leading textbooks for use in law schools, including International Law: Cases and Materials 241-243 (L. Henkin et al. eds, 3rd, ed. 1993).

3. See Advisory Opinion on the United Nations, 1949 I.C.J. 174 [hereinafter the Reparations Case]; Convention on the Law of Treaties Between States and International Organizations or Between International Organizations, March 20, 1986, 25 I.L.M. 543.

4. See M.V. Zakharova, The Individual as a Subject of International Law, 1989 Soviet State and Law, No. 11, at 118; J. Quigley, Law for a World Community, 16 Syracuse J. int'l L. & Com. 1 (1989); R.A. Mullerson, Human Rights and the Individual as Subject of International Law: A Soviet View, 1 Eur. J. Int'l. L. 33, 35 (1990); R.A. Mullerson, Human Rights: Ideas, Norms, Reality (Moscow, 1991).

5. Id. See also V.S. Vereshchetin & R.A. Mullerson, The Primacy of International Law in World Politics, 1989 Soviet St. & L., No. 7, at 10.

6. Robert Gilpin wrote that the nation-state is "losing control over economic affairs to transnational actors like multinational corporations. It cannot retain its traditional independence and sovereignty and simultaneously meet the expanding economic needs and desires of its people." R. Gilpin, Three Models of the Future, 29 Int'l Organizations, No. 1, at 41 (1975).

7. See N.V. Mironov, Eternal Relations of Ministries, Unions, and Enterprises (Jurid. Lit. 1986).

8. "[I]t is not particularly helpful, either intellectually or operationally, to rely on the subject-object dichotomy that runs through so much of the writings. It is more helpful and closer to perceived reality to return to the policy-science view of international law as a particular decision-making process. . . . In this model, there are no subjects or objects, but only participants." Higgins, Conceptual Thinking

About the Individual in International Law, 24 N.Y.L. Sch. L. Rev. 11, 15-16 (1978), citing D.P. O'Connell, International Law 117 (1965); McDougal, Some Basic Theoretical Concepts About International Law, 4 J. Conflict Resol. 337 (1960); McDougal et al., The World Constitutive Process of Authoritative Decision, 29 J. Legal Educ.253(1967).

9. U.N. Charter art. 1, para. 3. See also id., art. 55, 56.

10. Universal Declaration of Human Rights, G.A. Res. 217, art. 28 (1948).

11. See Final Document of the Vienna Meeting of the Conference on the Human Dimension of the Conference on Security and Cooperation in Europe, Principles 13.5 and 26, reprinted in 28 I.L.M. 527 (1989); Final Document of the Copenhagen Meeting of the Conference on the Human Dimension of the CSCE, Principles 10.3 and 11.3, reprinted in 29 I.L.M. 1305 (1990); and Final Document of the Moscow Meeting of the Conference on the Human Dimension of the CSCE, reprinted in 30 I.L.M. 1670 (1991). See also Final Act, Conference on Security and Cooperation in Europe, Basket III, reprinted in 14 I.L.M. 1292 (1975).

12. A. Cassese, International Law in a Divided World 4 (1986).

13. For an earlier review of many of the doctrines, tribunals, and trends discussed in this section of the chapter, see Brownlie, The Place of the Individual in International Law, 50 Va. L. Rev. 435 (1964).

14. Danzig Railway Officials (Jurisdiction), 1928 P.C.I.J. (ser. B) No. 15, at 17–18. Because it recognized the possibility of treaties creating individual rights and obligations, this decision has been said to have "dealt a decisive blow to the dogma of the impenetrable barrier separating individuals from international law." H. Lauterpacht, International Law and Human Right 28 (1968).

15. Mavrommatis Palestine Concessions (Jurisdiction), 1924 P.C.I.J. (ser.A) No. 2, at 11–12. See also Panevezys-Saldutiskis Railway Case (Estonia v. Lithuania), 1939 P.C.I.J. (ser. A/B) No. 76, at 16.

16. In our view, espousal is a legal fiction, as the national has no real claim. The state is asserting its own claim. A. D'Amato, International Law: Process and Prospect 194-198 (1987).

17. O'Connell, International Law 108 (2nd ed. 1970).

18. Lauterpacht, Revision of Oppenheim (1955), excerpted in the Human Rights Reader, 167, 169 (W. Laqueur & B. Rubin Eds. 1973).

19. Most notably, Filartiga v. Pena-Irla, 630 F.2d 876 (2nd Cir. 1980).

20. Feldman, International Personality, 2 R.C.A.D.I. 359 (1986), citing International Law 82 (G. Tunkin ed. 1982). See Restatement, supra note 2, para. 712, reporter's note 1.

21. 1 Y.B. Int'l L. Comm'n 173 (1953), cited in Przetacnik, The Socialist Concept of Human Rights: Its Philosophical Background and Political Justification, 13 Review Belge de Droit Int'l 238, 249 (1977).

22. See Geneva Convention Relative to the Protection of Civilian Persons in Time of War, 75 U.N.T.S. 287 (1949); Geneva Convention Relative to the Treatment of Prisoners of War, 75 U.N.T.S. 135 (1949), each ratified by both the U.S. and U.S.S.R.

23. The Convention on the Prevention and Punishment of the Crime of Genocide, 78 U.N.T.S. 277 (1948), ratified by the U.S.S.R. in 1954 and the U.S. in 1988, provides in Article VI that "Persons charged with genocide . . . shall be tried by a competent tribunal of the State in the territory of which the act was committed, or by such international penal tribunal as may have jurisdiction."

24. See e.g., Tokyo Convention on Offenses and Certain Other Acts Committed on Board Aircraft, 704 U.N.T.S. 219 (1963); Hague Convention of the Suppression

of Unlawful Seizure of Aircraft, 22 U.S.T. 1641, T.I.A.S. No. 7192 (1970); Montreal Convention for Suppression of Unlawful Acts Against the Safety of Civilian Aviation, 24 U.S.T. 565, T.I.A.S. No. 7570 (1971); International Convention Against the Taking of Hostages, U.N. Doc. A/Res/34/146 (1979).

25. See M. C. Bassiouni, International Crimes (1985).

26. Trial of the Major War Criminals Before the International Military Tribunal, Proceedings 34 (1947) [hereinafter Proceedings]. See also Trial of Japanese War Criminals, Documents 40 (1946).

27. Excluded from this discussion are human rights related petition procedures in specialized agencies of the U.N. such as the ILO and UNESCO. See, able, Valticos, The International Labour Organization and Saba, in The International Dimensions of Human Rights 363, 401 (K. Vasak & P. Alston eds. 1982). See generally United Nations Actions in the Field of Human Rights, U.N. Doc. ST/HR/2 Rev.1 (1983).

28. UN Commission on Human Rights—consideration of Gross Violations, 30 Review of the International Commission of Jurists 31, 34 (1983).

29. 213 U.N.T.S. 221 (1950), art. 25.

30. Id., art. 24.

31. Klass Case, 28 Eur. Ct. H.R. (ser A) at 18 (1978).

32. J. Merrills, The Development of International Law by the European Court of Human Rights 50 (1988).

33. United Nations Convention on the Law of the Sea, U.N. Doc. A/Conf.62/122 (1982) Annex VI, art. 20.

34. Parkinson, Admissibility of Direct Actions by Natural or Legal Persons in the European Court of Justice, 24 Tex. Int'l L., 456, 457, 460 (1989). See generally A. Arnull, The General Principles of EEC Law and the Individual (1990).

35. Van Gend and Loos Case, 1963 O.J. 1, at 23.

36. Advisory Opinion on Reparations for Injuries Suffered in the Service of the United Nations, 1949 I.C.J. 174 (1949).

37. Id. at 178.

38. Lukashuk citing G. Schwarzenberger, A Manual of International Law 40 (1960) as one such dreamer.

39. Lukashuk, Parties to Treaties: The Right of Participation, in Academie de Droit International, 1 Recueil Des Cours 1972 (1973), at 240. See the Reparations Case, supra note 3.

40. D'Amato, supra note 16, at 199. A pre-tribunal screening mechanism, functioning much like the European Commission on Human Rights, would be needed to screen out frivolous claims. See Higgins, supra note 8.

41. Case Concerning the Barcelona Traction Light and Power Co. (Belgium v. Spain)(Second Phase), 1970 I.C.J. 3, at 32 [hereinafter Barcelona Case].

42. We will use "transnational enterprise," as "multinational: wrongly implies ownership and control by investors in several states, whereas most such entities consist of parent companies based in industrialized states with affiliates or subsidiaries in developing countries. Moreover, "corporations" is too narrow, as some are co-operatives or partnerships, or state-owned or mixed-ownership entities.

43. Cassese, supra note 12. at 103.

44. Charney, Transnational Corporations and Developing Public International Law, 1983, Duke L.J., at 766.

45. Report of the Group of Eminent Persons, The Impact of Multinational Corporations on Development and on International Relations, U.N. Doc. E/5500/Add 1 (1974), at 9-10.

46. Rubin, Transnational Corporations and international Codes of Conduct: A Study of the Relationship Between International Legal Cooperation and Economic Development, 30 Am. U.L. Rev. 903, 914 (1981). Note that the Declaration on the Establishment of a New International Economic Order, G.A. Res. 3201 (S-VI), May 1, 1974, 13 I.L.M. 715, states in para. 4 that the new economic order shall be founded on full respect for, inter alia, "(g) Regulation and supervision of the activities of transnational corporation by taking full measures in the interest of the national economics of the countries where such transnational corporation operate on the basis of the full sovereignty of those countries."

47. Draft Res. II, Progress Made Towards the Establishment of the New International Economic Order, Obstacles that Impede It and the Role of Transnational Corporations, ECOSOC Res. 1980/60, para 6(a).

48. The problem is based on a proposal for litigation by Huraorani Indians against DuPont's subsidiary, Conoco Ecuador. In June 1990, the Sierra Club Legal Defense Fund and CONFENIAE, an NGO representing indigenous peoples in Ecuadoran Amozon, petitioned the Inter-American Commission on Human Rights, arguing that an oil-pipeline service road to be built by Conoco and state-owned Petroecuado through 100 miles of rainforest would breach international human rights law. A proposal to sue in U.S. federal district court was considered but dropped.

49. Unless it received almost universal ratification, it would be unlikely that the Code would be said to reflect customary law. It is hard to make a case that, under current jurisprudence, transitional corporations are already bound by customary international law. At any rate, developing countries have already taken the position that customary international law should not be used to amplify or interpret the Code.

PART 1.3

International Law as
Operating System:
Implementation and Compliance
with International Law

9

Compliance with International Agreements

BETH A. SIMMONS

A CENTRAL THEME IN MUCH RECENT INTERNATIONAL RELATIONS SCHOLARSHIP IS the growing role of formal international agreements and supranational authority in the ordering of relations among sovereign states. The growing range of authoritative commitments is evidenced by the movement since World War II to codify customary practices into explicit international legal instruments. The range of international agreements has grown rapidly over the past 40 years with the development of rules that regulate economic, social, communications, environmental, and human rights behavior. Evidence of the growth in supranational authority includes not only the number of international organizations that have mushroomed in the postwar years, but also, most strikingly, the growth and development of legally binding forms of third-party dispute settlement: The evolution of the dispute-settlement procedures of the General Agreement on Tariffs and Trade (GATT) into the more formal and less discretionary structure of the World Trade Organization (WTO), the 1996 inauguration of the International Maritime Court in Hamburg to handle disputes arising from the United Nations' Law of the Seas, the growing activism of the European Court of Justice, and the recent flurry of contentious case activity at the International Court of Justice[1] are all examples of states agreeing voluntarily to give up a portion of the most basic aspect of their sovereignty—the authority to act as the final judge of one's own actions—to authoritative international institutions.

These developments are a puzzle for the study of international relations, the traditional assumption of which has been that national governments generally desire to preserve their legal sovereignty, particularly the sole authority to judge the acceptability of their policies in the international

Reprinted with permission from the *Annual Review of Political Science*, Volume 1, © 1998, by Annual Reviews, www.annualreviews.org.

sphere. According to much mainline theorizing, states make commitments—especially formal legal commitments—either cautiously or cynically, and are reluctant to delegate decision making to supranational bodies. Over the past two decades, a good deal of theoretical and empirical work has been devoted to explaining why states have entered into this vast web of agreements voluntarily. Much of this work has examined issues relating to international economic and social interactions among states (the primary focus of this essay). Explanations have focused on the functional need for agreements due to the rising level of interdependence (Keohane 1984), the desire for greater regularity and predictability in actors' mutual relations (Brierly 1963), and growing state responsibility in the economic and social realm (Röling 1960, Friedmann 1964). Dominant international-relations paradigms generally hold that governments agree to sacrifice a degree of their legal freedom of action in order to secure policy changes from others or to gain influence over other states' policies (Keohane 1993).

Until recently, far less attention has been devoted to understanding why governments actually comply with such agreements, given that they can be costly in the short term and are not likely to be centrally enforced. Four broad approaches to this question are reviewed here: realist theory, rational functionalism, domestic regime–based explanations, and normative approaches. These perspectives are not mutually exclusive, and the less one is willing to straw-man the arguments of the major proponents, the clearer become the numerous points of overlap. For example, although realist theory has rarely been articulated in such as way as to take international legal constraints seriously, some of its major proponents would admit that international law compliance is fairly widespread (Morgenthau 1985). Similarly, scholars who focus on normative convergence as a source of compliance hardly rule out coercive processes to encourage such convergence (Bull 1977). Approaches that link domestic regime type with international rule compliance often tap into a deeper set of factors relating to the role of liberal principles and beliefs in securing international behavior consistent with the rule of law (Dixon 1993). Some functionalist arguments point to domestic regime characteristics as a source of "market failure" that make international agreements all the more necessary. Nonetheless, these four broad approaches diverge in important respects and provide a useful way to arrange the growing literature on compliance with international agreements.

Despite the recent interest in issues surrounding compliance, and more generally the effects of rules on international politics, the effort to link theory with evidence is still in its infancy. This is partly due to conceptual difficulties in identifying compliance itself. Another obstacle has been methodological: Difficulties in demonstrating causation remain, along with problems of selection bias in the use of cases and the analysis of data. Because the endeavor to understand compliance has been interdisciplinary,

involving legal scholars and sociologists as well as political scientists, differing methods of analysis, reasoning, and standards of proof pervade the
literature. Although these differences are enriching and have narrowed
through scholarly cooperation, they do help account for the disparate nature
of much of the relevant literature.

The first section discusses the concept of compliance and presents
strategies for its measurement. The second section reviews four strands of
international relations theory (inserting legal scholarship where arguments
are compatible, even if the authors are not self-consciously writing within
the tradition under examination) and culls from them a range of explanations and empirical findings regarding international legal commitments and
compliance. The third section of this essay draws some conclusions about
our knowledge of compliance with international agreements and suggests
directions for future research.

The Meaning and Measurement of Compliance

In his groundbreaking study on compliance with international public
authority, Oran Young (1979) suggested: "Compliance can be said to occur
when the actual behavior of a given subject conforms to prescribed behavior, and non-compliance or violation occurs when actual behavior departs
significantly from prescribed behavior." This definition distinguishes compliance behavior from treaty implementation (the adoption of domestic
rules or regulations that are meant to facilitate, but do not in themselves
constitute, compliance with international agreements). It also distinguishes
compliance from effectiveness; a poorly designed agreement could achieve
high levels of compliance without much impact on the phenomenon of concern (pollution levels for example). While compliance may be necessary for
effectiveness, there is no reason to consider it sufficient. The literature
reviewed here is almost exclusively concerned with the conformity of
behavior to rules, rather than the ultimate outcome of such conformity
(Jacobson & Weiss 1995, 1997).

Furthermore, most of the literature reviewed discusses compliance with
explicit rules or agreements, often of a legal character or of normative
import, and not "compliance" with the demands of an adversary or the
requests of an ally. The concern is typically with obligations that flow from
authoritative agreements, widely held normative prescriptions, or authoritative interpretations of proper behavior, rather than acquiescence to unilateral political demands based on the exercise of power alone. In practice, of
course, agreements among asymmetrically endowed actors are rarely per-
fectly voluntary, and the decision to "conform to prescribed behavior"
might rest on an amalgam of obligation and felt coercion. Fisher (1981) has

drawn an important distinction between "first order" and "second order" compliance. The former refers to compliance with standing, substantive rules often embodied in treaty arrangements (Downs & Rocke 1995, Chayes & Chayes 1995). Second-order compliance is compliance with the authoritative decision of a third party, such as a panel of the World Trade Organization, the United Nations Human Rights Committee, or the International Court of Justice (Bulterman & Kuijer 1996, Fisher 1981). The study of first-order compliance encounters difficulties in establishing an underlying "rate" of compliance, as it is far from clear how one could conceptualize a denominator for such a rate. As a result, researchers looking at the same set of behaviors can disagree vehemently over whether "most" foreign policy actions are effectively governed by law, rules, and agreements, or whether such considerations have little effect on state behavior (Henkin 1979). Studies of second-order compliance can often more convincingly establish such a rate and can narrow the range of behavior that would constitute compliance by focusing on a particular, often precisely rendered, decision (Fisher 1981). Unfortunately, rulings represent only the tip of the iceberg of the larger compliance problem, and are likely to represent a biased set of observations, especially since only governments willing to make concessions are likely to submit to authoritative decision-making processes (Coplin 1968).

Finally, most researchers admit it is difficult to judge whether a particular policy constitutes compliance at all (Jacobson & Weiss 1997). Often international agreements are written so as to permit a range of interpretations regarding the parties' obligations. Furthermore, compliance is rarely a transparent, binary choice. Actors' behavior is often intentionally ambiguous, dilatory, or confusing, and frequently takes place under conditions in which verification of compliance is difficult (Young 1979). In other contexts, actors may make good faith efforts to comply that nonetheless fall short of an agreement's prescribed behavior. Some researchers have dealt with these ambiguities by making such assessments in the context of generally prevailing expectations (Chayes & Chayes 1995). Going further, constructivist approaches assume that standards of compliance are socially constructed and must not be imposed by the analyst, making each assessment highly context-specific.

International Relations Theory and the Problem of Compliance

Compliance and the Realist Tradition

For realists, power, rather than law, has traditionally been the primary determinant of the course of interstate relations. Most realists—theoreticians and practitioners—tend to be highly skeptical that treaties or formal agreements significantly influence state actions (Boyle 1980, Bork 1989/90). Although Hans Morgenthau (1985) admitted that "during the four hundred years of its existence international law ha[d] in most instances been scrupulously observed," he thought that this could be attributed either to convergent interests or prevailing power relations. Governments make legal commitments cynically and "are always anxious to shake off the restraining influence that international law might have upon their foreign policies, to use international law instead for the promotion of their national interests" (Morgenthau 1985). Similarly, Hoffmann (1956) described the nation state as "a legally sovereign unit in a tenuous net of breakable obligations." In this formulation, what governments are legally bound to do or refrain from doing has little bearing on their actual behavior, except as provided by a coincidence of law and national interest. Aron (1981) put it succinctly: "International law can merely ratify the fate of arms and the arbitration of force."

To realists, the decentralized nature of the international legal system is its prime defect. International agreements lack restraining power, especially since governments generally retain the right to interpret and apply the provisions of international agreements selectively (Morgenthau 1985). Realists view the activities of major powers and the pursuit of important interests as highly unlikely to be constrained by legal authority or prior agreement.

In short, realists typically assume that international law is merely an epiphenomenon of interests or is only made effective through the balance of power (Oppenheim 1912). Aron and other realists have admitted that "the domain of legalized interstate relations is increasingly large" but argued that "one does not judge international law by peaceful periods and secondary problems" (Aron 1981). In the realm of high politics, realists have been especially skeptical about the rule of law and legal processes in international relations (see for example Diehl 1996, Fisher 1981, Bulterman & Kuijer 1996). For the most part, realist perspectives focus on the fundamental variables of power and interest, rarely inquiring further into states' compliance with international agreements.

Compliance and Rational Functionalism

A different set of expectations is suggested by a rational functional approach to the study of international institutions. Functionalist approaches view international agreements as a way to address a perceived need: International legal agreements are made because states want to solve common problems that they have difficulties solving any other way, e.g., unilaterally or through political means alone (Bilder 1989). Rational functionalism shares realists' concern with states' incentives to comply with or disregard international agreements, but is less likely to denigrate the cooperative problems that pervaded the realm of so-called low politics. By the mid 1980s it was increasingly difficult to relegate economic, social, and environmental issues to the status of "secondary problems," given the robustness of the postwar peace among developed countries. Unlike realist theorists, those taking a functional approach did not assume that these issues posed trivial problems for compliance. The initial assumption of rational functionalism is not that states cynically manipulate their legal environment, but that they "engineer" it in what are taken to be sincere efforts to affect an otherwise suboptimal outcome.

Both realism and rational functionalism are interest-driven approaches in which incentives play a crucial role.[2] The latter, however, views the particular agreements and even the international legal system in toto as a collective good, from which states collectively can benefit, but to which none wants to contribute disproportionately and by which none wants to be disadvantaged consistently. Rational functionalist analysis focuses on the perceived benefits of a system of rule-based behavior and on the individual incentives for states to contribute to, or detract from, such a system. Because they are often crucial to solutions, agreements are taken seriously. Therefore, in the absence of severe, unresolved collective-action problems or overwhelming, unaddressed incentives to defect, obligations are likely to be carried out.

Though functionalist theories concentrate on why states obligate themselves rather than why they comply with their obligations, theorists in this vein have suggested a number of mechanisms that potentially influence compliance behavior. The central mechanism for securing compliance is related to reputation: States anticipate paying a higher cost in the long run for breaking agreements in an effort to achieve immediate gain (Keohane 1984, Schachter 1991). Indeed, one function of international agreements is to enhance the reputational consequences of noncompliant behavior by providing mechanisms that increase transparency and therefore improve information regarding other states' behavior (Keohane 1984, Milgrom et al. 1990, Mitchell 1994). Some authors have argued that reputational explanations for compliance are especially relevant for new and developing countries, which have an interest in developing a reputation as "rule of law" countries (Shihata 1965). Greater transparency and opportunities for reciprocity also enhance compliance where there is repeated play within a small group, for example in the European Union (EU) or among the large countries in the WTO. Functionalist accounts often emphasize the crucial role of international institutions in providing a focal point for acceptable behavior (Garrett & Weingast 1993). These institutions facilitate the convergence of expectations and reduce uncertainty about other states' future behavior.

Like proponents of the normative research agenda discussed below, some functionalists point out that the standards or "focal points" created by international agreements or institutions can gain a high degree of legitimacy both internationally and domestically (Franck 1990, Peck 1996, Tacsan 1992). This legitimacy in turn can have important political consequences (Claude 1966). In this view, the search for a legitimate rule is a rational response to the need for a stable solution to an otherwise costly, intractable problem or dispute.

The starting point for functionalist explanations of international agreements and compliance is the inability of states to solve a problem without the institutional device. Like realist approaches, most functionalist approaches to international politics begin with the premise that states delegate sovereignty begrudgingly. Despite states' strong preference for solving international controversies through political means, even unilaterally if necessary, functional theories recognize that this may not be possible. Most functional theorizing has been systemic, focusing on international market failure and problems of collective action (Keohane 1984). Relatively little attention has been given to the domestic political reasons why international agreement may be impossible without an international institution, but in principle, the source of the "suboptimality" in functional theory could be either domestic or systemic.

One important exception to the systemic focus of most functional accounts of compliance is a theoretical study of the GATT rules by Downs & Rocke (1995). This work indicates that uncertainty regarding domestic politics and interest-group demands has a tremendous influence on the nature of international agreements undertaken, the severity of sanctions required, and hence the degree of compliance to be expected from participants in the GATT regime. Downs & Rocke argue that GATT's weak enforcement norm is a result of uncertainty about the future demands of interest groups: Most states do not want aggressive enforcement of the GATT because domestic conditions may arise under which they themselves will be compelled to violate GATT obligations (Downs & Rocke 1995). This uncertainty tilts preferences toward shorter and less stringent punishments, reducing the cooperative demands of the treaty agreement (as the costs of defection rise, a highly cooperative treaty becomes too risky to be practical). In this model, reached deductively through a game-theoretical representation, domestic uncertainty makes rule violation harder to punish, which makes compliance harder to secure. The expectation of these difficulties endogenizes the treaty commitment itself by contributing to a watering down of the initial agreement.

Other studies that locate the source of suboptimality at the domestic level have focused less on the implications for sanctioning and more on the role of international agreements or authoritative interpretations of obligations in

creating constraints that resonate in domestic politics. This approach begins
with the observation that domestic institutions can obstruct the realization
of benefits for society as a whole: Preference outliers can capture domestic
institutions and thus hold policies hostage to their demands; well-organized
interests can exert particularistic influences on policy, decreasing overall
welfare; decision makers can have time-inconsistent preferences that cause
them to pursue short-term interests at the expense of longer-term gains;
political polarization can lead to suboptimal outcomes or decisional paraly-
sis at the domestic level. Under these circumstances, actors may have
incentives not only to make international agreements (e.g., to freer trade,
fixed exchange rates, convergent macroeconomic policies), but also to comply with them in order to solve an intractable domestic problem. In this
view, international agreements place a desired constraint on policy where
domestic politics alone has proved socially suboptimal. Furthermore,
authoritative external decisions may reduce the domestic political costs of
particular courses of action—an argument regularly invoked to explain
compliance with the European Monetary Union (EMU) and the International Monetary Fund (IMF), for example. Those who have examined
bargaining in the context of legal-dispute settlement have argued that concessions tend to be easier to make, from a domestic political point of view,
when legally required by an authoritative third party (Fischer 1982, Merrills
1969). Thus the value of compliance flows as much or more from its
domestic political benefits as from the benefits of securing changes in the
behavior of other states in the system.

Finally, a large and growing literature has focused on one of the most
tangible sources of suboptimal social behavior: domestic administrative or
technical incapacities. A host of studies, many relating to compliance with
environmental accords, point to the inability (as distinct from unwilling-
ness) of governments to comply with their international obligations. A consortium of scholars headed by Jacobson & Brown Weiss (1995, 1997),
comparing the compliance performance of nine countries across five environmental accords in the past ten years, concludes that administrative
capacity has been a crucial variable. A country's administrative capacity
includes the knowledge and training of personnel responsible for environmental policy, adequate financial resources, the appropriate domestic legal
mandate/authority to accomplish program implementation, and access to
relevant information. Lacking such administrative or technical capacities,
rule-consistent behavior may simply not be within a signatory's choice set.
Outside agencies can help countries develop such capacities; the function
of international agreements, in this case, is not only to specify obligations
but to facilitate their attainment for certain classes of signatories deemed
unable, without external resources, to meet particular standards of behavior
(Haas et al. 1993).

Compliance and the Nature of the Domestic Regime

Another approach receiving attention in the study of interstate disputes, and more recently in legal circles, may be termed democratic legalism. (This appellation is not used by proponents of this approach but is convenient for the purposes of this article.) In this formulation, regime type is crucial to understanding the role of law in interstate relations (Slaughter 1995). While the domestically formulated functionalist literature focuses on the range of domestic conditions that can contribute to or detract from compliance, democratic legalism looks at the distinctive features of democratic regimes that tend to bind them into a "zone of law" in the conduct of their foreign relations.

The thrust of this literature is that democracies are more likely to comply with international legal obligations. One line of reasoning advanced to sustain this argument suggests that because liberal democratic regimes share an affinity with prevalent international legal processes and institutions, they tend to be more willing to depend on the rule of law for their external affairs as well. This argument depends on the notion that norms regarding limited government, respect for judicial processes, and regard for constitutional constraints carry over into the realm of international politics (Dixon 1993). Thus, countries with independent judiciaries are more likely to trust and respect international judicial processes than those lacking domestic experience with such institutions. Political leaders accustomed to constitutional constraints on their power in a domestic context are more likely to accept principled legal limits on their international behavior; therefore, governments with strong constitutional traditions, particularly those in which intragovernmental relations are rule governed, are more likely to accept rule-based constraints on their international behavior. This reasoning dovetails with a growing argument that liberal democracies are more likely than are other regime types to revere law, promote compromise, and respect processes of adjudication (Doyle 1986, Dixon 1993, Raymond 1994).

A specific mechanism that might tighten the link between the domestic rule of law and international behavior is the absorption of the latter into the corpus of domestic regulation itself. Assuming a close correlation between regime type and meaningful domestic legal restraints on the public exercise of authority, "[O]ne of the best ways of causing respect for international law is to make it indistinguishable from domestic law" (Fisher 1981). This parallels Keohane's 1992 notion of the "enmeshment" of international commitments into domestic politics and political institutions. One example of such absorption can be found in military manuals: Both Britain and the United States have imported international law concerning war fighting into their military handbooks. The idea is to make the two sets of law incentive compatible, such that "[p]atriotism and national loyalty will be aligned on the side of compliance" (Fisher 1981, p. 147). However, replication of international rules at the domestic level is no guarantee of their potency. Where international law is easily absorbed into the domestic system of rules one can wonder if behavior would have been much different in its absence; where international rules do not comport well with indigenous legal culture, expectations for compliance should not be high.

A second, distinct mechanism also supports the importance of democracy for law compliance. It rests on the observation that the leader of a liberal democracy may be constrained by the influence of international legal obligations on domestic groups, who are likely to cite such rules or rulings to influence their own government's policy. In one version of this argument, the mechanism of the compliance pull is domestic interest groups, who may have an interest in or preference for compliant behavior (Young 1979, Schachter 1991). Studies of compliance with environmental accords, for example, found that democracies provide more freedom for nongovernmental organizations (NGOs) to operate, allowing the formation and strengthening of transnational coalitions to influence government compliance efforts (Jacobson & Brown Weiss 1997). NGOs have been similarly crucial in the human rights area, and countries that have embarked on a transition to democracy have been influenced by their presence (Sikkink 1993). The weight of an international obligation or an authoritative legal forum may be vital in convincing domestic audiences actively to oppose a government policy, raising the political costs of noncompliance. Fisher (1981) has argued that these costs are likely to be especially heavy in the case of second-order compliance involving violation of an international authority's specific decision against a government, rather than a standing rule about which the government is likely to argue.

There is an affinity between this strand of democratic legalism and various kinds of functional reasoning that view international institutions as essential in influencing the domestic political debate surrounding a controversial foreign policy choice. The distinctive contribution of democratic legalism is its expectation of systematic differences between liberal democracies and nondemocracies: Domestic political constraints encouraging law-abiding behavior are assumed to be much stronger in democracies. Therefore, democratic countries are expected to be more willing to use legal institutions to regulate international behavior and settle disputes, and to comply more readily with these agreements once they are made.

Normative Approaches to Compliance

Normative considerations are present to some degree in the observation that democratic norms relating to the rule of law may influence governments' attitudes toward international law compliance. But a growing school of research places normative considerations at the center of its analysis of state behavior. This approach accepts that normative concerns are capable of driving perceptions of interest, and that the best way to understand normative influences is through a subjective rather than an analytically imposed-framework of meaning. In this view, normative standards of appropriate conduct are socially constructed reference points against which state behavior can be gauged.

Normative influences have a long tradition in the study of international law compliance. At the turn of the century, for instance, Root (1908) cited "moral force" as a reason for compliance with the decisions of arbitration panels. The predominance of realist theory in the study of international relations after World War II edged aside such arguments as naive, until a more subtle understanding of the relationship between international power and international society was articulated. Bull (1977) provided an early antecedent to what loosely can be termed a more constructivist approach to the problem of international law compliance. Although he believed in the ultimate importance of the balance of power in international politics, Bull's work emphasized the critical importance of international society (shared norms and beliefs) to the effective functioning of international law. Parting with such realist skeptics as Aron, Bull thought international law existed because actors in international relations assume that the rules under which they act are legal rules. This did not, however, justify "our treating them as a substantial factor at work in international politics" (1977, p. 137). Bull did not cite behavioral evidence, but drew on the discourse with which diplomats described, justified, and excused their actions: "What is a clearer sign of the inefficacy of a set of rules is the case where there is not merely a lack of conformity as between actual and prescribed behavior, but a failure to accept the validity or binding quality of the obligations themselves— as indicated by a reasoned appeal to different and conflicting principles, or by an unreasoned disregard of the rules."

Bull's work opened the way for a more interpretive, contextual approach to the understanding of compliance than that of his realist predecessors, with whom he shared a healthy respect for the balance of power. He believed that the primary function of international law is to help mobilize compliance with the rules of what he termed international society, but he remained skeptical that law could impose serious restraints on international behavior. Law could influence compliance only in the presence of a social system marked by shared norms and beliefs Bull (1977).

Bull's central insight was that actor behavior alone was inadequate to convey intersubjective meaning and hence was an insufficient indicator of the role of rules, norms and agreements in international politics. This insight was explicated by international regimes[3] theorists working in the constructivist mode in the 1980s, most brilliantly by Kratochwil & Ruggie

(1986). Rather than look to the violation of norms as the entire rule-compliance story, these scholars argued that analysts needed to understand state behavior as interpreted by other states and as intended by the actors themselves. Agreeing with Bull, they noted it was important to research how states justified their actions, and whether the international community responded to proffered rationales. "Indeed, such communicative dynamics may tell us far more about how robust a regime is than overt behavior alone" (Kratochwil & Ruggie 1986). In this view, even divergent practices of actors could express principled reasoning and shared understanding. What constitutes a breach of obligation is therefore not simply an objective description of a fact but an intersubjective appraisal. These observations comport well with the distinguishing features of social constructivism: its concern with the nature, origins, and functioning of social facts, the understanding of which is limited by more utilitarian approaches.

The implications for theory and research are profound. Kratochwil & Ruggie suggested that the emphasis on "rational institutional design"—a primary interest of the functionalist approaches discussed above—was fundamentally misplaced. Whereas such scholars as Downs & Rocke argued that relative incentives, rather than such concepts as fairness, drove the compliance decision, the more subjective, normative approach suggested that "rational institutions" can be undermined if their legitimacy is questioned (Kratochwil & Ruggie 1986). This assertion dovetailed with legal and sociological attempts to understand voluntary law compliance for individuals, groups, and organizations as a function of the perceived legitimacy of the law and legal processes themselves. (At the individual level, see Tyler 1990. With reference to collective organizations, see Knoke & Wood 1981.) The thrust of this literature is that perceived legitimacy of a legal rule or authority heightens the sense of obligation to bring behavior into compliance with the rule.

But if legitimacy is central to voluntary compliance, how can one explore this relationship in a non-tautological way? One approach is to locate the compliance pull of international norms in the nature of the norm itself. Franck (1990) has argued that the legitimacy of a rule—its ability to exert a pull toward voluntary compliance—should be examined in light of its ability to communicate, which in turn is influenced by the rule's determinacy and its degree of coherence. Similarly, Legro (1997) has proposed rule attributes such as specificity, durability, and concordance as one way to consider the effect of norms on outcomes. In his view, the clearer, more durable, and more widely endorsed a prescription, the greater will be its impact on compliance behavior.

Others have focused on the substance of the rule as underpinning its moral force and legitimacy. For example, Fisher (1981) asserted that rules will be better complied with when they follow commonly held notions of

fairness and morality; for example, proscribing killing rather than informing on friends, or prescribing reciprocal rather than uni-obligational behavior. He holds that the more "elemental" the rule—the more it reflects
malum in se rather than *malum in prohibitum*—the more first-order compliance should be expected. Similar arguments have been advanced in the
area of human rights compliance. Keck & Sikkink (1998) argue that among
the wide array of human rights standards embodied in international agreements, two kinds of prohibitions are most likely to be accepted as legitimate transnationally and cross-culturally: norms involving bodily integrity
and the prevention of bodily harm for vulnerable or innocent groups, and
norms involving legal equality of opportunity. These norms, they argue,
transcend culturally specific belief systems and resonate with basic ideas of
human dignity common to most cultures, enhancing their legitimacy as
behavioral prescriptions.

International, transnational, and nongovernmental organizations play a
significant role in normative processes described in some of this literature.
While the rational functionalist literature acknowledges that such entities
can provide focal points that narrow the range of equilibrium outcomes,
scholars in the normative vein would go much further: International institutions and organizations legitimate particular rules, enhancing their effectiveness through a heightened sense of obligation rather than through their
mere instrumental value as a convenient point of convergence (Claude
1966, Peck 1996). Tacsan (1992) for example, has written that the International Court of Justice (ICJ), as a producer and disseminator of new and
consensual knowledge, can establish a point where normative expectations
converge through an interactive bargaining process. He argued that the
ICJ's redefinition of self-determination, non-intervention, collective self-
defense, and regional use of force determined the normative expectations
that ultimately prevailed in Central America's peace settlement. The normative approach values authoritative institutions that review states' policies
for consistency with their international agreements, not because they have
the formal power of sanction, but because such procedures legitimate the
attempt to find a gap between governments' commitments (formal stances)
and their actions. Some have argued that this is why NGOs favored creating a Sustainable Development Commission at the 1992 UNCED in Rio de
Janeiro—not because it would have the formal power of sanction, which
realist and some functionalist perspectives would point out as a major weakness, but because it would legitimate the process of holding governments
accountable for their behavior and its relationship to their stated positions.

In short, normative approaches to the problem of compliance focus on
the force of ideas, beliefs, and standards of appropriate behavior as major
influences on governments' willingness to comply with international agreements. The hallmarks of this research are its departure from the radically

individualized methodology of some variants of realist and functionalist approaches and its embrace of international obligations as social constructs that must be understood and analyzed in an intersubjective framework of meaning. Scholars have attempted to marshal positive methodologies in the study of normative influences; Kacowicz (1994) looked at normative convergence as reflected in substantive treaty provisions and its effect on the prospects for peaceful territorial change, and Kegley & Raymond (1981) used "quasi-authoritative treatises" to draw correlations between prevailing legal norms and states' use of force. However, the intersubjective formulation of the problem has largely resisted such approaches. Scholars who have studied the social ideational influences on international politics submit that such factors as aspirations, legitimacy, and the notion of rights are reasons for actions, which are not the same as causes of actions (Ruggie 1998). Moreover, its explicitly inductive and high-contextual methodology distinguishes this approach from the (neo)realist and functionalist literature.

Conclusions

Research on compliance with international agreements encompasses a wide range of approaches to the study of international relations and crosses over into the disciplines of law and sociology. Yet despite an apparently sprawling literature, the empirical work that might link theory with observed behavior (or subjective understandings of such behavior, as constructivists would have it) has only begun to accumulate in recent years.

Part of the difficulty in the empirical study of compliance has been methodological. If the central analytical issue is to understand the conditions under which states behave in accordance with rules to which they have committed themselves or, more broadly, in accordance with prevailing norms of international behavior, then it is important to isolate the impact of those rules and norms. Several studies have tried to demonstrate a correlation between legal standards and state behavior, sometimes employing large databases and statistical techniques, but most are unconvincing in demonstrating causation, or even in providing an explanatory link between actions taken and the existence of agreements or normative considerations. It has been shown that much international behavior is consistent with international law, even in the conduct of hostilities between states (see for example Kegley & Raymond 1981, Tillema & Van Wingen 1982) it has been far more difficult, however, to show any causal link between legal commitments and behavior.

Establishing causation has been complicated by problems of selection bias and endogeneity. As realists have noted, selection bias proliferates rules in issue areas with minimal problems of strategic cooperation. From

Aron's 1981 complaint that it is no test of international law merely to look at "secondary" problems, to Downs et al.'s (1996) observation that compliance is not very interesting if international agreements are mere "flight control" agreements from which no one has much interest in defecting, there are good reasons to expect that the problem of compliance with treaties will be easier to resolve than the problem of international cooperation in general. This difference is due to the fact that treaty negotiation is endogenous: Governments are more prone to make agreements that comport with the kinds of activities they were willing to engage in anyway, and from which they foresee little incentive to defect. The endogeneity of treaty agreements also weakens the standards of behavior within agreements, which might be expected to improve compliance, but only because the rules are lax.

As a result, it is difficult to show that a rule, commitment, or norm per se influenced governments to take particular positions that represent compliance. In his account of compliance with the partial test ban treaty, Young (1979) gives away the reasons for compliance in the absence of enforcement mechanisms by admitting that the states involved had only extremely weak incentives to go against the agreement. It has been difficult to construct research around crucial case studies showing that agreements have created new and powerful incentives or have altered actors' perceptions of their interests.

The problem of selection bias creates inferential obstacles for the study of second-order compliance as well. Where significant national interests are involved, governments are arguably likely to resist or ignore international jurisdiction (Fischer 1982). As a result, cases in which third parties render authoritative rulings with which the parties are legally bound to comply are likely to be "easy" cases involving parties eager to settle their dispute and therefore willing to make concessions anyway (Coplin 1968, Schwarzenberger 1945), cases involving countries that tend to be law-abiding, or perhaps cases involving small countries whose weak negotiating position gives them little to lose by going through legal processes. However, the nature of the selection bias may differ across issue areas depending on the nature of the dispute-settlement mechanism in place. In the human rights area, the requirement of the "exhaustion of domestic remedies" might have the opposite effect on the pool of litigated cases: States with good domestic rules are not likely to produce many internationally reviewed cases. With respect to trade disputes under the GATT and now the WTO, incentives exist to sue the largest traders, as such suits offer much greater payoffs than going after small markets. In some issue areas, third parties themselves may act strategically, altering the nature of cases brought before them; for example, they may avoid taking jurisdiction for cases in which they anticipate a lack of compliance. The point is that in any given issue area the "litigation pool" is unlikely to be typical of the international community of states. The impact of these biases will influence our ability to draw inferences regarding compliance with authoritative third-party decisions. In some cases, adjudication or arbitration may complement what states would have done anyway; in other issue areas, its impact may vary.

Little has been done to determine whether selection bias is truly pervasive. For example, it should be possible to produce evidence that countries or country pairs that agree voluntarily to third-party arbitration or other judicial processes for settling their disputes are systematically different from a random sample of countries. Endogeneity of substantive agreements poses more difficulty and may require another strategy. One is to select cases in which there is evidence of a shift in state interests over time, rendering a previous commitment inconvenient or even costly to maintain, at least in the short run. The endogeneity problem would be minimized to the extent that compliance with earlier agreements is delinked from obvious explanations of strong, narrow, and immediate "interest-based" reasons to comply.

There are other ways to address the endogeneity of treaties themselves. One is to view the negotiation phase as an integral aspect of the compliance process. Scholars emphasizing the persuasive functions of legal agreements and discourse have also been interested in the contribution of participatory negotiation to eventual compliance. Taking a more constructivist approach to compliance, rather than worry about controlling for endogenous effects of treaty negotiation, one might incorporate its discursive elements into a fuller story of the compliance process. Governments persuade and become convinced of the value or appropriateness of particular standards of behavior over the months, years, and even decades they spend in their formulation. This research agenda might even call for an examination of the discourse used by participants as such negotiations unfold; attitudes toward compliance are shaped by and reflected in this discourse. This strategy uses the negotiation process as data on attitudes toward compliance, rather than viewing it as a source of bias in making inferences.

Despite the conceptual and methodological difficulties, research into the question of compliance with international agreements represents a substantial advance in the study of international law and institutions as important influences on international politics. Realism's assumption that such effects were marginal discouraged empirical investigation and broader theoretical innovations that might have addressed the variations that patently existed across issue areas, among nations, and over time. The current emphasis on the effects of rules on behavior has gone well beyond the functionalist studies of the 1980s, which were primarily concerned with the phenomena of rule creation and evolution rather than their behavioral effects. Nonetheless, we are a long way theoretically and empirically from an understanding of the conditions under which governments comply with international agreements. Pockets of progress mark particular issue areas, such as the environment and human rights, but more effort is needed to subject these findings to the broader concerns of international politics.

Notes

1. During the Cold War, the Court decided only one contentious case on average per year; in 1995, however, the Court had a record number of 13 cases before it.

2. The two approaches differ significantly regarding the role of sanctions versus the use of incentives to "manage" the process of compliance. Chayes & Chayes (1995) emphasize the persuasive function of international law. To enhance compliance, scholars and practitioners should move from an enforcement model that focuses on sanctions and punishments to a management model that focuses on positive incentives and negotiation. Critics respond that such a "managerial approach" to compliance will only go so far, arguing that deep cooperation—compliance with agreements proscribing behavior that is truly difficult to forswear or prescribing behavior that is costly in the short term—will require some form of enforcement (Downs et al. 1996). The distinction between enforcement and management approaches is often made in the context of domestic law enforcement (Hawkins & Thomas 1984, Snavely 1990).

3. "International regimes" were not conceived as isomorphic with international law, but the overlap is significant. International regimes were defined by Stephen Krasner (1983) as "principles, norms, rules, and decisionmaking procedures around which actor expectations converge in a given issue area.

References

Aron R. 1981. *Peace and War: A Theory of International Relations.* Malabar, FL: Robert E. Krieger. pp. 820.

Bilder R. B. 1989. International third party dispute settlement. *Denver J. Int. Law Policy.* 17(3):471–503.

Bork R. H. 1989/90. The limits of "international law." *Natl. Interest* 18:3–10.

Boyle F. A. 1980. The irrelevance of international law. *Calif. West. Int. Law J.* p. 10.

Brierly J. L. 1963. *The Law of Nations.* London: Sir Humphrey Waldock. 6th ed. p. 442.

Bull H. 1977. *The Anarchical Society: A Study of Order in World Politics.* New York: Columbia Univ. Press. p. 335.

Bulterman M. K., Kuijer M. 1996. *Compliance with Judgments of International Courts.* The Hague: Martinus Nijhoff. p. 172.

Chayes A., Chayes A. H. 1995. *The New Sovereignty: Compliance with International Regulatory Agreements.* Cambridge, MA: Harvard Univ. Press. p. 417.

Claude I. L. 1966. Collective legitimization as a political function of the United Nations. *Int. Organ.* 20(3):367–79.

Coplin W. D. 1968. The World Court in the international bargaining process. In *The United Nations and its Functions,* ed. R. W. Gregg, M. Barkin, pp. 313–31. Princeton, NJ: Princeton Univ. Press.

Diehl P. F. 1996. The United Nations and Peacekeeping. In *Coping with Conflict After the Cold War,* ed. E. Kolodziej, R. Kanet, pp. 147–65. Baltimore: Johns Hopkins Univ. Press.

Dixon W. J. 1993. Democracy and the management of international conflict. *J. Confl. Resol.* 37(1):42–68.

Downs G. W., Rocke D. M. 1995. *Optimal Imperfection? Domestic Uncertainty and Institutions in International Relations.* Princeton, NJ: Princeton Univ. Press. p. 159.

Downs G. W., Rocke D. M., Barsoom P. N. 1996. Is the good news about compliance good news about cooperation? *Int. Organ.* 50(3):379–406.

Doyle M. W. 1986. Liberalism and world politics. *Am. Polit. Sci. Rev.* 80:1151–69.

Fischer D. D. 1982. Decisions to use the international court of justice: four recent cases. *Int. Stud. Q.* 26(2):251–77.

Fisher R. 1981. *Improving Compliance with International Law.* Charlottesville: Univ. Virginia Press. p. 370.

Franck T. M. 1990. *The Power of Legitimacy Among Nations.* New York: Oxford Univ. Press. p. 303.

Friedmann W. 1964. *The Changing Structure of International Law.* London: Stevens & Sons. p. 410.

Garrett G., Weingast B. R. 1993. Ideas, interests, and institutions: constructing the EC's internal market. In *Ideas and Foreign Policy,* ed. J Goldstein, R. O. Keohane, pp. 173–206. Ithaca, NY: Cornell Univ. Press.

Haas P. M., Keohane R. O., Levy M. A. 1993. *Institutions for the Earth: Sources of International Environmental Protection.* Cambridge, MA: MIT Press. p. 448.

Hawkins K., Thomas J. M. 1984. *Enforcing Regulation.* The Hague: Kluwer Nijhoff. 198 pp.

Henkin L. 1979. *How Nations Behave: Law and Foreign Policy.* New York: Columbia Univ. Press and Counc. For. Relat. 2nd ed. p. 400.

Hoffmann S. 1956. The role of international organization: limits and possibilities. *Int. Organ.* 10(3):357–72.

Jacobson H. K., Weiss E. B. 1995. Compliance with international environmental accords. *Global Governance* 1:119–48.

Jacobson H. K., Weiss E. B. 1997. Compliance with international environmental accords: achievements and strategies. Presented at Harvard Univ. Sem. Law Int. Relat. Feb. 5.

Kacowicz A. M. 1994. The problem of peaceful territorial change. *Int. Stud. Q.* 38:219–54.

Keck M., Sikkink K. 1998. *Activists Beyond Borders: Advocacy Networks in International Politics.* Ithaca, NY: Cornell Univ. Press. p. 240.

Kegley C. W. Jr., Raymond G. A. 1981. International legal norms and the preservation of peace, 1820–1964: some evidence and bivariate relationships. *Int. Interact.* 8(3):171–87.

Keohane R. O. 1984. *After Hegemony: Cooperation and Discord in the World Political Economy.* Princeton, NJ: Princeton Univ. Press. p. 290.

Keohane R. O. 1992. Compliance with international commitments: politics within a framework of law. *Am. Soc. Int. Law Proc.* 86:176.

Keohane R. O. 1993. Sovereignty, interdependence, and international institutions. In *Ideas and Ideals: Essays on Politics in Honor of Stanley Hoffmann,* ed. L. B. Miller, M. J. Smith, pp. 91–107. Boulder, CO: Westview.

Knoke D., Woods J. R. 1981. *Organized for Action: Commitment in Voluntary Associations.* New Brunswick, NJ: Rutgers Univ. Press. p. 263.

Krasner S. D. 1983. Structural causes and regime consequences: regimes as intervening variables. In *International Regimes,* ed. S. D. Krasner, pp. 1–21. Ithaca, NY: Cornell Univ. Press.

Kratochwil F. V., Ruggie J. G. 1986. International organization: a state of the art on an art of the state. *Int. Organ.* 40(4):753–75.

Legro J. W. 1997. Which norms matter? Revisiting the "failure" of internationalism. *Int. Organ.* 51(1):31–63.

Merrills J. G. 1969. The justiciability of international disputes. *Can. Bar Rev.* 47:241–69.

Milgrom P. R., North D. C., Weingast B. R. 1990. The role of institutions in the revival of trade: the law merchant, private judges, and the champagne fairs. *Econ. Polit.* 2(1):1–23.

Mitchell R. B. 1994. Regime design matters: intentional oil pollution and treaty compliance. *Int. Organ.* 48(3):425–58.

Morgenthau H. J. 1985. *Politics Among Nations: The Struggle for Power and Peace.* New York: Knopf. 6th ed. p. 688.

Oppenheim, L. 1912. *International Law.* London: Longmans, Green. 2nd ed.

Peck C. 1996. *The United Nations as a Dispute Settlement System.* The Hague: Kluwer Law Int. 301 pp.

Raymond G. A. 1994. Democracies, disputes, and third-party intermediaries. *J. Confl. Resol.* 38(1):24–42.

Röling B. V. A. 1960. *International Law in an Expanded World.* Amsterdam: Djambatan. p. 126.

Root E. 1908. The sanction of international law. *Proc. Am. Soc. Int. Law* 2:14–17.

Ruggie J. G. 1998. *Constructing the World Polity: Essays on International Institutionalization.* New York: Routledge.

Schachter O. 1991. *International Law in Theory and Practice.* Dordrecht, Netherlands: Martinus Nijhoff. 431 pp.

Shihata I. F. I. 1965. The attitude of new states toward the International Court of Justice. *Int. Organ.* 19(2):203–22.

Schwarzenberger G. 1945. *International Law.* London: Stevens & Sons.

Sikkink K. 1993. Human rights, principled issue-networks, and sovereignty in Latin America. *Int. Organ.* 47(3):411–441.

Slaughter A. M. 1995. International law in a world of liberal states. *Eur. J. Int. Law* 6:503–38.

Snavely K. 1990. Governmental policies to reduce tax evasion: coerced behavior versus services and values development. *Policy Sci.* 23:57–72.

Tacsan J. 1992. *The Dynamics of International Law in Conflict Resolution.* Dordrecht, Netherlands: Martinus Nijhoff.

Tillema H. K., Van Wingen J. R. 1982. Law and power in military intervention. *Int. Stud. Q.* 26(2):220–50.

Tyler T. 1990. *Why People Obey the Law.* New Haven: Yale Univ. Press. p. 273.

Young O. R. 1979. *Compliance and Public Authority.* Baltimore: Johns Hopkins Univ. Press. p. 172.

10

The Princeton Principles of Universal Jurisdiction

THE PRINCETON PROJECT

The Challenge

During the last century millions of human beings perished as a result of genocide, crimes against humanity, war crimes, and other serious crimes under international law. Perpetrators deserving of prosecution have only rarely been held accountable. To stop this cycle of violence and to promote justice, impunity for the commission of serious crimes must yield to accountability. But how can this be done, and what will be the respective roles of national courts and international tribunals?

National courts administer systems of criminal law designed to provide justice for victims and due process for accused persons. A nation's courts exercise jurisdiction over crimes committed in its territory and proceed against those crimes committed abroad by its nationals, or against its nationals, or against its national interests. When these and other connections are absent, national courts may nevertheless exercise jurisdiction under international law over crimes of such exceptional gravity that they affect the fundamental interests of the international community as a whole. This is universal jurisdiction: it is jurisdiction based solely on the nature of the crime. National courts can exercise universal jurisdiction to prosecute and punish, and thereby deter, heinous acts recognized as serious crimes under international law. When national courts exercise universal jurisdiction appropriately, in accordance with internationally recognized standards of due process, they act to vindicate not merely their own interests and values but the basic interests and values common to the international community.

Universal jurisdiction holds out the promise of greater justice, but the jurisprudence of universal jurisdiction is disparate, disjointed, and poorly

Reprinted with permission of The Princeton Project.

understood. So long as that is so, this weapon against impunity is potentially beset by incoherence, confusion, and, at times, uneven justice.

International criminal tribunals also have a vital role to play in combating impunity as a complement to national courts. In the wake of mass atrocities and of oppressive rule, national judicial systems have often been unable or unwilling to prosecute serious crimes under international law, so international criminal tribunals have been established. Treaties entered into in the aftermath of World War II have strengthened international institutions, and have given greater clarity and force to international criminal law. A signal achievement of this long historic process occurred at a United Nations Conference in July 1998 when the Rome Statute of the International Criminal Court was adopted. . . . The jurisdiction of the International Criminal Court will, however, be available only if justice cannot be done at the national level. The primary burden of prosecuting the alleged perpetrators of these crimes will continue to reside with national legal systems.

Enhancing the proper exercise of universal jurisdiction by national courts will help close the gap in law enforcement that has favored perpetrators of serious crimes under international law. Fashioning clearer and sounder principles to guide the exercise of universal jurisdiction by national courts should help to punish, and thereby to deter and prevent, the commission of these heinous crimes. Nevertheless, the aim of sound principles cannot be simply to facilitate the speediest exercise of criminal jurisdiction, always and everywhere, and irrespective of circumstances. Improper exercises of criminal jurisdiction, including universal jurisdiction, may be used merely to harass political opponents, or for aims extraneous to criminal justice. Moreover, the imprudent or untimely exercise of universal jurisdiction could disrupt the quest for peace and national reconciliation in nations struggling to recover from violent conflict or political oppression. Prudence and good judgment are required here, as elsewhere in politics and law.

What is needed are principles to guide, as well as to give greater coherence and legitimacy to, the exercise of universal jurisdiction. These principles should promote greater accountability for perpetrators of serious crimes under international law, in ways consistent with a prudent concern for the abuse of power and a reasonable solicitude for the quest for peace.

The Princeton Project

The Princeton Project on Universal Jurisdiction has been formed to contribute to the ongoing development of universal jurisdiction. The Project is sponsored by Princeton University's Program in Law and Public Affairs and the Woodrow Wilson School of Public and International Affairs, the International Commission of Jurists, the American Association for the International Commission of Jurists, the Urban Morgan Institute for Human Rights, and the Netherlands Institute of Human Rights. The Project convened at Princeton University in January 2001 an assembly of scholars and jurists from around the world, serving in their personal capacities, to develop consensus principles on universal jurisdiction.

This assembly of scholars and jurists represented a diversity of viewpoints and a variety of legal systems. They are, however, united in their desire to promote greater legal accountability for those accused of committing serious crimes under international law.

The Princeton Principles on Universal Jurisdiction

The participants in the Princeton Project on Universal Jurisdiction propose the following principles for the purposes of advancing the continued evolution of international law and the application of international law in national legal systems.

Principle 1: Fundamentals of Universal Jurisdiction

1. For purposes of these Principles, universal jurisdiction is criminal jurisdiction based solely on the nature of the crime, without regard to where the crime was committed, the nationality of the alleged or convicted perpetrator, the nationality of the victim, or any other connection to the state exercising such jurisdiction.

2. Universal jurisdiction may be exercised by a competent and ordinary judicial body of any state in order to try a person duly accused of committing serious crimes under international law as specified in Principle 2(1), provided the person is present before such judicial body.

3. A state may rely on universal jurisdiction as a basis for seeking the extradition of a person accused or convicted of committing a serious crime under international law as specified in Principle 2(1), provided that it has established a prima facie case of the person's guilt and that the person sought to be extradited will be tried or the punishment carried out in accordance with international norms and standards on the protection of human rights in the context of criminal proceedings.

4. In exercising universal jurisdiction or in relying upon universal jurisdiction as a basis for seeking extradition, a state and its judicial organs shall observe international due process norms including but not limited to those involving the rights of the accused and victims, the fairness of the

proceedings, and the independence and impartiality of the judiciary (here-inafter referred to as "international due process norms").

5. A state shall exercise universal jurisdiction in good faith and in accordance with its rights and obligations under international law.

Principle 2: Serious Crimes Under International Law

1. For purposes of these Principles, serious crimes under international law include: (1) piracy; (2) slavery; (3) war crimes; (4) crimes against peace; (5) crimes against humanity; (6) genocide; and (7) torture.

2. The application of universal jurisdiction to the crimes listed in paragraph 1 is without prejudice to the application of universal jurisdiction to other crimes under international law.

Principle 3: Reliance on Universal Jurisdiction in the Absence of National Legislation

With respect to serious crimes under international law as specified in Principle 2(1), national judicial organs may rely on universal jurisdiction even if their national legislation does not specifically provide for it.

Principle 4: Obligation to Support Accountability

1. A state shall comply with all international obligations that are applicable to: prosecuting or extraditing persons accused or convicted of crimes under international law in accordance with a legal process that complies with international due process norms, providing other states investigating or prosecuting such crimes with all available means of administrative and judicial assistance, and undertaking such other necessary and appropriate measures as are consistent with international norms and standards.

2. A state, in the exercise of universal jurisdiction, may, for purposes of prosecution, seek judicial assistance to obtain evidence from another state, provided that the requesting state has a good faith basis and that the evidence sought will be used in accordance with international due process norms.

Principle 5: Immunities

With respect to serious crimes under international law as specified in Principle 2(1), the official position of any accused person, whether as head of state or government or as a responsible government official, shall not relieve such person of criminal responsibility nor mitigate punishment.

Principle 6: Statutes of Limitations

Statutes of limitations or other forms of prescription shall not apply to serious crimes under international law as specified in Principle 2(1).

Principle 7: Amnesties

1. Amnesties are generally inconsistent with the obligation of states to provide accountability for serious crimes under international law as specified in Principle in 2(1).

2. The exercise of universal jurisdiction with respect to serious crimes under international law as specified in Principle 2(1) shall not be precluded by amnesties which are incompatible with the international legal obligations of the granting state.

Principle 8: Resolution of Competing National Jurisdictions

Where more than one state has or may assert jurisdiction over a person and where the state that has custody of the person has no basis for jurisdiction other than the principle of universality, that state or its judicial organs shall, in deciding whether to prosecute or extradite, base their decision on an aggregate balance of the following criteria:

a. multilateral or bilateral treaty obligations;
b. the place of commission of the crime;
c. the nationality connection of the alleged perpetrator to the requesting state;
d. the nationality connection of the victim to the requesting state;
e. any other connection between the requesting state and the alleged perpetrator, the crime, or the victim;
f. the likelihood, good faith, and effectiveness of the prosecution in the requesting state;
g. the fairness and impartiality of the proceedings in the requesting state;
h. convenience to the parties and witnesses, as well as the availability of evidence in the requesting state; and
i. the interests of justice.

Principle 9: Non Bis In Idem Double Jeopardy

1. In the exercise of universal jurisdiction, a state or its judicial organs shall ensure that a person who is subject to criminal proceedings shall not be exposed to multiple prosecutions or punishment for the same criminal

conduct where the prior criminal proceedings or other accountability proceedings have been conducted in good faith and in accordance with international norms and standards. Sham prosecutions or derisory punishment resulting from a conviction or other accountability proceedings shall not be recognized as falling within the scope of this Principle.

2. A state shall recognize the validity of a proper exercise of universal jurisdiction by another state and shall recognize the final judgment of a competent and ordinary national judicial body or a competent international judicial body exercising such jurisdiction in accordance with international due process norms.

3. Any person tried or convicted by a state exercising universal jurisdiction for serious crimes under international law as specified in Principle 2(1) shall have the right and legal standing to raise before any national or international judicial body the claim of *non bis in idem* in opposition to any further criminal proceedings.

Principle 10: Grounds for Refusal of Extradition

1. A state or its judicial organs shall refuse to entertain a request for extradition based on universal jurisdiction if the person sought is likely to face a death penalty sentence or to be subjected to torture or any other cruel, degrading, or inhuman punishment or treatment, or if it is likely that the person sought will be subjected to sham proceedings in which international due process norms will be violated and no satisfactory assurances to the contrary are provided.

2. A state which refuses to extradite on the basis of this Principle shall, when permitted by international law, prosecute the individual accused of a serious crime under international law as specified in Principle 2(1) or extradite such person to another state where this can be done without exposing him or her to the risks referred to in paragraph 1.

Principle 11: Adoption of National Legislation

A state shall, where necessary, enact national legislation to enable the exercise of universal jurisdiction and the enforcement of these Principles.

Principle 12: Inclusion of
Universal Jurisdiction in Future Treaties

In all future treaties, and in protocols to existing treaties, concerned with serious crimes under international law as specified in Principle 2(1), states shall include provisions for universal jurisdiction.

Principle 13: Strengthening Accountability and Universal Jurisdiction

1. National judicial organs shall construe national law in a manner that is consistent with these Principles.

2. Nothing in these Principles shall be construed to limit the rights and obligations of a state to prevent or punish, by lawful means recognized under international law, the commission of crimes under international law.

3. These Principles shall not be construed as limiting the continued development of universal jurisdiction in international law.

Principle 14: Settlement of Disputes

1. Consistent with international law and the Charter of the United Nations states should settle their disputes arising out of the exercise of universal jurisdiction by all available means of peaceful settlement of disputes and in particular by submitting the dispute to the International Court of Justice.

Pending the determination of the issue in dispute, a state seeking to exercise universal jurisdiction shall not detain the accused person nor seek to have that person detained by another state unless there is a reasonable risk of flight and no other reasonable means can be found to ensure that person's eventual appearance before the judicial organs of the state seeking to exercise its jurisdiction.

Commentary on the Princeton Principles

Why Principles? Why Now?

The Princeton Principles on Universal Jurisdiction (Principles) are a progressive restatement of international law on the subject of universal jurisdiction. The Principles contain elements of both *lex lata* (the law as it is) and *de lege ferenda* (the law as it ought to be), but they should not be understood to limit the future evolution of universal jurisdiction. The Principles are intended to help guide national legislative bodies seeking to enact implementing legislation; judges who may be required to construe universal jurisdiction in applying domestic law or in making extradition decisions; governments that must decide whether to prosecute or extradite, or otherwise to assist in promoting international criminal accountability; and all those in civil society concerned with bringing to justice perpetrators of serious international crimes.

Participants in the Princeton Project discussed several difficult threshold questions concerning universal jurisdiction. How firmly is universal jurisdiction established in international law? It is of course recognized in treaties, national legislation, judicial opinions, and the writings of scholars, but not everyone draws the same conclusions from these sources. Commentators even disagree on how to ascertain whether universal jurisdiction is well established in customary international law: for some, the acceptance by states that a practice is obligatory *(opinio juris)* is enough; for others, the consistent practice of states is required.

When it is agreed that an obligation has been created in a treaty, legal systems differ in how they incorporate international obligations into domestic law. In many legal systems, the national judiciary cannot apply universal jurisdiction in the absence of national legislation. In other systems it is possible for the judiciary to rely directly on treaties and customary international law without waiting for implementing legislation. Accordingly, Principle 3 encourages courts to rely on universal jurisdiction in the absence of national legislation, so long as their legal systems permit them to do so. Principle 11 calls upon legislatures to enact laws enabling the exercise of universal jurisdiction. Principle 12 calls for states to provide for universal jurisdiction in future treaties and protocols to existing treaties.

Participants in the Princeton Project also carefully considered whether the time is ripe to bring greater clarity to universal jurisdiction. While it has been with us for centuries, universal jurisdiction seems only now to be coming into its own as a systematic means for promoting legal accountability. Universal jurisdiction was given great prominence by the proceedings in London involving former Chilean leader General Augusto Pinochet, and now courts around the world are seriously considering indictments involving universal jurisdiction.

In light of current dynamics in international criminal law, some supporters of universal jurisdiction question whether now is the time to clarify the principles that should guide its exercise. Might it not be better to wait to allow for unpredictable, and perhaps surprisingly progressive, developments? Is there a danger of stunting the development of universal jurisdiction by articulating guiding principles prematurely? . . . Our aim is to help guide those who believe that national courts have a vital role to play in combating impunity even when traditional jurisdictional connections are absent. These Principles should help clarify the legal bases for the responsible and reasoned exercise of universal jurisdiction. Insofar as universal jurisdiction is exercised, and seen to be exercised, in a reasoned, lawful, and orderly manner, it will gain wider acceptance. Mindful of the need to encourage continued progress in international law, these Principles have been drafted so as to invite rather than hinder the continued development of universal jurisdiction.

The Principles are written so as to both clarify the current law of universal jurisdiction and encourage its further development. As already noted, the Principles are addressed sometimes to the legislative, executive, or judicial branches of government, and sometimes to a combination of these.[1] The Principles are intended for a variety of actors in divergent legal systems who will properly draw on them in different ways. We acknowledge, for example, that in some legal systems, and according to some legal theories, judges are constrained in their ability to interpret existing law in light of aspirations to greater justice, or other principled aims. Nevertheless, judges on international and regional tribunals, and judges on national constitutional and supreme courts, often have greater interpretive latitude. Our hope is that these Principles might inform and shape the practice of those judges and other officials who can act to promote greater justice and legal accountability consistent with the constraints of their offices. We also offer these Principles to help guide and inform citizens, leaders of organizations in civil society, and public officials of all sorts: all of these different actors could benefit from a clearer common understanding of what universal jurisdiction is and when and how it may reasonably be exercised.

When and How to Prosecute Based on Universality?

In defining universal jurisdiction, participants focused on the case of "pure" universal jurisdiction, namely, where the nature of the crime is the sole basis for subject matter jurisdiction. There has been some scholarly confusion on the role of universal jurisdiction in famous prosecutions, such as the trial in Jerusalem of Adolph Eichmann.[2] In addition, it is important to recall that simply because certain offenses are universally condemned does not mean that a state may exercise universal jurisdiction over them.

Participants in the Princeton Project debated whether states should in general be encouraged to exercise universal jurisdiction based solely on the seriousness of the alleged crime, without traditional connecting links to the victims or perpetrators of serious crimes under international law. On the one hand, the whole point of universal jurisdiction would seem to be to permit or even encourage prosecution when states find within their territory a non-citizen accused of serious crimes under international law. In this way, universal jurisdiction maximizes accountability and minimizes impunity. The very essence of universal jurisdiction would seem, therefore, to be that national courts should prosecute alleged criminals absent any connecting factors (for example, even if the crimes were not committed against the enforcing states' citizens, or by its citizens).

There is, nevertheless, great concern that particular states will abuse universal jurisdiction to pursue politically motivated prosecutions. Mercenary governments and rogue prosecutors could seek to indict the heads of state or other senior public officials in countries with which they have political disagreements. Powerful states may try to exempt their own leaders from accountability while seeking to prosecute others, defying the basic proposition that equals should be treated equally. Members of peacekeeping forces might be harassed with unjustified prosecutions, and this might deter peacekeeping operations.

Should the Principles insist at least that the accused is physically present in the territory of the enforcing state? Should other connecting links also be required? Participants decided not to include an explicit requirement of a territorial link in Principle 1(1)'s definition. This was done partly to allow for further discussion, partly to avoid stifling the evolution of universal jurisdiction, and partly out of deference to pending litigation in the International Court of Justice.[3] Nevertheless, subsection (2) of Principle 1 holds that a "competent and ordinary" judicial body may try accused persons on the basis of universal jurisdiction "provided the person is present before such judicial body." The language of Principle 1(2) does not prevent a state from initiating the criminal process, conducting an investigation, issuing an indictment, or requesting extradition, when the accused is not present.

The Principles contain a number of provisions describing the standards that legal systems and particular prosecutions would have to meet in order to exercise universal jurisdiction responsibly and legitimately. Subsections (3) and (4) of Principle 1 insist that a state may seek to extradite persons accused or convicted on the basis of universal jurisdiction "provided that it has established a *prima facie* case of the person's guilt" and provided that trials and punishments will take place in accordance with "international due process norms" relevant human rights standards, and the independence and impartiality of the judiciary. Later Principles contain additional safeguards against prosecutorial abuses: Principle 9, for example, guards against repeated prosecutions for the same crime in violation of the principle of *non bis in idem,* or the prohibition on double jeopardy.[4] Principle 10 allows states to refuse requests for extradition if the person sought "is likely to face a death penalty sentence or to be subjected to torture" or cruel or inhuman treatment or sham proceedings in violation of international due process norms. The Principles reinforce proper legal standards for courts and should help guide executive officers considering extradition requests.

Of course, effective legal processes require the active cooperation of different government agencies, including courts and prosecutors. The establishment of international networks of cooperation will be especially important to the effective development of universal jurisdiction. Therefore, Principle 4 calls upon states to comply with their international obligations to either prosecute or extradite those accused or convicted of crimes under international law, so long as these legal processes comply with "international due process norms." Universal jurisdiction can only work if different states provide each other with active judicial and prosecutorial assistance, and all participating states will need to insure that due process norms are being complied with.

All legal powers can be abused by willfully malicious individuals. The Princeton Principles do all that principles can do to guard against such abuses: they specify the considerations that conscientious international actors can and should act upon.

Which Crimes Are Covered?

The choice of which crimes to include as "serious crimes under international law" was discussed at length in Princeton.[5] The ordering of the list of "serious crimes" was settled by historical progression rather than an attempt to rank crimes based upon their gravity.

- "Piracy" is a crime that paradigmatically is subject to prosecution by any nation based on principles of universality, and it is crucial to the origins of universal jurisdiction, so it comes first.[6]
- "Slavery" was included in part because its historical ties to piracy reach back to the Declaration of the Congress of Vienna in 1815. There are but a few conventional provisions, however, authorizing the exercise of universal jurisdiction for slavery and slave-related practices.[7] The phrase "slavery and slave-related practices" was considered but rejected by the Princeton Assembly as being too technical in nature. However, it was agreed that the term "slavery" was intended to include those practices prohibited in the Supplementary Convention on the Abolition of Slavery, the Slave Trade, and Institutions and Practices Similar to Slavery.[8]
- "War crimes" were initially restricted to "serious war crimes," namely "grave breaches" of the 1949 Geneva Conventions and Protocol I, in order to avoid the potential for numerous prosecutions based upon less serious violations.[9] The participants, however, did not want to give the impression that some war crimes are not serious, and thus opted not to include the word "serious." The assembly agreed, though, that it would be inappropriate to invoke universal jurisdiction for the prosecution of minor transgressions of the 1949 Geneva Conventions and Protocol I.
- "Crimes against peace" were also discussed at length. While many argue that aggression constitutes the most serious international crime, others contend that defining the crime of "aggression" is in practice extremely difficult and divisive. In the end, "crimes against peace" were included, despite some disagreement, in part in order to recall the wording of Article 6(a) of the Nuremberg Charter.[10]
- "Crimes against humanity" were included without objection, and these crimes have now been authoritatively defined by Article 7 of the

Rome Statute of the International Criminal Court.[11] There is not presently any conventional law that provides for the exercise of universal jurisdiction over crimes against humanity.

- "Genocide" was included without objection. Article 6 of the Genocide Convention provides that a person accused of genocide shall be tried in a court of "the State in the territory of which the act was committed."[12] However, Article 6 does not preclude the use of universal jurisdiction by an international penal tribunal, in the event that such a tribunal is established.

- "Torture" was included without objection though some noted that there are some disagreements as to what constitutes torture. "Torture" is intended to include the "other cruel, inhuman, or degrading treatment or punishment" as defined in the Convention Against Torture and Other Cruel, Inhuman or Degrading Treatment or Punishment.[13] Moreover, the Torture Convention implicitly provides for the exercise of universal jurisdiction over prohibited conduct.[14]

Apartheid, terrorism, and drug crimes were raised as candidates for inclusion. It should be carefully noted that the list of serious crimes is explicitly illustrative, not exhaustive. Principle 2(1) leaves open the possibility that, in the future, other crimes may be deemed of such a heinous nature as to warrant the application of universal jurisdiction.

When and Against Whom Should Universal Jurisdiction Be Exercised?

Among the most difficult questions discussed in the Princeton Project was the enforcement of universal jurisdiction, and the question of when if ever to honor immunities and amnesties with respect to the commission of serious crimes under international law. Especially difficult moral, political, and legal issues surround immunities for former or current heads of state, diplomats, and other officials (see Principle 5). Immunity from international criminal prosecution for sitting heads of state is established by customary international law, and immunity for diplomats is established by treaty. There is an extremely important distinction, however, between "substantive" and "procedural" immunity. A substantive immunity from prosecution would provide heads of state, diplomats, and other officials with exoneration from criminal responsibility for the commission of serious crimes under international law when these crimes are committed in an official capacity. Principle 5 rejects this substantive immunity ("the official position of any accused person, whether as head of state or government or as a responsible government official, shall not relieve such person of criminal responsibility nor mitigate punishment"). Nevertheless, in proceedings before national tribunals, procedural immunity remains in effect during a head of state's or other official's tenure in office, or during the period in which a diplomat is accredited to a host state. Under international law as it exists, sitting heads of state, accredited diplomats, and other officials cannot be prosecuted while in office for acts committed in their official capacities.

The Princeton Principles' rejection of substantive immunity keeps faith with the Nuremberg Charter, which proclaims: "The official position of defendants, whether as Heads of State or responsible officials in Government Departments, shall not be considered as freeing them from responsibility or mitigating punishment:"[15] More recently, the Statutes of the International Criminal Tribunal for the Former Yugoslavia (ICTY) and that of the International Criminal Tribunal for Rwanda (ICTR) removed substantive immunity for war crimes, genocide, and crimes against humanity.[16] Principle 5 in fact tracks the language of these statutes, which, in turn, were fashioned from Article 7 of the Nuremberg Charter.[17]

None of these statutes addresses the issue of procedural immunity. Customary international law, however, is quite clear on the subject: heads of state enjoy unqualified "act of state" immunity during their term of office. Similarly, diplomats accredited to a host state enjoy unqualified *ex officio* immunity during the performance of their official duties.[18] A head of state, diplomat, or other official may, therefore, be immune from prosecution while in office, but once they step down any claim of immunity becomes ineffective, and they are then subject to the possibility of prosecution.

The Principles do not purport to revoke the protections afforded by procedural immunity, but neither do they affirm procedural immunities as a matter of principle. In the future, procedural immunities of sitting heads of state, diplomats, and other officials may be called increasingly into question, a possibility prefigured by the ICTY's indictment of Slobodan Milosevic while still a sitting head of state.[19] Whether this unprecedented action will become the source of a new regime in international law remains to be seen. Participants in the Princeton Project opted not to try and settle on principles governing procedural immunity in order to leave space for future developments.

Another possible limit on the prosecution of "serious crimes under international law" are statutes of limitations.[20] Principle 6 reaffirms that statutes of limitations do not apply to crimes covered by universal jurisdiction. Conventional international law supports this position, at least as concerns war crimes and crimes against humanity.[21] Admittedly, the practice of states leaves something to be desired, here as elsewhere. Subsection (1) of Principle 13 provides that national judicial organs shall construe their own law in a manner "consistent with these Principles." If a nation's law is silent as to a limitations period with respect to a certain serious crime under international law, for example genocide, a local judge could draw on this subsection and legitimately *refuse* to apply by analogy another statute of limitations for a crime that was codified, e.g., murder. Because the laws of many nations include limitations periods, a number of participants suggested that the Principles should exhort states to eliminate statutes of limitations for serious crimes under international law; Principle 11 does this.

Another significant discussion took place on the topics of amnesties and other pardons that might be granted by a state or by virtue of a treaty to individuals or categories of individuals. Some participants were very strongly against the inclusion of any principle that recognized an amnesty for "serious crimes under international law." Others felt that certain types of amnesties, coupled with accountability mechanisms other than criminal prosecution, were acceptable in some cases: at least in difficult periods of political transition, as a second best alternative to criminal prosecution. Much controversy surrounds accountability mechanisms such as South Africa's Truth and Reconciliation Commission. We considered trying to specify the minimum prerequisites that should have to be satisfied in order for accountability mechanisms to be deemed legitimate (including such features as individualized accountability), but in the end those assembled at Princeton decided not to try and provide general criteria. Accordingly, Principle 7 expresses only a presumption that amnesties are inconsistent with a state's obligations to prevent impunity.[22] Subsection (2) recognizes that if a state grants amnesties that are inconsistent with obligations to hold perpetrators of serious international crimes accountable, other states may still seek to exercise universal jurisdiction.

Who Should Prosecute?

Principle 8 seeks to specify factors that should be considered when making judgments about whether to prosecute or extradite in the face of competing national claims. The list of factors is not intended to be exhaustive.[23] This Principle is designed to provide states with guidelines for the resolution of conflicts in situations in which the state with custody over a person accused of serious international crimes can base its jurisdiction solely on universality, and one or more other states have asserted or are in a position to exercise jurisdiction.

Originally, the drafters expressed a preference for ranking the different bases of jurisdiction so as to indicate which should receive priority in the case of a conflict. Almost without exception, the territorial principle was thought to deserve precedence. This was in part because of the longstanding conviction that a criminal defendant should be tried by his "natural judge." Many participants expressed the view that societies that have been victimized by political crimes should have the opportunity to bring the perpetrators to justice, provided their judiciaries are able and willing to do so.

Although it was decided not to rank jurisdictional claims, the Principles do not deny that some traditional jurisdictional claims will often be especially weighty. For example, the exercise of territorial jurisdiction will often also satisfy several of the other factors enumerated in Principle 8, such as the convenience to the parties and witnesses, as well as the availability of evidence.

What Protections for the Accused?

If universal jurisdiction is to be a tool for promoting greater justice, the rights of the accused must be protected. Principle 9 protects accused persons against multiple prosecutions for the same crime. There was no objection among the participants as to desirability of such safeguards. Several of the participants, however, questioned whether the prohibition on double jeopardy—*non bis in idem*—was a recognized principle of international law. Under regional human rights agreements, *non bis in idem* has been interpreted to apply within a state, but not between states. It was noted, however, that the importance of the doctrine of *non bis in idem* is recognized in almost all legal systems: it qualifies as a general principle of law and, as such, could be said to apply under international law.[24] Subsection (3) specifically grants an accused the right "and legal standing" to invoke the claim of *non bis in idem* as a defense to further criminal proceedings. This provision is designed to allow a defendant to independently raise this defense in jurisdictions that would otherwise only permit the requested state, in its discretion, to invoke the double jeopardy principle on an accused person's behalf.

Subsection (1) of Principle 10 requires that an extradition request predicated upon universality be refused if the accused is likely to face the death penalty, torture, or "other cruel, degrading, or inhuman punishment or treatment." This latter phraseology should be construed in accord with its usage as described in the Torture Convention.[25]

There was also some discussion about whether to include a provision on trials *in absentia* in the Principles. Although generally considered anathema in common law countries, such trials are traditional in certain civil law nations, such as France, and serve a valuable function with respect to the preservation of evidence. In the end it was decided not to refer to such trials in the Principles.

Conclusion: Promoting Accountability Through International Law

Several of the remaining principles have already been mentioned, and their import should be clear. Principles 11 and 12 call upon states both to adopt legislation to enable the exercise of universal jurisdiction and to include provisions for universal jurisdiction in all future treaties. The first sentence of Principle 13 was included by the drafters to memorialize their intention that nothing in the Principles should be construed as altering the existing obligations of any state under terrorism conventions. Subsection (1) of Principle 14 calls for states to peacefully settle disputes arising out of the application of universal jurisdiction.

Universal jurisdiction is one means to achieve accountability and to deny impunity to those accused of serious international crimes. It reflects the maxim embedded in so many treaties: *aut dedere autjudicare,* the duty to extradite or prosecute. All of the participants in the Princeton Project felt it important that the Principles not be construed to limit the development of universal jurisdiction or to constrain the evolution of accountability for crimes under international law, and this conviction is made explicit in Principle 13.

National courts exercising universal jurisdiction have a vital role to play in bringing perpetrators of international crimes to justice: they form part of the web of legal instruments which can and should be deployed to combat impunity. The Princeton Principles do not purport to define the proper use of universal jurisdiction in any final way. Our hope is that these Principles can bring greater clarity and order to the exercise of universal jurisdiction, and thereby encourage its reasonable and responsible use.

Notes

1. *See, e.g.,* Principle 3 which encourages judicial organs to rely on universal jurisdiction, Principle 11 which calls upon legislatures to enact laws enabling the exercise of universal jurisdiction, and Principle 12 which exhorts governments to include provisions for universal jurisdiction in new treaties and protocols to existing treaties.

2. *See Attorney General* of *Israel v. Eichmann,* 36 I.L.R. 5 (Isr. D.C., Jerusalem, 12 Dec. 1961), aff'd, 36 I.L.R. 277 (Isr. S. Ct., 29 May 1962), which is often cited as representing the exercise of universal jurisdiction by Israel, although many argue that the decision was more fundamentally predicated upon the passive personality doctrine and the protective principle under a unique Israeli statute passed by the Knesset in 1950. See Bass, *supra* note 3.

3. *See* the International Court of Justice's order in the case of *Arrest Warrant of 11 April 2000* (Congo v. Belg.) (Dec. 8, 2000), in which these issues feature prominently. In a recent development, on March 20, 2001, the Senegalese Cour de Cassation held that Hissene Habre, the former president of Chad, could not be tried on torture charges in Senegal. *See* Marks, *supra* note 3.

4. *See* Principle 9. Note also that the drafters intended the international due process norms in Principle 1(4) to be illustrative and not exhaustive. The right to reasonable bail (Cf. Principle 14[2]) and the right to counsel were also referred to as being included among the essential due process guarantees. *See also* Universal

Declaration of Human Rights, 10 Dec. 1948, arts. 10,11, G.A. Res. 217A (III), U.N. Doc. A1810 (1948); International Covenant on Civil and Political Rights, 19 Dec. 1966, arts. 14, 15,999 U.N.T.S. 171 [hereinafter ICCPR].

5. *See* Principle 2(1).

6. *See, e.g.,* Convention on the High Seas, 29 Apr. 1938, art. 19,450 U.N.T.S. 82, 13 U.S.T. 2312 ("On the high seas, or in any other place outside the jurisdiction of any state, every state may seize a pirate ship or aircraft, or a ship taken by piracy and under the control of pirates, and arrest the persons and seize the property on board."); United Nations Convention on the Law of the Sea, 10 Dec. 1982, art. 105, U.N. A/CONE62/122, 21 I.L.M. 1261.

7. *Cf* Convention for the Suppression of the Traffic in Persons and of the Exploitation of the Prostitution of Others, 21 Mar.1950, art. 11,96 U.N.T.S. 271 ("Nothing in the present Convention shall be interpreted as determining the attitude of a Party towards the general question of the limits of criminal jurisdiction under international law."); Convention Relative to the Slave Trade and Importation into Africa of Firearms, Ammunition, and Spiritous Liquors, 2 July 1890, art. 5,27 Stat. 886,17 Martens Nouveau Recucil (ser. 2) 345; Treaty for the Suppression of the African Slave Trade, 20 Dec. 1841, arts. 6,7,10, and annex B, Pt. 5,2 Martens Nouveau Recuell (ser. 1) 392.

8. 7 Sept. 1956, 266 U.N.T.S. 3,18 UST. 3201.

9. *See* Geneva Convention for the Amelioration of the Condition of the wounded and Sick in Armed Forces in the Field, 12 Aug. 1949, art. 50,75 U.N.T.S. 31,6 U.S.T. 3114, T.I.A.S. No. 3362; Geneva Convention for the Amelioration of the Condition of Wounded, Sick and Shipwrecked Members of Armed Forces at Sea, 12 Aug. 1949, art. 51,75 U.N.T.S. 85, 6 U.S.T. 3217, T.I.A.S. No. 3363; Geneva Convention Relative to the Treatment of Prisoners of War, 12 Aug. 1949, art. 130,75 U.N.T.S. 135,6 U.S.T. No. 3316, T.I.A.S. No. 3364; Geneva Convention Relative to the Protection of Civilian Persons in Time of War, 12 Aug. 1949, art. 147,75 U.N.T.S. 287,6 U.S.T 3516, T.I.A.S. No. 3365; Protocol I Additional to the Geneva Conventions of 12 August 1949, 12 Dec. 1977, art. 85, U.N. Doe. A/32/144, Annex I.

10. *See* Charter of the International Military Tribunal, 8 Aug. 1945, art. 6(a), 82 U.N.T.S. 284,59 Stat. 1546 [hereinafter Nuremberg Charter], annexed to Agreement for the Prosecution and Punishment of the Major War Criminals of the European Axis, 8 Aug. 1945,82 U.N.T.S. 279, 59 Stat. 1544.

11. 17 July 1998, art. 7, U.N. Doc. AICONF.183/9, 37 I.L.M. 999 [hereinafter ICC Statute].

12. Convention on the Prevention and Punishment of the Crime of Genocide, 9 Dec. 1948, art. 6, 78 U.N.T.S. 277.

13. G.A. Res. 39/46, Annex, U.N. GAOR, 39th Sess., Supp. No. 51, U.N. Doc. A/39/51 (1984), entered into force 26 June 1987 [hereinafter Torture Convention], draft reprinted in 23 I.L.M. 1027, modified 24 I.L.M. 535.

14. Id. arts. 5,7(1).

15. Nuremberg Charter, *supra* note 10, art. 7.

16. *See* Statute of the International Criminal Tribunal for the Former Yugoslavia, art. 7(2), S.C. Res. 808, U.N. SCOR, 48th Sess., 3175th mtg., U.N. Doc. S/RE51808 (1993), annexed to *Report of the Secretary-General Pursuant to Paragraph 2 of UN. Security Council Resolution* 808 (1993), U.N. Doc. S/25704 & Add.1 (1993) [hereinafter ICTY Statute]; Statute of the International Criminal Tribunal for Rwanda, art. 6(2), S.C. Res. 955, U.N. SCOR, 49th Sess., 3453d mtg., Annex, U.N. Doc. S/RES/955 (1994) [hereinafter ICTR Statute].

17. *See* ICTY Statute, *supra* note 16, art. 7(2); ICTR Statute, *supra* note 16, art. 6(2). Article 27 of the ICC Statute similarly provides: 1. This Statute shall apply equally to all persons without any distinction based on official capacity. In particular, official capacity as a Head of State or Government, a member of a Government or parliament, an elected representative or a government official shall in no case exempt a person from criminal responsibility under this Statute, nor shall it, in and of itself, constitute a ground for reduction of sentence. 2. Immunities or special procedural rules which may attach to the official capacity of a person, whether under national or international law, shall not bar the Court from exercising its jurisdiction over such a person.

ICC Statute, *supra* note 11, art, 27.

Article 98 of the ICC Statute, however, yields to the primacy of other multilateral treaties in assessing immunity:

1. The Court may not proceed with a request for surrender or assistance which would require the requested State to act inconsistently with its obligations under international law with respect to the State or diplomatic immunity of a person or property of a third State, unless the Court can first obtain the cooperation of that third State for the waiver of the immunity.
2. The Court may not proceed with a request for surrender which would require the requested State to act inconsistently with its obligations under international agreements pursuant to which the consent of a sending State is required to surrender a person of that State to the Court, unless the Court can first obtain the cooperation of the sending State for the giving of consent for the surrender.

Id. art. 98.

Note that Article 27 is located in Part III of the ICC Statute; while Article 98 is contained in Part IX of the Statute, which contains no prohibitions on immunities, and thus seems to permit a head of state, diplomat, or other official to invoke procedural immunity, where applicable.

18. *See* Vienna Convention on Diplomatic Relations, 18 Apr. 1961, 500 U.N.T.S. 95, 23 U.S.T. 3227; *see also* United States Diplomatic and Consular staff in Tehran (U.S. v. Iran), 1980 I.C.J. 3 (May 24). These temporary immunities are not revoked by this subsection. such doctrines, however, may be in the process of erosion. *See infra* note 25 and accompanying text.

19. Prosecutor v. Milosevic (Indictment) (24 May 1999), at http://www.un.org/icty/indictment!english/mil-ii990524e.htm.

20. *See* Principle 6.

21. *See* Convention on the Non-Applicability of Statutory Limitations to War Crimes and Crimes Against Humanity, 26 Nov. 1968, 754 U.N.T.S. 73; European Convention on Non-Applicability of Statutory Limitations To Crimes Against Humanity and War Crimes (Inter-European), 25 Jan. 1974, Europ. T.S. No. 82.

22. *See* Principle 7(1).

23. This method of listing relevant factors has been employed in other similar contexts, such as in determining jurisdictional priority over extraterritorial crime, *see* Restatement (Third) of Foreign Relations Law of the United States at 403 (1987), and in resolving conflict of laws problems, see Restatement (Second) of Conflict of 6 (1971).

24. It is also included in the ICCPR, *supra* note 9, art. 14(7), and the American Convention on Human Rights, 22 Nov. 1969, art. 8(4), 1144 U.N.T.S. 123, O.A.S. T.S. No.36.

25. *See* Torture Convention, *supra* note 13, art. 1.

PART 1.4

International Law
as Operating System:
International Legal Structures

11

The Impact of the International Legal System on the Growth of International Courts and Tribunals

JONATHAN I. CHARNEY

WHEN ONE BEGINS TO EXAMINE THE RECENT PROLIFERATION OF INTER-
national courts and other tribunals, this development must be put into its
proper historical context. Obviously, the existence of a standing international court of general jurisdiction is a creation of the twentieth century.
Prior to the establishment of the Permanent Court of International Justice
(PCIJ) after World War I, many ad hoc tribunals had been used. Even after
the PCIJ was established, a variety of international tribunals continued to
provide forums for third-party settlement of international disputes. After the
International Court of Justice (ICJ) was established at the conclusion of
World War II, ad hoc tribunals also continued to be used, albeit with less
frequency. Consequently, the International Court never has stood alone as
the sole tribunal to settle disputes in accordance with international law. It
always has coexisted with other third-party dispute settlement forums.
Recent developments are changing the international environment as a result
of the establishment of more permanent tribunals and, perhaps, the use of
fewer ad hoc tribunals. In very recent years, the rate of change from ad hoc
to permanent tribunals appears to be increasing dramatically.

Thus, states involved in international disputes have a greater range of
third-party dispute settlement vehicles than heretofore. Many legitimate
reasons help explain why states and other members of the international
community could prefer to have available a variety of international tribunals to resolve their disputes. They include, but are not limited to, the
desire for secrecy, control over the membership of the forum, panels with
special expertise or perceived regional sensitivities, preclusion of third state

Reprinted from Jonathan Charney, *The Impact of the International Legal System on
the Growth of International Courts and Tribunals,* 31 New York University's JOUR-
NAL OF INTERNATIONAL LAW AND POLITICS 697 (1999) with permission.

intervention, and forums that can resolve disputes in which non-state entities may appear as parties.

If states prefer a system with multiple options for third-party settlement
of international disputes, the question arises as to whether a hierarchy may
be established among them. It is clear to me that the international community will not and cannot establish such a hierarchy of international tribunals
that would place the ICJ or any other tribunal at the apex of international
law serving as the "Supreme Court of International Law." While the reasons may be many, two primary reasons are: (1) the fact that a universal,
or near universal, agreement of states to anoint any particular forum with
this status seems practically and politically impossible, and (2) such a
Supreme Court would undermine the community's desire for diverse
forums since many of the perceived advantages of such forums would
become impossible to attain within such a hierarchical structure. Review by
a court of general jurisdiction would compromise the very features that
make the alternative forums attractive in the first place, such as the special
qualities of the panel members. Thus, a significant number of independent
international tribunals will remain a part of the international legal system
for the foreseeable future.

Consequently, the question arises as to whether the proliferation of
international tribunals threatens the coherence of the international legal system. Not only may a cacophony of views on the norms of international law
undermine the perception that an international legal system exists, but if
like cases are not treated alike, the very essence of a normative system of
law will be lost. Should this develop, the legitimacy of international law as
a whole will be placed at risk. . . . Those doctrines included the law of
treaties, sources of international law, state responsibility, compensation for
injuries to aliens, exhaustion of domestic remedies, nationality, and international maritime boundary law. I considered the jurisprudence developed
by the ICJ, the European Court of Justice, the European Court of Human
Rights, the Inter-American Court of Human Rights, the dispute settlement
forums of the World Trade Organization (WTO) and General Agreement on
Tariffs and Trade (GATT), the Iran-United States Claims Tribunal, ad hoc
tribunals established to decide disputes involving international law, and
several administrative tribunals of international organizations, among others. I conclude that, in those core areas of international law, the different
international tribunals of the late twentieth century do share relatively
coherent views on those doctrines of international law. Although differences exist, these tribunals are clearly engaged in the same dialectic. The
fundamentals of this general international law remain the same regardless
of which tribunal decides the case.

However, an increase in the number of international law tribunals, absent
an effective hierarchical system that would produce definitive answers to

differences over norms of international law, means that complete uniformity of decisions is impossible. On the other hand, it is clear that ongoing international tribunals tend to follow the reasoning of their prior decisions. Furthermore, the views of the ICJ, when on point, are given considerable weight, and those of other international tribunals often are considered. Thus, the variety of international tribunals functioning today do not appear to pose a threat to the coherence of an international legal system.

The future is difficult to predict. Nevertheless, it is not clear that in the future significant numbers of new tribunals will be created. We may be approaching the end of the trend to establish new international tribunals, especially standing tribunals. Based on past lessons, however, the maintenance of a similar number of tribunals, or even an increase, should not present problems for international law, although risks do exist.

One strength of the multiplicity of international tribunals is that it permits a degree of experimentation and exploration, which can lead to improvements in international law. The lack of a strictly hierarchical system provides international tribunals with the opportunity to contribute collectively ideas that might be incorporated into general international law. It also facilitates the evaluation of those ideas by the international community as a whole. Ultimately, one would expect that the best ideas will be adopted widely, contributing to the body of international law. In some cases, however, unique solutions for special circumstances may be the better alternative. An overly strict hierarchical structure for international decisions could place undesirable constraints on the development of general international law and specialized law for specific areas.

It is also difficult to argue that these forums have taken cases away from the ICJ, thereby denying the Court its rightful role in the adjudication of international law. Nor does it appear likely that a decline of the ICJ is on the horizon, even with the increased number of forums deciding international legal issues. Instead, in recent years, the ICJ has had the heaviest caseload in its history.[1] Furthermore, during this period, the ICJ has been called upon to decide some of the hottest cases from the perspective of international politics that it ever has faced.[2]

Nonetheless, it is true that a comparison of the number of cases handled by the ICJ and those handled by the highest courts of states, or even several other standing international dispute settlement tribunals shows that the ICJ's caseload is relatively low.[3] Based on this fact, one can argue that the ICJ remains underutilized. Nevertheless, judges on the Court consider the number close to the limits of the Court's capacity. It is possible, however, for the Court to streamline its procedures in order to handle more cases. The schedule for submitting memorials, counter-memorials, and other documents is usually long and established specially for each case. There are no limits to the lengths of those documents. Hearings before the

Court can take many weeks. The Court's normal internal processes for reaching a decision and writing judgments is labor-intensive for all the judges and consumes considerable time. Furthermore, separate and dissenting opinions can be of enormous length.

It may be difficult to change the traditional procedures of the Court in fundamental ways. Even if the Court were willing to do so, it is not clear that states would be amenable to substantial changes that might promote such efficiency objectives. When sovereign states litigate against each other, they do not want to be constrained by procedures that restrict their ability to present their cases as fully and completely as they wish. The reasons for this attitude are closely related to international relations and domestic political sensitivities. Similarly, too much expedition on the part of the Court might derogate from the legitimacy that the Court's judgments must attract. In fact, the fullness and deliberative character of the ICJ may be essential to attracting certain cases to the Court as well as adding to the authority of its decisions.

That is not to say that the Court should not be able to proceed with dispatch as needed, or that its overall procedures can not be improved. It demonstrated recently, for example, that it could move quickly to issue an indication of provisional measures of protection in the *Vienna Convention on Consular Relations Case*.[4] This example also demonstrates the delicacy of the ICJ's authority. The Court did move rapidly to indicate provisional measures of protection instructing the United States to take all measures at its disposal to prevent the execution of Mr. Breard by the State of Virginia. Nevertheless, the U.S. Executive Branch did not take as forceful a position as it might have taken to obtain a delay of the execution, the United States Supreme Court declined to order a stay of the execution, and the Governor of Virginia refused to delay the execution.[5] An international culture that gives automatic and full authority to the ICJ's utterances does not exist. This suggests that substantial changes to expedite ICJ procedures in order to increase the Court's capacity may not be wise.

Indeed, the ICJ has taken steps to improve its procedures, but the international community has also implicitly resisted strengthening the Court. Thus, the Court has taken steps to increase the efficiency of its internal procedures, urged the litigating states to submit clearer, more succinct written pleadings, and made its orders and judgments quickly and easily accessible to all through its new web site.[6] On the other hand, the U.N. has placed significant budgetary constraints on the Court, thereby hampering its ability to manage its increased caseload. The gross disparity in the funds appropriated to the ICJ as compared to those appropriated for the International Criminal Tribunal for the former Yugoslavia appears to reflect a lack of interest on the part of the international community to strengthen the ICJ to a point where it might serve as the Supreme International Court.[7] Rather, it

reflects a continuing international support for a variety of international tribunals. The overwhelming support given to the establishment of the International Criminal Court (ICC) at the 1998 Rome Conference provides further confirmation of this conclusion.[8]

Despite limitations and setbacks as illustrated by the above case, we have
witnessed an overall expansion of third-party settlement of international disputes through law-based forums. This seems to reflect an increase in the role
of international law in the settlement of international disputes and a healthy
environment for this to take place. If it were otherwise, fewer states and other
entities would submit their disputes to international law forums. This may
reflect the fact that other international forums are necessary complements to
the ICJ, especially in matters that involve issues less central to core state concerns or involve parties that are incapable of being litigants before the ICJ.
The fact that only states may be parties before the ICJ may explain the creation of other tribunals and the fact that they attract so many cases.

The establishment and use of various third-party forums to decide
questions of international law means that more international issues are
being resolved pursuant to international law. This will add to the body of
decisions based on international law that are authoritative and can be relied
upon by the international community. Unfortunately, the ICJ is unequipped
and unable to address all of these numerous and sometimes highly specialized issues. As a whole, the other forums complement the work of the ICJ
and strengthen the system of international law, notwithstanding the risk of
some loss of uniformity.

Certainly, the primary objective of the international legal system is to
help the international community avoid disputes and, once a dispute arises,
to assist in its resolution. The many available forums serve both functions.
These forums usually are an integral part of international regimes. They
often have compulsory jurisdiction over disputes that may not be within the
ICJ's mandatory jurisdiction. In those situations, states know that if a dispute arises they could be forced to defend their actions before a tribunal.
Since states wish to avoid being brought before third-party tribunals, this
strengthens their motivation to avoid violations of their legal obligations. If
they are accused of a violation, they will try to negotiate a diplomatic settlement of the dispute. Due to the litigation potential, a negotiated settlement is likely to be influenced by the relevant international law. Finally, if
the dispute cannot be resolved diplomatically, the tribunal's jurisdiction
may be invoked and the dispute settled by an award or judgment based on
international law. As a consequence, the multiplicity of dispute settlement
forums increases the likelihood that disputes will be resolved in accordance
with international law, with or without litigation.

Notwithstanding determinations made by the other tribunals, the decisions of the ICJ are most significant when they address general international

law in well-reasoned judgments or advisory opinions. This is especially likely when there are few, if any, differing opinions by the participating judges. The fact is that the ICJ has a caché that makes its pronouncements on questions of general international law particularly significant. It is certainly within the ability of the Court to retain or even to build on this stature in order to provide the leading authoritative statements on general international law. The international community is predisposed to take the Court's views on this law quite seriously, and if the Court maintains a high level of competence and expresses its views in well-reasoned ways, it will continue to have an influence on the course of general international law that is well beyond its nominal jurisdiction. This is true notwithstanding the fact that the ICJ has not been endowed by the international community with the status of the Supreme Court of International Law with universal review authority. Thus, the Court has an important role to play in maintaining the coherence of international law even absent such jurisdiction. Both the members of the ICJ and the United Nations have the responsibility to assure that the Court continues to carry out this valuable function. Since the tribunals and attorneys involved in all of the international tribunals are usually well aware of the views of the other tribunals, especially those of the ICJ, these decisions are persuasive before other forums when the same legal issue arises. Thus, a significant amount of cross-fertilization occurs among international tribunals. In this environment, the ICJ remains a prodigious force. Judgments of the Court continue to be the most analyzed and the most frequently referenced of all the decisions by tribunals that address international law questions. This is unlikely to change in the foreseeable future.

Accordingly, it appears at present that the Court's salience is not at substantial risk, and it continues to play the leading role in weaving together the strands of international law. These strands are found not only in the traditional primary sources of the law, but also in determinations by the ICJ and other tribunals where questions of general international law are addressed. Certainly, the ICJ is the only international court of general jurisdiction. Thus, matters often come before it to be decided only on the basis of general international law. All other standing tribunals are only presented with cases arising within the context of the treaty regime within which they exist. This limited context constrains their ability to serve as the definitive forum for matters of general international law. That role is de facto reserved to the ICJ. It can take into account developments in international law across the entire spectrum of international relations. As a result, the ICJ's decisions reflect the perspective of a court unsullied by narrow limitations that a special regime may impose on a forum. Thus, its pronouncements on general international law necessarily are more persuasive than similar pronouncements given by tribunals with specialized jurisdiction and narrower perspectives. This strengthens the leadership role that the ICJ performs in the maintenance and development of general international law.

Other tribunals may decide disputes, but it remains for the ICJ to place its imprimatur on the law it examines, even if informed by decisions of other forums. In that sense, the other forums help to identify important issues of international law that deserve the attention of the ICJ. Even if it is not constitutionally established as the Supreme Court of International Law, by endorsing a particular interpretation of the law, the ICJ can strengthen a rule to the extent that states and other tribunals are likely to follow it.

Although the variations among tribunals deciding questions of international law are not so significant as to challenge the coherence of international law and its legitimacy as a system of law, the possibility that problems might develop in the future ought not be ignored. The various international tribunals other than the ICJ, which were examined in my Hague lectures, do have their own agendas. They were formed to serve the interests of the states that established them within the treaty regime for which they were created. The allegiance to that treaty regime may become greater than the allegiance to the international legal system as a whole. These specialized tribunals present the risk that their own centrifugal forces will drive them in directions away from the core of international law. As a result, these specialized tribunals could develop greater variations in their determinations of general international law and damage the coherence of the international legal system.

If a hierarchical judicial system for international law is not to be established, two factors will work as counter-forces against those centrifugal forces. First, the ICJ must continue to maintain its intellectual leadership role in the field. If it does so, the other tribunals will be under pressure to abide by the ICJ's determinations on international law. Second, the other tribunals and the ICJ should be encouraged to increase the dialogue that already exists among them. The idea that all of these tribunals are engaged in a common endeavor would be emphasized. This might provide strong pressures against the centrifugal forces at work, while still permitting the independence of these specialized tribunals.

Additionally, the ICJ might write its judgments and opinions so as to appear more like a Supreme International Court and overtly consider alternative theories on the international law as used by the various other tribunals. Based on such express analyses, the ICJ could issue well-reasoned decisions in which the views of the other tribunals are considered. It is likely that such rulings would attract even greater significance than heretofore. An interpretation of a rule of general international law that was produced by a tribunal and subsequently examined and rejected by the ICJ would make it difficult for that tribunal to continue to maintain its view. In addition, tribunals may adhere more strongly to their views if endorsed by the ICJ. Other tribunals may also be further encouraged to adopt the views endorsed by the ICJ. Certainly, increased inter-court dialogue and deference, whether it be explicit or implicit, is important to avoid the potential centrifugal forces in question.

Despite this optimistic prognosis, as we enter deeper into a period of a multiplicity of standing international tribunals, risks are present. These tribunals, and the states that create them, could produce such diversity in international law that the coherence of this system of law might be threatened. States and the tribunals created by them should be sensitive to this undesirable possibility. While diversity, experimentation, and competition have value, the coherence of international law is important to the maintenance of a peaceful and beneficial international legal system. All of the participants in this system should be sensitive to the maintenance of an appropriate degree of coherence in order to avoid unnecessary risks. For these reasons, I conclude that the coherence of international law does not appear to be significantly threatened by the increased number of international tribunals. However, all participants in the system need to be sensitive to the risks inherent in the decentralized system and be careful to avoid actions that might pull the system apart.

Notes

1. As of October 1998, twelve cases were pending before the ICJ. This is one case short of the highest number of cases the ICJ ever had on its docket, and it reflects the relatively high number of cases carried by the Court during the 1990s. *Address by the President of the International Court of Justice, Judge Stephen M. Schwebel, to the General Assembly of the United Nations* (visited Oct. 27, 1998) <http://www.icj-cij.org/icjwww/ipre. . ./SPEECHES/SpeechPresident GA98.htm>; *Consequences that the Increase in the Volume of Cases before the International Court of Justice has on the Operations of the Court,* Report of the Secretary-General, U.N. Doc. A/53/326/CORR.1 (Nov. 5, 1998) at 2 [hereinafter *Consequences*]. *See also* P. H. F. Bekker, *The 1995 Judicial Activity of the International Court of Justice,* 90 Am. J. Int'l. L. 328 (1996); R. Y. Jennings, *The International Court of Justice After Fifty Years,* 89 Am. J. Int'l. L. 493, 494 (1995); K. Highet, *The Peace Palace Heats Up: The World Court in Business Again?,* 85 Am. J. Int'l. L. 646 (1991).

2. *See, e.g., Application of Convention on Prevention and Punishment of Crime of Genocide (Bosn. & Herz. v. Yugo.)* 1996 I.C.J. 803 (Preliminary Objections of July 11); *Certain Phosphate Lands in Nauru (Nauru v. Austl.),* 1992 I.C.J. 240 (Preliminary Objections of June 26); *Military and Paramilitary Activities in and Against Nicaragua (Nic. v. U.S.),* 1986 I.C.J. 14 (Judgment on Merits of June 27); *United States Diplomatic and Consular Staff in Tehran (U.S. v. Iran),* 1980 I.C.J. 3 (May 24); *Territorial Dispute (Libya v. Chad),* 1994 I.C.J. 6 (Feb. 3); *Questions of Interpretation and Application of the 1971 Montreal Convention Arising from the Aerial Incident at Lockerbie (Libya v. U.K.),* <http://www.icj-cij.org/icjwww/idocket/iluk/

ilukjudgement> (Preliminary Objections of Feb. 27, 1998); *Oil Platforms (Iran v. U.S.* <http://www.icj-cij.org/icjwww/idocket/iop/iopframe> (Counter-claim Order of Mar. 10, 1998); *Legality of the Use by a State of Nuclear Weapons in Armed Conflict,* 1996 I.C.J. 4 (July 8); *Legality of the Threat or Use of Nuclear Weapons,* 1996 I.C.J. 226 (July 8); *Vienna Convention on Consular Relations (Para. v. U.S.),* <http://icj-cij.org/icjwww/idocket/ipaus/ipausframe> (Provisional Measures of Apr. 9, 1998).

3. Since its establishment in 1946, the Court has dealt with 77 contentious cases and 23 requests for advisory opinions. *Address by the President of the International Court of Justice, supra* note 2. See also *Consequences supra* note 2, at 2; A. Eyffinger, The International Court of Justice 1946–1996 369, 374–384 (1996).

4. Vienna Convention on Consular Relations (Para. v. U.S.), *supra* note 3.

5. *Para. v. Allen,* 949 F. Supp. 1269 (E.D.Va. 1996), *aff'd* 134 F. 3d 622 (4th Cir. 1998), *cert. denied sub nom. Breard v. Greene,* 523 U.S. 371 (1998); Brief for the United States as Amicus Curiae at 49–51, *Breard v. Greene,* 523 U.S. 371 (1998) (Nos. 97–1390 and 97–8214); *Statement by Governor Jim Gilmore Concerning the Execution of Angel Breard, Commonwealth of Virginia, Office of the Governor Press Office* (April 14, 1998); Letter from Madeleine K. Albright, Secretary of State to James S. Gilmore, III, Governor of Virginia (April 13, 1998). For a discussion of the legal issues arguing that the U.S. failed to take the actions it could under U.S. and international law, see Louis Henkin, *Provisional Measures, U.S. Treaty Obligations, and the States,* 92 Am. J. Int'l L. 679 (1998); Carlos Manuel Vázquez, *Breard and the Federal Power to Require Compliance with ICJ Orders of Provisional Measures,* 92 Am. J. Int'l. L. 683 (1998); Jordan Paust, *Breard and Treaty-Based Rights under the Consular Convention,* 92 Am. J. Int'l L. 691 (1998); Lori Fisler Damrosch, *The Justiciability of Paraguay's Claim of Treaty Violation,* 92 Am. J. Int'l. L. 697 (1998); Frederic L. Kirgis, *Zschernig v. Miller and the Breard Matter,* 92 Am. J. Int'l. L. 704 (1998). *But see* Curtis A. Bradley & Jack L. Goldsmith, *The Abiding Relevance of Federalism to U.S. Foreign Relations,* 92 AM. J. Int'l. L. 675 (1998). For a review of the entire facts of the case, see Jonathan I. Charney and W. Michael Reisman, *The Facts,* 92 Am. J. Int'l. L. 666 (1998).

6. *See* <http//www.icj-cij.org>; Schwebel, *Address by the President of the International Court of Justice, supra* note 2; *Consequences, supra* note 2, at 5–6.

7. *See Consequences, supra* note 2, at 7; Schwebel, *Address by the President of the International Court of Justice, supra* note 2.

8. Rome Statute of the International Criminal Court, A/CONF.183/9 (July 17, 1998) <http://www.un.org.icc>.

12

WTO Dispute Procedures, Standard of Review, and Deference to National Governments

STEVEN P. CROLEY AND JOHN H. JACKSON

Introduction

Increasing international economic interdependence is obviously becoming a growing challenge to governments, which are frustrated by their limited capacities to regulate or control cross-border economic activities. Many subjects trigger this frustration, including interest rates, various fraudulent or criminal activities, product standards, consumer protection, environmental issues and prudential concerns for financial services. Although it has been said that "all politics is local," it has also been said, with considerable justification, that "all economics is international."

The Uruguay Round's result (including the Agreement Establishing the World Trade Organization [WTO]) is one important effort to face up to some of the problems associated with interdependent international economic activity. Central and vital to the WTO institutional structure is the dispute settlement procedure derived from decades of experiment and practice in the GATT, but now (for the first time) elaborately set forth in the new treaty text of the Dispute Settlement Understanding, as part of the WTO charter. Over the last fifteen years, many countries have come to recognize the crucial role that dispute settlement plays for any treaty system. It is particularly crucial for a treaty system designed to address today's myriad of complex economic questions of international relations and to facilitate the cooperation among nations that is essential to the peaceful and welfare enhancing aspect of those relations. Dispute settlement procedures assist in making rules effective, adding an essential measure of predictability and effectiveness to the operation of a rule-oriented system in the otherwise relatively weak realm of international norms. Thus, the GATT contracting parties resolved at the 1986 launching meeting of the Uruguay Round (at Punta del Este) to deal with some of the defects and problems of existing dispute settlement rules. The result of that resolve was the new DSU.

Yet dispute settlement by an international body such as GATT or WTO panels treads on the delicate and confusing issue of national "sovereignty." Even if one recognizes that some concepts of "sovereignty" are out of date or unrealistic in today's interdependent world, the word still raises important questions about the relationship of international rules and institutions to national governments, and about the appropriate roles of each in such matters as regulating economic behavior that crosses national borders. The GATT dispute settlement procedures have increasingly confronted these questions, including the degree to which, in a GATT (and now WTO) dispute settlement procedure, an international body should "second-guess" a decision of a national government agency concerning economic regulations that are allegedly inconsistent with an international rule.

To pose a concrete example: Suppose that a government applies certain domestic product standards, perhaps for reasons of domestic environmental policy, in a manner that causes some citizens (or foreign exporters) to argue that the government action is inconsistent with certain WTO norms (such as rules in the WTO Technical Barriers to Trade Agreement). Suppose also, however, that a national government agency (or court) determines that the national action is *not* inconsistent with WTO rules, and another nation decides to challenge that determination in a WTO proceeding. It would seem clear that the international agreement does not permit a national government's determination *always* to prevail (otherwise the international rules could be easily evaded or rendered ineffective). But should the international body approach the issues involved (including factual determinations) *de novo*, without any deference to the national government? Certainly, it has been argued in GATT proceedings (especially those relating to antidumping measures) that panels should respect national government determinations, up to some point. That "point" is the crucial issue that has sometimes been labeled the "standard of review."

This issue is not unique to GATT or the WTO, of course; nor even to "economic affairs," as literature in the human rights arena indicates.[1] Even so, during the past several years the standard-of-review question has become something of a touchstone regarding the relationship of "sovereignty" concepts to the GATT/WTO rule system. Indeed, in the waning months of the Uruguay Round, the standard-of-review issue assumed such importance to some negotiators that it reached a place on the short list of problems called "deal breakers"—problems that could have caused the entire negotiations to fail. This was particularly odd, given that the issue was one that only a few persons understood, and that was virtually unnoticed by almost all the public or private policy makers concerned with the negotiation. Clearly, certain economic interests were deeply concerned, most notably those in the United States who favored greater restraints on the capacity of the international body to overrule U.S. government determinations on antidumping duties, and who were perceptive and economically endowed enough to carry their views deeply into the negotiating process. And those views cannot be easily dismissed. In many ways they go to a central problem for the future of the trading system—how to reconcile competing views about the allocation of power between national governments and international institutions on matters of vital concern to many governments, as well as the domestic constituencies of some of those governments. They also raise important "constitutional" questions about international institutions and the potential need for "checks and balances" against misuse or misallocation of power in and for those institutions.

For immediate purposes, however, we want to focus on the more particular question of proper standard of review for a WTO panel when it undertakes to examine a national government's actions or rulings that engage the issue of consistency with the various WTO Agreements and are subject to the WTO's DSU procedures. We will not here explore another interesting standard-of-review question—pertaining to the review by the new WTO Appellate Body established under the DSU of a report by a first-level panel acting under the DSU. In this appeal procedure, the Appellate Body's review is limited to "issues of law covered in the panel report and legal interpretations developed by the panel." The difficult question will be how to distinguish questions of law from other questions (fact?). But it seems clear that the standard of review of the first-level panel as it examines national government actions and determinations is a question of law, and so could very well come before the Appellate Body at some point, probably quite early in the evolution of the WTO.

Naturally, the standard-of-review issue is one that many legal systems face. Indeed, some negotiators drew on certain national-level legal doctrines for analogies to use in the GATT/WTO context. For example, the matter has been the subject of considerable litigation, and Supreme Court attention in the United States, and the European Union Court of Justice in Luxembourg has faced similar issues in its jurisprudence. In fact, one of the questions that interests us most is whether it is appropriate to draw an analogy from national-level jurisprudence—specifically, from U.S. jurisprudence—for help in determining the scope or standard of review of an international body over national-level activity.

We proceed here, then, as follows. In part II, we explore briefly the GATT context of the question, remembering that Article XVI:1 of the WTO Agreement mandates that GATT jurisprudence will "guide" the jurisprudence and practice of the WTO. In part III, we look at the new WTO Agreements relevant to the standard-of-review question, and consider their potential meaning against the backdrop of some of the history of the Uruguay Round negotiation. In part IV, we turn to the jurisprudence of U.S. administrative law, which has struggled for many decades with a somewhat similar standard-of-review question, associated in recent years with the U.S. *Chevron* doctrine, explained in part IV. In part V, we explore some of the basic policies underlying the *Chevron* doctrine and argue that those policies do not find easy application in the context of an international proceeding. Finally, in part VI we briefly draw some tentative conclusions and suggest some avenues that may be useful for considering the approach of the WTO panels.

Background: Illustrative GATT Panel Jurisprudence

Clearly, the desire of some negotiators to deal explicitly with this subject in the Uruguay Round was influenced by their reaction (or that of their constituencies) to some GATT panel cases, especially antidumping cases, in which observers felt the panels had overreached their authority and been too intrusive in disagreeing with national government authorities. Thus, it is worth noting some of the GATT panel reports that addressed this question or topics related to it.

In fact, a very early GATT working party discussed this subject in 1951 in a case involving a complaint by Czechoslovakia against a U.S. escape clause action that had raised tariff barriers on the importation of "hatter's fur." The working party concluded in favor of the United States, reasoning as follows:

> 48. These members were satisfied that the United States authorities had investigated the matter thoroughly on the basis of the data available to them at the time of their enquiry and had reached in good faith the conclusion that the proposed action fell within the terms of Article XIX as in their view it should be interpreted. Moreover, those differences of view on interpretation which emerged in the Working Party are not such as to affect the view of these members on the particular case under review. If they, in their appraisal of the facts, naturally gave what they consider to be appropriate weight to international factors and the effect of the action under Article XIX on the interests of exporting countries while the United States authorities would normally tend to give more weight to domestic factors, it must be recognized that any view on such a matter must be to a certain extent a matter of economic judgment and that it is natural that governments should on occasion be greatly influenced by social factors, such as local employment problems. It would not be proper to regard the consequent withdrawal of a tariff concession as *ipso facto* contrary to Article XIX unless the weight attached by the government concerned to such factors was clearly unreasonably great.[2]

By contrast, in a case brought by Finland against New Zealand's application of antidumping duties on imports of transformers, the panel ruled in 1985 that New Zealand authorities had not sufficiently established the validity of a "material injury" determination, a ruling that rejected New Zealand's contention that neither other contracting parties nor a GATT panel could challenge or scrutinize that determination. The panel said that to refuse such scrutiny "would lead to an unacceptable situation under the aspect of law and order in international trade relations as governed by the GATT."[3] The panel in this connection further noted that a similar point had been raised, and rejected, in the 1955 report of the panel on complaints relating to Swedish antidumping duties. The 1985 panel shared the view expressed by the 1955 panel that "it was clear from the wording of Article VI that no anti-dumping duties should be levied until certain facts had been established." The 1985 panel further pointed out, again quoting the 1955 panel: "As this represented an obligation on the part of the contracting party imposing such duties, it would be reasonable to expect that that contracting party should establish the existence of these facts when its action is challenged."[4]

To examine another example, in a case against Korea's antidumping duties on polyacetal resins, the United States challenged the Korean Government's determination of injury. Korea argued that "it was not the task of the Panel to second guess the KTC [Korean government body] . . . [T]he Panel's job was not to conduct a de novo investigation nor to attach its own weights to the different factors."[5] Nevertheless, relying on language in the relevant GATT antidumping agreement, the panel decided that the KTC's injury determination before the panel did not meet the requirements of the treaty language. Other cases have raised similar issues and, indeed, the criticism of the panel's approach in some cases is clearly what engendered the U.S. effort to obtain some limitations on the "standard of review" in the Uruguay Round negotiations.

Some later cases, however, seemed to take a more restrained view of a panel's authority. In the 1994 case of U.S. restrictions on imports of tuna, for instance, the panel noted:

> The reasonableness inherent in the interpretation of necessary was not a test of what was reasonable for a government to do, but of what a reasonable government would or could do. In this way, the panel did not substitute its judgement for that of the government. The test of reasonableness was very close to the good faith criterion in international law. Such a standard, in different forms, was also applied in the administrative law of many contracting parties, including the EEC and its member states, and the United States. It was a standard of review of government actions which did not lead to a wholesale second guessing of such actions.[6]

Similarly, in the prominent cases of twin complaints by Norway against the U.S. antidumping and countervailing duties on imports of Atlantic salmon, the panel in both cases ruled mostly in favor of the United States, finding that the U.S. action was not inconsistent with its GATT obligations, and seemed quite cautiously restrained in its approach (too restrained, some argue). The Government of Norway wrote a letter criticizing the panel's approach, to which the panel replied, saying, inter alia, that "the panel found it inappropriate to make its own judgement as to the relative weight to be accorded to the facts before the USITC."[7]

Thus it can be seen that the standard-of-review question is recurring and delicate, and one that to some extent goes to the core of an international procedure that (in a rule-based system) must assess a national government's actions against treaty or other international norms. Indeed, a more detailed review of these and other cases would show that quite a few concepts invoked by panels over the years relate to the broader question of the appropriate relationship of international dispute settlement proceedings to national government actions. With such broader questions in mind, we turn to the more particular question of the appropriate standard of review for GATT/WTO panels, focusing especially on antidumping.

The Law and Negotiating Context of the WTO

Relevant Texts

The Uruguay Round texts contain several different explicit or implied references to the standard-of-review question. The most prominent of these is found in the Anti-Dumping Agreement in Article 17.6. This provision, which applies *only* to antidumping measures, reads as follows:

> In examining the matter referred to in paragraph 5:
> (i) in its assessment of the facts of the matter, the panel shall determine whether the authorities' establishment of the facts was proper and whether their evaluation of those facts was unbiased and objective. If the establishment of the facts was proper and the evaluation was unbiased and objective, even though the panel might have reached a different conclusion, the evaluation shall not be overturned;
> (ii) the panel shall interpret the relevant provisions of the Agreement in accordance with customary rules of interpretation of public international law. Where the panel finds that a relevant provision of the Agreement admits of more than one permissible interpretation, the panel shall find the authorities' measure to be in conformity with the Agreement if it rests upon one of those permissible interpretations.

Article 17.6 is not the only provision bearing on the standard of review. Also relevant are two Ministerial Decisions taken at the final Ministerial

Conference of the Uruguay Round at Marrakesh, Morocco, in April 1994, and made part of the text of the Uruguay Round Final Act. These state, respectively:

> DECISION ON REVIEW OF ARTICLE 17.6 OF THE AGREEMENT ON IMPLEMENTA-
> TION OF ARTICLE VI OF THE GENERAL AGREEMENT ON TARIFFS AND TRADE
> 1994
>
> Ministers decide as follows:
>
> The standard of review in paragraph 6 of Article 17 of the Agreement on Implementation of Article VI of GATT 1994 shall be reviewed after a period of three years with a view to considering the question of whether it is capable of general application.

> DECLARATION ON DISPUTE SETTLEMENT PURSUANT TO THE AGREEMENT
> ON IMPLEMENTATION OF ARTICLE VI OF THE GENERAL AGREEMENT
> ON TARIFFS AND TRADE 1994 OR PART V OF THE AGREEMENT ON
> SUBSIDIES AND COUNTERVAILING MEASURES
>
> Ministers recognize, with respect to dispute settlement pursuant to the Agreement on Implementation of Article VI of GATT 1994 or Part V of the Agreement on Subsidies and Countervailing Measures, the need for the consistent resolution of disputes arising from anti-dumping and countervailing duty measures.

As both of these passages suggest, the antidumping provisions were not uncontroversial, for the Ministerial Decisions seem both to limit the application of those provisions, and to raise questions about how they fit into the overall jurisprudence of the WTO. To understand the source of that controversy, one must read these texts, Article 17.6 in particular, in the light of their negotiating context and history. That history, as we understand it, was briefly as follows.

Negotiating Context

Some government representatives thought it would be wise to have language constraining the standard of review by a GATT or WTO panel, and believed that U.S. administrative law jurisprudence provided a useful model for this constraint. As explained in more detail below, the U.S. jurisprudence seemed to suggest an approach whereby the courts (absent definitive statutory language to the contrary) would show deference to administrative actions by the executive branch of government, if those actions were based on a "reasonable interpretation" of the statute. Thus, negotiators suggested that the international rules of procedure should restrain WTO panels from ruling against a nation if its approach or interpretation was "reasonable."

This suggestion provoked opposition from at least two quarters. First, it drew opposition from many nations that felt such a rule would overly constrain panels while giving too much leeway to national governments to act in a manner inconsistent with the purposes of the WTO Agreements. In addition, many believed that a "reasonable" standard would allow different nations to develop different approaches to the international rules of the WTO Agreements, thus reducing consistency and reciprocity, and potentially allowing many different national administrative versions of the same treaty language.

Second, the "reasonable" standard worried certain other interests who wanted to ensure the effectiveness of many rules of the WTO, particularly those in the intellectual property area. These interests also believed that the "reasonableness criteria" would constrain panels too much, and make it difficult to successfully challenge objectionable practices that were inconsistent with various WTO rules.

In the tense moments of the final days of the negotiations, several compromises were reached. First, the text of Article 17.6 was reworded to use the word "permissible" rather than "reasonable" as justification for a national approach, *but* (a very big "but") this provision was preceded by the language of the first sentence in 17.6(ii), which we discuss below. No less important, the negotiators compromised so that the limiting language on standard of review would apply only to the antidumping text (which attracted the proposals in the first place), and not necessarily to other dispute settlement cases before the WTO panels. The Ministerial Decisions quoted above reflect the divisions of opinion on these issues by calling for consideration in three years of whether Article 17.6 "is capable of general application," and "recognizing" the "need for consistent resolution of disputes" with regard to "anti-dumping and countervailing duty measures." As to the general approach for panels (outside the antidumping area), while there are no provisions in the DSU explicitly concerning the "standard of review" as such, some language may be construed as relevant. The most interesting, perhaps, is found in DSU Article 3.2: "Recommendations and rulings of the DSB [Dispute Settlement Body] cannot add to or diminish the rights and obligations provided in the covered agreements." This language could be interpreted as a constraint on the standard of review, but possibly not to the extent of Article 17.6 of the Anti-Dumping Agreement.

The Fruits of Compromise

Now to focus on the structure of Article 17.6 of the Anti-Dumping Agreement itself. The key language is in paragraph 6(ii), quoted above. This was the compromise language of the Uruguay Round negotiators. What does it mean? A better understanding of its meaning must await future panel decisions. (Thus, early cases may be enormously important in this regard.) But, at least on the face of it, subsection (ii) seems to establish a two-step process for panel review of interpretive questions. First, the panel must consider whether the provision of the agreement in question admits of more than one interpretation. If not, the panel must vindicate the provision's only permissible interpretation. If, on the other hand, the panel determines that the provision indeed admits of more than one interpretation, the panel shall proceed to the second step of the analysis and consider whether the national interpretation is within the set of "permissible" interpretations. If so, the panel must defer to the interpretation given the provision by the national government.

Note that, in the first step of the analysis, subsection (ii) instructs the reviewing panel to consider the interpretive question, mindful of "the customary rules of interpretation of public international law." According to negotiators, this admonition is a direct albeit implicit, invocation of the Vienna Convention on the Law of Treaties. Interestingly, however, it is not clear in light of that Convention whether or how a panel could ever reach the conclusion that provisions of an agreement admit of more than one interpretation. This is true because the Vienna Convention provides a set of rules for the interpretation of treaties—defined as any "international agreement[s] concluded between States in written form and governed by international law" and thus clearly including the GATT/WTO—aimed at resolving ambiguities in the text. Articles 31 and 32 of the Vienna Convention are particularly relevant here. Article 31, "General rule of interpretation," sets forth a set of rules guiding the interpretation of the text of a treaty. Article 32, "Supplementary means of interpretation," provides additional guidelines for any case in which application of the rules in Article 31 still leaves the meaning of a provision "ambiguous or obscure," or when it renders a provision "manifestly absurd or unreasonable." Article 32 suggests, in other words, that the application of Article 31 should in many cases resolve ambiguities, and that where the application of Article 31 does not do so, Article 32's own rule—"[r]ecourse . . . to supplementary means of interpretation, including the preparatory work of the treaty and the circumstances of its conclusion"—will resolve any lingering ambiguities.

Thus, it is not clear what sort of ambiguity in an agreement's provision is sufficient to lead a reviewing panel to the second step of the analysis contemplated in Article 17.6(ii). Once a panel has invoked Articles 31 and 32 of the Vienna Convention, it presumably will have already settled on a nonambiguous, nonabsurd interpretation. Article 17.6 thus raises several questions about the relationship between it and Articles 31 and 32: Is any ambiguity whatsoever sufficient to move a panel to consider the range of permissible interpretations? Or does a provision admit of more than one interpretation for the purposes of Article 17.6(ii) after application of Article 31, but before application of Article 32? Or does a provision admit of more than one interpretation for the purpose of Article 17.6(ii) only after application of both

Articles 31 and 32? In short, just which sort of ambiguity is sufficient to trigger a panel's deference? Without answering these questions, Article 17.6(ii) does, at least on the surface, suppose that a panel could somehow reach the conclusion that a provision admits of more than one permissible interpretation, for the second sentence of paragraph 6(ii) would otherwise never come into play. Indeed, some of the negotiators seem to feel that this is precisely the case; there never can be resort to the second sentence. Others, however, mostly proponents of the original "reasonable" language who desire more constraint on panels, argue to the contrary.

The U.S. Jurisprudence: A Valid Source of Analogy?

As already suggested, an apparently similar standard-of-review issue, raising analogous questions, figures prominently in U.S. administrative law (the same is probably true for other countries as well). In U.S. law, that issue concerns the level of deference that federal courts reviewing decisions made by federal administrative agencies will exercise toward those decisions. Until fairly recently, and broadly speaking, reviewing courts exercised considerable deference with respect to agencies' "factual" determinations, and accorded less deference to agencies' "legal" decisions. This two-tiered approach reflected a familiar division of function between the separate branches of government, according to which agencies were to handle the more or less "technical" aspects of statutory implementation, while courts were to ensure that agencies exercised their authority within the boundaries of the law. This bifurcated approach also followed the U.S. Administrative Procedure Act's direction for courts to "decide all relevant questions of law," which itself reflected traditional understandings of the proper roles of courts and agencies. Traditionally, judicial deference to agencies' legal determinations required special justification, whereas deference to factual determinations did not. That general rule was altered, however, in 1984, when the U.S. Supreme Court handed down its decision in *Chevron U.S.A., Inc. v. Natural Resources Defense Council, Inc.*, in which the Court articulated a new standard of review for agencies' interpretations of law—the *Chevron* doctrine.

The Chevron Doctrine

Courts applying the *Chevron* doctrine face two sequential questions, often referred to as "step one" and "step two" of *Chevron*. First: Has Congress "directly spoken to the precise question at issue,"[8] or is the statute interpreted by the agency "silent or ambiguous"?[9] To answer this question, the reviewing court applies the "traditional tools of statutory construction."[10]

If, upon applying those traditional tools, the reviewing court concludes that Congress has indeed spoken to the precise issue in question, then "that is the end of the matter";[11] the court will hold the agency faithful to Congress's will, as unambiguously expressed in the statute.

If the court concludes instead that the statute is "silent or ambiguous" with respect to the interpretive question at issue, then the reviewing court proceeds to a second question—step two: Is the agency's interpretation of the statute a "reasonable" or "permissible" one? If the court determines that the agency's interpretation is not reasonable, then the court will supply one. If, however, the court determines that the agency's interpretation is reasonable, the court will defer to the agency's interpretation, even if—and this is the bite of the *Chevron* doctrine—the agency's interpretation is not one the court itself would have adopted had it considered the question on its own.

At least at first glance, then, the *Chevron* doctrine is straightforward: It instructs courts to defer to agencies' interpretations of law if and only if the statute in question is ambiguous and the agency's interpretation is reasonable. A close reading of *Chevron,* however, reveals that the doctrine itself is ambiguous, not least of all with respect to exactly how much interpretive ambiguity is necessary to proceed to step two. Will any statutory ambiguity suffice, or must the provision in question be utterly ambiguous, even after the reviewing court's application of the traditional tools of statutory construction, before the court will move on to address the reasonableness question? The best answer may be somewhere in between. What is clear is that *Chevron* provides sufficient leeway for lower courts to find ambiguities, or not, as they will. Accordingly, while lower courts cite and apply *Chevron* and its progeny routinely, their decisions vary widely with respect to what constitutes sufficient ambiguity to trigger step two of the doctrine.

According to many U.S. administrative law scholars, the *Chevron* doctrine constituted a significant shift of power from courts to agencies.[12] As explained shortly below, the shift is commonly justified by reference to some of the most important principles underlying U.S. administrative government—expertise, accountability and administrative efficiency. But, first, the important surface similarities between the *Chevron* doctrine in U.S. administrative law, on the one hand, and the standard of review set forth in Article 17.6 of the Anti-Dumping Agreement, on the other, deserve careful attention.

Chevron *and Article 17.6(ii)*

For one thing, *Chevron* requires a federal court to defer to an agency's interpretation of an ambiguous statutory provision so long as that interpretation is "reasonable" or "permissible," even if the reviewing court would have interpreted the statute differently had it considered the question in the first instance. Similarly, Article 17.6 requires a GATT/WTO panel to defer to a party's interpretation of an ambiguous Agreement provision so long as that interpretation is "permissible," even if (by direct implication) the reviewing panel would have adopted an alternative interpretation had it considered the question originally. Second, the *Chevron* doctrine instructs courts to employ the "traditional tools of statutory construction" when determining whether the statutory provision in question is "ambiguous" in the first place. Article 17.6, for its part, instructs panels to apply the "customary rules of interpretation of public international law" when determining whether the Agreement provision in question "admits of more than one permissible interpretation." Third, as noted, the *Chevron* doctrine is somewhat unclear about the level of ambiguity that is required to trigger step two of the *Chevron* analysis and, accordingly, lower courts vary widely on their approach to this issue. Article 17.6, similarly, is unclear about how panels will ever get to "step two" of the 17.6 standard, given the section's implicit invocation of the interpretive rules set forth in the Vienna Convention on the Law of Treaties.

Finally, and most fundamentally, both *Chevron* and the standard-of-review issue in Article 17.6 bear important implications about the distribution of legal and political authority. In the U.S. administrative regime, *Chevron* spelled an important shift of interpretive power from federal courts to agencies (and, thus, to the President). According to the conventional wisdom, whereas courts previously had most of the authority to resolve ambiguities in legislation, now agencies have significant authority to determine what Congress meant. Unless agencies exercise that authority unreasonably, courts must go along.

While this wisdom is sound so far as it goes, *Chevron*'s allocation of power is probably more complicated and more subtle than the conventional view suggests. Because reviewing courts have significant leeway to find, or not to find, a step-one ambiguity, courts retain significant power to vindicate or invalidate agencies' interpretive decisions. This is true because where courts' *Chevron* analyses end at step one, agencies often lose, and where the analyses proceed to step two, agencies usually win. Thus, courts retain an important check on agency authority, even though as a formal matter agencies and not courts have the authority to pass on the interpretive question initially. *Chevron* ties courts' hands only insofar as step one requires a court to defer to an interpretation it would have invalidated otherwise. *Chevron* shifts power *to* courts, however, insofar as step one allows a court to defer to what it considers a preferred interpretation of a statute that, under the pre-*Chevron* regime, the court would not have been able to support. In sum, *Chevron* comes with offsetting effects on federal judicial power: Reviewing federal courts "lose" in the sense that they must defer to unwelcome agency interpretations that, before *Chevron,* they could have invalidated; but they "gain" in the sense that they are permitted to vindicate welcome interpretations that, before *Chevron,* they would have been required to invalidate. What is more, courts hold the key to *Chevron*'s step two—given that the reviewing court itself decides at step one whether there is an ambiguity of sufficient proportions to proceed to step two.

While *Chevron*'s (re)allocation of interpretive authority between agencies and courts is complex, Congress's power almost certainly was curtailed as a result. This is so because, after *Chevron,* there are more interpretations of statutory provisions that courts can potentially uphold; again, some interpretations that courts would have been required to invalidate before *Chevron* will now be upheld. As a result, Congress must now speak with greater specificity, or run the risk that an agency will interpret a statute, with judicial blessing, in a manner that pre-*Chevron* courts would have said Congress did not intend.

Chevron-*Type Deference and Interpretive Authority in the GATT/WTO Context*

In the GATT/WTO context, the standard-of-review question implicates a similar allocation of interpretive power—among countries that first interpret a disputed provision of the Anti-Dumping Agreement, GATT/WTO panels hearing disputes, and members party to the Anti-Dumping Agreement. Here, too, the issue is complex and subtle. On the one hand, if panels were to interpret Article 17.6 as requiring considerable deference to a member's interpretation of a provision, disputing members would enjoy greater authority vis-à-vis GATT/WTO panels. On the other hand, if panels were to interpret Article 17.6 as requiring considerable deference where a provision admits of more than one interpretation, *and* as providing them with considerable leeway to determine whether a provision does admit of more than one interpretation, then panels themselves would enjoy significant power both to invalidate interpretations (under step one of 17.6) they deemed undesirable and to vindicate interpretations (under step two of 17.6) they deemed desirable. What is more, the power of WTO members, analogously to the power of Congress, would be compromised under a *Chevron*-like application of Article 17.6. Some of the members' intentions—specifically, those that were ambiguously, but nevertheless ascertainably, expressed in the Agreement—would not necessarily be vindicated under a *Chevron*-like interpretive framework. Indeed, beneficiaries of antidumping duty orders probably sought a *Chevron*-like standard of review for precisely this reason—so that panels would be less powerful. As suggested above, such interests no doubt thought that a *Chevron*-type standard, by making it more difficult for panels to invalidate a party's interpretation as contrary to the intent of the GATT/WTO membership, would effectively allocate power to

GATT/WTO disputants and away from the members collectively. But to reiterate, since panels will decide what is ambiguous, the result of the standard could conversely shift more power *to panels.*

None of this is to suggest, however, that Article 17.6(ii) should be interpreted like the *Chevron* doctrine, whatever hopes may or may not have motivated certain negotiators. At least two important differences distinguish the standard of review embodied in 17.6 from *Chevron* deference. First, Article 17.6(ii) uses the word "permissible," which may not be identical in meaning to "reasonable" or "permissible" as construed in U.S. law. In U.S. law, the essential test for step two of the *Chevron* analysis is whether the agency's interpretation is "rational and consistent with the statute," a test that agencies can quite easily pass. Second, the "customary rules of interpretation of public international law" referred to in Article 17.6 certainly are by no means identical to the "traditional tools of statutory construction" in U.S. domestic law, the latter being more quickly consulted and more open-ended than the former (especially, as indicated above, with regard to legislative history). As already explained, Articles 31 and 32 of the Vienna Convention aim at resolving any facial ambiguities in treaty text. In U.S. law, in contrast, it is well understood that application of the traditional tools of statutory construction can exacerbate as much as eliminate statutory ambiguities.

These important differences notwithstanding, at least some GATT/WTO disputants and negotiators have recognized both the analogy between *Chevron* and the standard of review for international panels, and the specific doctrinal and theoretical similarities between *Chevron*'s and Article 17.6's approaches to those analogous issues. In fact, the *Chevron* doctrine seems likely to shape the perspective of U.S. disputants in particular, for whom it is such a familiar and influential doctrine in their home regime. Thus the question arises, and will arise in future panel cases, about how far the *Chevron* analogy can be sustained in the context of GATT/WTO panel review. Should future GATT/WTO panels exercise *Chevron*-like deference? Or should they instead interpret the word "permissible" rather narrowly and/or apply the Vienna Convention's rules governing treaty interpretation in such a manner as to be very reluctant ever to conclude that an agreement provision "admits of more than one interpretation"? Part V is a first attempt to consider this crucial question.

Policy Consideration:
The Limits of the *Chevron* Analogy

Some Common Justifications for Chevron *Deference*

One traditional justification for greater judicial deference to agencies on legal questions in the U.S. administrative regime is that of agency expertise—the "expertise argument." This justification comports with traditional understandings about the respective roles of the different branches of government and agencies' place in modern government. Agencies, on this view, are the technical experts that put into operation the policy judgments made by legislators. Indeed, technical expertise is the raison d'être of agencies; by focusing on a particular regulatory field. or sector of the economy, agencies can do what Congress lacks the time and other institutional resources to do. *Chevron* itself, which presented the question whether the statutory term "stationary source" referred to an entire pollution emitting plant or, rather, to every single smokestack within such a plant, supplies an apt example of when an agency's special technical expertise can aid statutory interpretation. According to the expertise argument, agencies are deemed to understand even the legal ramifications of the problems agencies are created to work on. Admittedly, the dichotomy between legal and factual questions may at times be difficult to maintain, but that observation argues as much in favor of as it does against *Chevron* deference.

Agency expertise, however, is not the only common justification for *Chevron*-type deference. Sometimes the doctrine is justified also on democratic grounds. According to the argument from democracy, it is agencies, not courts, that are answerable to both the executive and the legislative representatives of the citizenry. Because judges are not elected, while presidents and legislators are, and because agencies but not judges are accountable to the President and to Congress, judicial deference to agency decisions enhances the political legitimacy of the administrative regime.

Finally, *Chevron* may be justified also in the name of administrative efficiency or coordination. Before *Chevron,* different federal courts in different jurisdictions could interpret the same statutory provision differently. Multiple interpretations by different federal courts would mean that the statute "said" different things in those different jurisdictions. Such confusion could be eliminated by appellate review, but agencies faced uncertainty pending review, and the possibility of different interpretations across different appellate circuits remained. Because multiple agencies do not typically interpret the same statutory language, however, *Chevron* deference allows the agency charged with administering a statute to interpret that statute. One agency, rather than many federal courts, now resolves ambiguities in the statute that the agency in question is charged to administer. Such interpretive streamlining not only reduces uncertainty but also promotes regulatory coordination. Once an agency has settled on a reasonable interpretation, it can act on the basis of that interpretation nationally.

These three arguments are not offered here to supply an unassailable normative defense of the *Chevron* doctrine; whether *Chevron* was a welcome development in U.S. administrative law is a debatable question beyond the scope of the present analysis. While these common justifications resonate with some of the most fundamental principles, underlying administrative government, they do not necessarily exhaust the argument that might be offered on behalf of *Chevron*. Each of the above justifications is subject to serious objection when applied to international review, however.

Chevron-*Type Deference and GATT/WTO Panels*

Whatever the doctrine's ultimate merits or demerits, *Chevron*'s central concept of "reasonableness" has at the very least a surface appeal. In fact, across many substantive areas of U.S. law, legal rules impose in one form or another requirements that are satisfied by reasonableness; where parties have acted in a reasonable way or have adopted reasonable positions, legal institutions and legal rules do not interfere. In the GATT/WTO context, the permissibility standard of Article 17.6 has a similar commonsense ring. The WTO Anti-Dumping Agreement will invariably raise many complicated interpretive questions involving a variety of underlying factual and legal issues. So long as a member's interpretation of the Agreement is permissible—within the realm of the plausible, in some general sense—deference on the part of reviewing panels may be sensible. After all, members may reasonably disagree about the meaning of the Agreement's provisions, and unless GATT/WTO panels have some privileged access to the meaning of the Agreement, there may be no reason to substitute a panel's interpretation for that of one authority. In addition, a deferential posture on the part of antidumping panels may help guard against panel activism more generally. Whatever the merits of *Chevron* in U.S. administrative law, then, do not the doctrine's general justifications also argue for a *Chevron*-like standard of review in the context of the Anti-Dumping Agreement?

Return first to the expertise argument, which justifies a deferential standard of review on the grounds that agencies are experts within their respective statutory domains. In the GATT/WTO context, there is probably no analogous rationale, certainly not one as strong. That GATT/WTO members have superior information to GATT/WTO panels about the meaning or ultimate aim of the Agreement's provisions seems implausible. Nor is any particular GATT/WTO member an "expert" relative to any other. GATT/WTO members undoubtedly have their own incentives to become experts about the meaning of the Agreement, but none can plausibly claim expertise over any other.

Granted, disputing parties who have made decisions facing a GATT/WTO panel challenge almost surely have vastly more *factual* information than reviewing panels do. Because panels themselves lack many fact gathering resources, they are ill-positioned to second-guess a party's factual determinations. Article 17.6(i), appropriately, reflects this reality by establishing a rather deferential standard of review of factual conclusions. That standard provides that panels shall ask only whether an authority's factual determinations were "proper" and whether an authority's evaluation of those facts was "unbiased and objective." If these conditions hold, a panel is to defer to the authority's view of the facts, "even though the panel might have reached a different conclusion." But parties' technical superiority over factual matters does not justify a deferential standard of review for authorities' interpretation of the Agreement's provisions. National authorities probably do not bring to a dispute any specialized understanding that renders them specially qualified to ascertain the legal meaning of *international agreements*, in the same way that the EPA's specialized understanding of environmental regulatory issues arguably renders that agency specially qualified to ascertain the meaning of "stationary source."

This leads to a second and related distinction between the posture of agencies and GATT/WTO members. In stark contrast to administrative agencies, GATT/WTO members are not specifically charged with carrying out the GATT/WTO. To be sure, members are obligated to fulfill their responsibilities under the WTO Agreement. In that limited sense, GATT/WTO members are charged with administering the GATT/WTO. But no country or combination of countries was ever delegated the responsibility of implementing the WTO Agreement in the way that administrative agencies are charged with implementing their statutes. Countries party to an antidumping dispute are not delegates whose technical expertise specially qualifies them to make authoritative interpretive decisions. They are, rather, interested parties whose own (national) interests may not always sustain a necessary fidelity to the terms of international agreements. Thus, while there may well be reasons for panels to defer to an authority's permissible interpretation of the WTO Agreement, expertise of parties to a panel dispute is probably not among them.

The same is true for the argument from democracy. Indeed, this argument cuts in the opposite direction from *Chevron*, once transplanted to the GATT/WTO context. Unlike agencies, national authorities that are parties to an antidumping dispute are not accountable to the GATT/WTO membership at large. GATT/WTO panels, not disputing parties, are the membership's delegates. Panels are delegated the authority to try to vindicate the political decisions—the compromises, the trade-offs—made by members as a whole. Therefore, while GATT/WTO panels resemble courts, and while they are asked to adjudicate claims between competing national parties, their interpretation of any WTO Agreement will *not* displace the interpretations of any body that is accountable to the membership—will not, in other words, displace interpretations by others who can plausibly be said to be representatives of the GATT/WTO membership. The argument in *Chevron* that judges should defer to the interpretive decisions made by those accountable to the citizenry's representatives simply has no analogue in the GATT/WTO antidumping context.

The observation that national authorities, unlike agencies, are not accountable to the membership at large speaks to the very purpose of the dispute settlement process, indeed the GATT/WTO Agreement itself—an agreement that, at bottom, seeks to overcome the significant coordination or collective-action problems that its membership otherwise faces. Absent the Agreement (or one like it), individual members have an incentive to erect trade barriers that may "benefit" them individually, to the greater detriment of other members. Furthermore, absent some dispute settlement process for keeping members faithful to the Agreement, members have similar incentives to apply the Agreement in ways "advantageous" to them. Further still, absent a standard of review for legal questions that prohibits self-serving interpretations of the Agreement that are *arguably* but not *persuasively* faithful to the text, members have an incentive to erode the Agreement through interpretation. In this light, respecting the policy preferences and judgments of the GATT/WTO constituency argues against, not in favor of, a *Chevron*-like standard of review.

Indeed, the fundamental problem with attempting to transplant a *Chevron*-like national standard of review to the GATT/WTO context is that such an approach overlooks the basic fact that in an international proceeding the underlying legal problem is rather different: Whereas in a national procedure the court is reviewing a national administrative action or determination under the national law, such as a statute, the international body has the task of ascertaining the meaning and application of an international norm. The question before the international body generally is whether the interpretation of an agreement underlying a national government's action is actually consistent or inconsistent with that agreement. This is not necessarily the same question as that faced by the national courts, at least in some legal systems. Of course, the international rule may be the applicable national rule if the treaty has direct "statutelike" application (if, for example, the treaty is self-executing), and the international rule may also have a role in influencing national interpretations of national law. But in many cases, at least in the United States, the courts are reviewing *national* law, which is determinative of the outcome of the national case, even if that determination proves to be inconsistent with *international* obligations. The international body, on the other hand, is charged with interpreting and applying the international norms engaged by the case. Accordingly, in almost all cases the parties to the dispute at the international process (nation-state governments) are different from the parties in the national case, which may be private firms, or subordinate parts of the government.

The efficiency argument fares no better in justifying a deferential standard of review. Whereas in the U.S. administrative law setting there is typically little danger of multiple interpretations of the statutory language by several different agencies, in the GATT/WTO setting multiple interpretations of agreement provisions is precisely one of the problems that panel review is designed to ameliorate. For in the GATT/WTO context it is highly likely that multiple countries will confront interpretive questions about one and the same GATT/WTO provision. The danger of multiple interpretations of the same provision as a threat to reciprocity thus seems considerable; as already observed, the Agreement itself is a response to a serious international coordination problem. At the same time, there seems to be little threat that the new GATT/WTO panels will render multiple and incompatible interpretations of the same agreement provision. Even though GATT/WTO panels are composed (at least at the initial stage) on an ad hoc basis, and even though, strictly speaking, GATT/WTO cases do not constitute binding precedent on subsequent GATT/WTO panels, the jurisdiction of these panels (in contrast to that of U.S. federal courts) is not confined to specific geographical regions. Moreover, while the principle of *stare decisis* does not govern GATT/WTO dispute settlement, panels very often make authoritative references to previous panels' decisions relating to the same or similar issues, and multiple panels' consistent treatment of a given issue over time can assume the force of a "practice" that guides panel interpretation of the Agreement. Here again, then, the GATT/WTO context presents an inverse situation as compared to U.S. administrative law: Whereas in the U.S. domestic context *Chevron* deference shifts interpretive power away from multiple courts and to one agency, similar deference in the antidumping context would shift interpretive power away from one institution and to multiple and varied parties to the GATT/WTO, each with a different culture and legal institution.

Of course, to argue that expertise, accountability and efficiency do not counsel in favor of a *Chevron*-like application of Article 17.6(ii) is not to argue that a *Chevron*-like approach is ultimately unjustifiable. Rather, the argument here is that some of the most common and most powerful justifications of the *Chevron* doctrine carry very little weight once transplanted to the context of GATT/WTO dispute settlement. To the extent that the *Chevron* doctrine influenced the drafting of Article 17.6, consideration of the appropriateness of that approach is in order. If Article 17.6 is to be applied in a *Chevron*-like way, its justification must come from outside the *Chevron* paradigm. We conclude with one possible justification.

Conclusion: Sovereignty and Standard of Review in International Law

While the analysis here has focused on scope of review in the GATT/WTO antidumping context specifically, the basic question considered reaches beyond the process of GATT/WTO dispute resolution itself. The standard-of-review question is faced at least implicitly whenever sovereign members of a treaty yield interpretive and dispute settlement powers to international panels and tribunals. Moreover, as national economies become increasingly interdependent, and as the need for international cooperation and coordination accordingly becomes greater, the standard-of-review question will become more and more important. The difficulty is clear: On the one hand, effective international cooperation depends in part upon the willingness of sovereign states to constrain themselves by relinquishing to international tribunals at least minimum power to interpret treaties and articulate international obligations. Recognizing the necessity of such power does not lessen the importance at the national level of decision-making expertise, democratic accountability or institutional efficiency. On the other hand, nations and their citizens—and particularly those particular interests within nation-states that are reasonably successful at influencing their national political actors—will want to maintain control of the government decisions.

Such parties may at times invoke the principle of national "sovereignty" to justify a deferential standard of review in the international context. At the same time, national authorities may also resist relinquishing interpretive power to GATT/WTO panels on the grounds that doing so compromises their sovereignty. Admittedly, the word "sovereignty" has been much abused and misused; nevertheless, if the term refers to policies and concepts that focus on an appropriate allocation of power between international and national governments, and if one is willing to recognize that nation-states *ought* still to retain powers for effective governing of national (or local) democratic constituencies in a variety of contexts and cultures—perhaps using theories of "subsidiarity"—then a case can be made for at least *some* international deference to national decisions, even decisions regarding interpretations of international agreements. After all, if the decisions and policy choices of national political and administrative bodies (such as the Commerce Department and the ITC in the United States) are too severely constrained by panel interpretation of the Agreement, those bodies and their constituencies will understandably resist. Important sovereignty values, in short, will inevitably come into conflict with the values underlying the newest embodiment of the GATT/WTO dispute settlement process. And there is no *a priori* reason why coordination values must in *every* case across every context, trump sovereignty values. Some trade-off is necessary.

Yet merely identifying important sovereignty values does not by itself provide a persuasive argument justifying deferential panel review. Standing alone, the argument that deferential review is necessary to protect authorities' national sovereignty fails to acknowledge that some balance between authorities' interest in protecting their sovereignty, on the one side, and the broader interest in realizing the gains of international coordination, on the other, must be struck. The argument proves too much, in other words, as it unwittingly challenges the very rationale of the GATT/WTO itself.

We thus approach the end of our analysis by identifying a major problem without recommending any easy solution. The problem is how to formulate and articulate the necessary mediating principle or principles between the international policy values for which a dispute settlement is desired, on the one hand, and the remaining important policy values of preserving national "sovereign" authority both as a check and balance against centralized power, and as a means to facilitate good government decisions close to the constituencies affected, on the other hand. Our appeal is to the dual propositions that the national-level approach to the standard-of-review issue, specifically a *Chevron*-like approach, does not provide appropriate analogies for the international approach, but that there is nevertheless an important policy value in recognizing the need for some deference to national government decisions. A reasonable, nuanced approach by the WTO panels is important for the credibility of the WTO dispute settlement system, and such an approach will lessen the dangers of inappropriate unilateral reactions by governments and citizen constituencies of nation-state members of the WTO. It should be obvious that this approach is needed for virtually all types of cases and not just those in antidumping or other specified categories.

Of course, we do not here prescribe any particular standard of review for panels considering national governments' interpretations of treaty obligations. Time and experience with particular cases will likely clarify the appropriate standard, or standards (since these may vary with different subject matters). Indeed, perhaps all that is required is that panels (including appellate panels) perceive and show sensitivity toward the issues involved when an international body reviews the legal appropriateness of national government authorities' actions. In this connection, panels should keep the relevant purposes, strengths and limitations of their institution in mind.

For example, panels should be cautious about adopting "activist" postures in the GATT/WTO context. For one thing, the international system and its dispute settlement procedures, in stark contrast to most national systems, depend heavily on voluntary compliance by participating members. Inappropriate panel "activism" could well alienate members, thus threatening the stability of the GATT/WTO dispute settlement procedure itself. Relatedly, panels should recognize that voluntary compliance with panel reports is grounded in the perception that panel decisions are fair, unbiased and rationally articulated.

Quite apart from these concerns, panels would be well advised to be aware also of the potential shortcomings of the international procedures, shortcomings that sometimes relate to a shortage of resources, especially (but not only) resources for fact-finding, as well as to the need for a very broad multilateral consensus. Moreover, panels should also recognize that national governments often have legitimate reasons for the decisions they take. At times, for example, such governments can justifiably argue that an appropriate allocation of power should tilt in favor of the national governments that are closest to the constituencies most affected by a given decision. More generally, panels should keep in mind that a broad-based, multilateral international institution must contend with a wide variety of legal, political and cultural values, which counsel in favor of caution toward interpreting treaty obligations in a way that may be appropriate to one society but not to other participants.

Notwithstanding these (and other) reasons for "judicial restraint," panels must at the same time understand the central role that the GATT/WTO adjudicatory system plays in enhancing the implementation, effectiveness and credibility of the elaborate sets of rules the WTO was created to maintain. Successful cooperation among national authorities to a large extent rests with the institutions given the responsibility to help carry out the WTO's dispute settlement procedures. Thus, when a particular national authority's activity or decision would undermine the effectiveness of WTO rules, or would establish a practice that could trigger damaging activities by other member countries, panels will undoubtedly show it less deference.

Notes

1. R. St. J. Macdonald, *Margins of Appreciation,* in European System for the Protection of Human Rights, ch. 6 (R. St. J. Macdonald, Franz Matscher & Herbert Petzold eds., 1993); *see also* Thomas A. O'Donnell, *The Margin of Appreciation Doctrine: Standards in the Jurisprudence of the European Court of Human Rights,* 4 Hum. Rts. Q. 474 (1982).

2. GATT Dispute Settlement Panel, "Hatter's Fur Case", Report on the Withdrawal by the United States of a Tariff Concession Under Article XIX of the GATT, 1951, paras. 8–14, GATT Sales No. GATT/1951–3 (1951), *portions reproduced in* John H. Jackson & William J. Davey, Legal Problems of International Economic Relations: Cases, Materials and Text 556 (2d ed. 1986).

3. GATT Dispute Settlement Panel, New Zealand—Imports of Electrical Transformers from Finland, GATT, Basic Instruments and Selected Documents [BISD], 32d Supp. 55, 67, para. 4:4 (1985) [hereinafter New Zealand Transformers].

4. New Zealand Transformers, *supra* note 3, at 68, para. 4:4.

5. GATT Dispute Settlement Panel, Korea—Anti-Dumping Duties on Imports of Polyacetal Resins from the United States, GATT Doc. ADP/92, para, 57 (1993) [hereinafter Korea Resins].

6. GATT Dispute Settlement Panel, United States—Restrictions on Imports of Tuna, GATT Doc. DS29/R, para. 3.73 (1994) [hereinafter Tuna II].

7. GATT Dispute Settlement Panel, United States—Imposition of Anti-Dumping Duties on Imports of Fresh and Chilled Atlantic Salmon from Norway, GATT

Doc. ADP/8, at 232 (1992); GATT Dispute Settlement Panel, United States—Imposition of Countervailing Duties on Imports of Fresh and Chilled Atlantic Salmon from Norway, GATT Doc. SCM/153, paras. 209–12 (1992). Many GATT panel cases discuss this question of "deference." *See, e.g.,* United States—Section 337 of the Tariff Act of 1930, BISD, 36th Supp. 345 (1990); Korea Resins, *supra* note 22, paras. 208–13; United States—Taxes on Automobiles, GATT Doc. DS31/R, paras. 5.11–5.15 (1994); United States—Imposition of Countervailing Duties on Imports of Fresh and Chilled Atlantic Salmon from Norway, GATT Doc. ADP/8, paras. 43–67 (1992).

8. *Chevron,* 467 U.S. at 842.

9. Id. at 843.

10. Id. n.9; *see also* KMart Corp. v. Cartier, Inc., 486 U.S. 218, 300 (1988) (Brennan, J., concurring); NLRB v. United Food & Commercial Workers Union, Local 23, 484 U.S. 112, 123 (1987); INS v. Cardoza-Fonseca, 480 U.S. 421, 446 (1987).

11. *Chevron,* 467 U.S. at 842.

12. *See, e.g.,* §3.3. Kenneth Culp Davis and Richard J. Pierce Jr., Administrative Law Treaties (3d. 3d. 1994).

13

The Rome Statute of the International Criminal Court

Mahnoush H. Arsanjani

The Negotiating Process

The Rome Conference was the culmination of a negotiating process that began in 1989 with a request by the General Assembly to the International Law Commission to address the establishment of an international criminal court.[1] In 1993 the Assembly asked the Commission to elaborate a draft statute for such a court as a matter of priority.[2] The Commission completed its draft in 1994.[3] In the same year, the General Assembly established an Ad Hoc Committee to review the major substantive and administrative issues arising out of the Commission's draft statute.[4] The Ad Hoc Committee was followed by a Preparatory Committee, which met in 1996, 1997 and finally in 1998, completing its work in April. While the negotiating process in the Ad Hoc Committee was of a general nature and focused on the core issue of whether the proposition to create a court was serious and viable, the discussions at the phase of the Preparatory Committee focused squarely on the text of the court's statute.[5]

The working text that the Preparatory Committee submitted to the Rome Conference[6] contained 116 articles, some of which were several pages long, with many options and hundreds of square brackets. Not only were the texts of most of the articles raw, but key policy issues about the jurisdiction and operation of the court had not yet been resolved.

At the Preparatory Committee, it became clear that the statute involved many areas of international and criminal law such as international humanitarian law, criminal procedure, extradition and human rights. Moreover, many of these areas touched on sensitive political issues relating to the UN

Charter and the competence of the Security Council. To avoid a long negotiating process similar to that of the Third UN Conference on the Law of
Sea, the Preparatory Committee divided the statute by subject matter into
sections, allocating each subject to a working group. The working groups
reported back to the plenary of the Preparatory Committee at the end of
each of the committee's sessions, and the task of coordination among the
different sections of the statute was primarily left to the coordinators.

The negotiating process at the Rome Conference was modeled on that
of the Preparatory Committee. The thirteen parts of the draft statute were
divided among different working groups of the Committee of the Whole,
which was ultimately responsible for negotiating the statute as a whole. The
coordinators and the Bureau of the Committee of the Whole became crucial
in the last two weeks of the conference. They provided advice on the technical questions of coordination between different parts and articles of the
statute, but even more important, were a strong, knowledgeable and dedicated negotiating team available to assist the chairman of the Committee of
the Whole, as he struggled to assemble a package containing compromises
on various aspects of the statute that would make it acceptable to an overwhelming majority of the participating states, including three permanent
members of the Security Council.

Parallel to the many working groups and informal consultations, discussions were conducted among political and regional groups, such as the
Non-Aligned Movement, the Arab Group, the Latin American and Caribbean Group, the European Union, the Western Europeans and others, and
the "like-minded states." The last group, comprising approximately fifty-
four states, played a significant role at the Preparatory Committee and the
Rome Conference. It had been formed during the preparatory work of the
Ad Hoc Committee by a handful of Western European and Latin American
states that were frustrated by the opposition of the major powers to the
establishment of the ICC. The group, which quickly grew in numbers and
soon included states from different regions, organized itself as an effective
and resourceful negotiating force. After the Labour Party's victory in the
British elections, the United Kingdom joined the like-minded states. That
was the first break in the ranks of the permanent members of the Security
Council and it proved to be an important step in the negotiation of the
statute. While the like-minded states did not agree on every issue, they
were committed, as a group, to the success of the Rome Conference and the
creation of the court.

Nongovernmental organizations played a significant role in the negotiation process at the Preparatory Committee and the conference. From the
beginning, a large group of NGOs committed themselves to the establishment of the ICC and lobbied intensively. Their influence was felt on a variety of issues, particularly the protection of children, sexual violence, forced

pregnancy, enforced sterilization and an independent role for the prosecutor. Throughout the Preparatory Committee's sessions and the Rome Conference, they provided briefings and legal memoranda for sympathetic delegations, approached delegations to discuss their points of view, and even assigned legal interns to small delegations. On occasion, they increased pressure on unsympathetic delegations by listing them as such in the media.

Two chairpersons, each with a different, but equally effective negotiating style, guided the negotiation of the statute. The Ad Hoc and Preparatory Committees were chaired by Adriaan Bos, the Legal Adviser of the Ministry of Foreign Affairs of the Netherlands. He became ill a few weeks before the Rome Conference and was replaced by Philippe Kirsch, Legal Adviser of the Department of Foreign Affairs of Canada, as the chairman of the Committee of the Whole.[7] Bos's style, incorporating the most detailed understanding of the positions of various governments and the political dynamics behind them, was reassuring and deliberate, a technique that was useful in keeping all sides engaged during the early phases of the negotiations. Kirsch is a consummate international parliamentarian, and his style is swift and creative in the formation of consensus. He was animated by a determination to assemble a final package by maintaining a consistent focus and negotiating both bilaterally and multilaterally. This style proved to be crucial in forging compromise texts for the statute. Both Bos and Kirsch relied on and effectively used the bureau and the coordinators of different parts of the statute.

The Structure of the Statute

The statute[8] is composed of a preamble and thirteen parts, including 128 articles.[9] Its structure remained unchanged from the one proposed by the Preparatory Committee. This structure had been assembled by the bureau and coordinators of the Preparatory Committee in a January 1998 meeting held in Zutphen, the Netherlands, when the theretofore disorganized articles were read from first to last, reshuffled, and given a form with parts and sequentially numbered articles.[10] The statute was deliberately not patterned after the Statute of the International Court of Justice.[11] The reason was concern for ratification. National legislatures, it was assumed, are more interested in the jurisdiction of the court than in such matters as its organization, the election of judges and their salaries. Hence, the jurisdictional section precedes the others. Neither the Preparatory Committee nor the Rome Conference reconsidered the structure of the statute.[12] Three principles underlie the statute. The first, the principle of complementarity, establishes that the court may assume jurisdiction only when national legal systems are unable or unwilling to exercise jurisdiction. Thus, in cases of concurrent jurisdiction between national courts and the international criminal court, the former, in principle, have priority.[13] The ICC is not intended to replace national courts, but operates only when they do not. The understanding of the majority of participating states was that states had a vital interest in remaining responsible and accountable for prosecuting violations of their laws. The international community had a comparable interest, inasmuch as national systems are expected to maintain and enforce adherence to international standards. The principle of complementarity was referred to in the preamble to the draft statute prepared by the International Law Commission: in the final Rome text, in addition to the preamble, it also found its way into Articles 1 and 17–19. The second principle is that the statute is designed to deal only with the most serious crimes of concern to the international community as a whole. This principle affected the selection of crimes, as well as the determination of their threshold of application. It was hoped that this principle would promote broad acceptance of the court by states and consequently enhance its credibility, moral authority and effectiveness. In addition, it would avoid overloading the court with cases that could be dealt with adequately by national courts, at the same time limiting the financial burden imposed on the international community. The selection of crimes was also related to the court's future role. Limiting the court's competence to a few "core crimes" would facilitate designing a coherent and unified approach to the exercise of jurisdiction and the requisite state cooperation. The third principle was that the statute should, to the extent possible, remain within the realm of customary international law. The reason for this approach was to make the statute widely acceptable. The proper place for adopting this approach was in the definition of crimes. With the exception of a few articles dealing with individual criminal responsibility, this principle could not have been applied to other provisions of the statute. Even in the provisions on defining crimes, there are matters that were not "international customary law," but had substantial, and in some cases overwhelming, support from the negotiating states. Conscious efforts were also made to harmonize the general principles of criminal law and rules of procedure of the common law and civil law systems in many of the articles in Parts 3, 5, 6, and 8. As a result, the provisions dealing with general principles and procedural issues are a hybrid of the common and the civil law. For example, while the adversarial character of trials is maintained, judges are assigned much broader competence in matters dealing with investigation and the questioning of witnesses.

Part 1, Establishment of the Court, comprises four articles dealing with the creation of the court. Article I expresses four cardinal points: the court is a standing institution; it is complementary to national criminal jurisdictions; it is intended to adjudicate the most serious crimes of international concern; and it is to exercise jurisdiction over persons and not legal entities.

The last issue is reinforced by Article 25(1), which provides that the court has jurisdiction over "natural persons." The seat of the court is The Hague (Article 3).

Part 2, Jurisdiction, Admissibility and Applicable Law, composed of seventeen articles (Articles 59721), is the heart of the statute and was the most difficult to negotiate. This part deals with the list and the definition of crimes, the trigger mechanism, admissibility and applicable law. The text of Part 2 was negotiated until the penultimate day of the conference.

Articles 12–19 deal with the jurisdiction of the court, the trigger mechanism and admissibility. Jurisdiction has a broad meaning in the statute and includes the competence of the prosecutor to investigate. The great majority of states wanted the court to have automatic jurisdiction regarding genocide, crimes against humanity, war crimes and the crime of aggression. A few states, including the United States, wanted automatic jurisdiction only for genocide. For other crimes, they preferred some form of a consent regime: either opting in or opting out, or consent on individual cases. The final text provides that the court may exercise jurisdiction with respect to the crimes listed in the statute, if it has the consent of the state of the territory where the crime was committed or the consent of the state of nationality of the accused (Article 12). But this requirement does not apply if a situation is referred to the court by the Security Council; the court will have jurisdiction regarding the crimes concerned even if committed in non-states parties by nationals of non-states parties and in the absence of consent by the territorial state or the state of nationality of the accused.

The requirement of consent by the state of nationality of the accused was strongly supported by the United States as a key condition for the court's jurisdiction. In the U.S. view, Article 12 is inconsistent with treaty practice, for it would enable the court to exercise jurisdiction over a national of a non-state party if the state where the crime was committed had consented to the court's jurisdiction. Hence, the statute purports to establish an arrangement whereby U.S. armed forces operating overseas could conceivably be prosecuted by the ICC even if the United States had not agreed to be bound by the treaty. The United States took the position that such overreaching by the ICC could inhibit the United States from using its military to meet alliance obligations and to participate in multinational operations, including humanitarian interventions to save civilian lives.

The overwhelming majority of states, however, could not agree to requiring the consent of the state of the nationality of the accused as a prerequisite for the court's jurisdiction for, in their view, it would paralyze the court. They also found it difficult to accept a situation, in terms of public policy, in which the nationals of a state party to the statute could be prosecuted for crimes committed in that state, while non-nationals of that state, committing the same crime in its territory, would be free from prosecution because their state of nationality was not party to the statute. These concerns, also shared by the United States, are partly addressed in the article dealing with admissibility and the primacy of national courts. In addition, the articles on judicial cooperation take into account the special situations of guest armed forces and require the consent of the state of nationality of the guest forces as a precondition to their release to the court by the host state. On the last day of the conference, the United States proposed another formula for jurisdiction. Under this formula, if the state of nationality of the accused declared that the accused had committed the crime in the pursuit of an official duty, the court would be precluded from exercising jurisdiction. Thus, a question of individual criminal responsibility would become one of state responsibility and would have to be addressed not under the statute, but under general international law. This proposal was not accepted.

One concern throughout the negotiations, expressed mostly by the permanent members of the Security Council, was the possibility of conflict between the jurisdiction of the court and the functions of the Council. There may be situations in which the investigation or prosecution of a particular case by the court could interfere with the resolution of an ongoing conflict by the Council. Hence the proposal for a provision that would automatically exclude the court's jurisdiction over any situation under consideration by the Council. Many states found the proposal too sweeping and feared it would undermine the court, for situations could remain pending before the Council indefinitely without its taking any final or serious action. A compromise formula was finally reached, which provided that the Security Council, acting under Chapter VII of the UN Charter, could adopt a resolution requesting deferral of an investigation or prosecution for a period of twelve months and that such a request could be renewed at twelve-month intervals (Article 16).

Under the statute, the court must satisfy itself that it has jurisdiction in any case brought before it (Article 19). Its jurisdiction is not retroactive to crimes committed before the entry into force of the statute. Even after that date, the court may exercise jurisdiction only with respect to a crime committed after the statute has entered into force for the state in question, unless that state agrees otherwise (Article 11). Since the court may only exercise jurisdiction if either the state where the crime was committed or the state of nationality of the accused is party to the statute or has consented to the court's jurisdiction, the application of this provision may not always be guaranteed.

A state party or the Security Council, acting under Chapter VII, may refer a "situation" to the Court (Article 13). The word "situation" is intended to minimize politicization of the court by naming individuals. The prosecutor may also initiate an investigation *proprio motu* subject to authorization by the pretrial chamber (Article 15). This power of the prosecutor was strenuously objected to by some states on the ground that the office might be over-whelmed by frivolous complaints and would have to waste the limited resources at his or her disposal to attend to them. In addition, concerns were expressed that the prosecutor might be placed under political pressure to bring a complaint even if the complaint might not be justifiable or help-ful in a particular political context. But a majority of states were of the view that, despite the potential for waste and abuse, it was better to em-power the prosecutor with such independence. In addition, they argued that the pretrial chamber will have broad competence with regard to the power of the prosecutor to use his or her own initiative and will be able to bar abuse. The NGOs strongly lobbied for this feature.

Where a situation has been referred by a state or the prosecutor has ini-tiated a case *proprio motu,* the prosecutor must inform all states parties to the statute, as well as non-states parties that would normally exercise juris-diction over the crimes concerned (Article 18). This provision was pro-posed by the United States. Many states accepted the article with great reluctance and as a compromise necessary for securing the prosecutor's power to bring a case on his or her own initiative. The prosecutor would have to defer to the state's investigation unless the pretrial chamber decided otherwise. Once having deferred an investigation to a state, the prosecutor may request that the state periodically inform him or her of the progress of its investigation. In addition, the prosecutor may review a state's investi-gation six months after the date of deferral or at any time when there has been a significant change of circumstances indicating the state's unwilling-ness or inability genuinely to carry out the investigation.

The court's complementary character to national jurisdictions is most clearly manifested in the provision dealing with admissibility. Article 17 on admissibility does something rather unusual in treaty practice. It refers to paragraph 10 of the preamble in addition to Article 1, which addresses the complementary character of the ICC with respect to national courts. It then identifies four grounds of inadmissibility: (1) the case is being investigated or prosecuted by a state that has jurisdiction over it; (2) the case has been investigated by a state that has jurisdiction over it and the state has decided not to prosecute the person concerned; (3) the person concerned has already been tried for the conduct in question; and (4) the case is not of sufficient gravity to justify action by the court. The first three grounds for inadmissi-bility, however, are subject to specific limitations: that the state is unwill-ing or unable genuinely to carry out the investigation or prosecution; that the national prosecution was conducted for the purpose of shielding the per-son concerned from criminal responsibility for crimes within the ICC's juris-diction; or that the national prosecution was not conducted independently or impartially in accordance with the norms of due process recognized by inter-national law and lacked a meaningful intent to bring the person concerned to justice. Paragraphs 2 and 3 of Article 17 provide guidelines on how to determine the "unwillingness" or "inability" of a state to conduct an investigation or prosecution. These were thorny issues that were skillfully negotiated by Canada during the negotiations in the Preparatory Committee.

The statute does not give any priority of jurisdiction to the court as against national courts, even if a matter is referred to it by the Security Council. Article 17 on admissibility and Article 90 on the obligation of the third state regarding competing requests by the court and by another state do not accord any priority to the court if the matter was referred to it by the Council. Thus, in such cases (when a situation has been referred to the court by the Security Council), national jurisdictions will still have priority over the court, if they meet the exceptions under Article 17. This result is not fully consistent with the original intention of empowering the Security Council with the right of referral which was to avoid the creation of ad hoc tribunals.[14]

The court's jurisdiction may be challenged by an accused; by the state that has jurisdiction over the case on the ground that it is investigating or prosecuting the matter or has investigated or prosecuted it or by the state in whose territory the crime was committed or the state of nationality of the accused, whose consent to the court's jurisdiction is required (Article 19). In principle, a challenge to jurisdiction may be brought only once at the beginning of the trial.

The statute prescribes a strict hierarchy among the rules of law to be applied by the court (Article 21). It must first apply the statute, the "Elements of Crimes" and its Rules of Procedure and Evidence. The Elements of Crimes must be read together with Article 9, in which they are included, so as to assist the court in the interpretation and application of articles on the definition of crimes. Second, the court must apply relevant "applicable treaties and the principles and rules of international law, including the established principles of the international law of armed conflict." The latter phrase was intended to include the *jus in bello*. In the third place, the court shall apply general principles of law that it has derived from the national laws of legal systems of the world including, as appropriate, the laws of the states that would normally have exercised jurisdiction over the case so long as they are consistent with the statute and international law. In addition to this hierarchy, the court *may* draw on its own jurisprudence from previous cases.

Even though the three categories were inspired by Article 38 of the Statute of the International Court of Justice, they are substantially and structurally different from that article. Moreover, Article 21(3) on applicable law provides its own rule of interpretation:

> The application and interpretation of law pursuant to this article must be consistent with internationally recognized human rights, and be without any adverse distinction founded on grounds such as gender . . . , age, race,

colour, language, religion or belief, political or other opinion, national, ethnic or social origin, wealth, birth or other status.

While the original intention behind this paragraph may have been to limit the courts powers in the application and interpretation of the relevant law, it could have the opposite effect and broaden the competence of the court on these matters. It provides a standard against which all the law applied by the court should be tested. This is sweeping language, and could apply to all three categories in Article 21. For instance, if the court decides that certain provisions of the Elements of Crimes or the Rules of Procedure and Evidence are not compatible with the standards set out in paragraph 3 of Article 21, it would not have to apply them. The provision also lays down special rules of interpretation for Article 21.

Crimes

One of the key issues throughout the negotiations, beginning during the deliberations of the Preparatory Committee, was which crimes should fall within the jurisdiction of the court. While there was virtually unanimous agreement on including genocide, other crimes had diverse supporters and opponents. An overwhelming majority of states supported the inclusion of war crimes, crimes against humanity, and aggression. Some states, in particular the Caribbean governments, supported inclusion of drug trafficking. Inclusion of the crime of terrorism also enjoyed some support. In addition, some states supported inclusion of crimes against the United Nations and associated personnel. During the latter part of the negotiations in the Preparatory Committee, however, support for the inclusion of drug trafficking, terrorism, and crimes against UN and associated personnel slackened, as it became clear that some states were unalterably opposed. The opposition was based on the fact that the nature of investigating the crimes of drug trafficking and terrorism, which requires long-term planning, infiltration into the organizations involved, the necessity of giving immunity to some individuals involved, and so forth, makes them better suited for national prosecution. Furthermore, their inclusion would have required revision of parts of the statute that had already been negotiated. In addition, it became clear that there was no time to secure a generally acceptable definition of terrorism and the Convention on the Safety of United Nations and Associated Personnel was not yet in force.[15] The inconclusive status of these crimes was indicated in the working document sent by the Preparatory Committee to the Rome Conference.[16]

The inclusion of the crime of aggression, which received overwhelming support in the Preparatory Committee, also faced definitional problems.

The intractable issue proved to be the role of the Security Council in the determination of aggression. While many states preferred a fixed and independent definition of aggression insusceptible to review by the Security Council, other states, including the five permanent members, took the position that the court could exercise jurisdiction with respect to this crime only after the Council determined that an act of aggression had occurred. By the end of the negotiations in the Preparatory Committee, there was a sense that the definition of aggression had become too complicated and divisive and could become a casualty in the context of a larger compromise.

The draft list of crimes that was forwarded to the Rome Conference by the Preparatory Committee listed "(a) the crime of genocide; (b) the crime of aggression; (c) war crimes; (d) crimes against humanity; and (e) [other crimes]."[17] The first four crimes were known as the "four core crimes."

At Rome, virtually all states supported inclusion in the statute of the crime of genocide, war crimes, and crimes against humanity. The conference did not have time to consider definitions of other crimes that would be acceptable to all, or to the majority of, states. As it was, even the definition of the core crimes took considerable time and ran into complications. The conference leadership appreciated that, to attract an overwhelming majority in support of the statute, some accommodation among the supporters of each of the other crimes was required. With regard to crimes against UN and associated personnel, Spain proposed language in the definition of war crimes that would have included crimes against UN personnel, obviating a separate category of crimes. This proposal was widely supported and language to that effect was eventually incorporated in Article 8(1), (b) (iii) and (e) (iii) of the statute. The crimes of terrorism and drug trafficking were included in a resolution adopted by the conference, which recommended that the Review Conference consider them with a view to arriving at an acceptable definition and their inclusion in the list of crimes within the court's jurisdiction.[18]

The crime of aggression was treated differently. At about the middle of the Rome Conference, it became clear that support for the inclusion of aggression was increasing despite the knowledge that no agreement could be reached at the conference either on its definition or on the role of the Security Council. The permanent members indicated that they could agree on the inclusion of the crime of aggression only if the proper role of the Security Council in accordance with the Charter were recognized. Many other states distinguished between the definition of aggression for the ICC and the competence of the Security Council to determine whether an act was aggression. Some of these states also contended that, while the Security Council had primary competence to determine whether an act constituted aggression, its competence on the subject was not exclusive. The support of the Non-Aligned Movement for inclusion of the crimes of aggression and the use of nuclear weapons was particularly strong. Many European states, including some NATO members, also insisted on the inclusion of aggression. Ultimately, a compromise was reached: Article 5(2) of the statute incorporates the crime of aggression, but the court may exercise jurisdiction in that regard only after the crime has been defined and the conditions for such exercise have been agreed upon. Furthermore, any provision on these issues must be consistent with the Charter of the United Nations. The latter text is intended to take account of the concerns of the permanent members of the Security Council that the statute not be used to amend the Charter by infringing on the competence of the Council to determine acts of aggression. In sum, Article 5 of the statute now lists the crime of genocide, crimes against humanity, war crimes and the crime of aggression as within the jurisdiction of the court.

Genocide, defined in Article 6, was the only crime that received a quick and unanimous consensus. Its definition follows verbatim Article II of the Convention on the Prevention and Punishment of the Crime of Genocide of 1948,[19] except for the replacement of the word "Convention" with the word "Statute" in the opening clause.

Contrary to the general expectation, crimes against humanity (Article 7) proved difficult to negotiate. In the earliest phase of negotiation in the Preparatory Committee, it became clear that a short article on crimes against humanity modeled after Article 5 of the Statute of the Yugoslav Tribunal[20] would be unacceptable to the majority of states. States also disagreed over whether the crime should be limited to acts occurring in time of armed conflict and what the threshold of gravity of the crime should be. At Rome, it was agreed that crimes against humanity are not limited to times of armed conflict but must be committed "as part of a widespread or systematic attack directed against any civilian population, with knowledge of the attack." At the earlier phases of negotiation, some states had insisted that the threshold should be raised so as to exclude crimes such as serial killings or a single murder. These states preferred that "widespread or systematic attack" be replaced with "widespread and systematic attack." Others were concerned that such a change would unnecessarily raise the threshold. Ultimately, it was agreed that the threshold would remain "widespread or systematic attack directed against any civilian population," but that the words "attack directed against any civilian population" would be defined in subparagraph 2(a) of the same article, which requires "multiple commission of acts . . . pursuant to or in furtherance of a State or organizational policy to commit such attack." Accordingly, crimes against humanity may be committed not only by or under the direction of state officials, but also by "organizations." The latter word is intended to include such groups as terrorist organizations and organizations of insurrectional or separatist movements. Therefore, the opening clause of Article 7 setting forth the general threshold for crimes against humanity should be read together with its sub-paragraph 2(a). This approach provided a basis for compromise on several other acts listed in Article 7 as crimes against humanity. Some attempts were made to include terrorism and economic embargo in the list of crimes against humanity. The proposals, however, did not generate sufficient support for acceptance.

Article 7 of the statute contains a much broader definition of crimes against humanity than those in the Statutes of the contemporary ad hoc international criminal tribunals.[21] It specifically includes rape, sexual slavery, enforced prostitution, forced pregnancy, enforced sterilization, and any other form of sexual violence of comparable gravity. The inclusion of "forced pregnancy" was passionately debated. A number of states were concerned that its inclusion could be misinterpreted to interfere with national laws concerning either the right to life of the unborn child or a woman's right to termination of pregnancy. Many Muslim states opposed it on the ground that forced pregnancy was not a new crime and was the consequence of the crime of rape, which was already included in the text. A compromise was reached to include "forced pregnancy" rather than the term "enforced pregnancy" and to define it in paragraph 2 of the article, with the hope that it could not be used in support of legalizing abortion.

Deportation or forcible transfer of population, enforced disappearance of persons and apartheid are also included in paragraph 1 and defined in paragraph 2. Deportation is defined in paragraph 2(d) as "forced displacement of the persons concerned by expulsion or other coercive acts from the area in which they are lawfully present, without grounds permitted under international law." The United States and Israel objected to the inclusion of "other coercive acts." The definition of "torture' in paragraph 2(e) excludes "lawful sanctions" to allay the concerns of some Muslim states that certain Islamic forms of punishment not be considered as "torture" within the meaning of the statute.

The act of "persecution" in paragraph 1 is defined to include acts against "any identifiable group or collectivity on political, racial, national, ethnic, cultural, religious, gender . . . , or other grounds that are universally recognized as impermissible under international law," but only in connection with other crimes and not as a separate crime. It was difficult to win consensus on persecution on grounds of "gender." Some states preferred to leave the word "gender" undefined and some delegations insisted that the word simply meant men and women as biologically defined. The issue came up in regard to other parts of the statute as well. A compromise was struck to provide a definition for "gender," applicable to the entire statute, in paragraph 3 of Article 7, where the word appears for the first time. Paragraph 3 provides: "For the purpose of this Statute, it is understood that the term 'gender' refers to the two sexes, male and female, within the context of society. The term 'gender' does not indicate any meaning different from the above."

War crimes are included in Article 8. From the start of the negotiations on the statute, war crimes proved to be one of the most intractable issues. Special difficulties arose in regard to the inclusion of certain topics: Protocol II Additional to the Geneva Conventions,[22] internal armed conflicts, nuclear weapons in the list of prohibited weapons, and child soldiers.

Some states took the position that only those war crimes that are recognized as such by customary international law should be included. This position therefore supported those crimes enumerated in the 1949 Geneva Conventions, the 1907 Hague Convention and the 1929 Geneva Convention.[23] Others pressed for extending the reach of the statute to crimes in the Protocols Additional to the Geneva Conventions. Some opposed inclusion of any crimes occurring in internal armed conflict, while others insisted that they be covered. As a result of these conflicting positions, the text of the article on war crimes was drafted in four sections: grave breaches of the 1949 Geneva Conventions, war crimes under Protocol I Additional to the Geneva Conventions,[24] violations of common Article 3 of the four Geneva Conventions, and breaches under Protocol II.[25] This structure, which had been created to facilitate negotiation, survived as the final structure of the article in the Rome statute. But the text that emerged does not always maintain the four distinct categories. It also drew from other treaties. Indeed, many of the provisions in the last category of war crimes are drawn from Protocol I, the Geneva Conventions and the Hague Conventions.[26] Although some of these norms were originally intended to apply to international armed conflicts, the drafters of the statute thought that they should also apply to internal armed conflicts.

Some states argued that the decision that the court was to have jurisdiction over serious crimes of concern to the international community necessarily implied that not every war crime would be included. "[O]nly" those crimes committed "as part of a plan or policy or as part of a large-scale commission of such crimes" would fall within its jurisdiction.[27] Some other states did not agree and felt that the word "only" would raise the threshold unnecessarily. The compromise language forged at Rome reads in Article 8(1) that "[t]he Court shall have jurisdiction in respect of war crimes in particular when committed as part of a plan or policy or as part of a large-scale commission of such crimes." The inclusion of the words "in particular" was intended to indicate the type of war crimes over which the court has jurisdiction. The language as drafted, however, does not exclude jurisdiction over a single war crime listed in the subsequent paragraphs of the article.

Paragraph 2 of Article 8 sets out four categories of war crimes: "(a) [g]rave breaches of the Geneva Conventions of 12 August 1949"; "(b) [o]ther serious violations of the laws and customs applicable in international armed conflict, within the established framework of international law"; "(c) [i]n the case of an armed conflict not of an international character, serious violations of article 3 common to the four Geneva Conventions"; and "(e) [o]ther serious violations of the laws and customs applicable in armed conflicts not of an international character, within the established framework of international law." Many of the provisions of subparagraphs 2(b) and (e) are parallel or identical.

The opening clauses of subparagraphs 2(b) and (e) are qualified by the words "within the established framework of international law." These words were intended to include implicitly considerations of the *jus in bello* such as military necessity and proportionality. Some delegations, however, expressed the view that these words also included requirements such as those in Article 85(3) and (4) of Protocol I, dealing with causing death or serious injury to body or health or when committed willfully and in violation of the Geneva Conventions or the Protocols.

The text of paragraph 2(b) (iii) and (e) (iii) of Article 8 deals with "[i]ntentionally directing attacks against personnel, installations, material, units or vehicles involved in a humanitarian assistance or peacekeeping mission in accordance with the Charter of the United Nations, as long as they are entitled to the protection given to civilians or civilian objects under the international law of armed conflict." This provision was included in place of a separate crime against United Nations and associated personnel. The latter part of the paragraph provides that the personnel, installations, material and other elements of humanitarian assistance and UN peacekeeping are protected so long as they remain civilian or civilian objects. It excludes situations in which UN personnel become involved or take part in hostilities.

The provisions in paragraph 2(b) (ix) and (e) (iv) cover "[I]ntentionally directing attacks against buildings dedicated to religion, education, art, science or charitable purposes, historic monuments, hospitals and places where the sick and wounded are collected, provided they are not military objectives." The text is based on Article 27 of Hague Convention No. IV of 1907, as well as the Convention for the Protection of Cultural Property of 1954[28] and Articles 85(4) (d) and 53 of Protocol I. The innovation in the text is the addition of "buildings dedicated to . . . education," which was originally proposed by New Zealand and Switzerland. A compromise was reached for the inclusion of these buildings by changing the last words of the paragraph from "military purposes" to "military objectives," which has a narrower reference.

Subparagraphs (e) (vi) and (b) (xxii) of Article 8(2) are parallel and deal with gender-based crimes. The difference is that the comparison in subparagraph (b) (xxii) is with the grave breaches of the Geneva Conventions, while that in subparagraph (e) (vi) is with violations of Article 3 common to the Geneva Conventions. In view of gender-based crimes in Bosnia and Rwanda, NGOs played an important role in securing the inclusion of this provision.

Subparagraphs (b) (xxvi) and (e) (vii) are parallel, dealing with enlisting children under the age of fifteen to participate in hostilities. These provisions are very much the result of inputs from NGOs. The texts are based on Article 38 of the Convention on the Rights of the Child[29] and Articles 77(2) of Protocol I and 4(3) (c) of Protocol II. The text in subparagraph (b) (xxvi) speaks of "national armed forces." The inclusion of the word "national" was intended to exclude situations like the intifada. The words "armed forces or groups" in subparagraph (e) (vii) are designed to take account of a frequent situation in internal armed conflicts, in which armed groups as well as armed forces are involved. Both subparagraphs set the age limit of children at "under the age of fifteen years," avoid the use of the word "recruited," and qualify the violation by "using them [children] to participate actively in hostilities." The word "actively" was inserted to exclude situations in which children are involved in support functions during hostilities. Attempts were made by some states and NGOs to raise the age of the children to eighteen to make it compatible with the definition under the Convention on the Rights of the Child, Article 1 of which defines the child as every human being below the age of eighteen. These attempts, however, faced strong resistance by other states, which relied on the age of below fifteen in Article 77 of Protocol I, as well as Article 38 of the Convention on the Rights of the Child.

Two issues concerning prohibited weapons raised problems: nuclear weapons and the inclusion of general language that could prohibit the use of future weapons with particular characteristics. The inclusion of nuclear weapons, which was supported by the majority of the participating states, was strongly opposed by some major nuclear powers. To encourage at least some of the major nuclear powers to support adoption of the statute, the reference to nuclear weapons was finally deleted. The inclusion of prospectively prohibitive language, which would have provided a general description of weapons that could be prohibited at some stage in the future, was opposed by more states. In their view, such a catchall and open-ended clause was incompatible with the principle of legality requiring absolute clarity in a criminal code. They insisted that the prohibition of any weapon should be clearly stated in the statute before its use becomes criminalized. As a compromise, subparagraph (b) (xx) prescribes three criteria for the inclusion of new weapons whose use will be considered war crimes. First, new weapons must be "of a nature to cause superfluous injury or unnecessary suffering or which are inherently indiscriminate in violation of the international law of armed conflict." Second, such weapons must be the "subject of a comprehensive prohibition." Third, such weapons must be "included in an annex to this Statute, by an amendment in accordance with the relevant provisions set forth in articles 121 and 123." The language of subparagraph (b) (xx) leaves open the possibility of including nuclear weapons. However, nuclear weapons or any new weapons can be included only through an amendment or review procedure of the statute, which cannot begin until the expiry of seven years after its entry into force (Articles 121 [1] and 123[1]). Moreover, even were a new weapon to be included among the list of prohibited weapons by amending the statute, its prohibition would be binding only on those states that had ratified the amendment.

Both subparagraphs 2(c) and (e) dealing with internal armed conflict had to be qualified to forge consensus. Subparagraph 2(d) qualifies subparagraph (c) by providing that it does not apply to "situations of internal disturbances and tensions, such as riots, isolated and sporadic acts of violence or other acts of a similar nature." Subparagraph 2(f), qualifying subparagraph (e), further provides that it applies "to armed conflicts that take place in the territory of a State when there is protracted armed conflict between governmental authorities and organized armed groups or between such groups." This language is based on Article 1(1) of Protocol II with the aim of further clarifying the scope of the subparagraph.

Paragraph 3 of Article 8 is based on Article 3 of Protocol II, dealing with nonintervention in the internal affairs of states. It was introduced to assuage the concerns of some states. Paragraph 3 provides that nothing in the subparagraphs dealing with internal armed conflicts "shall affect the responsibility of a Government to maintain or reestablish law and order in the State or to defend the unity and territorial integrity of the State, by all legitimate means."

In the latter part of the negotiations in the Preparatory Committee, the United States proposed the inclusion of elements of crimes. The proposal was first raised in connection with the definition of war crimes. Later, however, it was expanded to deal with genocide and crimes against humanity. The United States took the position that the crimes in the statute are not sufficiently defined and that the principle of legality dictated a further and full definition of their elements. The majority of states opposed the inclusion of the elements of crimes on two grounds: it would delay the adoption of the statute, its coming into force and the establishment of the court; and it was superfluous, since all the necessary elements were already included in either the definition of crimes or Part 3, General Principles of Criminal Law. Many delegations were concerned that it would be extremely difficult to reach an agreement on detailed elaborations of the elements of crimes, taking into account, among other factors, the differences in the criminal laws of civil and common law countries, as well as the different approaches to criminal law of individual states. A further concern was that any detailed elaboration of the elements of crimes might narrow their definition in the statute and thus introduce a substantive change into the statute.

As a compromise, it was agreed to include elements of crimes in Article 9, on the condition that their preparation and adoption should be separate from those of the statute, and should not affect its adoption, its entry into force or the operation of the court. Article 9, Elements of Crimes, provides that these elements shall assist the court in the interpretation and application of Articles 6, 7 and 8—which define the three crimes. "Elements of Crimes" and any subsequent amendments to it must be approved by a two-thirds majority of the members of the Assembly of States Parties. Furthermore, the Elements of Crimes and its amendments must be consistent with the statute. . . .

During the preparatory phase, in 1997, a number of states were concerned about what they considered a "conservative" approach to the definition of war crimes and feared that such an approach might prevail and, as a result, hamper the development of international law in this area. This concern led to a suggestion that language be included somewhere in the statute to the effect that nothing in it "shall be interpreted as limiting or prejudicing in any way existing or developing rules of international law."[30] During the Rome Conference, however, the tenor of negotiations over war crimes changed substantially. The war crimes definition is anything but conservative and the definition of crimes against humanity is much broader than what was anticipated during the earlier phases of the negotiations.[31] The interest in the safeguard language now shifted from protecting the future development of international law to shielding the statute from such developments. Article 10 deals with jurisdiction *ratione temporis* and reads: "Nothing in this Part [part 2 of the statute] shall be interpreted as limiting or prejudicing in any way existing or developing rules of international law for purposes other than this Statute."[32]

The crimes under the statute, because of their seriousness, are not subject to any statute of limitations (Article 29).

General Principles of Criminal Law

Part 3, General Principles of Criminal Law, composed of twelve articles, sets out the statute's substantive criminal law, including the basis for individual criminal responsibility and grounds for excluding criminal responsibility. This part states clearly that the court has jurisdiction over "natural persons" (Article 25[1]). But the court lacks jurisdiction over any person under the age of eighteen at the time the crime was committed (Article 26). During the preparatory phase, France proposed extending the court's jurisdiction to organizations. That proposal was addressed at Rome but could not gather sufficient support and was dropped. Articles 22 and 23 deal with the principles of *nullum crimen sine lege* and *nulla poena sine lege*.

An individual is responsible for an act or omission. The word "conduct" is used throughout the statute as including acts and omissions. An individual is criminally responsible for the commission of the crime, whether as an individual or jointly; ordering, soliciting or inducing the commission of a crime that in fact occurs or is attempted; or facilitating the commission of a crime, or aiding, abetting or otherwise assisting in its commission or attempted commission (Article 25). An individual may also be criminally responsible for, in any other way, intentionally contributing to the commission or the attempted commission of a crime by a group of persons acting with a common purpose, when that contribution is made with the "aim of furthering the criminal activity or criminal purpose of the group, where such activity or purpose involves the commission of a crime within the jurisdiction of the Court," or is "made in the knowledge of the intention of the group to commit the crime."[33] This language is intended to include other forms of participation, including conspiracy, a concept that does not exist as such in civil law systems. It was taken verbatim from Article 2(3) (c) of the International Convention for the Suppression of Terrorist Bombings,[34] which in turn was taken from a treaty on extradition of the European Union.[35] In cases of genocide, an individual would also have criminal responsibility for direct and public incitement.[36] The attempt to commit a crime is also a criminal act so long as the individual has taken substantial steps toward commission of the crime, even if the crime does not occur because of circumstances independent of the individual's intention.[37]

The official position of the individual or any immunity or special procedural rules that may attach to the individual because of his or her official capacity will not bar the jurisdiction of the court (Article 27). During the preparatory phase of the negotiations, two basic issues were raised in relation to command responsibility: first, whether command responsibility was a form of criminal responsibility in addition to other forms of responsibility or whether it expressed a different principle, to the effect that commanders are not immune from responsibility for the acts of their subordinates; and second, whether command responsibility should extend to any superior in a nonmilitary setting. The Rome Conference answered both questions in the affirmative. Article 28 deals with the responsibility of commanders and other superiors with respect to the criminal acts of subordinates under their effective authority and control. The words "effective authority and control" are intended to superimpose in a civilian setting the requirements of the same types of relationships between superior and subordinate in the military.

Articles 31 and 32 address grounds for excluding criminal responsibility. Superior orders and prescription of law are not grounds for excluding criminal responsibility unless the person was under a legal obligation to obey such orders, the person did not know that the order was unlawful, *and* the order was not manifestly unlawful (Article 33). The first part of this three-part exception is included because a superior order, under the statute, applies to civilians, as well as to the military. Orders to commit genocide or crimes against humanity are manifestly unlawful.[38]

Organization of the Court

Part 4, Composition and Administration of the Court, comprises nineteen articles. The court will be composed of four organs: the Presidency; an Appeals, a Pre-Trial and a Trial Division; the Office of the Prosecutor; and the Registry (Article 34). The court is to have eighteen judges, nominated and elected by states parties (Article 36). They will be elected as full-time personnel and shall be available to serve on that basis (Article 35). But the statute anticipates that some of the judges, other than the president and vice-presidents, may be part-time depending on the court's workload.

As regards the qualification of judges, there were extensive discussions on the relative proportion between judges with criminal law experience and those with international and humanitarian law experience. At the end, a compromise was reached, dividing the bench between at least nine judges with a criminal law background and at least five with an international and humanitarian law background (Article 36). Throughout the preparatory phase of negotiations, there was support for placing an age limit on the nominees. The age requirement was dropped at the Rome Conference. Some states preferred to have a system of screening the nominations of judges by which a short list could be prepared. Other states did not find the idea appealing. At the end, there was a compromise, by which the Assembly of States Parties may decide to establish an Advisory Committee on nominations.[39] While the judges must be the nationals of states parties, there is no such restriction on the prosecutor, who will also be elected by states parties, and the registrar, who will be elected by the judges.[40] The official languages of the court will be the official languages of the United Nations, but the working languages will be English and French.[41]

At the first election, one-third of the judges (six judges) will serve by lot for a term of three years, one-third for a term of six years, and the remainder for a term of nine years. Except for the judges who will serve for a three-year term, the other judges may not stand for reelection (Article 36).

The Rules of Procedure and Evidence will enter into force when adopted by a two-thirds majority of states parties (Article 51). In case of conflict between the Rules of Procedure and Evidence and the statute, the statute will prevail. The court's regulations will be adopted by an absolute majority of the judges (Article 52).

Investigation, Prosecution and Trial

Part 5, Investigation and Prosecution, consists of nine articles. It addresses the steps to be taken to initiate investigations, the rights of the person under investigation, and other requirements to be complied with before trial. During the preparatory phase, the question of how to address amnesties and truth commissions was never seriously discussed, in part because of pressure from the human rights groups. The same evasive approach was taken at Rome. The statute does not preclude the court's competence over criminal conduct of individuals covered by amnesties or truth commissions. But it allows the prosecutor not to proceed with an investigation if it would not serve the interests of justice (Article 53). Such a decision by the prosecutor may be reversed by the pretrial chamber.[42] This chamber may issue an arrest warrant on the prosecutor's application if it is satisfied that there are reasonable grounds to believe that the person committed a crime within the court's jurisdiction (Article 58). The custodial state is expected to comply with the order (Article 59). The pretrial chamber must hold hearings to confirm charges in the presence of the person charged. However, in exceptional circumstances, the chamber may hold a hearing in the absence of the person charged (Article 61). At the request of the prosecutor, the pretrial chamber may also take measures necessary to avail itself of a unique opportunity to collect evidence that may not be available subsequently for the purposes of a trial (Article 56). These measures must take into account the efficiency and integrity of the proceedings and the rights of the defense.

Part 6, The Trial, contains fifteen articles. It addresses the conduct of the trial, rights of the accused, protection of victims and witnesses, and admissibility of evidence. Trial must be in the presence of the accused (Article 63). Due process for the accused and his or her rights are fully recognized. The presumption of innocence is established in Article 66. The accused is entitled, inter alia, to having a public and fair hearing conducted impartially and without delay; being promptly informed of the charges in a language he or she fully understands and speaks; having adequate time and facilities to prepare a defense and to examine witnesses against him or her before and during the trial; having the free assistance of a competent interpreter and necessary translations; and not being compelled to testify or confess guilt.[43] The question of protection of national security information was of particular concern to major powers. The text that emerged leaves the final decision on whether the disclosure of information would prejudice its national security to the state itself (Article 72). The state, however, is obliged to cooperate with the court to see how the matter can be resolved. Use of *in camera* or *ex parte* proceedings, summaries or redactions of disclosure of the information, as well as other permissible protective measures, is allowed. But the state still has wide latitude in deciding on the disclosure of evidence in any form.

Reparation to victims was raised during the preparatory phase of the negotiations. There was some opposition to the idea on the ground that the statute establishes a criminal court that will not be equipped to address reparations. There were also concerns about the sources from which reparation may be made and enforcement of an order of reparations by the court. At Rome, the subject attracted more interest, particularly from France, the United Kingdom and many NGOs. The result was the inclusion of Article 75, which requires the court to establish principles relating to reparations to victims, including restitution, compensation and rehabilitation. The court may make an order directly against a convicted person for reparations. States parties to the statute are required to enforce the court's order.[44] To the same effect, the statute provides for a trust fund to be established for the benefit of the victims and their families (Article 79). Forfeiture of proceeds, property and assets derived directly or indirectly from the crime may be imposed as a penalty, subject to the rights of bona fide third parties. The statute does not define bona fide third parties or specify under what system of law it should be defined. Presumably, conflict-of-laws methods would have to determine that question. The fines or forfeiture ordered by the court may be transferred to the trust fund for the benefit of victims and their families (Article 79). When reparations to victims were taken up, some states raised the question of reparations for individuals who are unlawfully arrested or detained. Article 85 was included to address this concern. It provides that anyone "who has been the victim of unlawful arrest or detention shall have an enforceable right to compensation." Similarly, when a person has been wrongly convicted of a crime and subsequent evidence shows a clear miscarriage of justice, that person is entitled to compensation.

Part 7, Penalties, is composed of four articles. The question of the death penalty was difficult to negotiate because its supporters could not agree to its exclusion from the statute, lest it undermine their own national laws permitting capital punishment. With the leadership of Norway, a compromise formula was reached (Article 77): the death penalty was excluded from the statute, but the President of the Rome Conference read a statement in the plenary to the effect that there was no international consensus on the inclusion or exclusion of the death penalty. That statement indicated that, by virtue of the principle of complementarity, national jurisdictions have the primary responsibility for investigating, prosecuting and punishing individuals in accordance with their own laws.[45] Under this compromise, one may note, a person convicted of a crime under the statute may receive the death penalty in a national court, but not under the statute if that person was convicted for the same crime by the ICC. This understanding is confirmed by Article 80 on nonprejudice to the national application of penalties and national laws.

Part 8, Appeal and Revision, consisting of five articles, allows for the decision of the trial chamber to be appealed by either the prosecutor or the convicted person. Other decisions that may be appealed include those regarding jurisdiction and admissibility, the grant or denial of release of the person investigated or accused, the fair and expeditious conduct of proceedings, and functions and powers of the pretrial chamber.[46] Some of the proceedings will be heard on an expedited basis (Article 82). The appeals chamber may reverse or amend the decision or a sentence or may order a new trial before a different trial chamber (Article 83).

Judicial Assistance

Part 9, International Cooperation and Judicial Assistance, contains seventeen articles. States parties to the statute are obliged to cooperate with the court and they shall ensure that their domestic laws provide for the forms of cooperation specified under the statute (Articles 86 and 88). The articles of this part, however, recognize that compliance with the court's requests should be in accordance with domestic procedural law. When a state party receives a request from both the court and another state to surrender an indicted person for the same crime, it shall give priority to the court's request if the court has already determined that the case is admissible. Otherwise, the state is free to decide which request to execute. In cases where the competing requests are for the same person but not for the same crime, the state party shall give priority to the court's request (Article 90). States parties are obliged to cooperate with the court in respect of other matters, such as the service of documents, facilitating the appearance of witnesses or experts, the examination of sites, execution of searches and seizures, the protection of victims and witnesses, and the preservation of evidence (Article 93). A state party may postpone execution of a request from the court, if it decides that it will interfere with an ongoing investigation or prosecution or the admissibility of the case is being challenged before the court (Articles 94 and 95). While the rule of speciality is recognized in the statute, a state party may waive it, either on its own initiative or at the court's request (Article 101). The court is to report noncooperation by states parties to the Assembly of States Parties or the Security Council, if the matter was referred to the court by the Council.

Article 98 deals with a conflict between the obligations of a state toward the ICC and toward another state under international law. In this context, two issues were of particular concern to the negotiators of the Rome statute: first, the ICC's request for surrender of a person or property that enjoys diplomatic immunity in the territory of the requested state; and second, the ICC's request for surrender of a non-national and the obligation of the requested state toward the state of nationality of that person, which requires the consent of that state. Paragraph 1 of Article 98 addresses the first issue by barring the ICC from requesting a surrender or assistance that would require the requested state to act inconsistently with its obligations under international law with respect to immunity of a person or property of a third state, unless the court can first obtain the consent of the third state for the waiver of the immunity. Paragraph 2 addresses the second question. The main concern in this paragraph is to respect the obligations of host states under status-of-forces agreements. Under these agreements, the forces of a sending state may remain under its jurisdiction for some or all matters, and not under that of the host state. In accordance with paragraph 2, where there are such international agreements, unless the court first obtains the consent of the sending state, it may not request a surrender of its nationals from the host state.

Other Matters

Part 10, Enforcement, includes nine articles. A sentence of imprisonment shall be served in a state chosen by the court from a list of states that have indicated their willingness to accept sentenced persons (Article 103). The court shall supervise the enforcement of conditions of imprisonment, which is governed by the law of the state of enforcement and must be consistent with widely accepted international treaty standards governing the treatment of prisoners (Article 106).

Part 11 consists of a single article establishing the Assembly of States Parties.[47] The function of the Assembly of States Parties is to provide oversight for the court and its operation. Non-states parties that have signed the statute or the Final Act may be observers in the assembly. The assembly is to approve the budget of the court, decide on the number of judges, and deal with noncooperation, or perform any other function consistent with the statute and the Rules of Procedure and Evidence. The Assembly of States Parties will meet once a year at the seat of the court or at the headquarters of the United Nations. Decisions on matters of substance shall be taken by a two-thirds majority of those present and voting, provided that an absolute majority of states parties constitutes the quorum for voting. On procedural matters, decisions of the assembly may be taken by a simple majority of states parties present and voting.

Financing of the court is addressed in the six articles of part 12. Expenses shall be paid from assessed contributions made by states parties and funds provided by the United Nations, subject to the approval of the General Assembly, in particular in relation to expenses incurred in cases of referral by the Security Council (Articles 114 and 115). The court may also receive funds from governments and nongovernmental entities and individuals.

The ten articles of part 13 constitute the final clauses. The court has competence to decide on any dispute regarding its "judicial functions" (Article 119). This broad competence encompasses not only the court's jurisdiction, but also other matters, including requests for judicial cooperation. Any other dispute between states parties relating to the interpretation or application of the statute that is not settled through negotiations within three months shall be referred to the Assembly of States Parties. It is for the assembly to decide how to settle the matter, including whether it should be referred to the International Court of Justice.[48]

The question of reservations was discussed intensely during the preparatory phase. Some states preferred the possibility of reservations to some articles or no provision on reservations, in which case the Vienna Convention on the Law of Treaties would apply.[49] The majority of states, however, felt that reservations could undermine the statute. Consequently, no reservations are allowed (Article 120), but a state party may opt out of the provision giving the ICC jurisdiction over war crimes for a period of seven years (Article 124). However, there may be situations in which a conflict of jurisdiction may arise as between two states parties in relation to war crimes. For example, the territorial state has consented to the court's jurisdiction unconditionally, while the state of nationality of the accused has opted out of the court's jurisdiction over war crimes for seven years. The statute is silent on the interpretation of Article 12 on the jurisdiction of the court in the event of such a conflict.

Seven years after the entry into force of the statute, any state party may propose amendments to it. Amendments, if not adopted by consensus, require a two-thirds majority of states parties (Article 121). One year after the deposit of instruments of ratification by seven-eighths of the state parties, the amendments will become binding on all states.[50] States that do not accept an amendment have one year to withdraw from the statute with immediate effect.[51] However, any amendments to the articles dealing with the list of crimes and their definitions will be binding only on those states that have ratified them.[52] Amendments to a limited number of articles of an institutional nature will enter into force for all states parties six months after their adoption by a two-thirds majority of states parties (Article 122). The first Review Conference of the statute will take place seven years after its entry into force and, thereafter, at the request of any state party with the approval of the majority of states parties (Article 123).

In addition to the articles on amendments to the statute, Articles 9 and 51 require a two-thirds majority of states parties for the adoption of the Elements of Crimes and Rules of Procedure and Evidence. The Rules of Procedure and Evidence will enter into force once adopted as such. The Elements of Crimes, however, requires ratification by seven-eighths of states parties.[53] States may withdraw from the statute. Withdrawal will take effect one year after the date of notification of withdrawal (Article 127). . . .

Notes

1. GA Res. 44/39, UN GAOR, 44th Sess., Supp. No. 49, at 311, UN Doc. A/44/49 (1989). The revival of the idea of establishing an international criminal court was initiated by Trinidad and Tobago in 1989 in connection with illicit trafficking in narcotic drugs across national frontiers and other transnational criminal activities. *See* Letter dated 21 August 1989 from the Permanent Representative of Trinidad and Tobago to the Secretary-General, UN GAOR, 44th Sess., Annex 44, Agenda Item 152, UN Doc. A/44/195 (1989).

2. GA Res. 47/33, UN GAOR, 47th Sess., Supp. No. 49, at 287, UN Doc. A/47/49 (1992); and GA Res. 48/31, UN GAOR, 48th Sess., Supp. No. 49, at 328, UN Doc. A/48/49 (1993).

3. *See* Report of the International Law Commission on the work of its forty-sixth session, UN GAOR, 49th Sess., Supp. No. 10, at 44, UN Doc. A/49/10 (1994).

4. GA Res. 49/53, UN GAOR, 49th Sess., Supp. No. 49, at 239, UN Doc. A/49/49 (1994).

5. For a record of the discussions in the Preparatory Committee, see the series of reports by Christopher Keith Hall in 91 AJIL 177 (1997), and 92 AJIL 124, 331, and 548 (1998).

6. UN Doc. A/CONF. 183/2/Add.1 (1998).

7. An account of the negotiating process at the Rome Conference by Mr. Kirsch and John T. Holmes appears *supra* at p. 2.

8. After its adoption, the statute was found to contain a number of technical and typographical errors. In accordance with established practice, the depository circulated a note to governments, correcting the statute.

9. For the text, see Rome Statute of the International Criminal Court, July 17, 1998, UN Doc. A/CONF.183/95 <www.un.org/icc> *reprinted in* 37 ILM 999 (1998) [hereinafter ICC statute].

10. UN Doc. A/AC.249/1998/L.13 (1998).

11. The first chapter of the Statute of the International Court of Justice begins with the organization of the Court and the jurisdiction of the Court begins with Article 34 as chapter 2.

12. Partly owing to time constraints, the International Law Commission's approach to the draft statute was to prepare a slim statute dealing with the essentials. The Commission also set aside the question of substantive criminal law and criminal procedure in the belief that the definition of crimes and other substantive criminal law were addressed in another topic before it, the draft Code of Crimes against the Peace and Security of Mankind. In addition, the Commission took the

view that rules of criminal procedure will be covered in a separate document that will be prepared by the judges of the court. The General Assembly's Sixth Committee, however, after receiving the Commission's report, took a different position. It preferred a more elaborated statute that would leave less to interpretation by judges. It also preferred to separate the statute from the project on the draft code and decided that states and not judges should write the articles dealing with procedure. As a result, the statute grew substantially in size. At the latter phases of the preparatory negotiations, a sentiment formed that it would have been preferable to move some of the provisions of the statute, particularly those dealing with procedural issues, to the Rules of Procedure and Evidence and address them in only a general fashion in the statute.

13. This is one of the important differences between the ICC and the two ad hoc Tribunals on the former Yugoslavia and Rwanda. Under Article 9 of the Statute of the Yugoslav Tribunal and Article 8 of that of the Rwanda Tribunal, in case of concurrent jurisdiction by the Tribunals and national courts, the Tribunals have primacy over national courts.

In the original request for the establishment of an international criminal court. Trinidad and Tobago's concern was the inadequacy of national criminal laws and jurisdiction to deal with drug trafficking. *See* Letter from the Permanent Representative of Trinidad and Tobago, *supra* note 1. Some of the concerns of smaller states were that, in relation to certain crimes such as drug trafficking and terrorism, the fragile national courts could not withstand the power and terror that those involved in such activities could bring about, which could destabilize even governments themselves. An international criminal court could replace national courts on such prosecutions and remove the pressure from those courts. This idea was not acceptable to the great majority of the states negotiating the statute.

14. Article 103 of the UN Charter, in accordance with which the member states' obligations under the Charter prevail over any other international obligations, will not directly overcome this problem. Article 103 binds the states but not the court. The court, under Article 17 of its statute, is obliged to determine that a case is inadmissible when certain conditions are met. The states in whose favor a decision of admissibility is made may then renounce their rights under the statute and consent to the court's exercise of jurisdiction.

15. GA Res. 49/59, UN GAOR, 49th Sess., Supp. No. 49, at 299, UN Doc. A/49/49 (1994), *reprinted in* 34 ILM 482 (1995). Under Article 27, 22 ratifications were necessary for the Convention to enter into force. The 22d instrument of ratification was deposited by New Zealand on December 16, 1998, and the Convention entered into force on January 15, 1999.

16. UN Doc. A/CONF.183/2/Add.1 n.18 (1998).

17. Id. Art. 5, at 11.

18. *See* Final Act of the United Nations Diplomatic Conference of Plenipotentiaries on the Establishment of an International Criminal Court, Res. E, UN Doc. A/CONF.183/1O*, at 7 (1998) [hereinafter Final Act].

19. Dec. 9, 1948, 78 UNTS 277.

20. UN Doc. 5/25704, annex, *reprinted in* 32 ILM 1192 (1993). For additional discussion, see the report by Darryl Robinson on the negotiation of the article on crimes against humanity, *infra* p. 43.

21. The Statute of the Yugoslav Tribunal in its Article 5 and the Statute of the Rwanda Tribunal in its Article 3 list the following acts as crimes against humanity: murder; extermination; enslavement; deportation; imprisonment; torture; rape; persecutions on political, racial, and religions grounds; and other inhumane acts. For

the Rwanda Statute, see SC Res. 955, annex (Nov. 8, 1994), *reprinted in* 33 ILM 1602 (1994).

22. Protocol Additional to the Geneva Conventions of 12 August 1949, and Relating to the Protection of Victim of Non-International Armed Conflicts, June 8, 1977, 1125 UNTS 609 [hereinafter Protocol II].

23. *See,* respectively, [Geneva] Convention for the Amelioration of the Condition of the Wounded and Sick in Armed Forces in the Field, Aug. 12, 1949, 6 UST 3114, 75 UNTS 31; [Hague] Convention [No. IV] Respecting the Laws and Customs of War on Land, with annexed Regulations, Oct. 18, 1907, 36 Stat. 2277, 1 Bevans 631; and [Geneva] Convention Relative to the Treatment of Prisoners of War, July 18, 1929, 118 LNTS 303.

24. Protocol Additional to the Geneva Conventions of 12 August 1949, and Relating to the Protection of Victims of International Armed Conflicts, June 8, 1977, 1125 UNTS 3 [hereinafter Protocol I].

25. The four Geneva Conventions deal with the law of armed conflict of an international character and the protection of civilians. The Geneva Conventions are mostly concerned with the protection of persons in the power of a party to the hostilities. Article 3 of the four Geneva Conventions establishes standards for noninternational armed conflicts. Protocol I supplements the four Geneva Conventions for international armed conflicts. Protocol II deals with noninternational armed conflicts.

26. For the 1907 Hague Convention No. IV, see *supra* note 23. [Hague] Convention [No. II] with Respect to the Laws and Customs of War on Land, with annexed Regulations, July 29, 1899, 32 Stat. 1803, 1 Bevans 247; [Geneva] Convention for the Amelioration of the Condition of the Wounded and Sick in Armed Forces in the Field, *supra* note 23; [Geneva] Convention for the Amelioration of the Condition of the Wounded, Sick, and Shipwrecked Members of Armed Forces at Sea, Aug. 12, 1949, 6 UST 3217, 75 UNTS 85; [Geneva] Convention Relative to the Treatment of Prisoners of War, Aug. 12, 1949, 6 UST 3316, 75 UNTS 135; [Geneva] Convention Relative to the Protection of Civilian Persons in Time of War, Aug. 12, 1949, 6 UST 3516, 75 UNTS 287. For Protocol I, see *supra* note 24; and for Protocol II, see *supra* note 22.

27. *See* "Elsewhere in the Statute," UN Doc. A/CONF.183/2/Add.1, at 25 (1998).

28. Convention for the Protection of Cultural Property in the Event of Armed Conflict, May 14, 1954, 249 UNTS 240.

29. GA Res. 44/25, UN GAOR, 44th Sess., Supp. No. 49, at 166, UN Doc. A/44/49 (1989), *reprinted in* 28 ILM 1448 (1989), 29 id. at 1340 (1990).

30. *See* UN Doc. A/CONF.183/2/Add.1, at 25, Art. Y (1998).

31. Crimes against humanity are not limited to those occurring during armed conflicts but also include those committed in time of peace and encompass other crimes covered by the Statutes of the two ad hoc Tribunals. Despite the original intention of including only war crimes under customary international law, some of the crimes found in Article 8 had not theretofore been recognized as customary. See the discussion on crimes against humanity and war crimes above.

32. Article 10 was negotiated at the last minute and is the only article in the statute without a title.

33. *See* ICC statute, *supra* note 9, Art. 25, para. 2(d).

34. GA Res. 52/164, UN GAOR, 52d Sess., Supp. No. 49, at 389, UN DOC. A/52/49 (1998). It was adopted on Jan. 9, 1998.

35. Convention drawn up on the basis of Article K.3 of the Treaty on European Union relating to Extradition between the Member States of the European Union, Sept 27, 1996. 1996 O.J. (C 313) 3.

36. ICC statute, *supra* note 9, Art. 33, para. 2.

37. Id., Art. 25. para. 5(f).

38. Id., Art. 33, para. 2.

39. Id., Art. 36, para. 4(c).

40. Id., Art. 43, para. 4.

41. Id., Art. 50.

42. The pretrial chamber may review the decision by the prosecutor not to proceed with prosecution either at the request of the state concerned or the Security Council, if they had referred the matter to the court, or on its own initiative. Id, Art. 53, para. 3.

43. Id, Arts. 63–67.

44. Id., Art. 75, para. 2.

45. The following statement with regard to the noninclusion of the death penalty in the statute was read by the President of the Rome Conference on July 17, 1998, at the last meeting of the plenary:

> The debate at this Conference on the issue of which penalties should be applied by the Court has shown that there is no international consensus on the inclusion or non-inclusion of the death penalty. However, in accordance with the principle of complementarity between the Court and national jurisdictions, national justice systems have the primary responsibility for investigating, prosecuting and punishing individuals, in accordance with their national laws, for crimes falling under the jurisdiction of the International Criminal Court. In this regard, the Court would clearly not be able to affect national policies in this field. It should be noted that not including the death penalty in the Statute would not in any way have a legal bearing on national legislation and practices with regard to the death penalty. Nor shall it be considered as influencing the development of customary international law or in any other way the legality of penalties imposed by national systems for serious crimes.

46. ICC statute, *supra* note 9, Art. 81.

47. Id., Art. 112.

48. 1d., Art. 119.

49. Opened for signature May 23, 1969, Art. 19, 1155 UNTS 331.

50. ICC statute, *supra* note 9, Art. 121, para. 4.

51. Id., Art. 121, para. 6.

52. Id., Art. 121, para. 5.

53. Id., Art. 121, para. 4.

PART 2.1

International Law
as Normative System:
To Regulate the Use of Force

14

International Law
and the Recourse to Force:
A Shift in Paradigms

ANTHONY CLARK AREND AND ROBERT J. BECK

> The point is that international law is not higher law or better law; it is
> *existing* law. It is not a law that eschews force; such a view is alien to the
> very idea of law. Often as not it is the law of the victor; but it is law withal
> and does evolve.[1]
>
> Daniel Patrick Moynihan

Introduction

When the framers of the United Nations Charter met in San Francisco, they
hoped to establish a new world order—one in which the recourse to force
would be severely restricted. To this end, they formulated the United
Nations Charter paradigm for the *jus ad bellum*. Three components set the
parameters of this paradigm: 1) a legal obligation; 2) institutions to enforce
the obligation; and 3) a value hierarchy that formed the philosophical basis
of this obligation.

The first of these components, the legal obligation, was embodied in
Article 2(4) of the Charter. States were to refrain from any threat or use of
force against the political or territorial status quo or in any other way
against the principles of the United Nations. The only exceptions to this
general prohibition were 1) force used in self-defense as defined in Article
51, and 2) force authorized by the Security Council in accordance with the
provisions of Chapter VII.

The second component, the international institutions, were established
under Chapter VII of the Charter. Under these provisions, the Security

Anthony Clark Arend and Robert J. Beck, *International Law and the Use of Force,*
London: Routledge, 1993, pp. 177–202. Reprinted with permission of Routledge
and the authors.

Council is empowered to investigate international conflicts and determine if there is a threat to the peace, a breach of the peace, or an act of aggression. If the Council so determines, it is further authorized to take collective action against the recalcitrant state.

The third element of the Charter paradigm is the underlying value hierarchy. When the Charter was drafted, even though the framers proclaimed many goals for the new international organization, its preeminent goal was the maintenance of international peace and security. This goal of peace was to take priority over other goals of justice. Justice was to be sought, but not at the expense of peace. Given the experience of the first two world wars, the framers believed that more damage was done to the international system by taking up arms to fight for justice than by living with a particular injustice.

The preceding analysis reveals, however, that since the Second World War, a number of significant developments have challenged the validity of this Charter paradigm. These include such problems as the failure of international institutions and the emergence of new values concerning the recourse to force. Although most international legal scholars would contend that these post-war developments represent serious threats to the Charter paradigm, few would claim that they are indicative of a paradigmatic shift. We reject this contention. Our conclusion is that in the world since 1945, a new legal paradigm has indeed emerged: a 'post-Charter self-help' paradigm. This paradigm, we argue, is at present the best framework for understanding the contemporary law relating to the recourse to force. But even as this second paradigm may currently describe existing law, recent events in the Middle East, Eastern Europe, Central America, Africa, and elsewhere suggest that a third paradigm may be emerging, a 'prodemocratic' paradigm.

This chapter will attempt to provide an analytical framework for understanding these conclusions. In order to do so, the first section will outline the contours of the post-Charter self-help paradigm. The second section will explore the possible emergence of a new, pro-democratic paradigm. Finally, the third section will examine the future direction of the *jus ad bellum* and make recommendations for its development.

The Post-Charter Self-Help Paradigm

Not long after the Charter was adopted, changes in the international system began to challenge the efficacy of this framework for the recourse to force, leading ultimately to the emergence of a new paradigm. In order to understand the nature of this paradigm, let us examine three elements: 1) the failure of Charter institutions; 2) the emergence of a new value hierarchy; and, 3) the changed legal obligation.

The Failure of Charter Institutions

Since 1945 several major problems have developed with the system for the collective use of force established by the Charter. These include the veto, the inability to establish formal mechanisms for collective action, and the general rejection of limited collective security. Even though world leaders and scholars made efforts to respond to these problems, these efforts showed little promise. Using the General Assembly as a substitute for the Security Council only really worked in the case of Korea. And in that case, the Security Council has already authorized the initial action. In subsequent uses of force, the Assembly has not been able to respond effectively to challenge an act of aggression. Similarly, the use of regional arrangements has not proved very successful. Such arrangements have responded only selectively to uses of force by states and have frequently been perceived as little more than a fig leaf for great power actions. Finally, peacekeeping, which developed in the wake of the failure of limited collective security, cannot be considered as a substitute. Peacekeeping explicitly recognizes that collective action to fight aggression is unlikely. It comes into play only after the hostilities have ceased and the parties consent to international supervision. Peacekeeping is thus not a legitimate alternative to the Chapter VII approach to collective enforcement.

In short, in the post-Charter period, international institutions have failed to deter or combat aggression. The international community has faltered in its efforts to address this profound problem.

A New Value Hierarchy

As observed previously, the Charter paradigm for the recourse to force was predicated upon the assumption that 'peace' was more important than justice. In the post-1945 world, however, states have repudiated this hierarchy of values. In many diverse sectors of the international system, claims have been made that force against the existing political and territorial order may, at times, be justified. These claims seem to have manifested themselves in three different ways: 1) claims to use force to promote self-determination; 2) claims to resort to 'just' reprisals; and, 3) claims to use force to correct past 'injustices.'

These claims suggest that the members of the international system have rejected the philosophical underpinnings of the Charter paradigm. Rather than believing that more injury to world order occurs when force is used to pursue just goals, states have come to believe that, at certain times, it is better to break the peace in the name of justice, than to live with the injustice. At times, justice must take precedence over peace.

A Changed Legal Obligation

The Death of Article 2(4)

The failure of Charter institutions to enforce norms relating to the recourse to force and the changing value hierarchy have obliged many scholars to rethink the status of the contemporary *jus ad bellum*. In short, scholars have been compelled to ask whether Article 2(4) is still good international law. We have argued that a putative norm is a rule of international law only if it is authoritative and controlling. As a consequence, for Article 2(4)'s proscription to be regarded as genuine law, its authority and control must be clearly demonstrated.

A review of scholarship and practice suggests three fundamental approaches to this question. The first has been labelled the 'legalist' approach; the second the 'core interpretist' approach; and the third the 'rejectionist' approach.[2] This section will examine each of these three approaches in turn and conclude that the 'rejectionist' approach reflects most accurately the reality of the international system.

The Legalist Approach. A significant number of international publicists might be considered 'legalists.'[3] These legal scholars, while recognizing that problems exist, adhere to the basic belief that the principle enunciated in Article 2(4) is still good law. To make this argument, they stress several points. First, they argue that the norm remains authoritative since no state has explicitly suggested that Article 2(4) is not good law. As Professor Louis Henkin has explained '[n]o government, no responsible official of government, has been prepared to pronounce it dead.'[4] Thus, because states have not explicitly repudiated Article 2(4), its authority continues.

Second, legalists argue that despite the problems of Article 2(4), the norm remains controlling of state behavior. Here, they contend that despite violations of the norm, it has *for the most part* exerted a restraining influence on state behavior. In the words of Professor Henkin, 'the norm against the unilateral national use of force has survived. Indeed, despite common misimpressions to the contrary, the norm has been largely observed'.[5] One aspect of this legalist argument seems to be that while it is easy to count the times that a particular norm is violated, it is quite difficult to identify the times when a norm exerted a controlling influence, when states refrained from forcible action because of Article 2(4)'s proscription. Another aspect of this argument is that since most states are not, in fact, using force in violation of the Charter, the norm is generally controlling of behavior.

Finally, the legalists argue that Article 2(4) must be understood as a *treaty* obligation for those states that have ratified the United Nations Charter and not just as an obligation under customary international law. Hence, the procedure for a normative change is much more specific and defined. Professor Edward Gordon has argued that

> [t]he rule embodied in Article 2(4) is not just a freestanding rule of customary law; it is also a formal treaty obligation. States may withdraw their consent to be bound by treaty obligations, but may not simply walk away from them.[6]

Explains Gordon, '[t]he existence of an operational code [read 'state practice'] different from the formal commitment may be cause for withdrawing state consent, but it does not supplant the process for withdrawing consent called for by the treaty or by treaty law generally.'[7] Although recognizing that treaties may be 'replaced' if they are 'not followed,' Gordon contends that 'an observer's inference that they are lagging behind actual practice is too subjective and fragile a criterion to replace the formal evidence of withdrawal of state consent as an indicator of the continuing force of treaty obligations.'[8] In other words, states must formally terminate a treaty for it to cease to binding; mere non-compliance is insufficient.

While there is a certain logic in these arguments advanced by the legalists, there are also problems. First, although it may be true that no state has explicitly declared that Article 2(4) is not good law, this fact alone does not mean that the norm is necessarily authoritative. For obvious political reasons, states have not overtly argued that the Charter norms are invalid. States have on numerous occasions claimed the right to use force in circumstances that are, nevertheless, clearly antithetical to the principle enshrined in Article 2(4). Given these claims, it seems incorrect to contend that states still hold 2(4) in very high esteem. Admittedly, the provision may still command some perceptions of legitimacy, but they seem to be far below those required for a healthy rule of law.

Second, the arguments advanced by the legalists for the controlling nature of Article 2(4) also seem to be inconsistent with realities of the international system. Certainly not every state violates Article 2(4), and certainly it is difficult to judge when a particular state's behavior was influenced by the existence of 2(4). Nevertheless, the norm has been violated frequently and with impunity in some of the most important cases of state interaction. Even though legal scholars may disagree as to the precise list of such violations of Article 2(4), there is broad agreement that numerous violations have taken place. . . .

Even Professor Henkin, in arguing that Article 2(4) is still valid, was forced to deal with a number of these instances. He explains:

> the norm against unilateral force has been largely observed. With the exception of Korea (in some respects an 'internal war'), the brief, recurrent Arab–Israel hostilities in 1956, 1967, and 1973, the flurry between

India and Pakistan over Kashmir in September 1965, the invasion of
Czechoslovakia by Soviet troops in 1968, [and in the footnote he says:
'One might add, unhappily, Ethiopia–Somalia and Vietnam–Cambodia–
China in 1978–79'], nations have not engaged in 'war,' in full and sus-
tained hostilities or state-to-state aggression even in circumstances in
which in the past the use of force might have been expected.'[9]

These 'exceptions,' and others that have taken place since the time Henkin's book was written, are profound exceptions, not simply minor incidents. These uses of force would seem rather clearly to indicate that when
a state judges other foreign policy goals to be at stake, it will generally *not*
allow itself to be circumscribed by the prohibition of Article 2(4).

Finally, the legalists' use of the treaty-nature of Article 2(4) is problematic. Even though Article 2(4) is a treaty provision, the same test for
determining the validity of customary international law can also be
employed. If a treaty provision is greatly lacking in authority and control,
it seems quite logical to argue that the provision is no longer authentic
'international law.' In the decentralized system that exists today, international law is constituted through state practice. In 1945, fifty-one states
chose to enunciate a particular rule relating to the use of force by ratifying
the United Nations Charter. Since then, these states and over one hundred
additional ones have, through their actions, chosen to change this rule.
Even though there have been no formal acts that have attempted to change
the written words of Article 2(4), the behavior of these states has been sufficient to effect a change.

The 'Core Interpretist' Approach. Another approach to understanding the
status of Article 2(4) has been called the 'core interpretist' approach. The
'core interpretists' argue that although the narrow, legalistic interpretation
of Article 2(4) no longer represents existing law, a 'core' meaning of the
Article that is still authoritative and controlling can nevertheless be identified.[10] Naturally, these scholars differ as to what represents this 'core'
meaning. Some suggest that the 'core' is very large. They contend that the
basic prohibition contained in Article 2(4) is still valid, except as modified
by authoritative interpretations confirmed in state practice. Thus, every unilateral use of force is prohibited unless it can be demonstrated that the
accepted interpretation of the Charter allows for an exception. These 'core
interpretists' argue that permissible exceptions would include such uses of
force as anticipatory self-defense, intervention to protect nationals, and
humanitarian intervention.

Other 'core interpretist' scholars take a slightly different approach.
They contend that the 'core' of Article 2(4) is much smaller. For example,
Professor Alberto Coll suggests that

insofar as there is a remnant of a legal, as opposed to a moral obligation left in article 2(4), it is a good faith commitment to abstain from *clear aggression* that involves a disproportionate use of force and violates other principles of the Charter.[11]

According to Coll,

[c]lear aggression and the content of article 2(4) and article 51 would, in turn, be defined by reference to established traditions of normative reasoning, such as prudence and just war doctrine, in an open interpretative process similar, in fact, to that already underlying state decisionmaking on the use of force in many situations.[12]

He explains that '[u]nder this interpretative process, *clear aggression* would encompass different typologies of coercive acts which various traditions of ethical reasoning, throughout different periods of history, have condemned in the strongest terms as unlawful and morally reprehensible.'[13] Thus using Coll's approach, 'clear aggression' could include the use of force to gain territory, to achieve political domination, and to perpetrate genocide. The activities of Nazi Germany and Imperial Japan that inaugurated the Second World War would be the most obvious examples of such 'clear aggression.'

But whatever the precise nature of the 'core' that the various scholars identify, the important aspect of this approach is that it continues to affirm Article 2(4) as the existing *jus ad bellum*. All the writers of this school would contend that *some* version of Article 2(4) represents the law, and would reject arguments that 2(4) is now dead. One reason for this desire to hold on to even a shred of Article 2(4) is a belief that rejecting the norm entirely might be premature because states do refrain from certain uses of force. Consequently, such rejection could actually contribute to the dissolution of whatever restraining influence 2(4) still exerts. Another reason seems to be the symbolic nature of 2(4). For many 'core interpretists,' Article 2(4) represents a goal, an aspiration of the post-Second World War era. To claim that it is no longer law, would be to claim that prohibiting the unilateral resort to force was no longer a noble goal worth pursuing.

But despite these laudable aspirations, there is one major problem. Holding on to Article 2(4) may actually be doing more harm than good to the international legal system. Given the severely weakened authority of 2(4) and its manifest lack of control, to use Article 2(4) in any way to describe the law relating to the recourse to force may simply be perpetrating a legal fiction that interferes with an accurate assessment of state practice. It may indeed be true that some 'core' of the Article 2(4) prohibition may remain, such as a prohibition on the use of force for territorial aggrandizement. But the problem is that Article 2(4) was designed to be much more than simply a prohibition on the use of force for that narrow purpose. One of the radical aspects of 2(4) was that it went beyond the Kellogg-Briand Pact, which prohibited recourse to 'war,' by prohibiting *all* uses of *force* that were against the territorial integrity or political independence of a state or otherwise inconsistent with the purposes of the United Nations. Moreover, it even prohibited *threats* of force. In other words, the Article 2(4) prohibition was much broader than simply the 'core.' If only this small sub-set of Article 2(4) still remains, it does not seem appropriate to describe the law by reference to the full set.

The 'Rejectionist' Approach. The third possible approach to the status of Article 2(4) has been called the 'rejectionist' approach. To take this approach would be to argue that Article 2(4) does not in any meaningful way constitute existing law. The contention would be that because authoritative state practice is so far removed from any reasonable interpretation of the meaning of Article 2(4), it is no longer reasonable to consider the provision 'good law.'

The classical elaboration of the rejectionist approach can be found in Professor Franck's 1970 article on the death of Article 2(4).[14] At the time, Professor Franck argued that '[t]he prohibition against the use of force in relations between states has been eroded beyond recognition.[15] This erosion, according to Franck, was due to three main factors: 'the rise of wars of "national liberation",' 'the rising threat of wars of total destruction,' and 'the increasing authoritarianism of regional systems dominated by a super-Power.[16] But, he explained, '[t]hese three factors may . . . be traced back to a single circumstance: the lack of congruence between the international legal norm of Article 2(4) and the perceived national interests of states, especially the super-Powers.[17] In short, as states have come to value goals other than those expressed in Article 2(4), the authority and control of the norm have essentially disappeared. As Professor Franck put it in 1970: 'The practice of these states has so severely shattered the mutual confidence which would have been the *sine qua non of* an operative rule of law embodying the precepts of Article 2(4) that, as with Ozymandias, only the words remain.'[18]

Twenty years later, in his *The Power of Legitimacy Among Nations,* Franck reaffirmed his 'rejectionist' understanding of Article 2(4). Acknowledging the egregious lack of control of putative rules dealing with the use of force, he commented:

> the extensive body of international 'law,' oft restated in solemn texts, which forbids direct or indirect intervention by one state in the domestic affairs of another, precludes the aggressive use of force by one state against another, and requires adherence to human rights standards simply, if sadly, is not predictive of the ways of the world.[19]

Later, Franck compared Article 2(4) and the one-time US Government mandated 55-mile per hour national speed limit. Observing that while both rules possess 'textual clarity,' they, nevertheless, 'do not describe or predict with accuracy the actual behavior of the real world.'[20] He explained that

> their determinacy is undermined by a popular perception that they can't mean what they so plainly say. The irrationality of the rules—their incoherence: a failure to be instrumental in relation to the purposes for which they were devised—causes us to believe, and act on the belief, that they have become indeterminate. The rules, therefore, have lost some of their compliance pull.[21]

Apart from Professor Franck, no other major international legal scholar has *explicitly* taken this approach. Yet despite this lack of support, the 'rejectionist' approach seems to offer the most accurate description of the contemporary *jus ad bellum*. The legalist approach seems too removed from the realities of the international system and the core interpretist approach seems to do little more than perpetuate a legal fiction. Based on what states have been saying and what they have been doing, there simply does not seem to be a *legal* prohibition on the use of force against the political independence and territorial integrity of states as provided in even a modified version of Article 2(4). The rule creating process, authoritative state practice, has rejected that norm.

The Post-Charter Obligation

If Article 2(4) is in fact dead, a larger question remains: what norms have developed in the post-Charter era to replace it? In other words, what rules of behavior have states constituted that *are* regarded as authoritative and are, in practice, controlling? Based on state behavior, several conclusions can be drawn about legal principles that seem to have emerged to fill the gap caused by the death of Article 2(4). The following section will set out these conclusions. We will employ here a 'positivist' approach to international law. That is, we assume that unless a restrictive norm of law can be established prohibiting a particular use of force, states are permitted to engage in that use of force. In short, for any use of force to be prohibited, an authoritative and controlling *proscription* must exist.

Our proposal does not purport to offer the only acceptable formulation of the law; rather, it seeks merely to present one possible description of the post-Charter *jus ad bellum*. In order to do so, we will first discuss those circumstances under which recourse to force seems to be lawful. Then, we will examine those circumstances under which recourse to force appears to be unlawful.

Lawful uses of force

1. Self-defense (including anticipatory self-defense and reprisals). The first circumstance in which the unilateral use of force would seem to be lawful in a post-Article 2(4) legal system would be self-defense. This is not particularly controversial. Individual and collective self-defense has always been explicitly permitted under Article 51 of the Charter. The major change would be the addition of anticipatory self-defense and reprisals.

Before the Charter was adopted, states had the right under customary international law to use force in self-defense even before an armed attack occurred if it could be demonstrated that such an attack were imminent and that no other recourse was available. With the demise of Article 2(4), it is reasonable to assume that this preexisting right would be rehabilitated. There seems to be no consensus on a rule prohibiting force undertaken for that purpose.

In addition to anticipatory self-defense, it would also seem that reprisals would be permissible. States have also been suing a broadened definition of self-defense to justify reprisals. There seems to be a belief on the part of states conducting such actions that they are proper to punish and deter certain prior illegal acts of the target state, even though such initial acts do not rise to the level of an armed attack. While not all states have endorsed the use of force for these purposes, there appears to be no clear agreement on an authoritative norm prohibiting reprisals.

2. Promotion of self-determination. In light of the growing preference for 'just' uses of force, the use of force to promote self-determination would also seem to be lawful. But since different states have defined self-determination in different ways, it would be impossible to restrict this right to the promotion of a particular 'type' of self-determination. It would, in other words, be difficult to claim that using force to promote 'pro-democratic' self-determination would be permissible, but using force to promote 'pro-socialist' self-determination would be impermissible. Consequently, there would seem to be a right for states to use force to promote self-determination *however* they define it. This would mean that such action as the Soviet 'liberation' of Czechoslovakia and the American 'liberation' of Panama would be lawful. It would also mean that it would be permissible to provide assistance to either side in a civil conflict, with the determination being made by the intervening party as to which side was acting in the true interests of self-determination.

This use of force to promote self-determination is obviously much more controversial than self-defense. It actually constitutes a clear use of force against the political independence and territorial integrity of a state. Nevertheless, as demonstrated earlier, states have come to regard a just pursuit of

self-determination as a proper use of force, at least when it is their definition of self determination. Once again, there seems to be no restrictive rule
prohibiting such use of force.

3. *Correction of past injustices.* Finally, it would seem to be lawful to
employ force to correct injustices that had been inflicted on a particular
state at a particular time in the past. This means that if one state had previously seized the territory of another state, had endangered the nationals of
that state, or had violated some other major norm of international law, the
aggrieved state could use force to rectify the situation. This new rule would
legalize such actions as the Argentine invasion of the Falklands and, if they
had been done today, the British, French, and Israeli invasion of Egypt in
1956, and the Arab invasion in 1973.

This use of force to correct past injustices also clearly involves action
against the political and territorial status quo. States seem to feel, however,
that the status quo is often unjust, and that in the absence of other effective
means to correct the situation, they have the right to take the matter into
their own hands.

Unlawful Uses of Force: Territorial Annexation

If states have come to acknowledge that force may properly be used to promote self-determination and to correct past injustices, very little would
seem to be prohibited. In fact, in a world without Article 2(4), the only
thing that does seem to be proscribed is the use of force for pure territorial
aggrandizement. States still appear to believe that it is illegitimate to use
force solely for the purpose of gaining territory.

Perhaps the most dramatic example of this belief can be seen in the
response of the international community to the August 1990 Iraqi invasion
of Kuwait. When Iraq invaded and annexed Kuwait, it justified its actions
on the basis of Arab unity. Claiming that colonial borders had been unjustly
drawn, the Iraqi Revolutionary Command Council proclaimed that it had
'decided to return the part and branch, Kuwait, to the whole and origin,
Iraq, in a comprehensive, eternal and inseparable merger unity.' Yet despite
this apparent claim of correcting a past injustice, the international community squarely condemned the invasion and annexation. On August 2, the
United Nations Security Council adopted Resolution 660 condemning
the invasion by a vote of 14–0, with Yemen not voting. Four days later the
Council acting under Chapter VII of the Charter, imposed economic sanctions on Iraq by a vote of 13–0, with Cuba and Yemen abstaining. Shortly
thereafter, following Iraq's claim of annexation, the Council unanimously
adopted Resolution 662. This Resolution reiterated the Council's demand
'that Iraq withdraw immediately and unconditionally all its forces' from

Kuwait, and decided 'that annexation of Kuwait by Iraq under any form and whatever pretext has no legal validity, and is considered null and void' and demanded 'that Iraq rescind its actions purporting to annex Kuwait.' On November 30, after much negotiation, the Council adopted Resolution 678 authorizing states to use force in Iraq did not comply with the demanded withdrawal.

The Security Council's actions in this case are quite telling. Even though Iraq's actions were veiled in claims of 'justice,' the Council did not hesitate in condemning the invasion and purported annexation. The justification undoubtedly was too much of a transparent 'pretext' for a simple effort at territorial aggrandizement, reminiscent of justifications used at the beginning of the Second World War. The reaction would indicate a strong perception on the part of the overwhelming majority of states that uses of force for pure territorial aggrandizement are impermissible. Moreover, the fact that such uses of force have been quite rare in the post-War era, indicate that this norm does have a high degree of control.

But what all this suggests is that the legal structure that has emerged from the ashes of Article 2(4) may simply be a modified regime of 'self-help.' Under such a regime, states can lawfully use force to promote self-determination as they define it and to correct what they perceive to be injustices. For these purposes they possess a *competence de guerre,* akin to that possessed by states before the adoption of the League of Nations Covenant. Under this paradigm, however, one use of force *is* prohibited—force for territorial annexation. Of course even here, state could claim that they were acing for other 'just' reasons when their actual goal was pure territorial acquisition.

An Assessment of the Post-Charter Obligation

If the international legal system has moved toward a modified regime of self-help in the post-Charter period, is this evolution good? Does this type of legal arrangement further the general goals of international law? Assuming that one of the main purposes of international law is to promote stability and regularity in the relations among states, the answer would quite clearly be *no.* Self-determination and justice are extremely subjective terms. They can mean virtually anything a particular state chooses them to mean, and they can be used to justify virtually any use of force. In the world of 'just' causes, one person's liberator is another person's oppressor, and one person's freedom fighter is another person's terrorist.

The problem, however, is that while self-determination can mean almost anything, Article 2(4) has already been stripped of any real meaning. In light of state practice, to contend that it is still good law is to make *it mean* virtually anything. Recognizing that Article 2(4) is dead may not be very satisfying, but it may be accurate. The normative framework suggested above certainly does not represent the most desirable legal regime, but it may reflect the *existing* legal regime.

The Post–Cold War Era: A New Paradigm?

Critics of the preceding analysis of the post-Charter self-help paradigm might contend that the discussion has assumed the existence of a particular type of international system. The paradigm, it could be argued, seems to assume the continuance of the Cold War and its attendant evils—lack of superpower cooperation, widespread superpower intervention, and the like. Now that the tumultuous year of 1989 has brought an end to the Cold War, the paradigm no longer depicts reality. With the collapse of the Soviet Union, increased cooperation among the permanent members of the Security Council, the rising capital of the United Nations, and the great movements toward democracy, a *laissez-faire* approach to the use of force no longer seems accepted. Instead, it could be argued, a new 'pro-democratic' paradigm is coming to describe the law relating to the recourse to force.

    This section will examine the arguments supporting the existence of this would-be paradigm. It will do so by exploring the possible emergence of a new value hierarchy and a 'new' legal obligation. . . .

The Emergence of a New Value Hierarchy?

In the Post-Charter Self-Help paradigm, justice is valued above peace. States are claiming the right to use force to promote certain 'just' goals. The major difficulty with this formulation is that different groups of states have: offered differing and often contradictory definitions of what a 'just' goal is. With the ending of the Cold War, however, it could be contended that an international consensus is emerging around certain acceptable 'just' goals. Specifically, it could be argued that in light of recent developments, there is a consensus that it is proper to use force to promote democratic self-determination in the western sense of the term.

    This argument could be made in two steps. First, with the decline of the ideological confrontation between the East and the West, there is growing international agreement on what constitutes an 'illegitimate' regime. Such a regime would be one that engages in gross violations of human rights as enumerated in the Covenant on Civil and Political Rights or one which has come to power in total disregard of constitutional processes. Hence, the pre-1989 regimes in Panama, East Germany, Bulgaria, Czechoslovakia, and Romania, to name a few, could be regarded as illegitimate. In support of the notion that agreement on the illegitimacy of certain regimes transcends the East-West divide, proponents of this contention would cite Gorbachev's attitude regarding the Eastern European regimes. They would argue that in his calls for change in Eastern Europe and his tacit acceptance of such change, he reflected a new thinking on the part of the Soviet Union's leadership that those regimes were, in fact, illegitimate. Second, because there could be near universal agreement that a particular government is illegitimate, it could be contended that there is an emerging belief that it is becoming permissible to use force against such regimes to promote the self-determination of the peoples.

Although this argument is only in the initial stages of development, one American scholar, Thomas Franck, has attempted to suggest its contours. Professor Franck argued that states 'are gradually coming to agree on a *right* to democratic governance, or freedom from totalitarianism.'[22] He explained that

> [w]hatever decent instincts came to cluster around the magnet of 'self-determination,' creating a widely-accepted exception to article 2(4), must now carry forward, in the post-colonial era, to imbue a new inter-nationally-recognized human right to political freedom.[23]

And, according to Franck,'[k]in to such a right would be another: a right of the democratic members of the international community to aid, directly or indirectly, those fighting for their democratic entitlement.'[24] These 'democratic entitlements,' explained Franck, 'are already spelled out in international instruments, in particular the Covenant on Civil and Political Rights, which may now be regarded as customary international law.'[25] But Franck believes that

> [w]hen the most basic of these rights have been found to have been violated—and *only* then—an enunciated international consensus might now be ready to form around the proposition that the use of some levels of force by states could be justified to secure democratic entitlements for peoples unable to secure them for themselves.'[26]

In short, justice would still be valued over peace, but the definition of justice would not be as subjective as in the self-help paradigm.

The Emergence of a 'New' Legal Obligation?

Based on these institutional and attitudinal changes, it could be argued that a 'new' legal obligation regarding the recourse to force is in the process of emerging. Following Franck, it could be contended that the international community is coming to accept one just cause for the recourse to force aside from self-defense—intervention to remove an 'illegitimate' regime. With the decline of competing ideologies, there is developing a consensus around what constitutes such an illegitimate regime and a growing accept- ance of the permissibility to use force, if necessary, to remove such a regime. If this is indeed becoming the case, then the paradigm depicting the *jus ad bellum* may be shifting away from the post-Charter self-help para- digm to a new pro-democratic paradigm. Under such a paradigm, force would be permissible in two circumstances: to engage in individual and collective self-defense and to promote 'pro-democratic' self-determination.

While such a paradigmatic shift may occur at some point in the future, at present, it seems exceptionally premature to assert its imminent arrival. This is true for a number of reasons. First, despite the dramatic develop- ments in Eastern Europe and the former Soviet Union, there still seems to be no real international consensus as to what constitutes an 'illegitimate' regime. While it is true that an apparent agreement developed regarding the illegitimacy of certain Eastern European governments, there seems to be no such consensus with respect to the rest of the world. If fidelity to the Inter- national Covenant on Civil and Political Rights is used as a determinant of legitimacy, a substantial number of countries fall short. Even following the remarkable developments of 1989, the human rights organization Freedom House lists fifty-nine states as 'not free.'[27] These states comprise over two billion people and come from nearly every area of the world. Clearly, if over one-third of the states in the international system maintain regimes in which significant political rights and civil liberties, as defined in the West, are denied, it is impossible to argue that there is some consensus on demo- cratic legitimacy.

Second, even assuming there were some emerging agreement on legit- imacy, there is clearly no consensus developing on the efficacy of the use of force to remove such a regime. A case in point would be the invasion of Panama by the United States. Even though one argument raised by the United States centered around the illegitimacy of the Noriega regime, there was near universal condemnation for the American action. While certain states believed that the government of Manuel Noriega was indeed illegiti- mate, there seemed to be a general rejection of US contentions that this ille- gitimacy gave rise to a unilateral right to invade the country. If this was the case with respect to Panama, it is difficult to envision many other cases in which there could be agreement on the permissibility of force to remove an anti-democratic regime.

In short, despite the dramatic changes that have taken place in inter- national politics over the last several years, there does not yet seem to be the international consensus necessary to support the existence of a pro- democratic paradigm. States have not yet come to accept a *jus ad bellum* that permits intervention for only one particular type of self-determination aimed at removing illegitimate, anti-democratic regimes.

The Future of the *Jus Ad Bellum*

Three Possible Scenarios

In light of the preceding analysis, it is contended that there has been a definite paradigm shift in the post-Charter period. The Charter prohibition on the recourse to force as established in Article 2(4) is simply no longer authoritative and controlling. States have chosen to reject this strict proscription in favor of a more permissive norm that prohibits force only in cases of action aimed at territorial aggrandizement and allows forcible efforts to promote self-determination as it is variously defined, to carry out a just reprisal, and to correct a past injustice. Despite the changes that have taken place in the international system, states have not yet reached a consensus on a more restrictive norm limiting permissible intervention to cases involving 'pro-democratic' self-determination. In other words, the post-Charter self-help paradigm, for good or ill, still describes the existing law relating to the initiation of force.

Given this conclusion, where is the law going? Is the international system evolving toward a pro-democratic paradigm or not? While it is impossible to answer this question with any certainty, three scenarios seem plausible.

First, it is conceivable that there will be no significant change in the post-charter self-help paradigm. States may continue to claim the right to use force to correct injustices and promote self-determination as they determine.

While there may be increased great power cooperation, this does not necessarily indicate that all states will refrain from acting to promote self-determination. It should be noted, for example, that even while the Soviet Union was allowing the East European states to go their own way, the United States was acting forcefully in Panama. Moreover, the changed nature of Europe may have little to do with the actions of states in other parts of the world. Islamic states, African states, and others may continue to be motivated by diverse definitions of self-determination and justice and may, when appropriate, use force to realize these claims.

A second possible scenario involves the ultimate acceptance of the pro-democratic paradigm. Even though the international system has not yet come to accept a definition of a legitimate regime, it is possible that the international community is evolving toward such definition. Before 1945, human rights was not even a legitimate topic of conversation in international discourse; now, even though definitions of human rights vary greatly, the notion that individuals have certain rights in the international system is generally accepted. It is possible that over time more refinements will be made in this area of the law and the provisions of instruments such as the Covenant on Civil and Political Rights will begin to be reflected in practice. This may then give rise to an accepted notion of legitimacy and a concomitant right to intervene to promote such legitimacy.

Finally, there is even a possibility that Article 2(4) could be rehabilitated. The recent actions by the United Nations in the Gulf may indicate a willingness to return to a more restrictive approach to force. Even though the Iraqi invasion is an easy case because it involved obvious aggression for territorial aggrandizement, it is possible that the effect of the UN response will be a reinvigoration of the norm. With the world apparently rallying around the Charter in this case, the effect may be to encourage states to be more supportive of Charter norms in the future. Having committed themselves as a matter of principle in this case, states may be more inclined to defend the honor of Article 2(4) in the future. If this were to occur, it could lead to a new consensus on the unilateral use of force. Article 2(4) could actually become reflective of authoritative state practice.

A Recommended Jus Ad Bellum

Whether these or other plausible scenarios will come about is likely to remain unclear for some time. What is clear, however, is that the current post-Charter self-help regime leaves much to be desired. A system that provides very little in normative restraints on the recourse to force, that allows states to use force to promote self-determination and justice as they may choose to define them, is destructive of world order. For policy makers, a course of action that would promote the return to something more closely resembling Article 2(4) would seem to make sense.

Given the recent developments in the United Nations system, the greater potential for great power cooperation, and the commitment of the international community in the Iraqi conflict, the possibility of reestablishing the Charter framework for the recourse to force seems greater than at any other time since 1945. In consequence, we would recommend the following framework for the law relating to the recourse to force. This proposal, we believe, would move the international system closer to a more stable and predictable normative structure. First, we will set out our suggestions for lawful uses of force. Next, we will examine what we believe should be regarded as unlawful uses of force. Finally, we discuss four advantages of our proposal: its clarity of language; its treatment of the changed nature of international conflict; its recognition of the need for limited self-help; and its capacity to enhance international order.

Lawful Uses of Force

Self-defense

As under the Charter paradigm, self-defense would be a permissible ground for states to take recourse to force. Our proposal sets out three explicit circumstances under which a state may lawfully use force to defend itself: armed attack; imminent attack; and indirect aggression.

1. Armed attack. First, states would be allowed to use force in response to an overt armed attack. This would simply reaffirm the language of Article 51. When one state engaged in a clear, obvious armed attack against another, the victim state would have the right to respond with force. The only restriction on this right of the aggrieved state would be the traditional requirements of necessity and proportionality.

2. Imminent attack. Second, states would be allowed to use force to respond to an 'imminent' armed attack. It seems only logical to assert that states need not be required to wait until the bombs drop or the troops cross their borders before they can take defensive action. Given the technology of modern weaponry, the right of *effective* self-defense could become meaningless if a state were required to weather a first hit before it could respond. In accepting anticipatory self-defense as a permissible ground for the use of force, we posit that the burden of proof should fall upon the state exercising this right. The state must demonstrate that an armed attack is truly 'imminent' and that its preemptive action is necessary.

3. Indirect aggression. The International Court of Justice held in the *Nicaragua* case that indirect aggression could rise to the level of an 'armed attack,' engendering a right of self-defense under Article 51. One of the main difficulties with the Court's decision was that it set the threshold of armed attack unduly high.

We accept the notion that indirect aggression can, in some cases, be tantamount to an armed attack. We would, however, propose a lower threshold than that suggested by the International Court of Justice. In our view, indirect aggression (subject to certain qualifications) can be regarded as an armed attack in three instances: covert actions, interventions in civil/mixed conflicts, and certain terrorist actions.

Covert action. While every covert action not undertaken in self-defense is delictual, not every one constitutes an 'armed attack.' It is impossible to determine with absolute precision when a covert action rises to the level of an armed attack. We nevertheless believe that a reasonable assessment of a covert action's character can be made on the basis of three interrelated factors: the nature of the activities; the severity of the effect of the activities; and the temporal duration of the activities.

Nature of activities. We believe that a host of covert activities could rise to the level of an armed attack. These would include such state actions as assassination, destruction of buildings, attacks against military and civilian targets, sabotage, and other acts of violence. The critical common denominator in all these would be their fundamentally *violent* nature. Covert actions such as bribery of public officials and financial support for political movements would be excluded from this category. Although these non-violent actions would be illegal violations of the sovereignty of the target state, we do not consider them to be equivalent to an armed attack. In short, the necessary precondition for an armed attack is *violence.*

Severity of effect. The effect of the violent covert activities in question should be comparable in severity to the effect of an overt armed attack. This level of severity would obviously vary with the nature of the action. Sabotaging a single small building that contained a limited amount of military equipment would not rise to the level of an armed attack. Assassinating a state's president, destroying a major military compound with explosives, or poisoning a water filtration plant would.

Temporal duration. A third factor to be weighed is the temporal duration of covert activities. A one-time covert act producing an effect of great severity might by itself be sufficient to constitute an armed attack. Activities producing effects of lesser severity, however, might only constitute an armed attack if they were part of an ongoing pattern of behavior. If the head of state were assassinated, that one act per se could be equated to an armed attack. The isolated destruction of a single small building might not be sufficient to be considered an armed attack; nevertheless, the destruction of a number of such structures over a period of time could be sufficient

Support of rebels. At what point does outside state support of a rebel movement rise to the level of an armed attack? This question proved to be one of the most contentious ones debated during the Central American conflict of the 1980s. In order to answer this inherently difficult question, three interrelated factors must be weighed: the nature of outside support; the severity of the effects of outside support; and the attributability of the effects to the intervening state.

Nature of support. As noted above, the International Court of Justice in Nicaragua set the 'armed attack' threshold at a very high level. Specifically, it held that only the introduction of 'armed bands' or 'mercenaries' into a target state would rise to the level of armed attack. We disagree. We contend that a whole *range of actions* could cross the armed attack threshold: a state's provision to rebels of significant financial support; a state's provision of weapons and ocher equipment, intelligence, command and control support, and training; and, of course, a state's introduction of armed bands and mercenaries.

Severity of effect. In determining whether a state's actions constitute an armed attack, the *intention* of the intervening state is not dispositive. Nor, moreover, is the *amount of aid* provided by the intervening state to the rebels. The key element in determining whether a state's support of rebels engenders the right of self-defense is the *effect on the target state* of the outside support. The degree of outside support for rebels must be sufficient to produce 'substantial effects' within the target state. Any 'effects' akin to those caused by a conventional attack by regular armed forces should be regarded as 'substantial' ones. As with covert actions, a temporal factor should affect the determination of what constitutes substantiality. 'Substantial effects' could be the result of a single prominent action or of a series of lesser actions undertaken over a period of time.

Attributability of effects to the intervening state. Unlike effects produced by covert action, effects produced by a state's support of rebels are not directly caused by the intervening state. The intervening state merely provides various forms of assistance to the rebels; the rebels, in turn, undertake actions producing effects within their state. Accordingly, for an 'armed attack' to be attributable to the intervening state, the effects within the target state must be demonstrated to be *directly linked* to the intervenor's assistance. For example, if it were proven that an intervening state provided munitions and logistical support to rebel forces, and that those forces employed that assistance in raids against government targets tantamount to an overt armed attack, then the intervening state should be considered to have effectively committed an 'armed attack.' Under such circumstances, the victim state could use force in self-defense against the intervening state.

Terrorist action. As with covert action, every terrorist act is delictual, though not every terrorist act constitutes an 'armed attack.' It is impossible to determine precisely when a terrorist act rises to the level of an armed attack. We nevertheless believe that a host of terrorist acts can do so. Depending on the attendant circumstances, these might include such actions as assassination, destruction of buildings, attacks against military and civilian targets, and sabotage.

A terrorist act is distinguished by at least three specific qualities:

a. actual or threatened *violence;*
b. a *'political'* objective; and
c. an *intended audience.*

Random acts of violence performed without deliberate political objectives should not be considered 'terrorism,' even if they do inspire 'terror.' Neither should non-violent acts, done for political purposes and directed at a specific target group. Nor, properly speaking, should politically-motivated acts of violence, when undertaken without any particular audience in mind. Accordingly, an 'act of terrorism' should be considered *'the threat or use of violence with the intent of causing fear in a target group, in order to achieve political objectives.'*

In order to justify a forcible state response, the effect of the terrorist act or acts in question must be comparable to the effect of an overt armed attack. This 'armed attack threshold' varies with three interrelated factors: the *locus* of the terrorist act; the *temporal duration* of the terrorist act; and the *severity of injury* the act inflicts upon the state.

Locus. The locus of a terrorist act may be either within a responding state's territory or outside it. Though scholars have generally not isolated this factor, we believe that it is a critical variable for determining the 'armed attack threshold.' Because it violates a state's 'territorial integrity,' a terrorist act occurring within a state's borders constitutes an inherently greater injury to that state's sovereignty than does an identical act abroad.

Temporal duration. A second factor to be weighed is the temporal duration of terrorist acts. A terrorist act can be a single, isolated occurrence or part of an on-going pattern of behavior. The latter variety of act, irrespective of its locus or severity, is more likely to rise to the level of an 'armed attack' because it causes a continuing injury to the state.

Severity of injury to the state. The 'severity' of injury to the state caused by a terrorist act can range across a broad spectrum of acts, although where precisely an act should be placed on this spectrum is debatable. At one end of the spectrum are acts causing injuries of minor severity to the state. We believe that these acts would include ones such as the temporary detention of a private citizen, the destruction of a private citizen's property, or the destruction of a limited amount of government property. Even the killing of a single national could be considered an act inflicting an injury of minor severity upon the state. To contend this is not to diminish the tragic results of such an act; rather, it is to underscore that the severity of the act should ultimately be evaluated in terms of its effect upon the state *per se*.

At the other end of the spectrum are acts causing injury of major severity to the state. We believe that these acts would consist of ones which strike at the core of a state's sovereignty. These would include the assassination of a government official, the destruction of a major government installation, or the killing of a large group of nationals *qua* nationals. While we believe that the killing of one national, or perhaps a small number of them, should not be regarded as inflicting severe injury to the state, we nonetheless contend that the killing of a large group of nationals should be so regarded. When a large number of nationals are attacked solely on the basis of their nationality, such an attack on what can reasonably be considered an embodiment of the state's sovereignty would seem to cause the state an injury of major severity.

In assessing whether the 'armed attack threshold' has been reached, the locus of the act, its temporal duration, and the severity of injury it inflicts upon the state must be considered simultaneously. As each of these three factors varies, so, too, will the assessment of whether an 'armed attack' has occurred. For example, an attack of a given severity occurring abroad might not be tantamount to an 'armed attack,' while one of equal severity occurring within a state's territory might be. Because an act within a state's borders self-evidently violates that state's 'territorial integrity,' it is reasonable to posit a lower standard for 'severity' for terrorist acts occurring there than for acts occurring outside a state's territory. Similarly, a single act producing an injury of great severity to the state might by itself be sufficient to constitute an armed attack, whereas activities producing injuries of lesser severity might only constitute an armed attack only if they were part of an ongoing pattern of behavior. In addition to the question of which terrorist acts engender a right of forcible response is the question of what entities constitute permissible *targets for a self-defense response.* There are two such possible targets: the terrorist actor itself; or a state related in some way to the terrorist actor.

We submit that a self-defense response should be permitted against a terrorist actor under three circumstances. First, force may be employed by a victim state if the terrorist actor is located in that state's jurisdiction or in an area beyond the jurisdiction of any state: for example, the high seas or the airspace over the high seas. Second, a state may take forcible action against a terrorist actor located in another state's jurisdiction if that 'host state' is unable or unwilling to take steps to suppress that actor. Lacking evidence of 'host state' support or sponsorship of the terrorist actor, a victim state may not use force against host state targets *per se.* Rather, its action must be limited to the terrorist actor alone. Third, a victim state may employ force against a terrorist actor located in a state which is supporting or sponsoring the activities of the terrorist actor.

Depending on the circumstances, a self-defense response should also be permitted against a state involved with a terrorist actor. Here, we propose an 'attributability' requirement similar to that which we advanced for state support of rebels. A state may support or sponsor terrorist actors. In either of these cases, the effects produced by a state's action are not *directly* caused by the state. Instead, the state merely provides various forms of assistance to the terrorist actors; the terrorists, in turn, undertake actions producing effects on the victim state. Accordingly, for an 'armed attack' to be attributable to the sponsoring or supporting state, the effects on the victim state must be demonstrated to be *directly linked* to the state's assistance.

For example, if it were proven that a state provided munitions and logistical support to terrorist actors, and that those terrorists employed that assistance in an action reaching the 'armed attack threshold,' then the sponsoring or supporting state should be considered itself to have effectively committed an 'armed attack.' Under such circumstances, the victim state could use force in self-defense against the terrorist-linked state.

Intervention to protect nationals

Provided that four criteria are satisfied, a state should be permitted to intervene to protect its nationals. First, the nationals of the intervening state must be in imminent danger of loss of life or limb. Second, the target state must be unwilling or unable to protect the nationals of the intervening state. Third, the purpose of the intervention must be limited to the removal of the threatened nationals. The intervention must not be used as a pretext for any other activities in the territory of the target state. Fourth, the force used in the intervention must be proportionate to the mission of removing the nationals. No force may be used beyond that which is required to accomplish that limited task.

Force authorized by the Security Council

Finally, as in the Charter paradigm, force authorized by the Security Council would be permissible.

Unlawful Uses of Force

Aside from the uses of force detailed above, all other uses of force by a state would be prohibited. This would include the use of force to gain territory, to correct past injustices, and to promote self-determination. As noted above, there is virtually universal agreement that the use of force for territorial aggrandizement is currently illegal. To permit such a use of force would be to destroy all vestiges of international order. In addition, even though the post-Charter self-help paradigm seems to allow the use of force to correct injustices and to promote self-determination, we believe that the terms 'injustice' and 'self-determination' are excessively subjective. Were states allowed to use force to promote their own brands of justice and self-determination, nearly any use of force could be legitimized.

Advantages of Our Proposed Jus Ad Bellum

Our proposed *jus ad bellum* may not constitute the 'ideal' regime. Nevertheless, it represents a significant improvement over both the Charter paradigm and the existing post-Charter self-help paradigm. The advantages of our proposal can be evaluated in the light of four criteria: its clarity of language; the degree to which it addresses the nature of international conflict; the degree to which it recognizes the need for limited self-help; and its capacity to enhance international order.

First, our suggested *jus ad bellum* eliminates some of the interpretation problems of the Charter framework. In particular, the proposal attempts to deal with the meaning of Article 51 and the nature of an 'armed attack.' It allows for an explicit recognition of several categories of action that may give rise to the right of self-defense including imminent attack and indirect aggression. Our approach includes a number of subjective elements; nevertheless, we believe that it contains fewer than other approaches.

Second, our proposal addresses the changed nature of international conflict. It responds to both civil and mixed conflicts and to the problem of state-sponsored terrorism. As noted throughout our work, these types of conflict have been prominent features of the post-Second World War system. Any legal framework must specifically address these varieties of conflict if it is to be effective.

Third, our framework recognizes the need for self-help for the protection of nationals. It acknowledges that states are frequently unable to receive the cooperation of the target state when their nationals are in danger and that sometimes they may be required to engage in unilateral action to extricate their citizens. Our proposal would legitimize such action, subject to the criteria set out above.

Fourth, our proposal recognizes the critical importance of a restrictive *jus ad bellum* for international order. As we have consistently emphasized, the post-Charter self-help paradigm is destructive. It is far too subjective and allows states excessive justifications for the resort to force. If international law is to promote international stability, the normative framework for the recourse to force must be as limited and objective as possible. In our proposal, we consider all uses of force to correct past injustices and to promote self-determination to be impermissible. Although any given use of force for these purposes could indeed be just, it seems impossible to devise any realistic criteria that would be both reasonably objective and acceptable to all states. Accordingly, we support a strict prohibition on the unilateral recourse to force for these purposes.

If a particular incident were to arise in which states claimed that force should be used either to correct an injustice or to promote self-determination, we believe that the Security Council would be the most appropriate body to consider the issue. If the Council determined then that the matter were so grave that it constituted a threat to the peace, the Council could authorize forcible measures. Such a multilateral approach would, in our view, be far more preferable to the unilateralism of the post-Charter self-help paradigm. It would not eliminate the subjective aspects of defining justice or self-determination. However, before any forcible action could be undertaken, it would require Security Council endorsement.

Notes

1. D. Moynihan, *On the Law of Nations*. 19 (1990).

2. Arend, 'International Law and the Recourse to Force: A Shift in Paradigms,' *Stan J. Int'l L.* 27: 1 (1990).

3. Although it is nearly impossible to categorize scholars as *absolutely* falling into a particular school, some individuals seem to be more clearly 'legalists.' Such scholars would include: Michael Akehurst, Ian Brownlie, and Louis Henkin. See, M. Akehurst, *A Modern Introduction to International Law:* 256–261 (6th ed. 1987); I. Brownlie, *International Law and the Use of Force by States* (1963); L. Henkin, *How Nations Behave:* 135–164 (2nd ed. 1979).

4. Henkin, 'The Reports of the Death of Article 2(4) Are Greatly Exaggerated,' *Am. J. Int'l L.* 65: 544, 547 (1971).

5. L. Henkin, *How Nations Behave:* 146 (2nd ed. 1979).

6. Gordon, 'Article 2(4) in Historical Context,' *Yale J. Int'l L.* 10: 271, 275 (1985).

7. Ibid.

8. Ibid.

9. L. Henkin, op. cit.: 146.

10. This seems to be the approach taken by the majority of international legal scholars. Such scholars would include Derek Bowett, Myres McDougal, John Norton Moore, W. Michael Reisman. See, D. Bowett, *Self-Defence in International Law* (1958); M. McDougal and F. Feliciano, *Law and Minimum World Public Order* (1961); Moore, 'The Secret War in Central America and the Future of World Order,' *Am. J. Int'l L.* 80: 43, 80–92 (1986); Reisman, 'Coercion and Self-Determination: construing Charter Article 2(4),' *Am. J. Int'l L.* 78: 642 (1984).

11. Coll, 'The Limits of Global Consciousness and Legal Absolutism: Protecting International Law from Some of its Best Friends,' 27 *Harv. J. Int'l L.* 27: 509, 613 (1986).

12. Ibid.: 620.

13. Ibid.

14. Franck, 'Who Killed Article 2(4)? Or: Changing Norms Governing the Use of Force by States,' *Am. J. Int'l L.* 64.

15. Ibid.: 835.

16. Ibid.

17. Ibid.

18. Ibid.: 809.

19. T. Franck, *The Power of Legitimacy Among Nations:* 32 (1990) (footnotes omitted).

20. Ibid.: 78.

21. Ibid.

22. Franck, 'Secret Warfare: Policy Options for a Modern Legal and Institutional Context,' Paper presented to the Conference on Policy Alternatives to Deal with Secret Warfare: International Law, US Institute of Peace, March 16–17, 1990: at 17.

23. Ibid.: 17–18.

24. Ibid.: 18.

25. Ibid.

26. Ibid. Professor Franck has further developed these ideas. See, Franck, 'The Emerging Right to Democratic Governance,' *Am. J. Int'l L.* 86: 46 (1992).

27. 'Survey Update,' insert in *Freedom at Issue* 112 (1990).

28. Professor John Norton More has consistently emphasized the point that for the right of self-defense to be meaningful, it must be a 'real' right. States must be able to provide for 'effective' self-defense. See Moore, 'The Use of Force in International Relations: Norms Concerning the Initiation of Coercion,' in J. Moore, F. Tipson and R. Turner, *National Security Law:* 85, 87–89 (1991).

15

Legal Control of
International Terrorism:
A Policy Oriented Assessment

M. CHERIF BASSIOUNI

TERRORISM HAS EXISTED, IN ONE FORM OR ANOTHER, IN MANY SOCIETIES for as long as history has been recorded. The differences between its various manifestations, however, have been as to methods, means, and weapons. As the means available to inflict significant damage to society improve, the harmful impact of terrorism increases. And as weapons of mass destruction become more accessible, the dangers to the world community increase.

This essay assesses substantive international norms and their enforcement, and highlights the weaknesses of the international system's effectiveness in combating transnational crime generally, and terrorism in particular. It starts with defining the phenomenon of terrorism, before proceeding into a critical assessment of the modalities of interstate cooperation in penal matters and offering a few recommendations thereto. It is necessarily more a survey than an in-depth study of the questions addressed. . . .

Terrorism is a strategy of violence designed to instill terror in a segment of society in order to achieve a power-outcome, propagandize a cause, or inflict harm for vengeful political purposes. That strategy is resorted to by state actors either against their own population or against the population of another country. It is also used by non-state actors, such as insurgent or revolutionary groups acting within their own country or in another country. Lastly, it is used by ideologically motivated groups or individuals, acting either inside or outside their country of nationality, whose methods may vary according to their beliefs, goals, and means.

State and non-state actors who commit terrorist acts can be distinguished, *inter alia,* on the basis of their participants, their goals, their methods, and the means they have at their disposal. But these actors all resort

---

to a strategy of terror-violence in order to achieve goals that include a power-outcome. The quantum or level of violence employed by actors in each category will usually depend on their access to means of terror-inspiring effects, and on whether these effects are likely to cause consequences conducive to attaining the desired power-outcome.

The advent of globalization has helped terrorist groups such as Al Qaeda. Globalization is characterized by the elimination of time and distance barriers and the increased popular access to information, technology, and communications. These characteristics have been exploited by both legitimate and illegitimate enterprises. They have particularly benefited terrorist groups by allowing the groups' members and supporters to cross state borders, acquire and move equipment, obtain information, communicate with one another, and transfer funds transnationally with much greater ease, all the while relying on the worldwide media to broadcast both their message and the success of their operations. Globalization has also allowed terrorist groups to network with one another, permitting terrorist groups to develop strategic alliances with other groups engaged in transnational criminality in order to develop synergetic connections and to maximize respective capabilities and effectiveness. These networks have particularly developed between terrorist groups and organized crime; in Colombia, for example, the Revolutionary Armed Forces of Colombia (FARC) funds its rebellion by protecting the drug traffickers.[1] Terrorist groups also rely on techniques perfected by organized crime, particularly their methods of and sources for obtaining funding, arms, and military equipment on the illegal market. Because of economic globalization and the lack of international control of arms trafficking, terrorist groups seldom lack access to weapons and military equipment; the so-called "black market" is quite open and accessible to those with funds. For example, with arms purchased from funds obtained in the illegal diamond trade and laundered in European financial institutions, the Liberian and Sierra Leone rebels have terrorized their respective peoples for a decade, leaving an estimated 200,000 and 300,000 people dead, thousands of children mutilated, and thousands of women raped.[2] These rebels, particularly their leaders, have benefited from the loopholes in financial and criminal controls that have resulted from globalization.

The Weaknesses of Existing International Law in Addressing Terrorism

Non-Specific Conventional and Customary International Law Applicable to Terrorism

Given the advent of globalization and the development of international terrorism, the international community must establish effective means of punishing such international criminal acts. Currently, the conduct of state actors and insurgent or revolutionary groups is governed by the 1948 Genocide Convention,[3] customary international criminal law governing crimes against humanity (since there is no applicable international convention other than the 1998 Statute of the International Criminal Court), the 1984 Convention against Torture,[4] and the various norms against war crimes as reflected in the customary law of armed conflict, and the four 1949 Geneva Conventions and their two 1977 Protocols.[5]

There is significant overlap between conventions and custom within the international criminal framework. The Convention against Torture, the Genocide Conventions, and the prohibitions on crimes against humanity apply in times of war and peace. However, the customary law of armed conflict and the Geneva Conventions apply only in times of war or armed conflict, either of an international or non-international character. These norms, applicable in the context of armed conflict, while sufficient, are seldom enforced against state actors and even less often enforced against non-state actors.[6] Furthermore, none of them makes distinctions in criminal responsibility between decision-makers and senior executors and lesser rank personnel.[7]

In addition, these conventions lack an enforcement mechanism to truly deter and punish criminal behavior on an international scale. Certain international attempts have been made in the course of the last decade to provide effective enforcement. The Security Council established the International Criminal Tribunal for the Former Yugoslavia (ICTY) in 1993 and the International Criminal Tribunal for Rwanda (ICTR) in 1994 to prosecute persons charged with the first three of these crimes (genocide, crimes against humanity, and war crimes), committed in the context of these two conflicts. In no other conflict since World War II has such a post conflict justice mechanism been established. When the ICC enters into effect, it will in time become a universal accountability mechanism for these three crimes. The extent to which the existence of such a system of international criminal justice can be an effective deterrent is, however, to be seen. Further, universal jurisdiction of international conventions has spurred domestic attempts at enforcement of such laws against international crime.[8] Indeed, the Torture Convention may become more effectively enforced as the Pinochet experiment in the United Kingdom[9] provides the precedent for increased state use of universal jurisdiction for national prosecutions. Universal jurisdiction can also be relied upon by national legal systems to prosecute genocide, crimes against humanity, war crimes, and torture. However, as crimes against humanity are not yet posited in conventional international criminal law other than in the two *ad hoc* tribunals of the JCTY and JCTR, and in the ICC Statute, it would be useful to have a specialized international convention on crimes against humanity, which, like Article 7 of the

ICC Statute, would include non-state actors. In that way, crimes against humanity would encompass certain forms of terrorism committed by an "organization" which, on the basis of a "policy," engages in "widespread" or "systematic" attack upon "a civilian population," by means of killing and other specified acts.[10] An international convention prohibiting such crimes would likely allow for universal jurisdiction of the acts committed and thus increase national prosecution of terrorist acts.

The lack of coordinated international control of other dangerous and international criminal conduct also prevents effective enforcement. There is a significant legal gap, for example, in the control of weapons of mass destruction, such as nuclear, chemical, and biological weapons. For instance, there are no conventions on the prohibition of the use of nuclear weapons, whether by state or non-state actors. In addition, the 1993 Chemical Weapons Convention[11] lacks effective enforcement provisions applicable to unlawful terrorist use, and the 1972 Bacteriological Convention[12] does not criminalize the use of such agents for terrorist attacks. The Bacteriological Convention had been in the process of being amended for years, only to have a final draft opposed by the United States in 2001 as a result of pressures from the chemical and pharmaceutical industries. Thus, progress toward adopting a new convention with effective criminal provisions has been forestalled.

There is, in short, no normative fabric to international criminal law, just bits and pieces of overlapping norms with significant gaps as to their coverage. Even those norms that could be enforced, are subject to the recurring problem of a lack of effective enforcement by states. When states are permitted to rely on universal jurisdiction to enforce such norms, through their national legal systems, they fail to do so, even though such enforcement is required by international humanitarian law and other norms. International criminal law, therefore, suffers from both substantive and enforcement deficiencies, leading to a substantial lack in deterrence.

Specific Treaty-Based International Law Applicable to Terrorism

Treaty-based international legal efforts to combat terrorism have suffered from similar problems in enforcement and deterrence, and are characterized in particular by the absence of a comprehensive convention governing the international dimensions of the fight against terrorism. Instead, the legislative international legal framework is comprised of thirteen international conventions,[13] adopted over a span of thirty-two years (1969–2001), that apply to different types of terrorist acts, including: airplane hijacking (4);[14] piracy on the high seas (2);[15] attacks or kidnappings of internationally protected persons, U.N. personnel, and diplomats (2);[16] attacks upon civilian maritime vessels;[17] attacks upon platforms on the high seas;[18] the taking of civilian hostages;[19] the use of bombings and explosives in terrorist acts;[20] the financing of terrorism;[21] and nuclear terrorism (pending).[22] Several regional intergovernmental organizations have established anti-terrorism conventions as well, including the Organization of American States (1971);[23] the Council of Europe (1977);[24] the South Asian Association for Regional Cooperation (1987);[25] the League of Arab States (1998);[26] the Organization of African Unity (1999);[27] and the Organization of the Islamic Conference (2000).[28]

As mentioned earlier, there is no comprehensive convention on terrorism that even modestly integrates, much less incorporates into a single text, these thirteen conventions so as to eliminate their weaknesses. The logic of such a comprehensive convention on terrorism is compelling, as is the logic against the current piecemeal approach taken by the separate conventions. Nevertheless, the United States has consistently opposed such a convention since 1972, ostensibly so that it can pick and choose from these disparate norms those that it wishes to rely upon. Above all, the United States does not want to have an effective multilateral scheme that would presumably restrict its unfettered political power to act unilaterally.

International Institutions

International legal crime-fighting institutions, in place to facilitate prevention of transnational crime, have also been ineffective. The United Nations has a Centre for International Crime Prevention in Vienna whose mandate includes fighting terrorism;[29] but the Centre has historically been underfunded, understaffed, and bereft of political influence within the U.N. system. Furthermore, in recent years it has suffered from disastrous leadership, further reducing its effectiveness.[30] Therefore, not only does it need new leadership, staff, and resources, but it needs a new mandate that better incorporates the fight against terrorism in this globalization-induced era of increased international and transnational criminal activity. In October 2001, the Security Council established a committee to deal with terrorism, at the behest of the United States, following the adoption of Security Council Resolution 1373.[31] Because the Security Council deals only with international "peace and security" threats under its powers contained in Chapter VII of the U.N. Charter, the new committee's focus is necessarily confined to a limited set of terrorist acts (those that threaten international peace and security).[32] The ad hoc nature of this Committee also portends that it may not outlive its present usefulness.

The International Criminal Police Organization (INTERPOL) has been only marginally effective in combating terrorism because major powers, like the United States, do not fully trust it. Furthermore, INTERPOL is a police association and does not include intelligence agencies. It is self-evident that combating international terrorism cannot succeed while beholden to the same bureaucratic boundaries that exist between law enforcement and intelligence agencies in domestic contexts. In this sense, INTERPOL merely reflects a political and bureaucratic reality that exists in almost all countries of the world, and which inevitably reduces its effectiveness. In fact, until 1993, INTERPOL was effectively precluded from dealing with terrorism altogether because its Charter prohibited it from dealing with such "political" matters.[33] While INTERPOL has since changed, it remains ineffective for the reasons expressed above.

Certain regional intergovernmental organizations have bodies or committees that deal with transnational criminal activity, including terrorism;[34] but not one of these bodies has any intelligence or law enforcement function.[35] Instead, they essentially do research, develop policy recommendations, and prepare draft treaties—functions that only indirectly contribute to combating terrorism.

Interstate Cooperation in Penal Matters

There are presently 190+ member-states of the United Nations, with significant variation among them in intelligence, law enforcement, prosecutorial, and judicial capabilities. Thus, it is easy for groups that engage in transnational criminality, including terrorism, to find countries where they can seek refuge, obtain support, or operate without much concern of detection.

Experience in combating transnational criminal activity, including terrorism, reveals that the first and most important stage in interdiction is intelligence and law enforcement cooperation. Such cooperation serves primarily as a means of prevention and deterrence, and only ultimately as a means of bringing perpetrators to justice. National systems, however, distribute these functions between competing bureaucratic agencies, thus reducing their individual and combined effectiveness. Furthermore, each separate national agency tends to develop *ad hoc* relationships with its counterparts in a select number of countries; so whatever information that is shared between corresponding agencies of different countries runs into the same intra-national bureaucratic impediments to information sharing and cooperation.

There is so far no international treaty that governs interstate law enforcement and intelligence cooperation. Thus, the international cooperation that does exist takes place outside international and national legal scrutiny. Therefore, there exists no protection of citizens against abuse of power and invasion of privacy, leading to a greater risk that those who are the victims of mistaken identity will have fewer means of protection at their disposal. International criminal law has so far developed six modalities for international cooperation in penal matters. Agreements, in some form, exist covering extradition, legal assistance, transfer of criminal proceedings, recognition of foreign penal judgments, transfer of sentenced persons, and freezing and seizing of assets. These six modalities, however, are not contained in a single international convention that integrates them in a way that makes them more effective. Instead, they are scattered in the provisions of a number of multilateral regional conventions.[36] There are no U.N.-sponsored international conventions dealing with any of these areas.[37]

In dealing with cooperation in international criminal enforcement, states rely on a web of bilateral treaties, each dealing with a separate modality of interstate cooperation in penal matters. While multilateral conventions dealing with substantive international criminal law, such as the thirteen aforementioned conventions dealing with terrorism,[38] do contain provisions on extradition and mutual legal assistance, these provisions are not consistent from convention to convention, and are usually limited to a few lines.[39] Instead, the United States, for example, has 137 bilateral extradition treaties applicable to 103 states, and 34 bilateral treaties on mutual legal assistance.[40] Worldwide, there are hundreds of bilateral treaties on extradition and mutual legal assistance. Other modalities, such as recognition of foreign penal judgments and transfer of criminal proceedings are seldom the subject of such bilateral agreements, while others still, such as the freezing and seizing of assets, are used only by a few states. Even the most significant for combating terrorism, the freezing and seizing of assets, until now has seldom been used except in connection with drug trafficking, due to the financial incentives that governments have in seizing assets derived from drug sales and then distributing them among their prosecutorial and law enforcement agencies.

States also rely on domestic legislation to enact these six modalities of interstate cooperation into law; as stated above, with the exception of Austria, Germany, Italy, and Switzerland, all other states deal with each of these modalities separately, thus precluding the integration of these modalities in order to make them more effective. For instance, the United States only has statutory provisions that deal with extradition and transfer of sentenced persons.[41] The extradition statute was drafted in 1825 with some recent modification.[42] At present, however, the provision is ridden with gaps that treaties and court decisions attempt to fill with considerable variation, rendering enforcement cumbersome, lengthy, and costly.[43]

The absence of both multilateral and domestic enforcement regimes that integrate the six modalities mentioned above has resulted in making interstate cooperation in penal matters cumbersome, lengthy, and, more often than not, ineffective. Developing countries, in particular, lack not only the legislative resources to engage in these modalities of interstate cooperation, but also the required expertise in their ministries of justice, interior, and foreign affairs to deal adequately with these processes. The

United Nations' efforts to train experts in these areas, for instance, through its Crime Prevention Centre in Vienna, have been few and far between. Regional organizations such as the Council of Europe, the Organization of American States and the Commonwealth Secretariat, have been better about undertaking such efforts. But these actions, too, have been limited.

In sum, the international community has not undertaken the effort of codifying international criminal law, either in its substantive or procedural aspects. Academic efforts in this direction have been sporadic,[44] and have not received significant governmental attention. As a result, there is a substantial weakness in the normative and procedural framework that is necessary to provide the bases for international cooperation in penal matters. Even reliance on national legal systems, for both the reasons stated above and those left unaddressed, were proved weak and inefficient.

State Responsibility for the Sponsorship or Failure to Take Appropriate Preventative Measures of Terrorism

International law establishes a principle whereby states that breach their international obligations are held responsible for their breaches. That responsibility has historically been of a civil nature. The remedy for a state that is aggrieved by such a breach is to bring an action before the International Court of Justice, and to obtain damages or reparations. A breach based on omission occurs where a state's failure to take appropriate action to carry out its obligations, or to prevent harm from occurring to other states, can trigger liability.

Since the late 1970s, the International Law Commission, which had been working on the codification of the Principles of State Responsibility,[45] has also considered the concept of state criminal responsibility.[46] But the concept of state criminal responsibility has met with a great deal of opposition, as evidenced by the fact that the ICC Statute does not contain such international criminal responsibility. Nevertheless, in recent years the Security Council has imposed sanctions on both Libya[47] and Sudan[48] on the basis that these states have permitted terrorist organizations to operate from within their respective territories, but with the implication that these countries may have even been involved in more direct support for such organizations, both within and beyond their own territories. The imposition of sanctions, which have the effect of collective punishment on a given population, are certainly punitive. Consequently, even though state criminal responsibility has not been officially recognized, punitive consequences have been attached to states whenever the Security Council has determined that such state action constitutes a breach of peace under Chapter VII of the U.N. Charter.

International criminal law since the Nuremberg judgment has, however, recognized the concept of criminal responsibility for organizations such as the S.S. and S.A. of Nazi Germany.[49] The events of September 11 should raise the question of whether or not state responsibility should include the concept of state criminal responsibility, much in the same way as it includes breaches of other international obligations, including failure to act. Failure to act should encompass the failure to develop appropriate national legislation to prevent and suppress terrorism—and all other international crimes as well—and to enforce both international law and national legislation in connection with such crimes. The area of state criminal responsibility is an area of international law that has not so far been adequately developed, probably for the reason that international criminal law has not sufficiently evolved as a new discipline which bridges international and criminal law.

Old and New Concepts of Conflicts of a Non-International Character

Conflicts of a non-international character are regulated in conventional international humanitarian law by Common Article 3 of the four Geneva Conventions of August 12, 1949;[50] and further developed in Additional Protocol II of 1977.[51]

These norms were originally intended to give some protection to combatants and civilians in the context of wars of national liberation, which reached their height during the decolonization era of the 1950s to the 1970s. In turn, this period of national liberation insurgency was followed by a period of uprisings by revolutionary groups who fought their governments for regime-change. These insurgents and revolutionary groups[52] resorted to acts of terror-violence against colonizers/settlers and domestic regimes, acts which led to their being referred to as terrorists. While the term "terrorism" clashed with the legitimacy of such a right to engage in a war of national liberation or to topple dictatorial regimes, it properly described the means employed to those ends. This legitimacy-versus-means issue is still with us today.

The Geneva Conventions and Additional Protocols are based on the unarticulated premise that even legitimate ends do not justify certain means. Insurgents and revolutionaries, though not without right to resort to armed conflict, must nonetheless abide by the rules of armed conflict applicable to combatants and non-combatants in the context of non-international armed conflicts. The same applies to state forces fighting against such groups.[53] Violations by one side do not allow reprisals in kind by the other.[54] Thus, symmetry in legal obligations is established.

Insurgent and revolutionary groups, however, do not have the same military means and capabilities available to conventional state forces, and therefore feel that they cannot abide by the same rules if they are to succeed. They are reinforced in their disregard of these norms by the fact that state forces also seldom respect these rules. In addition, these groups are not professional combatants and have neither the command and control nor the training that regular and well-disciplined armed forces have. Additional Protocol II tried to take some of these factors into consideration by inducing compliance of insurgent and revolutionary groups with international humanitarian law through the relaxation of conditions for prisoner of war status under the 1949 Conventions.[55] This inducement—essentially one of status recognition—has naturally been met with considerable resistance on the part of states, who fear that this gives such groups misplaced legitimacy.

These problems were seldom resolved in the many conflicts of a non-international character that have occurred since World War II, where neither governments nor insurgent and revolutionary groups abided by either the terms of Common Article 3 or those of Additional Protocol 11.[56] In fact, there has almost always been a premium for insurgent and revolutionary groups to increase their violence, including terror-violence, to levels that will garner them recognition and legitimacy, and eventually political settlements.[57] The result is that in conflicts of a non-international character the norms exist but are neither followed nor enforced.

This situation of lawlessness in the non-international context still exists. Governments do nor want to give legitimacy to insurgent and revolutionary groups, while the latter are unwilling to abide by international humanitarian law in view of the imbalance of power that exists between them and the states or regimes they are fighting against. They claim that legitimacy is on their side and that a double standard is used against them. Thus, they legitimize their terror-violence in their own perception.

With few exceptions, until September 11, conflicts of a non-international character occurred between an insurgent or revolutionary group and a state or regime. Probably the first conflict that at least began as one of a non-international character was the Vietnam conflict. The Viet Cong used Laos as a base and a travel route for operations in South Vietnam, which was deemed to be another country.[58] Another example is that of the U.S.-sponsored Nicaragua Contras whose base of operation was in Honduras. In the first case, the United States bombed Laos in violation of that state's sovereignty but the United States considered it an exercise of a legitimate right of self-defense. In the second case, the United States had no such legal justification.[59]

The operations of Al Qaeda against the interests of the United States, including both domestic[60] and foreign-based[61] actions, emanated from Afghanistan but with a support network in several countries. This raises novel questions in international humanitarian law. The first of these is whether a state can be at war with a group operating from another country (or from more than one country) with membership consisting of multiple nationalities, whose members comprise various nationalities. The second regards the legal implications of such an armed conflict.

The answer to the first question is in the negative, because only states can be at war. Clearly, however, a state can be engaged in an armed conflict with an insurgent or revolutionary group, irrespective of that group's legitimacy, and vice versa. This is reflected in Common Article 3 and Additional Protocol II[62] The fact that, historically, such conflicts were confined to the territory of a given state does not alter the legal status of the participants in that conflict and the international humanitarian law applicable to them. The laws of armed conflict are not geographically bound. They relate to the conduct of combatants with clear limits and inderrogable prohibitions with respect to what these norms refer to as "protected targets." Thus, under no circumstances can, *inter alia,* non-combatant civilians, POWs, the sick, the wounded, and the injured at land, at sea, and in hospitals, be attacked. The rationale is simply a humanitarian one and the prohibition is absolute. The only available exonerating circumstance is a reasonable mistake of fact. But no rule of military necessity exonerates those who commit such violations from criminal responsibility.[63] International humanitarian law opted for a neutral rule that protects certain targets, but by implication it favors state forces over insurgent or revolutionary forces in light of the balance of power. Regardless, however, the law is binding on both state and insurgent or revolutionary forces.[64]

Al Qaeda's attacks against the United States on September 11 and earlier fall within this paradigm: they are subject to the strictures of international humanitarian law, regardless of the legitimacy of their perpetrators' cause. If Al Qaeda violates such norms (as it has), those who committed such acts may properly be considered war criminals. Furthermore, a country such as Afghanistan that has given such a group a base of operation is also responsible for the actions of that group, and the United States is entitled to use force based on its "inherent right of self-defense" under Article 51 of the U.N. Charter. If combatants from that group are seized in the field, that is, in Afghanistan, they can be tried by a Military Commission established by the Commander of U.S. forces in the field. This is permissible under the customary law of armed conflict, and there certainly is precedent. The United States did so in the Far East after World War II, and one case reached the United States Supreme Court, *In re Yamashita.*[65]

With respect to combatants from a foreign state with which the United States is formally at war and who are caught within the United States, the only precedent for a Military Commission was in 1942 when President Roosevelt established one to try eight German saboteurs. The validity of such a Commission was recognized by the Supreme Court in *ex parte*

Quinn,[66] even if its jurisdiction in this case applied to U.S. citizens.[67] But these combatants were also nationals of a state with which the United States was at war in accordance with a proper declaration of a state of war by Congress in accordance with Article I of the Constitution.

There is therefore a valid legal basis for the Presidential Military Order of November 13, 2001, with respect to Military Commissions in the field that are outside the United States, and for Military Commissions in the United States for Violations of the Laws and Customs of War.[68] Not so for jurisdiction over persons in the United States or outside the United States who do not fall within these categories. With respect to persons within the United States, other than those mentioned above, the Military Order violates the Constitutional doctrine of separation of powers, and in particular, Article 1, Section 8, Clause 4; Article III, Section 2; and the due process clauses of the Fourteenth and Fifth Amendments and the Fourth, Fifth, Sixth and Eighth Amendments. Regrettably, this type of legal analysis and resort to the norms of international humanitarian law have not been sufficiently aired in the post–September 11 context.

Finally, it should be noted that the attacks upon the United States of September 11 constitute "Crimes Against Humanity" as defined in Article 7 of the Statute of the International Criminal Court (ICC).[69] The provisions of the ICC Statute are not applicable to the United States, as the treaty establishing the ICC has not yet entered into effect and the United States has not ratified it. Further, the United States, unlike other countries, does not have a domestic statute on "Crimes Against Humanity," and the Uniform Code of Military Justice does not apply to acts committed by civilians in the United States.[70] This is an opportunity to pass appropriate legislation to include these crimes in Title 18 U.S.C. and make them subject to the jurisdiction of Federal Courts.[71]

Conclusion

"Terrorism" is a value-laden term. Consequently, it means different things to different people, a characteristic that perhaps is best expressed in the saying, "What is terrorism to some is heroism to others," and has never been satisfactorily defined. Yet the phenomenon is as old as history, even as its manifestations have changed as a result of new technology. Both state and non-state actors have resorted to the same approaches in terrorizing civilian populations, while using different weapons and techniques. For both, the goals of terror-violence are political. However, where non-state actors are often ideologically motivated, state actors, soldiers and police personnel who are either conscripts or persons seeking a career or temporary job in these bodies, are usually not.

The need for a comprehensive convention on terrorism that is, as much as possible, value-neutral, encompassing all actors, and covering all modalities and techniques of terror-violence, is self-evident. Such a convention, though, has been politically elusive. Governments understandably seek to exclude state actors from the definition of terrorism, and reject the notion that a causal connection even exists between state-sponsored acts of terror-violence and terror-violence committed by non-state actors. Since governments inevitably prevail in the international arena, the definition of terrorism has been limited to encompass unlawful conduct by non-state actors. Even with respect to this confined definition, however, governments have avoided developing an international legal regime to prevent, control, and suppress terrorism, preferring instead the hodgepodge of thirteen treaties that currently address its particular manifestations. The absence of a coherent international legislative policy on terrorism is consistent with the *ad hoc* and discretionary approach that governments have taken toward the development of effective international legal responses to terrorism. Thus, international legal norms governing terrorism rest essentially on the identification of certain types of conduct or means employed. To date, there is no international initiative to systematize, update, integrate, or even harmonize these international norms.

Interstate cooperation in penal matters is also limited due to this lack of a coherent and cohesive international legal regime. National legal systems are therefore left with whatever jurisdictional and resource means they have at their disposal, making them ineffective in dealing with terrorism's international manifestations. The exclusion of state actors' unlawful terror violence acts from inclusion in the overall scheme of terrorism control highlights the double standard that non-state actors lament and use as a justification for their own transgressions. This disparity of treatment between state and non-state actors is plainly evident, and constitutes one of the reasons for the attraction of adherents to non-state terrorist groups.

Since the current renewed interest in the subject of terrorism is due to the tragic events of September 11, 2001, it may be useful to confront certain controversial questions. First, these attacks were not only criminal, but unconscionable as to their harmful consequences, both human and economic. Additionally, the incidents were a blow to the invulnerability of the world's only superpower. But in comparative terms, the estimated 3000 casualties of September 11 pale in contrast to some 5,000–23,000 people killed by other forms of violence, and the 15,000 people killed by drunk driving in the United States every year.[72] The effect of the reaction on many throughout the Arab and Muslim world, which consists of 1.3 billion people worldwide is to ask why, applying the same legal and moral standards, is the U.S. sponsored embargo on Iraq, which has caused the deaths of an estimated five hundred thousand innocent children, acceptable? Of course, there are several valid distinctions between the embargo and the attacks upon the United States, but not in comparative human terms. In the end, the United States bears an indirect responsibility for that outcome in Iraq. Similarly, a large segment of the world population asks why Israel's repression of the Palestinian people, which includes the commission of "grave breaches" of the Geneva Convention and what the customary law of armed conflict considers "war crimes," is deemed justified, while Palestinians' unlawful acts of targeting civilians are condemned? These are only some contemporary examples of the double standard that fuels terrorism. All these acts are unjustifiable, and one wrong does not make another right.

Terrorism springs our of despair and injustice; it is the weapon of the weak, not the coward; it is indiscriminate and a crime against its innocent victims. It must he addressed with effective and legitimate means by law enforcement and the national justice systems of all countries of the world. The control of its manifestations depends on international cooperation, but its prevention requires addressing its causes.

In 1961, President John F. Kennedy, addressing an Organization of American States heads of states meeting in Punta del Esre, Uruguay, said "those who make peaceful evolution impossible, make violent revolution inevitable."[73] If we want to put an end to the forms of violence that we call terrorism, then we need an effective international legal regime with enforcement capabilities that can, as Aristotle once said, apply the same law in Athens as in Rome.[74] This is the only alternative to Mao Tse-Tung's exhortation, to paraphrase, that truth comes out of the barrel of a gun.[75]

Notes

1. M. Cherif Bassiouni & Edoardo Vetere, *Organized Crime and Its Transnational Manifestations,* in International Criminal Law 883 (M. Cherif Bassiouni ed., 2d ed. 1999).

2. *See* Human Rights Watch, Sierra Leone: A Call Lot Justice, http://www.hrw.org/campaigns/sleone.

3. Genocide Convention, *supra* note 1.

4. Torture Convention, *supra* note 4.

5. Geneva Convention I, *supra* note 3; Geneva Convention II, *supra* note 3; Geneva Convention III, *supra* note 3; Geneva Convention IV, *supra* note 3. Note that only Additional Protocol I applies to conflicts of a non-international character, while Additional Protocol II applies to conflicts of a non-international character. *See* Additional Protocol I, *supra* note 3; Additional Protocol II, *supra* note 3.

6. There is an absence of criminal prosecutions after conflicts occur, as evidenced by the fact that the Security Council had to establish the ICTY and ICTR in order to bring about the prosecution of crimes committed in, respectively, the former Yugoslavia and Rwanda. See M. Cherif Bassiouni, *Searching for Peace and Achieving Justice: The Need for Accountability* 59 L. & Contem. Props. 1, 99728 (1996); Steven Ratner & Jason Abrams, Accountability for Human Right Atrocities

in International Law: Beyond the Nuremberg (26 ed. 2001); Diane F. Orentlicher, *Settling Accounts: The Duty to Prosecute Human Rights Violations of a Prior Regime*, 100 Yale L. J. 2537 (1991).

7. *See* Bassiouni, *supra* note 2, at 369–446.

8. *See* International Law Association. Final Report on the Executive of University Jurisdiction in Respect of Gross Human Rights Offenses, 404 (2000); M. Cherif Bassiouni, *Universal Jurisdiction for International Crimes: Historical Perspectives and Contemporary Practice*, 42 VA. J. Int'l. L. (2001). *See also* Princeton University Progress in Law and Public Affairs, The Princeton Principles of Universal Jurisdiction (2001) (prescribing principles to govern the application of universal jurisdiction in light of its potential for abuse).

9. Regina v. Bow Sr. Metro. Stipendiary Magistrate, *parte* Pinocher Ugarte (No. 3), 1 A.C. 147 (2000); Christine M. Chinkin, *Congressional Decision, Regina v. Bow Street Siependiary Magistrate, Ex Parte Pinochet Ugarte (No. 3)*, 93 Ass. J. Int'l. L. 703, 704 (1999).

10. ICC Statute, *supra* note 1, art. 7. *See also* M. Cherif Bassiouni, Crimes Against Humanity in International Law (2d rev. ed. 1999).

11. Convention on the Prohibition of the Development, Production, Stockpiling and Use of Chemical Weapons and on their Destruction, Jan. 13, 1993, S. Treaty Doc. No. 103–21, 1974 U.N.T.S. 3.

12. Convention on the Prohibition of the Development, Production and Stockpiling of Bacteriological (Biological) and Toxin Weapons and on their Destruction, Feb. 25, 1972, 26 U.S.T. 583, 1015 U.N.T.S.

13. *See* M. Cherif Bassiouni, International Terrorism: Multilateral Conventions 1937–2001 (2001).

14. Montreal Convention for the Suppression of Unlawful Acts Against the Safety of Civil Aviation, Sept. 23, 1971, 24 U.S.T. 564, 974 U.N.T.S. 17 Montreal Protocol for the Suppression of Unlawful Acts of Violence at Airports Serving Civil Aviation, Feb. 24, 1988, S. Treaty Doc. No. 100–19, 27 I.L.M. 627; Hague Convention for the Suppression of Unlawful Seizure of Aircrafts, Dec. 16, 1970, 22 U.S.T. 1641, 860 U.N.T.S. 105; Tokyo Convention on Offences and Certain Other Acts Committed on Board Aircraft, Sept. 14, 1963, 20 U.S.T. 2941, 704 U.N.T.S. 219.

15. Convention on the Law of the Sea, Dec. 10, 1982, 1833 U.N.T.S. 3; Convention on the High Seas, Apr. 29, 1958, 13 U.S.T. 2312, 430 U.N.T.S. 11.

16. Convention on the Safety of United Nations and Associated Personnel, Dec. 9, 1994, G.A. Res. 49/59, U.N. GAOR, 49th Sess., Supp. No. 49, at 299, U.N. Doc. A/49/49 (1994); Convention on the Prevention and Punishment of Crimes Against Internationally Protected Persons, Including Diplomatic Agents, Dec. 14, 1973, 28 U.S.T. 1975, 1035 U.N.T.S. 167.

17. Convention for the Suppression of Unlawful Acts Against the Safety of Maritime Navigation, Mar. 10, 1988, S. Treaty Doc. No. 101–1, 27 I.L.M. 668.

18. Protocol for the Suppression of Unlawful Acts Against the Safety of Fixed Platforms Located on the Continental Shelf, Mar. 10, 1988, S. Treaty Doc. No. 101–1, 27 I.L.M. 685.

19. Convention Against the Taking of Hostages, Dec. 17, 1979, T.I.A.S. No. 11,081, 1316 U.N.T.S. 205.

20. International Convention for the Suppression of Terrorist Bombings, Jan. 9, 1998, S. Treaty Doc. No. 106–6, 37 I.L.M. 251.

21. International Convention for the Suppression of the Financing of Terrorism, G.A. Res. 109, U.N. GAOR, 54th Sess., Supp. No. 49, Agenda Item 160, at 408, U.N. Doc. A/54/109 (1999).

22. Draft Convention on the Suppression of Acts of Nuclear Terrorism, Jan. 28, 1997, U.N. Doc. A/AC.252/L.3.

23. Organization of American States: Convention to Prevent and Punish Acts of Terrorism Taking the Form of Crimes Against Persons and Related Extortion that Are of International Significance, Feb. 2, 1971, 27 U.S.T. 3949, 1986 U.N.T.S. 195.

24. European Convention on the Suppression of Terrorism, Jan. 27, 1977, Europ. No. 90, 1979 U.N.T.S. 94 [hereinafter European Terrorism convention].

25. South Asian Association for Regional Cooperation Convention on Suppression of Terrorism, U.N. GAOR, 44th Sess., U.N. Doc. A/S1/136 (1989).

26. The League of Arab States, The Council of Arab Interior and Justice Ministers: The Arab Convention on the Suppression of Terrorism, Apr. 22, 1998, http://www.leagueofarabstates.org/W..NewsAntiterrorism.asp.

27. Organization of African Unity: Convention on the Prevention and Combating of Terrorism, July 14, 1999. http://untreaty.un.org/English/Terrorism.asp.

28. Organization of the Islamic Conference: Convention of the Organization of the Islamic Conference on Combating International Terrorism, Oct. 11, 2000, *reprinted in* UN. Doc. A154/637, Annex, http://www.oic-un.orgi2fiicfmlc.html.

29. Operated within the United Nations' Office for Drug Control and Crime Prevention, the Center works closely with the United Nations' Terrorism Prevention Branch, also based in Vienna.

30. *See* Report of the Office of Internal Oversight Services, U.N. GAOR, 56th Sess., Agenda Item 130, U.N. Doc. A/56/381 (2001), http://www.un.org/Depcs/oios/reports/a5fi...38I.pdf. Report of the Office of Internal Oversight Services on the Inspection of Programme Management and Administrative Practices in the Office for Drug Control and Crime Prevention, U.N. GAOR, 56th Sess., Agenda Items 123, 124, 134, 143, U.N. Doc. A156/83 (2001), http://www.un.orgiDeprsloios/reports/a5&83.htm; Triennial Review of the Implementation of the Recommendations Made by the CPC at its Thirty-Eighth Session on the In-Depth Evaluation of the U.N. Crime Prevention and Criminal Justice, U.N. ESCOR, 41st Sess.

31. S.C. Res. 1373. U.N. SCOR, 56th Sess., 4385th mtg., U.N. Doc. S/Res/1373 (2001).

32. *See* id. 76.

33. *See* Interpol Const., art. 3, http://www.interpol.int/Publit/ICPO/LegalMaterialS/Constitution..asp ("It is strictly forbidden for the organization to undertake any Intervention or activities of a political, military, or religious or racial character."). However, the organization recognized the role it could play in combating international terrorism as early as 1985. *See* International Terrorism and Unlawful Interference with Civil Aviation, Interpol G.A. ass. No. AGN/54/RES/1 (1985), http://www.interpol.intipobiic/terrorism/default.55p. *See also, Mary Jo Grotenroth, Interpol's Role in International Law Enforcement* in Legal Responses To International Terrorism: U.S. Procedural Aspects 375, 381 (1988) (Interpol's resolution on terrorism); Nepore, *The Role of International Criminal Police (INTERPOL),* in A Treatise on International Criminal Law: Crimes and Punishment 676 (M. Cherif Bassiouni & Ved P. Nanda eds., 1973).

34. These organizations include the Commonwealth Secretariat, the Council of Europe, the European Union, the League of Arab States, and the Organization of American States.

35. *See* M. Cherif Bassiouni, *Policy Considerations on Interstate Cooperation in Criminal Matters,* in International Criminal Law, *supra* note 13, at 3.

36. *See, e.g.,* Inter-American Convention on Extradition, O.A.S. T.S. No. 60 (February 25, 1981), http://www.oas.org/iuridico/eng1ish/sigsfb..47 html; Inter-American Convention on Mutual Assistance in Criminal Matters, O.A.S. T.S. No. 75

(May 23, 1992); European Convention on Extradition, Dec. 13, 1957, 359 U.N.T.S. 273. *See also*, Ekrehart Mollor Rappard & M. Cherif Bassiouni, European Inter-State Co-operations in Criminal Matters: The Council of Europe's Legal Instruments (2d ed. 1991) (for a discussion on the Council of Europe's Conventions). The League of Arab States also has a convention on extradition and one on mutual legal assistance.

37. *See* U.N. Model Treaty on Extradition, G.A. Res. 116, U.N. GAOR, 45th Sess., Annex, at 21197 15, U.N. Doc. A/RES/45/1 16 (1990); U.N. Model Treaty on Mutual Assistance in Criminal Matters, G.A. Res. 117, 45th Sess., Annex, at 21549, U.N. Doc. A/RES/117 (1990).

38. *See supra* notes 26–34 and accompanying text.

39. *See* M. Cherif Bassiouni & Edward M. Wise, Aut Dedere Aut Judicare: The Duty to Prosecute or Extradite in International Law 79719 (1995). *See also* M. Cherif Bassiouni, International Extradition in United States Law and Practice 295–382 (3d ed. 1996).

40. *See* 18 U.S.C. 3181–3196 for a listing of these treaties.

41. Id. 3181–3195.

42. Antiterrorism and Effective Death Penalty Act of 1996, Pub. L. No. 104–132, at 443(a), 110 Stat. 1280(1996).

43. A 1984 proposal for comprehensive revision of the statute was rejected because it was deemed to contain too many individual guarantees. *See also* M. Cherif Bassiouni, *Extradition Reform Legislation in the United States: 1981–1983, 17 Akron L. Rev. 495 (1984); United States and United Kingdom Supplementary Extradition Treaty: Hearings Before the Subcomm. on Foreign Relations, United States Senate,* 99th Cong. (1985).

44. *See* M. Cherif Bassiouni, A Draft International Criminal Code and a Draft Statute for an International Criminal Tribunal (1987).

45. The International Law Commission concluded its work in 2001. *See* International Law Commission, Report by the International Law Commission on the Work of its Fifty-Third Session, Apr. 2397 June 1 July 297Aug. 18, 2001, U.N. GAOR, 53d Sess., Supp. No. 10, U.N. Doc. A/56/10 (2001).

46. *See* M. Cherif Bassiouni, *The Sources and Content of International Criminal Law: A Theoretical Framework,* in 1 Int'l. Crim. L. 3, *supra* note 13, at 27 (2d ed. 1999).

47. S.C. Res. 748, U.N. SCOR, 42d Sess., 3063d mtg., U.N. Doc. S/Res.f 748 (1992).

48. S.C. Res. 1054, U.N. SCOR, 1 Crh Sess., 3660th mtg., U.N. Doc. S/Rest 1054 (1996).

49. *See* Bassiouni, *supra* note 58, at 24.

50. *See* Geneva Convention I, *supra* note 3, art. 3; Geneva Convention II, *supra* note 3, art. 3; Geneva Convention III, *supra* note 3, art. 3; Geneva Convention IV, *supra* note 3, art. 3. *See also,* Documents on the Laws of War (Adam Roberts & Richard Gucif eds., 3d ed. 2000). With respect to the customary law of armed conflict, *see* International Committee for the Red Cross, International Law Concerning the Conduct of Hostilities (1996).

51. *See* Additional Protocol II, *supra* note 3.

52. The terms "insurgents" and "revolutionary groups" are just two of the terms used to describe groups of this type. *See* The International Law of Civil War (Richard Falk ed., 1971); Elizabeth Chadwick, Self-Determination, Terrorism, and the International Humanitarian Law of Armed Conflict (1996); Restructuring the Global Military Sector: New Wars (Mary Kaldot & Basket Vaske eds., 1997).

53. *See, e.g.,* Howard S. Levie, Terrorism in War: The Law of War Crimes (1993). *See also* Hans-Peter Gasser, *Prohibition of Terrorist Attacks in International Humanitarian Law,* 1985 Int'l. Rev. Red Cross 200, 203 (1985).

54. *See* Frits Kashoven & Liesbeth Zeoveld, Constraints on the Waging of War: An Introduction to International Humanitarian Law (3d ed. 2001).

55. *See* Additional Protocol II, *supra* note 3, art. 43. *See also,* Commentary on the Protocols of 8 June 1977 to the Geneva Convention of 12 August 1949 (Yves Sandoz et al. eds., 1987).

56. The failure to resolve these problems has generated considerable harm in those conflicts. For a survey of such harm, see Jennifer Balint, *Conflict Victimization and Legal Redress,* 14 Nouvelles Etudes Penales 101 (1998).

57. This was the case with recent rebellions in Liberia and Sierra Leone, which resulted in approximately 200,000 and 300,000 victims, respectively, most of whom were innocent civilians, and many of whom had their limbs cut off or were raped.

58. North Vietnam and South Vietnam were legally deemed two different countries, but North Vietnam rejected that contention and argued that all of Vietnam was one country. *See* The Vietnam War and International Law (Richard Falk ed., 1976).

59. *See* Military and Paramilitary Activities in and Against Nicaragua (Nicar. v. U.S.) (1986) I.C.J. 14.

60. With respect to the September 11 attacks, both the hijacking and the subsequent destruction of the four airplanes occurred within the continental United States.

61. Foreign-based actions include attacks upon the U.S. Embassies in Kenya and Tanzania and against a U.S. naval vessel the *U.S. Cole,* in Yemen.

62. *See* George Aldrich, *The Laws of War on Land,* 94 Am. J. Int'l. L. 42 (2000).

63. *See, e.g.,* Christopher Greenwood, A Manual of International Law (1995); Leslie C. Green, Essays on the Modern Lawn of War (2d ed., 1999); The Law of War Crimes: National and International Approaches (Timothy L. H. McCormack & Gary J. Simpson eds., 1997) [hereinafter Law of War Crimes].

64. *See* Law of War Crimes, *supra* note 18.

65. 327 U.S. 1 (1946) (upholding the authority of Supreme Allied Commander General Douglas MacArthur to establish such Commissions). *See also* 327 U.S. 759 (1946) ("The motion for leave or file petition for writ of habeas corpus and writ of prohibition is denied and the petition for writ of certiorari is also denied on authority of Application of Yamashita, and Yamashita v. Styer); Lawrence Taylor, A Trail of Generals: Homma, Yamashita, MacArthur (1981).

66. 317 U.S. 1 (1942).

67. Id. at 37.

68. Military Order, *Detention, Treatment and Trial of Certain Non-Citizens in the War Against Terrorism,* 66 Fed. Reg. 57, 833 (Nov. 13, 2001). *See* Jordan Paust, *After My Lai: The Case for War Crimes Jurisdiction over Civilians in Federal District Courts,* 50 Tex. L. Rev. 6 (1971).

69. *See* ICC Statute, *supra* note 1; Bassiouni, *supra* note 1; *International Criminal Court Ratification and National Implementing Legislation,* 71 Rev. Int'l. Detroit Penal (2000).

70. *See* 10 U.S.C. 801–946 (2000). *See also* Jordan Paust, M. Cherif Bassiouni et al., International Criminal Law: Cases and Materials (2d. rev. ed. 2000).

71. *See* Paust, *supra* note 80.

72. 23,040 cases in 1990, and 15,530 cases in 1999. See Federal Bureau of Investigation, Uniform Crime Reports: Crime in the United States 1999, Index of Crime, http://www.fbi.gov/urr/99cius.htm.

73. The Law of Dissent and Riots (M. Cherif Bassiouni ed., 1971).

74. *See* Aristotle, the Nicomachean Ethics (David Ross trans., Oxford Univ. Press, 1998).

75. Quotations from Chairman Mao Tse-Tung 33 (Stuart Schram ed., 1967) ("Every communist must grasp the truth, 'Political power grows out of the barrel of a gun.'").

PART 2.2

International Law
as Normative System:
For the Protection
of Individual Rights

16

Protecting Human Rights in a Globalizing World

DINAH SHELTON

Introduction

International human rights law aims primarily to protect individuals and groups from abusive action by states and state agents. Recent developments throughout the world, including failed states, economic deregulation, privatization, and trade liberalization across borders—components of what has come to be known as globalization—have led to the emergence of powerful non-state actors who have resources sometimes greater than those of many states. Two opposing views of globalization and its relationship to human rights have emerged: some see the two topics as mutually reinforcing and positive in improving human well-being, while others view globalization as posing new threats not adequately governed by existing international human rights law. . . .

The article concludes that responses to globalization are significantly changing international law and institutions in order to protect persons from violations of human rights committed by non-state actors. To the extent that these changes have brought greater transparency to and participation in international organizations, globalization has produced unintended benefits and further challenges to the democratic deficit in global governance.[1] At the same time, an emphasis on subsidiary and a strengthening of weak states and their institutions may be necessary to ensure that globalization does not mean a decline in state promotion and protection of human rights. To ensure that such strengthening does not lead to further human rights violations, the international community should make concerted multilateral efforts to enhance its ability to respond to human rights violations, rather

Reprinted with permission of Boston College International and Comparative Law Review.

than unleashing each state to control what it views as the sins of the private sector.

The Meanings of Globalization

Globalization is a multidimensional phenomenon, comprising "numerous complex and interrelated processes that have a dynamism of their own."[2] It involves a deepening and broadening of rapid transboundary exchanges due to developments in technology, communications, and media. Such exchanges and interactions occur at all levels of governance and among non-state actors, creating a more interdependent world.

Globalization is not new,[3] although its forms and the technology that spurs it have changed. Globalization today is most often associated with economic interdependence, deregulation, and a dominance of the market-place that includes a shifting of responsibilities from state to non-state actors.[4] Economic globalization has been accompanied by a marked increase in the influence of international financial markets and transnational institutions, including corporations, in determining national policies and priorities.[5] In addition, information and communications technology has emerged as a dominant force in the global system of production, while trade in goods, services, and financial instruments are more prevalent than any time in history.[6]

Some see this emergence of cross-border networks of production, finance, and communications as posing profound challenges to traditional concepts of state sovereignty. Richard Falk has spoken of the "disabling of the state as guardian of the global public good"[7] in the face of a shift of power and autonomy from the state to markets. Kenichi Ohmae refers to a "borderless world" in which "[m]ore than anything else, the burgeoning flow of information directly to consumers is eroding the ability of governments to pretend that their national economic interests are synonymous with those of their people."[8] He adds that, "[i]n today's world there is no such thing as a purely national economic interest."[9] Perhaps the same may be said for national political interests. Other authors refer to the decline of the western nation state.[10] The presence of weakened and failed states is an undeniable modern phenomenon,[11] yet there is no clear causal link between globalization and failed states.[12] Moreover, state sovereignty remains the international frame of reference, even if the exact contours of sovereignty change over time, as they have throughout history.

Paul Streeten has pointed out that globalization can come "from above," in the form of multinational firms, international capital flows, and world markets, or it can come "from below," reflecting the concerns of individuals and groups throughout the world.[13] It seems evident that globalization has enhanced the ability of civil society to function across borders and promote human rights. The past two decades have seen a shift to multi-party democratic regimes, as more than 100 countries ended rule by military dictatorships or single parties. Pressed by an international network of nongovernmental organizations and activists, the international protection of human rights itself can be seen as an aspect of globalization, reflecting universal values about human dignity that limit the power of the state and reduce the sphere of sovereignty.

Global technology and the information revolution have limited the ability of governments to control the right to seek, receive, and transmit information within and across boundaries. Ideas and information can circulate more freely, as can individuals. The number of televisions per 1000 persons doubled between 1980 and 1995, while the number of Internet subscribers exceeds 700 million persons. Free circulation enhances the ability to inform all persons about rights and avenues of redress. It also makes it more difficult for governments to conceal violations and allows activists more easily to mobilize shame in order to induce changes in government behavior.[14] Information technology and the media also can be used, however, to violate human rights when the government is weak. In Rwanda, the radio and television channel "Radio-Télévision Libre des Mille Collines" was an important avenue for inciting genocide.[15] Internet too has been used for hate speech.[16]

The multiple and sometimes contradictory impacts of globalization are reflected in the complete disagreement of views over the pattern and direction of globalization. Proponents point to a rise in average incomes for the world as a whole. Opponents note that there is persistent inequality and poverty. The World Bank Development Report estimates that, at purchasing power parity, the per capita GDP in the richest twenty countries in 1960 was eighteen times that of the poorest twenty countries.[17] By 1995, the gap had widened to thirty-seven times.[18] According to the International Labour Organization (ILO), only 24% of the world's foreign direct investment (FDI) went to developing countries in 1999, down from 38% over the period 1993–1997, and 80% of recent investment went to only ten developing countries.[19] Wealth concentration is not only seen among countries, but among individuals as well. According to the *UNDP Human Development Report 1999,* the assets of the three wealthiest individuals in the world is more than the combined gross national product of all least developed countries, while the annual sales of one transnational corporation exceeds the combined gross domestic product of Chile, Costa Rica, and Ecuador.[20]

Globalization, thus, has created powerful non-state actors that may violate human rights in ways that were not contemplated during the development of the modern human rights movement.[21] This development poses challenges to international human rights law, because, for the most part, that law has been designed to restrain abuses by powerful states and state agents, not to regulate the conduct of non-state actors themselves or to allow intervention in weak states when human rights violations occur.[22] An increasingly globalized civil society is likely to respond to economic globalization by opposing liberalized trade and investment regimes that are not accompanied by accountability, transparency, public participation, and respect for fundamental rights.

The result may be viewed as a "clash of globalizations."[23] The clash plays out in the international institutional and normative system that has separated human rights matters from economic policy and regulation, creating distinct institutions, laws, and values for each field. Integrating them is no easy task; indeed, some commentators view a conflict as inevitable. . . . [24]

Is Globalization Good for Human Rights?

There is considerable debate over the question of whether or not globalization is good for human rights. One view is that globalization enhances human rights, leading to economic benefits and consequent political freedoms.[25] The positive contributions of globalization have even led to the proposal that it be accepted as a new human right.[26] In general, trade theory predicts a significant increase in global welfare stemming from globalization, indirectly enhancing the attainment of economic conditions necessary for economic and social rights. Many thus believe that market mechanisms and liberalized trade will lead to an improvement in the living standards of all people. Some also posit that free trade and economic freedom are necessary conditions of political freedom, or at least contribute to the rule of law that is an essential component of human rights.[27] Certainly, globalization facilitates international exchanges that overcome the confines of a single nation or a civilization, allowing participation in a global community. There is also the possibility that economic power can be utilized to sanction human rights violators more effectively.[28] Ease of movement of people, goods, and services are enhanced. Increased availability and more efficient allocation of resources, more open and competitive production, and improved governance could lead to faster growth and more rights. In sum, Judith Bello argues that:

> Trade liberalization promotes the growth of stability-promoting middle class all over the globe; trade enhances efficiency and wealth and thereby creates potential revenue for environmental protection. Trade creates jobs in developing as well as developed countries, thereby reducing the pressure on both illegal immigration and illicit drug trafficking. Trade liberalization is not a panacea for the world's problems, but it can be part of a solution for many of them.[29]

The pro-globalization assumption that globalization is in the common good and market forces will achieve general well being is not a consensus view. Anne Orford, for example, argues that, "[t]he trade and investment liberalization furthered by the Uruguay Round agreements entrenches a relationship between states and transnational corporations that privileges the property interests of those corporations over the human rights of local peoples and communities."[30] As such, the economic and technological changes associated with globalization may lead to a world in which the state is no longer the principal threat to human rights, but one where the threats are more posed by multinational corporations, multilateral intergovernmental organizations, and transnational criminal syndicates or organized terrorists. The U.N. Development Program devoted its 2000 *Human Development Report* to "Human Development and Human Rights" in which it pointed out that, "global corporations can have enormous impact on human rights—in their employment practices, in their environmental impact, in their support for corrupt regimes or in their advocacy for policy changes."[31]

It has been argued that values associated with human rights emerge with multinational free market growth, as the rule of law follows investors who seek predictability and safeguarding of investments, leading to strengthened independent institutions for civil and political rights, but human rights advocates assert that liberalization in trade, investment, and finance does not necessarily lead to general economic development or better human rights performance. According to the Oxfam Poverty Report:

> Trade has the power to create opportunities and support livelihoods; and it has the power to destroy them. Production for export can generate income, employment, and the foreign exchange which poor countries need for their development. But it can also cause environmental destruction and a loss of livelihoods, or lead to unacceptable levels of exploitation. The human impact of trade depends on how goods are produced, who controls the production and marketing, how the wealth generated is distributed, and the terms upon which countries trade. The way in which the international trading system is managed has a critical bearing on all of these areas.[32]

Opponents of globalization see it as a threat to human rights in several ways. First, local decision-making and democratic participation are undermined when multinational companies, the World Bank, and the IMF set national economic and social policies. Second, unrestricted market forces threaten economic, social, and cultural rights such as the right to health, especially when structural adjustment policies reduce public expenditures for health and education. Third, accumulations of power and wealth in the hands of foreign multinational companies increase unemployment, poverty, and the marginalization of vulnerable groups.

Some criticism has been particularly strong. In resolution 1997/11, the U.N. Sub-Commission on the Promotion and Protection of Human Rights asked El Hadji Guissé to prepare a working document on the impact of the activities of transnational corporations on the realization of economic, social, and cultural rights. The report, delivered in June, 1998, is a wholesale condemnation of economic globalization.[33] It begins, "[t]oday's economic and financial systems are organized in such a way as to act as pumps that suck up the output of the labour of the toiling masses and transfer it, in the form of wealth and power, to a privileged minority."[34] Given this opening, it is not surprising that Guissé finds little in globalization that assists in the realization of human rights. Yet, he agrees that the pursuit of profit is not necessarily incompatible with the promotion and protection of human rights.

Globalization is leading to greater problems of state capacity to comply with human rights obligations, particularly economic, social, and cultural rights,[35] such as trade union freedoms,[36] the right to work, and the right to social security. It also may have a disproportionate effect on minorities.[37] Cooperation internationally and from non-state actors is needed in the face of an undoubted concentration of wealth in the hands of multinational enterprises, greater than the wealth of many countries. Globalization is a particular issue for women, because they often bear a disproportionate burden of poverty, which may be exacerbated by economic restructuring, deregulation,[38] and privatization.[39] Investors have demonstrated a preference for women in the "soft" industries such as apparel, shoe- and toy-making, data-processing, and semi-conductor assembling—industries that require unskilled to semi-skilled labor, leading women to bear the disproportionate weight of the constraints introduced by globalization.[40] The process of economic liberalization has also led to growth in the informal sector and increased female participation therein. Employment in the informal sector generally means that employment benefits and mechanisms of protection are unavailable.[41] Underemployment seems to be as big a problem as open unemployment. It also has been asserted that states feel compelled to ease labor standards, modify tax regulations, and relax other standards to attract foreign investment,[42] seen especially in the export production zones (EPZs) where employment may be plentiful, but working conditions poor. Labor unions claim that EPZs are sometimes designed to undermine union rights,[43] deny or restrict rights to free association, expression, and assembly.[44] There are some twenty-seven million workers employed in such zones worldwide.[45] It is estimated that the number of developing countries with EPZs increased from twenty-four in 1976 to ninety-three in 2000, with women providing up to 80% of the labor force.[46]

Another impact observed in many countries is a shift from companies hiring permanent employees with job security and benefits, to the use of contingent or temporary workers lacking health care, retirement, collective bargaining arrangements, and other security available to the permanent work force.[47] As with other negative impacts of globalization, this one also has more severe impacts on women,[48] minorities, and migrant workers.[49] Women comprise the largest segment of migrant labor flows, both internally and internationally. States often do not include migrant workers in their labor standards, leaving women particularly vulnerable.[50] Overall, only some 20% of the world's workers have adequate social protection.[51] In addition, some 3000 people a day die from work-related accidents or disease.[52]

Globalization also has produced an important new type of transboundary criminal enterprise. International crimes that involve or impact human rights violations are increasing: illegal drug trade, arms trafficking, money laundering, and traffic in persons are all facilitated by the same technological advances and open markets that assist in human rights. Traffic in women for sexual purposes is estimated to involve more than $7 billion a year, but the sex trade is not the only market for humans. Coercion against agricultural workers, domestic workers, and factory workers also is evident.

Crime syndicates are rivaling multinational corporations for economic power, threatening the security and well being of large numbers of persons. The free movement of capital, which is a prior condition to the growth in foreign investment, permits money laundering in the absence of exchange controls or other appropriate regulation. The free circulation of goods can bring stolen automobiles, smuggled sex workers, and torture implements, as well as fresh fruit and vegetables. At the same time, new technologies also permit the easier pirating of intellectual property. Indigenous groups and local communities challenge the very foundations of intellectual property protection, particularly when applied to pharmaceuticals necessary to ensure the right to life and to health.

Certain human rights are particularly threatened by globalization. Respect for private life needs protection against personal data collection. Cultural and linguistic rights can also suffer under global assault, but the evidence seems contradictory. There is no doubt that globalization facilitates the transfer of cultural manifestations and cultural property. A study by the U.N. Economic and Social Council (UNESCO) indicates that commerce in cultural property tripled between 1980 and 1991 under the impulse of satellite communications, Internet, and videocassettes.[53] Yet, in this field, as in others, mergers and acquisitions have concentrated ownership to the detriment of local industry. The Hollywood film industry represented 70% of the European market in 1996, more than double what it was a decade earlier, and constituted 86% of the Latin American market. In the opposite direction, traditional cultures across the world are being transmitted and revived in multiethnic states through the movement of peoples, their languages, and their beliefs.

Economic globalization has been criticized for protecting investors to the detriment of local people, arguably increasing unemployment and underemployment. To make conditions better for investors, the World Bank and IMF impose economic "reform" that may lead to human rights violations, including an increase in infant and child mortality rates.[54] In addition, structural reform usually mandates trade liberalization, something industrialized countries have not been similarly pressured to do. States may or may not be weakened, but the weakest within states are further marginalized. Lack of accountability results from the inability to exercise rights of political participation or information about key decisions. Structural adjustment may require cutting public expenditure for health and education, social security, and housing. Labor deregulation, privatization, and export-oriented production increase income disparity and marginalization in many countries.[55] This leaves the main function of the state to be policing and security, which may lead either to increased political repression or to violent protests and political destabilization. According to the independent expert appointed by the U.N. to study the impact of structural adjustment programs on human rights, there are two main consequences of such programs. First, they have led to a significant erosion of the living standards of the poor and investment in the productive sectors of many countries; second, such countries have ceded their right to independently determine their country's development priorities. According to the expert, structural adjustment shifted from being a mechanism to handle national debt into a vehicle for deregulation, trade liberalization, and privatization—all reducing the role of the state in national development. Properly structured debt relief is essential to alleviate poverty and build democratic institutions.[56]

The formation and enhancement of transboundary religious, tribal, corporate, or associational allegiances are aspects of globalization that have both positive and negative aspects. They may challenge the nationality link and loyalty of individuals towards the territorial state. Networks of human rights activists forming an international civil society are an important component in the protection of human rights. Their formation and work is enhanced by information technology and ease of movement. Networks linked by air, telecommunications, media, and the Internet allow shared ideas and the formation of shared values. The human rights activists of the world share values with each other and a commitment to universal compliance with human rights norms that transcend nationality and particular cultural values. These activists have in turn pressured corporations to accept social responsibility in their global dealings. On the negative side, international criminal syndicates and terrorist groups form the same transboundary allegiances and threaten the security of all. The problems then become those of states that are too weak, not states that are too strong.

Are Human Rights Good for Globalization?

The dominant view among economists and policy makers in multilateral financial institutions appears to be that any hindrances to global trade and investment are bad for development in general. Recent studies, however, suggest that business and economic indicators are better in developing countries that have more favorable civil and political rights than in repressive regimes.[57] Mancur Olson explains that the majority in whose interests a democratic government is ruling demand smaller growth-retarding exaction from the minority and pay greater attention to the supply of growth-promoting public goods than does a dictatorship, even when the majority is acting out of pure self-interest.[58] According to his analysis, the dispersal of political power and the emergence of representative government have often been the trigger for faster economic growth. So, prosperity is not only good for democracy, but democracy seems good for prosperity. A feature in the poorest countries is the absence or poor enforcement of contract and property rights, which are necessary for advanced markets and rapid growth.

It also seems clear that establishment of the rule of law with protection for contracts and property rights is essential to maintaining security for international investment and trade. Tourism is the world's fastest-growing industry, generating more than 10% of total international GNP, and is particularly harmed by images of repression, acts of terrorism, and the political instability that usually result from widespread human rights abuses. Judicial reform and the establishment of the rule of law with respect for human rights should be a priority, even if only for the instrumental reason to secure investment, property, contracts, debts, and profits. As the U.N. Development Program's *Human Development Report 2000* proclaims, "[r]ights make human beings better economic actors."[59]

Like human rights, economic liberalization is concerned with restraining the power of the state. At the special session of the U.N. General Assembly to review progress since the 1995 Copenhagen World Summit for Social Development, the final document, adopted on July 1, 2000, makes special reference to the role and responsibilities of the private sector to work with governments to eradicate poverty, promote full employment and universal access to social services, and ensure that everyone has equal opportunities to participate in society. In turn, democratic rule and the rule of law inspires further global business activity, generating an upward spiral in rights protection. The text encourages corporate social responsibility and promotes dialogue among government, labor, and employer groups. It also expresses a belief in the relationship between economic growth and social development.[60] The Copenhagen Declaration and Program of Action affirmed that social development and social justice cannot be attained in the absence of respect for all human rights and fundamental freedoms. The Sub-Commission on Promotion and Protection of Human Rights finds in major human rights instruments "obligations and goals which are fundamental to the development process and to economic policy."[61]

None of the international human rights instruments imposes an economic model, free trade, or deregulation. Yet, as Anne Orford points out, there is a link between human rights and a liberal economic regime that may facilitate globalization.[62] Liberal concepts of human rights identify the individual with property ownership and are linked with the emergence of capitalism.[63] In contrast, the failure by some governments to respect core labor standards is likely to provoke trade tensions and lead to protectionist efforts. The stability of the world's trading system may thus depend upon ensuring that an open trading system does not come at the price of human rights.

International Responses to the Problems of Globalization and Human Rights

Globalization has led to an increased concern about the responsibility of all international actors to ensure the promotion and protection of human rights. International institutions and scholars have responded with various proposals for strengthening the international regime. First, human rights activists and institutions have begun to posit the primacy of human rights law. The Committee on Economic, Social and Cultural Rights (CESCR) has emphasized that, "the realms of trade, finance and investment are in no way exempt from these general principles [on respect for human rights] and that international organizations with specific responsibilities in those areas should play a positive and constructive role in relation to human rights."[64] The CESCR also asserts that competitiveness, efficiency, and economic rationalism must not be permitted to become the primary or exclusive criteria against which governmental and inter-governmental policies are evaluated.[65]

Second, state responsibility for failing to control the actions of private parties has received considerable attention in the case law of international tribunals[66] and the work of the U.N.[67] Third, international law is increasingly regulating non-state behavior directly. Fourth, private market mechanisms such as codes of conduct or consumer purchasing schemes have sought to influence corporate behavior. Finally, restructured international governance mechanisms are bringing a variety of international actors together to achieve common goals.

The first general trend, seen particularly among human rights advocates, has been to affirm the priority of human rights over other international legal regimes. According to this view, international economic policies cannot be exempt from conformity to international human rights law.

States and international organizations are directly obliged to comply with those principles and obliged to ensure that private economic actors within their jurisdictions do not act in violation of those rights.[68] In a 1998 statement on globalization and economic, social, and cultural rights, the CESCR expressed its concerns over the negative impact of globalization on the enjoyment of economic, social, and cultural rights, and called on states and multilateral institutions to pay enhanced attention to taking a rights-based approach to economic policy-making.[69] The CESCR declared that the realms of trade, finance, and investment are in no way exempt from human rights obligations. Those concerns were raised again in the statement the CESCR addressed to the WTO Third Ministerial Conference in Seattle in November, 1999. The CESCR urged WTO members to adopt a human rights approach at the conference, recognizing the fact that, "promotion and protection of human rights is the first responsibility of Governments."[70] The CESCR's language echoes that of the Vienna Declaration and Program of Action,[71] which affirmed that, "the promotion and protection of human rights and fundamental freedoms is the first responsibility of government" and that, "the human person is the central subject of development." Similarly, the Copenhagen Declaration and Program of Action[72] recommended to states the need to intervene in markets to prevent or counteract market failure, promote stability and long-term investment, ensure fair competition and ethical conduct, and harmonize economic and social development. The Sub-Commission on Promotion and Protection of Human Rights has expressly asserted the "centrality and primacy" of human rights obligations in all areas of governance and development, including international and regional trade, investment and financial policies, agreements, and practices.[73] The Commission on Human Rights, for its part, has affirmed that, "the exercise of the basic rights of the people of debtor countries to food, housing, clothing, employment, education, health services and a healthy environment cannot be subordinated to the implementation of structural adjustment policies and economic reforms arising from the debt."[74] The special rapporteurs on globalization and its impact on the full enjoyment of human rights flatly assert that, "the primacy of human rights law over all other regimes of international law is a basic and fundamental principle that should not be departed from."[75]

Can the primacy of human rights be justified in international law? An argument can be posited on the basis of treaty law. The U.N. Charter refers to human rights in its second preamble paragraph and lists human rights as the third of its purposes in Article 1, after maintenance of peace and security, and the development of friendly relations among nations based on equal rights and self-determination of peoples.[76] The Charter not only makes human rights an aim of the organization, it obligates all member states to take joint and separate action with the U.N. to achieve universal respect for and observance of human rights and fundamental freedoms, as in Articles 55 and 56.[77] Article 103 of the Charter provides that, "in the event of a conflict between the obligations of the members of the United Nations under the present Charter and their obligations under any other international agreement, their obligations under the present Charter shall prevail."[78] This "supremacy clause" has been invoked to suggest that the aims and purposes of the U.N., maintenance of peace and security, and the promotion and protection of human rights, constitute an international public order to which other treaty regimes must conform.[79] It may be argued, however, that there is no conflict between human rights and the international trade and financial regime because they regulate separate areas of human activity. In addition, some may point to the "later in time" rule of the Vienna Convention on the Law of Treaties.[80] However, the Vienna Convention is not retroactive and, in any case, the provisions of Article 30 expressly provide that the later in time rule is "without prejudiced to [A]rticle 103 of the United Nations Charter."[81] As with domestic bills of rights, international human rights law may limit the implementation of other social goals to means and methods compatible with its contents. In practice, states and international organizations are taking action to increase the responsibility of state and non-state actors when their economic activities impact on human rights.

The second response to globalization is found in efforts to insist on state responsibility for the behavior of non-state actors. As far as human rights are concerned, this means the state is responsible for its acts and its omissions. The Restatement of U.S. Foreign Relations Law makes it clear that a state violates international law if it commits, encourages, or condones genocide, slavery, torture, or inhuman or degrading treatment.[82] Complicity in human rights violations between state and non-state actors is a growing subject of interest and litigation.

The next question posed is whether or not a state is responsible for the acts of international organizations in which it participates. The International Covenant on Economic, Social and Cultural Rights (ICESCR),[83] Article 2(1), provides that each state party will "take steps, individually and through international assistance and cooperation" to achieve the rights in the Covenant.[84] This means that voting in the World Bank or IMF for programs or policies that will lead to human rights regression in one or more states could be deemed to violate the voter's obligations under the Covenant.[85]

Traditional interpretations of the ICESCR, Article 2, permit states to determine how and when they allocate resources for the realization of economic, social, and cultural rights.[86] However, in its General Comment No. 3 on the nature of the states parties' obligations under the ICESCR, the CESCR declared that concrete legal obligations are imposed by the Covenant under Article 2.[87] State parties are obliged to realize minimum standards relating to each of the rights utilizing available resources in an effective manner. Violations can occur either through commission or omission.

The jurisprudence of the CESCR also recognizes "minimum core obligations" on the part of state parties that have to be fulfilled irrespective of resource or other constraints. In determining whether a state party has utilized the "maximum of its available resources," attention shall be paid to the equitable and effective use of and access to available resources. States also may be responsible if they fail to exercise due diligence in controlling the behavior of non-state actors, such as transnational corporations, over which they exercise jurisdiction, when such behavior deprives individuals of their economic, social, and cultural rights.

The CESCR has consulted with multilateral institutions, specialized agencies, and non-governmental organizations (NGOs) in developing its approach to the issue of globalization. Other treaty-based human rights mechanisms have also shown concern over rising economic disparities that impact on their individual mandates. For example, the Committee examining periodic country reports under the Convention on the Elimination of All Forms of Discrimination against Women (CEDAW), has shown great concern over the evidence of the feminization of poverty and the impact of economic policies on the rights of women.[88] The Human Rights Committee, in General Comment No. 28 dealing with equality of rights between men and women, gives some consideration to issues such as the feminization of poverty, declining social indicators, and gender inequity in employment within the framework of globalization.

A number of U.N. specialized agencies have also addressed the question of globalization. The ILO has long tackled the phenomenon. From the Copenhagen Social Summit in 1995 to the 1998 Declaration on Fundamental Principles and Rights at Work, the ILO has pressed for an international consensus on the content of the core labor standards that provide a social floor to the global economy.[89] In 1998, the ILO adopted the Convention concerning the Prohibition and Immediate Action for the Elimination of the Worst Forms of Child Labour (Convention No. 182).[90] It also adopted its Declaration on Fundamental Principles and Rights at Work together with a follow-up procedure based upon technical cooperation and reporting. The principles have been incorporated into codes of conduct by the private sector and also used as a basis for action by various regional communities, such as the Southern African Development Community, MERCOSUR, and the Caribbean Community. U.N. bodies and specialized agencies, such as the U.N. Children's Fund (UNICEF), the U.N. Educational, Scientific and Cultural Organization (UNESCO), the Office of the U.N. High Commissioner for Refugees (UNHCR), and the U.N. Environment Programme (UNEP), have all carried out work that has implications for the overall response by the U.N. to the phenomenon of globalization. On the regional level, the European Union, in the context of negotiations for the fourth Lomé Agreement with countries of Africa, the Caribbean, and the Pacific (ACP states), sought to include good governance in public affairs, democracy, respect for human rights, and respect for the rule of law, essential in the elements of the accord, with the termination of assistance for non-respect of any of the elements.

Finally, it may be asserted that both the home and the host states have obligations to regulate the conduct of multinational companies. The *Trail Smelter Arbitration,*[91] the *Corfu Channel Case,*[92] and the U.N. Survey of International Law all state the same principle: every state's obligation not to allow knowingly its territory to be used contrary to the rights of other states.[93] The *Trail Smelter Arbitration* involved a privately owned Canadian company that caused harm through its activities to farmers in the United States.[94] Corporate decisions in one state to undertake activities in another state that involve human rights violations could similarly lead to recognition that both states have a duty to control the conduct of the multinational company.

In a third approach, the international community has been moving towards greater ascription of individual responsibility for human rights violations, both by state and by non-state actors. While states remain primarily responsible for ensuring the promotion and protection of human rights, increasing attention is being given to the responsibility under international law of inter-governmental organizations, business enterprises, and individuals. In this regard, the international legal system can no longer be described as one governing states alone. The Universal Declaration of Human Rights opened the door to this development by providing, in Article 30, that, "[n]othing in this Declaration may be interpreted as implying for any [s]tate, group or person any right to engage in any activity or to perform any act aimed at the destruction of any of the rights and freedoms set forth herein."[95] Conceptually linked to this, the preceding article stipulates that, "everyone has duties to the community in which alone the free and full development of his personality is possible."[96]

The special rapporteur on the relationship between the enjoyment of human rights, in particular economic, social, and cultural rights, and income distribution, views economic, social, and cultural rights as "the set of basic rights which determines the limits of globalization."[97] In Bengoa's view, "lack of education, early school leaving and structural poverty are not only general ethical issues but also violations of the human rights proclaimed by international law."[98] He concludes that the great legal, political, and ethical challenge for the coming century will be the codification and enforceability of human rights in an internationalized market.[99] Such an action requires taking into consideration the fact that the state is neither the sole agent nor the sole economic actor, despite its central responsibility, for the realization of economic, social, and cultural rights. Other important actors are transnational corporations, international organizations, trading and financial enterprises, and even such groups as private agencies providing assistance to the poor and needy.[100] He suggests further development of codes of conduct for these non-state actors and in particular the formation of a "Social Forum" with the participation of all such actors. It is somewhat surprising that the suggestion is this modest, given his characterization of the globalized world as one where:

> There is not only the enormous wealth of a few thousand, but also the corruption of many [s]tate authorities, the failure of [s]tate mechanisms and services to discharge their functions, the unregulated and uncontrolled presence of transnational corporations and companies, the authoritarian and unconsidered operation of international financial institutions, and the frequently futile action of organizations and institutions which are well-intentioned but which do not coordinate their activities in a stable and sustained manner.[101]

Another special rapporteur has remarked upon the lack of effective mechanisms to enforce the accountability of non-state actors.[102] He asserts that enforcing respect for codes of conduct, trade union laws, and rights of association and expression may prove difficult, citing the example of the code on marketing breast milk substitutes.[103]

In respect to intergovernmental organizations, the theoretical basis for insisting that they adhere to human rights standards in their programs derives from their international legal personality.[104] International organizations are entities created by states delegating power to achieve certain goals and perform specified functions. While not states, and not having the full rights and duties of states, international organizations take on rights and duties under international law. It would be surprising if states could perform actions collectively through international organizations that the states could not lawfully do individually.[105] In other words, if states cannot confer more power on international organizations than they themselves possess, international organizations are bound to respect human rights because all the states that create them are legally required to respect human rights pursuant to the U.N. Charter and customary international law. The Commission on Human Rights has begun to suggest, albeit very cautiously, that multilateral institutions must conform their policies and practices to human rights norms. In its Resolution 2001/32, the Commission recognized:

> that multilateral mechanisms have a unique role to play in meeting the challenges and opportunities presented by globalization and that the process of globalization must not be used to weaken or reinterpret the principles enshrined in the Charter of the U.N., which continues to be the foundation for friendly relations among states, as well as for the creation of a more just and equitable international economic system.[106]

The resolution affirms not only the individual responsibility of states for human rights but "also recognizes that, in addition to [s]tates' separate responsibilities to their individual societies, they have a collective responsibility to uphold the principles of human dignity, equality and equity at the global level."[107] Subsequent to this, and in the most recent statement of the human rights bodies on the issue, the Sub-Commission adopted a resolution in which it considers that, "attention to the human rights obligations of governments participating in international economic policy formulation will help to ensure socially just outcomes in the formulation, interpretation and implementation of those policies."[108] The Sub-Commission expresses its gratitude for discussions with the WTO, the IMF, and the World Bank, and attempts to walk a difficult line in reaffirming "the importance and relevance of human rights obligations in all areas of governance and development, including international and regional trade, investment and financial policies and practices, while confirming that this in no way implies the imposition of conditionalities upon aid to development."[109] It urges all governments and "international economic policy forums" to take international human rights obligations fully into account in international economic policy formulation.[110]

In its 1998 comment on globalization, the CESCR called for a renewed commitment to respect economic, social, and cultural rights, emphasizing that international organizations, as well as governments that have created and managed them, have a strong and continuous responsibility to take whatever measures they can to assist governments to act in ways that are compatible with their human rights obligations, and to seek to devise policies and programs that promote respect for those rights.[111] The CESCR addressed itself in particular to the IMF and the World Bank, calling upon them to pay enhanced attention to human rights, including "through encouraging explicit recognition of these rights, assisting in the identification of country-specific benchmarks to facilitate their promotion, and facilitating the development of appropriate remedies for responding to violations."[112] The WTO also should "devise appropriate methods to facilitate more systematic consideration of the impact upon human rights of particular trade and investment policies."[113] The CESCR's recent General Comment on the right to food concerns food security within the context of globalization.[114] It draws attention to the responsibilities of private actors, aside from the obligation of states parties to regulate appropriately their conduct, in the realization of the right to adequate food.[115] The comment goes on to stipulate that, "[t]he private business sector—national and transnational—should pursue its activities within the framework of a code of conduct conducive to respect of the right to adequate food, agreed upon jointly with the Government and civil society."[116] Furthermore, it calls upon the IMF and the World Bank to pay attention to the protection of the right to food in drawing up lending policies, credit, and structural adjustment programs.[117] This approach by a treaty-based mechanism, focusing on the responsibilities of multilateral organizations as well as private actors in protecting human rights, is a significant step in international law.

International conferences also have called on international financial institutions to pay greater attention to human rights, through promotion and through assisting in the development of benchmarks to monitor compliance and remedies to respond to violations.[118] In particular, "social safety nets should be defined by reference to these rights and enhanced attention should be accorded to such methods to protect the poor and vulnerable in the context of structural adjustment programs."[119] Social monitoring and impact assessments, similar to that done for the environment, are recommended to international financial institutions and to the WTO. Labor unions have called for including core labor standards in the future WTO work program.[120]

For individuals, international responsibility is also increasing. The U.N. Development Program *Human Development Report 2000* calls for greater accountability of non-state actors, pointing out that, "global corporations can have enormous impact on human rights—in their employment practices, in their environmental impact, in their support for corrupt regimes or in their advocacy for policy changes."[121] The most egregious acts are proscribed as international crimes. The Nuremberg Military Tribunal[122] and subsequent principles prepared by the U.N. International Law Commission[123] made clear that neither government position nor government orders will free an individual from responsibility for the commission of an international crime.[124] As was said in the Nuremberg judgment: "crimes against international law are committed by men and not by abstract entities and it is only by punishing individuals who commit such crimes" that international law can be upheld.[125] The U.N. Security Council also has made clear the international liability of non-state as well as state actors who commit war crimes and other international crimes.

The list of international crimes at Nuremberg were war crimes, crimes against peace, and crimes against humanity.[126] The Convention on the Prevention and Punishment of the Crime of Genocide affirms that genocide, whether committed in peacetime or wartime, is a crime under international law and that, "[p]ersons committing genocide . . . shall be punished, whether they are constitutionally responsible [rulers], public officials, or private individuals."[127] In 1973, the U.N. similarly declared apartheid a crime against humanity and broadly imposed responsibility on "individuals, members of organizations, institutions and State representatives."[128] The International Law Commission's Draft Code of Crimes against the Peace and Security of Mankind holds that systematic or widespread violations of human rights constitute international crimes for which non-state as well as state actors may be responsible.[129] Article 21 of the Draft Code of Crimes imposes individual responsibility for the commission of "murder; torture; establishing or maintaining over persons a status of slavery, servitude, or forced labor; persecution on social, political, racial, religious, or cultural grounds in a systematic manner or on a mass scale; and deportation or forcible transfer of the population."[130]

Recently, member states of international organizations have sought to reach misconduct that is transnational in character, but not specifically designated as an international crime. The Inter-American Convention on Violence against Women calls on state parties thereto to take action against state and non-state actors that commit violence against women in the public and private spheres, including family violence.[131] On November 15, 2000, the U.N. General Assembly adopted a Convention against Transnational Organized Crime and a Protocol to Prevent, Suppress and Punish Trafficking in Persons, Especially Women and Children.[132] This Convention calls on states to criminalize listed offenses, including money laundering and corruption, and to cooperate to combat transnational crime and to protect victims of crime.[133] The Protocol on Trafficking expressly refers to the human rights of victims[134] and to various human rights abuses such as forced labor, slavery, or practices similar to slavery.[135] Natural and legal persons may be liable, and the proceeds of crimes confiscated and seized are to be used for the benefit of victims.

International organizations have taken up several problems where trade and human rights are linked, in the process enhancing global governance by bringing together state and non-state actors. The U.N. Security Council has expressed its concern about the role of the illicit diamond trade supporting the conflict in Sierra Leone and called upon the international diamond industry to cooperate on a ban on all rough diamonds from Sierra Leone.[136] The Council requested the U.N. Secretary-General to appoint a panel of experts to monitor implementation of the ban.[137] In addition, the resolution calls upon states, international organizations, the diamond industry, and other relevant entities to assist the government of Sierra Leone to develop a well-structured and well-regulated diamond industry.[138] The World Diamond Congress, meeting in 2000 in Antwerp, proposed the creation of an international diamond council made up of producers, manufacturers, traders, governments, and international organizations to oversee a new system to verify the provenance of rough diamonds.

If the behavior of non-state actors violates international norms directly applicable to their conduct, they may be held responsible to their victims. Efforts to hold corporations accountable for conduct occurring in overseas operations have recently become prevalent in U.S. courts. Using the Alien Tort Claims Act, plaintiffs have sought to hold multinational companies liable for customary human rights violations and environmental harm in

Burma, Nigeria, Ecuador, and India. In England as well, the House of Lords has upheld an action brought against an English-based multinational company by South African mineworkers suffering from asbestos related diseases. The use of international human rights law in presenting claims directly against industry is a relatively recent phenomenon and reflects the growing attention being paid to non-state actors in international law and the expectations that their behavior will be tested by norms previously directed at states and state agents. The draft Hague Convention on Jurisdiction and Foreign Judgments in Civil and Commercial Matters refers to human rights in Article 18, in reference to war crimes and grave violations of fundamental rights.

Further action is being taken by human rights bodies. In 1998, the U.N. Sub-commission for the Prevention of Discrimination and Protection of Minorities voted to establish a Working Group to examine over three years the effects of the working methods and activities of transnational corporations on human rights.[139] The mandate of the Working Group is extensive and includes identification and examination of the effects of the activities of transnational corporations on the enjoyment of civil, cultural, economic, political, and social rights, the right to development, the right to a healthy environment, and the right to peace.[140] It is to gather and examine information and reports, and prepare an annual list of transnational corporations to provide examples of the positive and negative impacts on human rights of their activities in the countries in which they operate.[141] In addition, the Working Group is to assess how existing human rights standards apply to transnational corporations, including private initiatives and codes of conduct, and collect for study international, regional, and bilateral investment agreements.[142]

The Working Group has prepared a draft code of principles relating to the human rights conduct of companies, based upon relevant language from the codes of conduct by the U.N., the Organization for Economic Co Operation and Development (OECD), the ILO, corporations, unions, and non-governmental organizations.[143] The principles address a wide range of human rights issues, including non-discrimination, and freedom from harassment and abuse, slavery, forced labor and child labor, healthy and safe working environments, fair and equal remuneration, hours of work, freedom of association, and the right to collective bargaining, as well as war crimes and other international crimes.[144] The fundamental rationale for the draft principles was to impose responsibility on companies commensurate with their increased power.[145] During the meetings of the Working Group leading up to the principles, many non-governmental organizations argued in favor of drafting a legally binding instrument, on the basis that another voluntary code of conduct would be insufficient.[146]

The ILO remains the key institution concerned with the rights of workers throughout the world. To the extent that other organizations have become involved, the ILO seeks to determine whether or not their standards conform to those of the ILO and adopt a similar human rights approach. The ILO Tripartite Declaration of Principles Concerning Multinational Enterprises and Social Policy addresses the obligations of four groups: the enterprises themselves; workers' groups; employers' organizations; and governments. Its aims are to encourage the positive contributions of multinational companies to economic and social progress and to minimize the negative consequences that might accompany their activities. The Declaration provides that all four groups should respect the Universal Declaration of Human Rights and the two U.N. Covenants on Human Rights. The ILO also surveys the positive and negative effects of multinational activities based on information from workers, employers, and governments.

The OECD became a focus of controversy during its unsuccessful efforts to draft a Multilateral Agreement on Investment (MAI), a process that ended in December, 1998.[147] Strikingly, both the investors pressing the MAI and those opposed to it were part of the globalized community and, according to one view, "compromise the concept of national sovereignty and local control."[148] Many of the issues raised concerned human rights, including some related to the negotiating process itself and its lack of transparency.[149] In addition, NGOs were concerned about several substantive areas that seemed to seriously limit the sovereignty of states in favor of foreign investors.

Before and after the MAI negotiations, the OECD addressed issues of human rights. First, in 1995, it published guidelines on participatory development and good governance[150] in which the members reiterated their adherence to international human rights norms.[151] In 1996, OECD studied trade and labor standards, looking at core worker rights.[152] Later, it adopted revised Guidelines for Multinational Enterprises on June 27, 2000,[153] supported by follow-up procedures in the twenty-nine member states and four non-member states participating in the process.[154] The Guidelines concern multinational enterprises operating in or from the thirty-three countries and apply to all operations worldwide. The revision added a human rights obligation, stating that, "enterprises should . . . [r]espect the human rights of those affected by their activities consistent with the host government's obligations and commitments." It is significant that the Guidelines do not refer to policies or practices, but rather to the legal obligations of the host state. Every state has such obligations under the U.N. Charter, customary international law, and such human rights treaties as the state has ratified. The Guidelines impose a duty upon businesses to inform themselves of the relevant obligations and conform their conduct to them. The follow-up foresees a series of procedures involving consultations, good offices, conciliation, and mediation.

The U.N. Declaration Against Corruption and Bribery in International Commercial Transactions encourages social responsibility and ethical behavior, calling on partners to international transactions to observe the laws of the host countries, and take into account the impact of their activities on economic and social development and protection of the environment and human rights.

Yet another response to the intersecting issues of globalization and human rights has been to utilize market mechanisms and other forms of private regulation to impact corporate behavior. Pressure from international and national groups, as well as perceived long term interests, have led many companies to take up the issue of human rights. A survey by the Ashridge Centre for Business and Society found that human rights issues caused more than one in three of the 500 largest companies to abandon a proposed investment project and nearly one in five to divest its operations in a country. Nearly half have codes of conduct that refer to human rights. The record is not clear, however, on implementation. The U.N. Development Program *Human Development Report 2000* calls for better implementation of corporate codes of conduct, stating that, "many fail to meet human rights standards, or lack implementation measures and independent audits."[155] It suggests that the use of human rights indicators be extended to include the role of corporations.

Codes of conduct for human rights often result from pressure on companies to divest from countries with widespread and systematic human rights violations.[156] Consumer boycotts and labeling initiatives such as "Rugmark"[157] provide a means for persons concerned with labor conditions and human rights to use their purchasing power to influence corporate policy. Effective mobilization of international consumer pressure can substitute for regulation.[158] A writer in the *Economist* has observed that, "a multinational's failure to look like a good global citizen is increasingly expensive in a world where consumers and pressure groups can be quickly mobilised behind a cause."[159] Such marketplace regulation has been criticized as lacking in the accountability and transparency that normally accompany the formation of laws.[160]

The final approach concerned with enhancing human rights in a globalized world is one that has broad implications for global governance generally. It seeks to enhance non-state participation in international organizations and other fora concerned with international regulation. While international organizations other than the ILO have limited participation for non-governmental entities, efforts are being made to develop more collaborative efforts between state and non-state actors within the framework of international organizations.

The U.N. Millennium Declaration[161] resolves to give greater opportunities to the private sector, NGOs, and civil society in general "to contribute to the realization of the Organization's goals and programs."[162] The U.N. Global Compact Initiative aims to develop policy networks of international institutions, civil society, private sector organizations, and national governments to further human rights.[163] The Initiative has taken up such issues as trade in diamonds in zones of conflict, corporate social responsibility generally, the inclusion of corporate behavior in the studies conducted by U.N. special rapporteurs on various human rights issues, and the impact of national litigation on corporate liability for human rights abuses in countries where the companies have operations.[164] It is also concerned with the work of international financial institutions like the World Bank and regional organizations, such as the OECD.[165]

U.N. special rapporteurs have held discussions with private actors in exercising their mandates. The special rapporteurs on Sudan and on Afghanistan held dialogues with oil companies conducting activities in these countries; the special rapporteur on toxic waste met with a pharmaceutical company.[166] The special rapporteur on the sale of children has worked with the International Chamber of Commerce requesting information about company initiatives benefiting children that could be proposed for action in various parts of the world.

Multinational companies also have been important in conflict resolution, especially in mobilizing information and communications technology. This was the case with the U.N. High Commissioner for Refugees in, for example, Kosovo.[167] Successful partnership will require companies to shun corrupt leaders and work to build viable states that respect human rights.[168] The joint U.N.–World Bank effort in East Timor demonstrates a broad engagement in rebuilding, including the development of judicial institutions and processes.[169] Given the insecurity in many conflict and post-conflict areas, the cooperation of the U.N. and the World Bank with private enterprise will be necessary to ensure that the risks are properly shared, perhaps through more favorable terms for political-risk insurance.[170] Humanitarian and human rights NGOs also must be part of the coalition, with the aim of overcoming the mutual distrust with which the business sector and NGOs view each other. To fully work, such a coalition may require restructuring international institutions to allow more effective participation by non-state actors.

Several multinational agreements have been concluded between international industry associations and workers' organizations.[171] These include the collective agreement between the International Transport Workers Federation and the International Maritime Employers' Committee, an agreement that covers wages, minimum standards, and other terms and conditions of work, including maternity protection. In January 2001, the two partners agreed upon the future development of labor standards in the international shipping industry to permit such standards to become the third pillar of the shipping industry, alongside maritime environmental and safety standards.[172] The Spanish based telecommunications company Telefonica and the Union Network International (UNI) similarly signed an agreement that covers some 120,000 workers represented by eighteen labor unions affiliated to UNI. Both sides agreed to respect ILO core labor standards covering freedom of association and the right to collective bargaining, non-discrimination, and freedom from forced labor and child labor. In all, the agreement referred to some fifteen ILO conventions and recommendations.

The question of whether or not non-economic, e.g., human rights values, are or should be incorporated in the trade regime remains debated. Richard Shell has proposed a "stakeholder model" of international government in which "private commercial parties, indigent citizens in developing countries with weak governments, environmentalists, labor interests, . . . consumer groups," and others affected by trade would have a role in economic policy-making and dispute settlement in order to integrate non-economic values with economic ones.[173] Human rights interest groups and other NGOs having consultative status[174] have been prominent in various U.N. human rights meetings and in other international fora, but have had far less success in participating in the WTO.[175] In general, more transparency and participation are needed.

Conclusion

The key international legal developments that appear to be emerging as a result of globalization, as discussed above, seem to be the following. First, human rights institutions and activists are asserting a primacy of human rights law over other fields of international law. Whether or to what extent this assertion will be accepted remains to be seen. Second, the international legal personality of inter-governmental organizations is seen to carry with it the obligation to conform to general international law norms, above and beyond the requirements of the constituting charters or constitutions of the organizations. Third, the imposition of responsibility for human rights violations on non-state actors appears to be increasing. This all leads to asking: does the state need strengthening?

Globalization has created centers of power that are alongside, even in competition with the power of states. Accountability for human rights violations and prevention of future ones must today and in the future take into account these non-state actors: the media, corporations, and international organizations such as the WTO and the World Bank. States and their agents are no longer the only or sometimes even the key actors responsible for ensuring that human rights and freedoms are guaranteed. As recent international developments have shown, there are multiple avenues to respond to this problem. The first is to strengthen the state and to insist on its responsibility for ensuring that non-state actors do not commit human rights violations.

There is no doubt a need to strengthen weak states that lack the institutions necessary to protect and ensure human rights. Institutions such as independent judiciaries must be formed and executive power, including the police and military, must be brought under the rule of law. At the same time it must be recognized that there are two problems with solely relying on strengthened individual state action. First, it raises the specter of powerful state agents again capable of and perhaps willing to use and abuse state power to prolong their time in office. The wisdom of political philosophers who called for a balance of and restraints on power must not be forgotten because "the good old rule, [s]ufficeth them, the simple plan, [t]hat they should take, who have the power, [a]nd they should keep who can."[176] The second problem is that even strong states are unable to deal unilaterally with all the challenges posed by globalization, especially when dealing with international crime, including terrorism. The amount of individual state strengthening that would be necessary to combat these problems would probably require an unacceptable retreat from basic human rights.

The alternative is to strengthen the weak states to enable them to protect human rights, while at the same time imposing increased international obligations on non-state actors through multilateral mechanisms. Thus, even though states will retain the primary responsibility for ensuring the promotion and protection of human rights, non-state actors will be held accountable when they undermine state efforts to do so or are complicit in violations undertaken by the state. Non-state actors have always had a pivotal role in developing the law of human rights; they now may take a further role as a result of globalization.

Notes

1. *See* Eric Stein, *International Integration and Democracy: No Love at First Sight,* 95 Am. J. Int'l. L. 489, 489 (2001).

2. *Globalization and its Impact on the Full Enjoyment of All Human Rights: Preliminary Report of the Secretary-General,* U.N. GAOR, 55th Sess., para. 5, U.N. Doc. A/55/342 (2000). On the various meanings of globalization, *see* Wolfgang H. Reinicke & Jan Martin Witte, *Interdependence, Globalization and Sovereignty: The Role of Non-binding International Legal Accords,* in Commitment and Compliance: The Role of Non-Binding Norms in the International Legal System 75 (Dinah Shelton ed., 2000). *See generally* A. G. McGrew et al., Global Politics: Globalization and the Nation States (1992); States Against Markets: The Limits of Globalization (R. Boyer & D. Drache eds., 1996); J. N. Rosenau, *The Dynamics of Globalization: Toward an Operational Formulation,* 27 Sec. Dialogue 247 (1996).

3. Some see globalization as beginning around the end of the fifteenth century, with Europe's expansion through mercantile capitalism into America and Asia. *See*

Statement of Rubens Ricupero, Secretary-General, UNCTAD, *Financial Globalization and Human Rights: Written Statement Submitted by the International Organization for the Development of Freedom of Education to the Commission on Human Rights*, U.N. Doc. E/CN.4/1998/NGO/76 (1998). Others consider it to be a phenomenon with even longer roots, beginning with the invention of money and the emergence of trade links around the Mediterranean. *See* Grzegorz W. Kolodko, *Technical Paper No. 176: Globalisation and Transformation: Illusions and Reality*, at 7, *available at* http://www.oecd.org/dev/publication/tpla.htm (last visited Dec. 12, 2001).

4. *See* W. H. Reinicke, Global Public Policy: Governing Without Government 11–18 (1998).

5. *See* Philip Alston, *The Universal Declaration in an Era of Globalization*, in Reflections on the Universal Declaration of Human Rights: A Fiftieth Anniversary Anthology 29 (Barend van der Heijden & Bahia Tahzi-Lie eds., 1998).

6. *See, e.g.*, John O. McGinnis, *The Decline of the Western Nation State and the Rise of the Regime of International Federalism*, 18 Cardozo L. Rev. 903, 918 (1996). The rate of information exchange has drastically reduced transaction costs, enabling expansion of transboundary communications. In 1860, sending two words across the Atlantic cost the equivalent of $40 in current money. Today this amount would be enough to transmit the contents of the entire Library of Congress. Kolodko, *supra* note 8, at 11–12.

7. Richard Falk, Law in an Emerging Global Village: A Post-Westphalian Perspective, at xxiv (1998); *see also* Enrico Colombatto & Jonathan R. Macey, *A Public Choice Model of International Economic Cooperation and the Decline of the Nation State*, 18 Cardozo L. Rev. 925, 925 (1996).

8. Kenichi Ohmae, The Borderless World 185 (1991).

9. Id. at 197.

10. McGinnis, *supra* note 11, at 918; Kenichi Ohmae, The End of the Nation State: The Rise of Regional Economies 1 (1995).

11. "An estimated five million people died in intrastate conflicts in the 1990s. In 1998, there were more than ten million refugees and five million internally displaced persons," U.N. Development Programme, Human Development Report 2000, at 6 (2000), available at http://www.undp.org/hrd2000/english/hdr2000.htm [hereinafter UNDP]. On Internal conflicts, race, and ethnicity, *see* New Tribalisms: The Resurgence of Race and Ethnicity 1 (Michael W. Hughey ed., 1998).

12. Dinah Shelton, *Droit et justice pour chaque citoyen de la planète?*, in Marina Ricciardelli et al, Mondialisation et Sociétés Multiculturelles: L'incertain du Future 305, 313 (2000). The weakening of the state is at the origin of numerous ethnic conflicts, sustained by unregulated commerce in conventional arms and by the growth in numbers of armed mercenaries. Id. Of the sixty-one conflicts that appeared during the years 1989–1998, all but three were internal armed conflicts. In states where the government has collapsed, armed tribes, and ethnic and political groups control territories without the rule of law and in the absence of public authorities. *Id.* In those states, human rights, like other legal constraints, have given way to anarchy and the exercise of unlimited power. Id.

13. Paul Streeten, *Globalization and its Impact on Development Co-operation*, 42 Dev. 11, 11 (1999).

14. *See, e.g.*, Upendra Baxi, *Voices of Suffering and the Future of Human Rights*, 8 Transnat'l L. & Contemp. Probs. 125, 159–61 (1998).

15. *See* Jamie Frederic Metzl, *Rwandan Genocide and the International Law of Radio Jamming*, 91 Am. J. Int'l. L. 628, 629 (1997).

16. *See* Christiane Chombeau, *Des Juifs D'extrême Droite Déversent Leur Haine Antiarabe Sur Internet,* Le Monde, Oct. 12, 2001, at 11.

17. International Labor Office, Reducing the Decent Work Deficit: A Global Challenge—Report of the Director General 49 (2001), available at http://www. ilo.org (citing World Bank, World Bank Development Report 2000/2001: Attacking Poverty [2001]) (last visited Jan. 29, 2002) [hereinafter ILO Report of the Director General].

18. Id. The 1998 U.N. Development Program report has even more extreme figures, focusing on individual wealth: the 20% of the world's people who live in the richest countries had thirty times the income of the poorest 20% in 1960, and by 1995, had eighty-two times as much income. U.N. Development Programme, Human Development Report 1998, at 29 (1998).

19. *See* ILO Report of the Director General, *supra* note 25, sec. 3.1.

20. U.N. Research Institute for Social Development, States of Disarray: The Social Effects of Globalization, Report on the World Summit for Social Development 13 (1995), *available at* http://www.unrisd.org (last visited Mar. 11, 2002).

21. Although there were issues such as the slave trade and war crimes that were raised during the nineteenth century and concern for some economic and social rights emerged in the early twentieth century, most human rights law developed in the period following World War II.

22. *See generally* Louis Henkin, The Age of Rights (1990).

23. Stephen Kobrin, *The MAI and the Clash of Globalizations,* 112 Foreign Pol'y. 97, 97 (1998).

24. *See* Philip M. Nichols, *Trade Without Values,* 90 Nw. U. L. Rev. 658, 672–73 (1996) (noting that the basic values of globalization may conflict with other values of society); *see also* Frank Garcia, *The Global Market and Human Rights: Trading Away the Human Rights Principle,* 25 Brook. J. Int'l. L. 51, 51 (1999); Alex Seita, *Globalization and the Convergence of Values,* 30 Cornell Int'l. L. J. 429, 470 (1997).

25. *See* Anthony Giddens, Runaway World: How Globalization Is Reshaping Our Lives 30–35 (1999).

26. M.D. Pendleton, *A New Human Right—The Right to Globalization,* 22 Fordham Int'l. L. J. 2052, 2052 (1999).

27. *See* Garcia, *supra* note 32, at 60.

28. *See* Patricia Stirling, *The Use of Trade Sanctions as an Enforcement Mechanism for Basic Human Rights: A Proposal for Addition to the World Trade Organization,* 11 Am. U. J. Int'l. L. & Pol'y. 1, 42–45 (1996).

29. Judith Bello, *National Sovereignty and Transnational Problem Solving,* 18 Cardozo L. Rev. 1027, 1029 (1996).

30. Orford, *supra* note 37, 169.

31. UNDP, *supra* note 16, at 1.

32. Kevin Watkins, The Oxfam Poverty Report 109–110 (1995).

33. El Hadji Guisse, *The Realization of Economic, Social and Cultural Rights: The Question of Transnational Corporations,* U.N. ESCOR, 50th Sess., U.N. Doc. E/CN.4/Sub.2/1998/6 (1998).

34. Id. para. 1.

35. *See* Statement by the United Nations Committee on Economic, Social and Cultural Rights, *Globalization and Economic, Social and Cultural Rights* (May, 1998), at http://www.unhchr.ch/tbs/doc.nsf/385c2ad...a?OpenDocument&Highlight= O, globalization (last visited Oct. 22, 2001); *see also* UNCTAD, World Investment Report 1994: Transnational Corporations, Employment and the Workplace 260 (1994).

36. ILO Report of the Director General, *supra* note 25, at 9. According to the 2001 report of the ILO Director General, close to two of every five countries have serious or severe problems of freedom of association. Id.

37. *See* Marc W. Brown, *The Effect of Free Trade, Privatization and Democracy on the Human Rights Conditions for Minorities in Eastern Europe: A Case Study of the Gypsies in the Czech Republic and Hungary,* 4 Buff. Hum. Rts. L. Rev. 275, 275 (1998).

38. *See* Lin Lean Lim, More and Better Jobs for Women: An Action Guide 18–20 (Int'l. Labour Office 1999). Deregulation and the privatization of state enterprises have been key components of structural adjustment programs (SAPs) introduced by multilateral lending agencies as conditionals attached to aid packages to developing countries. Id.

39. *See generally* Bharati Sadasivam, *The Impact of Structural Adjustment on Women: A Governance and Human Rights Agenda,* 19 Hum. Rts. Q. 630 (1997).

40. For more information on these effects, see Riham el-Lakany, *WTO Trades off Women's Rights for Bigger Profits,* 12 Women's Env't. & Dev. Org. 1, 32 (1999), available at www.wedo.org/news/Nov99/wtotradeoff.htm.

41. Lim, *supra* note 104, at 19–20.

42. *See* Deborah Spar & David Yoffie, *Multinational Enterprises and the Prospects for Justice,* 52 J. Int'l. Aff. 557, 557 (1999).

43. International Confederation of Free Trade Unions, *Background Paper: Implementation of International Covenant on Economic, Social and Cultural Rights,* para. 4, U.N. Doc. E/C.12/1998/4 (1998) [hereinafter ICFTU].

44. *See, e.g.,* John Eremu, *Uganda Warned on EPZ Strategy,* New Vision, Dec. 7, 1998, at 54 (noting that exclusive protection zones in many African countries are characterized by human rights abuses).

45. ILO Report of the Director General, *supra* note 25, at 10.

46. Lim, *supra* note 104, at 30.

47. *See* Aaron B. Sukert, Note, *Marionettes of Globalization: A Comparative Analysis of Protections for Contingent Workers in the International Community,* 27 Syracuse J. Int'l. L. & Com. 431, 431 (2000).

48. *See 1999 World Survey on the Role of Women in Development: Globalization, Gender and Work: Report of the Secretary General,* at 9, 54th. Sess., U.N. Doc. A/54/227, U.N. Sales No. E.99.IV.8 (1999). Women have entered the workforce in large numbers in states that have embraced liberal economic policies. Id. "It is by now considered a stylized fact that industrialization in the context of globalization is as much female-led as it is export led." The overall economic activity rate of women for the age group 20–54 approached 70% in 1996. Id. at 8. One estimate is that 90% of the twenty-seven million people employed in EPZs worldwide are women. *See* John Hilary, Globalization and Employment: New Opportunities, Real Threats 1 (1999).

49. Hilary, *supra* note 114, at 440–41.

50. *See generally* Laurie Nicole Robinson, *The Globalization of Female Child Prostitution: A Call for Reintegration and Recovery Measures Via Article 39 of the United Nations Convention on the Rights of the Child,* 5 Ind. J. Global Legal Stud. 239 (1997).

51. ILO Report of the Director General, *supra* note 25, at 9.

52. Id.

53. *See generally* U.N. Economic and Social Council, Study on International Flows of Cultural Goods Between 1980–1998 (2000).

54. *See* Danilo Turk, *The Realization of Economic, Social and Cultural Rights,* U.N. GAOR, Hum. Rts. Comm., 44th Sess., Agenda Item 8, para. 1–37, U.N. Doc.

E/CN.4/Sub2/1992/16 (1992); *see also* Statement by the Committee on Economic, Social and Cultural Rights, *Globalization and Economic, Social and Cultural Rights* (May, 1998), at http://www.unhchr.ch/ html/menu2/6/cescrnote.htm#note18h [hereinafter Statement, *Globalization*].

55. *See* Sadasivam, *supra* note 105, at 630.

56. The debt burden of the thirty-three poorest countries of the world collectively amounts to $127 billion owed to industrialized countries and institutions. In Mozambique, one of the poorest countries in the world, 30% of all revenue goes to debt servicing.

57. *See* A. Bernstein, *Labor Standards: Try a Little Democracy,* Bus. Wk., Dec. 13, 1999, at 42.

58. *See generally* Mancur Olson, Power and Prosperity: Outgrowing Communist and Capitalist Dictatorships (2000). On development and human rights, see generally Amartya Sen, Development as Freedom (1999).

59. UNDP, *supra* note 16, at iii.

60. For clarification on this relationship, see United Nations, *Copenhagen+5 Review,* at http://www.un.org/esa/socdev/geneva2000/index.html (last visited Mar. 10, 2002).

61. Res. 1999/30, *supra* note 57.

62. Orford, *supra* note 81.

63. *See* John Locke, Second Treatise of Government ch. V, sec. 27 (C. B. McPherson ed., Hackett Publishing Co. 1980) (1690).

64. Statement, *Globalization, supra* note 120, para. 5.

65. Id. para. 4.

66. *See, e.g.,* Inter-Am. C.H.R., Velasquez Rodriguez Case, Judgment of July 29, 1988, Ser. C, No. 4, para. 159–77, available at http://www.corteidh.or.cr/sericing/C_4_Eng.html (last visited Mar. 11, 2002). *See generally,* Dinah Shelton, *Private Violence, Public Wrongs, and the Responsibility of States,* 13 Fordham Int'l. L. J. 1, 1 (1990).

67. The General Assembly has affirmed that while globalization, by its impact on the role of the state, may affect human rights, the promotion and protection of all human rights is first and foremost the responsibility of the state. The Assembly has called for an environment at both the national and global levels that is conducive to development and to the elimination of poverty through, *inter alia,* good governance within each country and at the international level, transparency in the financial, monetary, and trading systems and commitment to an open, equitable, rule-based, predictable, and non-discriminatory multilateral trading and financial system. G.A. Res. 102/54, U.N. GAOR, 54th Sess., U.N. Doc. A/RES/54/102 (2000).

68. According to Diller and Levy, referring specifically to the issue of coercive forms of child labour, where fundamental human rights norms are implicated, "international law requires that treaty obligations, such as trade undertakings, be maintained only to the extent of consistency with these norms." Janelle Diller & David Levy, *Child Labor, Trade and Investment: Toward the Harmonization of International Law,* 91 Am. J. Int'l. L. 678, 678 (1997).

69. Statement, *Globalization, supra* note 120.

70. *Statement of the United Nations Committee on Economic, Social and Cultural Rights to the Third Ministerial Conference of the World Trade Organization,* Committee on Economic, Social and Cultural Rights, 21st Sess., Agenda item 3, para. 6, U.N. Doc. E/C.12/1999/9 (1999).

71. World Conference on Human Rights, *Vienna Declaration and Programme of Action,* U.N. Doc. A/CONF.157/23; *see also* Commission on Human Rights,

Globalization and its Impact on the Full Enjoyment of All Human Rights, U.N. Doc. E/CN.4/RES/1999/59 (1999) ("While globalization by its impact on, *inter alia,* the role of the State, may affect human rights, the promotion and protection of all human rights is first and foremost the responsibility of the State.").

72. *Final Act, World Summit for Social Development: Report of the World Summit for Social Development,* U.N. Doc. A/CONF.166/9 (1995) [hereinafter *Final Act*].

73. Sub-Commission on Promotion and Protection of Human Rights, *Human Rights as the Primary Objective of Trade, Investment and Financial Policy,* U.N. Doc. E/CN.4/Sub.2/ RES/1998/12 (1998); *Report of the Sub-Commission on its 50th Sess.,* U.N. ESCOR, 50th Sess., at 39, U.N. Doc. E/CN.4/Sub.2/1998/45 (1998).

74. Commission on Human Rights, *Effects of Structural Adjustment Policies and Foreign Debt on the Full Enjoyment of All Human Rights, Particularly Economic, Social and Cultural Rights,* U.N. Doc. E/CN.4/RES/2000/82 (2000).

75. Oloka-Onyango & Udagama, *Globalization* I, *supra* note 50.

76. U.N. Charter pmbl., art. 1.

77. Id. arts. 55–56.

78. Id. art. 103.

79. *See* id.

80. Vienna Convention on the Law of Treaties, May 27, 1969, art. 59, 1155 U.N.T.S. 331, 8 I.L.M. 679 (1969).

81. U.N. Charter art. 30.

82. Restatement (Third) of the Foreign Relations Law of the United States art. 601–02 (1987).

83. *International Covenant on Economic, Social, and Cultural Rights,* G.A. Res. 2200A (XXI), U.N. GAOR, Supp. No. 16, at 49, U.N. Doc. A/6316 (1966), reprinted in 6 I.L.M. 360.

84. Id. art. 2(1). Other references to international cooperation are found in Articles 11, 15, 22, and 23.

85. Id.

86. Id. art. 2.

87. *See* Committee on Economic, Social and Cultural Rights, *Report on the Fifth Session, Economic and Social Council,* U.N. ESCOR, Supp. No. 3, Annex III, General Cmt. No. 3, U.N. Doc. E/1991/23–E/C.12/1990/8 (1991).

88. *See Report of the Committee on the Elimination of Discrimination against Women,* U.N. GAOR, 52d Sess., Supp. No. 38, paras. 295, 345, U.N. Doc. A/52/38/ Rev.1 (1997); *see also* Committee on the Rights of the Child, *Report on the Twentieth Session,* U.N. ESCOR, paras. 211–13, U.N. Doc. CRC/C/84 (1999) (recording a statement made by a representative of the IMF at the session acknowledging the link between child rights and a stable macroeconomic environment).

89. The rights guaranteed are: freedom of association and the effective recognition of the right to collective bargaining; elimination of all forms of compulsory or forced labor; effective abolition of child labor; elimination of discrimination in occupation and employment. For more information, see the ILO website, at http://www.ilo.org.

90. *See generally* Michèle Jackson, *A New Convention to Eliminate the Economic Exploitation of Children,* 6 Tribune des Droits Humains 36 (1999).

91. 3 U.N. R.I.A.A. 1905 (1931–41) [hereinafter *Trail Smelter Arbitration*].

92. 1949 I.C.J. 22.

93. Id. *See generally supra* notes 158–159.

94. *Trail Smelter Arbitration, supra* note 158.

95. Universal Declaration, *supra* note 42, art. 30.

96. Id. art. 29.

97. Jose Bengoa, *Poverty, Income Distribution and Globalization: A Challenge for Human Rights, Addendum to the Final Report,* at para. 28, U.N. ESCOR, 50th Sess., U.N. Doc. E/CN.4/Sub.2/1998/8 (1998).

98. Id.

99. Id. para. 29.

100. Id. para. 31. Bengoa also notes that it is very important that development NGOs, international cooperation agencies, and charitable foundations participate, "as they are acquiring ever greater relevance in relations between north and south, as part of the growing 'privatization' of cooperation." Id.

101. Id. para. 30.

102. Oloka-Onyango, *Racism, supra* note 51, para. 35.

103. Id.

104. *See* Reparation for Injuries Suffered in the Service of the United Nations, Advisory Opinion, 1949 I.C.J. 174, 178–79. *See generally,* Louis Henkin, *Responsibility of International Organizations,* in Henkin et al., International Law, Cases and Materials 359–60 (3d ed. 1993).

105. The U.N. Charter, Chapter VII, does allow international peace-keeping actions, however, for threats to the peace, breaches of the peace, and acts of aggression—actions that would generally not be legal if performed unilaterally except in self-defense.

106. Commission on Human Rights, *Globalization and its Impact on the Full Enjoyment of All Human Rights,* U.N. Doc. E/CN.4/RES/2001/32 (2001).

107. Id.

108. Id.

109. *See* id.

110. *See* id.

111. Statement, *Globalization, supra* note 120, para. 5.

112. Id. para. 7.

113. Id.

114. *The Right to Adequate Food: Report of the Committee on Economic, Social and Cultural Rights,* General Comment No. 12, at 102, 106, U.N. ESCOR., Supp. No. 2, U.N. Doc. E/2000/22 (2000).

115. Id.

116. Id. para. 20.

117. Id. para. 41.

118. *See Final Act, supra* note 139 (calling for a reorientation of the work of the international community including the IMF and the World Bank to establish full employment, the eradication of poverty and popular participation as the primary goals of global development policy); ICFTU, *supra* note 109.

119. ICFTU, *supra* note 109, para. 7.

120. Id. para. 17.

121. UNDP, *supra* note 16, at 10.

122. *See* Charter of the International Military Tribunal, Aug. 8, 1945, 82 U.N.T.S. 280, 58 Stat. 1544 [hereinafter *London Charter*].

123. *Principles of International Law Recognized in the Charter of the Nuremberg Tribunal and in the Judgment of the Tribunal,* [1950] Y.B. Int'l. L. Comm'n. 374–78, para. 95–127, U.N. Doc. A/1316; *Draft Code of Crimes Against the Peace and Security of Mankind: Report of the International Law Commission on the Work*

of its Forty-third Session, [1991] 2 Y.B. Int'l. L. Comm'n. 79, U.N. Doc. A/CN.4/L 464.Add.4 (1991) [hereinafter *Draft Code of Crimes*].

124. *London Charter, supra* note 189, arts. 7–8; *Draft Code of Crimes, supra* note 190, arts. 11, 13.

125. International Military Tribunal, 22 Trials of the Major War Criminals Before the International Military Tribunal 466 (1948).

126. *London Charter, supra* note 189, art. 6.

127. Convention on the Prevention and Punishment of the Crime of Genocide, Dec. 9, 1948, 78 U.N.T.S. 277 (entry into force Jan. 12, 1951).

128. International Convention on the Suppression and Punishment of the Crime of Apartheid, Nov. 30, 1973, art. III, G.A. Res. 3068 (XXVIII), 28 U.N. GAOR, Supp. No. 30, U.N. Doc. A/9030 (1974), reprinted in 13 I.L.M. 50.

129. *Draft Code of Offenses Against the Peace and Security of Mankind: Report of the Int'l. Law Comm'n on the Work of its 48th Session,* U.N. GAOR, 51st Sess., art. 21, U.N. Doc. A/51/10 (1996).

130. Id.

131. Inter-American Convention for the Prevention, Punishment and Eradication of Violence against Women, June 9, 1994, 33 I.L.M. 1334 (1994) (entry into force Mar. 3, 1995).

132. United Nations Convention Against Transnational Organized Crime; Protocol to Prevent, Suppress and Punish Trafficking in Persons, Especially Women and Children, Protocol Against the Smuggling of Migrants by Land, Sea and Air, Nov. 15, 2000, U.N. Doc. A/55/383 (2000), reprinted in 40 I.L.M. 335 (2001).

133. Id. arts. 14(2), 25.

134. Id., pmbl., art. 2(b)6.

135. *See* Id. art. 3(a).

136. S.C. Res. 1306, U.N. SCOR, 55th Sess., 4168th mtg., U.N. Doc. S/RES/ 1306 (2000).

137. Id.

138. Id.

139. Sub-Commission Resolution 1999/8, *supra* note 49.

140. Id.

141. Id.

142. Id.

143. *See* Commission on Human Rights, *Report of the Working Group on the Effects of the Working Methods and Activities of Transnational Corporations on Human Rights,* at 4, U.N. Doc. E/CN.4/Sub.2/2000/WG.2/WP.1 (2000).

144. Id.

145. Id.

146. Commission on Human Rights, *The Realization of Economic, Social and Cultural Rights: The Question of Transnational Corporations: Second Report of the Working Group,* para. 52, U.N. Doc. E/CN.4/Sub.2/2000/12 (2000).

147. For differing accounts about why the effort was unsuccessful, see Kobrin, *supra* note 31, at 97.

148. Id. at 99.

149. *See* Milloon Kothari & Tara Krause, *Human Rights or Corporate Rights? The MAI Challenge,* 5 Tribune des Droits Humains 16 (1998).

150. *See generally* Development Assistance Committee of the Organization for Economic Co-operation and Development, *Final Report of the Ad Hoc Working Group on Participatory Development and Good Governance,* at 1, OECD Doc.

OCDE/GP/93/191 (1997), available at http://www.oecd.org/dac [hereinafter OECD, *Working Group*].

151. Id. para. 66.

152. *See generally* Organization for Economic Co-operation and Development, Trade, Employment and Labour Standards: A Study of Core Workers' Rights and International Trade (1996).

153. OECD, *Working Group, supra* note 217, paras. 12–13.

154. The revision process demonstrated the impact of the Internet on prospects for participation in international organizations. A draft text of the guidelines were posted on the web with an invitation for the public to comment. After comments were received from businesses, labor unions, environmental groups, academic institutions, individuals, and non-member states, the draft was revised and the second version also posted on the Internet. A second round of public comment followed before the Guidelines were finalized. *See* James Salzman, *Labor Rights, Globalization and Institutions: The Role and Influence of the Organization for Economic Cooperation and Development,* 21 Mich. J. Int'l. L. 769, 847 (2000).

155. UNDP, *supra* note 16, at 80.

156. Examples are the Sullivan Principles concerning South Africa during apartheid and the McBride Principles for Northern Ireland. *See* Lance Compa & Tashia Hinchliffe-Darricarrère, *Enforcing International Labor Rights Through Corporate Codes of Conduct,* 33 Colum. J. Transnat'l. L. 663, 671 (1995); *see also* J. Perez-Lopez, *Promoting International Respect for Worker Rights Through Business Codes of Conduct,* 17 Fordham Int'l. L. J. 1, 47 (1993).

157. "Rugmark" is a program to label carpets that have been made free from child labor. *See* J. Hilowitz, *Social Labelling to Combat Child Labor: Some Considerations,* 136 Int'l. Lab. Rev. 215, 224 (1997).

158. Peter J. Spiro, *New Global Potentates: Nongovernmental Organizations and the "Unregulated",Marketplace,* 18 Cardozo L. Rev. 957, 959 (1996).

159. *See Multinationals and Their Morals,* Economist, Dec. 2, 1995, at 18.

160. Spiro, *supra* note 225, at 962–63 (criticizing NGOs for lack of accountability and transparency).

161. *United Nations Millennium Declaration,* G.A. Res. 55/2, U.N. GAOR, 55th Sess., U.N. Doc. A/Res/55/2 (2000) (issuing on behalf of the heads of state and government attending the U.N. Millennium General Assembly).

162. Id. para. 30.

163 *See* Office of the High Commissioner for Human Rights, *Business and Human Rights: An Update* (June 26, 2000), at http://www.unhchr.ch/businesupdate.htm.

164. Id.

165. Id.

166. The mandate of the special rapporteur on toxic waste includes complaints brought by and against states and non-state actors for the transboundary movement of toxic wastes and she is to identify specific companies and states involved in such traffic.

167. *See* Jane Nelson, The Business of Peace: The Private Sector as a Partner in Conflict Prevention and Resolution 20 (2000), available at http://www.international-alert.org/corporate/Pubs.htm (last visited Dec. 22, 2001).

168. *See* Jonathan Berman, *Boardrooms and Bombs: Strategies of Multinational Corporations in Conflict Areas,* 22 Harv. Int'l. Rev. 28, 28 (2000), available at http://www.hir.harvard.edu (last visited Mar. 11, 2002).

169. *See generally* Hansjörg Strohmeyer, *Collapse and Reconstruction of a Judicial System: The United Nations Missions in Kosovo and East Timor,* 95 Am. J. Int'l. L. 46 (2001).

170. Id.

171. In addition to the two agreements mentioned here, other international agreements signed include the code of labor practice signed between the International Federation of Association Football (FIFA) and the International Confederation of Free Trade Unions (ICFTU), the International Federation of Commercial, Clerical, Professional and Technical Employees (FIET) and the International Textile, Garment and Leather Workers' Federation (ITGLWF). ILO, Report of the Director General, *supra* note 25, at 43–44.

172. Id. at 42.

173. *See* G. Richard Shell, *Trade Legalism and International Relations Theory: An Analysis of the World Trade Organization,* 44 Duke L. J. 829, 908–09 (1995).

174. Article 71 of the U.N. Charter authorizes ECOSOC to consult with NGOs concerned with matters within ECOSOC competence. Article 71 has been implemented through procedures adopted in ECOSOC resolutions. *See General Review of Arrangements for Consultations with Non-Governmental Organizations: Report of the Secretary-General, Open-ended Working Group on the Review of Arrangements for Consultation with Nongovernmental Organizations,* U.N. GAOR, 1st Sess., U.N. Doc. E/AC.70/1994/5 (1994).

175. *See* Kenneth W. Abbott, *"Economic" Issues and Political Participation: The Evolving Boundaries of International Federalism,* 18 Cardozo L. Rev. 971, 1005–06 (1996).

176. Wordsworth, *Rob Roy's Grave,* stanza 9, available at http://www.bartleby.com/145/ ww242.html (last visited Mar. 10, 2002).

17

Beyond Kosovo:
The United Nations
and Humanitarian Intervention

RALPH ZACKLIN

Introduction

A deadly century has ended. It was, in the words of historian Eric Hobs-bawm, "without doubt the most murderous century of which we have record, both by the scale, frequency, and length of the warfare which filled it."[1] In the last [decade], ethnic conflicts in Kosovo, East Timor and Chechnya were added to numerous international conflicts in the Horn of Africa, the Great Lakes region and Kashmir, [with] civil wars in Afghanistan, Colombia, Sudan, Sri Lanka and Angola. This enumeration is not exhaustive.

What is particularly significant is the nature of these wars. Wars are increasingly fought within states, not between them. Civilians rather than soldiers are the victims, and among the civilians, the most vulnerable are children, the poor and the elderly. As Mary Kaldor has pointed out in her recent book, *New and Old Wars*, the ratio of military to civilian casualties at the beginning of the twentieth century was eight to one; by the 1990s, the ratio had been almost exactly reversed.[2]

In *Twentieth Century*, a single volume history of the world from 1901 to 2000, Professor J. M. Roberts tells a story that most thinking people would like to forget and that those of us who are professionally engaged in the practice of international law and international relations must regard with dismay.[3] If the century has seen unimaginable and unparalleled progress in science, technology and medicine, this very progress seems paradoxically to have created more, rather than less, conflict. The laws of human nature appear to be infinitely more difficult to tame than the laws of science.

Reprinted with permission of the *Virginia Journal of International Law.*

For the United Nations, the second attempt in the twentieth century to create an international organization of universal competence and authority to maintain international peace and security, the last decade of the century proved to be tumultuous. Beginning with the end of the Cold War and the successful reversal of Iraq's aggression against Kuwait, the fulfillment of the organization's role in maintaining peace and security through an engaged and, finally, relatively cohesive Security Council appeared to be realizable. A "New World Order" was proclaimed.

Then, in swift succession, came Somalia, Bosnia and Rwanda. The Security Council's credibility and, by extension, the credibility of the United Nations as a whole, was grievously damaged. In Somalia, what began as a humanitarian mission ended in ignominious withdrawal after a succession of failed operations. The casualties sustained by the United States and other contingents blighted peacekeeping and peace-enforcement in Bosnia, and led directly to the inability to deal with the single worst crime of the second half of the century, the genocide in Rwanda. The United Nations will live with the consequences of these failures for a very long time, even as it strives to learn from them.

By the end of the last decade, with U.N. credibility hugely diminished, if not entirely destroyed, the Security Council was unable to find a working consensus on Kosovo. A NATO-led coalition undertook an enforcement action without the prior authorization of the Security Council and not in self-defense, in violation of U.N. Charter principles, including the prohibition on the use of force,[4] thereby plunging the organization into a political, legal, institutional, and moral crisis. The decade ended with the utility and the future of the U.N. very much in doubt.

The Challenge of Kosovo

NATO's actions in Kosovo presented a serious threat to the United Nations and the conception that had prevailed since 1945: that as the only universal political organization, it represented the international community of states, and that the principles contained in its Charter formed the cornerstone of international relations. Quite suddenly, fundamental principles, such as the respect for sovereignty, territorial integrity and the prohibition on the use of force except in self-defense or when authorized by the Security Council, were cast into doubt. The very fabric of organized international society as we knew it appeared to have been dissolved.

What was particularly worrisome about the NATO-led action in Kosovo was that the decision to proceed with the use of force without U.N. authorization was so overt—more so than the closest precedent at the end of the Gulf War, when the coalition intervened in northern and southern Iraq on the basis of Security Council Resolution 688.[5] Moreover, among the countries most politically and militarily engaged in Kosovo were those who historically have most consistently upheld the principles of the U.N. Charter and the importance of the authority of the United Nations as the foundation of the present system of peace and security.

The NATO-led action in Kosovo caused considerable unease not only among member states, but also among senior U.N. Secretariat officials. This unease deepened as the bombing was stepped up, as civilian installations such as the bridges across the Danube were destroyed, innocent civilians were killed and injured, and questions began to surface about the means and method of warfare and the lack of proportionality in the use of force. It was impossible for Secretary-General Kofi Annan to remain silent. He had the difficult task of trying to defend the Charter principles and its institutional framework, while at the same time recognizing that massive and systematic violations of human rights could not be permitted to unfold without an appropriate response from the United Nations. With its credibility already severely damaged in Somalia, Bosnia, and especially in Rwanda, the U.N. could not afford to be seen as indifferent to the human suffering in Kosovo. In brief press statements at the beginning of the hostilities, the Secretary-General deplored that the situation in Kosovo had not been resolved by peaceful means, and that the Security Council had not been able to fulfill its role. However, he also made it clear that, in his view, there were circumstances in which unauthorized force could legitimately be used in the defense of peace, and in the prevention of massive and systematic violations of human rights.

As events in Kosovo unfolded, the need for an authoritative and more comprehensive statement on humanitarian intervention became necessary. The occasion for such an address presented itself in The Hague on May 18, 1999, during the centennial commemoration of the first International Peace Conference.[6]

The Secretary-General's Address, The Hague, May 18, 1999

The Secretary-General began his address by noting that the meeting was taking place during a time of war, a reference to the then-ongoing armed intervention regarding Kosovo. He stated that a renewal of the effectiveness and relevance of the Security Council was a cornerstone in protecting and preserving the legal regime of the U.N. Charter. It was, therefore, a cause for concern that the Security Council had been disregarded on such matters as mandatory sanctions, cooperation in disarmament and non-proliferation, and the implementation of the decisions of the Yugoslav and Rwanda war crimes tribunals. The case of Kosovo, he said, "has cast into sharp relief the fact that member states and regional organizations sometimes take enforcement action without Security Council authorization."[7] He believed that such marginalization of the Council was regrettable. The inability of the Security Council in the case of Kosovo to unify two equally compelling interests—its primary responsibility for the maintenance of peace and the legitimacy on the use of force in the pursuit of peace and the defense of human rights—was a source of great danger. It was clear that "unless the Security Council is restored to its preeminent position as the sole source of legitimacy on the use of force, we are on a dangerous path to anarchy."[8]

The core challenge of the Security Council and the United Nations as a whole was "to unite behind the principle that massive and systematic violations of human rights conducted against an entire people cannot be allowed to stand."[9] The choice, thus, should not have been between Security Council unity and inaction in the face of genocide, as in Rwanda, and Council division and regional action, as in Kosovo.

The Secretary-General's Address to the General Assembly, September 20, 1999

Between the Hague address and the Secretary-General's address at the opening of the 54th session of the General Assembly on September 20, 1999,[10] two significant events occurred regarding the ongoing debate on sovereignty vs. humanitarian intervention. First, the use of force against Yugoslavia in relation to Kosovo was brought to an end and the situation was brought back into the fold of the Security Council, which authorized a far-reaching military and civilian operation in Kosovo.[11] Second, violence erupted in East Timor in the immediate aftermath of a popular consultation favoring independence from Indonesia, resulting in large-scale violations of human rights. Like Kosovo, this situation yet again confronted the United Nations with the problem of how far it could, or should, go in intervening militarily in the eventuality that the state exercising sovereignty rejected such intervention. Unlike Kosovo, however, the United Nations was able to act expeditiously in East Timor. In doing so, the U.N. authorized first a military intervention under Chapter VII[12] which obtained Indonesia's acquiescence and, subsequently, a comprehensive military and civilian operation, with very broad powers of governance, to act as an interim civilian administration pending full independence for East Timor.[13] The extent to which the lessons learned in Kosovo influenced the decision-making on East Timor is unclear. What is clear is that the Secretary-General was determined in this situation to exercise all the powers at his disposal in order to ensure that action to halt the human rights violations be immediate and that the framework of the United Nations be respected.

In light of these dramatic events, the Secretary-General's speech to the General Assembly took on added significance. Placing the problem of what he termed, "the prospects for human security and intervention,"[14] in the wider context of the need to adapt the United Nations to a transforming world—transformed by global geo-political, economic, technological and environmental changes—in which new actors, responsibilities and possibilities for peace and progress were emerging, the Secretary-General put forward two propositions: (1) that state sovereignty, which for all of the twentieth century had been regarded as the very foundation of organized international society as enshrined in the U.N. Charter, was being redefined by the forces of globalization and international cooperation, that "[t]he State is now widely understood to be the servant of its people, and not vice versa";[15] and (2) that "individual sovereignty . . . , the human rights and fundamental freedoms of each and every individual as enshrined in . . . [the U.N.] Charter . . . has been enhanced by a renewed consciousness of the right of every individual to control his or her destiny."[16]

These "parallel developments" demanded a "willingness to think anew about how the United Nations responds to political, human rights, and humanitarian crises," the means employed and the "willingness to act."[17] While genocide in Rwanda defined "for our generation the consequences of inaction," the conflict in Kosovo prompted "important questions about the consequences of action in the absence of complete unity on the part of the international community."[18] Kosovo demonstrated the "dilemma of . . . humanitarian intervention": the questionable legitimacy of an action taken without U.N. authorization, on the one hand, and the imperative of "halting gross violations of human rights," on the other.[19] It had been the "inability of the international community" (namely the United Nations) in Kosovo to reconcile these two competing interests that resulted in the "tragedy" in Kosovo.[20]

Some commentators and scholars attacked the U.N. Charter system as being outmoded or irrelevant.[21] The Secretary-General took issue with this view.[22] The Charter's principles still defined the "aspirations of peoples everywhere."[23] "Nothing in the Charter preclud[ed] a recognition that there are rights beyond borders."[24] The source of the dilemma lay not in deficiencies in the U.N. Charter, but in its application—more precisely applying its principles in an era during which sovereignty and human rights had taken on new meanings in relation to one another.[25] The Secretary-General concluded by affirming that:

> Just as we have learned that the world cannot stand aside when gross and systematic violations of human rights are taking place, so we have also learned that intervention must be based on legitimate and universal principles if it is to enjoy the sustained support of the world's peoples. This developing international norm in favour of intervention . . . will no doubt continue to pose profound challenges to the international community. Any such evolution in our understanding of state sovereignty and individual

sovereignty will, in some quarters, be met with distrust, scepticism [sic], and even hostility. But it is an evolution that we should welcome.[26]

The Secretary-General's speech achieved its principal goal: to encourage an internal and public debate on the issue of humanitarian intervention. The debate, however, also revealed a substantial polarization of views, largely along north-south lines, which does not augur well for the early evolution of a norm of international law.

While the events in Kosovo, East Timor and Chechnya have focused renewed attention on the role of the United Nations and humanitarian intervention, and while the Secretary-General's address was a timely, even bold, attempt on his part to frame the debate and provoke new thinking about a doctrine of humanitarian intervention, which may or may not be evolving normatively, thus far, very little clarity has emerged. The debate has predictably given rise to much political posturing, but it has also served to highlight a number of underlying issues, such as the imperative need for reform of the Security Council, which lies at the heart of the disenchantment of a great majority of member states. It is, therefore, a good opportunity to take a closer look at the question of humanitarian intervention, and to analyze it from a legal, as distinct from a purely political, point of view. The questions then become: (1) what exactly does humanitarian intervention entail; (2) what might its elements be; and (3) is it possible to envisage the emergence of a norm of humanitarian intervention or, in other words, a binding rule of international law, either through the development of a customary rule, or through a codified international instrument?

Humanitarian Intervention and the Legality of the Use of Force

Definition of Humanitarian Intervention

Historically, "humanitarian intervention" has had several meanings, or has come to encompass different concepts, not all of which have the same legal significance. It is important, therefore, at the outset of any discussion of an evolving norm of humanitarian intervention, to define its specific meaning. It may be noted that in his General Assembly speech, the Secretary-General quite deliberately placed his remarks within a broad definition of humanitarian intervention, including a wide spectrum of action from the most pacifistic to the most coercive, placing a good deal of emphasis on preventive diplomacy through the peaceful dispute settlement mechanisms of Chapter VI of the U.N. Charter. There is little doubt today as to the legal standing of these consensual forms of intervention, which trace their origins to The

Hague Peace Conferences of 1899 and 1907, and which have acquired a normative value which is largely uncontested.[27]

However, the recent debates on intervention, whether in the General Assembly or the public at large, have focused almost exclusively on coercive humanitarian intervention. Since the use of force is permissible under the Charter in certain well-defined circumstances, it is situations such as Kosovo, East Timor and Chechnya, which get to the core of the issue. In other words, the question is whether, in the absence of a specific authorization of the Security Council, it may be legitimate for a state or group of states to intervene in the territory of a third state, through the threat or use of force, to halt massive and systematic violations of human rights within that state. Humanitarian intervention, in this sense, does not have the same meaning as other forms of intervention with which it is sometimes confused, such as the protection of foreign nationals (e.g., Grenada, Panama) or humanitarian assistance offered through international non-governmental organizations (NGOs). These forms of intervention pose somewhat different legal problems, and have attained a relative degree of recognition under international law.

A good starting point in the legal analysis of humanitarian intervention as understood in the narrow sense outlined here is, therefore, the U.N. Charter itself, in order to see to what extent its principles and mechanisms might permit such intervention. From the perspective of the U.N. Charter and international law in general, the development of a norm of humanitarian intervention would have to overcome two major obstacles: (1) the prohibition on the use of force; and (2) the principle of non-intervention in the internal affairs of states.

Non-Use of Force: Principles and Mechanisms

The fundamental rule under which any examination of humanitarian intervention must proceed is Article 2(4) of the U.N. Charter, according to which all U.N. member states must "refrain in their international relations from the threat or use of force against the territorial integrity or political independence of any state, or in any other manner inconsistent with the Purposes of the United Nations."[28] It is generally understood that the prohibition on the use of force in international relations contained in this article was intended at the time of its adoption and is still regarded today to be comprehensive in nature. Indeed, it is this provision of the Charter which marked the historic evolution of organized international relations in the twentieth century, prior to which no general prohibition on the use of force existed.

The Hague Peace Conferences—the centenary of which ironically enough took place during the Kosovo intervention—are considered to be the beginning of the process to prohibit the use of force in international relations. The 1907 Hague Convention,[29] however, did not prohibit the use of force; it merely formalized resort to it. The Covenant of the League of Nations likewise failed to establish a general prohibition of war, a step that was not achieved until the Kellog-Briand Pact in 1928.[30] Although the Kellog-Briand Pact soon came to be regarded as part of customary international law, it too had its shortcomings. For instance, it did not contain a general prohibition on the use of force (as distinct from war), and it was not linked to a system of sanctions.

Article 2(4) of the U.N. Charter, therefore, represented a considerable advancement in international law by prohibiting the use and threat of force in general. The Charter provides for only two exceptions to this rule: (1) the inherent right of individual or collective self-defense if an armed attack occurs against a member;[31] and (2) the ability of the Security Council, if it determines that a threat to the peace, breach of the peace or act of aggression has occurred, to take (or authorize) military enforcement action involving the armed forces of member states.[32] This second exception is the foundation of the entire U.N. collective security system. Thus, any threat or use of force that is neither justified as self-defense against an armed attack nor taken or authorized by the Security Council is a violation of the U.N. Charter and is, therefore, contrary to international law.

Viewed in this perspective, it is clear that what is illegitimate unilaterally may be legitimate if it is the subject of a collective decision of the United Nations. Also, it is clear that coercive humanitarian intervention is not excluded by the Charter, provided that the Security Council determines that massive and systematic violations of human rights occurring within a state constitute a threat to the peace, and then calls for or authorizes an enforcement action (i.e., a collective U.N. action or an authorized coalition of member states).

As correct as this conclusion may be from the standpoint of *lex lata*,[33] the question arises whether this view of the law is morally acceptable today. Can we really accept that a collective or authorized action to halt massive and systematic violations of human rights is entirely dependent upon the political ability of the Security Council to make a determination that such violations constitute a threat to the peace—a determination which, at a minimum, requires the affirmation or acquiescence of all five permanent members of the Security Council? The choice, as the Secretary-General has identified it, must surely be more than unity and inaction, as in Rwanda, or division and unauthorized action, as in Kosovo.[34]

The Principle of Non-Intervention

The second major obstacle to be overcome is the principle of nonintervention in the internal affairs of states, a customary principle which, in the eyes of the overwhelming majority of international lawyers, has the character of *jus cogens,* a peremptory norm from which no derogation is possible. This principle is reflected in numerous international instruments adopted by the U.N. General Assembly, including the Declaration on Friendly Relations,[35] and has been affirmed on several occasions by the International Court of Justice, most notably in *The Corfu Channel* case[36] and in the *Nicaragua* case.[37] In the context of the debate regarding humanitarian intervention, *The Corfu Channel* case is particularly instructive, since the de-mining operation carried out by the Royal Navy in the Corfu Channel which gave rise to the dispute could be characterized as having a humanitarian objective.[38] Is it possible then to envisage a deviation from the principle of non-intervention on the grounds of a competing norm of humanitarian intervention?

Today, it is frequently observed that human rights are no longer the exclusive concern of the sovereign state, that they have become a core concern of the international community, and that obligations to respect such rights are *erga omnes*—obligations of a State toward the international community as a whole. To some degree, this has always been the case. For instance, consider the attempts to impose sanctions on the Spanish Fascist regime of Franco, or the use of comprehensive mandatory sanctions to end the racist policies in Rhodesia and South Africa. The trend has become far more pronounced in the last decade, which has witnessed the remarkable institutional development of the establishment of two ad hoc war crimes tribunals by the Security Council acting under Chapter VII. Whether the trend might be said to constitute a deviation from, or an exception to, the principle of non-intervention, is a question that must be approached with great caution for the reasons advanced by the International Court of Justice (i.e., the risk of abuse).

The principles of the non use of force and non-intervention represent serious obstacles to the development of a norm of humanitarian intervention. However, such principles are not immutable, and their meaning may change over time through the practice of states. In order to overcome these obstacles, an emerging norm of humanitarian intervention would have to accommodate these principles or, as the case may be, be able to demonstrate that state practice has achieved what amounts to a de facto amendment of the controlling principle.

The Question of an Emerging Norm of Humanitarian Intervention

In his statements on various occasions, the Secretary-General has clearly and expressly aligned himself with those scholars and members of civil society who, for some time now, have advocated what has been perceived as the embryo of a rule of humanitarian intervention in international law. In

April 1999, in an address to the U.N. Human Rights Commission, he stated that: "[e]merging slowly, but I believe surely, is an international norm against the violent repression of minorities that will and must take precedence over concerns of State sovereignty."[39]

As we have seen, the Secretary-General returned to this vision in his address to the General Assembly on September 20, 1999. However, in this address, he acknowledged that the evolution in our understanding of state and individual sovereignty would almost certainly be met with distrust, skepticism, and hostility. There is no doubt about the commitment of the Secretary-General to the promotion of human rights, which has become a cornerstone of his administration. His advocacy of humanitarian intervention is both courageous and far-sighted, but as his address to the General Assembly shows, his idealism is tempered by realism. A norm of humanitarian intervention may be a desirable goal—what international lawyers would refer to as *lex ferenda*—but it is far from acquiring the character of a rule *lex lata*.

To those who are familiar with the formation of rules of international law through customary or conventional means, the notion of an emerging norm is a familiar one. There are numerous areas of international law where today's rules "emerged" over time through a developing practice of states, which achieved wide recognition either as customary principles or became codified in conventions. The development of the law of the sea, in particular in relation to such concepts as the continental shelf, the territorial sea, and the exclusive economic zone, is one example of an emerging norm that has developed through the practice of states. The current state of the emerging norm of humanitarian intervention, and the many difficulties which it poses, may be gauged from the reactions of member states to the Secretary-General's address to the General Assembly.

As was to be expected, the Secretary-General's address provoked a lively debate among member states, fifty-one of whom took part.[40] An analysis of the various positions demonstrates that the views of states can be grouped into three major tendencies: (1) the smallest group, represented by Germany and Sweden, strongly advocated immediate intervention in situations of grave human rights violations; (2) a larger group, composed of states from Africa, Asia and Latin America, expressed strong opposition to humanitarian intervention and defended national sovereignty as an unchallengeable principle; and (3) a third and, by some margin, the largest group, aligned itself somewhere between the other two. Many of the states in this third group, while not opposed outright to humanitarian intervention, nevertheless emphasized the need to provide clear and consistent criteria to ensure that the doctrine of humanitarian intervention is applied on an equitable basis. Overall, of the states that took an explicit position on the issue, approximately thirty-two states were either against or negatively inclined, while only eight states were generally supportive. Equally significant, and an indication of the perceptions underlying the positions, the polarization of those generally in favor and those generally against was strictly along north-south geographic lines. Importantly, among those overtly opposed or negatively inclined towards a doctrine of humanitarian intervention were both China and the Russian Federation—two of the five permanent members of the Security Council.

While the views expressed by member states in a general debate such as this one may be regarded as essentially impressionistic, nevertheless, it is almost certainly a reasonably reliable guide as to current state thinking. Although not encouraging to those inclined toward the view of an evolving norm of humanitarian intervention, some encouragement may be drawn from the fact that the largest group of states did not reject the idea of humanitarian intervention, but rather, expressed the need to build a political consensus in the General Assembly, and the necessity of establishing clear and consistent criteria if such a doctrine were to be developed.

Kosovo as a Catalyst for Change

The late Georg Schwarzenberger[41] stated in his Manual of International Law that "the totality of the rules of international law can be explained as a constantly changing and dynamic interplay between the rules underlying the principles of sovereignty and those governing the other fundamental principles of international law."[42] Nowhere is this more apparent than in the interplay between the principles of sovereignty and the principles underlying the promotion and protection of fundamental human rights. Law, whether domestic or international, is, by nature, a conservative discipline, and change usually comes about slowly. But there are crises or events of such magnitude that they produce tectonic changes, not only in the political landscape, but also in the legal landscape. Thus, we can see how the two world wars brought lasting changes on international law. The U.N. Charter was, of course, a product of the Second World War, and remains so to this day with its emphasis on state sovereignty. Yet, as the Secretary-General has frequently pointed out, the Charter was issued in the name of "the peoples," rather than the governments of the United Nations, and its aim is not only to maintain international peace and security, but also to encourage "respect for human rights and for fundamental freedoms." Furthermore, the Charter has proved to be a flexible instrument, responsive to change more readily than its purely formal amendments would lead us to believe.[43]

It is undeniable that as slow and painstaking as it may have been, there has been a steady evolution of the human rights principles in the Charter; first, with the elaboration of the fundamental human rights instruments such

as the Universal Declaration of Human Rights[44] and the Covenants, and subsequently, through the various mechanisms for their implementation. Side-
by-side with this normative and institutional development, we have witnessed
the rise and growth of civil society and what might be called humanitarian
action at both the inter-governmental and non-governmental levels.

The question of whether the intervention in Kosovo will recede into
history as a singular exception to the prevailing law, or whether it will
prove to be an event which acts as a catalyst for change resulting in a new
norm of humanitarian intervention, remains to be seen. Judging by the
intensity of the debate that it has already provoked, it may come to be
regarded in the future as such a catalytic event. The challenge for the international lawyer is to seize the opportunity created by the particular con-
juncture of policy and practice, represented in a general sense by the
Kosovo conflict, and to explore the possibilities for achieving that elusive
common ground that could provide a basis on which the international community can develop a norm of humanitarian intervention. One must do this
without at the same time eroding the principles and purposes of the Charter. This is, to say the least, a daunting task, but, as the General Assembly
debate has demonstrated, there is substantial consensus among states that
the issues underlying new dynamics in the relationship between sovereignty
and human rights must be discussed. This is only a starting point. While we
are largely removed from a definitive framework of a normative doctrine of
humanitarian intervention, it is possible to outline some of the legal and
institutional elements of such a doctrine, which, if it is to become a rule of
law, must be clear, equitable, principled, and authoritative.

Toward a Norm of Humanitarian Intervention

The degree of hostility or suspicion with which the intervention in Kosovo
was received in many countries, particularly among the nonaligned—who
perceived it as a form of neo-interventionism under humanitarian pre-
texts—underscores the necessity of agreeing on certain criteria for humanitarian intervention linked to the U.N. Charter's substantive and institutional framework. Nothing short of this is likely to overcome the deeply
held view that, as presently conceived, humanitarian intervention is an
instrument of dubious legality, inequitable in implementation, and represents a weakening of the foundations of organized international society. A
number of substantive and institutional criteria or pre-conditions have
already been suggested by governments and scholars, or have emerged
from the debate in the General Assembly.[45] It is around these elements that
the eventual formation of a norm might develop.

Primacy of Preventive Measures

Since the use of force in international relations must always be treated as an exceptional measure and is an extremely grave matter under any circumstances, every effort must be made to exhaust all possible peaceful means of resolving humanitarian crises. Primacy must, therefore, be given to preventive measures, including the greater use and development of early warning systems and preventive diplomacy, deployment and disarmament. As the Secretary-General has said, "Even the costliest policy of prevention is far cheaper, in lives and in resources, than the least expensive use of armed force."[46] The primacy of resort to, and the exhaustion of preventive measures, must be made an integral part of any humanitarian intervention doctrine.

A Demonstrated Inability or Unwillingness
to Uphold the Law by the State Concerned

If violations of human rights are the result of a breakdown in the organs of the state, it must be ascertained that the governmental authorities are not only incapable of ending these violations but, at the same time, have refused assistance from other states or international organizations. If, on the other hand, the violations are in fact attributable to the government, it must be shown that the authorities concerned have consistently withheld their cooperation from the U.N. or other international organizations, or have systematically refused to comply with appeals, recommendations or decisions of such organizations.

The Primary Role and Responsibility
of the Security Council Must Be Recognized

Under the U.N. Charter, the Security Council has the primary and exclusive authority to authorize the collective use of force.[47] The inability of the Security Council to fulfill this primary function because of disagreement among the members, or because one or more of the permanent members exercises its veto, must be clearly established.

The Violations of Human Rights
Must Be Massive and Systematic

In order to give rise to intervention involving the threat or use of force, the violations must be massive and systematic. Examples of such egregious violations include genocide, as in Rwanda, large-scale ethnic cleansing, as in Bosnia and Kosovo, and crimes against humanity, as defined in the relevant international instruments or by the jurisprudence of the international criminal tribunals for the former Yugoslavia and Rwanda. The threat posed to civilian life must be overwhelming and immediate, thus allowing no alternative action.

Action Must Be Collective or Collectively Legitimized

Humanitarian intervention must have the support or acquiescence of the international community at large. Such support may be demonstrated in a number of ways, but obtaining the views and support of the overwhelming majority of states in an organ such as the General Assembly of the United Nations would be a clear indication of the necessary support.

Limitations on the Use of Force

The use of force must be limited to the purpose of halting the violations and restoring respect for human rights. The intervention must be discontinued once this limited goal has been achieved. It must not undermine the territorial integrity of the state concerned. Finally, it must be proportionate in the use of means and be conducted in accordance with international humanitarian law. It should be noted that these criteria are not the product of any one group of states, but represent a broad cross-section of positions advanced by states of all regional groupings.[48]

The criteria, taken individually, reflect, for the most part, the existing Charter-based law and practice. They re-affirm the central goal of the non-use of force by emphasizing the basic principles of the Charter: (1) the primacy of preventive measures and the primary role of the Security Council; (2) the exceptional nature of humanitarian intervention is invoked by requiring that the violations of human rights that give rise to intervention must be massive and systematic; (3) the limitations of intervention are strictly confined through the express reaffirmation of the principle of territorial integrity; and (4) the exceptional use of force is subject to the rules governing proportionality and respect for international humanitarian law.

Notes

1. Eric J. Hobsbawm, The Age of Extremes: A History of the World, 1914–1991, 13 (1994).

2. Mary Kaldor, New and Old Wars: Organized Violence in a Global Era 8 (1999).

3. J. M. Roberts, Twentieth Century: The History of the World, 1901–2000 (1999). "Reprinted by permission of the Virginia Journal of Law."

4. U.N. Charter art. 2, para. 4.

5. S.C. Res. 688, U.N. SCOR, 46th Sess., 2982d mtg., at 31, U.N. Doc.S/ RES/688 (1991).

6. *Secretary-General Says Renewal of Effectiveness and Relevance of Security Council Must Be Cornerstone of Efforts to Promote International Peace in Next Century,* Press Release, SG/SM/6997 (visited Apr. 5, 2001) <http://www.un.org/ News/Press/docs/1999/19990518.SGSM6997.html>.

7. Id.

8. Id.

9. Id.

10. Report of the Secretary-General on the Work of the Organization, U.N. GAOR, 54th Sess., 4th plen. mtg., at 1, U.N. Doc. A/54/PV.4 (1999) [hereinafter Report of the Secretary General].

11. S.C. Res. 1244, U.N. SCOR, 54th Sess., 4011th mtg., U.N. Doc. S/RES/ 1244 (1999).

12. U.N. Charter arts. 39–51.

13. S.C. Res. 1272, U.N. SCOR, 54th Sess. 4057th mtg., U.N. Doc. S/RES/ 1272 (1999).

14. Report of the Secretary-General *supra* note 10, at 1.

15. Id.

16. Id. at 1–2.

17. Id. at 2.

18. Id.

19. Id.

20. Id.

21. See Id. The Secretary General said. "In response to this turbulent era of crises and interventions, there are those who have suggested that the Charter itself— with its roots in the aftermath of global inter-State war—is ill-suited to guide us in a world of ethnic wars and intra-State violence. I believe they are wrong." Id.

22. See Id.

23. Id.

24. Id.

25. See Id.

26. Id. at 4.

27. See U.N. Charter arts. 33–38.

28. Id. art. 2, para 4.

29. Convention with Other Powers Respecting the Laws and Customs of War on Land (Hague Convention), Oct. 18, 1907, 36 Stat. 2277, T.S. No. 539, 1 Bevans 631.

30. The General Treaty for the Renunciation of War (Kellog-Briand Pact), Aug. 27, 1928, 46 Stat. 2343, T.S. No. 796, 94 L.N.T.S. 57.

31. See U.N. Charter art. 51.

32. See id. arts. 39–51.

33. Defined as "[e]xisting law, the law which is presently in force." Encyclopedia Dictionary of International Law 214 (1986).

34. See *supra* note 10.

35. Declaration of Principles of International Law Concerning Friendly Relations and Cooperation Among States in Accordance with the Charter of the United Nations, G.A. Res. 2625 (XXV), annex, U.N. GAOR, 25th Sess., Supp. No. 28, at 121, U.N. Doc. A/8028 (1970).

36. The Corfu Channel Case (U.K. v. Alb.), 1949 I.C.J. 4 (Apr. 9).

37. Military and Paramilitary Activities (Nicar. v. U.S.), 1986 I.C.J. (June 27).

38. See Corfu Channel Case, 1949 I.C.J. 4.

39. *World Expects United Nations to Take Stand Against Atrocities, Secretary-General Tells Commission on Human Rights,* Press Release, HR/CN/899 (visited Apr. 10, 2001) <http://www.un.org/News/Press/docs/1999/19990407.hrcn899.htm>.

40. For an analysis of this debate, I am indebted to an internal U.N. Secretariat paper prepared by a group of interns in the Policy Planning Unit of the Department of Political Affairs (unofficial document).

41. Professor of International Law at University College, London. Professor Schwarzenberger was known for his inductive approach to international law—a form of strict empiricism in which state practice, as evidenced through the decisions of international courts and tribunals, was elevated to a high degree.

42. Georg Schwarzenberger & E. D. Brown, A Manual of International Law 77 (6th ed. 1976).

43. U.N. Charter art. 1, para. 3.

44. G.A. Res. 217 (AIII), U.N. GAOR, 3rd Sess., at 71, U.N. Doc. A/810 (1948).

45. One of the first and most notable scholars to outline the elements of an emerging customary rule was Antonio Cassese, then a presiding judge of Trial Chamber II of the International Criminal Tribunal for the formed Yugoslavia (ICTY) and its president from 1993–1997. See Antonio Cassese, Ex iniuia ius oritur: *Are We Moving Towards International Legitimation of Forcible Humanitarian Countermeasures in the World Community?* 10 Eur. J. Int'l. 23 (1999).

46. Speech of Secretary-General, *supra* note 10.

47. U.N. Charter art. 2, para. 4.

48. The British Government has espoused a set of ideas along similar lines in an effort to encourage the development of what it calls "a set of pragmatic understandings on action in response to humanitarian crises," which it believes could assist the Security Council to reach consensus when such crises occur.

PART 2.3

International Law
as Normative System:
For the Protection of
the Environment

18

Why Domestic Environmental Law Needs a Robust International Environmental Law Regime

A. Dan Tarlock

DO DOMESTIC ENVIRONMENTAL LAW REGIMES NEED INTERNATIONAL ENVI-ronmental law? I argue that the answer to this question is yes, but for many this is a counter-intuitive answer. There is great resistance to the incorporation of international environmental law into domestic law even in Australia, New Zealand and the United States. All three nations have been leaders in the development of comprehensive domestic environmental protection regimes. United States environmental law, because it was developed early, has served as the world model. Australian and New Zealand law has served as the model for South Pacific and Asian environmental law regimes[1] and for integrated resource management.[2] All three nations have equally been at the forefront of the development of international environmental law, and each country has made substantial contributions to the development of international law. Nonetheless, the degree of integration of the two regimes varies among the countries and there is continued resistance to integration.

The United States has contributed both core principles and political will to the development of international environmental law, but has resisted integration. Australia and New Zealand have been comparatively more receptive to integration. United States law is the basis for the four principles of international environmental law: state responsibility for transboundary harm[3] and the duty to prevent pollution. There is widespread consensus, at least in theory, that all states have a duty not to allow state agencies and private parties subject to the state's regulatory jurisdiction[4] to use its territories in a manner that causes substantial harm to other states and their nationals.[5] The basic duty is now firmly grounded in modern *international* law,[6] although like many international rules it is more often invoked than applied.[7] The United States, along with Germany, has also played a leading role in developing the emerging precautionary principle[8] which posits that states have the power, if not the duty,[9] to prevent serious risks from materialising in the absence of provable environmental harm, if there is evidence of significant environmental risks. The principle is still vague[10] but it probably includes a duty to avoid foreseeable, significant risks, although the burden of proof issue is unresolved.[11] Precaution projects the substitution of risk for provable harm that underlies United States and European toxic pollutant regulation as an international duty among states and *erga omnes*.[12]

Australia and New Zealand's geography has pushed them to expand state power to manage both its sovereign resources and regional commons in which they have a special interest. International environmental law is evolving toward the recognition that states have the right (if not the duty) to minimize ecological risks both within their territories and outside their territories if the conduct of other states in common areas harms the interests of a state. Australia and New Zealand are world leaders in defining and expanding these rights and duties before international tribunals and in other appropriate fora to advance both national and international environmental interests. Australia and Japan's use of the United Nations Convention on the Law of the Sea (UNCLOS) arbitration procedures to protect migratory fishing stocks in the South Pacific and Australia's exploration of UNCLOS to protect marine biodiversity reserves in the South Pacific are excellent examples of adjuration as a method of international law creation. Domestically, Australia and New Zealand's High Court jurisprudence are models of how international environmental law can be integrated into domestic law.[13]

This article sets out both a positive and normative case for the integration of domestic and international environmental law. The positive case, in brief, is that integration is inevitable in the post–second world war "decentred" world of environmental law where multiple private and public actors are necessary to implement protection regimes. The normative case is that both regimes are mutually re-enforcing and thus serve as a check, however weak, against the inevitable domestic tendency to discount protection duties when they conflict with a "higher" state priority. The article recognises, however, that integration will be the exception rather than the norm and thus it starts with the case against integration.

The Case For and Against Integration

The Case Against Integration

The basic case is that international environmental law is either unnecessary or unwelcome. It is unnecessary because domestic environmental law has flourished in almost all countries as a parallel regime to international environmental law. This is especially true in developed as opposed to developing countries. In the latter, international law can empower both the state and non-governmental officers (NGOs), but in developed countries international law is often seen as an unwelcome constraint on the formulation and implementation of state policy that will conform to international norms.

The case against integration starts from the dualist theory of international law. This theory posits that there are two parallel regimes each performing discrete but separate functions. Thus, international environmental law should be limited to the redress of transboundary harm or to the protection of true commons such as the oceans, the stratospheric ozone layer, and the earth's climate. Outside of these relatively narrow "true" international spheres, states have sovereign prerogatives to manage their territorial resources as they choose. This position is supported by four separate, and somewhat inconsistent, arguments: (1) "realpolitik," (2) redundancy, (3) the "race-to-the-bottom" and (4) equity.

Realpolitik. The "realpolitik" argument is a positive one. It asserts that since states fear that international law will interfere with their sovereign prerogative to manage their territorial resources, they will inevitably resist integration. Thus, integration will be a futile exercise and should be foregone as a costly waste of scarce political resources. Integration will be unsuccessful and scarce political capital will be diverted from more productive domestic environmental protection initiatives.

The race to the bottom. The race to the bottom is a traditional justification for central government environmental standards to curb the tendency of subordinate units of government to compete for industry through lower pollution standards. In this context, it refers to the central problem of international law. The only basis of international law is consensus among sovereign nation states, and the price for consensus is agreement on the lowest common denominator. Students of international law know that the race to the bottom is a product of efforts to overcome the positivist paradox (the lack of a sovereign to enforce the law). From the perspective of modern Anglo-American and civil law jurisprudence, international law gains its legitimacy through consensus among states. In international environmental law, this consensus is generally reflected in treaties. The principal alternative basis of consensus, customary law, is a generally backward-looking doctrine that contributes little to international environmental law. Environmental law seeks to reverse past state practices not enshrine them into law.[14] To secure consensus on a treaty, it is often necessary to accept the lowest common denominator. In short, international environmental law will cause a downward rather than upward pressure on environmental standards, at least in developed countries. International environmental law is generally rejected by states either because of a fear that it will lower a state's level of environmental protection or require the state to raise it above the existing domestic level. In either case, strong state resistance will undermine the project of integration.

The trade environmental interface is an example of race-to-the-bottom concerns. General Agreement on Tariffs and Trade (GATT) and the North American Free Trade Agreement (NAFTA) preserve the right of the state to apply their own health and safety regulations to imported products, but the trade specialists and less-developed exporting states have expressed concern that strong public and ISO 14000 standards are disguised trade barriers.[15] This, in turn, has led to fears among developed countries that trade dispute settlement procedures can be used as *a forum* for countries to accept lower environmental standards. The World Trade Organization's (WTO) trade-environment jurisprudence fuels these fears because the WTO Appellate Panels have invalidated several United States efforts to control the process by which protections are manufactured. The race-to-the-bottom is frequently raised by developed countries against participation in an environmental law regime. This argument was, and continues to be, raised by United States NGOs to oppose participation in NAFTA. Mexico is a one-half first world country with a long, and continuing history of minimal environmental protection. Concern is not limited to the possibility that a United States law will hold NAFTA illegal. For example, trade has profound potential effects on the concentration of adverse environmental impacts. An analytical study of the costs and benefits of NAFTA noted that:

> NAFTA-generated trade may create choke points that generate local environmental stress should trade increase or concentrate more rapidly than new transportation/transmission infrastructure can be constructed to service it . . . 40% of total US exports to Mexico move south along Texas highways and railways.[16]

Redundancy. The redundancy argument case makes a different assumption from the race-to-the-bottom argument. The redundancy argument posits that domestic and international regimes are converging on a common core of principles and that multi-national corporations are formulating a set of uniform environmental standards that all countries will be forced to adopt as the price for participating in global markets. Specifically, the argument asserts that domestic environmental law has developed and can continue to develop these principles independently of international environmental law. Domestic environmental law rests on universal rather than national or local norms and thus there is no need for an international norm. Environmental law is more universalist than human rights because it is driven by science and scientific imperatives tend to minimize cultural and political differences among nations.[17]

This is a powerful argument because the most distinctive feature of environmental law is that it is fundamentally science-based. I define science broadly to include both the physical and social sciences. The physical sciences, especially ecology, have defined the field of environmental law by disclosing the social costs of unrestrained use of natural resources. The social sciences, primarily economics, have provided the justification for public intervention to protect the environment and increasingly structure the debate about the best institutions to do so. The environmental dialogue about the nature of problems is remarkably similar from country to country. The differences come in debates about the proper *level* of environmental protection and in the enforcement of mandates.

This argument does not deny that there is an ethical or "cultural" component to environmental law, but it does argue that environmentalism is grounded in the western rational tradition and that any ethical or cultural claim must be supported by scientific basis.[18] The scientific analysis of problems holds throughout the world. The case for a universal environmental ethic is weaker given the religious and cultural diversity in the world. However, as is the case for human rights, the western case for a shift from human domination to human stewardship has been widely accepted throughout the world and no counter-environmental ethic has emerged. Asian religious and philosophical value systems have often been put forward as superior to the Judeo-Greco-Christian world view because they lack the duality between human and nature. But, with the possible exception of India,[19] these traditions have not played a significant role in Asian domestic environmental law. Thus, there is a powerful convergence argument that all legal systems will converge on a common set of principles and policy instruments without the necessity for a central coordinating system.

This convergence is manifest in the similarity of environmental law throughout the world. Environmental impact assessment is practised in most countries. The level of public participation may vary but there is a quite uniform consensus on what constitutes an adequate impact statement or assessment. Most countries have accepted the idea that law formation and enforcement should be shared between NGOs and the state. Some form of the citizen suit to review administrative action or to enforce a protection mandate can be found in both civil and common law countries. Many legal systems have a form of the precautionary principle which allows regulators to act in the face of present scientific uncertainty to protect the public from low probability but potentially severe risks of human health or ecosystem impairment. This list goes on.

Equity. Equity is the reverse of the race-to-the-bottom argument. The equity argument is a normative rather than positive one. The central premise is that international environmental law will tend to higher standards to the detriment of less-developed countries. International law, including environmental law, is a western construct and the values it advocates are those of developed, wealthy countries with the luxury to atone for the sins of the exploitation. Therefore, it is unjust to impose these standards on developing usually post-colonial countries. They often argue that international environmental law is a new form of western colonialism which saddles developing countries with high protection standards and thus deprives them of the resource exploitation and development opportunities enjoyed by Europe, America, Australia and New Zealand in the seventeenth to nineteenth centuries. Equity takes the form of either a plea for the recognition of uniform standards but differential compliance capabilities or north-south wealth transfers.

Equity is a hard argument for developing countries because it flies in the face of scientific imperatives that the ecological and human adverse impacts of resource degradation are often worse in developing countries and uneven protection regimes undermine the protection of global commons. The 1998 Indonesian forest fires are a manifestation of the regional impact of under-protection of the environment. The west has tried to side step this argument by the umbrella concept of environmentally sustainable development, but environmentally sustainable development has not yet established itself as a sustainable legal principle capable of constraining resource use.

The Case for Integration

The case for integration is both jurisprudential, positive and normative. The jurisprudential case adopts the monistic theory of the relationship between domestic and international law. It does so not only on the general principle that the separation of domestic from international is artificial but because increasingly both NGOs and corporations see legal systems as seamless systems that incorporate both international and domestic elements. Many private actors will find it to their advantage to conform their conduct to a single public or private international norm. The normative case starts from the proposition that international law has important roles to play in strengthening domestic protection regimes. It can help prevent back-sliding and re-enforce domestic protection efforts. International environmental law plays the latter role in many developing countries. It is vital for NGOs and public officials to invoke international norms to advocate new positions or to justify official positions. However, international environmental law is equally important in developed countries where the idea of environmental protection remains legally marginal and subject to being factored out of the policy equation when it conflicts with economic development or another traditional state interest.

Environmental law is universally marginal because the basic idea that humans should subordinate themselves to two communities, ecosystems and future generations, is a radical one in the dominant western liberal tradition. The grand objectives of environmental law are only partially related to the protection of human dignity, property and the maintenance of social order. Environmental law is both anthropocentric and non-anthropocentric; it seeks to protect society from future risks of serious health problems, such as cancer, genetic mutation and disease epidemics, and the irreversible impairment of ecosystem services. But the actual human benefits of environmental protection are hard to demonstrate and much protection is done on the belief that nature should be protected for intrinsic reasons. Thus, much of environmental law remains a very contested, radical idea which is outside the western constitutional and common law tradition.[20]

Paradoxically, the central defect of international environmental law which is that it is soft rather than hard may actually strengthen and promote integration. International environmental law is a new idea and it has been necessary to articulate first principles compared to domestic environmental law which is positive and fragmented. Thus, international environmental law often more clearly articulates the protection fundamental values at stake, such as justice between generations,[21] biodiversity conservation and inter-generational equity compared to domestic environmental law which remains media rather than principle focused. International environmental law can thus inform, shape and ultimately strengthen the foundations of domestic environmental law.

"Realpolitik" and redundancy. The "realpolitik" argument is a substantial one, but it has its limits. The convergence argument advanced above as a reason for non-integration can be turned around. Developed countries have comparatively little to fear from international environmental law. They largely control the treaty-making process and, equally as important, principles that treaties reflect. Stripped to essentials, international environmental law is a projection of western law, with the possible exception of the wild card of environmentally sustainable development. Thus, developed countries have already made the adjustment to the addition of environmental protection as a relevant factor in public and private decisions. More importantly private actors are making the adjustment faster than nation states.

There is a deeper problem with the "realpolitik" justification and that is simply that international law is too useful to reject. Countries will continue to select it when it furthers their interests and reject it when it does not. But, on balance, I think that developed countries such as Australia, New Zealand and the United States will find it more often to their advantage to invoke and apply. As is well-known, United States efforts to conserve species in its territorial waters have been found to be GATT-illegal by the WTO and its predecessor. The Vice President of the International Tribunal for the Law of the Sea has made the provocative suggestion that extra-territorial conservation can be justified as an effort to enforce international rather than domestic environmental law.[22]

Race-to-the-bottom. The race-to-the-bottom argument reflects a real problem but it is not a compelling reason to reject integration. The race-to-the-bottom reflects the painful reality that globalization produces costs and benefits and that countries must develop new cost minimization strategies. In the United States, the legal cases rest on the two GATT *Tuna-Dolphin* decisions and the WTO *Reformulated Gasoline* and *Shrimp Turtle* decisions. In the *Tuna-Dolphin* and *Shrimp Turtle* decisions, United States efforts to control fishing processes to protect marine resources outside of its territorial jurisdiction were invalidated. *Reformulated Gasoline* upheld Venezuela's challenge to Environmental Protection Agency's (EPA) calculation of the baseline for reformulated gasoline on the ground that it favoured domestic over foreign refiners. The GATT-WTO decisions are the subject of enormous debate in the United States, Canada and elsewhere.[23] These are important issues but they are problems to be solved in the international and domestic arenas. Integration can in fact aid in the solution of these issues. International environmental law supports the assumption of environmental protection duties for areas of global commons, and eventually this expanded protection duty must be factored into WTO jurisprudence.

Equity. Equity is a substantial reason for non-integration in developing countries, but it cannot serve as a legitimate basis for non-integration in developed countries. There is no serious case that it is unfair to make developing countries redress the social and environmental costs of unrestrained development. There are, of course, real fairness questions about how the responsibility should be distributed within the country. More generally, the case for non-integration is weak in developing countries. Environmental protection is a universal value which is based on science.

Conclusion

Integration is necessary and, I think, inevitable because the ultimate objective of both international and domestic environmental law is to move from sovereignty as a basis for unrestrained resource use to stewardship sovereignty. This will require that nations internalize and enforce universal standards of restraint and sustainability. Those that do will flourish and those that do not will not. The idea of limited rather than absolute sovereignty is now widely accepted by developed and developing nations. In the *Tasmanian Dam Case,* the Australian High Court accepted the World Heritage Convention as a restraint on its internal resource use. Stewardship sovereignty applies a basic principle of post-modern environmental ethics to international law. There is a lively debate about the source and scope of environmental ethics, but there is an emerging global consensus that we must replace the Greco-Judeo-Christian tradition that humans are despots over nature[24] with the principle that we are stewards of the earth,[25] and thus we must approach all exploitation decisions with much more caution than we have in the past.

Stewardship is an evolving concept, but it contains three core consensus building principles. The first is the principle of intergenerational equity articulated by Professor Edith Brown Weiss.[26] This standard permits resource exploitation subject to the constraint that we leave the resource in no worse shape than when we started. As a leading environmental philosopher has noted:

> environmentalists will achieve more by appealing to the relative noncontroversial and intuitive idea that the use of natural resources implies an obligation to protect them for future users—a sustainability theory based on inter-generational equity, rather than exotic appeals to hereto unnoticed inherent values in nature.[27]

Notes

1. B. Boer, R. Ramsay and D. R. Rothwell, *International Environmental Law in the Asia Pacific* (1998).

2. See D. E. Fisher and N. McNamara (eds.), *Integrated Water and Land Management: Essays on Comparative Approaches to the Integration of Water and Land Management* (2000).

3. D. Caponera, "The Role of Customary International Water Law," in *Water Resources Policy for Asia*, 365, 367–68, 372, 380–81 (M. Ali G. Radosevich, and A. Ali Khan eds. 1985) cited in *International Environmental Law and World Order*, L. D. Guruswamy, Sir G. W. R. Palmer, B. H. Weston (herein after G. P. W.), West Publishing Co, St. Paul, Minn., 1994, 630.

4. State responsibility for the conduct of private parties who cause injury to the territory of another state is widely asserted in international law, although the basis for the duty and its scope remain disputed. The basic principle posits that a state must exercise due diligence to prevent conduct, if performed by the state, which would breach its primary international duties. This is thought to include the duty to regulate and to enforce regulations. "Developments in the Law: International Environmental Law" (1991) 104 *Harvard Law Review* 1494. Publicists continue to debate whether the standard is negligence or strict liability and sometimes assert, incorrectly, that the complaining state must show a breach of a prior duty. *See* A. E. Boyle, "State Responsibility and International Liability for Injurious Consequences of Acts Not Prohibited by International Law: A Necessary Distinction?" (1990) 39 *International and Comparative Law Quarterly* I. The general duty to prevent is endorsed in section 601 of the United States Restatement of Foreign Relations, although the scope is narrower than the general duty. Section 601 limits the state duty to take necessary environmental protection measures to "the extent practicable under the circumstances." D. Caron, "Reviews of the Restatement (Third) of the

Foreign Relations of the United States, The Law of Environment: A Symbolic Step of Modest Value" (1989) 14 *Yale Journal of International Law* 528 describes this standard as conservative compared to the fault-based due diligence standard of international law. Australia and New Zealand invoked the doctrine in *Australia v France* and *New Zealand v France* (1974) ICJ Rep 457.

5. *The Trail Smelter Arbitration (U.S. v Canada)* (1949) 3 UNRIAA 1938, is the basis for the two most authoritative statements of state liability which extends to the failure to police and regulate those acting within a state's territory. State liability for acts which injure the other is re-enforced by the *Corfu Channel* decision. *United Kingdom v Albania* (1949) ICJ Rep 4.

6. Among the best discussions are I. G. Lammers, "International and European Community Law Aspects of Pollution of International Watercourses in Environmental Protection and International Law" in W. Lang, H. Neuhold, and K. Zemanek (eds.), *Environmental Protection and International Law* (1991) 115.

7. But cf *Commission v Greece.* Case *C-387197* ECI (2000) (EU member state liable for monetary penalties for failing to comply with European Commission order requiring adequate waste disposal measures.).

8. *See* E. Hey, "The Precautionary Concept in Environmental Policy and Law: Institutionalizing Caution" (1992) 4 *Georgetown International Environmental Law Review* 303. E.g., in 1983, the German government took the position that there was no need to wait until harm had been proved before North Sea pollution was regulated, and this review is reflected in the Second North Sea Declaration. This approach has been adopted in principle at other marine conventions, in United Nations sustainable development declarations, in the ozone convention, and in regional hazardous waste treaties, but the idea of ecological risk prevention remains underdeveloped.

9. G. Handl, Environmental Security and Global Change: The Challenge to International Law (1991) in W. Lang, H. Neuhold, and K. Zemanek (eds.), *Environmental Protection and International Law* (1991) 59, 99.

10. For a sceptical view see G. Handl, "Environmental Security and Global Change: The Challenge to International Law" (1990) 1 *Yearbook of International Environmental Law* 3, 22–24.

11. J. E. Hickey Jr, "Refining The Precautionary Principle in International Environmental Law" (1995) 14 *Virginia Environmental Law Journal* 424.

12. H Hohmann, *Precautionary Legal Duties and Principles of Modern International Environmental Law* (1994) 314–45 argues that the precautionary principle is a logical product of the trend toward planned environmental management and that it has been so widely adopted in binding and non-binding agreements that it has become an "instant" doctrine of customary international law. See P. Sands, *Principles of International Environmental Law* Vol 1 (1995) 120–121.

13. *Commonwealth of Australia & Anor v State of Tasmania & Ors (The Tasmanian Dams Case)* (1983) 158 CLR I.

14. Some commentators have posited the doctrine of instant custom.

15. *See,* e.g., Patricia Motta Veiga, "Environment-related Voluntary Market Upgrading Initiatives and International Trade: Eco-labelling Schemes and the ISO 14000 Series" in D. Tussie (ed.), *The Environment and International Trade Negotiations: Developing Country Stakes* (1999) 53.

16. Commission for Environmental Cooperation, "Assessing Environmental Effects of the North American Free Trade Agreement (NAFTA): An Analytic Framework (Phase II) and Issue Studies" (1999).

17. Human rights must deal with the argument from culture, whereas it is harder for non-western countries to make an ethical rather than economic and political case

for environmental degradation. See M. C. Nussbaum, "In Defense of Universal Values," (2000) 36 *Idaho Law Review* 379.

18. I have argued this point at length in A. D. Tarlock, "Environmental Law: Ethics or Science?" (1996) 7 *Duke Environmental Law & Policy Forum* 193.

19. *See* C. M. Abraham, *Environmental Jurisprudence in India* (1998).

20. The western legal tradition identifies "constitutionalism" as the fundamental legal basis for organising society. The basic norm of western constitutionalism is the recognition of negative liberties against the government. Governmental action is always measured against two standards: (1) consistency with delegated authority and (2) the non-infringement of fundamental *individual rights*. Law is also primarily negative: it gives back what was taken away. It is also a regime which treats all persons equally, recognises and protects their fundamental rights, and does so by the application of clear standards in a consistent and fair manner against both private parties and the state. The Constitution, for example, is a source of environmental rights and the duties, because the values that environmentalism promotes are not primarily those of the Enlightenment. The Constitution is frequently defined as a negative charter of liberties, but environment protection requires the affirmative exercise of regulatory power, but the expert consensus is that constitutions should be confined to negative rather than affirmative rights. R. L. Posner, "The Costs of Rights: Implications for Central and Eastern Europe and for the United States" (1996) 32 *Tulsa Law Journal* I. J. B. Ruhl, "The Metrics of Constitutional Amendments: And Why Proposed Environmental Quality Amendments Don't Measure Up" (1999) 74 *Notre Dame Law Review* 245. The efforts of an indigenous group in Indonesia to seek redress for the cultural and environment degradation caused by mining is instinctive. The group's *Alien Tort Act* claims were dismissed because the Actor applies to shockingly egregious violations of international law that have been generally recognised. The sources cited by the plaintiff were dismissed as "merely . . . a general sense of environmental responsibility . . . [which] state abstract rights and liberties devoid of articulable or discernible standards and regulations to identify practices that constitute international environmental abuses or torts." Principle 2 of The Rio Declaration was not applicable because it confirms state sovereignty over natural resources and (2) only prohibits acts which injure another nation. *Beanal Freeport-Moran, Inc.*, 969 F. Supp. 362 (E.D.La. 1997), aff'd, 1999. U.S. App. Lexis 31365 (11th Cir. 1999).

21. Professor Edith Brown Weiss's book, *In Fairness to Future Generations: International Law, Common Patrimony, and Intergenerational Equity* (1989) is foundational.

22. R. Wolfrum, "Means of Ensuring Compliance With and Enforcement of International Environmental Law" (1998) 272.

23. *Recueil des Cours, Academie de Droit Internationale* 62. See also A. Rueda, "Tuna, Dolphins, Shrimp & Turtles: What About Environmental Embargoes Under NAFTA" (2000) 12 *Georgetown International Environmental Law Review* 647.

24. *See*, e.g., L. Guruswamy, "The Annihilation of Sea Turtles: World Trade Organization Intransigence and U.S. Equivocation," *The Environmental Law Reporter*, News & Comment, 30 ELR 10261, April 2000.

25. J. Passmore, *Man's Responsibility for Nature* (1974) remains the leading exponent of this position. *See* R. Attfield, *The Ethics of Environmental Concern* (2nd ed, 1991) for a forceful exposition of this provocative thesis.

26. E. Brown Weiss, *In Fairness to Future Generations* (1989).

27. B. G. Norton, "Why I Am Not a Nonanthropocentrist: Callicott and the Failure of Monistic Inherentism," (1995) 17 *Environmental Ethics* 341, 356.

19

Searching for the Contours of International Law in the Field of Sustainable Development

INTERNATIONAL LAW ASSOCIATION

The Inception of Sustainable Development in International Law

The phrase "sustainable development" as launched in the Rio Declaration has found recognition in international legal instruments remarkably soon. Various environmental treaties incorporate it, for example, the Climate Change Convention, the Convention on Biological Diversity, and the Anti-Desertification Convention. It also features in the World Fisheries/Straddling Stocks Convention as well as in the preamble of the 1995 Agreement on the Establishment of the World Trade Organization. The WTO includes among its goals the "optimal use of the world's resources in accordance with the objective of sustainable development." The Doha Declaration of the Fourth Ministerial Conference of 14 November 2001 states: "International trade can play a major role in the promotion of economic development and the alleviation of poverty . . . " and since "the majority of WTO Members are developing countries . . . we seek to place their needs and interests at the heart of the WTO Work Programme . . . " (para. 2). Furthermore, the Ministers strongly confirmed their commitment "to the objective of sustainable development, as stated in the Preamble of the Marrakesh Agreement": "We are convinced that the aims of upholding and safeguarding an open and non-discriminatory multilateral trading system, and acting for the protection of the environment and the promotion of sustainable development can and must be mutually supportive" (para. 6).[1]

Reference may also be made to the prominent place of sustainable development as an objective in the law of the European Union. For example, the Treaty on European Union, as amended through the 1997 Treaty of

Amsterdam, includes objectives such as "economic and social progress and a high level of employment and to achieve balanced and sustainable development" (Art. 2). Sustainable development is also elevated as a general objective in Article 2 of the revised EC Treaty, albeit in not entirely identical terms.[2] These new objectives are a clear policy response to the call for sustainable development as adopted during the UN Conference on Environment and Development, held in Rio de Janeiro in 1992. Obviously, the Community aims at fostering a type and pace of economic growth which does not lead to exhaustion of non-renewable natural resources and to irreparable damage to the physical and natural environment. This goal should be viewed in conjunction with the social objectives of the Community such as promoting a high level of employment and social cohesion. Furthermore, Article 6 of the revised EC Treaty stipulates the integration of environmental protection requirements in all Community policies and activities "with a view to promoting sustainable development."

Sustainable development is also an objective in the ACP-EU development co-operation treaties.[3] In the new ACP-EU Partnership Agreement of Cotonou (2000) the pursuance of sustainable development is clearly linked to poverty reduction (art. 1). Furthermore, sustainable utilization and management of natural resources is identified as one of the three cross-cutting issues, alongside with gender and institutional capacity building.[4]

It is interesting to note that sustainable development and related concepts also feature in a number of international judicial decisions of the 1990s.[5] Reference should first of all be made to the International Court of Justice. In the aborted New Zealand v. France *Nuclear Tests Case* (1995) the Court pronounced that its Order was "without prejudice to the obligations of States to respect and protect the natural environment."[6] In its Advisory Opinion to the UN General Assembly on *The Legality of the Threat or Use of Nuclear Weapons* the Court made reference to Principle 24 of the Rio Declaration on Environment and Development (on protection of the environment in times of armed conflict). The Court stated that "the environment is not an abstraction, but represents the living space, the quality of life and the health of human beings, including generations unborn." Moreover, the Court concluded: "The existence of the general obligation of States to ensure that activities within their jurisdiction and control respect the environment of other States or of areas beyond national control is part of the corpus of customary international law relating to the environment."[7]

In its judgment in the case concerning the *Gabcikovo Nagymaros* project between Hungary and Slovakia the Court re-emphasized and elaborated on this principle: " . . . new norms and standards have been developed, set forth in a great number of instruments during the last two decades. Such new norms have to be taken into consideration, and such standards given proper weight, not only when States contemplate new activities, but also when continuing activities begun in the past. *This need to reconcile development with protection of the environment is aptly expressed in the concept of sustain able development.*"[8] Judge Weeramantry, in his separate opinion, went a few steps further by stating that sustainable development is "part of modern international law by reason not only of its inescapable logical necessity, but also by reason of its wide and general acceptance by the global community," reaffirming that "in the area of international law . . . there must be both development and environmental protection, and that neither of these rights can be neglected."[9]

Second, reference can be made to the pronouncements by the WTO Appellate Body, most notably in the *United States–Import Prohibition of Certain Shrimp and Shrimp Products Case* (1998), commonly known as the *Shrimp Turtle* case between the U.S. and India, Malaysia, Pakistan and Thailand. In its interpretation of exception article XX(g), which permits, in deviation of the GATT rules, the taking of measures "relating to the conservation of exhaustible natural resources," the Appellate Body referred to "contemporary concerns of the community of nations about the protection and conservation of the environment" and to the fact that the Preamble of the WTO Agreement explicitly acknowledges the objective of sustainable development, a concept which in its view "has been generally accepted as integrating economic and social development and environmental protection." Hence, the Appellate Body deemed U.S. legislation "provisionally justified" under Article XX(g). Although the Appellate Body ultimately decided that the U.S. measures constituted unjustifiable discrimination, the various references to sustainable development and legitimate environmental concerns differ from earlier decisions of GATT panels, especially the Tuna/Dolphin panels.[10]

From this brief review of significant recent developments it follows that sustainable development has become an established objective of the international community and a concept with some degree of normative status in international law.[11] This is not to say that its contents are clear. For example, Professor Lowe goes as far as to claim that sustainable development "is rooted in theoretical obscurity and confusion, and it suffers from the same reluctance to test theoretical principles for their practical utility that impedes the development of many other areas of international law." The author also states that sustainable development "is clearly entitled to a place in the Pantheon of concepts that are not to be questioned in polite company, along with democracy, human rights, and the sovereign equality of states."[12]

The Various Dimensions of Sustainable Development

It seems imperative to provide a somewhat more precise description of the concept of sustainable development, in addition to the concise but admirable one of the Brundtland Commission: " . . . development to ensure that it meets the needs of the present without compromising the ability of future generations to meet their own needs."[13] In its various reports the Committee made an effort to distinguish various dimensions of the concept of sustainable development,[14] including:

- sustainable use of natural resources;
- sound economic development, both of developing countries and of industrialised countries which in the case of particularly the latter necessitates reducing and eliminating unsustainable patterns of consumption and production;
- integration of developmental and environmental concerns;
- inter- and intra-generational equity;
- the time dimension;
- respect for human rights; and
- public participation.

Building on the description of "development" in the UN Declaration on the Right to Development (1986), on the Universal Declaration of Human Rights (1948) and on the Stockholm and Rio Declarations (1972 and 1992), we may well arrive at describing sustainable development as a comprehensive economic, social and political process, which aims at the sustainable use of natural resources of our planet and the protection of the environment on which nature and human life as well as social and economic development depend and which seeks to realize the right of all human beings to an adequate living standard on the basis of their active, free and meaningful participation in development and in the fair distribution of benefits resulting there from, with due regard to the needs and interests of future generations.

The Contours of an International Law Relating to Sustainable Development

Some general and some specific principles of international law are at the core of international law relating to sustainable development. Taken together, they may well be viewed as a framework of an international law in the field of sustainable development.

General Principles

Obviously, a first general principle is the *rule of law in international relations, including international economic relations.* This entails a duty incumbent on States (and on international institutions and other main actors in international economic relations as well) to abstain from measures of economic policy that are incompatible with their international obligations and which are detrimental to the sustainable development opportunities of third countries and peoples. Treaties and binding decisions by international institutions have to be observed and fulfilled in good faith by all parties concerned.[15]

This brings us to the principle of the *duty to co-operate* towards global sustainable development and protection of the global environment. The duty to co-operate is well-established in international law, as exemplified by Chapter IX on International Economic and Social Co-operation of the UN Charter and Principle 4 of the 1970 Declaration on Friendly Relations.[16] It applies at the global, regional and bilateral levels and often requires prior information, consultation and negotiation. It is also embodied in Principle 27 of the Rio Declaration, where it provides: "States and peoples shall co-operate in good faith and in a spirit of partnership in the fulfillment of the principles embodied in this Declaration and in the further development of international law in the field of sustainable development." Similarly, Rio Principle 7 states that "States shall co-operate in a spirit of global partnership to conserve, protect and restore the health and integrity of the Earth's ecosystem . . . ," while its Preamble refers to the goal of establishing a new and equitable global partnership through the creation of new levels of co-operation among States, key sectors and people." Indeed, in today's world this principle does no longer exclusively relate to States, but also applies to international institutions, civil society and the business community as contracted in this mission by UN Secretary-General Kofi Annan through his Global Compact to promote sustainable growth and good citizenship through committed and creative leadership. Calling to observe nine universal principles in the areas of human rights, labour standards and the environment, it brings together companies with business organizations, UN organizations, international trade unions, non-governmental organizations and other parties to foster partnerships and build a more inclusive and equitable global marketplace.[17]

Third is the principle of the *observance of human rights* both economic, social and cultural rights and civil and political rights.[18] This principle is instrumental for integrating human rights concerns and the discourse on sustainable development as well as for emphasizing the preponderant role of public participation in promoting development, social progress and environmental conservation. First of all, the fundamental human right to a life in dignity is at stake to which the right to development as the synthesis of existing human rights, such as the rights to an adequate living, food, education and primary health care, is closely related. Secondly, the principle now also includes participatory rights, access to information and justice.

The fourth and last general principle with a prominent place in this effort is that of *integration*. It could even be argued that the principle of integration serves as the very backbone of the concept of sustainable development. As to its content, inspiration can be sought from various principles of the Stockholm and Rio Declarations, the World Charter for Nature, the IUCN Covenant, the Earth Charter as well as from important multilateral treaties such as the UN Convention on the Law of the Sea and the EC Treaty.[19] Principle 3 of the Rio Declaration stipulates that "environmental protection shall constitute an integral part of the development process and cannot be considered in isolation from it." Furthermore, the Declaration integrates not only the concepts of environment and development, but also the needs of generations, both present and future (see Rio Principle 4). Earlier, Principle 13 of the Stockholm Declaration provided that "States should adopt an integrated approach to their development planning so as to ensure that development is compatible with the need to protect and improve the human environment for the benefit of their population."

As regards treaty law, the Law of the Sea Convention, for example, states: " . . . the problems of oceans and space are closely interrelated and need to be considered as a whole." Article 6 of the revised EC Treaty mandates the integration of environmental protection requirements in all Community policies and activities "with a view to promoting sustainable development." Similar, albeit somewhat weaker, wording is also employed in the only real "coherence" and "integration" article in the field of development co-operation, namely Article 178 EC Treaty according to which: "The Community shall take account of the objectives referred to in Article 177 [listing the EC development objectives, rapp.] in the policies that it implements which are likely to affect developing countries." The importance of an integrated approach features also prominently in the Anti-Desertification Convention and the Straddling Stocks Agreement. Various international regimes are a process towards enhanced integration, as can be noted from the efforts of the fourth Ministerial Conference of the WTO, held in Doha in 2001, to mainstream labour standards, environment and development in WTO arrangements as well as from the jurisprudence of its dispute settlement bodies in the *Hormones, Shrimp Turtle* and *Asbestos* cases.

Specific Principles of International Law in the Field of Sustainable Development

Amongst more specific principles, the first to be mentioned is the established principle of *sovereignty over natural resources* according each State the right to possess and determine freely the management of its natural resources for its own development within the limits of international law. The particular meaning of this principle dominated the discussions in the context of the United Nations during the 1960s and 1970s as well as those of the former NIEG Committee of the International Law Association.[20] This principle is a natural corollary of the traditional principle of territorial sovereignty which implies a duty of a territorial State to protect, within its territory, the rights of other States, as pointed out by the *Island of Palmas* arbitration (1928).[21] During recent decades this has been supplemented by an obligation incumbent upon territorial States to protect not only the environment of areas beyond national jurisdiction, but also their own environment. Indeed, resource sovereignty has increasingly been interpreted as giving rise to a series of duties as well, most notably the duty of sustainable and prudent use of natural resources, protection of biological diversity and elimination or reduction of the effects of over-exploitation of soil, deforestation, over-fishing and pollution.[22] It should be noted that the Stockholm Declaration was among the first documents which stipulated that the principle of sovereignty over natural resources must be exercised in an environmentally responsible way. Especially its Principle 21 called for the prevention of extraterritorial effects causing environmental damage in other countries or in areas outside national jurisdiction. This is repeated in Principle 2 of the Rio Declaration, with the notable addition of the words "and developmental needs" in the phrase that all States have the sovereign right to exploit their natural resources "pursuant to their environmental and developmental needs." The principle of sovereignty over natural resources and the corollary responsibility not to cause transboundary damage is included in various treaties, including UNCLOS, the Climate Change Convention, the Convention on Biological Diversity and the European Energy Charter Treaty.

A result of this development is the emergence of the principle of *the duty to ensure sustainable use of natural resources*. It requires States and peoples to pay due care to the environment and to make prudent use of the natural wealth and resources within their jurisdiction. To a certain extent this was already reflected in paragraph 1 of the 1962 Declaration on Permanent Sovereignty over Natural Resources: "The right of peoples and nations to permanent sovereignty over natural resources must be exercised in the interest of their national development and the well-being of the people of the State concerned."[23] Principle 2 of the Stockholm Declaration also pointed out that careful planning and rational management are required for safeguarding the natural resources of the earth. Ever since, UN resolutions have gradually elaborated standards for nature conservation and utilization of natural resources. Reference can be made to Article 30 of the Charter of Economic Rights and Duties of States (1974),[24] the UNEP Principles on Conservation and Harmonious Utilization of Shared Natural Resources (1978)[25] and the World Charter for Nature (1982).[26] This principle of sustainable use of natural resources is also amply reflected in treaty law, including in the fields of the law of the sea (through the notion of "maximum sustainable yield"), natural resource exploitation (e.g. Tropical Timber Agreement), nature conservation and the environment. The Convention on Biological Diversity provides a clear definition of sustainable use: "the use of components of biological diversity in a way and at a rate that does not lead to the long-term decline of biological diversity, thereby maintaining its potential to meet the needs of the present and future generations."[27]

In this way the principle of sustainable use is closely related to the principle of *intergenerational equity,* perhaps still an emerging one in international law. According to this principle, States must take into account the interests of both present and future generations. The principle of equity is a principle of international law of a rather more general nature, enabling the international community to take into account considerations of justice and fairness in the formation, application and interpretation of international law. Treaty law refers frequently to equity or equitable principles, both in the environmental field (e.g., Climate Change Convention) and the law of the sea (e.g., as regards maritime delimitation). On various occasions, the ICJ has applied the principle of equity, for example, in the *Continental Shelf* case (Tunisia *v.* Libya, 1982) with a view to balancing up "the various considerations which it regards as relevant in order to produce an equitable result."[28] The principle of intergenerational equity has been well defined by Edith Brown Weiss, reflecting the view that as "members of the present generation, we hold the earth in trust for future generations," while "at the same time we are beneficiaries entitled to use it."[29] The Stockholm Declaration referred in its Principle 1 already to a "solemn responsibility to protect and improve the environment for present and future generations," while Rio Principle 2 includes the objective "to equitably meet developmental and environmental needs of present and future generations."

Intergenerational equity as a principle has found recognition in the law of the sea, outer space law, international wildlife law (early applications are the Whaling Convention and the World Heritage Convention) and international environmental law, albeit that here sustainability and preservation are also based—and ought to be—on the intrinsic value of nature and fauna and flora rather than on the needs and interests of future generations of humankind. However, outside these fields the status of the principle of intergenerational equity is still uncertain. It is interesting to note the landmark decision of the Supreme Court of the Philippines in the *Minor Oposa* case when it provided *locus standi* and acceded to the claims of NGOs on behalf of children and future generations against drastic deforestation plans and actual logging licenses,[30] but this decision on its own cannot accord the principle of intergenerational equity a firm status in international law with respect to the management of natural resources and the environment *within* national jurisdiction.

It is often argued that the principle of equity includes *intragenerational equity* relating to members of the current generation of humankind, necessitating assistance by the industrialised States to developing States by way of distributive justice and global partnership. This may be reflected in various stipulations aimed at a fair and equitable utilisation of natural resources as well as at financial assistance and access to environmentally sound technology. This concept of intragenerational equity is crucial to achieving sustainable development, if the global partnership for sustainable development is to secure both participation of developing countries and effective implementation.[31] While various treaty provisions and some State practice can be noted, in general terms intragenerational equity has as yet received an inadequate follow-up in practice. Hence, it must be concluded that, so far, intragenerational equity is at best an emerging principle of international law in the field of sustainable development.

By contrast, the principle of *common but differentiated responsibilities* has a firm status in various fields of international law, including human rights law, international trade law and international environmental law.[32] Principle 7 of Rio reads in part: "In view of the different contribution to global environmental degradation, States have common but differentiated responsibilities. The developed countries acknowledge the responsibility they bear in the international pursuit of sustainable development in view of the pressures their societies place on the global environment and of the technologies and financial resources they command." An obvious example is climate change. The Climate Change Convention and its Kyoto Protocol seek to achieve the stabilisation of greenhouse gas concentrations in the atmosphere at a level which would prevent dangerous anthropogenic interference with the world's climate system and they commit industrialised countries to take measures with the aim of returning, by the years 2008–2012, to the 1990 emission level of greenhouse gases. The rationale for differentiation is twofold. Firstly, it is recognised that so far the bulk of global emissions of greenhouse gases originated in industrialised countries and they should therefore bear the main burden for combating climate change. Secondly, developing countries need access to resources and technologies in order to be able to achieve sustainable development. The principle of common but differentiated responsibilities is being implemented in various ways, including different standards for developing countries (no quantitative reduction commitments in the field of climate change), delayed compliance time tables (ozone layer arrangements) and undertakings conditioned upon receipt of additional financial assistance and access to technology (biological diversity).

Recently, it was also acknowledged in the context of WTO dispute settlement proceedings, in which a WTO Panel urged "Malaysia and the United States to co-operate fully in order to conclude as soon as possible an agreement which will permit the protection and conservation of sea turtles to the satisfaction of all interests involved and taking into account the principle that States have common but differentiated responsibilities to conserve and protect the environment."[33] While we have thus noted a hole in the traditional bulwarks of the principle of sovereign equality, the principle of differentiation goes even one step further through the principle of the recognition of *the special needs and interests of countries with economies in transition and developing countries, with special regard to least developed countries*. The first group of countries, those with economies in transition, may be a temporary one with particular relevance in the fields of international financial, monetary and environmental law. It includes especially the countries which belonged to or were within the sphere of influence of the former Soviet Union and which suffered from inefficient and wasteful production patterns, outdated technologies and extreme pollution levels and consequent public health problems in heavily industrialised areas. Particularly international climate law provides these countries with considerable "flexibility" in meeting the commitments under the Convention and the Kyoto Protocol.[34]

The category of the "least developed countries," currently numbering fifty, has a somewhat longer history and roots in some other fields of international law as well, including the law of the sea, international trade law and international development co-operation arrangements (e.g., the Lome conventions). Yet, what that actually means in practice is subject to erosion as illustrated by the lack of clear results of the recent UN Conference on the Least-Developed Countries, held in Brussels in May 2001.[35] In essence, the same goes for other sub-categories of developing countries affected adversely by environmental, social and developmental circumstances, such as small island developing States and islands supporting small communities or particularly environmentally fragile developing countries, which are, for example, low-lying or with mountainous eco-systems.

A principle which has gained some currency is that of the *common heritage of humankind*. Considerable attention has been given to the regulation and control of the global commons, most notably the deep sea-bed and its resources, outer space and its celestial bodies such as the moon, and perhaps Antarctica. Principles of non-appropriation, non-exclusive and peaceful use, international management, equitable sharing of benefits and reservation for intergenerational equity have been agreed to for these areas beyond national sovereignty or jurisdiction. Most notably, the principle of common heritage of humankind has been codified in Part XI of the Law of the Sea Convention and the 1979 Agreement Governing the Activities on the Moon and Other Celestial Bodies. On various occasions it has been proposed that these principles could also be extended to, for example, tropical rain forests, wetlands of international importance, or the environment as such, and what belongs to all of us, such as major ecological systems of our planet. Currently, this is at best called *common concern of humankind* (see the Climate Change and Biodiversity conventions). This is a somewhat vaguer notion than the common heritage principle, obviously not implying non-appropriation and an international regime, but it still carries the connotations of global interest in preserving the environment and needs of future generations.

Next, [we refer] to two key principles especially of international environmental law: the principle of the "precautionary approach" and the principle of "public participation." The *precautionary principle* is often quoted in general terms, but also more concretely applied in various environmental regimes at both international and national levels. There is increasing emphasis on the duty of States to take preventive measures to protect the human health, natural resources and the environment, for example, through environmental impact assessment. The emergence of this "precautionary approach" is also clearly reflected in Principles 15 and 19 of the Rio Declaration and multilateral treaty law, most notably in international fisheries law, international water law and physical planning. The Rio Declaration provides unequivocally in its Principle 15: "In order to protect the environment, the precautionary approach shall be widely applied by States according to their capabilities. Where there are threats of serious or irreversible damage, lack of full scientific certainty shall not be used as a reason for postponing cost-effective measures to prevent environmental degradation." The principle of the precautionary approach builds on older principles such as the principle of due care and the preventive principle. The principle has been expressed in various multilateral treaties, most notably the Vienna Convention on the Ozone Layer and its Montreal Protocol, the Biological Diversity Convention and the Fish Stock Agreement. Furthermore, it is quickly gaining firm ground in numerous regional regimes and domestic laws.[36]

One of the novel features of the Rio Declaration was its call for *public participation and access to information and justice.* It coincided with the call of many citizens movements for more participatory processes of national and international decision-making and with the increased status of human rights. In international environmental law this has received a certain response, most notably in the Treaty of Aarhus on Access to Information, Public Participation in Decision-making and Access to Justice in Environmental Matters concluded in 1998 under the auspices of the UN Economic Commission for Europe. Similarly, participatory processes in development efforts are widely viewed as to be of prime importance.[37]

Last but not least, the new international law of sustainable development also embraces *good governance, including democratic accountability.* Its exact contents may not be very clear in the discourse of politics and development studies. Yet, as a legal concept it has found a place in, among other legally relevant documents, the EU-ACP co-operation treaties (1995 and 2000). The concept of good governance can well be instrumental in integrating the various dimensions of the concept of sustainable development, including global good governance in the sense of the participation of States in international law-making, conference diplomacy and decision-making within international institutions, participation of non-State entities in national and international decision-making and good national governance.[38] As to the latter, the 1997 UNDP policy document *Governance for Sustainable Development* defines the concept in the following terms: "Good governance ensures that political, social and economic priorities are based on a broad consensus in society and that the voices of the poorest and the most vulnerable are heard in decision-making over the allocation of development resources." The Cotonou Convention of June 2000 incorporates a further interesting definition: " . . . good governance is the transparent and accountable management of human, natural, economic and financial resources for the purposes of equitable and sustainable development. It entails clear decision-making procedures at the level of public authorities, transparent and accountable institutions, the primacy of law in the management and distribution of resources and capacity building for elaborating and implementing measures aiming in particular at preventing and combating corruption.[39] This anti-corruption element is also emphasised in the IMF Guidelines on Good Governance (1997).[40]

Notes

1. Text Doha Declaration, 14 November 2001, available at website www.wto.org and published in *ILM*.

2. It is notable that the Title on Environment in the Maastricht and Amsterdam Treaties (currently Title XX) did not refer explicitly to the objective of "sustainable development." However, the EU Nice Conference held in December 2000 adopted an interesting Declaration on Article 175 EC Treaty: "The High Contracting Parties are determined to see the European Union play a leading role in promoting environmental protection in the Union and in international efforts pursuing the same objective at global level. Full use should be made of all possibilities offered by the Treaty with a view to pursuing this objective, including the use of incentives and instruments which are market-oriented and intended to promote *sustainable development.*" (emphasis added)

3. For a discussion of European development co-operation policies see K. Arts, *Integrating Human Rights into Development Co-operation: The Case of the Lome Convention,* The Hague, 2000, and J. A. McMahon, *The Development Co-operation Policy of the EC,* London, 1998.

4. See Articles 36–38 of the ACP-EU Partnership Agreement, signed in Cotonou, 23 June 2000.

5. See in particular P. Sands, "International Courts and the Application of the Concept of Sustainable Development," in 3 *Max Planck UNYB* (1999), pp. 389–403.

6. ICJ Order of 25 September 1995, *ICJ Reports 1995,* para. 64.

7. *ICJ Reports 1996,* para. 29.

8. *ICJ Reports 1997,* para. 140 (emphasis added).

9. Ibid., pp. 85–119.

10. See the case note by F. Weiss, "The Second Tuna Panel Report," in *Leiden Journal of International Law*, vol. 8 (1995), pp. 135–150.

11. See among other publications P. Sands (ed.), *Greening International Law*, London, 1993; ibid., "International Law in the Field of Sustainable Development," in *British Year Book of International Law*, vol. 65 (1994), pp. 303–381; ibid., *Principles of International Environmental Law: Frameworks, Standards and Implementation*, Manchester, 1995; D. Hunter, J. Salzman, and D. Zaelke, *International Environmental Law and Policy*, New York, 2nd ed., 2002; A. Boyle and P. Birnie, *International Environmental Law*, Oxford, 2nd ed., 2002.

12. See V. Lowe, "Sustainable Development and Unsustainable Arguments," in A. Boyle and D. Freestone (eds.), *International Law and Sustainable Development*, Oxford, 1999, pp. 30–31. Similarly, Brownlie writes: "For the present, the concept remains problematic and nebulous, appearing more as a statement of the issues than as a resolution of the basic problems." I. Brownlie, *Principles of Public International Law*, Oxford, 5th ed., 1998, p. 287.

13. World Commission on Environment and Development, *Our Common Future*, Oxford, 1987, p. 43.

14. See especially the Committee's reports to the ILA Conferences in Buenos Aires (1994) and Helsinki (1996). See also M. C. W. Pinto, "The Legal Context: Concept, Principles, Standards and Institutions," in F. Weiss, E. Denters, and P. de Waart (eds.), *International Economic Law with a Human Face*, The Hague, 1998, pp. 13–14; A. Boyle and D. Freestone, "Introduction," in ibidem (eds.), *International Law and Sustainable Development: Past Achievements and Future Challenges*, Oxford, 1999, pp. 8–16; M. Fitzmaurice, "The Principle of Sustainable Development in International Development Law," forthcoming in *UNESCO Encyclopaedia on Environment and Life Support Systems*.

15. See Seoul Declaration Principle I, referred to in note 1 above.

16. GA Res. 2625 (XXV), 24 October 1970. Declaration on Principles of International Law Concerning Friendly Relations and Co-operation among States in Accordance with the Charter of the United Nations.

17. See the website un.org/globalcompact. See also the paper of Paul de Waart to the Committee's research seminar, *Sustainable Development in the Global Markets Principle and Practice*, Amsterdam, 2001.

18. Cf. The Vienna Declaration of the World Conference on Human Rights, 1993.

19. See Preamble UN Convention on the Law of the Sea, 1982 and Art. 6 revised EC Treaty.

20. See K. Hossain and S. R. Chowdhury (eds.), *Permanent Sovereignty over Natural Resources: Principle and Practice*, London, 1984. See also ILA, *Report of the Seoul Conference*, London, 1987, p. 409.

21. *Island of Palmas* case (The Netherlands/United States of America), 4 April 1928, 2 *UNRIAA* 829, extracts in C. R. R. Robb (ed.), *International Environmental Law Reports*, Cambridge, vol. I *(Early Decisions)*, 1999, pp. 141–146.

22. See N. J. Schrijver, *Sovereignty over Natural Resources: Balancing Rights and Duties*, Cambridge, 1997.

23. GA Res. 1803 (XVII), 14 December 1962.

24. GA Res. 3281 (XXIX), 12 December 1974.

25. UNEP Principles on Conservation and Harmonious Utilization of Natural Resources Shared by Two or More States, 1978.

26. GA Res. 37/7, 28 October 1982.

27. Article 2 of the UN Convention on Biological Diversity, 1992. See also preamble and Art. 5 of the UN Watercourses Convention.

28. *ICJ Reports 1982*, p. 60.

29. This principle was coined by Edith Brown Weiss, *In Fairness to Future Generations: International Law, Common Patrimony, and Intergenerational Equity*, New York, 1989. See also C. Redgwell, *Intergenerational Trusts and Environmental Protection*, Manchester, 1999.

30. Text in 33 *ILM (1994)*, p. 173.

31. See the thorough analysis by D. A. French, "International Environmental Law and the Achievement of Intragenerational Equity," in *The Environmental Law Reporter*, vol. 31 (2001), pp. 10469–10485.

32. See on this principle D. A. French, "Developing States and International Environmental Law: The Importance of Differentiated Obligations," in 49 *International and Comparative Law Quarterly* (2000), pp. 34–60 and Y. Matsui, *Some Aspects of the Principle of Common but Differentiated Responsibilities*, paper to the ILA92s research seminar, Amsterdam, 2001.

33. *United States–Import Prohibition of Certain Shrimp and Shrimp Products: Recourse to Art. 21.5 by Malaysia*, Report of the Panel, WT/D558/AB/RW, 22 October 2001.

34. Text Kyoto Protocol in 37 *ILM (1998)*, p. 32 and Marrakesh Agreement in 41 ILM (2001/2002). See the Committee's report to the ILA Conference in Taipeh, London, 1999, pp. 700–703; J. Gupta, *The Climate Change Convention and Developing Countries: From Conflict to Consensus?* Dordrecht, 1997. See also O. Yoshida, *The International Legal Regime for the Protection of the Stratospheric Ozone Layer*, The Hague, 2001.

35. See the Brussels Declaration in UN Doc. AICONF.191/12 as well as the Programme of Action for Least Developed Countries in UN Doc. AICONF.191/11, 8 June 2001.

36. See F. Hey, "The Precautionary Concept in Environmental Policy and Law: Institutionalizing Caution," in *Georgetown International Environmental Law Review* IV (1992), pp. 303–318.

37. See Declaration on the Right to Development, *UN Doc*. AIRES/4 1/128, 4 December 1986 and the UN Secretary-Generals' *Agenda for Development*, in UN Doc. A148/935, 1994.

38. See Commission on Global Governance, *Our Global Neighbourhood*, Oxford, 1995; P. Sands, "International Law in the Field of Sustainable Development," in 65 *British Year Book of International Law* (1994), pp. 303–381 and pp. 355–360.

39. Article 9 of the Cotonou Convention.

40. IMF, Guidelines Regarding Governance Issues, published in *IMF Survey* (1997), 5 August 1997.

20

Responsibility for Biological Diversity Conservation Under International Law

CATHERINE TINKER

Introduction

The international law on biological diversity has developed along with scientific understanding and now embodies an ecosystem approach to the conservation of the variety of life. The ecosystem concept and a basic sense of state responsibility not to harm the environment was formulated in 1972 in the Stockholm Declaration and later, in the World Charter for Nature. Since Principle 21 of the Stockholm Declaration, the concept has crystallized in customary international law, but it did not appear in binding treaty law until the United Nations Convention on Biological Diversity (the Convention or Treaty) entered into force in 1993. Earlier wildlife protection treaties contained some aspects of the approach that was later adopted in the Biodiversity Convention. For example, the Ramsar Convention adopted a habitat and sustainable use approach to the conservation of wetlands; the World Heritage Convention has been a factor in some national development plans that were altered to avoid damage to listed sites.

The nature of state responsibility under Principle 21, which is not to harm the territory of other states or the territory beyond national jurisdiction, is still evolving. One way of implementing the goals contained in Article 3 of the Biodiversity Convention is to apply the precautionary principle, which requires restraint of any human activity that may adversely affect biodiversity. The precautionary principle in international environmental law is one response to the popular recognition that preventive action in the face of scientific uncertainty about future harm is necessary. The precautionary principle lowers the burden of proof required for blocking proposed or existing activities that may have serious long-term harmful con-

Reprinted with permission of *Vanderbilt Journal of Transnational Law*.

sequences. There is no agreement on the content of the precautionary principle nor is there consensus on whether a principle, rather than an approach, has actually emerged. "Nevertheless, countries have begun to develop precise and useful formulations of the principle in specific contexts."[1]

There is tremendous scientific uncertainty about the loss of biodiversity caused by various human activities, both lawful and unlawful. The numbers and types of life forms that exist as genes, species, sub-species, microorganisms, and bacteria in various ecosystems and habitats are a vast unknown. In the face of this, the precautionary principle requires an even greater degree of restraint in human activity to conserve and sustainably use biodiversity. Perhaps, for now, the precautionary principle should mandate a policy of "no action." Such an interpretation would be consistent with those who have called for a clarification of the notion of responsibility and prevention in environmental concerns. As one author has asserted, "[i]t is no longer sufficient to talk of state responsibility for environmental damage. The context must change to reflect state responsibility for the preservation of global environmental well-being."[2]

Traditional international lawmaking or standard-setting is an inherently slow process. This is particularly true in international environmental law where there is very little consensus surrounding existing norms. Soft law, customary law, and treaties are needed to set standards and define legally-binding duties and obligations based on the precautionary approach. Existing environmental treaties need to be enforced and additional states urged to ratify them. To ensure the highest degree of compliance, the principle of precautionary action to avoid environmental harm must be recognized in international law as a means of fulfilling states' obligations to conserve, sustainably use, and equitably share biodiversity.

The United Nations Convention on Biological Diversity codifies a line of soft law and international custom to create hard law in the treaty. The obligations accepted by states party to the Convention are threefold: conservation of biodiversity; sustainable use of biological diversity; and equitable sharing of biodiversity benefits. States party to the Convention are mandated to establish national legislation and plans. In order to fully comply with the treaty, these internal laws and development plans must take into account the responsibility accepted under the Principle 21 language and the jurisdictional scope article, Article 4. Arguably, to fully comply with the letter and spirit of the Convention, states must apply the precautionary principle in their decision-making processes and whenever they take action under national legislation and development plans.

Full application of the principle of precautionary action may require states to forego the short-term financial opportunities available from resource depletion and loss of biodiversity in order to secure long-term human benefits for the planet and future generations. For those developing countries in which poverty, disease, and starvation make it almost impossible to forego short-term but destructive gains, the Convention offers means of financing biodiversity conservation projects and the transfer of appropriate technology. In the meantime, the Convention requires states to monitor, study, and catalogue the rich storehouse of genetic variety contained in their rainforests, coral reefs, wetlands, deserts, and coastal zones. When greater scientific certainty about the effect of human activity on ecosystems and habitats is achieved, planners, lawyers, and diplomats may be better able to balance conservation and sustainable use of biological diversity. In the meantime, the lack of full scientific certainty should not be used as a reason for postponing measures to avoid or minimize a threat of significant reduction or loss of biological diversity.

International attention should be drawn to formulating global responsibility for biodiversity conservation and sustainable use. The Convention on Biological Diversity echoes Principle 22 of the Stockholm Declaration with a weak reference to the need to study state liability. It may be fruitful for such a study to follow the guidance of two other Stockholm Declaration principles. Principle 4 states that "[humanity] has a special responsibility to safeguard and wisely manage the heritage of wildlife and its habitat, which are now gravely imperiled by a combination of adverse factors. Nature conservation, including wildlife, must therefore receive importance in planning for economic development." Principle 5 states that "[t]he non-renewable resources of the earth must be employed in such a way as to guard against the danger of their future exhaustion and to ensure that benefits from such employment are shared by all [humanity]." The arguments for global conservation of biological diversity are weighted in favor of intangibles: aesthetics or preservation of open space or potential value for generations not yet born, based on equity or fairness.

This article analyzes the legal issues that attend fulfillment of the ambitious objectives of the Convention on Biological Diversity. This article also notes areas of ambiguity in the Convention, which remain to be clarified, and emphasizes responsibility for loss of biodiversity and prevention of that loss. Part II explores the failure of the traditional international law of state responsibility and liability to adequately protect the environment. Part II also reviews the U.N. International Law Commission's work on draft articles that incorporate a preventive or precautionary approach, specifically the draft articles on state responsibility and liability for environmental harm from lawful activities. This article suggests that a more appropriate legal approach is the application of the precautionary principle, which seeks to prevent harm rather than determine liability and damages after harm has occurred.

Part III argues that as greater scientific knowledge is achieved, the precautionary principle should be applied to all proposed human actions that may cause a loss of biodiversity, alter ecosystem and habitats, or affect genetic material. The article concludes that the principle of precautionary action may be seen as the means of enforcing the Biodiversity Convention and used as a procedural test to decide whether a proposed use of biodiversity is sustainable. Ultimately, the real test of the Convention on Biological Diversity will be the extent to which its provisions safeguard the planet's rich biological diversity, and the extent to which humans can undertake development projects without irrevocably destroying their global genetic heritage.

State Responsibility and Liability

Under traditional concepts of international law, the doctrine of state responsibility developed to address the relationship between a given state and citizens of other countries. The concept of state responsibility presupposes a clear legal duty or international plane or an obligation arising under treaty or the customary law. The state-alien example implicates the international principle of nondiscrimination against aliens and treaty obligations involving the treatment of diplomatic persons or the right of innocent passage. In the early 1970s, the concept of state responsibility was broadened to include any internationally wrongful acts.

The problem for international law is to interpret the concept of state responsibility in the environmental context. The U.S. understanding of international law is codified in the *Restatement (Third) of the Foreign Relations Law of the United States,* which states that a nation is obligated to take necessary measures to ensure that activities within the jurisdiction or control of that state conform to "generally accepted" international rules or standards. Even in the absence of an injury, a state is responsible to all other states for any violation of this obligation and for any resultant significant injury to "the environment of another state or to its property, or to persons or property within that state's territory or under its jurisdiction or control." The application of the broad language of Section 601, however, is limited by the state's obligation to take only "such measures as may be necessary, to the extent practicable under the circumstances. . . ."

"Generally accepted" international obligations and rules of conduct related to international environmental law now require, inter alia, the conservation and sustainable use of biological diversity and nonrenewable natural resources. At the same time, pressures for resource development and short-term economic gain encourage a broad range of public and private activities that adversely affect the environment, either now or in the future. In the area of generally accepted international obligations, state responsibility is triggered by the *de minimis* duty to observe the principle of *sic utere tuo ut alienum non laedas*.[3] Thus, states have a general duty to prevent uses of their territory that cause significant harm to other states. A state causing transboundary pollution is obligated to take reasonable measures to protect neighboring states from harm and to compensate them for damage. In addition, there may be obligations *erga omnes;*[4] the *Restatement* contemplated these obligations as they apply to areas beyond national jurisdiction and they are described by the International Court of Justice in the *Barcelona Traction* case.

The International Law Commission's Approach: State Responsibility for Internationally Wrongful Acts

The United Nations International Law Commission (I.L.C.) differentiates internationally wrongful acts from activities not contrary to international law. The first give rise to state responsibility. The second give rise to liability for injurious consequences. It is well established in international law that breach of a rule of international law entails state responsibility for an internationally wrongful act. The I.L.C.'s 1980 Draft on State Responsibility specified: "There is an internationally wrongful act of a State when conduct consisting of an action or omission is attributable to the State under international law; and that conduct constitutes a breach of an international obligation of the State."

The I.L.C. approach to state responsibility is to differentiate between "primary rules" and "secondary rules" of conduct that specify the action or refusal to act, which triggers state responsibility. Primary rules are obligations, secondary rules determine the legal consequences of failure to abide by primary rules. Secondary rules "specifically [deal] with the issues of responsibility and liability, although these issues cannot always actually be separated from the operation of the primary rules."[5] Allott has taken issue with the possibly meaningless distinction between primary and secondary rules and with the amount of time that has been invested over the past four decades in belaboring the point. Allott charges that the resultant delay in the formulation of the I.L.C. draft on state responsibility, "is doing serious long-term damage to international law and international society."[6] Even more seriously, Allott charges that the I.L.C.'s process and states' substantive approach to state responsibility virtually assure that states will not be held accountable for their actions.[7]

Under traditional public international law, three threshold questions are used to determine state responsibility: Was there a duty under international law? Was the duty breached? Can responsibility be attributed to a state for the violation of international law? Acts by nonstate entities, such as a citizen or official for whose acts a state is not responsible, do not give rise to state responsibility. Through the doctrine of attribution, however, a state can be responsible for the acts of its own citizens against another state.

The I.L.C. maintains that state responsibility attaches only to internationally wrongful acts. Although the violation of a clearly-defined treaty obligation or an unequivocally recognized norm of customary law clearly constitutes an internationally wrongful act, the I.L.C. has neither listed nor defined other potentially wrongful acts. Under the I.L.C. rubric, state responsibility is triggered when a state commits an international delict, regardless of whether any injury results. Once a state accepts binding duties, any failure to observe them necessarily amounts to a breach of international obligations. The breach may provoke a variety of responses, ranging from state protests to formal diplomatic expressions of displeasure and censure throughout the world community.

A state may raise a defense to its breach of an international obligation; in I.L.C. parlance, these defenses are known as 'conditions precluding wrongfulness." The defenses include necessity, prior consent, self-defense, and *force majeure*. They may be raised in many situations, including a failure to observe the precautionary principle that causes transboundary pollution or degradation of biological diversity. Because the international obligation at issue is one that requires the state to balance competing interests, almost every state can be expected to raise a defense such as necessity. Here the difficulty of defining and applying the precautionary principle becomes apparent. If the precautionary principle is merely a guideline to actions that may accomplish other goals, then it cannot be a primary rule or an obligation for purposes of state responsibility analysis. The application of the precautionary principle may be seen as a consequence of attempting to fulfill a primary obligation.

Although state responsibility does not arise unless there is a breach of an international obligation, the breaching action or inaction must be attributable to the state. Difficulties of attribution are inherent in the concept of objective responsibility, because a state is always liable for the acts of its officials and organs, even when they act *ultra vires*.[8] Brownlie notes that Grotius viewed the *culpa* as the proper basis of state responsibility.[9] Brownlie, however, moved beyond the confines of fault to a more realistic test when he wrote that one 'need not qualify responsibility of a state for an internationally wrongful act by the negligence (*culpa*) or intention (*dolus*) of the actor."[10] In the I.L.C.'s consideration of objective state responsibility, negligence or fault is not generally important for determining state responsibility or establishing an internationally wrongful act. After several years of inattention to the topic of state responsibility, in 1993 the I.L.C. formally adopted articles on cessation, reparation, restitution in-kind, compensation, satisfaction and assurances, and guarantees of nonrepetition, and included exceptionally detailed commentaries to the articles.

Consideration of whether to include a draft article on "international crimes" was postponed until the I.L.C.'s 1994 session. International crimes include internationally wrongful acts that are considered "essential for the protection of the fundamental interests of the international community" as a whole.[11] In its list of proposed international crimes, draft Article 19(3)(d) includes the serious breach of an international obligation of essential importance for the safeguarding and preservation of the human environment. Thus, according to the proposal, massive pollution of the atmosphere or of the seas would constitute an international crime. The I.L.C. remains divided on this controversial subject. Some members consider the same serious acts to be wrongful acts or to be violations of *erga omnes* obligations. From this perspective, there is no need to use the label "crimes." In contrast, other I.L.C. members consider the same acts to be crimes and believe that "crimes" is an appropriate label.

The International Law Commission's Approach: Liability of States for Injurious Consequences of Acts Not Contrary to International Law

If an exporting state—or a company within its jurisdiction or control—failed to obtain prior informed consent from the importing state and shipped hazardous biotechnology products, such an activity could be considered an internationally wrongful act, and thus trigger state responsibility regardless of whether any harm occurred. On the other hand, the shipment could be considered an activity not contrary to international law, which could only trigger liability for the exporting state if there were injurious consequences. The need to fit the facts of a given situation into these particular categories—whether the distinction is meaningful or not—arises from the decision of the I.L.C. to split the issue into two separate topics: state responsibility for internationally-wrongful acts, consisting of both primary and secondary obligations; and international liability for injurious consequences of activities not contrary to international law.

On a theoretical level, it is not clear that the conceptual basis on which it—liability for injurious consequences of activities not contrary to international law—is distinguished from state responsibility is either sound or necessary. On a more practical level, it is questionable whether it represents a useful basis for codification and development of existing law and practice relating to environmental harm, the field in which the Commission has mainly located the topic. From either perspective, it is liable to seem at best a questionable exercise in reconceptualising an existing body of law or, at worst, a dangerously retrograde step that may seriously weaken international efforts to secure agreement on effective principles of international environmental law.

The I.L.C. draft on liability for the injurious consequences of activities not contrary to international law states that civil liability will attach when four factors are present. There must be: (1) human activity; (2) the activity must be within the territory or control of a state; (3) the activity must be capable of giving rise to harm; and (4) there must be actual harm to persons or things within the territory or control of another state. Unlike the doctrine of state responsibility, which can attach even in the absence of harm, the concept of liability requires actual harm. Most commentators agree that the harm must be "substantial" or "serious," because state liability should not attach to minor incidents. There are several unanswered questions surrounding the draft. These questions include the draft's intended meaning of "control" and whether the draft applies when a state fails to act to remove a natural danger.

The I.L.C.'s current approach to liability is to "focus on prevention of harm from activities that constitute a particular risk." The I.L.C. begins by clarifying that the scope of the article includes lawful activities that "create a risk of causing significant transboundary harm through their physical consequences." The I.L.C. defines risk to include both "a low probability of causing disastrous harm and a high probability of causing other significant harm." The I.L.C. then goes on to address prior authorization, risk assessment, and measures to minimize risks.

States are most likely to be deterred from causing environmental harm if some standard of liability is imposed. Whether the system is grounded in strict liability or negligence is of considerably less importance. If international law adopts a liability system, states will be liable for environment damage caused by both public and private actors, regardless of whether the harm occurs within another state or beyond the boundaries of national jurisdiction. The liability approach best protects the rights of innocent victims of environmental harm because it shifts the burden of proof and makes it possible to collect prompt, adequate, and effective compensation once injury is established. Of course, the most effective way to protect the rights of the innocent is to prevent the harm or destruction from occurring in the first place.

One of the most difficult issues facing the I.L.C. is whether to impose a strict liability system or a fault-based system. For a number of obvious political and financial reasons, states are reluctant to adopt strict liability and therefore lack the will to negotiate an environmental liability protocol.[12] On the other hand, "the very absence of responsibility or liability provisions may be essential to the success of many environmental protection agreements."[13]

The meaning of strict liability and absolute liability in the context of activities affecting the environment is particularly relevant to hazardous or ultrahazardous activities and has created substantial problems for the I.L.C. The most visible ultrahazardous activity is nuclear and there is precedent for finding liability in cases where nuclear operations have caused environmental damage. The treaties pertaining to nuclear accidents have adopted a variety of approaches. Other treaties have addressed the harms caused by such specialized problems as objects that fall to earth from outer space.

The I.L.C. has had considerable difficulty addressing ultrahazardous activities. The I.L.C. created a working group and later adopted the group's recommendations. In essence, the I.L.C. is attempting to create consensus within itself on the basic issues of prevention and remediation.[14] If general consensus does develop, the I.L.C. will be able to move on to consideration of the specific mechanisms that should be used to address ultrahazardous risks.[15]

The Precautionary Principle and the International Law of Biological Diversity

Traditional models of international law and state responsibility focus upon ensuring compensation for transboundary damages and do not adequately address the challenges arising in international environmental law. The classic model poses a bilateral conflict between one state as actor and another state as victim, with significant physical harm occurring across national boundaries attributable to the first state. Emerging conflicts over the fundamental assumptions and value choices inherent in the "sustainable development" and "sustainable use" of nonrenewable natural resources located within a given state do not fit the bilateral paradigm. Presently, unless some transboundary damage is implicated, no state may raise a legal objection to the domestic environmental policies of any other state. Within the confines of their own borders, international law permits each state to deplete or injure its natural resources, to destroy its gene pool, species, and habitats, and to otherwise harm its environment. Thus, the traditional model of international environmental law creates a jurisdictional problem.

A second problem is that the long-standing "duty and damages for breach" model is inherently reactive and simply cannot prevent the loss of biological diversity, the despoliation of Antarctica, or the destruction of the ozone layer. Although the reactive model once may have been an appropriate response to transfrontier air or water pollution, today a growing number of environmental problems do not fit the mold of narrowly-defined transfrontier pollution and duties imposed on single states. International relations in the field of environmental protection have developed mostly in multilateral frames.

A new, more preventive model is needed to protect transnational ecosystems and the global commons. Under the new model, proponents of development will bear the burden of proving, before they proceed, that the planned use is sustainable and that no harm will result from proposed development. Only compliance with standards based on the precautionary principle and international cooperation will provide the necessary protection for the planet. Ultimately, achieving conservation and sustainable use of biodiversity and nonrenewable natural resources will require changes in human production and consumption. Certain groups or individuals in society will have to sacrifice short-term gains for long-term benefits and to consider meeting the basic needs of future generations as well as those of the present. International law and state responsibility doctrines must necessarily expand to reflect this new imperative for precautionary approaches to human activity and their regulation.

The Precautionary Principle

The precautionary principle has been defined in two ways. It has been defined as an international application of the German law principle of precautionary action (*vorsorgeprinzip*). It has also been defined as the variety of regulatory approaches adopted by governments to implement the *vorsorgeprinzip* principle; efforts to control emissions at their source by using best available technology are one example of this definition in practice. The precautionary principle can be used as a theory and justification for environmental strict liability; this perspective is rooted in the tort law goal of providing compensation to victims of harm. The precautionary principle also may be understood more broadly as a duty to take precautionary action and to avoid risk. In practice, the precautionary principle informs a substantive duty of care that requires environmental impact assessments or other regulatory investigations prior to permitting given actions.

The phrase "the precautionary principle" has appeared in a number of international instruments. Its meaning varies from "its weakest formulations ... to its strongest [in which] it can be seen as a reversal of the normal burden of proof, as in the Oslo Convention Prior Justification Procedure."[16] Several recent United Nations documents, including the 1992 Rio Declaration, have articulated the precautionary principle: "In order to protect the environment, the precautionary approach shall be widely applied by States according to their capabilities. Where there are threats of serious or irreversible damage, lack of full scientific certainty shall not be used as a reason for postponing cost-effective measures to prevent environmental degradation." In another formulation, the preamble to the U.N. Convention on Biological Diversity also refers to the precautionary principle, but omits phrases such as "according to their capabilities" and "cost-effective" measures, which qualify the language of the Rio Declaration. The Biodiversity Convention declares its intentions by, "[n]oting also that where there is a threat of significant reduction or loss of biological diversity, lack of full scientific certainty should not be used as a reason for postponing measures to avoid or minimize such a threat." In the Biodiversity Treaty, the language of obligation has been softened by using "should" to replace the mandatory "shall" used in the Rio Declaration. Other references to the precautionary principle appear in recent multilateral treaties, conference declarations, and regional agreements, especially in agreements related to oil pollution of the North Sea. It has been noted that the precautionary principle turns away from the "assimilative capacity" approach to environmental pollution, and recognizes the limitation to scientific knowledge on ecosystems.

Each of these formulations of the precautionary principle gives rise to different applications of the international law of state responsibility and liability. At its strongest, the precautionary principle may be interpreted to prohibit virtually all uses of natural resources and all human activities in certain ecosystems. Such a moratorium could continue indefinitely, until sufficient scientific knowledge developed about the effects of proposed activities or uses. At its weakest, the precautionary principle may be merely hortatory language that is intended to guide states as they adopt national legislation and plans. This permissive approach to resource use and human activity creates a balancing of interests that makes it possible for developmental and quality of life considerations to outweigh the need to conserve biodiversity and take other preventive action. Although the international community may strive to achieve an expansive application of the precautionary principle in the future, the permissive interpretation dominates the status quo.

The precautionary principle has appeared as soft law in numerous conference declarations and other statements of what governments think international law should be. In the absence of strong evidence of state practice and *opinio juris*,[17] such as an explicit statement from a high-level government minister that precautionary measures were adopted because they are mandated under international law, it is difficult to conclude that the precautionary principle is currently customary international law. Examples of national legislation that refer to the precautionary principle or that are implicitly based on such a principle are insufficient to demonstrate a binding international legal obligation.

Apart from any sense of legal obligation under international law, there are many subjective variables that may affect a state's choice of precautionary action. Precautionary actions may save money in several situations: when there is a great likelihood that damages will occur; when damages, while unlikely, will be of great magnitude should they occur; and when a large number of people are likely to be injured if the harm is not prevented. The type or degree of damage contemplated and the ease of adopting precautionary measures may also induce precautionary action, particularly if there is public demand or political support for precautionary action. A state may act voluntarily based on a moral or ethical imperative. It may also voluntarily adopt a precautionary course for economic reasons. Sometimes it is more cost-efficient to prevent damage than to wait for damage to occur and pay the resulting costs.

It is never easy to say precisely when a rule crystallizes into customary international law. There is no convenient bright line test or formula to apply; the number of years that have elapsed since the original articulation of the principle and the number of times the principle has been quoted in soft law documents are not dispositive. To find the *opinio juris,* it is always necessary to locate the reasons for state practice. Similarly, if states adopt the language of international instruments that are neither binding nor intended to be binding upon the parties, then the mere fact that states have adopted that language is insufficient to prove that a customary rule of international law exists.

If a state happens to follow such a nonbinding principle, it may not necessarily believe that it was under a legal compulsion to do so and may not accept that it could be liable for breach under international law for failing to follow the law. To structure the definition of customary international law otherwise would be to erase the difference between nonbinding and binding international law, and to eliminate the incentive for states to join the soft law declarations from which international environmental law frequently evolves. For purposes of this article, it is not necessary to definitively state whether the precautionary principle is or is not customary law. Rather, the question is whether the precautionary principle affects the international law of state responsibility and liability when the principle is or becomes law, either through treaty obligations or through the future development of customary international law.

The relationship between state responsibility and the precautionary principle has yet to be fully defined. The first element of state responsibility is the existence of a clear legal duty or obligation that gives rise to the concept of an "internationally wrongful act." The second element is a breach of the legal duty. The next step is evaluation of possible defenses to the breach. Finally, compensation for victims of the breach must be determined.

The first element is the crux of the relationship between the precautionary principle and state responsibility. If the precautionary principle has not yet risen to the level of a legal duty or obligation, then it is difficult or even impossible to move on to the problems of breach, defenses, and compensation. Certainly, it may also be impossible to deter harmful behavior.[18] Because the concept of environmental harm is relatively new international law, there are few clearly-defined internationally wrongful acts that could trigger state responsibility. As principles of international environmental law become recognized as binding law through customary law and treaty law, more obligations will exist. Breach of those obligations may then lead to state responsibility. At present, a state's failure to follow the precautionary principle is not an internationally wrongful act that can trigger state responsibility.

Even when a state is obligated by treaty to observe the precautionary principle, an internationally wrongful act has not necessarily occurred. It is necessary to examine the precise language of the treaty obligation. If the treaty says "should" instead of "shall," the offending state is not bound. Similarly, state obligations are often conditioned by phrases such as "to the extent practicable" and "according to their capabilities." Treaties frequently require adoption of only those preventive measures that are "cost-effective." Another problem in the relationship between the precautionary principle and the law of state responsibility is that some treaties referring to the precautionary principle are quite new and have not entered into force. In such situations, it is impossible to gauge the extent of compliance to be expected from states parties, or to imagine extending the obligation to states not party to the treaty. If the treaty is regional, it is difficult to draw out a clear rule of international law with "global applicability." Furthermore, the problem remains: how to determine what action must be taken to fulfill the obligation.

One starting point is to consider the relationship between the ' precautionary principle and Principle 21 of the Stockholm Declaration. It may be possible to achieve compliance with Principle 21 through observation of the precautionary principle. Principle 21 of the Stockholm Declaration is an example of an international environmental text containing the principle of state responsibility. It states that all nations have a responsibility to ensure that activities under their jurisdiction or control do not cause damage to the environment of other states or to areas beyond national jurisdiction. Principle 21 should be read in conjunction with Principle 22, which calls for the development of international law "regarding liability and compensation for the victims of pollution and other environmental damage. . ."

The Stockholm Declaration can also be read as a policy shift. Some developed nations addressed newly-recognized global environmental problems and, at the same time, some developing nations asserted sovereignty over their own natural resources. The broadening of the responsibility concept can be seen both in the second clause of Principle 21 and in the World Charter for Nature, in which states accepted the responsibility principle in relation both to other states and to nature itself. Perhaps the notion of state responsibility to nature will be further extended in the future to include a state's responsibility to international civil society. The foregoing discussion demonstrates that the principle of precautionary action may be considered a secondary obligation or a consequence of the states' primary responsibility not to harm the territory of another state or the territory beyond national jurisdiction. It remains to be seen whether Principle 21 applies to harms that occur within a state's own territory.

Efforts to link Principle 21 to states' responsibility not to breach international obligations are supported by the recommendations of the World Commission on Environment and Development. The Brundtland Report noted that "recognition by states of their responsibility to ensure an adequate environment for present as well as future generations is an important step toward sustainable development." The Brundtland Report defined international environmental obligations the breach of which triggers the duty to pay compensation by saying that states have a responsibility toward their own citizens and to other states. While the Brundtland Report provides a road map for the future development of general principles of international environmental law, it is not a source of binding legal duties or obligations for states.

The Brundtland Commission convened a group of legal experts that drafted one obligation on state responsibility and a second obligation on "liability for transboundary environmental interferences resulting from lawful activities"; the International Law Commission divided consideration of the two subjects in a similar manner. The main object of the liability article clearly is payment of compensation for transboundary environmental harm. Indeed, the article seems to assume that the cost of preventing harm or reducing the risk is so great that prevention is realistically impossible. In Article 11, the state responsibility article of the Brundtland Commission's legal experts group report, the mandate is much broader than in Article 21. Under Article 11, the state must cease the internationally wrongful act and restore the *status quo ante* as far as possible. Where appropriate, the state must give satisfaction and pay compensation for harm caused by its breach of international obligations.

In order to identify the possible impact of the precautionary principle upon the international law of state responsibility, it is necessary to examine the nature of the obligations that the precautionary principle as international law would create. Given the uncertainty over the scope and meaning of the precautionary principle and the extent to which it obligates a state to act, violation of the precautionary principle presently does not constitute a breach of international law. This section suggests that the precautionary principle may develop into its own treaty and customary norm. If this occurs, the precautionary principle will be analytically similar to the duty to warn and the duty to mitigate; through these duties a link will be forged between state responsibility and the obligation not to harm the territory of another state or the territory beyond national jurisdiction.

The Precautionary Principle and Biological Diversity

International biodiversity law and policy objectives are strongly affected by ideas concerning the value of biodiversity and the root causes of biodiversity loss. These same value judgments affect related national and regional policies and laws. Valuing biodiversity is difficult because little is understood about genes, species, and ecosystems. First, biodiversity has direct economic value from products derived from biodiversity, such as medicines or new breeds of animals or plants. Second, biodiversity has indirect value, such as ecotourism.

Third, biodiversity possesses options value, because it offers uses not yet known but of value to future generations. Fourth, biodiversity possesses existence value, which is drawn from the mere continuance of life forms in and of themselves, without regard for their economic utility. In addition to these economic, aesthetic, and ethical values, biodiversity has ecological and scientific value, because it is a storehouse of genes and micro-organisms that may permit organisms and ecosystems to recover from various afflictions. The World Charter for Nature recognized humanity's powerful impact upon the environment, the benefits of biodiversity, and the causes of biodiversity destruction.

Given the potential transboundary impact of the loss of biodiversity and the attendant mitigation costs, loss of biodiversity is clearly a matter of international concern. Furthermore, human activity is undeniably responsible for the accelerating loss of global biodiversity. Human activity is rapidly altering both terrestrial and aquatic ecosystems at an unprecedented and alarming rate. Human impact far exceeds the impact of catastrophic natural events, such as periodic fires, floods, and pestilence, that have occurred since prehistoric times. Although the planet possesses a remarkable ability to recuperate from natural disasters and even some human-made disasters, many authorities agree that the planet has reached the limits of its endurance.

Conditions of poverty are the impetus for the governments of developing countries to seek an improved quality of life for their citizens. This legitimate and worthy goal must be counterbalanced by the need to prevent further loss of biodiversity or, at the least, to make informed choices reflecting both long-term and short-term costs and benefits. Importantly, the Rio Declaration repeated the World Charter for Nature's concern for unsustainable consumption and production patterns.

The Convention on Biological Diversity requires party states to draw up national plans and legislation to achieve the Convention's objectives. If a state produces a plan claiming to address the conservation and sustainable use of biological diversity, that state has fulfilled its Convention obligations. At present, no mechanism exists to assess the substantive adequacy and consistency of national plans with the goals of the Convention. Without this important oversight mechanism, it is nearly impossible to charge a state party with breach of its Convention obligations. Similarly, until clear international standards of sustainability are developed, it is impossible to gauge the effects of a state's plan or a proposed activity on the long-term conservation and sustainable use of biological diversity.

The Convention also failed to explain its relationship to other treaties, such as the Convention on International Trade in Endangered Species and the Ramsar Convention. Under the specific language of the treaty, the general "last in time rule"[19] of treaty interpretation and preemption does not apply. Determining the effect of an action taken under multiple international instruments is difficult. The Law of the Sea Treaty clearly trumps the Biodiversity Convention according to the Convention itself. But under earlier conservation and wildlife treaties, it is much less certain whether a decision from the Conference of the Parties (COP) overrides a decision by the treaty body of a different instrument. The interrelationship and overlapping jurisdiction of various U.N. bodies also creates problems. For example, the location of the forests issue is being debated in numerous fora including the COP to the Convention on Biological Diversity; the U.N. Commission on Sustainable Development (CSD); the Global Environment Facility (GEF); the U.N. Food and Agriculture Organization (FAO); and other treaty bodies. Although this may be a salutory multi-fora approach to a complicated problem, it may also permit special interests to "forum-shop" for a receptive audience.

New treaties and soft law declarations of the past two decades and states' increasingly serious reports on their environmental protection activities have created an international environmental law that is strong and growing. The goals of conservation, sustainable use, and equitable benefit-sharing have at last elicited common efforts at the local, national, and international levels that are mutually reinforcing, as will be seen in the next subsection's examination of the international law on biodiversity.

"Soft Law," Customary International Law, and Treaty Law Related to Responsibility for Biodiversity

Commentators frequently refer to international conference statements that represent international consensus or aspiration as "soft law,"[20] a legal form that is not actually binding on states. Soft law is the newest and most common form of law-making in the international system; it frequently appears in new areas of international law-making in which obligations are not dependent upon custom. International soft law states global goals and public expectations. Once the expectations are stated, they may lead to increased public pressure, and ultimately states may recognize the soft law goals as enforceable international prohibitions. Examples of soft law include declarations and resolutions by conferences on the ministerial level or head of state level, multi-disciplinary meetings of scholars or professionals, and U.N. General Assembly resolutions. Even if soft law declarations are not initially binding, they indicate the direction in which the international community is interested in moving and how far states are willing to go.

The U.N. World Charter for Nature, adopted by the General Assembly in 1982, is a good illustration of a "soft law" that formulated a rule and caused some countries to follow the rule as a matter of policy. The General Assembly "expressed its conviction that the benefits which could be obtained from nature depended on the maintenance of natural processes and on the diversity of life forms and that those benefits were jeopardized by the excessive exploitation and the destruction of natural habitats." The General Assembly also "solemnly invited Member States, in the exercise of their permanent sovereignty over their natural resources, to conduct their activities in recognition of the supreme importance of protecting natural systems, maintaining the balance and quality of nature and conserving natural resources, in the interests of present and future generations."

The World Charter for Nature was adopted against this background as a statement of aspirations. The Charter contained a number of far-reaching significant statements regarding the relationship of human beings to other forms of life and the consequences of human activity for natural resources. Some of these statements were dropped or altered significantly in the UNCED documents and in the Biodiversity Treaty ten years later. The general principles in the World Charter for Nature included respect for nature, preservation of global genetic resources, global conservation, and sustainable use.

Customary international law is another recognized method of international lawmaking. The central problem in customary international law is determining whether and when a rule has reached the point of universality and legality. Although the traditional two-pronged test of customary international law searches for evidence of state practice and evidence of *opinio juris*, the test does not necessarily provide a simple answer. Principle 21 of the Stockholm Conference on the Human Environment provides a useful case study of the long road leading to becoming customary international law. Principle 21 provides that "[s]tates have . . . the sovereign right to exploit their own resources pursuant to their own environmental policies, and the responsibility to ensure that activities within their jurisdiction or control do not cause damage to the environment of other states or of areas beyond the limits of national jurisdiction." This statement is the result of a long progression that began with the appearance of the general idea of the principle in the *Trail Smelter* arbitration, a decision with no precedential value in any judicial forum. *Trial Smelter's* principle was repeated in a decision of the International Court of Justice in the *Corfu Channel* case, and later included as part of the declaration of the 1972 Stockholm Conference. The principle was repeated more strongly in the "soft law" World Charter for Nature resolution. Each of these steps was evidence that at some point, Principle 21 had become customary law. Finally, the principle became hard law when it was included in the U.N. Convention on Biological Diversity.

The language that became Principle 21, and later Article 3 of the Convention on Biological Diversity, changed slightly through its various incarnations. The *Trail Smelter* arbitration decision said that no state has the right "to use or permit the use of its territory in such a manner as to cause injury by fumes in or to the territory of another or the properties or persons therein, when the case is of serious consequences and the injury is established by clear and convincing evidence." The *Corfu Channel* case expanded the general principle to recognize every state's obligation not to knowingly allow its territory to be used for acts contrary to the rights of other states. The Stockholm Declaration was much more specific and prohibited states from activities that, "cause damage to the environment of other States or of areas beyond the limits of national jurisdiction." The U.N. General Assembly revised the principle's language somewhat. The "soft law" World Charter for Nature appeared and announced that "[s]tates and, to the extent they are able, other public authorities, international organizations, individuals, groups and corporations shall . . . [e]nsure that activities within their jurisdictions or control do not cause damage to the natural systems located within other States or in the areas beyond the limits of national jurisdiction. . . ."

Although the World Charter for Nature changed the term "environment" to "natural systems," it still limited the prohibition against harm to areas "within other States or in the areas beyond the limits of national jurisdiction." This jurisdictional scope limitation persisted in later formulations, including the Biodiversity Treaty. The addition of a phrase referring to both nations' developmental and environmental policies emphasizes the concern for sustainable development that was articulated first, and most effectively, in the Brundtland Report. This concern for sustainability characterized the UNCED documents, including the Rio Declaration, Agenda 21, and the U.N. Convention on Biological Diversity.

In its next incarnation, Principle 21 appeared in the Rio Declaration, and said:

> States have, in accordance with the Charter of the United Nations and the principles of international law, the sovereign right to exploit their own resources pursuant to their own environmental and developmental policies, and the responsibility to ensure that activities within their jurisdiction or control do not cause damage to the environment of other States or of areas beyond the limits of national jurisdiction.

The recognized test for whether Stockholm Principle 21 has become customary law is the traditional inquiry of evidence of both state practice and *opinio juris*. Evidence of state practice can be found in the presence of statements made by governments since 1972 that support Principle 21; in the inclusion of the principle in other treaties or formal declarations; and in the decisions of arbitral panels and judicial bodies that cite or rely on the principle. *Opinio juris* is evidenced by the writing of jurists who claim to have found an acceptance of Principle 21 in major legal systems around the world, as well as by a number of bilateral and regional agreements that have referred specifically to the Stockholm Declaration in their texts. Each of these documents establishes that states are following Principle 21 in practice and believe themselves to be obligated.

Statements and declarations by the U.N. General Assembly and other multilateral conferences that include the text of Principle 21 can also be cited as proof that the principle has indeed crystallized into customary law. Principle 21's language has been copied countless times in other declarations and resolutions. Moreover, when Principle 21 was codified in the Biodiversity Treaty, it earned international acceptance. Once codified in a treaty, Principle 21 is separately binding on all parties to the treaty, regardless of whether it is customary law.

Since Principle 21 was codified in the Biodiversity Treaty, it becomes necessary to define the meaning of Principle 21 in that context. The existence of states' rights implies that states have a corresponding moral, ethical, and increasingly legal responsibility. The principle of sovereignty guarantees the right of a state to act. Principle 21 balances that right with a state's duty to protect the environment within its jurisdiction or control and to prevent transboundary harm. This responsibility necessarily limits a state's right to use its natural resources with unfettered discretion. Similarly, international law restricts a state's right to use force at will through the requirements of necessity and proportionality. States' absolute sovereignty is already restricted by the global imperative to survive in the face of grave threats to the planet's soil, water, and air. Absolute freedom of consumption without regard for environment costs and nonsustainable means of production are also becoming the target of restrictions under international law and policy.

States may find themselves increasingly under prohibitions regarding the protection or sharing of scarce natural resources, under both permissive and prohibitive systems of laws. As described above, in a permissive system, everything that is not prohibited is permitted and states' sovereignty is absolute. In a prohibitive system, everything not explicitly permitted is assumed prohibited unless clear pension can be found from some supranational source. Principle 21 as binding customary law appears to be a permissive system, tempering states' absolute rights with only the responsibility not to harm the territory of another or territory beyond national jurisdiction. Both the precautionary principle and Principle 21 of the Stockholm Declaration as contained verbatim in the Biodiversity Convention embody the concept of responsibility and need to consider sustainability.

The shift toward prevention and responsibility, and away from the notion of liability and compensation after harm occurs, is a crucial step in accepting the fundamental concept of international biological diversity.

Once the basic premises of responsibility and sharing are accepted, resources can be redirected to find the means to achieve these ends. Some
possible solutions include transfer of environmentally-sound technology,
access to genetic resources, and distribution of some of the royalties from
successful genetically-derived products to the source countries and local
communities. Greater international cooperation will benefit those who participate; countries may choose not to share, but they will be denied access
to valuable resources.

Protection of biological diversity requires more than species preservation. Scientists have discovered the importance of ecosystems; they act both
as corridors between habitats that support endangered species and as rich
depositories of unidentified organisms. It is inadequate to measure the
value of an "ecosystem by reference to its utility for human beings, because
it is impossible to value uses that have not yet been imagined. Utility valuation also fails to account for the intrinsic value of ecosystems and life
forms. The degree of environmental harm and the true cost of biodiversity
loss are important in decision-making and risk analysis; they also have
implications for any future liability and compensation regime. Given the
present inability to accurately value biodiversity, it is best to adopt a preventive approach rather than to risk unknown harm. The precautionary principle does not require absolute scientific certainty as a prerequisite to
preservation of an area or species that may be irreparably harmed before it
is fully understood.

The new United Nations Convention on Biological Diversity attempts
to balance interests on a global level and represents a general commitment
to the conservation and sustainable use of biodiversity. In an effort to clarify the interests being balanced, the Convention carefully defines biological
diversity, biological resources, and biotechnology. Although the Convention
codifies Principle 21, it does not resolve the problem of liability for the loss
of biodiversity.

The parties to the Biodiversity Convention accepted a binding obligation to conserve biodiversity and received an affirmation of their sovereign
right to use forests, wetlands, and other ecosystems for development, tempered by the requirement of sustainable use. This obligation was a new
departure for developing countries. In return for guaranteed access to the
genetic resources located in genetically rich developing countries, developed countries accepted an obligation to share the benefits of biotechnology. The final compromise, then, endorsed both the conservation of biodiversity and its sustainable use. To some, this trade-off has ominous
overtones. The Third World Network, an Indian nongovernmental organization, fears that the North is attempting to preserve its access to the
South's genetic resources. Thus, the South would supply the "raw material
for the [North's] next industrial revolution," in the North's privately-held
biotechnology industry.

International law does not yet possess state responsibility or means of calculating appropriate damages for the accidental or willful destruction of biodiversity. Nevertheless, since the Convention on Biological Diversity entered into force in December 1993, it is plausible that the international law of precautionary action may rise to the level of a duty, which can trigger state responsibility when breached. The breach may occur when states fail to regulate activities within their jurisdiction or control or cause damage in areas beyond national jurisdiction. In order to achieve the conservation and sustainable use of biological diversity, it may be necessary to use the international legal system to regulate or restrict development patterns in accordance with the precautionary principle.

When a state breaches its duty to uphold the precautionary principle, Article 3 of the Convention on Biological Diversity offers a basis for assessing the state's responsibility. Although the duty applies only to extraterritorial harm, the Convention's article on jurisdictional scope may give rise to responsibility for a state's activities, regardless of where the effect occurs. The Convention's jurisdiction varies somewhat. The Convention's jurisdiction over components of biodiversity is consistent with Principle 21 and extends only to harms caused in the territory of other states or in the territory beyond national jurisdiction. The Convention's jurisdiction over processes and activities is considerably broader and leaves room for further interpretation of responsibility beyond the transborder context. Such an extension of jurisdictional scope is inherently necessary to the conservation of biological diversity.

New principles of international environmental law have developed quickly in recent years in response to global imperatives for sustainable development; nowhere is that trend more noticeable than in the formation of international law on biodiversity. The United Nations Convention on Biological Diversity, which entered into force as binding international law on December 29, 1993, has been ratified by 127 nations. The first Conference of the Parties took place in late 1994, formally adopting many of the interim institutional and financial mechanisms for the operation of the treaty established when the treaty was opened for signature during the United Nations Conference on Environment and Development in June, 1992. A declaration adopted at the close of the first COP noted that states party to the Convention on Biological Diversity regard it "as much more than just a set of rights and obligations: it is a global partnership with new approaches to multilateral cooperation for conservation and development. . . ."

The U.N. Convention on Biological Diversity represents a new style of treaty negotiation, in that the Convention's subject matter is very broad and the Convention was negotiated with unusual speed and openness. Other features also contribute to the treaty's uniqueness. First, the treaty pioneers an ecosystem approach to conservation that moves beyond the species-specific or habitat-specific approaches of earlier conservation treaties, including those on migratory birds, wetlands, and trade in endangered species. Second, both the preamble and the body of the treaty emphasize the participation of women, local communities, and nongovernmental organizations (NGOs) in biodiversity protection. This language is a significant departure from most other multilateral instruments, which address only the role of the states party to the treaty. The Convention's identification of nonstate actors is a recognition that successful implementation of the treaty will require cooperation from many sectors.

Third, the initial formulation of the treaty was marked by the initiative and contributions of NGOs; indeed, the first draft of the treaty was prepared by an NGO. Fourth, the Biodiversity Treaty is unique, because the text of Stockholm Principle 21 appears verbatim as Article 3; marking the first time this language has appeared in binding international law, rather than in "customary law" or "soft law." The idea of national sovereignty over resources is balanced or tempered to some degree by the requirement that each state accept its responsibility not to harm the territory of any other state or the territory beyond its own national jurisdiction. Finally, the treaty represents a trade-off of mutually beneficial goods, a trade-off that is possible because both developing and developed states have something of value that the other group wants.

Although it is too early to tell how effectively the treaty will be implemented, there is cause for some optimism. The Convention calls for the study of the creation of a Clearinghouse Mechanism for Technical and Scientific Cooperation, which would share knowledge on biological diversity and promote cooperation. In addition, the Convention establishes the Subsidiary Body on Scientific, Technical, and Technological Advice (SBSTTA). On-going discussions at the two meetings of the Intergovernmental Committee on the Convention on Biological Diversity and at the first COP centered on the institutional and organizational entities needed to implement the Convention, as well as on related concerns such as financial mechanisms, intellectual property rights, and biosafety. Most of the NGOs in attendance at the meetings on the Convention in 1993 and 1994 called for efforts to address the relationships between poverty, unsustainable production and consumption, unequal trade relations, and biodiversity; the discussions did not, however, directly address these underlying causes of biodiversity loss.

By the end of the first COP, many of the organizational issues required to set up a new treaty were resolved. The United Nations Environment Programme (UNEP) was designated the appropriate institutional body to function as the Secretariat, and the rules of procedure were established. Finally, the work of the next three years was divided into topics and compiled as the Medium Term Programme of Work of the Conference of the Parties 1995-1997. Despite progress at the first COP, many aspects of the Biodiversity

Treaty remain open to interpretation. These gray areas include: state responsibility for prevention of loss of biodiversity; the meaning of "sustainable use" of biological diversity; the extent of a party's obligations to enforce the treaty's objectives through domestic laws; the relationship of the Convention to other wildlife and habitat treaties; and the relationship of the COP and Secretariat to other U.N. bodies whose mandates include aspects of biodiversity.

Conclusion

New international environmental law principles, including sustainable development and recognition of serious human threats to the global environment, have created new applications for the doctrines of state responsibility and liability, although states' environmental obligations under international law remain ill-defined. It is difficult to reconcile most activities threatening loss of biological diversity with the I.L.C.'s language on state responsibility for "primary" and "secondary" obligations and "internationally wrongful acts." Furthermore, the concept of "injurious consequences arising from acts not contrary to international law" appears to be of limited use when only ultrahazardous activities are examined. The concept's use is limited, because biodiversity loss most frequently occurs through the accumulation of ordinary human activities that affect an ecosystem.

Principle 21's concept of state responsibility links sovereign power and privilege with general obligations not to harm the territory of another state or the area beyond national jurisdiction. The legal principles relevant to air, space, aircraft, and maritime boundary disputes are considerably less relevant to problems involving micro-organisms and migratory species. Similarly, territorially-based concepts are not very useful in assessing states' responsibility when they fail to regulate multinational commercial entities that destroy or unsustainably exploit biodiversity resources. One option is to define such commercial activities as internationally wrongful or otherwise prohibited under international law. Unfortunately, this step is unlikely to occur. Another option is to recognize the precautionary principle as a means to comply with state responsibility not to harm the environment. Failure to adopt national plans or procedures incorporating a precautionary approach may then trigger international responsibility or liability.

In other words, a state's duty to take precautionary action may be seen as one of a cluster of procedural norms similar to the duties to warn other states, to mitigate damages, and to assist in case of emergency. For example, the Rio Declaration reaffirms a state's obligation to provide early notification in an emergency and when activities may have a significant transboundary impact. The Rio Declaration also affirms a state's obligation to assist in the event of such emergencies. Moreover, some states are required by treaty to provide both early notification of risk to other states and assistance to other states in the event of a nuclear accident. The goal of these procedural norms is to make information widely available to local communities and to the international community so that states can make informed choices and undertake appropriate responses. A state wishing to comply with the principle of precautionary action may do so by incorporating environmental impact assessment procedures in national planning and legislation.

At the 1992 United Nations Conference on Environment and Development (UNCED), participating states affirmed the importance of environmental impact assessment (EIA) procedures as an integral part of the development process. Currently, more than fifty nations require EIA as a matter of domestic law; and sixteen states of the United States have adopted laws that are more substantive than the National Environmental Protection Act (NEPA). In addition, international organizations, such as the World Bank, have adopted EIA procedures as part of their decision-making process. The popularity of EIAs is due in large measure to their proven effectiveness in anticipating and mitigating the adverse environmental impacts of development projects, and their usefulness in providing environmental information to decision-makers. Moreover, EIA procedures often give potentially affected local communities an opportunity to participate in the decision-making process.

The widespread acceptance of environmental impact assessments is demonstrated by the passage of the Espoo Convention on Environmental Impact Assessment in a Transboundary Context, which was opened for signature in 1991. As of mid-1995, twenty-eight states have signed the convention; a majority of Western and Eastern European states, the United States, and Canada are among the signatories. The Convention requires parties to "take all appropriate and effective measures to prevent, reduce, and control significant adverse transboundary environmental impact from proposed activities." To comply with the Convention, states must notify potentially affected states of environmental dangers, and must consult with affected states to reduce or eliminate adverse environmental effects. The use of EIAs, then, may be one way to implement the precautionary principle in national and international law and policy. It is an approach with particular relevance to the conservation and sustainable use of biological diversity.

Another conceptual way to approach the goal of biodiversity conservation under international law, as explored *supra* in Part II, is through state responsibility and liability. The current limitation of obligations not to harm territory within the jurisdiction of another state or beyond the national jurisdiction does not fully protect global biodiverse resources, for states may still destroy such resources within their territorial boundaries under existing international law. What is needed in the future, then, is to extend responsibility to all states to conserve and sustainably use such resources as a global storehouse of genetic information or medicine chest, separate and apart from claims of sovereign rights, unless subject to the balances and tradeoffs negotiated in the Convention on Biological Diversity.

Applying the principle of state responsibility in areas beyond national jurisdiction, such as Antarctica and the high seas, creates an opportunity to apply the doctrine of state responsibility in a context free from the claims of sovereign rights. The U.N. Convention on the Law of the Sea (LOS) offers a plan that is tailored for the maximum preservation of humanity's common heritage. Similarly, Antarctica offers the chance to preserve a unique ecosystem of "enormous scientific, ecological, spiritual, and aesthetic importance."[21] The Madrid Protocol to the Antarctic Treaty "implicitly adopts the precautionary principle of environmental planning."[22] In the concept of pollution on the high seas, "[d]octrine and practice . . . now evidence the existence of a parallel obligation to prevent harm to the shared resource of the high seas environment. . . . The 1982 LOS Convention [codifies a duty] as the obligation to act with 'due regard' for other states."[23]

The concept of "internationally wrongful act" creates problems for the application of traditional notions of state problems responsibility for environmental damage. Because clear norms of international environmental law have not yet been fully and universally recognized, the application of the doctrine of state responsibility is not particularly useful at this time. Thus, "[i]t may be concluded that, with respect to transfrontier pollution, the principle of state responsibility is undergoing a process of development and consolidation, but it is not yet to be considered to have hardened into a rule of international law."[24] As discussed by the I.L.C., much serious environmental harm can result from activities that are not "wrongful" in themselves, but whose cumulative effect is disastrous. The international system still awaits the development of an international law on liability and compensation for victims and a broader concept of state environmental responsibility. Obviously, the best strategy for a state that is mindful of its responsibility is to avoid a breach of international obligations entirely or to adopt preventive measures. It is the duty of the international community to develop a full understanding of those obligations.

The creation of international environmental law has led to the recognition of certain legal obligations, such as states' responsibility not to harm the territory of another state and the territory beyond national jurisdiction. This responsibility should be expanded to address threats to global resources and biodiversity even when the threats occur within the territory of individual states. The new international environmental legal system should encourage states to observe their obligations to conserve and sustainably use the environment. In cases where it is difficult to know whether an activity is sustainable the best course for legislators and policy makers is to apply the precautionary approach and prevent environment harm. States that take their environmental responsibilities seriously, comply with their treaty obligations, and strengthen their national regulatory systems need not fear the establishment of international standards and an extended notion of state environmental responsibility. The international community soon must formulate a clear understanding of state environmental responsibility that is proactive and designed to minimize risk. The duty to take precautionary action is becoming customary international law. As such, it offers one way for states to undertake sustainable development, to uphold Stockholm Principle 21, to conserve and sustainably use biological diversity, to protect areas beyond national jurisdiction, and to meet other global obligations. In the process, states' and citizens' self-interest in adopting precautionary measures will become apparent as the Biodiversity Convention is implemented and other sources of international law develop.

Notes

1. Edith Brown Weiss, *International Environmental Law: Contemporary Issues and the Emergence of a New World Order*, 81 Geo. L.J. 675, 690 (1993).

2. Susan H. Bragdon, *National Sovereignty and Global Environmental Responsibility: Can the Tension Be Reconciled for the Conservation of Biological Diversity?*, 33 Harv. Int'l L.J. 381, 391 (1992).

3. This phrase is roughly translated as a form of the golden rule or good neighborliness—an injunction to use one's property in a manner that does not injure another's property. It is related to the civil law concept of "abuse of rights." One classic example of the principle is the idea that neighbors may not build "spite fences" to separate themselves from one another.

National laws also contain "the doctrine that makes an otherwise proper exercise of one's property rights wrongful unless the use [sic] compensates the person who is injured by the use." Louis Henkin et al., International Law: Cases and Materials 1380 (3d ed. 1993). *See also* James Barros & Douglas M. Johnston, The International Law of Pollution 74–76 (1974).

4. *Erga omnes* obligations are obligations owed to the international community as a whole, rather than just to another state.

5. Francisco O. Vicuña, *State Responsibility, Liability, and Remedial Measures Under International Law: New Criteria for Environmental Protection*, in Environmental Change and International Law 124, 128 (Edith Brown Weiss ed., 1992).

6. Philip Allott, *State Responsibility and the Unmaking of International Law*, 29 Harv. Int'l L.J. 1, 1 (1988).

7. *Id.* at 16.

8. [T]he public law analogy of the *ultra vires* act is more realistic than a seeking for subjective *culpa* in specific natural persons who may, or may not, 'represent' the legal person (the state) in terms of wrongdoing. . . . the state also bears an international responsibility for all acts committed by its officials or its organs which are delictual according to international law, regardless of whether the official organ has acted within the limits of his

competency or has exceeded those limits." Ian Brownlie, Principles of Public International Law 437–40 (4th ed. 1990) (citing Estate of Jean-Baptiste Caire v. United Mexican States, 5 R.I.A.A. 516, 529–31 [1929]).

[T]here is no need to show fault in the sense of malicious intent or negligence on the part of the state officials responsible for the action of inaction. . . . [O]pinions of eminent authorities such as Lauterpacht, Verdross and Eagleton . . . have favoured the Grotian view that State responsibility rests on "the conception of States as moral entities accountable for their acts and omissions in proportion to the *mens rea* of their agents, the real addressees of international duties. . . ."

Oscar Schachter, International Law in Theory and Practice 203 (1991) (quoting Hersh Lauterpacht, Private Law Sources and Analogies 173 [1970]).

9. Brownlie, *supra* note 8, at 437.

10. *Id.* at 437–39. Negligence and fault are, however, pertinent when determining reparations. *Id.*

11. *Report of the International Law Commission on the Work of its Twenty-Eighth Session,* U.N. GAOR, 28th Sess., Supp. No. 10, U.N. Doc. A/28/10 (1976), *reprinted in* 2 Y.B. Int'l L. Comm'n 95, U.N. Doc. A/CN.4/SER.A/1976/Add.1 (pt. 2) (1976).

12. In fear of possible liability for environmental harm from their own activities, no state is leading the charge to impose international liability. For example, following the Chernobyl accident, one might have expected states such as Sweden to bring a case against the U.S.S.R. at the International Court of Justice for damage suffered within their state. In reality, no such case was brought. This suggests Sweden is concerned that it too could be subject to third party claims, such as those resulting from acid rain pollution damage.

13. Jutta Brunnée, *The Responsibility of States for Environmental Harm in a Multinational Context—Problems and Trends,* 34 Les Cahiers de Droit [C. de D.] 827, 845 n.96 (citing A. Rest, *New Tendencies in Environmental Liability/Responsibility Law,* 21 envtl. Pol'y & L. 135 [1991] [supporting the adoption of instruments of legal responsibility and liability]).

14. In other words, the Commission will focus first on preventive measures in respect of activities creating a substantial risk of harm, and then on remedial measures after harm has occurred. The goal is to create, in this manner, agreement in the Commission on basic elements of its work on the topic.

15. It remains to be seen whether this procedure will enable the Commission to free itself of the difficulties it has faced. If so, the Commission may be able to focus on various approaches, including insurance schemes of the type contained in the International Convention on Civil Liability for Oil Pollution Damage and the 1971 International Convention on the Establishment of an International Fund for Compensation for Oil Pollution Damage. These instruments reflect a market-oriented socialization of the risk with regard to one class of undeniably useful, indeed essential, activities known to be ultrahazardous in terms of their potential damage.

16. David Freestone, *The Precautionary Principle,* in International law and Climate change 21, 30 (Robin Churchill & David Freestone eds., 1991).

17. The *opinio juris communis,* or expression of a legal obligation, relates to a nation's perception of its duties. Proof of obligation can be found in decisions of national courts, and in statements by leaders and jurists as to the legal effect of a declaration, etc.

18. Deterrence theory posits that a change in behavior will occur when the threatened consequences of an act become too painful or expensive, and when it is clear that such consequences will occur. Deterrence works only if the consequences are sufficiently unpleasant.

19. The "last in time rule" provides that in the case of a direct conflict between a treaty and a federal statute, the last in time will prevail.

20. Alexandre C. Kiss, Survey of Current Developments in International environmental Law 23 (1976) (citing Rene J. Dupuy, *Droit déclaratoire dt Droit Programmatoire: de la Coutume Sauvage à la Soft Law, in* l'élaboration Du Droit International Public 132 (1975)). See also Christine M. Chinkin, *The Challenge of Soft Law: Development and Change in International Law,* 38 Int'l & Comp. L.Q. 850 (1989); Panel, *A Hard Look at Soft Law,* 82 Proc. Am. Soc'y Int'l L. 317 (1988).

21. David J. Bederman, *The Antarctic and Southern Ocean Coalition's Convention on Antarctic Conservation,* 4 Geo. Int'l Envtl. L. Re. 47, 47 (1991).

22. Bederman, *supra* note 21, at 49.

23. *See* Brian D. Smith, State Responsibility and the Marine Environment: the rules of Decision (1988), at 89.

24. Jutta Brunnée, Acid Rain and Ozone Layer Depletion: International Law and Regulation (1986). at 113 (citing Lothar Gündling, *Verantwortlichkeit der Staaten für grezüberschreitende Umweltbeeintäctigungen,* 45 Zeitschrift Fur Auslandisches Offentliches Recht und Volkerrecht [Zaörv] 265, 273 [1985]).

PART 2.4

International Law
as Normative System:
Managing the Commons

21

Looking Back to See Ahead: UNCLOS III and Lessons for Global Commons Law

CHRISTOPHER C. JOYNER AND ELIZABETH MARTELL

IN DECEMBER 1973 THE PREPARATORY CONFERENCE FOR THE THIRD UNITED Nations Conference on the Law of the Sea (UNCLOS III) convened in New York. Representatives from 150 states were in attendance as the Conference was charged by the United Nations General Assembly with preparing a comprehensive international agreement on the law of the sea, by consensus if possible.

On December 10, 1982, after nearly 9 years, the product of 11 substantive UNCLOS III sessions—a treaty of some 200 single-spaced pages, consisting of 17 parts with 320 articles and 9 annexes—was opened for signature in Montego Bay, Jamaica.[1] UNCLOS III negotiations formally came to a close with a new instrument for governing the world's oceans proffered for legal adoption by the international community. Yet while 117 states became signatories to the new 1982 Convention on that December day, many other governments continued to harbor real frustration and dissatisfaction with the final legal product. Included among those disgruntled governments were several of the most important international maritime actors, including the United States, the United Kingdom, Italy, and the Federal Republic of Germany.

The UNCLOS III experience has been aptly described as "the largest, most technically complex, continuous negotiation attempted in modern times."[2] The Conference was negotiated on the basis of consensus, as a package deal, with the understanding by participants that such an approach required that no reservations to the final treaty be permitted. Appreciating this, several aspects of the 1982 United Nations Convention on the Law of the Sea (1982 Convention) have already entered into customary international law. It also is true that the treaty itself entered into force in late

1994 with the requisite 60 ratifications deposited. Nevertheless, the Convention did not embody a wholly successful outcome. In retrospect, the 1982 Convention fell victim to a North-South, developed-developing world ideological schism that detracted from the participating governments' ability to make it universally accepted conventional law. Certain political and economic residues of that schism remain to complicate the implementation of contemporary ocean law.

This article examines precedents for making future international global commons law that can be derived from the experience of the UNCLOS III negotiations and their progeny, the 1982 Convention. To this end, the following section undertakes a brief historical review of UNCLOS III. In so doing, those provisions in the Convention deemed offensive to the developed world are analyzed. The next section, "Lessons for Future Commons Law Negotiations," appraises the status of the law of the sea today, in light of the promulgation of the 1994 Implementation Agreement.[3] In particular, an assessment is made to determine if consensus exists among governments on whether the seas are properly deemed *res nullius* or *res communis*. Further, a comparison is made of the intent of the UNCLOS III participants regarding the customary international legal effects of the Convention's provisions with the current understanding and application of those provisions, especially the concept of the exclusive economic zone (EEZ).

Lessons that have applicability for the creation of future commons law creation can clearly be drawn from the UNCLOS III negotiations. In the section, "Rethinking Approaches to Commons Law Negotiations," a number of important lessons are presented, as are several options that might be contemplated by states in negotiating future commons law. Clearly, the consensus method used to formulate the 1982 Convention is not the only means available to states, and it remains arguable whether the global conference is the most appropriate means to negotiate a treaty of such a sweeping, universal character.[4] In the conclusion, the query is posed as to whether a binding global commons regime can be negotiated by all states, accepted and ratified by all states, and then actually be made to fulfill its stipulated, multifaceted purpose. Admittedly, the conclusion may be hardheaded and even less than optimistic. Still, the UNCLOS III experience suggests cause for caution in this regard.

It is important at the outset to appreciate what is meant by the notion of a global commons area. A *global commons* is an area beyond the limits of national jurisdiction to which all peoples have free and open access. Such commons are generally meant to include the oceans, outer space, and Antarctica. In environmental policy, the "tragedy of the commons" is a much-repeated metaphor of what can happen when a common resource is overexploited by too many people.[5] The long-term result of a short-run strategy of overuse is exhaustion of the common area's resources, to the detriment of everyone. While the traditional accounting of the tragedy of the commons tells of herdsmen grazing their sheep on a village green, today the exploitation frequently is performed by large corporations and governments, with a critical component of the (over)exploitation of the global commons being technological. Until technology reaches a level where resources of the global commons areas can be profitably and easily exploited, such exploitation will remain limited. Harvesting marine living resources in this century exemplifies the point. Since the 1940s, technological developments have made it possible for ocean fisheries to be overharvested. Today, only a half-century later, the world's fisheries have been severely depleted. Whereas the living resources of the ocean were once viewed by Hugo Grotius as inexhaustible, in 1995 they are so threatened that a "usually quiet player on the world stage" may feel compelled to take unilateral and legally suspect action to protect stocks off its coasts, as the recent tension between Canada and Spain so dramatically illustrates.[6]

A vital element of the global commons problem is environmental. As long as the oceans are regarded as a commons, users have scant incentive to accept responsibility for their pollution or other degradation, or at most, will accept only a modicum of the costs imposed on the entire global community. The traditional view of Grotius held that the resources of the seas were inexhaustible. The oceans would remain forever free of being polluted in wholesale fashion since human activities could affect the seas to a limited degree.[7] This view held that the seas were so vast and so fluent, with such extraordinary remedial capabilities, that they could be used safely as a toilet for the world's wastes. Today, this view seems hopelessly naive. Again, the issue of marine pollution is inextricably linked with technological advances. Between 1964 and 1974, for example, the world commercial deadweight shipping tonnage doubled from 150 million tons to more than 308 million tons.[8] With increased maritime traffic came increased marine pollution.

The accepted legal definition of a commons area rests on the notion of *res communis,* that is, something belonging to all. During the UNCLOS III negotiations, the developing states endeavored to have the seas beyond the limits of national jurisdiction legally declared—in the 1967 phrase of Malta's representative to the United Nations, Arvid Pardo—the "common heritage of mankind."[9] This understanding of the concept of common heritage rests on *res communis* and refers to "an undivided asset to be shared by all nations irrespective of their technological capabilities and to be managed by the United Nations," rather than by any particular state.[10] Pardo's original conception of the high seas and deep seabed as the common heritage of mankind was intended to operationalize *res communis* for all of the world's people. The oceans and their bounty were to be shared by all, and everyone was to share in the benefits derived from use of the oceans.[11]

With regard to ocean resources, the legal notion of *res communis* is set against the concept of *res nullius,* which holds that things belonging to no one are available for appropriation by anyone capable of recovering them. The distinction here is important, simply because if the ocean belongs to all people and all people have the right to use the oceans, how could any particular person or state legally justify a special right of exploiting and consuming ocean resources for their own personal gain? If the oceans belong to all, how could only a few lawfully exploit and profit from marine resources? The conflict became drawn between contrary conceptions of ocean property rights and the technological ability to exploit resources of the seas.

The *res nullius* interpretation traditionally has been applied to high seas resources and it was this conception that the developed states applied to the seabed during the UNCLOS III negotiations. With regard to the deep seabed, the practical difficulties of obtaining effective occupation (particularly the requirement of establishing permanent settlement) make it highly unlikely that any one state could stake a sovereign claim to any portion of the ocean floor. Consequently, the debate over whether the ocean floor is legally *res nullius* versus *res communis* may have been overstated. Whichever precept applies in principle, developed states obviously retain a great advantage over the developing world in exploitation capacity, unless and until their technological and capital advantage is somehow offset. The distinction between *res communis* and *res nullius* as applied to the deep seabed proved to be irreconcilable at UNCLOS III. While developed states espoused laissez-faire, free-trade principles, Third World states denounced the fact that in the modern era, "open access meant equal access to the valuable resources of the commons in name only."[12] The philosophical lines had been drawn for a protracted ideological confrontation.

UNCLOS III Revisited

By the mid-1960s, when several governments began seriously discussing the possibility of a new conference to standardize sea law, the need for an updated convention had become clear. Although the first and second Geneva Conference meetings had taken place less than a decade earlier, they had proved ineffective in establishing a lasting, much less universal, regime for the oceans. The most pressing maritime issue seen by the two superpowers at the time was the threat to over 100 strategic straits posed by the proliferation of unilateral state claims to territorial seas and economic zones beyond the then accepted 3-mile territorial sea limit. The United States and the former Soviet Union both wanted to maintain the largest possible extent of high seas area as the first substantive session of UNCLOS III began in Caracas in June 1974.

For their part, the states of the developing world welcomed the opportunity to participate in negotiating a new law of the sea. Many of them had achieved independent status subsequent to UNCLOS I and II, and thus had been unable to exercise their sovereignty in fashioning ocean law during those earlier conferences.[13] Additionally, developing countries were driven by the ideological imperative during the mid-1970s of establishing a new international economic order (NIEO) that would address the perceived inequities inherent in the current global distribution of resources. As one authoritative commentator has observed, "Consistent with their criticism of the laissez-faire ideology of traditional international law, Third World countries challenged its corollary, the principle of the freedom of the seas, as developed by the more powerful and now technologically superior maritime states."[14] Even before the UNCLOS III negotiations began, the ideological clash had begun to take shape. This schism had been foreshadowed in 1970 by the split 62 in favor, 28 in opposition, with 28 abstentions vote in the UN General Assembly on Resolution 2574D, the so-called "Moratorium Resolution."[15] This resolution, which had aimed to forestall the national freedom of seabed mining pending establishment of an international regime, was opposed by major maritime powers and others as "the declaration of a mere 'paper majority.'"[16]

The agenda of UNCLOS III was impressive in legal scope and issue-area breadth. The scope of the items negotiated at the Conference is unprecedented in international negotiations, as it encompassed a variety of disparate themes—political, legal, economical, technological, informational, and military, among others. The agenda also revealed a split between the developed states, led by the United States and the former Soviet Union as global maritime powers, and the developing world. Initially the United States would have preferred only a limited review of ocean law issues, since its main interests involved expanded coastal state jurisdiction. By 1970, however, the United States had realized that the newly independent developing countries refused to consider the question of "creeping jurisdiction" in isolation from ocean resource issues. Consequently, the United States acceded to a comprehensive conference.[17] The capacity to set the agenda for international negotiations may well be an instrument of state power that developed nations can wield to ensure that their environmental concerns are addressed, as some observers have suggested.[18] In the case of UNCLOS III, however, that ability seems to have been wanting by the two superpowers, to their eventual regret.

A gentleman's agreement at the outset among participants decided that the negotiations at UNCLOS III should proceed on a consensus basis.[19] It was understood by the participants that all governments involved might well be obliged to sacrifice one goal in favor of gaining others. Indeed as Robert Friedheim has noted, "Both the United States and the Soviet Union recognized that under the basic consensus rule the treaty would have to be a package, and they would therefore have to offer trade-offs on issues of lesser salience to get favorable outcomes of issues of higher salience."[20] Thus the Convention was negotiated as a "package deal," with the stipulation in Article 309 that no reservations to the final draft would be permitted. While the issue linkages contained in the Convention served to enlarge the potential scope of the new regime for the seas,[21] the terms of the package were ambiguous. Many governments came to view the original package deal as being a trade-off of navigational rights for expanded coastal state jurisdiction. Others perceived the trade-off in more general terms, especially as navigational guarantees in exchange for access to resources.[22] These differing perceptions led to a breakdown in communications and eventually to diplomatic deadlock as the negotiations drew to a close in 1982.

It should be noted that in the corpus of international environmental law, UNCLOS III provides a somewhat unusual case owing to the actual degree of scientific certainty about its environmental provisions. Other negotiations designed to protect some aspect of the environment often have been compelled to operate under a cloud of uncertainty and without consensus in the scientific community about either the causes of or the optimal solutions to a recognized problem. In some cases, the very existence of a real environmental threat has been questioned.[23] Negotiations at UNCLOS III took place in a very different atmosphere, largely because the period between the late 1960s and the late 1970s was an era marked by several prominent disasters for the ocean environment, including the wrecks of the tankers *Torrey Canyon* in 1967 and *Amoco Cadiz* in 1978.[24] International attention became riveted on the fate of the oceans from man-made pollution. Yet while protection of the marine environment and the preservation of the ocean's living resources certainly are components of the 1982 Convention, and extensive ones at that,[25] the Convention does not endeavor to establish specific provisions aimed at protection. Rather, it relies on statements of general principles.[26] It directs states to enact national laws to protect the marine environment and its inhabitants from land- and sea-based sources of pollution,[27] as well as to establish and work within regional and global institutions, including the International Maritime Organization, to preserve the ocean environment.[28]

There was, of course, a considerable body of international environmental law dealing with conservation and pollution control already on the books. Yet the 1982 Convention itself is remarkably short on specifics, given the clarity about the issues involved. This lack of specifics likely reflects the suspicions and doubts in the North-South debate over the proper assignment of state responsibility for shouldering the costs of conservation: Should there be equal assignment of responsibility, or proportional assignment based on level of development?[29] While a deliberately ambiguous approach may be preferred by governments negotiating a treaty so as to ensure its acceptability by all participants, a convention that merely "invites states to be good citizens, but does not define what good citizenship means, beyond not polluting,"[30] leaves much to be desired in terms of policy implementation and its actual international enforcement.

Scientific uncertainty can undermine the chances for successfully negotiating an international environmental protection regime. Still, even absent the difficulty of having to deal with scientific uncertainty, the treaty product of UNCLOS III was compromised for other reasons. The final draft of the Convention was rejected largely on ideological grounds by the Reagan administration early in 1982, leaving other Conference delegates stunned and frustrated. After nearly a decade of negotiations, the desire to conclude the Conference was strong. Representatives of the Group of 77, while persistently adamant on seabed issues, had made compromises in the recent sessions and were not willing to make further concessions to the United States.[31] The Conference concluded without agreement to its composite negotiated product by the most visible and important global maritime actor, the United States.

Although the United States had entered into the UNCLOS III negotiations with the preeminent goals of securing navigational freedom and straits passage for its military and commercial ships—goals which were realized in the language of the 1982 Convention—the entire package was jettisoned by the United States because of Part XI, which concerned deep seabed mining. Mining resources of the deep seabed initially had not been a major objective for the United States in the negotiations, and in fact both the U.S. Navy and the Department of Defense had entered the negotiations with a willingness to compromise on other aspects of sea law in order to obtain navigational security. Indeed, these departments had "preferred linkage because it appeared to permit trading other issues for assurances of free access for military forces."[32] By 1982, however, ideological forces had coalesced in the new administration to sink the agreement. In a real sense, a more fervent, committed kind of conservative political ideology had risen to power with the Reagan administration. It affected every issue of domestic and foreign policy, and the law of the sea proved no exception.[33]

The North-South debate first hinted at in the 1969 General Assembly vote on the Moratorium Resolution had now grown into an ideological impasse. Under the leadership of the Group of 77, land-based producers of the minerals found in the polymetallic nodules of the sea—most of them from developing countries—joined with other Third World states against prospective deep seabed mining states, particularly the United States. On April 30, 1982, the first, only, and final vote on the Convention was taken, with 130 states in favor, 4 opposed, and 17 abstaining.[34] As one analyst tersely put it, "The end of UNCLOS could hardly be called its finest hour."[35] The treaty for the law of the sea had been consummated, at a cost of turning off participation by most Western states.

The ideological confrontation thus had been joined. There were on the one hand the Western industrialized states, led by the United States, who advocated private, free-enterprise capitalism. For them, the deep seabed retained its traditional legal status of being *terra nullius*. On the other hand, there were the developing countries in the Group of 77, who wanted an international authority to manage and regulate deep seabed mining. For this group the seabed was the common heritage of mankind, the resources of which should be exploited, with derived revenues being distributed to poor, needy governments.

The unanimous 1970 Declaration of Principles (G.A. Resolution 2749) and the eventual law of the sea instrument confirmed that the seabed beyond the limits of national jurisdiction is not a *res nullius*. The Declaration of Principles also affirmed that it has become an unchallengeable principle of international ocean law that this area cannot be appropriated unilaterally. This fiat is explicitly set out and secured by Article 137 of the 1982 Convention.[36] The question, of course, turns on allocation of the resources of the seabed. Today the sea, "including the surface of the water, the water column, the seabed, and all minerals and organisms found therein, is regarded as a juridical unity, subject to a single constitutive regime governing its use, a view supported by traditional jurisprudence as well as by the language of the 1958 and 1982 conventions."[37] The clear conclusion suggests that if the oceans are viewed as *res communis*—something held in common by all—then it follows that legal restrictions on the exploitation of exhaustible resources are mandated. The key question then is whether these restrictions apply to third parties outside the juridical obligations of the 1982 Convention.

Before the 1994 Implementation Agreement was produced, a debate arose over whether the 1982 Convention constituted an "objective regime" that would have applicability to third parties. One argument went that since the United States had participated in the UNCLOS III negotiations with the acknowledged recognition that the end product would be a package deal, that government was bound by the principle of estoppel. The United States and its allies "implicitly represented to other States that they would accept Part XI along with the other new rules in the Convention, or they would forego these rules entirely."[38] Since other governments had made concessions in their interests based on this assumption, the United States and its allies should be estopped from rejecting Part XI while accepting the other sections of the treaty. Nonetheless, referring to Article 35 of the Vienna Convention, which affirms that treaties require consent to be binding, some observers have suggested that until a treaty is ratified by the "specially affected states," it cannot be said to "constitute a binding customary regime."[39] With particular regard to ocean law,

> |w|hile UNCLOS, in many respects, represents a codification of prior cus-
> tomary international law, and in some cases, a progressive development
> now probably on its way to establishing new customary norms [including
> the concept of the exclusive economic zone], this cannot be said of
> UNCLOS' seabed regime.[40]

Thus strong support surfaced for the U.S. contention that while many aspects
of the 1982 Convention might be exercised as customary international law,
such was not the case with respect to the deep seabed mining regime. The law
of the sea in the Convention was clearly customary and universally applicable. The law of the seabed was new, untested, and nascent in state practice.

On the other hand, the *res communis* principle might be viewed as a
peremptory norm, as defined under Article 53 of the Vienna Convention.[41]
This situation would suggest that the Convention did indeed establish an
objective regime for the seabed that would be binding on the United States,
even without its consent. As James Morell opined, "The nonappropriation
element of the *res communis* principle—mandatory in nature regardless of
whether an ocean use is exhaustible or not, although some exclusive rights
of use may be allocated under an international regulatory regime in the former case—is thus a true peremptory norm."[42] The implication here is that,
because manganese nodules are an exhaustible resource found in an area
designated *res communis,* they should be properly governed under a multilateral regulatory regime. Consequently the proposed establishment of an
alternative competitive mining regime would contravene the status of *res
communis,* and thus violate the peremptory norm.[43]

In any event, shortly after the Convention was opened for signature in
December 1982, several of its aspects already were deemed reflective of
customary international law, including the innovative concept of the EEZ
contained in Part V of the Convention.[44] The *travaux preparatoire* for the
1982 Convention suggest that this interpretation runs contrary to what the
negotiators had intended.[45] Indeed when the U.S. intention not to sign the
Convention became known, the president of UNCLOS III, Tommy Koh,
insisted that the Convention was an integral package and that "it is not possible for a State to pick what it likes and to disregard what it does not
like."[46] Even so, as one legal scholar has noted, "[T]here is actual evidence
supporting the view that the 'package deal' argument will not carry great
weight before an international tribunal."[47] By way of example, in both the
Tunisia/Libya and *Malta/Libya* cases,[48] the International Court of Justice
accepted that the EEZ exists as customary law quite apart from the EEZ
regime that was created in Part V of the 1982 Convention. This probably
was attributable in large part to the broad acceptance of 200-nautical-mile
fishery and conservation zones implemented by many coastal states during
the 1970s, before the EEZ had become accepted as a legal construct.

Lessons for Future Commons Law Negotiations

A number of lessons that may supply insight into the most effective ways and means to negotiate global commons regimes can be realized from the UNCLOS III experience. These lessons also suggest where problems may be confronted and how opportunities may be seized in the course of future commons negotiations.

1. To be successful, agreements cannot exclude specially affected states. Article 34 of the Vienna Convention on the Law of Treaties asserts that "a treaty does not create either obligations or rights for a third State without its consent."[49] Accordingly, to achieve their intended purposes, commons law agreements cannot exclude specially affected states (i.e., those governments that have particular national stakes in the treaty's purpose and effects). That the 1994 Implementation Agreement to the 1982 Convention was felt necessary substantiates this realization. This addendum was negotiated to permit United States participation basically on its own terms, by eliminating or negating the offensive provisions of Part XI.[50] Only decisions that take into consideration the interests of those states particularly affected by the treaty are likely to generate sound and acceptable norms of behavior. As one authoritative commentator put it, "Decisions that emerge largely from the rhetorical imperatives of multilateral bodies or national ideologies are likely to produce fustian and divergent practices."[51] This is no doubt true. The latter sort of decision appears more likely to emerge when a large multilateral conference convenes and "creates a temptation to regard the assembled participants as representatives of all mankind dispatched to enunciate global community policy on its behalf. . . . The result is a rhetorical pressure to cast issues in terms of community values."[52] Such self-imposed global responsibility expands the realm of states that conceivably could be "specially affected"—at least in a philosophical sense—by a commons agreement.

Whether a state is specially affected by an international agreement largely becomes a matter of self-definition. The most important considerations in the law of the sea, from the early vantage point of the United States, were those that dealt with navigational freedom and straits passage. As the UNCLOS III negotiations continued, however, the U.S. delegation reformulated its hierarchy of national interests until the issue of deep seabed mining took on greater salience. While the seabed mining companies themselves clearly had an interest in negotiating a favorable convention, most outside observers disagreed with the Reagan administration's perception of the balance of U.S. interests.[53] Of course, such observers were not making U.S. foreign policy decisions. While many scholars may question and disagree with the U.S. government's own notions of its interest hierarchy, self-perception by the decision-makers of a special interest remains the most important factor.[54]

This lesson, if carefully applied to future commons law negotiations, may result in fewer binding treaties being presented for signature. It may also foster an increase in the number of nonbinding statements of principle or similar documents that permit a specially affected state to put on a show of support for the effort while not committing itself to be bound by the terms of the agreement. For example, at the United Nations Conference on Environment and Development (UNCED) in Rio de Janeiro in 1992, the negotiations did not produce a treaty on deforestation but rather a statement of principles on forestry issues.[55] This reflected the reluctance of the major affected states, particularly Indonesia, Malaysia, and Brazil, to accept a binding treaty with any restrictive substance. Yet UNCLOS III also illustrated the potential liability that comes with the exclusion of such states, particularly when specially affected states are also the ones that would bear substantial costs of the regime. In April 1982, those governments that abstained or voted against the draft law of the sea convention contributed some 60% of the total United Nations budget,[56] an economic consideration that cannot be ignored.

2. *Issue linkage may improve the chances of success if used judiciously, but it can backfire.* The 1982 Convention was, of course, negotiated as a "package deal." Evidence emerges from the UNCLOS experience that issue linkage can work as a sound negotiating strategy to expand the zone of agreement for participants.[57] Elliott Richardson, the U.S. representative to UNCLOS III during the Carter administration, agrees and put it neatly: "Where a country is asked to do more or give up more than its self-interest would warrant, it must be offered positive incentives to sacrifice for the larger good."[58] That suggestion seems quite reasonable, especially if the country is also a state specially affected by the agreement.

The difficulties involved in negotiating the 1982 ocean law instrument suggest, however, that it may not be an ideal paradigm to use for all other environmental negotiations. With regard to establishing a climate change convention, for example, the UNCLOS III negotiations model appeared to suggest that the political, economic, and diplomatic costs of covering all aspects of climate change in one agreement far exceeded the benefits of the comprehensiveness obtained.[59] It was the very comprehensiveness of the 1982 Convention that ultimately eroded its support. This realization has prompted the conclusion that the elimination of issues may serve as a means to preserve and strengthen negotiating blocs.[60] This, of course, is the principal intent and design of the 1994 Implementation Agreement: to remove the objectionable seabed mining portions of the Convention so that the rest of the instrument could be considered and implemented on its own considerable merits.

Another suggestion on the question of issue linkage and delinkage might be to increase the incentive structure for parties. Instead of subtracting issues that could undermine a comprehensive convention, the provision of greater economic incentives by one side could thereby encourage the other side to accept the treaty or at least make constructive compromises. Such incentives might include linking loans to environmental protection, or establishing environmental assistance programs, or pursuing debt-for-nature swaps.[61] Such linkages could be established on a bilateral or multilateral basis and integrated into the formal provisions of the agreement.

When the United States walked away from the 1982 Convention, the Third World was in no mood to renegotiate the sensitive terms of the treaty. It appeared as though the United States had attempted to use a shake-down tactic rather than a linkage tactic. Whereas the latter is a quid pro quo approach and should produce a mutual advantage, the former is "one-sided extortion by means of threats,"[62] with the express intent of producing a winner at the expense of the other side. Since the United States recognized that its status as a specially affected state would undermine the establishment of an effective, universal regime for the seas if it did not participate, the Reagan administration sought to use that leverage to gain concessions from the developing states majority. It is possible that the incoming U.S. negotiators in the Reagan administration were not aware that other governments were weary of negotiating and thus they miscalculated the degree to which further concessions might be wrung. It also is possible that the Reagan administration concluded that might makes right and the United States did not need a law of the sea treaty containing an internationally socialistic seabed mining regime. Though plainly a cynical view, that is the impression left by the administration's ultimate legal attitude and policy position.

The basic lesson is that a bird in the hand is probably worth two in the bush. Pressing issue linkage too hard and too far can lead to mutual loss. As one commentator on negotiations has observed,

> There is a risk that constantly pushing to find additional value through linkages can create a climate that Roger Fisher describes as a "stingy bargaining environment"—in which each side always holds out for more, even after satisfying their fundamental interests. This stance can become self-defeating if the parties turn down "good" agreements that they actually have in hand in favor of theoretically superior outcomes.[63]

The lesson is that, at a certain point, governments must recognize that they have gained all that can be won from issue linkage. This realization, of course, is a subjective calculation. Accordingly, since governments frequently fail to act as fully rational actors and misperceptions by policymakers can happen, miscalculations are bound to occur. The fact that so many commentators feel that the United States should have accepted the 1982 Convention supports the conclusion that the Reagan administration miscalculated the extent to which other states were willing to exchange further concessions for U.S. participation.

3. The consensus approach to negotiation tends to expand the time and effort required to reach a successful agreement. The consensus approach to negotiations recognizes the sovereign equality of states and, in theory, that collective choice can be a useful means to achieve a positive sum outcome without the alienation and divisiveness that come with casting votes to formally declare positions. An agreement based on consensus also may acquire special status as being reflective of customary law. While the UNCLOS III negotiations proceeded on a consensus basis for nearly 9 years, in April 1982 the United States forced a vote on the acceptability of the Convention text. This act reflected the fundamental understanding by the U.S. government that an international agreement reached by consensus carries relatively greater weight in creating customary international law than an agreement that proceeds according to a majority-rule procedure.[64] When a formal opportunity is presented for "objectors" to officially assert their view, the case is made for those governments to elude being legally bound to an international agreement without their consent.

At the same time, consensus decision making attributes disproportional influence to critics and can be very costly in time and effort.[65] The consensus approach allows all participants to share a voice in the final product of the negotiations. This means that in formulating a global ocean regime, the disparate interests of nearly 160 states had to be taken into consideration. Clearly these 160 states did not share a common agenda, a fact attributable to conflicting ideological, political, and economic interests. The dilemma for all international negotiations is that in most cases, as it was at UNCLOS III, some issues are of particular importance to all states, which reduces the possibility for compromise and increases the complexity of the process. As one authority on ocean law and policy observed, "On any issue of importance, no state [is] willing to be excluded from a negotiation or to allow its interests to be represented by others."[66] Governments cannot be condemned for exercising caution when confronted with a possible loss of their sovereignty. Still the result of such a sentiment is an increase in the effort, patience, and time required to reach an agreeable consensus outcome.

4. Protracted, drawn-out negotiations risk being overtaken by technological and political changes. When negotiations are conducted over a prolonged period of time, they may be outstripped by technological and political changes in the international milieux. There are at least two elements to this impact of change. First, the problem of "foreseeability" of technological developments suggests that to remain relevant, international negotiations must be both timely and appropriate for the issue at hand. Because the pace of technological developments is so rapid today, it is understandable why the Group of 77 countries were acutely concerned that the potential bonanza of mineral riches on the seabed would be harvested before those developing governments were able to participate and share in that exploitation. Even so, the intensity of objections to the provisions in Part XI ultimately helped to undermine U.S. support for the entire Convention. James Sebenius pointed out that, "In the earlier days of the LOS negotiations the official view generally held that, in the absence of a treaty, navigational rights would erode and conflict would generally increase."[67] As negotiations continued, however, the United States elected a succession of new leaders until one took office who believed that there was a viable alternative to the Convention. That alternative did not include U.S. participation in the Convention, either as a party or even as a signatory.

On the other hand, technological or other circumstances that arise during the course of a negotiation or before it comes into force might make concluding an agreement easier. In the case of deep seabed mining, the United States has only limited economic and security interests, since both the demand for and prices of the nodular minerals have declined over the past decade. Thus at present the market does not appear likely to make deep seabed mining commercially viable before 2030, and in all probability, even much later than that." In theory this change in the international setting should have made the Convention more economically palatable to the United States by the early 1990s, even without the 1994 Implementation Agreement. The implementation instrument, however, supplied the legal guarantees necessary to protect U.S. interests in a future regime for mining the deep seabed, whenever that might occur.

5. *The ideological divide between the North and the South must be given due weight.* Since the 1982 Convention entered into force in late 1994, the concept of the common heritage of mankind has become fixed as a part of conventional international law. The association of the common heritage of mankind with the NIEO during the 1970s made it repulsive to many industrialized states, but its inclusion in the 1982 Convention was necessary to secure Third World cooperation. Similar compromises probably will be required in future international commons law negotiations and therefore must be anticipated. The fact remains, as Lawrence Susskind points out, that more than 2 decades after its formulation, the NIEO aspiration has not been fully abandoned by developing countries. Susskind logically believes that continued pressure on the North by the South to achieve the NIEO agenda could give the less developed world sufficient leverage to temper demands of the industrialized world.

> If the South makes meeting its earlier economic goals a quid pro quo for its willingness to participate in collective efforts to respond to environmental threats, all progress on the environmental front will come to a halt. If, however, the South's objectives can be linked strategically (perhaps *opportunistically* is a better word) with Northern efforts to achieve environmental protection and sustainable development, then the impetus for sustained global cooperation may finally be provided.[69]

This possibility suggests that the governments of the South can play their ideological trump card, but should do so only with due caution. While the industrialized governments of the North must recognize the needs and goals of their neighbors to the South, the Third World also has an obligation to be willing to compromise. Sustainable development must be a two-way street, if it is to work for the betterment of national economies and the protection and preservation of global commons areas.

6. *Since national interest and global equity open conflict, governments most consider the long-term consequences of their immediate actions.* This lesson is similar to the previous one, but it places the onus squarely on the developed world, which is the chief beneficiary of global inequity today. The text of the 1982 Convention is notable for its efforts to incorporate the notion of global equity into its provisions. For example, the treaty recognizes the needs of geographically disadvantaged and landlocked states. The Convention text in Part XI attempted to redress the balance of interests between the technologically advanced states and the less-developed world in the sea-bed mining regime, although it went too far in the view of the United States and other miners. The upshot, of course, was the Implementation Agreement 12 years later. Even so, its assertion that the deep seabed and its resources are the common heritage of mankind underscores the precept that "first-come, first-served" is not an acceptable principle of economic justice. Obtaining global equity implies genuine acknowledgment that a principal source of First World wealth was colonial or imperial exploitation, and that all peoples have the right to enjoy a certain, minimal standard of living, regardless of whether they live in Northern Europe or sub-Saharan Africa. A just international arrangement "nullifies the contingencies and biases of historical fate," in the words of philosopher John Rawls.[70] Instead of calling for the equitable distribution of resources yet to be exploited, as the 1982 Convention does, conceptions of global equity frequently mandate redistribution of resources today.[71] This is a debate that goes beyond the scope of this study, however, though it no doubt will impact heavily on future commons law negotiations.

In the future it is conceivable that sets of treaties may have to be considered simultaneously, or individual treaties might have to be placed in the context of a larger North-South global bargain. To a certain extent, this was the road taken to the Rio Summit in 1992. Negotiating such a bargain would require taking considerations of global equity into account. Hence the evolution of "sustainable development" as a critical component of a new global environment order. The key point in the fifth lesson above was that North and South must recognize each other's ideological agendas and be truly willing to compromise on certain points. The key point in the sixth lesson is that at times producing global equity may demand more concessions from the developed states than from the Third World. Yet because governments often view their national interests in utilitarian, zero-sum terms, it may be difficult for leaders to rally the political will necessary to transcend immediate goals and recognize a long-term interest in creating a global community based on principles of justice.[72] That is to be expected in an international system composed of sovereign states motivated by self-serving national interests.

An example from the Convention illustrates this point. Since the EEZ concept is customary international law today, it is fair to conclude that the United States benefited greatly in economic terms from the UNCLOS III process, without paying any economic or ideological costs that the Reagan administration associated with Part XI and the international regulation of deep seabed mining. In this case it is easy to recognize that certain economic benefits were obtained by an apparently inequitable policy. On the other hand, there were long-term costs incurred by the United States in terms of international political tension and ill will. These costs had come in relationships with the Third World, which had sought to use the UNCLOS III negotiations to redress global inequities, as well as with a number of Western allies, who might have gone along with the treaty absent U.S. pressure. Obviously, the long-term costs are less tangible and more difficult to empirically measure than are the economic gains reaped by the United States. They are costs nonetheless. When making international policy, leaders should define their national interests to take into account the costs incurred when global equity is undermined.

Rethinking Approaches to Commons Law Negotiations

Approaches to negotiating global environmental law for the commons fall into two categories. The first involves a comprehensive strategy that links several issue areas under one negotiating umbrella.[73] This view toward international environmental law is bolstered by the emerging understanding that ecosystems must be preserved as systems for environmental action to be optimally effective. Such a holistic approach also may help overcome the North-South problems discussed above. The incremental approach to crafting environmental regimes puts pieces of the ecological puzzle together, though not in either a uniform or unitary fashion. Problems are dealt with on an ad hoc basis. A comprehensive strategy would aim for an overarching relationship between North and South—one that could link together issues of process and substance through a comprehensive international negotiation. The second strategy instead takes a more piecemeal approach to negotiations. The philosophy behind this approach is that issue linkage may increase the benefits for all participants in a negotiation, but it also may undermine the possibility for consensus. The UNCLOS III negotiations illustrate the potential for difficulty and obstruction that may result from linking too many issues.

As one of some 200 sovereign actors, an individual state, even a large and influential one, often has little control over setting the agenda for international negotiations. This is illustrated well by the UNCLOS III process, where the unified South through the Group of 77 was able to include agenda items that the North would have preferred to leave out. Further, the forum for negotiations is also usually removed from the control of individual governments. In the early, prenegotiation stage of UNCLOS III, for example,

> many governments initiated studies on a large number of the ocean-use problems, many of which required more than unilateral acts for solution. In dealing with particular problems—fisheries, the continental shelf, pollution—shipping and naval rights analysts often recommended technically sound solutions which they hoped could be achieved unilaterally, bilaterally, or regionally. They recommended going to a universal conference only if unilateral, bilateral, or regional efforts had failed, or were likely to fail, and they preferred returning to a universal forum only if the issues could be grouped into "separate packets."[74]

All this notwithstanding, the developing countries seized the time and opportunity to convene a near-universal conference. The intimation here suggests that the selection of agenda items for consideration and the type of negotiating found to be used can be of critical importance in producing a successful outcome for parties.

As already mentioned, the opinions of specially affected states should be given due regard in the negotiations. One can compare the eagerness of states to gain control over the zones off their coasts with the relatively small number of states that perceived a direct interest in Part XI of the Convention. Where the negotiations focused on food, energy, and military issues, the assembled states were able to reach a near consensus. The fact that consensus broke down over polymetallic nodules implies that multilateral negotiations have greater chances for success when the immediate national stakes are both high and broadly distributed.[75] Recognizing the ideological basis of this breakdown in consensus, resort to issue-linkage could raise the stakes so high for all parties that abandoning negotiations will be seen as producing a net loss for both North and South. The likelihood is that future environmental treaties may well have to be tied to explicit pledges about aid flows, trade, and debt in ways unlike the past. Perhaps given the recent global acceptance of free market principles exemplified in the 1994 Implementation Agreement, ideological aversion to such linkages will wane in the developed world as states in the South learn to frame their demands in liberal, rather than socialist, terms.

At least five approaches are available for pursuing commons law negotiations and each has its own strengths and deficiencies. Each approach, or combinations of them, can provide strategies for negotiating international agreements affecting the oceans, outer space, or the Antarctic. Much obviously depends on the nature of the commons agreement, the particular governments involved, and the international circumstances affecting the negotiations.

1. Construct a framework convention, with provisions for additional protocols. One strategy involves negotiating a framework convention with the understanding that one or more additional related protocols eventually will be attached to it. In many instances, a piecemeal approach may make agreement more likely than would a comprehensive approach to the same agenda, such as the UNCLOS III strategy on the law of the sea. By breaking the general subject down into manageable pieces, the convention-cum-protocols strategy can sidestep the negative results of issue-linkages experienced in the course of the law of the sea negotiations. The more ambitious the goals are, the more issues upon which participating governments must reach agreement. A strategy designed to augment a framework agreement allows for more gradual, deliberate piece-by-piece commons law to evolve. In this manner, governments have more time to appreciate the legal and political merits in adding new measures later to the new regime.

The initial framework convention may be lacking in specifics. Still, it can become the first step in involving a government in the negotiating process on an important issue. Subsequently, a negotiating history among states may make future negotiations on the issue area more likely. In many cases the framework convention requires governments to demonstrate serious intent to participate in subsequent protocol arrangements in order to become a party to the general agreement. Even so, separate parts may be negotiated without any specific requirement to become party to all of them.[76]

The open-ended nature of this approach permits negotiators more flexibility in taking future developments into account. Such a strategy might have helped overcome the difficulties encountered with the seabed mining provisions of the 1982 Convention. While the Convention as a whole deals with contemporary marine activities, the seabed regime focuses with great specificity on future contingent activities. In such a case, a more suitable approach might have been to establish a framework regime. Later when serious interest in resource development surfaces, an international regulatory system could then be set up to manage any anticipated development. One example of an agreement that did use the framework convention-plus-protocols approach was the 1976 United Nations Environment Programme's (UNEP's) Regional Seas Convention, which has been followed in subsequent UNEP regional seas conventions.[77] Similarly the 1985 Vienna Convention for the Protection of the Ozone Layer set out a general framework for monitoring, exchanging information, and facilitating scientific research.[78] It was succeeded by the 1987 Montreal Protocol, a more detailed document that established a sophisticated regime for controlling chemical depletion of the ozone layer.[79]

2. *Encourage and improve international coordination of national plans.* International coordination of national conservation plans allows governments to retain a certain functional sovereignty over global commons environmental protection. Unlike the above-mentioned strategy of negotiating a framework convention plus protocols, under this coordination approach future protocols are not anticipated when the framework agreement is established. Instead states merely agree to establish their national plans within a structure of international oversight, perhaps complemented with an international monitoring component. This approach could be especially useful when governments agree on the need to deal with an environmental problem, but cannot reach agreement even on a vague framework convention calling for future protocols, or on who should bear how much of which burdens. Examples of such an approach being utilized include the 1992 Framework Convention on Climate Change[80] and the 1992 Convention on Biological Diversity.[81]

One element in the debate over the preservation of global commons areas and their resources turns on the issue of whether governments are more likely to adopt forward-looking, conscientious policies in zones that are formally recognized as falling under their exclusive jurisdiction, as opposed to the policies they adopt toward the commons areas. The establishment of the system of EEZs put under national jurisdiction and control the environmental management of a substantial portion of what in large part formerly had been high seas areas, as well as 90% of the world's fisheries. Depletion of fish stocks has continued apace, however, even though international agreements outside the 1982 Convention have been negotiated to curb unsustainable harvesting of stocks. Continued overfishing suggests that state governments have difficulty controlling the actions of their own nationals. It also indicates that such a loose arrangement that allows governments to set their own quotas (within "reasonable" limits or similar such language) may be too weak. While it is necessary to be cognizant of state sovereignty, if states are unwilling to take on the responsibility for implementing needed conservation measures, the commons environment ultimately will suffer. This realization suggests that incentives, perhaps through issue-linkages, might be sought to make reluctant states more amenable to agreeing to and upholding a more binding convention.

3. *Pursue regional arrangements.* Regional arrangements have been established to deal with many environmental issue areas, including fishing on the high seas,[82] outer space law,[83] and conservation in the Antarctic.[84] A regional approach could help to avoid cultural and ideological conflicts

that have emerged in the past when governments at different levels of economic development have met for discussions in an international forum. Regionalism might improve the chances for achieving a successful outcome to the negotiations. On the other hand, because levels of economic development of states within a geographical region tend to be similar, a regional approach to negotiating multilateral agreements also could solidify the schism of the world into haves and have-nots.

Resort to a regional arrangement might be more viable in situations where a global convention is perceived as being too unwieldy or too time-consuming to negotiate. In such a situation, "[r]ather than wait for universal consensus, groups of countries with analogous interests and capabilities may wish to pursue agreements among themselves,"[85] perhaps but not necessarily under the aegis of a framework treaty. Active involvement of the United States in the ocean law negotiations began in a regional setting, under the umbrella of the Organization of American States (OAS) in the 1940s. The United States was badly outnumbered in the OAS forum, however, and so shifted negotiations to the United Nations framework.[86] This strategy eventuated into the 1958 and 1960 Geneva Conferences on the Law of the Sea, then to the UNCLOS III experience, and ultimately the negotiations that led to promulgation of the 1994 Implementation Agreement.

4. Pursue a strictly unilateral approach. In certain circumstances, states might be better off if they opt to pursue an independent course of action rather than adhere to a wider convention or international regime. A government considering unilateral action may be in a situation where there is no international agreement to which it can become a party.[87] If there is in fact no global regime in a certain issue area, a unilateral approach might be the only option for a government that feels the need to take some constructive action and is unable to garner support for an international treaty on that issue. Paradoxically, a state can be punished for pursuing a unilateral approach to environmental protection if its action is seen to interfere with trade practices under the General Agreement on Tariffs and Trade (GATT).[88] Moreover even if the provisions of GATT are not at issue, a government pursuing an independent policy of environmental protection may find itself at a distinct economic disadvantage relative to less "green" states. A government also may be concerned that a subsequent international agreement will require further action without giving the proactive state credit for its previous environmental accomplishments.[89] Clearly, there are both costs and benefits for a government considering unilateral action when no international agreement exists for dealing with the environmental problem in question.

A government confronts different considerations when an international regime is already in place. A precedent now exists demonstrating the advantages of unilateral action in the UNCLOS III negotiations. The United States was able to reap the current benefits of its EEZ and continental shelf resources while avoiding the costs of acceding to Part XI of the Convention. In retrospect, this strategy appears successful since the 1994 Implementation Agreement substantially revised the offensive portions of the 1982 text to be more compatible with a free market economic philosophy. As one authority has tersely posited, "[R]ejection of the Convention by the United States reflects a belief that unilateralism is a viable policy alternative when backed by military force, the *res communis* principle and budget deficits notwithstanding."[90] The United States was fortunate and seems to have emerged relatively unharmed from its solo ocean law course throughout the past decade. It is not unreasonable to conclude, however, that pursuing a unilateral approach in place of participating in a complex international regime such as the Convention might well carry high costs, as many observers had predicted the United States would discover soon after its refusal to sign the agreement in 1982.[91]

While it might be possible for a government to establish bilateral and multilateral arrangements that obtain benefits or rights analogous to those contained in a broader agreement, without paying the legal costs of being obligated to that general agreement, certain political advantages and economic benefits may be lost in exchange for those rights. Moreover, the government acting unilaterally may encounter contrary states who are disinclined to grant such rights or who insist on asserting their own interpretation of that international law.[92] A government considering such a unilateral approach would have to conduct its own cost-benefit analysis to determine if the costs involved in participating in the regime truly outweigh the costs it would incur by taking a solo national approach. The fact remains that for any government, be it a maritime power or a geographically disadvantaged state, the fundamental problems of ocean law essentially are global, not national or regional. Sooner or later, law of the sea questions will have to be resolved on a global basis if maritime commerce and use of ocean resources are to proceed in a peaceful, stable international climate.

5. Pursue a parliamentary diplomacy approach. The last realization leads back to the negotiating strategy pursued at UNCLOS III, namely what Friedheim termed "parliamentary diplomacy."[93] Of course, there are certain problems of international relations that cannot be effectively resolved absent securing universal or near-universal consent among states. Although many environmental problems can be addressed on a regional or even a unilateral basis, the world's commons areas present a special case and often require a more comprehensive and global strategy.

A parliamentary diplomacy approach works by consensus based on the sovereign equality of all states. It also assumes that outcomes can be bargained, which will increase the benefits for all participants; that is, outcomes of parliamentary diplomacy are not zero-sum. To increase their bargaining power, states with common interests often join together and create the opportunity for shaping "complementary (overlapping) and contradictory interests (cross-cutting cleavages)."[94] Given the complexity associated with large-scale, multilateral conferences that adopt a universal approach, parliamentary diplomacy frequently involves the use of a package deal—a trade-off strategy that simplifies the process of achieving consensus on key issues without adopting a majority-rule procedure,[95] as seen in UNCLOS III. Consensus permits obtaining agreement without having to vote on an issue, an act that inevitably casts a formal split between parties in a negotiation.

The high issue-density of establishing a comprehensive maritime regime revealed to governments that a universal approach was necessary to avoid uneven participation in the ocean regime as evinced after the first two UNCLOS meetings. The failure to reach universal agreement on the final text of the 1982 Convention strongly suggested that a convention on global climate change would be better pursued by using another approach. The parliamentary diplomacy approach appears most successful when governments are formulating new law, since an extensive body of existing law frequently can complicate the process of codifying norms in one document.

Conclusion

In the absence of a universally accepted regime for the oceans, governments are forced to conclude limited bilateral and multilateral agreements or to act unilaterally to achieve their national interests. For example, in lieu of the protections offered by the Convention, the United States adopted the Freedom of Navigation Program in 1979 to globally protect navigational rights. The program

> combines diplomatic action and the operational assertion of navigational rights. [It] emphasizes the use of naval exercises to discourage state claims inconsistent with customary international law, as reflected in the Convention, and to demonstrate the U.S. resolve to protect navigational freedoms proclaimed in that agreement.[96]

Given what is currently known about the costs and benefits accrued from seabed mining, pursuing such a unilateral strategy now seems to involve substantial military, financial, and political costs in return for minimal economic benefits. Further in an era of diminishing naval strength, "the United States is confronted with increasingly diverse claims to sovereignty over ocean areas by coastal and island states, claims that are inconsistent with the terms of the 1982 Convention."[97] These claims are asserted by a diverse collection of states and pertain to a wide assortment of maritime issues, affecting all regimes of the oceans.

It remains arguable whether the current proliferation of unilateral claims is comparable to the cacophony of claims asserted during the period between the World War II and the 1960s. In this regard the 1982 Convention has stabilized ocean law, even without universal ratification. It also is probably true that had the Convention been more widely accepted in 1982, the costs confronting the United States today in protecting its freedom of navigation would be much lower. The United States chose to reject the Convention out of a belief that the most important provisions already were customary law. This assumption is being challenged today.

As a maritime superpower, the United States, and all states for that matter, benefit most when ocean law is stable and regular. Widespread ratification of the 1982 Convention undoubtedly will increase order and predictability by facilitating international adaptability to new circumstances, fostering accommodation of interests among states, narrowing the scope of maritime disputes to more manageable proportions, and providing the ways and means to resolve these disputes. If not binding on all states, the influence of the 1982 Convention will be gravely weakened and the U.S. interest in order and stability will be undermined. The Convention is a framework agreement for ocean law. If governments are unwilling to participate even within that general framework, the prospects for cooperation on narrow issue-areas would seem to be diminished.

The basic question that must be addressed is whether a global commons regime can be negotiated, accepted by all or most states, and then actually be made to fulfill its agenda. There are tools that can be used to facilitate negotiation of such an agreement, such as the resort to linking and subtracting issues. The fact that commons areas are best governed by a regime in which all states participate is obvious. It is equally true that environmental issues are best dealt with systemically, by recognizing the complexity and interdependence of the web of life in a particular ecosystem. The dilemma turns on reconciling the need for universal participation by states with conflicting interests. It also comes down to satisfactorily resolving the vast array of issues that must be considered in concluding such a regime.

While each case obviously is different, a spate of environmental treaties has been promulgated in recent years that reveals a clear trend. Transboundary air pollution, acid rain, biological diversity, transboundary movement and disposal of hazardous wastes, global warming, protection of wetlands, conservation of species, ozone depletion, and many other environmental issues have been addressed through special international agreements. A progressive attitude has evolved stemming from a steep learning curve in the international community, which seems to suggest great promise for future negotiations on global commons issues. If governments can incorporate the lessons of UNCLOS III into their negotiating strategies, and then prudently employ those strategies to keep international law genuinely applicable to managing the commons areas, that optimism may prove to be warranted.

Notes

1. *The Law of the Sea: United Nations Convention on the Law of the Sea with Index and Final Act of the Third United Nations Conference on the Law of the Sea* (New York: United Nations, 1983), [hereinafter cited as 1982 Convention]

2. Robert L. Friedheim, *Negotiating the New Ocean Regime* (Columbia, SC: University of South Carolina Press, 1993), 5.

3. G.A. Res. 48/263 (July 28, 1994), Agreement relating to the Implementation of Part XI of the United Nations Convention on the Law of the Sea of 10 December 1982.

4. The meaning of "appropriate" in this context simply refers to the likelihood of a successful outcome (i.e., the promulgation of a widely ratified international legal instrument).

5. See Garrett Hardin, "The Tragedy of the Commons," *Science* 162 (Dec. 13. 1968), 1243–1248.

6. Anne Swardson, "Canada, EU Reach Agreement Aimed at Ending Fishing War," *Washington Post,* April 16, 1995, A21.

7. Friedheim, *Negotiating the New Ocean Regime,* 14.

8. United Nations Department of Public Information, *A Quiet Revolution: United Nations Convention on the Law of the Sea* (New York: United Nations, 1984). 34.

9. See U.N. GAOR 22d Sess., U.N. Doc. A/6695 (17 August 1967). Pardo suggested that the General Assembly should internationalize the seabed beyond a narrow territorial sea by either reinterpreting or amending the 1958 Continental Shelf Convention, and that this international seabed should be placed under international management.

10. Robert L. Bledsoe and Boleslaw A. Boczek, *The International Law Dictionary* (Santa Barbara: ABC-Clio, 1987), 189.

11. See Arvid Pardo, "Who Will Control the Seabed?," *Foreign Affairs* 47 (1968), 123–137.

12. Friedheim, *Negotiating the New Ocean Regime,* 17.

13. See, e.g., United Nations. *A Quiet Revolution,* 4, 6.

14. Boleslaw Boczek, "Ideology and the New Law of the Sea," *Boston College International and Comparative Law Review* 7 (1984), 10.

15. U.N.G.A. Res. 2j74 (XXV), text reprinted in 9 I.L.M. 419–423 (1970).

16. Dennis W. Arrow, "Seabeds, Sovereignty, and Objective Regimes," *Fordham International Law Journal* 7 (1984). 169. 179.

17. Markus Schmidt, *Common Heritage or Common Burden?* (Oxford: Clarendon Press, 1989). 43.

18. See Andrew Hurrell and Benedict Kingsbury, "Introduction," in Andrew Hurrell and Benedict Kingsbury, eds., *The International Politics of the Environment* (Oxford: Clarendon Press, 1992), 37.

19. "Declaration Incorporating the 'Gentleman's Agreement' made by the President and Endorsed by the Conference at its 19th Meeting on 27 June 1974," in Rules of Procedure, U.N. Doc. A/Conf. 62/36 (July 2. 1974), Appendix.

20. Friedheim, *Negotiating the New Ocean Regime*, 33.

21. See Lawrence Susskind, *Environmental Diplomacy: Negotiating More Effective International Agreements* (New York: Oxford University Press, 1993), 87.

22. Schmidt, *Common Heritage or Common Burden?*, 29.

23. For example, Wilfred Beckerman argued that "according to the latest scientific consensus, such as it is, the damage done by the predicted climate change will be nothing like as great as is widely believed and certainly not the inevitable global catastrophe scenario hawked around. . . . There is plenty of time to think and to weigh up the costs and benefits of alternative courses of action." "Global Warming and International Action: An Economic Perspective," in Hurrell and Kingsbury, *International Politics of the Environment*, 288. Compare another article from the same volume: "If it is important to prevent climate change, it is important to begin now." The article offered several approaches to negotiating an agreement and suggests essential elements to the eventual treaty. Elliot L. Richardson, "Climate Change: Problems of Law Making," in ibid., 170.

24. United Nations, *A Quiet Revolution*, 3.

25. See 1982 LOS Convention, arts. 192–237.

26. 1982 Convention, art. 194(1), for example, illustrates the point. While asserting that states "shall" take action, the passage is quite general in describing what states "shall" actually do, leaving the specific obligations of states wide open to interpretation.

27. For example, 1982 Convention, arts. 207–212.

28. For example, 1982 Convention, arts. 197, 200, 202, 207–212.

29. Friedheim, *Negotiating the New Ocean Regime*, 181.

30. Ibid., 183.

31. Ibid., 39.

32. Joseph S. Nye, Jr., "Political Lessons of the New Law of the Sea Regime," in Bernard H. Oxman, et al., eds., *Law of the Sea: U.S. Policy Dilemma* (San Francisco: Institute for Contemporary Studies, 1983), 115.

33. Schmidt, *Common Heritage or Common Burden?*, 259.

34. The four votes in opposition were cast by Israel, Turkey, the United States, and Venezuela. The abstentions came from Western European states and the Soviet Eastern European bloc.

35. Schmidt, *Common Heritage or Common Burden?*, 254.

36. 1982 Convention, art. 137.

37. James B. Morell, *The Law of the Sea: An Historical Analysis of the 1981 Treaty and Its Rejection by the United States* (Jefferson, N.C.: McFarland & Co., Inc., 1992), 175.

38. Stephen Vasciannie, "Part XI of the Law of the Sea Convention and Third States: Some General Observations," *Cambridge Law Journal* 48 (March 1989), 1, 97.

39. Arrow, "Seabeds, Sovereignty, and Objective Regimes," 215.

40. Ibid., 226.

41. Vienna Convention on the Law of Treaties, May 23, 1969, U.N. Doc. A/CONF.39/27, reprinted in 8 I.L.M. (1969). See Morell, *The Law of the Sea Convention*, 183.

42. Morell, *The Law of the Sea Convention*, 185.

43. Ibid., 189.

44. As Bernard Oxman, a former vice-chairman of the U.S. Delegation to the Conference, stated in 1983, "Except perhaps for the provisions on deep seabed mining and the settlement of disputes, the stipulations of the convention are already regarded by some government and private experts as generally authoritative statements

of existing customary international law applicable to all states." Bernard Oxman, "Summary of the Law of the Sea Convention," in Oxman, et al., *Law of the Sea,* 148.

45. See Vasciannie, "Part XI of the LOS Convention," 94 (at note 43) for examples.

46. Quoted in James K. Sebenius, *Negotiating The Law of the Sea* (Cambridge: Harvard University Press. 1984), 93.

47. Vasciannie, "Part XI of the LOS Convention," 95. See also Schmidt, *Common Heritage or Common Burden?,* 12.

48. *Case Concerning the Continental Shelf (Tunisia/Libyan Arab Jamahiriya)* 1982, reprinted in 21 I.L.M. 225 (1982) and *Case Concerning The Continental Shelf (Libyan Arab Jamahiriya v. Malta),* 1985, reprinted in 24 I.L.M. 1189 (1985).

49. Vienna Convention. art. 34.

50. See Christopher C. Joyner. "The United States and the New Law of the Sea," *Ocean Development and International Law,* 27 (1996), pp. 41–58.

51. Bernard Oxman, "The Two Conferences," in Oxman, et al., *Law of the Sea,* 140.

52. Ibid., 134.

53. Ken Booth, Law, Force and Diplomacy at Sea (London: George Allen & Unwin, 1985). 29.

54. See "Statement by Expert Panel: Deep Seabed Mining and the 1982 Convention on the Law of the Sea," *American Journal of International Law* 82 (1988), 367, which concluded that, *"[T]he United States has limited economic and security interests in deep seabed mining.* But the United States shares the compelling interests in all states in achieving universal agreement on a comprehensive law of the sea, which requires agreement also on a regime for the deep seabed." (authors' emphasis). Compare with Sebenius, *Negotiating the Law of the Sea,* 82, who observed that, "[A]fter noting that 'those extensive parts dealing with navigation and overnight and most other parts of the convention are consistent with United States interests,' President Reagan said that he rejected the treaty because of his 'deep conviction that the United States cannot support a deep seabed mining regime with such major problems.'"

55. Statement of Principles for a Global Consensus on the Management, Conservation, and Sustainable Development of All Types of Forests adopted at the United Nations Conference on Environment and Development Rio de Janeiro, June 13, 1992.

56. Obviously. this is explained by the fact that the largest United Nations contributors—the United States, Western Europe, and Japan—fell into this category. Note, however, that both Japan and France signed the Convention within a short period of time, so they cannot properly be said to have been excluded.

57. Susskind, *Environmental Diplomacy,* 87.

58. Richardson, "Climate Change," 176.

59. Susskind, *Environmental Diplomacy,* 89.

60. Ibid.

61. Richardson, "Climate Change," 176.

62. Susskind, *Environmental Diplomacy,* 98.

63. Ibid., 93.

64. Morell, *The Law of the Sea,* 83.

65. Friedheim, *Negotiating the New Ocean Regime,* 33.

66. Ann Hollick, U.S. *Foreign Policy and the Law of the Sea* (Princeton, NJ: Princeton University Press, 1981). 378.

67. Sebenius, *Negotiating the Law of the Sea,* 83.

68. See Jonathan I. Charney, "The United States and the Revision of the 1982 Convention on the Law of the Sea," *Ocean Development and International Law* 23 (1992), 286.

69. Susskind, *Environmental Diplomacy*, 94 (emphasis in original).

70. John Rawls, *A Theory of Justice* (Cambridge, MA: Harvard University Press, 1971), 378.

71. See, e.g., Charles Beitz, *Political Theory and International Relations* (Princeton, NJ: Princeton University Press, 1979).

72. Obviously, scholars and practitioners who view international politics through a classical realist or a neorealist lens would dispute the basic point that normative considerations should play a role in formulating so-called national interest. They would not agree that a "just" (i.e., incorporating notions of equity such as we have mentioned) global arrangement ipso facto, must be in any given state's long-term best interests. For discussion of these considerations, see Christopher C. Joyner, "International Law and Foreign Policy: Rethinking the Academic Relevance of Normative Reality," paper prepared for the Conference on International Law and Australian Foreign Policy, University of New South Wales Australian Defense Force Academy, Canberra, July 10, 1995.

73. Gareth Porter and Janet W. Brown, *Global Environmental Politics* (Boulder, CO: Westview Press, 1991), 145–152.

74. Friedheim, *Negotiating the New Ocean Regime*, 29.

75. Oxman, "Summary of the LOS Convention," 139.

76. Edith Brown Weiss, "International Environmental Law: Contemporary Issues and the Emergence of a New World Order," *Georgetown Law Journal* 81 (1993), 675, 688.

77. See Barcelona Convention for the Protection of the Mediterranean Sea Against Pollution, February 16, 1976, in 15 I.L.M. 290; Barcelona Protocol Concerning Cooperation in Combatting Pollution of the Mediterranean Sea by Oil and Other Harmful Substances in Cases of Emergency, February 16, 1976, in 15 I.L.M. 306; Barcelona Protocol for the Prevention of Pollution of the Mediterranean Sea by Dumping from Ships and Aircraft, February 16, 1976, in 15 I.L.M. 300.

78. Convention for the Protection of the Ozone Layer, March 22, 1985, in 26 I.L.M. 1529 (entered into force September 22, 1988).

79. Montreal Protocol on Substances that Deplete the Ozone Layer, September 16, 1987, 26 I.L.M. 1550 (entered into force January 1, 1989).

80. Framework Convention on Climate Change, opened for signature June 4, 1992, 31 I.L.M. 849 (1992).

81. Convention on Biological Diversity, opened for signature June 5, 1992, 31 I.L.M. 818 (1992).

82. For example, the 1982 Convention for the Conservation of Salmon in the North Atlantic, done at Reykjavik March 2, 1982, entered into force October 1, 1983, T.I.A.S. No. 10789. The 1966 International Convention for the Conservation of Atlantic Tunas established regional commissions to coordinate state activities. See International Convention for the Conservation of Atlantic Tunas, done May 14, 1966, 20 U.S.T. 2887, T.I.A.S. No. 6767, 673 U.N.T.S. 63.

83. For example, the Convention of 1976 for the Establishment of a European Space Agency, adopted by several states in Western Europe, and the Agreement of 1976 on Cooperating in the Exploration and Use of Outer Space for Peaceful Purposes, adopted by nine communist states.

84. See Christopher C. Joyner, "Fragile Ecosystems: Preclusive Restoration in the Antarctic," *Natural Resources Journal* 34 (Fall 1994), 879–904.

85. Richardson, "Climate Change," 178.

86. Hollick, *U.S. Foreign Policy and the Law of the Sea,* 377.

87. See, e.g., Peter M. Haas, "Protecting the Baltic and North Seas," in Peter M. Haas, Robert O. Keohane, and Marc A. Levy, eds., *Institutions for the Earth: Sources of Effective International Environmental Protection* (Cambridge, MA: Massachusetts Institute of Technology Press, 1994), 134–141 (discussion of leader and laggard states).

88. 61 Stat. Part 5, A12, 5j U.N.T.S. 187, T.I.A.S. No. 1700. For instance, in 1991 a GATT panel found against the United States for its imposition of trade restrictions (under the U.S. Marine Mammal Protection Act of 1972 [86 Stat. 1027 (1972), as amended by 104 Stat. 4467 (1990) and codified at 16 U.S.C. 1361 ff] against Mexico for that country's continued use of purse-seine nets to catch tuna. and in the process taking incidental catches of dolphins. See "General Agreement on Tariffs and Trade: Dispute Settlement Panel Report on United States Restrictions on Imports of Tuna," 30 I.L.M. 1594 (1991).

89. Lawrence Susskind and Connie Ozawa. "Negotiating More Effective International Environmental Agreements," in Hurrell and Kingsbury, *International Politics of the Environment,* 162.

90. Morell, *The Law of the Sea,* 206. It is not clear that this belief in "right through might" was as uniform as Morell suggests. See, e.g., Schmidt *Common Heritage or Common Burden?,* 266, who notes the Department of Defense's recognition that a unilateral policy based on force (i.e., that "might makes right") may carry diplomatic and political costs.

91. For example, Sebenius in his *Negotiating the Law of the Sea,* 93–94, opines that "It is . . . conceivable that certain states would seize on U.S. repudiation of the convention as an excuse to impose selectively special costs, taxes, requirements, or regulations on vessels flying the U.S. flag. . . . Beyond outright discrimination, however, lies the prospect that without its support for the whole treaty, the very consensus [on navigational freedoms] the United States is relying on will erode."

92. Kathryn Surace-Smith, "Note: United States Activity Outside of the Law of the Sea Convention," *Columbia Law Review* 84 (1984), 1032, 1058.

93. Friedheim, *Negotiating the New Ocean Regime,* 5.

94. Ibid., 47.

95. Ibid., 73–74.

96. George Galdorisi, "The United Nations Convention on the Law of the Sea: A National Security Perspective," *American Journal of International Law* 89 (1995), 208, 210.

97. Ibid., 211.

22

Towards a New Regime
for the Protection of Outer Space
as a Province of All Mankind

DAVID TAN

THE NOTION OF STATES SHARING A COMMON INTEREST IN THE EXPLORATION
and use of outer space has led the international community to declare outer
space to be the "province of all mankind."[1] There is a preponderance of literature largely preoccupied with the freedom of exploration and use of
outer space[2] and comparatively little on the need to protect it from environmental damage.[3] The concept of outer space as the "province of all
mankind" is not confined merely to the prohibition on national appropriation of resources in outer space or the sharing of benefits derived from
exploitation of the space environment. Despite criticisms of its amorphous
and ideologically abstract nature, the "province of all mankind" has the
potential to acquire a legal prescription within a new regime that requires
states to conserve and preserve the outer-space environment for all of
humanity—for present and future generations. However, this will not be
achieved by resorting to hard law, like conventional rules, customary
norms, or principles of *jus cogens*. On the contrary, the solution may be
found in a softer but more sophisticated regime formation and elaboration
process with a clear goal of environmental orientation. . . .

Article I of the Outer Space Treaty declares outer space to be the
"province of all mankind" without endowing that phrase with a precise definition,[4] while Article III requires that states conduct their space programs
"in accordance with international law."[5] [This essay] will advance the
proposition that the concept of the "province of all mankind" limits
the freedom of exploration and use of outer space, drawing support from
the notions of common interest and *res communis*. . . . A new regime will

Reprinted from David Tan, "Towards a New Regime for the Protection of Outer
Space as the Province of All Mankind." *Yale Journal of International Law,* 25
(2000) with permission.

only emerge after decades of information-building, clarification, elaboration, refinement, and international cooperation. An essential first step is to make the notions of sustainable development and intergenerational responsibility applicable to the outer-space environment, and to clarify the meaning of the "province of all mankind" in order to provide a new language for dialogue within a regime building framework.

The conclusion will demonstrate that, while the precise definition of the "province of all mankind" may be unclear, the very nature of the outer-space environment demands special recognition by the international community as a whole—that it must be transmitted in a substantially unimpaired state to future generations. The common interest of states and the freedom of exploration and use of outer space will be jeopardized unless the international community takes immediate steps to protect the space environment from pollution. In balancing delicate political and economic interests, the protection of the outer-space environment from pollution would best be achieved by the adoption of a Framework Convention on the Protection of the Space Environment and the establishment of an International Space Agency. . . .

Understanding Pollution in the Outer-Space Environment

The issues of pollution in outer space are more complex than environmental pollution on Earth, and may appear to many as far-fetched or too insignificant to merit the attention of international lawyers and jurists. This article argues that space pollution is a problem that deserves closer scrutiny, both under the classical international law approach (focusing on sources and hard-law obligations), as well as under a soft-law regime (focusing on the role of institutions, non-governmental organizations, and the active management of compliance). But first, we need a better understanding of the *sui generi* character of pollution in the outer-space environment.

Nuclear Power Sources

The use of nuclear power sources (NPS) in outer space is aimed at providing electric power for spacecraft sub-systems such as altitude control, communications, and command, as well as for the operations of various equipment on board. There are two types of NPS presently in use in outer space. The first is the isotopic source in which energy is obtained from the decay of a radioactive isotope like plutonium-238. The second is the nuclear reactor, which derives its thermal energy from a controlled fission process. The advantages of NPS over other non-nuclear sources of power, such as long life, compactability, and the ability to operate independently of solar radiation, seem to entrench its position as a preferred technical choice for space missions. The escalating use of nuclear energy to power an increasingly wide variety of spacecraft is perhaps inevitable, and the trend continues unabated.[6] However, the hazards associated with the increasing utilization of NPS have raised widespread concern in the international community. The interconnectedness of the Earth's environment and outer space means that any damage or harm to the space environment is likely to have a spillover effect on Earth.[7] This is evidenced by the Cosmos-954 incident in 1978, where a nuclear-powered satellite disintegrated upon re-entry, scattering a significant amount of highly radioactive debris across Canadian territory. Similarly, in 1983, Cosmos-1402, carrying 45 kilograms of uranium-235, malfunctioned and broke into three parts upon re-entry.[8] The hazards to humankind from NPS in outer space will primarily be radiological, arising from radiation exposure through "both direct external radiation and internal radiation from inhalation or ingestion."[9] The freedom of exploration and use of outer space must be "for the benefit and in the interests of all countries."[10] It is in the interest of states that the space environment be free from the radioactive pollution caused by NPS since any radiological contamination of outer space is likely to have an adverse effect on the Earth's environment. The problem is exacerbated by the direct effect the increasing use of NPS has on the accumulation of space debris. Upon the malfunctioning of a nuclear-powered-satellite usually stationed in the geostationary orbit, not only do the component parts contribute to the space debris, but the radioactive materials pose an additional hazard to human life, in particular to manned space stations.

In view of such possible dangers, the Scientific and Technical Sub Committee of COPUOS has discussed the possibility of establishing international standards and safety regulations governing the use of NPS in the outer-space environment.[11] The efforts of this Committee are paralleled by studies of legal implications by the Legal Sub-Committee of COPUOS.[12] After repeated discussions and informal consultations, the Legal Sub-Committee has developed a proposal containing seven draft principles on the use of NPS in outer space.[13] Unfortunately, the consensual approach adopted by COPUOS fails to address the problems in a satisfactory and expedient manner; after almost two decades, many issues still remain unresolved.[14]

Space Debris

In recent years, man-made space debris or space refuse has been an environmental hazard whose seriousness is a shared concern of many scientists and policy-makers in the international community.[15] The deployment of an ever-increasing number of man-made objects into outer space has created

a potential for malfunctioning and decay. It has also resulted in a concomitant rise in the number of defunct, damaged, or abandoned objects, which,
together with other debris caused by explosions and collisions, has fast
become a threat to space activities. It has been estimated that there are over
7000 trackable man-made objects in space and a substantially larger number of untrackable objects.[16] Most of the trackable objects are located in
low-earth-orbit (LEO) with a significant number in geosynchronous orbit
(GEO)—an area of intense space activity.[17] The limited empirical data
reveal that objects of sizes between 0.01 and 1 centimeter can cause significant damage upon impact. Objects larger than 1 centimeter can produce
catastrophic effects.[18] Present spacecraft systems are particularly vulnerable as they have not been designed with these threats in mind.[19] If the
growth in numbers is permitted to continue without adequate measures to
safeguard active space objects from damage caused by explosion, collision,
or harmful radiation, it could easily result in serious accidents involving the
loss of human lives or substantial property damage. Collision and interference are the major risks space debris poses to human life and active payloads. Perhaps the most serious consequence of collisions with space debris
is the cascade effect: (1) As the number of space objects in earth-orbit
increases, the probability of collisions between them also increases; (2) collisions would produce new orbiting fragments (secondary debris), each of
which would heighten the risk of further collisions; (3) collisions and any
ensuing cascading would lead to an exponential increase of debris flux and
could lead to the formation of a debris belt around the Earth by the end of
this century; and (4) the near-earth environment could become so populated
with space debris that portions of LEO would be unusable.[20] Moreover the
majority of NPS satellites reside in the most densely populated regions of
LEO, thereby enhancing the danger of collision with space debris.[21] The
impact of a spent NPS fuel core colliding with a space station could cause
devastating radioactive contamination in addition to structural damage,
because the half-life of uranium-235 is in excess of 700,000 years. Russia,
as successor state to the Soviet Union, has unofficially acknowledged that
space debris poses a hazard to the outer-space environment.[22] . . . Ironically, the abandonment in 1999 of Mir, the "rust-stained, raffling, 13-year-
old Russian space station,"[23] will only exacerbate this problem. . . .

Since as early as 1987, it has been noted in COPUOS that increased
pollution of the outer-space environment resulting from the proliferation of
NPS and space debris is creating a global hazard.[24] In COPUOS's Fifteenth
Scientific-Legal Roundtable, held on October 20, 1993, on the "Scientific
and Legal Aspects of Space Debris,[25] various well-known experts in this
area advocated that policy-makers should support an international legal
regime that has as its principal purpose the minimization of the presence
of man-made debris." Although a completely accurate picture of the dangers

posed by space debris is currently unavailable, there are already compelling scientific data available to ascertain the emerging threat of identifiable space debris.[26] It is with these environmental hazards in mind that we next assess the adequacy of the existing principles in international law in the protection of the space environment.

An Overview of the Principles of the Law of Outer Space

. . . Many skeptics question what role legal rules really play in a highly politicized international arena.[27] An international treaty or convention is the most basic multilateral document that attempts to secure agreement among sovereign nations to act in a particular manner, or to refrain from certain behavior. The closest parallels to the treaties relating to outer space are those that regulate the use of the Earth's environment and resources. The reasons why states ratify and comply with environmental treaties generally fall into three categories: (a) because the signatory states have a "genuine concern for the issue or a stake in the regulated industry and want to influence treaty rulemaking;"[28] (b) because the cost of compliance is relatively low compared to the higher cost of noncompliance;[29] and (c) because of fear of the consequences of noncompliance.[30] In the case of the negotiation and ratification of the space treaties from the late 1950s to the 1970s, the spacefaring nations were competing to optimize the use and exploration of outer space, while the nonspacefaring states were concerned with influencing rulemaking to constrain the activities of those states and to protect their own future interests. Perhaps it is true that the incentive to deploy weapons in outer space was originally low, but it was not inconceivable that in the absence of these treaties, one or the other superpower would have begun experimenting with such deployments. These fascinating geopolitical forces resulted in the birth of five space treaties. . . .

A Brief History of the International Space Treaties

The Ad Hoc Committee on the Peaceful Uses of Outer Space was established by the U.N. General Assembly at its thirteenth session in 1958,[31] and was replaced a year later by a permanent body.[32] The preliminary work of COPUOS resulted in the adoption of the 1963 Declaration of Legal Principles Governing the Activities of States in the Exploration and Use of Outer Space.[33] This declaration formed the basis for the 1967 Outer Space Treaty,[34] which introduced many fundamental principles of outer-space law and has been regarded by numerous scholars as the "Magna Charta" of outer space.[35]

The 1967 Outer Space Treaty laid down broad fundamental principles pertaining to the exploration and use of outer space.[36] It was understood that further conventions would have to be negotiated to provide more specific rules. Thus, the impetus provided by the Outer Space Treaty led to the successful conclusion of four other major international conventions, which provide the international legal framework regulating the conduct of space activities. They are:

1. the 1968 Agreement on the Rescue of Astronauts, the Return of Astronauts, and the Return of Objects Launched into Outer Space;[37]
2. the 1976 Convention on the Registration of Objects Launched into Outer Space;[38]
3. the 1977 Convention on the International Liability for Damage Caused by Space Objects;[39] and
4. the 1979 Agreement Governing the Activities of States on the Moon and Other Celestial Bodies.[40]

None of the five major space treaties deals with the protection of either the space environment or the Earth's environment in a satisfactory fashion. Any protection of the environment appears to be incidental. Other treaties that govern space activities and have some bearing on environmental protection are the 1963 Partial Nuclear Test Ban Treaty,[41] the 1972 ABM Treaty,[42] and the 1977 ENMOD Convention.[43]

In broad terms, international space law enables a kaleidoscope of activities to be conducted in the space environment. They include the launch of satellites, the performance of scientific research and experiments, and the operation of commercial telecommunication services. . . . The five space treaties were not formulated to address, and did not foresee, the complex problems of space pollution we face in the twenty-first century. The next section illustrates the underlying inadequacies and the need for a new approach to treaty-making and regime building that allows states to take account of longer-term consequences.

The Space Treaties

The 1967 Outer Space Treaty. In addition to proclaiming outer space to be the "province of all mankind," article I of the Outer Space Treaty also declares that outer space is "free for exploration and use by all states without discrimination of any kind, on a basis of equality," and that "[t]here shall be free access to all areas of celestial bodies."[44] Article II states that outer space, including the Moon and other celestial bodies, is not subject to national appropriation "by claim of sovereignty, by means of use or occupation, or by any other means."[45] States are thus barred from extending to outer space, and exercising within it, those rights that constitute attributes of territorial sovereignty. Although Article II prohibits national appropriation, states are allowed free access to all areas of celestial bodies; this access includes the collection of mineral samples, scientific research, and the exploitation of geostationary orbits.[46] Article VII imposes international liability on states for damage caused by an object launched into space, while Article IX makes no direct reference to the need to protect the space environment against harm, requiring only that space activity be undertaken "with due regard to the corresponding interests of all other States Parties to the Treaty."[47] Finally, apart from the freedom of exploration, another fundamental principle is laid down in Article III—the exploration and use of outer space shall be governed by international law and the U.N. Charter. This is not a simple question of applying existing norms of international law to this new environment *in toto*. The *sui generis* space environment demands the revision and adaptation of numerous principles of transboundary harm and state responsibility, and inevitably in many situations, new principles, destined purely for outer space, must be created. The content of international law in this area is difficult to determine with any useful clarity. . . .

The 1968 Astronaut Agreement. The 1968 Astronaut Agreement establishes specific procedures to provide assistance to distressed astronauts who may be victims of environmental or other adversities.[48] Moreover, Article 5(4) of the Astronaut Agreement stipulates that if a state party "has reason to believe that a space object or its component parts discovered in territory under its jurisdiction, or recovered by it elsewhere, is of a hazardous or deleterious nature,"[49] it may so notify the launching authority, which is immediately required to take effective measures to eliminate possible danger of harm.[50]

The 1972 Liability Convention. The 1972 Liability Convention provides specific rules as an elaboration of Article VII of the Outer Space Treaty and determines liability for damage caused by a space object.[51] The definition of "space object"[52] is controversial; a major issue is whether a space object remains a space object after its breakup, deterioration, loss, or abandonment, or whether it becomes space debris. Moreover, the "damage" as defined by the Convention may involve loss of life, personal injury, or damage to property, but no mention is made of damage to the environment.[53]

The 1976 Registration Convention. The primary purpose of the Registration Convention is to facilitate the identification of the space object causing damage. The launching state party is required to maintain a national registry and enter into it each object launched into space.[54] Furthermore, information must be furnished to the U.N. Secretary-General on each space object launched for the purposes of international registration[55] Notice must also be given regarding objects on which information has previously been provided and which have been but are no longer in earth-orbit.[56]

The 1979 Moon Agreement. The Moon Agreement is intended to supplement the 1967 Outer Space Treaty. It is not intended to derogate from or restrict the provisions of the Outer Space Treaty; the Outer Space Treaty will continue to apply where the Moon Agreement does not enunciate more specific provisions.[57] Although Article IX of the Outer Space Treaty already provides for the protection of the environment, both in space and on Earth, Article VII of the Moon Agreement further requires states parties to take measures to prevent the "disruption of the existing balance" of the celestial bodies and avoid harm to the environment of the Earth.[58] The Moon Agreement also refers to the applicability of international law and the U.N. Charter in Articles 2, 6(1), and 11(4). In addition to the prohibition on national appropriation by occupation in Article 11(2), the Moon Agreement further requires an "equitable sharing" by all states parties in the benefits derived from the resources, taking into account the interests and needs of developing countries as well as the contributions made by the developed nations in their operational activities.[59] The possibility of establishing a new international legal regime designed to facilitate exploitative and sharing activities when such exploitation becomes feasible is recognized in Article 11(5).

The Outer Space Treaty and the Moon Agreement are far more concerned with the exploration and use of the outer-space environment than with its preservation in a substantially unimpaired condition for future generations. The non-renewable resources of outer space should be protected from abuse by the developed nations; international law must "maximize the interests and values of all peoples."[60] The question is how we determine the "interests and values of all peoples." Is there such a thing as "common interest"? Is the concept of the "province of all mankind" in Article I of the Outer Space Treaty predicated on the "common interest"?

The Meaning of "Common Interest" and the "Province of All Mankind" in International Law

The concept of common interest becomes relevant when one considers claims to resources located in areas outside territorial sovereignty or beyond national jurisdictions.[61] The *res nullius* concept was associated with the view that no national sovereignty existed in certain areas and that states had the right to assert sovereignty. The alternative view is that some resources, like airspace, the deep sea-bed, solar energy, and radio spectra, are commonly needed by humanity as a condition of survival and are to be used for the common benefit *(res communis);* such resources cannot be subject to private ownership or state sovereignty.[62] In pursuit of the common benefit, the members of the international community are able to determine the conditions under which the exploitation or use of such resources is to take place. . . . Such a theory assumes that states share a common interest in the exploitation and use of the indicated commons.

The notion of *res communis humanitatis* was introduced by Aldo Armando Cocca. It is based upon the rights of mankind and is derived from "the community of interests and benefits recognized in favour of mankind in outer space and celestial bodies."[63] The *res communis liumanitatis* principle was refined to the CHM, which proposes that certain common areas and their resources are open to inclusive use and that there may not be exclusive uses. Furthermore it asserts that the benefits and values so derived must be shared. CHM is defined in the Moon Agreement; according to Article XI(1) of the Moon Agreement, "the Moon and its natural resources are the common heritage of mankind,"[64] and the CHM principle has been interpreted to have limited spatial coverage—it applies only to the Moon and the Moon's orbits and intrajectories, but not to the outer-space environment generally.[65]

On the other hand, the exploration and use of outer space as the "province of all mankind" in Article 1(1) of the Outer Space Treaty is not defined by the Treaty but is, according to Article III, governed by "international law and the Charter of the United Nations."[66] Does the "province of all mankind" then have a particular meaning in international law? First it may be argued that "mankind" in Article 1(1) of the Outer Space Treaty may be understood to be a beneficiary of space exploration and may be considered a new legal subject of international law. There are numerous statements on the definition of "mankind," but only Professor Stephen Gorove has come close to a working definition of the term:

> [M]ankind as a concept should be distinguished *from that* of man in general. The former refers to a collective body of people, whereas the latter stands for individuals making up that body. Therefore, the rights of mankind should be distinguished, for instance, from the so-called human rights. Human rights are rights to which individuals are entitled on the basis of their belonging to the human race, whereas the rights of mankind relate to the rights of the collective entity and would not be analogous with the rights of the individuals making up that entity.[67]

In contrast, there has been no attempt to define the word "province"; this has made the task of discovering the meaning of the phrase the "province of all mankind" an uphill battle. Some have argued that the CHM principle is designed to replace the abstract "province of all mankind" with a more meaningful legal framework,[68] but the remarkably poor ratification of the Moon Agreement by only ten states and the specificity of various provisions in the Agreement weigh against this conclusion. . . .

The meaning that may have been ascribed to the phrase in 1967 may be different from the understanding that should be accorded to it today. The Outer Space Treaty was concluded over thirty years ago in a political climate dominated by a superpower arms race and a great ideological divide, where both spacefaring and non-spacefaring nations alike were determined not to allow any state to colonize space for strategic weapons deployment or commercial exploitation. It was thus agreed that space was the "province of all mankind" and could not be subverted under the exclusive sovereignty of any state. In the new millennium, while these same nations are now cooperating on the ISS and various space initiatives and scientific research, the "province of all mankind" must mean something different. The lofty aspirations of the expression as understood in 1967—the freedom of use and exploration for the benefit of all nations—must be brought down to Earth.[69]

The meaning of the "province of all mankind" should include the concept of sustainable development. Our exploration and use of the outer-space environment should leave it in a substantially unimpaired condition for the enjoyment and benefit of future generations. The purpose of the existing space treaties was to ensure that no state would arrogate exclusive rights to itself or use them at the expense of others. The freedom of action of states in outer space or on celestial bodies is neither unlimited, absolute, or unqualified, but is determined by the rights and interests of other states and all humanity: "The freedom to use outer space which is granted to everyone must find its limits in the freedom of others."[70] Perhaps this limit is found in Article III of the Outer Space Treaty, which requires that the exploration and use of outer space be "in accordance with international law."[71]

The Protection of the Space Environment: An Analysis of Conventional Law and Customary International Law

In theory, the role of legal norms—whether conventional or customary—in classical international law appears to be a fairly straightforward one. To put it succinctly, they are prescriptions for action in situations of choice, carrying a sense of obligation that they ought to be followed. Where the conduct in question is in an area governed by a treaty or custom, the choice of governing principle may be simplified, though it will not necessarily be clear. Even then, there is no precise linear path that dictates the application of a norm to a specific conduct. As Chayes and Chayes so aptly stated, "the need to operate in a multifaceted, interacting, and interdependent international environment with relatively diffuse power tends to lengthen the time horizon of states and lead them to take account of longer-term."[72]

The Adequacy of the Existing Space Treaties in the Control of Space Pollution

Article VI of the Outer Space Treaty states:

States Parties to the Treaty shall bear international responsibility for national activities in outer space, including the moon and other celestial bodies, whether such activities are carried on by governmental agencies or by non-governmental entities, and for assuring that national activities are carried out in conformity with the provisions set forth in the present Treaty.[73]

The general terms of Article VI resulted in the 1972 Liability Convention and the 1975 Registration Convention. However, both treaties fail to refer directly to the problem of space debris or nuclear power sources. In orbit, situations endangering property and life may be brought about by the overcrowding of space objects in a particular area, the close proximity of two or more space objects, the conduct of military maneuvers and weapons testing, and the release of harmful radiation from NPS.

Nuclear Power Sources

Article IV of the Outer Space Treaty specifically forbids *only the stationing of nuclear weapons or any other weapons of mass destruction* in outer space. It does not regulate the use of NPS. It provides: "States Parties to the Treaty undertake not to place in orbit around the Earth any objects carrying nuclear weapons or any other kinds of weapons of mass destruction, install such weapons on celestial bodies, or station such weapons in outer space in any other manner."[74] Similarly, Article III of the Moon Agreement carries the same prohibition relating to the Moon and other celestial bodies.[75] Regrettably, the restrictions in the Outer Space Treaty apply only to space objects in orbit and to the stationing of identified kinds of weapons in space.[76] Furthermore, although Articles IV and IX of the Outer Space Treaty and Articles III and VII of the Moon Agreement require states parties to avoid the harmful contamination of outer space and the Moon environment and forbid the deployment of nuclear weapons, they do not require states to transfer space objects with NPS on board to a nuclear-safe orbit (NSO).

Other treaties that are not strictly part of the current space treaties framework can also impose some control on radioactive pollution in space. For example, the testing and deployment of a space-based anti-missile system envisioned by the Strategic Defense Initiative (SDI) program would certainly violate the provisions of the U.S.-Soviet ABM Treaty.[77] Russia has put a series of proposals before the United Nations that have the effect of imposing a prohibition on the testing, deployment, and use of space weapons.[78] Such an effort to demilitarize the space environment is commendable. But because NPS is usually used for non-military purposes in communication satellites and in space stations, where research and manufacturing take place, the regulation of its use falls outside the ambit of the various space weapons treaties. Satellite remote sensing is continuing to make valuable contributions to environmental monitoring, planning sustainable development, water-resource development, monitoring crop conditions, and predicting and assessing drought. Meteorological and atmospheric research satellites are similarly important to the study of global climate change, the greenhouse effect, the degradation of the ozone layer, and other oceanic and global environmental processes.[79] Studies of human and animal psychology conducted in space led to important advances in medical knowledge, in such areas as "blood circulation, hypertension, osteoporosis, cardiovascular physiology, sensory perception, immunology, and the effects of cosmic radiation."[80] Hence the threat to the outer-space environment from nuclear power sources remains largely unchecked, perhaps masked by the significant advances that NPS has made possible.

Space Debris

The specificity of damage, the requirement of fault, and the difficulty of identification all contribute to the impotence of the Liability Convention and the Registration Convention in the protection of the outer-space environment from debris pollution.

In order to ascertain whether the present space treaties are applicable to space debris, a determination must be made whether space debris can be classified as a space object. Under the 1972 Liability Convention, in order for liability to arise, there must be "damage" caused by a "space object." Without damage, there can be no state liability for environmental risks, much as there is no liability if damage is not caused by a space object. "Damage," as defined in Article 1(a), is limited to physical and direct damage, and does not cover indirect damage or non-physical damage, i.e., it does not deal with environmental dangers created by space activities, particularly radioactive hazards presented by NPS. The term "damage" means loss of life, personal injury, or other impairment of health; loss of or damage to property of states or of persons, natural or juridical; or damage to property of international intergovernmental organizations.[81] If damage is to the elements of the space environment that are not property of states, persons, or international intergovernmental organizations, for example, radioactive leakage from nuclear reactors in space, there appears to be no legitimate recourse under the Liability Convention.

Under Article II of the Liability Convention, the absolute liability of the launching state is limited to damage caused by the fall of a space object "on the surface of the Earth or to aircraft in flight."[82] There is no absolute liability for any damage to objects in the outer-space environment; fault must be proved by the state seeking compensation.[83] This requirement of fault for damage caused in outer space presents a significant impediment to a successful claim under the Liability Convention. Moreover, the potential recovery for damage caused by space debris is often seriously hampered by the identification of the launching state associated with the space object.[84] Arguably, Articles VI, VII, and XI of the Outer Space Treaty, Articles IV and VI of the Registration Convention, and Article 5 of the Astronaut Agreement all contribute in varying degrees to the imposition of international responsibility for dangers created by space debris. But the identification problem remains an insurmountable hurdle to any compensation claim.[85]

Many of the treaty provisions are outdated and incapable of coping adequately with the emerging threats of space debris. For example, under a strict interpretation of Article XI of the Outer Space Treaty, if the space activity results in space debris, the launching state is required to inform the U.N. Secretary-General and the international scientific community of the debris resulting from the activity.[86] Provisions of the Registration Convention require the state of registry to give notice of objects that are no longer in earth-orbit and to assist in the identification of hazardous or deleterious space objects.[87] These existing treaty provisions unfortunately are not preventive in character: There is no system of obligatory safety assessment prior to launching, and no appropriate quality-control program in place. Finally, piecemeal treaty provisions relevant to environmental protection in outer space are present in the Partial Nuclear Test Ban Treaty, the ENMOD Convention, and the International Telecommunication Convention.[88] These treaties, however, do not protect the outer-space environment per se, and their provisions only apply to the few signatory states. The inadequacies of the existing multilateral treaty regime in the regulation of pollution in space should be ameliorated by the adoption of a framework convention that deals specifically with the pollution of the space environment. Part VI will provide the outline of such a convention.

Customary International Law—and Its Problems

International Custom in Relation to the Space Environment

The principle of the "province of all mankind" as a limitation on the freedom of exploration appears to lack the requisite *opinio juris* to attain the status of a customary norm. It does not "constitute a principle sufficiently normative in character that it becomes capable of generating specific legal effects or enhancing particular value expectations."[89]

According to Jonathan Charney's criteria,[90] one could contend that the preservation of the outer-space environment has merited international attention and generalized concern as evidenced in the numerous U.N. General Assembly declarations and the formation of COPUOS and its integral role in the making of international space treaties. However, none of the treaty obligations under the framework of the present space treaties contains a discrete, well-defined customary rule that imposes a duty on states to avoid harm to the space environment.

Nevertheless, the generalized concern for the protection of the space environment is reflected in the Sixty-Sixth Conference of the TLA, which adopted the Buenos Aires International Instrument on the Protection of the Environment From Damage Caused by Space Debris,[91] and in the Scientific Subcommittee of COPUOS. It appears that protection of the space environment is currently a pressing issue on the agenda of many expert groups and international bodies. As discussed above, existing treaty rules and custom do not impose concrete obligations on states to prevent pollution to the space environment. Is there some other way that the outer-space environment may be protected from pollution by NPS or debris?

The International Law Commission took the view that "[i]t is not the form of a general rule of international law but the particular nature of the subject-matter with which it deals that may . . . give it the character of *jus cogens*."[92] This statement seems to suggest that the very nature of a subject matter, independent of any reference to custom, may qualify it as a norm of *jus cogens*. What the current literature fails to address is whether the protection and conservation of the outer-space environment as the "province of all mankind" qualifies as a norm of *jus cogens*.[93] Discussions center around the application of the "province of all mankind" and the CHM principles to the use and exploitation of outer space, and rarely address environmental concerns specific to the preservation of the outer-space environment. The notion of *jus cogens* is supported by the view that the satisfaction of the higher interest of the entire community should prevail over often contradictory national preference.[94]

It appears from the foregoing analysis that international law presently does not recognize the "province of all mankind" as possessing any legal prescription pertaining to the protection of the space environment from pollution flowing from space activities. However, it is in the common interest of all states that the exploration and use of outer space should, at the bare minimum, be "sustainable."

The Emerging Norm of Sustainable Development

Concern for future generations figured prominently in the 1972 Stockholm Declaration of the U.N. Conference on the Human Environment, which was adopted by the U.N. General Assembly by 112 votes in favor and none against (with ten abstentions).[95] Principle 1 of the Declaration declares that we have a "solemn responsibility to protect and improve the environment for present and future generations."[96] Since the Declaration, about 300 multilateral agreements and 900 bilateral treaties have been concluded on the environment.[97] On October 29, 1982, the U.N. General Assembly—with 111 votes in favor and 1 against (the United States)—proclaimed the World Charter for Nature, which explicitly states that governments have a duty to pass on humanity's natural heritage to future generations.[98] In 1987 the World Commission on Environment and Development (WCED) published its report on environment and sustainable development, known as the "Brundtland Report."[99] The main guidelines of the Report were *unanimously* endorsed by the U.N. General Assembly in 1987 as a framework for future environmental cooperation.[100] Unfortunately, the contours of many concepts are blurred and the precise contents of the customary rules are unclear.[101]

Two decades after the Stockholm Declaration, over 170 countries gathered at the Rio Convention to reaffirm their commitment to the protection of the environment for present and future generations, and to implement the goals of sustainable development.[102] Although such international declarations were focused primarily on the protection of the Earth's environment, the theoretical justifications for intergenerational responsibility and sustainable development that underpin the U.N. declarations relating to the human environment are no different from the concept of the transmission of the outer-space environment substantially unimpaired to future generations under the "province of all mankind" principle. Hence such environmental policies should apply equally to the outer-space environment.

Edith Brown Weiss has advanced the theory of "intergenerational equity," which provides for generational rights and obligations.[103] Her thesis consists of a normative framework of intersecting theories of intergenerational and intragenerational equity that are derived from an underlying planetary trust, embodying the notion that generations act as stewards to sustain the welfare and well-being of all generations. . . . Unfortunately, Weiss's model generally rests upon an intertemporal human rights model for preserving the global environment. This presents *many* problems, ranging from the questionable existence of the right to a decent environment to the issue of remedies in respect of claims made by future generations against present generations.[104]

Whether the global awareness of the harm to our sense of intergenerational identity, as evidenced by the various U.N. General Assembly resolutions and numerous international conventions, will be sufficient to mobilize the implementation and enforcement of effective legal measures on behalf of future generations is doubtful. But more importantly, the notions of intergenerational identity and sustainable development will prove to be invaluable concepts in framing the discussion in Part VI. Current literature has concentrated on the notion of sustainable development as involving the integration of economic and environmental considerations at all levels of decision-making.[105] But the outer-space environment has been largely ignored, as if it were simply economic development on Earth that must be environmentally sound. There is no reason, however, why the precautionary principles that emerge from the concept of sustainable development in the Stockholm Declaration, the Rio Declaration, and the World Charter for Nature should not apply equally to the outer-space environment. One might even ultimately find that the uniqueness and vulnerability of the outer-space environment demand that the international community as a whole recognize sustainable development as a "global ethic"[106] that transcends terrestrial boundaries, as a peremptory norm that prohibits "policies and practices that support current living standards by depleting the productive base, including natural resources, and that leaves future generations with poorer prospects and greater risks than our own."[107]

We should not confine our actions to those we are now able to determine as directly or indirectly benefiting ourselves or our descendants. On the contrary, we should "cultivate our natural sense of obligation not to act wastefully or wantonly even when we cannot calculate how such acts would make any present or future persons worse off."[108] It seems impossible to find universally agreed-upon limits on the freedom of exploration and use of outer space. Rather than focus on indeterminate rules of custom-formation, we should concentrate on establishing fair and workable arrangements and institutions that can successfully accommodate the competing interests of all nations. With these guidelines in mind, we will now examine new methods of treaty-making that will enhance the willingness of states to participate in an environmental program that seeks to achieve an acceptable balance between pollution control and freedom of space exploration.

Some Proposals: New Principles of International Environmental Law-Making

Soft Law and a Regime-Building Approach

Environmental regimes are not static structures. Like human rights treaty regimes, they evolve along a continuum from dialogue to the sharing of information and expertise, to more defined framework conventions for cooperation, to more precise binding legal norms contained in protocols. . . . This continuum of regime formation, in both a substantive and a procedural sense, is not always linear, as it allows for "overlapping cycles of cooperation and competition."[109] A space environment regime must include the concepts of sustainable development and intergenerational equity and, at the same time, respect the sovereign interests of states. The regime is like a living organism: When a regime is established through practice and a convergence of interests and expectations around that practice, its interests and expectations may persist even after the forces that shaped its evolution have changed.[110]

In order for the space environment regime to be successful, we must emphasize implementation as a measure of effectiveness and overcome our obsession with mechanisms of dispute settlement. The traditional rhetoric of enforcement will not ensure compliance. Instead, the framework-protocol approach is the best model for the protection and preservation of the space environment, and is well tested in international environmental law.[111] . . . Thus it is important to concentrate on finding the right balance between political exigencies and the need for precise legal wording that imposes obligations on signatory states. The acceptable balance may be found in "soft law."

Soft law, "where international law and international politics combine to build new norms,"[112] has become a fashionable phrase in international environmental law, as it acknowledges the inextricability of law and politics. Treaty-making in an environmental context goes beyond the consideration of traditional treaty-making techniques and cannot be viewed in isolation from international declarations and recommendations that have not yet attained the binding force of international law, but which embody a certain degree of political commitment and hence give rise to expectations for future behavior.[113] The advantages of soft law include range, flexibility, and frequent adherence by the governments that made such declarations. Its shortcomings include the lack of precision in such political commitments and the absence of enforceable legal sanctions.[114] . . . Yet in the absence of *lex lata,* soft law may succeed.[115] Soft-law instruments have been said to include the Stockholm[116] and Rio Declarations,[117] and the 1989 Hague Declaration on the Environment,[118] where the establishment of a comprehensive regulatory regime is contemplated. These should be distinguished from "soft provisions" of treaties, where the treaty in its final form imposes vague and imprecise obligations.[119]

Perhaps one can avoid the rule of unanimous consent by adopting a Framework Convention on the Protection of the Outer Space Environment (the Space Environment Framework Convention or SEFC), much like the 1985 Vienna Convention for the Protection of the Ozone Layer,[120] which established general obligations to cooperate. The Vienna Convention paved the road toward the 1987 Montreal Protocol on Substances that Deplete the Ozone Layer,[121] the 1989 Helsinki Declaration on the Protection of the Ozone Layer,[122] and the 1990 London Amendments,[123] each adding an element of specificity to the general obligations contained in the framework Ozone Layer Convention. This successful regime-building approach has its genesis in a contextual framework and then moves effectively through the continuum to eventuate in a legally binding regime with a convergence of interests. . . .

The process begins with political consensus in multilateral fora, leading to the formation of soft-law obligations. The constellation of political interests are then accommodated in a framework convention that expresses the commitment of signatory states to cooperate in knowledge sharing in a setting in which binding normativity can emerge. Subsequent protocols would supplement and elucidate the content of the fundamental norms in the framework convention.[124] Protocols represent the real operational part of such a regime, and are undoubtedly the cornerstone of the proposed Space Environment Framework Convention. By ratifying the SEFC, states would express their commitment to the protection and preservation of the space environment as the "province of all mankind." These declarations would reflect political commitments toward a common interest that may at some later stage, through the development of specific protocols, acquire the full force of law.

The current configuration of space treaties does not contemplate such a regime-building approach in relation to the protection of the space environment from pollution. The regime-building approach as understood in international relations theory is most conducive to furnishing the fundamental building blocks for the ultimate grand architecture of a more specific holistic regime with binding legal obligations.[125] To facilitate the drafting of the Protocols—the next point in the regime-building continuum after establishing the framework convention—scientific and technical issues relating to the threats posed by space debris and nuclear power sources must be worked out over time by an International Space Agency comprising experts from both spacefaring and non-spacefaring nations. Indeed, this approach allows a framework embodying general aspirations and principles to come into force in a cooperative regime where the consensus necessary for a more detailed agreement is immediately lacking. However, it requires repeated negotiation and identification of protocols, and can only succeed with centralized active management.

A Framework Convention on the Protection of the Space Environment

The SEFC must be grounded in a cooperative paradigm where the focus is on sharing the exploration and use of the "province of all mankind." The SEFC must aim to secure a dynamic universal cooperation and must resist the allure of succumbing to any attempts to impose a normative code of conduct from the outset. In this regime-building approach, in order to acknowledge the unique nature of the outer-space environment, the SEFC must first encompass all states whose activities can affect or be affected by, in the present or future, the exploration and use of outer space. It should also emphasize the "common interest" of all states in the protection and preservation of the space environment for the common benefit," rather than their competing sovereign interests, it must also speak the new rhetoric of "compliance" and avoid the offensive language of "breach" and "dispute settlement."

In order for the regime to be effective, the SEFC must be able to grow in both the substantive and the procedural sense. At the bare minimum, states should also undertake, in accordance with the means at their disposal and their capabilities, to

1. cooperate by means of systematic observations, research, and information exchange in order better to understand and assess the short-term and long-term effects of human activities on the outer-space environment through epistemic communities coordinated by a central agency;[126]
2. be guided by the emerging principles of sustainable development, intergenerational equity, equitable allocation, and the precautionary principle in their dialogues and in the formulation of agreed measures, procedures, and standards for more precise implementation of the SEFC through the adoption of future protocols;[127] and
3. identify and develop implementation, compliance, and dispute-avoidance mechanisms.[128]

As the emphasis shifts from state interests to common environmental interests in the sharing of knowledge and identification of problems by the epistemic communities,[129] the resulting depoliticization can lead to important substantive evolution of the regime into normative frameworks of law.[130] In the formulation of more concrete binding obligations in future protocols, it is possible to involve different parties in issues of especial concern to them. As protocols are usually focused on relatively narrow issues, each has the capacity to flesh out the broad principles embodied in the SEFC and can crystallize into custom. The main strength of this framework-protocols regime lies in its intrinsic ability to involve both contextual and normative aspects in a creative synergy from formation to maturation at all points in its dynamic continuum.[131] The three broad working principles proposed above provide a wide ambit for procedural cooperation and ample room for epistemic communities to interact and flourish.

Experience may be gleaned from the regime-building approach to climate change, which began with the 1992 U.N. Framework Convention on

Climate Change (FCCC).[132] Further elaboration of rules and guidelines through intergovernmental cooperation moved the regime along the continuum that adequately addresses the problem of global climate change, resulting in the adoption of the Kyoto Protocol by over 160 parties to the FCCC in December 1997.[133] The FCCC was designed as a first step in dealing with the threat of anthropogenic climate change, explicitly recognizing that countries have "common but differentiated responsibilities."[134] In the same manner, both spacefaring and non-spacefaring nations have the common responsibility of conserving, protecting, and restoring the integrity of the outer-space environment. The policies that each state adopts—for example, reporting, communication, research, and mitigation measures—will vary depending on their individual space capabilities. . . .

Critics of the Kyoto Protocol may argue that it has no effective compliance regime because it affords member states too much flexibility with respect to how it implements its obligations, at both the national and international levels. Indeed, one of the hallmarks of the regime-building approach—and its ultimate success in securing "compliance"—is this very flexibility. An authoritarian uniform treaty rule that fails to recognize the uniqueness of each member state is destined only for obsolescence. When the framework convention and its subsequent protocols are all driven by a single vision—in the case of the SEFC, the protection of the outer-space environment as the "province of all mankind"—each state party can still comply with its obligations when each designs its own approach in light of its unique economic, technological, social, and political situation. The Antarctic Treaty system is another unusual international regime that has experienced great success in maintaining a balance between international interests and national interests in Antarctica. While once believed to be impossible, the Protocol on Environmental Protection to the Antarctic Treaty is now a reality.[135]

Like the FCCC and the 1992 Convention on Biological Diversity,[136] the SEFC should also contain provisions for funds to finance capacity-building and "compliance."[137] It should specifically require that the commitments of states parties developing space capabilities are contingent on the provision of resources by present spacefaring nations to meet the full agreed incremental costs of compliance. At the same time, in order to secure regime transparency, verification and monitoring functions should be actively managed by a central organization like the International Space Agency.

The aim of the SEFC will be to protect and preserve the outer-space environment as the "province of all mankind," and all subsequent protocols should build upon the structural and institutional components of the SEFC, beginning with reporting and review requirements and potentially culminating in binding implementation norms. While one would not expect substantive obligations to be present in the SEFC, nevertheless the Preamble should begin with a firm commitment by signatory states:

> While we recognize our freedom of the use and exploration of outer space as stated in Article I of the Outer Space Treaty, we also acknowledge our responsibility for conserving the outer-space environment and for using its resources in a sustainable manner for the benefit of present and future generations. . . .

Coercive enforcement of a hegemony of norms is as misguided as it is costly, as we are faced with varying degrees of capability and priority. At the most fundamental level, the new regime assumes a primary managerial role at its genesis and a secondary regulatory role as it matures. The management of this new regime must:

1. ensure transparency in the generation and dissemination of information about the requirements of the SEEC and the parties' performance under it;
2. coordinate the scientific research and data reporting of epistemic communities, national governments, and international organizations;
3. assist in capacity-building by coordinating technical assistance for enabling countries; and
4. establish a multilateral consultative process and dispute-resolution procedure that focuses more on fulfilling the spirit of the SEFC (through mediation, negotiation, or compulsory conciliation) than on sanctions and fault attribution.

These guiding principles are by no means exhaustive, but could provide a fertile ground for further debate and action in the new millennium. The success of this regime-building approach will depend much on the level of collective political will, and the efforts of bureaucratic alliances and interdisciplinary cooperation.

The Need for an International Space Agency

At present, regional and interregional coordination of space science and technical assistance for developing countries is coordinated by the U.N. Programme on Space Applications, through its Office for Outer Space Affairs.[138] However, the Programme's main focus is in making the benefits of space technology available to all countries by such cooperative activities as sharing payloads, ensuring compatibility of space systems, educating in remote sensing, and providing access to launch capabilities.[139] The Programme pays scant attention to the conservation of the space environment. In spite of the establishment of the U.N. Conference on Environment and Development (UNCED) and the U.N. Environment Program (UNEP), the United Nations still lacks any coherent institutional mechanism for dealing effectively with environmental issues. At present, environmental responsibilities are divided among numerous international organizations, but the existing institutions suffer from poor coordination and the lack of real power and authority. In order to offer any credible protection to the outer-space environment a U.N. International Space Agency (UNISA) should be established, and should be managed by COPUOS. NASA (United States), CNES (France), BNSC (United Kingdom), NASDA (Japan), ASI (Italy), DARA (Germany), RKA (Russia), the International Telecommunication Union (ITU), the International Astronomical Federation (JAY), and other international space organizations should be brought under UNISA's umbrella.[140] The presence of one single international agency to coordinate international negotiations on the regulation of space activities is crucial to the success of any program that has the goal of the protection and preservation of the space environment as the "province of all mankind."

A truly inter-disciplinary approach must be undertaken under the auspices of the proposed UNISA. The role of UNISA would be to coordinate the Scientific and Technical Subcommittee and the Legal Subcommittee of COPUOS, and the participation of experts from the areas of science, technology, economics, health, national security, law, and other fields. The contribution of these "communities of shared knowledge" or "epistemic communities"[141] plays a crucial role in influencing the space regime formation, particularly in identifying and developing policy options. . . . The proposed UNISA would also be the international agency in charge of making recommendations to the United Nations to adopt internationally binding norms and enforceable regulations in appropriate international agreements, in the form of protocols to the proposed Space Environment Framework Convention. In order to promote the protection of the space environment and the associated earth environment, states parties should be obliged to arrange for members of UNISA to have access to all parts of stations, installations, equipment, and spacecraft for the purpose of inspection to ensure effective implementation of the Space Environment Framework Convention and its subsequent protocols.

The proposed UNISA is crucial to the success of the regime-building approach to be adopted in the formation of the Space Environment Framework Convention. The following guidelines are instrumental to the effectiveness and success of UNISA as a strategic manager:

1. the formulation of a clear mission, agreed to by the signatories to the SEFC;
2. the acceptance of the role of UNISA in an organizational structure that reflects the interest, power, and capabilities of member states;
3. the minimization of bureaucratic inefficiency through the establishment of an able and professional Secretariat within UNISA to coordinate transnational scientific, technical, technological, and legal matters, maintaining at all times an apolitical agenda;

4. the authority to engage in research on the effects of all space activities on both the outer-space environment and the Earth's environment;

5. the authority to recommend, from time to time and without the need to achieve consensus, relevant principles to be included in a protocol to the Space Environment Framework Convention; and

6. the guarantee of funding from the United Nations.

We have to recognize that UNISA, like all international organizations, will ultimately be a political institution. Like all politics, there will be a fair share of political bargaining and power-brokering. But as long as we have an active management strategy in place—which is as much a part of the bargaining process—commitments will eventuate and performance will ensue. Efforts are already underway to establish regional centers for space science and technology education, led by the U.N. Programme on Space Applications.[142] As mentioned earlier, the establishment of UNISA would harmonize the myriad initiatives and programs undertaken by the spectrum of organizations and agencies involved in the exploration and use of outer space.[143] It will be in a better position to coordinate uniform policies among the many states to implement SEFC rules for the protection of the "province of all mankind." UNISA will draw together COPUOS, its Legal as well as its Scientific and Technical Subcommittees, and the administrators of the U.N. Programme on Space Applications, to work more closely with the governments of member states at the policy-making level. The above criteria may seem like a millennial wish list, but the fact is they have been surfacing as agenda items at numerous meetings, colloquia, conferences, and symposia.

Conclusions

Any attempt to establish a new space order can only be successful if it is based on a realistic assessment of the existing power structures within the international community.[144] Experience indicates that, when the developing countries that lack spacefaring capabilities but possess numerical superiority in the General Assembly attempt to control the process of hard-law formation, the result is a farrago of impractical propositions and vague obligations in multilateral conventions. For example, the CHM regime declared in Article XI of the Moon Agreement finds few supporters, particularly amongst the developed nations, and appears condemned to a philosophical existence.[145] The ephemeral notions of "equitable access" and "equitable distribution" require a delicate balance of the special needs of developing nations with the largely commercial and military interests of the spacefaring states. On the other hand, the protection of the outer-space environment as the "province of all mankind" transcends the politics of technological and economic asymmetry—it affects all individuals, present and future.

As discussed . . . , the current space treaties regime fails to offer satisfactory protection to the space environment. Customary international law can hardly be said to possess adequate content or scope to prevent damage and furnish sufficient sanctions to be directed against the perpetrators when damage to the outer-space environment occurs. It is "not a regulatory system and cannot be turned into one."[146] A unique Space Environment Framework Convention, created within a regime-building approach, still recognize[s] the prohibition on damage or harm to the outer-space environment and overcome[s] "the tyranny of realism"[147] to protect the "province of all mankind." The desirability of this recommendation is supported by the principle of sustainable development as recognized by the international community in the Stockholm Declaration, the Rio Declaration, and various multilateral international fora; it is also grounded in the jurisprudential notions of intergenerational equity and responsibility. The proposals on the possibility of negotiating the Framework Convention on the Protection of the Outer Space Environment and the establishment of a U.N. International Space Agency should be considered seriously. Commitments made within an organizational framework regime as such, no matter how insignificant the skeptics may lead one to believe they are, are visible to the participants and part of the kaleidoscope of favors, promises, and patronage exchanged over time.[148] It has been said that the notion of the outer-space environment as the "province of all mankind" was adopted as a result of "concrete political interests and social or economic requirements involved in the struggle and cooperation of states in pursuit of solutions to compelling problems of the moment."[149] The compelling problems of space debris and the increasing use of nuclear power sources must be addressed immediately. The protection of the space environment in the new millennium is in the interest of all states, developing and developed, and it is in the interest of all human beings, present and future.

Notes

1. Treaty on Principles Governing the Activities of States in the Exploration and Use of Outer Space, Including the Moon and Other Celestial Bodies, Jan. 27, 1967, art. 1, 18 U.S.T. 2410, 610 U.N.T.S. 205 [hereinafter Outer Space Treaty].

2. *See, e.g.,* Bin Cheng, *The 1967 Space Treaty,* 95 Journal Du Droit International [3.Droit- Int'l] 532 (1968); Stephen Gorove, *Property Rights in Outer Space: Focus on the Proposed Moon Treaty,* 2 J. Space L. 27 (1974); He Qizhi, *Certain Legal Aspects of Commercialization of Space Activities,* 15 Annals Air & Space L. 333 (1990); Vladimir Kopal, *The Question of Defining Outer Space,* 8 J. Space L. 154 (1980); H. A. Wassenbergh, *Speculations on the Law Governing Space Resources,* 5 Annals Air & Space L. 611 (1980).

3. . . . *See, e.g.*, Albert Gore, Jr., *Outer Space, the Global Environment, and International Law: Into the Next Century,* 57 Tenn. L. Rev. 329 (1990); Nicolas Mateesco Matte, *Environmental Implications and Responsibilities in the Use of Outer Space,* 14 Annals Air & Space L. 419 (1989); D. E. Reibel, *Environmental Regulation of Space Activity: The Case of Orbital Debris,* 10 Stan. Envt'l. L. J. 97 (1991).

4. *See* Outer Space Treaty, art. I, 18 U.S.T. at 2410, 610 U.N.T.S. at 205.

5. Id. art. III, 18 U.S.T. at 2413, 610 U.N.T.S. at 208.

6. . . . *See* Warren E. Leary, *String of Rocket Mishaps Worries Industry,* N.Y. Times, May 12, 1999, at A1.

7. *See generally* P. U. R. Abeyratne, *The Use of Nuclear Power Sources in Outer Space and Its Effect on Environmental Protection,* 25 J. Space L. 17 (1997) . . . and Stanley B. Rosenfield, *Where Air Space Ends and Outer Space Begins,* 7 J. Space. L. 137 (1979). . . .

8. *See* Abeyratne, *The Use of Nuclear Power Sources,* at 17; He Qizhi, *Towards a New Legal Regime for the Use of Nuclear Power Sources in Outer Space,* 14 J. Space. L. 95, 97 (1986).

9. *Question Relating to the Use of Nuclear Power Sources in Outer Space,* U.N. GAOR, COPUOS, 15th Sess., at 14, U.N. Doc. AIAC.1051220 (1978).

10. Outer Space Treaty, art. I, 18 U.S.T. at 2412, 610 U.N.T.S. at 207.

11. *See Summary Record of the 188th Meeting,* U.N. GAOR, COPUOS, 15th Sess., at 6, U.N. Doc. AJAC.IOSIC.115R188 (1978); *Proposed Terms of Reference for Ad Hoc Working Group of Scientific and Technical Sub-Committee on "Questions Relating to the Uses of Nuclear Power Sources in Outer Space,"* U.N. GAOR, COPUOS, 15th Sess., U.N. Doc. AIAC.105/C.l/L.103 (1978). . . .

12. *See Use of Nuclear Power in Outer Space,* U.N. GAOR, COPUOS, 15th Sess. U.N. Doc. A/AC.105/C.2iL.115 (1978).

13. *See The Elaboration of Draft Principles Relevant to the Use of Nuclear Power Sources in Outer Space,* U.N. GAOR, COPUOS, 26th Sess., U.N. Doc. A/AC.1051C.21L.154 Rev. 2 (1987) [hereinafter *NPS Principles*]. . . .

14. *See* Howard A. Baker, Space Debris: Legal and Policy Implications 107 (1989). . . .

15. *See, e.g.*, Howard A. Baker, *Current Space Debris Policy and Its Implications,* in Proceedings of The Thirty-Second Colloquium on The Law of Outer Space 59 (1990); Howard A. Baker, *The Sci-Lab Perception: Its Impact on Protection of the Outer Space Environment,* in Proceedings of The Thirtieth Colloquium of The Law of Outer Space 121 (1988); Nicholas L. Johnson, *Hazards of the Artificial Space Environment,* in Proceedings of The Thirtieth Colloquium of The Law of Outer Space at 482. The International Aeronautical Federation recognized in a 1984 study that space debris was a "particularly serious" and "real" problem in the low-earth-orbit (LEO) and that international action was "imperative" in order to resolve the problem. *Implications to International Cooperation of Large-Scale Space Systems,* U.N. GAOR, COPUOS, at 19, U.N. Doc. AIAC.105I349 (1984).

16. *See* Stephen Gorove, Developments in Space Law: Issues and Policies 156, 164 (1991).

17. The term "geosynchronous" applies to all orbits having a period of rotation corresponding to that of Earth (about 23 hours, 56 minutes). It is a unique natural resource of vital importance for myriad space activities, including communications, meteorology, broadcasting, remote sensing, data relay, and tracking. Presently the entire civil telecommunication satellite industry is located in GEO. The presence of space debris makes GEO an "endless shooting gallery"; active payloads, otherwise known as functioning space objects, are "sitting ducks." David H. Suddeth,

Debris in the Geostationary Orbit Ring: "The Endless Shooting Gallery"—The Necessity for a Disposal Policy, in Orbital Debris 349, 356 (Donald J. Kessler & Shin-Yi Su eds., 1985).

18. . . . *See* D. M. Wanland, *Hazards to Navigation in Outer Space: Legal Remedies and Salvage Law* 8979 (research prepared for the NASA-AMES/University Consortium for Astrolaw Research, Hastings College of Law, University of California), cited in Baker, Space Debris: Legal and Policy Implications at 127 nn. 104 & 106. . . .

19. *See* Craig Fishman, *Space Salvage: A Proposed Treaty Amendment to the Agreement on the Rescue of Astronauts, the Return of Astronauts and the Return of Objects Launched into Space,* 26 Va. J. Intl'l. 965, 995 (1986).

20. *See* Baker, Space Debris: Legal and Policy Implications at 13 and . . . Vladimir Bogomolov, *Prevention of an Arms Race in Outer Space—Developments in the Conference on Disarmament in 1994,* 235. Space L. 43, 46 (1995).

21. *See* Baker, Space Debris: Legal and Policy Implications at 23–24, 35–37.

22. U.N. Press Release, *Outer Space Committee Considers Agenda of Legal Sub-Committee,* 05/1259 (Jun. 11, 1986) 3, cited in Baker, Space Debris: Legal and Policy Implications at 146 n. 482.

23. *Last Full Crew Leave Mir, To Be Abandoned After 13 Years,* N.Y. Times, Aug. 28, 1999, at A6.

24. *See Thirtieth Session of the Committee on the Peaceful Uses of Outer Space,* U.N. GAOR, COPUOS, para. 18, U.N. Doc. A/AC.1OS/5R.294 (1987) (remarks by the Pakistani representative on the effects of NPS and space debris).

25. *See* Gorove, Space Debris Issues at 178 (summarizing Carl Christol, *Scientific and Legal Aspects of Space Debris*).

26. . . . *See Draft Technical Report on Space Debris of the Scientific and Technical Subcommittee,* U.N. GAOR, COPUOS, 35th Sess., U.N. Doc. AIAC.105/707 (1998); *Report of the Scientific and Technical Subcommittee on the Work of Its Thirty-Fifth Section,* U.N. GAOR, COPUOS, U.N. Doc. IAC.1051697 (1998); *Report of the Scientific and Technical Subcommittee on the Work of Its Thirty-Fourth Session,* U.N. GAOR, COPUOS, U.N. Doc. AIAC.1051672 (1997). In 1999, the final draft technical report on space debris was adopted by the Subcommittee at its 36th Session in Vienna. *See Report of the Scientific and Technical Subcommittee on the Work of Its Thirty-Sixth Session. See also Thirtieth Session of the Committee on the Peaceful Uses of Outer Space,* U.N. GAOR, COPUOS, U.N. Doc. A/AC.1OS/5R.294 (1987) para. 35.

27. For a brief account of how legal norms work in the international arena, are Abram Chayes & Antonia Handler Chayes, The New Sovereignty: Compliance with International Regulatory Agreements 112–24 (1995).

28. Daniel Vice, *Implementation of Biodiversity Treaties: Monitoring, Fact-Finding, and Dispute Resolution,* 29 N.Y.U. 3. Int'l L. & Pol. 577, 631 (1997).

29. *See* Vice, *Implementation of Biodiversity Treaties* at 632.

30. *See* Vice, *Implementation of Biodiversity Treaties.*

31. *See Question of the Peaceful Use of Outer Space,* G.A. Res. 1348, U.N. GAOR, 13th Sess., 792 plen. mtg., U.N. Doc. AIRES 11348 (1958).

32. *See International Co-operation in the Peaceful Uses of Outer Space,* G.A. Res. 1472, U.N. GAOR, 14th Sess., 856th plen. mtg., U.N. Doc. AIRES/1472 (1959).

33. G.A. Res. 1962, U.N. GAOR, 18th Sess., 1280th plen. mtg., U.N. Doc. AIRES/1962 (963); *see also* G.A. Res. 1721, U.N. GAOR, 16th Sess., 1085th plen. mtg., U.N. Doc. AIRES/1721(1961) (setting expectations and reviewing progress of COPUOS); G.A. Res. 1802, U.N. GAOR, 17th Sess., plen. mtg., U.N. Doc.

AIRES1I8O2 (1962) (same); G.A. Res. 1884, U.N. GAOR, 18th Sess, 1244th plen. mtg., U.N. Doc. A1RES/1884 (1963) (calling upon states not to deploy weapons of mass destruction in outer space).

34. The Outer Space Treaty has entered into force for over 90 states, including the United States, Russia, and the People's Republic of China. It has been signed but not yet ratified by about 30 countries. See 18 U.S.T. at 2410, 610 U.N.T.S. at 205.

35. See Walter W. C. de Vries, The Creation of a Concept of the Law of Outer Space, in Space Law: Views of the Future, 21, 29 (Tanja Zwaan et al. eds., 1988) [hereinafter Views of the Future].

36. These consist of, inter alia, the freedom of exploration and use of outer space in accordance with the fundamental principles of international law, including the Charter of the United Nations. See Ida Bagus R. Supancana, The Contribution of the Developing Countries to the Legal Formulation of Future Space Law, in de Vries, Views of the Future at 113, 117.

37. Apr. 22, 1968, 19 U.S.T. 7570, 672 U.N.T.S. 119 (entered into force Dec. 3, 1968) [hereinafter Astronaut Agreement]. It has entered into force for over 75 countries. The European Space Agency is also a party.

38. Opened for signature Jan. 14, 1975, 28 U.S.T. 695, 1023 U.N.T.S. 15 (entered into force Sept. 15, 1976) [hereinafter Registration Convention]. It has been ratified by 37 states.

39. Mar. 29, 1972, 24 U.S.T. 2389, 961 U.N.T.S. 187 (entered into force Oct. 9, 1973) [hereinafter Liability Convention]. It is presently binding in over 70 countries.

40. Opened for signature Dec. 18, 1979, 1363 U.N.T.S. 3 (registered ex officio July 11, 1984) [hereinafter Moon Agreement]. The Moon Agreement has been ratified by Austria, Australia, Chile, the Netherlands, Pakistan, the Philippines, and Uruguay; it has also been signed by France, Guatemala, India, Morocco, Peru, and Romania. It is perhaps unsurprising that the Moon Agreement has not been ratified by the major developed states, namely, Canada, France, Germany, Japan, Russia, the United Kingdom, and the United States. Because they possess the technological capabilities to engage in ongoing space activities, the regime of equitable sharing and distribution as proposed in the Agreement remains highly unsatisfactory to the spacefaring nations.

41. Treaty Banning Nuclear Weapon Tests in the Atmosphere, in Outer Space and Under Water, Aug. 5, 1963, 14 U.S.T. 1313, 480 U.N.T.S. 43 (entered into force Oct. 10, 1963) [hereinafter Partial Nuclear Test Ban Treaty].

42. Treaty on the Limitation of Anti-Ballistic Missile Systems, May 26, 1972, U.S.-U.S.S.R., 23 U.S.T. 3435 (entered into force Oct. 3, 1972) [hereinafter ABM Treaty].

43. Convention on the Prohibition of Military or Any Other Hostile Use of Environmental Modification Techniques, May 18, 1977, 31 U.S.T. 333, 1108 U.N.T.S. 151 (entered into force Jan. 17, 1980) [hereinafter ENMOD Convention].

44. Outer Space Treaty, art. I, 15 U.S.T. at 2413, 610 U.N.T.S. at 207–08.

45. Id., art II, 18 U.S.T. at 2413, 610 U.N.T.S. at 208.

46. See Bogota Declaration, Dec. 3, 1976, reprinted in 6 J. Space L. 193 (1978).

47. Outer Space Treaty, art. IX, 18 U.S.T. at 2416, 610 U.N.T.S. at 210.

48. See Astronaut Agreement, arts. 1975, 19 U.S.T. at 75739775, 672 U.N.T.S. at 121–23.

49. Id., art. 5(4), 19 U.S.T. at 7575, 672 U.N.T.S. at 123.

50. Outer Space Treaty, art. V, 18 U.S.T. at 2414, 610 U.N.T.S. at 209.

51. *See* Liability Convention, art. 11, 24 U.S.T. at 2392, 961 U.N.T.S. at 189.

52. "Space object" is defined as "component parts as well as the launch vehicle and parts thereof." Id., art. I.

53. Id.

54. *See* Registration Convention, art. 11, 28 U.S.T. at 698–99, 1023 U.N.T.S. at 17.

55. *See* id., art. IV(1), 28 U.S.T. at 699, 1023 U.N.T.S. at 17.

56. *See* id., art. IV(3), 28 U.S.T. at 700, 1023 U.N.T.S. at 17.

57. *See* H. A. Wassenbergh, Speculations on the Law Governing Space Resources, 5 *Annals Air & Space L.* (1998) at 617.

58. Moon Agreement, art. 7, 1363 U.N.T.S. at 24.

59. *See* id., art. 11(2), 1363 U.N.T.S. at 25.

60. Carl Christol, Space Law: Past, Present, and Future 347 (1991).

61. *See* G.A. Res. 1348, U.N. GAOR 13th Sess. (recognizing "the common interest of mankind in outer space"); *see also* G.A. Res. 1472, U.N. GAOR 14th Sess. (calling for international cooperation in the peaceful use of outer space); G.A. Res. 1721, U.N. GAOR, 16th Sess., 1085th plen. mtg., U.N. Doc. AIRES/1721 (1961) (asserting that the use and exploration of outer space should be "for the benefit of mankind").

62. See A. O. Adede, *The System for the Exploitation of the "Common Heritage of Mankind" at the Caracas Conference,* 69 Am. J. Int'l. L. 31(1975). *See also* Declaration of Principles Governing the Sea-Bed and the Ocean Floor, and the Subsoil Thereof, Beyond the Limits of National Jurisdiction, G.A. Res. 2749, U.N. GAOR, 25th Sess., 1933 plen. mtg., U.N. Doc. 1RE512749 (1970). . . .

63. Aldo Armando Cocca, *The Principle of the "Common Heritage of All Mankind" as Applied to Natural Resources from Outer Space and Celestial Bodies,* in Proceedings of the Sixteenth Colloquium on the Law of Outer Space 172, 174 (1974) (quoting the Conclusion of the VITA Hispano-Luso-American Congress on International Law, Buenos Aires, 1969); *see also* Ernst Fasan, "The Meaning of the Term 'Mankind' in Space Legal Language," 2 J. Space L. (1974) at 129.

64. . . . Moon Agreement, art. 11(1), 1363 U.N.T.S. at 25. . . . *See* id., art. 11(5), 1363 U.N.T.S. at 25.

65. *See* Christol, Space Law: Past, Present, and Future, at 406–26.

66. Outer Space Treaty, art. III, 18 U.S.T. at 2413, 610 U.N.T.S. at 208.

67. Stephen Gorove, *The Concept of "Common Heritage of Mankind": A Political, Moral or Legal Innovation?* 9 San Diego L. Rev. 390, 393 (1972).

68. *See* Aldo Armando Cocca, *The Advances in International Law Through the Law of Outer Space,* 9 J. Space L. 13, 16 (1981). . . .

69. . . . Richard H. Fallon, Jr., *Reflections on Dworkin and the Two Faces of Law,* 67 Notre Dame L. Rev. 553, 554 (1992); *see also* Friedrich V. Kratochwil, Rules, Norms and Decisions: On the Conditions of Practical and Legal Reasoning in International Relations and Domestic Affairs 97 (1989) ("The prescriptive force of norms appears then as a claim to validity which is mediated by language and which can be validated discursively.").

70. Ogunsola Ogunbanwo, International Law and Outer Space Activities 66 (1975).

71. Outer Space Treaty, 18 U.S.T. at 2413, 610 U.N.T.S. at 208. *But see* Shyom Brown et al., Regimes for the Ocean, Outer Space and Weather 130 (1977), *quoted in* Young, Law and Policy in the Space Station's Era at 193. . . .

72. Chayes & Chayes, The New Sovereignty: Compliance with International Regulatory Agreements at 124.

73. Outer Space Treaty, art. VI, 18 U.S.T. at 2415, 610 U.N.T.S. at 209.

74. Id., art. IV, 18 U.S.T. at 2413, 610 U.N.T.S. at 208.

75. See Moon Agreement, art. 3, 1363 U.N.T.S. at 23. . . .

76. See Christol, Space Law: Past, Present, and Future at 471–72. Such restrictions are on weapons systems that can be classified as nuclear weapons or weapons of mass destruction. See Gennady Danilenko, *The Progressive Development of Space Law: New Opportunities and Restraints,* in de Vries, *The Creation of a Concept of the Law of Outer Space* at 99, 109.

77. For a discussion of the effect of the ARM Treaty on the SDI, see V. S. Vereshehetin, *"Strategic Defense Initiative" and International Law,* in Proceedings of the Twenty-Ninth Colloquium on the Law of Outer Space (1987).

78. See, e.g., *Draft Treaty on the Prohibition of the Stationing of Weapons of Any Kind in Outer Space,* U.N. GAOR, 36th Sess., Annex, U.N. Doc. A/36/192/ Annex (1981) (annex to a request for the inclusion of a supplementary item on the agenda); *Draft Treaty on the Prohibition of the Use of Force in Outer Space and From Space Against the Earth,* U.N. GAOR, 38th Sess., Annex, U.N. Doc. A/38/194/Annex (1983) (same).

79. See *Report of the Scientific and Technical Subcommittee on the Work of Its Thirty-Fifth Session,* U.N. Doc. IAC 1051697 (1998), paras. 126–27.

80. Id., para 131

81. See Liability Convention, art. 1(a), 24 U.S.T. at 2397, 961 U.N.T.S. at 189. Damage may be caused on the surface of the Earth, *see* id., art 11, 24 U.S.T. at 2392, 961 U.N.T.S. at 189, to aircraft in flight, *see* id., or elsewhere other than on the surface of the Earth, *see* id., arts. III and IV, 24 U.S.T. at 23929793, 91 U.N.T.S. at 189–90.

82. Id., art. 11, 24 U.S.T. at 2392, 961 U.N.T.S. at 189.

83. See id., art. 111, 24 US.T. at 2392, 961 U.N.T.S. at 190.

84. See Gorove, Developments in Space Law: Issues and Policies at 154.

85. The Registration Convention does not even provide for any obligatory marking of space objects. See Vladimir Kopal, *Some Considerations on the Legal Status of Aerospace Systems,* 22, 3. Space L. 57, 62 (1994).

86. See Outer Space Treaty, art. XI, 18 U.S.T. at 2418, 610 U.N.T.S. at 210.

87. See Registration Convention, 28 U.S.T. at 700–01, 1023 U.N.T.S. at 17–18.

88. See Partial Nuclear Test Ban Treaty, ENMOD Convention, International Telecommunication Convention, Oct. 25, 1973, 28 U.S.T. 2495, 1209 U.N.T.S. 32.

89. Christopher Joyner, *Legal Implications of the Concept of the Common Heritage of Mankind,* 35 Int'l. & Comp. L. Q. 190, 197 (1986).

90. See Jonathan I. Charney, *Universal International Law* 87 Am. J. Int'l L. at 543–47.

91. See Buenos Aires International Instrument at 112.

92. *Reports of the Commission to the General Assembly,* U.N. Doc. A/6309/ Rev.1 (1966), reprinted in [1966] 2 Y.B. Int'l L. Comm'n. 169, 248, U.N. Doc. A/CN.4/5ER.A/1966/Add.1.

93. See, e.g., Christol, Space Law: Past, Present, and Future at 443.

94. See Alfred von Verdross, *Forbidden Treaties in International Law,* 31 Am. J. Int'l L. 571, 574 (1937).

95. See G.A. Res. 2994, U.N. GAOR, 27th Sess., 2112 plen. mtg., U.N. Doc. A/RE5/2994 (1972).

96. United Nations Conference on the Environment: Final Documents, U.N. Doc. AICONF.45114, reprinted in 11 I.L.M. 1416, 1418 (1972).

97. See Veit Koester, From *Stockholm to Brundtland,* 20 Envt'l. Pol'y & L. 14, 15 (1990).

98. *See* G.A. Res. 3717, U.N. GAOR, 37th Sess., 48th plen. mtg., U.N. Doc. A/RES/37/7 (1982).

99. World Comm'n on Env't and Dev, Our Common Future, (1987).

100. *See* G.A. Res. 42/186, U.N. GAOR, 42d Sess., U.N. Doc. AIRE5142/186 (1988); G.A. Res. 42/187, U.N. GAOR, 42d Sess., 96th plen. mtg., U.N. Doc. A/RES/42/187 (1988).

101. *See* Gunther Handl, *Environmental Security and Global Change: The Challenge to International Law,* 1 Y.B. Int'l. Envt'l. L. 3, 3974 (1990); Louis Sohn, *The Stockholm Declaration on the Human Environment,* 14 Harv. Int'l. L. J. 423 (1973).

102. *See* Rio Declaration on Environment and Development, adopted June 14, 1992, U.N. Doc. A/CONF/15 1/26, vol. I, reprinted in 31 I.L.M. 874 (1992) [hereinafter Rio Declaration].

103. *See generally* Edith Brown Weiss, In Fairness to Future Generations at 17–46 (arguing that each generation is obliged to conserve the planet in trust for the next). An alternative theory of our responsibility to future generations was recently put forward in Christopher Stone, Earth and Other Ethics: The Case for Moral Pluralism 84–91 (1987) and was further developed in Gary P. Supanich, *The Legal Basis of Intergenerational Responsibility: An Alternative View—The Sense of Intergenerational Identity,* 3 Y.B. Int'l. Envt'l. L. 94, 99–105 (1992). . . .

104. *See, e.g.,* Christopher Stone, Earth and Other Ethics: The Case for Moral Pluralism (1987) at 85–89; Philip Alston, A Third Generation of Solidarity Rights: Progressive Development or Obfuscation of International Human Rights Law?, 29 Num. Int'l. L. Rev. 307 (1982); Brian Bany, Justice Between Generations, in Law, Morality and Society 270–76 (P. Hacker & J. Raz eds., 1977). . . .

105. *See, e.g.,* Patricia Birnie & Alan Boyle, International Law and the Environment 119 (1992) ("The protection of common spaces . . . is thus a complex issue in which scientific, moral, ethical, political, economic, social, and technological issues are inextricably intertwined and on which these interests do not always coincide."); *see also* Alexandre S. Timosbenko, *From Stockholm to Rio: The Institutionalization of Sustainable Development,* in Sustainable Development and International Law 143 (Winfried Lang ed., 1995) (chronicling the development and legitimization of the notion of sustainable development beginning with the Stockholm Conference in 1972).

106. Gary P. Supanich, *The Legal Basis of Intergenerational Responsibility: An Alternative View—The Sense of Intergenerational Identity,* 3 Y.B. Int'l. Envt'l. L. (1992) at 107.

107. Robert Repetto, World Enough and Time: Successful Strategies for Resource 15 (1986), quoted in Supanich, *The Legal Basis of Intergenerational Responsibility* at 107.

108. Anthony D'Amato, *Do We Owe a Duty to Future Generations to Preserve the Global Environment?* 84 Am. J. Int'l. L. 190, 198 (1990).

109. Jutta Brunnee & Stephen Toope, Environmental Security and Freshwater Resources: Ecosystem Regime Building, 91 Am. J. Int'l. L. (1997) at 28. . . .

110. *See* Stephen D. Krasner, *Regimes and the Limits of Realism: Regimes as Autonomous Variables,* 36 Int'l. Org. 497, 500 (1982).

111. A detailed examination of the various approaches to treaty-making is beyond the scope of this article. For a comprehensive treatise on the merits of different approaches to treaty-making, see Chayes & Chayes, The New Sovereignty: Compliance with International Regulatory Agreements (1995).

112. Geoffrey Palmer, New Ways to Make International Environmental Law (1992) at 269; *see also* John Gerard Ruggie, *International Regimes, Transactions,*

and Change: Embedded Liberalism in the Postwar Economic Order, 36 Int'l. Org. 379, 382 (1982). . . .

113. *See* Military and Paramilitary Activities (Nicar. v. U.S.), 1986 I.C.J. 14, 99 (June 27); Alexandra Kiss & Dinah Shelton, *Systems Analysis of International Law: A Methodological Inquiry,* 17 Neth. Y.B. Int'l. L. 45, 67 (1986).

114. *See* C. M. Chinkin, *The Challenge of Soft Law: Development and Change in International Law,* 38 Int'l. & Comp. L. Q. 850, 859–62 (1989) (commenting on the choice of soft-law forms); Blaine Sloan, *General Assembly Resolutions Revisited (Four Years Later),* 58 Brit. Y.B. Int'l. L. (1987) at 106–25 (analyzing the difficulties of measuring or even categorizing the force of a given norm, as well as the problems involved in attempting to measure its effects). . . .

115. *See, e.g.,* the 1989 Langkawi Declaration on the Environment, in which the Commonwealth heads of government committed themselves to a program of action that stresses the need to promote "economic growth and sustainable development, including the eradication of poverty." Reprinted in 5 Am. U. I. Int'l. I.. & Poly 589, 589 (1990). . . .

116. *See* G.A. Res. 2994, U.N. GAOR, 27th Sess., 2112 plen. mtg., U.N. Doc. A/RES/2994 (1972).

117. *See* Rio Declaration on Environment and Development, adopted June 14, 1992, U.N. Doc. A/CONF/151/26m vol. I, reprinted in 31 I.L.M. 874 (1992).

118. The Hague Declaration was signed by 24 nations at the International Summit on the Protection of the Global Atmosphere, March 11, 1989. *See* Hague Declaration on the Environment, 28 I.L.M. 1308 (1989).

119. *See* Winfried Lang, *Diplomacy and International Environmental Law-Making: Some Observations,* 3 Y.B. Int'l. Envt'l. L. (1992) at 109, 116 [hereinafter *Diplomacy and International Environmental Law-Making*]. Examples of soft obligations include articles 2 and 6 of the 1979 Convention on Long-Range Transboundary Air Pollution, Nov. 13, 1979, 34 U.S.T. 3043, 3046 47, 18 I.L.M. 1442, 1443–44 (1979).

120. Ozone Layer Convention.

121. Sept. 16, 1987, S. Treaty Doc. No. 100 10, 26 I.L.M. 1541 (1987) (entered into force Jan. 1, 1989) [hereinafter Montreal Protocol].

122. May 2, 1989, 28 I.L.M. 1335 (1989).

123. Adjustments to the Montreal Protocol on Substances that Deplete the Ozone Layer, June 29, 1990, S. Treaty Doc. No. 102–4, 30 I.L.M. 537 (1991) [hereinafter London Amendments].

124. Such an approach to international environmental law-making has the support of Abram Chayes & Antonia Handler Chayes, The New Sovereignty Compliance with International Regulatory Agreements (1995) at 225–27; Lang, *Diplomacy and International Environmental Law-Making* at 117–22; Palmer, *New Ways to Make International Environmental Law* at 273–78; and Donald Rothwell, *International Law and the Protection of the Arctic Environment,* 44 Int'l. & Comp. L. Q. 280, 308 (1995).

125. *See, e.g.,* Keohane, *The Demand for International Regimes* at 334. . . .

126. *See, e.g.,* Alan E. Boyle, Saving the World? Implementation and Enforcement of International Environmental Law Through International Institutions, 3 J. Envm. L. 229, 231 (1991); Katharina Kummer, Providing Incentives to Comply with Multilateral Environmental Agreements: An Alternative to Sanctions?, 3 Eur. Envn'l. L. Rev. 256, 257 (1994). . . .

127. *See, e.g.,* UNCLOS, art. 192, 21 I.L.M. at 1308, 1315 ("States have the obligation to protect and preserve the marine environment."); id., art. 235(1) ("States are responsible for the fulfillment of their international obligations concerning the protection and preservation of the marine environment. They shall be

liable in accordance with international law."); *see also* Elizabeth P. Barratt Brown, *Building a Monitoring and Compliance Regime Under the Montreal Protocol,* 16 Yale Int'l. L. 519, 544–70 (1991). . . .

128. *See, e.g.,* Andronico Adede, *Management of Environmental Disputes: Avoidance Versus Settlement,* in Sustainable Development and International Law at 115 (distinguishing between "dispute avoidance" and "dispute settlement"); Martti Koskenniemi, *Breach of Treaty or Non-Compliance? Reflections on the Enforcement of the Montreal Protocol,* 3 Y.B. Int'l. Envt'l. L. 123, 150–55 (1992) (assessing the effectiveness of the Meeting of the Parties under the Montreal Protocol). . . .

129. *See, e.g.,* Oran R. Young & Gail Osherenko, Polar Politics: Creating International Environmental Regimes (1993); Peter M. Haas, *Do Regimes Matter? Epistemic Communities and Mediterranean Pollution Control,* 43 Int'l. Org. (1989).

130. This effect was observed by the Intergovernmental Panel on Climate Change. *See* Oran R. Young, International Governance: Protecting the Environment in a Stateless Society 41–42 (1994); Daniel B. Bodansky, *The Emerging Climate Change Regime,* 20 Ann. Rev. Energy & Env't. 425, 443–44 (1995); Brunnee & Toope, *Environmental Security and Freshwater Resources* at 43 n A02.

131. At the 66th Conference of the International Law Association in Buenos Aires, Aug. 20, 1994, the Buenos Aires International Instrument on the Protection of the Environment from Damage Caused by Space Debris was adopted by consensus. *See* Maureen Williams, *The ILA Finalizes Its International Instrument on Space Debris in Buenos Aires, August 1994* Space L. (1995) at 77. . . .

132. United Nations Framework Convention on Climate Change, opened for signature June 4, 1992, S. Treaty Doc. No. 102–38 (1992), 31 I.L.M. 849 (1992) (entered into force Mar. 21, 1994) [hereinafter FCCC].

133. Kyoto Protocol to the FCCC, Conference of the Parties, 3d Sess., U.N. Doc. FCCC/CP/19971L.7/Add.l (1998), reprinted in 37 I.L.M. 22 (1998) [hereinafter Kyoto Protocol].

134. FCCC, art. 3(1), 31 I.L.M. 854. . . .

135. *See* Rodney R. McColloch, *Protocol on Environmental Protection to the Antarctic Treaty—The Antarctic Treaty—Antarctic Minerals Convention—Wellington Convention—Convention on the Regulations of Antarctic Mineral Resource Activities,* 22 G.A. 3. Int'l. & Comp. L. 211, 231 (1992). . . .

136. The Biodiversity Convention, June 5, 1992, 31 I.L.M. 818 (1992) [hereinafter Biodiversity Convention], signed at the U.N. Conference on Environment and Development (UNCED) by 153 states and the European Community, is aimed at conserving and protecting ecosystems and biodiversity. . . .

137. *See* FCCC, art. 11, 31 I.L.M. at 864–65; Biodiversity Convention, arts. 209721, 31 I.L.M. at 830–32.

138. *See Report of the Scientific and Technical Subcommittee on the Work of Its Thirty-Sixth Session,* paras. 65–76.

139. *See* id.

140. Extending the activities of the International Atomic Energy Agency (IAEA) to safeguarding the use of NPS in outer space has also been suggested. *See Report of the Legal Subcommittee on the Work of Its Twenty-Third Session (19 March–April 1984),* U.N. GAOR, COPUOS, at 26, U.N. Doc. AIAC.1051337 (1934); *see also* Hilary F. French, *Reforming the United Nations to Ensure Environmentally Sustainable Development,* 4 Transnat'l. L. & Contemp. Probs. 559, 586 (1994). . . .

141. *See, e.g.,* Oran R. Young & Gail Osherenko, Polar Politics: Creating International Environmental Regimes 245 (1993); Peter M. Haas, *Do Regimes Matter?*

Epistemic Communities and Mediterranean Pollution Control, 43 Int'l. Org. 377, 380, 384 (1989). . . .

142. *See Report of the Scientific and Technical Subcommittee on the Work of Its Thirty-Sixth Session,* U.N. GAOR, COPUS, U.N. Doc. A1AC,105/719 (1999).

143. Similar principles, but in relation to the equitable sharing of benefits from the exploitation of outer space, have been highlighted in Christol, Space Law: Past, Present, and Future (1991) at 440–42.

144. . . . *See* Suzanne C. Massey, *Global Warming—International Environmental Agreements—The 1992 United Nations Conference on the Environment and Development Most Likely Will Not Culminate in a Successfully Preventive Global Warming Treaty Without the United States' Support,* 22 G.A. 3. Int'l. & Comp. L. 175, 208 (1992).

145. *See* Douglas Barritt, *A "Reasonable" Approach to Resource Development in Outer Space,* 12 Loy. L.A. Int'l. & Comp. L. 615, 627–35 (1990); Barbara Ellen Heiin, *Exploring the Last Frontiers for Mineral Resources: A Comparison of International Law Regarding the Deep Seabed, Outer Space and Antarctica,* 23 Vano. 3. Transnational, 819, 834–35 (1990); *see also* Carl Q. Christol, *The 1979 Moon Agreement: Where Is It Today?,* 27 J. Space L. . . .

146. Palmer, *New Ways to Make International Environmental Law* at 266.

147. Don B. Kash, The Politics of Space Cooperation 126, 130–31 (1967) ("Given the weight of evidence put forward by our present reality one could hardly expect the government generally or a government agency to accept the innovative approach."). In the new millennium, a different reality of international cooperation faces us. *See, e.g.,* Aldo Armando Cocca, *Prospective Space Law,* 26 J. Space L. 51 (1998). . . .

148. *See* Lisa L. Martin, *Credibility, Costs and Institutions: Cooperation on Economic Sanctions,* 45 World Pol. 406, 418 (1993).

149. Merlin M. Magallona, *The Concept of Jus Cogens in the Vienna Convention on the Law of the Treaties,* 51 Phil. L. J. 521, 526 (1976).

PART 3

The Future of International Law

23

International Law—
New Actors and New Technologies:
Center Stage for NGOs?

John King Gamble and Charlotte Ku

Anyone whose head is not planted deeply in the sand must recognize that momentous changes are afoot with this phenomenon called the information age. . . . Will the information age have a significant effect on international law? International law has shown itself capable of moving along at its own lethargic pace, often influenced only marginally by the external world for which it is developing norms. Behavior occurs at so many individual and institutional levels that profound change at the human level can be blunted, distorted or blocked entirely before its influence is felt on the international law-making plane. These reservations notwithstanding, evidence exists that international law and the systems and assumptions that undergird it will be transformed by the information age.

Technology and the information age are changing the allocation of power and authority in the international system, with non-state actors such as intergovernmental organizations (IGOs) and nongovernmental organizations (NGOs) assuming decision-making roles previously reserved primarily to states.[1] Professor David Johnston sees the information age as "creating deep and broad disruptive breaches in our society, disruptions equal to those of the agricultural or industrial revolution."[2] Professors Keohane and Nye believe that the information age will alter the power structure of governments.[3] Jessica Mathews's stimulating article in *Foreign Affairs* argues both that the information revolution is shaking the foundations of state authority, the principal tenet of international law since 1648, and that the scholarly community has been slow to understand the profound ramifications of these changes.

> The most powerful engine of change in the relative decline of states and the rise of non-state actors is the computer and telecommunications revolution,

whose deep political and social consequences have been almost completely ignored. Widely accessible and affordable technology has broken
governments' monopoly on the collection and management of large
amounts of information and deprived governments of the deference they
enjoyed because of it. In every sphere of activity, instantaneous access to
information and the ability to put it to use multiplies the number of players who matter and reduces the number who command great authority.
The effect on the loudest voice—which has been the government's—has
been the greatest.[4]

Mathews's analysis forces us to re-examine our assumptions about the
allocation of authority and decision-making in international relations and
international law. The changes she describes have been accelerated by the
end of the Cold War and the bursting of the bipolar dam that for fifty years
constrained and simplified the international system. Observations like these
challenge the 300-year-old fundamental operating assumption of the international system that the authority and structure of states will dwarf all other
elements. Reacting to this new authority structure, Professor James Rosenau recommends moving beyond *governments,* which are tied too closely to
states, and instead focusing on the broader concept of *governance,* which
he thinks will be "transcendent" in the late twentieth century.[5]

A key element of this challenge to state authority is globalization.
Wolfgang Reinicke describes "the integration of a cross-national dimension
into the very nature of the organizational structure and strategic behavior of
individual companies."[6] Because these activities are undertaken to overcome the constraints of national boundaries, they pose a direct challenge
to states that derive their authority by maintaining territorial boundaries to
define the reach of their authority. Reinicke foresees a "threat to a government's ability to exercise internal sovereignty" and perhaps even a threat to
democracy itself[7] In response to this challenge, he proposes a partnership
between public and private entities to formulate a global public policy
using "cross-national structures of public interest" and the creation of
"more dynamic and responsive institutions of governance."[8] . . .

We [have] argued that the context within which international law operates has been shaped by two broad forces: (1) the state-centric character of
the post-Westphalian international system; and (2) the Gutenberg global
information system dominated by the printed word.[9] The former has been
analyzed extensively; the latter, at least so far as it affects international law,
largely has been ignored.

The Role of Information in the International Arena

Professor Ethan Katsch, one of the first scholars to address broad normative questions about the information age, explained why the revolution in

information would be much more significant than other technological changes that have influenced the law:

> Other new technologies, such as nuclear power or biotechnology or medical advances, have caused a reassessment of several areas of legal doctrine. Yet, information technology is different and presents the law with a very different challenge. It is different because . . . the law runs on information and because much of law is information. . . . Changes in our information environment are important for all institutions in society. They may, however, be particularly important for law. Law is not only a process that touches all other societal institutions but it is, as I have stressed, an institution that is fundamentally oriented around information and communication.[10]

The pace and complexity of life in the late twentieth century has set dramatically higher standards for the amount of information needed for decision-making. When analyzing the twentieth century from the vantage of the information age that drove its last decade, historians may see the leit-motif of the development and use of information on the structures and modes of that information. The NGOs that are our focus have heightened awareness of the information age they helped to create in the first place. The importance of information is hardly limited to recent scholarship in international relations, international institutions, and international law; however, the volume of information and variety of subjects covered have expanded drastically, demanding new modes to deal with the information. Further, "privatizing" of the sources of information has significant implications for governance and law-making. Professor Inis Claude's classic treatment of the development of international organizations noted,

> The third major stream of the development in the organization of international life arose from the creation of public international unions agencies concerned with problems in various essentially nonpolitical fields. Whereas both the Concert [of Europe] and the Hague [Peace Conferences] reflected the significance of the quest for security and the importance of high political issues, this third phenomenon was a manifestation of the increasing complexity of the economic, social, technical, and cultural interconnectedness of the peoples of the modern world.[11]

The growth of international institutions—both IGOs and NGOs—in the twentieth century is attributable, in part, to the need for information necessary for collective action.

In his seminal introduction, Professor Harold Jacobson describes the major functions of international organizations, the first of which is informational. The others are normative, rule-creating, rule-supervisory, and operational.

> *Informational* functions involve the gathering, analysis, exchange, and dissemination of data and points of view. The organization may use its

staff for these purposes, or it may merely provide a forum where representatives from constituent units can do these things. . . .

This article focuses on NGOs to test their newly achieved prominence
in international law-making by examining their role in the Landmines Convention and in the thwarting of the Multilateral Agreement on Investment.
Are NGOs a manifestation of new governance structures emerging in the
information age? Can they be a check against non-democratic, unaccount-
able, and aloof intergovernmental institutions that may complicate, rather
than solve, problems?[12] So that our discussion will be rooted in international law as usually understood we examine both international law's
encounters with NGOs and how NGOs relate to the sources of international
law. . . .

Especially in the 1990s, NGOs seem to have taken an almost Hegelian
leap in significance. A typical example of this expanded awareness of
NGOs can be seen in the views of former UN Secretary-General Boutros
Boutros-Ghali:

> Nongovernmental organizations are now considered full participants in
> international life. . . . Today, we are well aware that the international com-
> munity must address a human community that is transnational in every
> way. . . . The movement of people, information, capital, and ideas is as
> important today as the control of territory was yesterday [P]eace in the
> largest sense cannot be accomplished by the United Nations system or by
> Governments alone. Nongovernmental organizations, academic institu-
> tions, parliamentarians, business and professional communities, the media
> and the public at large must all be involved."[13]

. . . There is agreement that one of the major contributions of NGOs is
communicating information to governments, individuals, IGOs, and other
NGOs.[14] Recently, information technology has transformed communications so that it has become possible to mobilize worldwide political networks almost overnight to address specific issues. . . .

New technologies such as the Internet have created enormous opportunities for NGOs. Enterprising individuals with little institutional infrastructure beyond a computer can mobilize thousands of people over huge
distances. The drawing power of computers is enormous because it allows
individuals who are similarly equipped (set up with computers) to join a
cause based on their own interests without active solicitation. Technology
permits NGOs to organize large numbers from multiple sectors, and to do
so quickly, empowering NGOs in the international political and international law-making arenas. Even assuming good intentions, this new
power will not necessarily have positive results. It may become so cheap to
start new NGOs that competition for scarce resources will become more
intense. NGOs can coalesce around many different causes, good and evil.[15]

New Governance Structures, NGOs, and the Information Age

The Evolving Perception of the Role of the NGO

Professor James Rosenau's description of the nature of change can be applied to NGOs: "Change means the attrition of established patterns, the lessening of order, and the faltering of governance, until such time as new patterns can form and get embedded in the routines of world politics."[16] This creates the daunting challenge of discerning what "new patterns" will emerge when change is occurring at many levels and involves many centers of power, actors, and systemic assumptions.

In 1648, when the current state system emerged, decision-making authority in international relations was given to autonomous states that were expected to control activities within their borders and to function as equals on the international plane. A secular, hierarchical model was rejected—understandable in the context of the religious wars of that period—leaving power in the hands of states. Three hundred and fifty years later a new possibility has arisen, that governance which has "been usurped by governments" needs to expand beyond those governments.[17]

The new routine of international relations that is emerging will see an expanded and qualitatively different role for NGOs. Networks of information providers are formed by individuals drawn together by a shared interest. The importance of information to contemporary governance means those with information will influence political and legal processes.

Rosenau's concept of governance that "embraces governmental institutions, but . . . also subsumes informal, non-governmental mechanisms whereby those persons and organizations within its purview move ahead, satisfy their needs, and fulfill their wants"[18] encapsulates the new milieu within which international law will operate. How will international law, which has centered on the state as the principal actor as well as the locus of authority and power, respond in this new era? Rosenau asks "whether the emergent, successor order rests on new systemic foundations or whether it derives from the reconstitution of the existing system."[19] His answer is that it is too early to tell. "[M]uch depends on how the key concepts are defined, thus enabling different analysts to offer different interpretations as they accord greater or lesser weight to the post–Cold War competence of states, the strength of transnational issues, the power of sub-group dynamics, and the changing skills of citizens."[20]

It would be inaccurate to imply that international law—primarily as described by leading scholars—has ignored NGOs. Before World War II, NGOs were thought to play only a secondary role. Even those international law scholars who seemed most progressive and willing to extend the reach of the law showed a certain hesitance about NGOs. Twenty years ago, Professor Louis Henkin wrote,

> While international society today recognizes other entities—intergovernmental and other international organizations (the United Nations, the International Committee of the Red Cross), national and multinational companies with major transnational activities, even individual human beings—these are normally of concern only when, and because, their actions and the effects of their actions spill over national boundaries. Even to the extent that the individual has become a "subject" of international law, it is *international law* he is a subject of. Even the new concern for the human rights of individuals finds expression to date only through treaties and practices between nations, or through organizations of nations or bodies created by nations.[21]

In his more recent writings, Professor Henkin saw new possibilities presented as information technology facilitated the extension of international law to the individual. "States can control physical penetration, as by overflight in their airspace, but they cannot easily prevent communication or exclude information, they cannot prevent inspection by satellite from outer space, and national frontiers can do little to keep out or combat a growing number of environmental threats."[22]

An early theme about NGOs—made even before the term NGO was widely used—dealt with the formation of groups, often technical experts, to assist policy makers. Professor Malcolm Shaw discussed the nineteenth century origins of these groups:

> The nineteenth century also witnessed a considerable growth in international nongovernmental associations. . . . These private international unions, as they have been called, demonstrated a wide ranging community of interests on specific topics, and an awareness that co-operation had to be international to be effective. Such unions created the machinery for regular meetings and many established permanent secretariats. The work done by these organizations was, and remains, of considerable value in influencing governmental activities and stimulating world action.[23]

In describing the immediate post–World War I period, Professor Ellery Stowell observed that states had expanded the scope of their "voluntary cooperation through the establishment of international unions and commissions, and have recently organized the League of Nations and the World Court which give promise of better things to come."[24]

A recurring emphasis in scholarly writing about NGO activity has been on groups of experts who provided an objective scientific basis to guide the development of international law. Professor Quincy Wright described the positive role of NGOs:

Private organizations have many advantages over official organizations in the scientific exposition of international law. . . . Today the need for "an eye to the welfare of society at large" is greater than ever. Private institutions, whose members combine legal wisdom with wisdom in the other social disciplines and who view the problems of the world as a whole, can serve this need.[25]

. . . Contemporary international law is much less rigid and more inclusive—NGOs have benefited from this disposition. This outlook found early expression in the work and ideas of Professor (later World Court Judge) Philip Jessup and is captured in the phrase "transnational law."

The term "transnational law" [includes] all law which regulates actions or events that transcend national frontiers. Both public and private international law are included, as are other rules which do not wholly fit into such standard categories. . . . Transnational situations, then, may involve individuals, corporations, states, organizations of states, or other groups.[26]

Today, international law scholars and practitioners have taken Jessup's concept much further. A good example is the widely-used Weston, Falk, and D'Amato text, which states: "More and more nongovernmental transnational actors . . . are becoming primary actors in this human rights sphere, manifesting their primary allegiance to world order values with no territorial constraints."[27] The most recent version of this text finds a qualitative change in NGOs reaching the point where they "exert pressures, and [are] increasingly capable of ensuring constructive results through direct action."[28]

A good example of this broader view is presented by Judge Rosalyn Higgins, who wrote: "[I]nternational law is not rules. It is a normative system . . . harnessed to the achievement of common values."[29] She rejects the traditional concept of "subjects" and "objects" of international law as too narrow and prefers the phrase "international legal participants," which includes individuals, corporations and NGOs.[30] The law-making process in which all these participants are engaged is open and competitive. "Everyone is entitled to participate in the identification and articulation as to what they perceive the values to be promoted. Many factors, including the responsive chords struck in those to whom the argument is made, will determine whether particular suggestions prevail."[31]

NGOs already engage actively in issue identification and value setting, steps towards the "authoritative decision-making" that is definitive of international law. However, NGOs have had difficulty finding a seat at the table of authoritative decision-making. This is somewhat ironic because states long have relied on NGOs to provide the information that is essential to the entire process of decision-making. Their influence on governments or organs of intergovernmental organizations have brought them closer to the source of authoritative decision-making, but, important as this role has become, NGOs are not yet authoritative decision-makers. A principal question for this analysis is whether globalization and technology will elevate the status of NGOs.

The Expanding Role of NGOs in the Information Age

Contemporary circumstances have created opportunities for NGOs to play more direct roles in international law-making. This stems in part from international law's shift in focus from concerns of the state to those of the individual. One theory attributes the shift to the fact that little additional progress was being made in the state centric mode. As Professor Henkin put it: "More states, diversity of states, have slowed the movement from state values ('sovereignty') to human values, as in the law of human rights or law for the environment."[32] These are areas where states acting alone seemed not only incapable of solving problems, but seemed to have become part of the problem, e.g., in their failure to protect the environment, weak economic and political development, and abuses of human rights. This results in an expanded "band of activism" within which NGOs operate. For example, the second report from the International Law Association's Committee on Cultural Heritage Law discussed "the role of NGOs . . . both in defining the larger process of regulation and in implementing the harder law forged by intergovernmental agreement and custom."[33]

The technical character of many issues now facing policy-makers continues to make them, as they have been for decades, if not centuries, receptive to expert information. "New technology and the increasingly complex and technical nature of issues of global concern not only increase decision makers' uncertainty about their policy environment but also contribute to the diffusion of power, information, and values among states, thereby creating a hospitable environment for epistemic communities."[34] Thus, NGOs starting in the 1990s see their traditional nineteenth century–based role enhanced at the same time as technology permits a new range of functions that can bypass state borders.

Intergovernmental organizations have contributed to the prominence of NGOs by circumventing governments. As governments seem less able or willing to meet the financial needs of intergovernmental organizations, IGOs have tapped the vast private wealth available through the intermediation of NGOs. One result of this practice, however, may be an exaggerated perception of the ability of NGOs to carry out a wide range of activities. The potential fragmentation in information, resources, and decision-making may, in the long run, be a serious threat to the order and authority that are requisite to civil society. The hesitancy of international law to accord full participatory rights to NGOs in the law-making process stems in part from this situation.

Structurally, international law remains constrained by a preoccupation with territorial states that conduct activities across borders. Change is occurring, albeit slowly, to accommodate new actors and new voices. Pressure from complex new issues and the intense involvement of non-state actors like NGOs accelerate the change. NGOs do not operate in a vacuum; they often gain stature by cooperating with states. Although there are manifestations of new actors in areas previously reserved to states, a new structure for law-making has yet to emerge. Our work here is an assessment of how far the traditional law-making structure has been stretched as NGOs operate in a new information environment.

Most scholars acknowledge the positive influence NGOs have had on contemporary international law in areas such as the well being of individuals, human rights, gender and race equality, environmental protection, sustainable development, indigenous rights, nonviolent conflict resolution, participatory democracy, social diversity, and social and economic justice.[35] In the broadest sense, we may be moving towards the point where effective and sustained attention to these issues requires the political and financial mobilization of resources at all levels from local to global. This is where the voluntary, local, and issue specific character of NGOs make them a useful link between the sub-national community and national and international communities and institutions. By providing a link, NGOs supplement the human and financial resources of governments and intergovernmental organizations. . . .

Successful NGOs combine enlightened policies with the ability to mobilize constituents and the expertise to add to the competition. For international law, the contributions of NGOs need to be tested against this need for authoritative decision-making. "[A] crucial factor in the effectiveness of organizations is their perceived legitimacy, [which] is linked to participation and transparency in their decision-making processes and to the representative nature of bodies that exercise authority."[36] Although consideration of these factors may help to develop a role for NGOs as authoritative decision-makers, the diffuse and varied structure as well as the process of international law-making makes an across-the-board law-making role for NGOs difficult to formulate. Nevertheless, opportunities for NGO involvement and their information collection capacities are likely to increase as international law-making becomes a more continuous, iterative process in moving towards a common objective rather than merely establishing a specific, static norm.

NGOs have been extending their activities from issue identification to the monitoring of state and IGO compliance with and implementation of international legal obligations. Professor Christine Chinkin described this new role in terms of soft law: "The international legal order is an evolving one that requires a wide range of modalities for change and development, especially into new subject areas. They must draw upon the entire contin-uum of mechanisms ranging from the traditional international legal forms to the soft law instruments."[37]

NGOs have achieved a measure of recognition at UN-sponsored inter-governmental conferences through participation in preparatory activities and, to a degree, the conferences themselves. Participation has varied with the recent addition of separate NGO fora that parallel and complement the inter-governmental effort. The controversy over the location and role of the NGO Forum at the Beijing Women's Conference provided a pointed reminder of the ambiguity of the NGO role in authoritative decision-making.[38]

Traditionally, NGOs have helped to mold treaty language, although usually working through national delegations. Increasingly, they are also assisting with monitoring, compliance, and implementation of those instru-ments.[39] NGOs can enter the picture at many points from creating pres-sure—making demands—for norm change, to participating in treaty-drafting conferences. As treaties increasingly are seen not as static statements of norms, but as organic entities constantly changing and meeting new con-tingencies, NGOs have a wider range of opportunities to influence norms. This new situation is clear in the myriad of roles for NGOs in the fifty-year history of the International Whaling Commission.[40]

Proposals to allow NGOs some level of representation in the UN Gen-eral Assembly illustrate a new mode. UN organs like the General Assembly aid in "the creation and shaping of contemporary international law."[41] Pro-fessor Jonathan Charney wrote,

> Today, major developments in international law often get their start or substantial support from proposals, reports, resolutions, treaties or proto-cols debated in such forums. There, representatives of states and other interest groups come together to address important international problems of mutual concern. Sometimes these efforts result in a consensus on solv-ing the problem and express it in normative terms of general application. At other times, the potential new law is developed through the medium of international relations or the practices of specialized international institu-tions and at later stages is addressed in international forums. The process draws attention to the rule and helps to shape it and crystallize it.[42]

Models of NGO Influence on the Sources of International Law

This section will use the sources of international law to assess the influence exerted by NGOs. It examines three case studies of NGO influence: (1) the

1982 UN Convention on the Law of the Sea (UNCLOS III), (2) the 1997 Convention on the Prohibition of the Use, Stockpiling, Production, and Transfer of Anti-Personnel Mines and Their Destruction (the Ottawa Convention), and (3) the "false start" of the Multilateral Agreement on Investment (MAI) in 1998. These three cases demonstrate how technology has enhanced the political capacity and power of NGOs and what might be expected in the future.

The Sources of International Law

The four sources of international law, recognized in the Statute of the International Court of Justice and taught in every course in international law, are:

a. international conventions, whether general or particular, establishing rules expressly recognized by the contesting states;
b. international custom, as evidence of a general practice accepted as law;
c. the general principles of law recognized by civilized nations; and
d. subject to the provisions of Article 59, judicial decisions and the teachings of the most highly qualified publicists of the various nations, as subsidiary means for the determination of rules of law.[43]

. . . Although there is a voluminous literature on the sources of international law,[44] we have found no diagrammatic representation of the sources, except for a few that do nothing more than list the four.[45] Understanding possible interrelationship patterns among the sources, along with the possible information flows and roles for NGOs is greatly enhanced through the use of diagrams. The four main sources— treaty, custom, general principles of law, and judicial decisions/teachings of publicists— do not stand in isolation, as is often implied by a ranked list. While the two preeminent sources, treaty and custom, certainly are the clearest and most frequently used, often all four work as an interrelated system to develop international law.

The ability of NGOs to influence the sources of international law. Figure 23.1 represents the most general case and illustrates interrelationship patterns among states, IGOs, NGOs, and the four main sources of international law. The most important question addressed in the diagram is the directness of the link between NGOs and international law. Is there any instance where NGOs *directly* influence a source that, in turn, "creates" international law? The answer appears to be "yes," but with debilitating qualifications. It is almost impossible to make a case for a direct link between NGOs and the three most important sources, treaty, custom, and

Figure 23.1 General Case

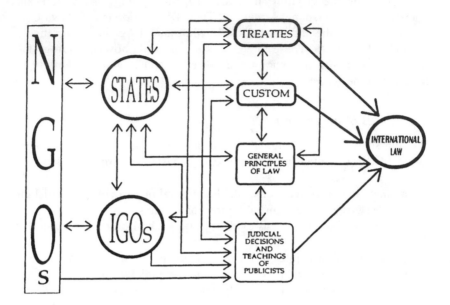

general principles. Each of the three sources is cast almost exclusively in terms of state action. The definition of treaty provided in the 1969 Vienna Convention on the Law of Treaties, "an international agreement concluded between states in written form and governed by international law,"[46] does not seem to leave the door open for a direct NGO role. One could argue that entities other than states are entitled to be parties to treaties, but when that envelope has been expanded it almost never has included NGOs. Prospects for direct NGO participation through custom are hardly more promising. Customary international law must meet two requirements: habituality and a feeling of legal obligation *(opinio juris)*. A rule of customary international law comes into existence when almost all states behave almost exactly the same way for a long time and feel a legal obligation to do so.

It is clear that states, and states alone, dominate in the creation and legitimization of customary international law. This does not mean that NGOs have no influence, but that they must work through intermediate entities, principally states and IGOs.

A direct link between general principles and NGOs is equally difficult to establish. Professor Georg Schwarzenberger listed general principles as the last "subsidiary" of three "law-creating processes,"[47] with the following three requirements that must be met:

1. it must be a *general* principle of law as distinct from a legal rule of more limited functional scope;
2. it must be recognized by *civilised* nations as distinct from barbarous or savage communities;
3. it must be shared by a fair number of civilised nations, and it is arguable that these must include at least the principal legal systems of the world.[48]

Perhaps a case could be made that NGOs help to clarify when a principle has become general enough to fit within this definition, but again NGOs, at most, help to apply icing to a cake prepared and baked by states and IGOs.

Figure 23.1 shows a direct link between NGOs and the fourth source, "judicial decisions and the teachings of the most highly qualified publicists." In interpreting this link, one must remember this is a much less significant source than the first three. Professor Schwarzenberger went so far as to call it a "subsidiary law-determining agenc[y]," in contrast to the first three which he characterized as "law-creating agencies."[49] Within this already devalued category, there is an additional hierarchy with international courts first, municipal courts second, and the writings of publicists bringing up the rear.[50] It *is* possible to conceive of groups of scholars and experts, working through NGOs, having direct access to this fourth source.[51] But opportunities for NGOs to affect any of the sources directly remain marginal.

NGO participation in negotiating the 1982 UN Convention on the Law of the Sea. Figures 23.2 and 23.3 illustrate how this model of sources and NGOs might be applied to a specific situation, the negotiation of the 1982 UN Convention on the Law of the Sea.[52] UNCLOS III, stretching from Ambassador Pardo's speech in 1967, through a decade-long conference, to the entry into force of the Convention in 1992, was the last great pre-information age, law-making conference. Figure 23.2 shows the elements of the model to highlight factors especially important to this treaty-creating exercise. The NGO portion of the model (far left) identifies six important clusters of NGOs[53] active in the law of the sea.

In Figure 23.2, the way NGOs exert influence is identical to Figure 23.1, i.e., through states and IGOs. However, there have been major changes to other portions. Although four IGOs have been specified, the UN is the preeminent IGO because it had administrative responsibility for this huge conference.[54] Of course, virtually all specialized agencies of the UN had some interest in the conference, but two, the Food and Agriculture Organization and the International Maritime Organization, had the most salient interests. The European Community was also actively involved and is included in the diagram.

Figure 23.2 The Case of the 1982 UN Convention on the Law of the Sea

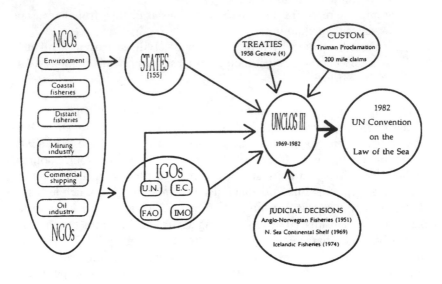

Figure 23.3 The Case of the 1982 UN Convention on the Law of the Sea
(conference-induced additional opportunities for NGOs)

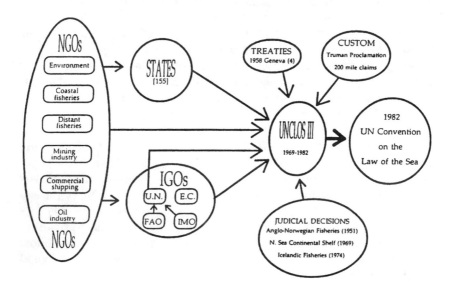

The most significant change from Figure 23.1 to Figures 23.2 and 23.3 is the insertion of the conference that created the 1982 Convention labeled "UNCLOS III." This changed the dynamic completely. The sources of international law—concretized for this example—had a direct impact on the conference in the form of existing international law such as the Truman Proclamation,[55] the 1958 Geneva Convention on the Continental Shelf,[56] and the Icelandic Fisheries Case.[57] The model illustrates that these manifestations of existing international law permeated the conference; after all, existing law has been made, followed, interpreted, and enforced by the very states negotiating the treaty.

Figure 23.3 differs from Figure 23.2 principally in that it indicates an important, *direct* link between NGOs and UNCLOS III. On what basis do we infer such a link? Multilateral conferences are strange phenomena. Their goal is to negotiate treaties, they have "no regular sessions, no permanent venue and no constitutional infrastructure."[58] In the case of UNCLOS III, the conference was so complex, so lengthy, and had so many participants (at times more than 5,000 people), it developed its own character that was more hospitable to NGOs. . . .

How was it that NGOs were able to gain access? First, the size and complexity of the conference gave NGOs many points of access to those charged with deciding on the treaty. Access could come through the UN or a specialized agency. Furthermore, NGO representatives often were part of national delegations. Once access to conference sessions was achieved, NGOs could exert influence on more than just the entity (usually a government) that got them through the door. The highly technical nature of the conference increased the potential role for NGOs.[59] For example, when trying to negotiate Part XI, the provision for mining the deep sea-bed, the parties needed assistance in understanding technical issues such as mining operations and geological factors affecting the distribution of polymetallic nodules. This help was available from NGOs representing the mining industries in North America, Europe, and Japan. These interests were part of national delegations and could form informal coalitions within the conference.

Two ironies should be acknowledged. First, if NGOs did play a more significant, direct role, it was because sources, a major part of the model, were moved to the periphery. NGOs were important in spite of sources rather than operating through them. Second, UNCLOS III was not an immediate success. It took more than a decade to negotiate, needed another decade to garner the requisite sixty ratifications and accessions to enter into force, and had to be renegotiated on the fly (essentially suspending most of Part XI) to become widely acceptable to key maritime states.[60] It could be argued that the increased access given to NGOs made negotiations less efficient and more protracted.

We do not wish to skirt an important issue, to wit, how different is the situation with UNCLOS III than that occurring constantly within the UN system? A myriad of interests, including those of NGOs, are represented every time the UN hosts a meeting or conference and, to a lesser extent, during regular sessions of the General Assembly and its committees. We believe that the combination of length and size of the conference, the huge number of participants, and the highly technical subject matter provided an increased opportunity for NGOs to have a fairly direct influence on the formulation of a major treaty. Further, political bargains struck early in the conference, e.g., the package deal and consensus decision-making, helped to produce a lengthy, protracted conference with a concomitant increase in opportunity for NGO influence.[61]

NGO participation in negotiating the Ottawa Convention. The 1982 UN Convention on the Law of the Sea generally was viewed as involving a massive, highly technical set of issues that were difficult for governmental leaders to interpret and almost impossible to explain to the general public. One is hard pressed to think of a greater contrast than the 1997 Ottawa Convention on Land Mines. Professors Ramesh Thakur and William Maley described the process as "social networking across national frontiers."[62] The way massive public support was mobilized for this treaty is astounding given the slow pace usually characterizing the treaty-making process. . . .

The Ottawa Convention's final result seems superficially comparable to UNCLOS III in that 120 states went to Ottawa in December 1997 to sign the convention. But the process leading up to this event was much different. As explained by Professor Kenneth Anderson, the NGO presence was much more prominent:

> The landmines campaign . . . combined together from the beginning several areas of international law and affairs that had traditionally been thought of as conceptually very far apart. . . . Several features of the NGO movement's strategy bear noting. First, much of the campaign's early impetus came from strongly organized national campaigns that pushed in the first place for a unilateral governmental or legislative ban.[63]

Earlier efforts by NGOs to participate in a review conference encountered a traditional roadblock, i.e., "NGOs were excluded from full participation . . . because conference members considered discussions to be matters of disarmament and therefore national security."[64] The saga of the Ottawa Convention depended on unprecedented cooperation and mobilization of political forces that would not have been possible before the information age. The international network that was created served many functions, the most important of which was linking activists around the world. Other complementary roles included "spotlighting recalcitrants, whether they be governments or private industries that produce (land)mines."[65] A driving force was Ms. Jody Williams, who brought order to an umbrella NGO confederation, the International Campaign to Ban Landmines (ICBL), "making full and innovative use of the Internet, prodding coordination between groups with agendas that often had no other common ground."[66] The magnitude of NGO involvement is astounding; it has been estimated that 225 NGOs actively lobbied the U.S. government.[67] Success came from Ms. Williams's effectiveness and commitment, on the one hand, and new technologies on the other:

> The other key factor was electronic mail, which enabled Ms. Williams and other campaign workers to keep in regular contact with their far-flung ground troops.
> Some observers say that such a global campaign involving hundreds of grassroots groups would have been impossible as recently as five years ago, when most organizations would have lacked that technical capability. . . . [B]y using the Internet . . . organizations could stay in close contact with one another and with campaign organizers, whether based in Washington or in rural Vermont, which is where Ms. Williams spent much of her time. Electronic mail also enabled organizations to control costs.[68]

There was a flurry of activity in national capitals. The Canadian federal government was a prime mover and is credited with convincing states *not* to use the consensus approach so common in international treaty making.[69] Within Canada, the principal architect was Foreign Minister Lloyd Axworthy,[70] although in the early stages it can be assumed Axworthy had at least the tacit support of Prime Minister Jean Chrétian. Axworthy's approach, which sought to remove landmine issues from the usual secrecy of disarmament negotiations, has been termed "unconventional diplomacy."[71] As momentum built and public opinion—both in Canada and in most other countries—became very favorable, Chrétian was handed a dream issue for a Canadian prime minister. Canada legitimately could claim to be a world leader, staking out a position clearly different from the United States, but not a position likely to jeopardize the overall bilateral relationship between Ottawa and Washington.

Figure 23.4 is quite complex but still illustrates only a fraction of activity that coalesced very quickly to build support for the treaty. The model attempts to use the same general elements from the earlier figures; however, the shoe is not a very good fit, which is probably indicative of the uniqueness of the landmines issue and the effect of new information technologies. NGOs are more prominent than in the UNCLOS III example, having a more substantial and direct influence on the treaty-making sequence. The group of conferences shown at the bottom of the figure illustrates the mingling of NGO and IGO meetings that characterized this process. Further, NGOs were far more important at IGO meetings— NGO fora had a more prominent role than ever and NGOs came much closer to getting seats at the negotiating table.

**Figure 23.4 The Case of the Convention on the Prohibition of the Use,
Stockpiling, Production and the Transfer of Anti-Personnel Mines
and Their Destruction (the Ottawa Convention)**

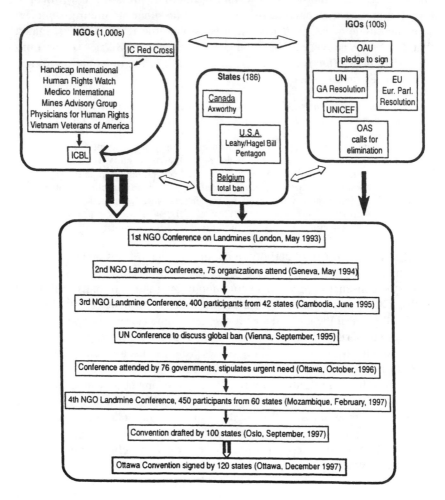

The state portion of the model (center) shows only a few examples from a massive amount of activity. Although Canada's lead role is acknowledged, Belgium was the first state to pass legislation comparable to the provisions that would later be included in the Convention.[72] United States support was lukewarm. President Clinton tried to reconcile Pentagon pressure with his desire to stay on the comfortable side of public opinion. Senators Patrick Leahy and Chuck Hagel led an effort in the U.S. Senate to "ban new deployments of antipersonnel mines after January 2000."[73] While full U.S. support was unlikely, at least opposition was fragmented.

IGOs were active in myriad ways on many levels. One explanation for NGO success is that human interest issues made issue cohesion easier.[74] The contrast between the Ottawa Convention and UNCLOS III is clear. In the latter case, the UN was *the* driving force. In the instance of the Ottawa Convention support was more broadly manifest. The General Assembly and the European Parliament passed resolutions endorsing the treaty's provisions. In May 1997, the Organization of African Unity pledged their twenty-five members to sign the Ottawa Convention.[75] Austrian Chancellor (then Foreign Minister) Wolfgang Schussel described the process in the following terms: "Lessons learned from the Ottawa Process are that public opinion must be the driving force and NGOs form with states one team. Their synchronous action will row the boat. Together and amplified by the media we can do it."[76]

The NGOs' defeat of the Multilateral Agreement on Investment. A recent example of the influence of information on treaty-making is the Multilateral Agreement on Investment.[77] This is a very complicated, lengthy "treaty" in some ways reminiscent of UNCLOS III. Professor Stephen Kobrin wrote an excellent, yet concise, summary of the substantive terms of the "treaty:"

• A broad definition of investment to include investment in stocks and bonds, as well as foreign direct investment and contract rights, intellectual property, real estate, and "claims to money."
• Very strict limits on "performance requirements"—laws governing such matters as the obligation to have a certain level of local content . . . and domestic equity participation. . . .
• Limits on expropriation subject to the "usual" justifications and conditions: a public purpose; nondiscriminatory application; due process; and prompt, adequate and effective compensation. The phrasing, however, is quite broad, including "measures having equivalent effect."
• Free transfer or repatriation of capital, profits, interest payments, expropriation settlements, and the like.
• Dispute settlement provisions that establish an international tribunal to arbitrate between countries and give private investors standing to sue a country in its courts for breach of the agreement or to bring action in an international tribunal.
• Provisions that require countries to "roll back" existing laws or regulations that are not in accordance with the MAI and refrain from passing new laws that contradict it.
• Specific application of nondiscrimination or national treatment to privatization, monopoly regulation, and access to minerals and raw materials.[78]

Jumping ahead to the climax (or, more accurately, the anticlimax), in April 1998, after three years of negotiations, the MAI was stopped dead in its tracks. The Organization for Economic Cooperation and Development (OECD), under whose auspices the MAI was negotiated, tried to put a positive face on developments by asking for a six-month delay.[79] OECD Secretary-General Donald Johnston, finally realizing that his organization had been outmaneuvered, remarked, "It's clear we needed a strategy on information, communication, and explication."[80] Some held out hope the negotiation would be revived. However, on December 3, 1998, the OECD announced that after "[a]n informal consultation among senior officials . . . [n]egotiations on the MAI are no longer taking place."[81] This experience represents one of the fastest, most resounding defeats for a treaty—a defeat attributable to the efforts of NGOs. The history of the MAI under the OECD was only about three years. . . .

The desirability of negotiating the MAI under OECD auspices was controversial. The OECD, based in Paris, represents twenty-nine major economic powers: all of Western Europe plus Japan, the United States, Canada, Korea, Australia, and New Zealand. Reasons for using the OECD include the fact that its membership accounts for about ninety percent of the world's direct foreign investment.[82] Further, the OECD has broad experience in drafting investment treaties.[83] However, many developing countries are suspicious of the OECD, believing it to be a club of rich countries that would give priority to the interests of multinational enterprises headquartered in member countries.[84] Eventually, the negotiations may be taken over by the WTO, but consensus seems to be that with its membership of 132— five times that of OECD—it would be even harder to reach agreement.

It is understandable how many "outsiders" might view this process as secretive and unresponsive to the needs of developing countries.[85] OECD carried on the negotiations largely oblivious to mounting opposition. A notable example occurred in October 1997. The negotiations were nearly completed when OECD Secretary-General Donald Johnston presided over an "informal" consultation with NGOs.[86] Mr. Johnston's remarks clearly show that he believed matters were moving along well. He began by enumerating NGO concerns, including national sovereignty, treatment of foreign personnel, labor practices, and accommodating the interests of countries not participating in the negotiations.[87] Although not totally oblivious to opposition, Johnston grossly underestimated that opposition. He commented that the "OECD has always taken a balanced approach to foreign direct investment."[88] At the end of his remarks, Johnston announced that "a broad framework is now in place" and that he was ready to review the MAI with NGO representatives in attendance.[89] Poor communications, a process perceived to be secretive, and this *fait accompli* attitude set the stage for opposition to rise up and overwhelm the MAI.[90]

Lawrence Herman, apparently unaware of the Ottawa Convention, wrote: The MAI was the first real Internet negotiation. Never before was so much information on an international negotiation available from so many different sources to so many different people. Interest groups and average citizens came armed with massive amounts of cyberspace information about the MAI.[91]

In this instance, a coalition of groups used the Internet to stop the treaty cold. Hundreds of advocacy groups, attempting to galvanize opposition to the MAI, used terms and examples that brought their message home to the public. Their sites on the World Wide Web were colorful and easy to use, offering primers on the MAI that anyone could understand. . . ,[92]

The unprecedented influence of a large group of disparate NGOs was due to more than flashy, state-of-the art web sites. Some estimates place the number of opposition NGOs at more than 600.[93] Professor Rugman argued convincingly that the United States' failure to pass trade legislation and to give President Clinton fast-track negotiating authority created a "vacuum the NGOs were able to step [into] and steal the agenda."[94]

The case of the MAI may presage a new era where justification to a wider audience—certainly a democratic principle—will be an essential part of treaty making. But it would be simplistic and premature to proclaim global grassroots democracy Are some issues too complex to explain to a mass audience? Canada spawned one of the most active anti-MAI NGO efforts lead by Maude Barlow, head of the Council of Canadians, a major global influence against the MAI. But Ms. Barlow did *not* have broad popular support in Canada. In 1993, she campaigned actively for a number of candidates in the federal election—those whom she supported receiving less than one percent of the votes cast.[95] The situation in Canada confirms the observation of reporter Reginald Dale: "NGOs often display none of the transparency they seek in others, hide the sources of their funding and represent only narrow special interests, not the wider public."[96] The negotiating process for treaties often needs a degree of secrecy to facilitate delicate political bargains. Will Internet diplomacy make this impossible?

We believe these three examples—the MAI, the Ottawa Convention, and UNCLOS III—illustrate important aspects of contemporary NGO influence. It may be premature to generalize from only three cases, but the reasons for NGO influence are telling. In the case of the Law of the Sea Convention, the duration of the conference, the complexity of the issues, including the need for technical expertise, created a rare opportunity for NGO influence because states needed information often available only from NGOs. In the case of the Ottawa Convention, the issue was concrete, the human dimension palpable, and states had an existing legal and institutional platform on which to place the issue as soon as popular momentum began to build—the speed and scope of mobilizing political support through technology was evident. Finally, in the case of the MAI, political opposition came from a host of issues ranging from human rights to environmental protection. Again, technology permitted fast and broad mobilization of an unprecedented nature.

Notes

1. See David Held, *Democracy and Globalization,* 3 Global Governance, 251, 261 (1997).

2. David Johnston, *Challenge of the Highways,* Maclean's, Oct. 12, 1998, at 58, 58.

3. See Robert O. Keohane & Joseph S. Nye, Jr., *Power and Interdependence in the Information Age,* Foreign Aff., Sept./Oct. 1998, at 81, 93–94.

4. Jessica T. Mathews, *Power Shift,* Foreign Aff., Jan./Feb. 1997, at 50, 51.

5. James N. Rosenau, *Governance, Order and Change in World Politics,* in Governance Without Government: Order and Change in World Politics 1, 1 (James N. Rosenau & Ernst-Otto Czempie eds., 1992).

6. Wolfgang H. Reinicke, *Global Public Policy,* Foreign Aff. Nov./Dec. 1997, at 127, 127.

7. Id. at 130.

8. Id. at 137.

9. The panel was entitled "The Effect of New Electronic Technologies on the Sources of International Law," part of the Fourth Joint Conference (American Society of International Law/Nederlandse Vereniging voor International Recht) held in The Hague. Participants were Professor John King Gamble (Pennsylvania State University); Professor Alfred Soons (University of Utrecht); Judge Gilbert Guillaume (International Court of Justice); Professor Donald McRae (University of Ottawa); Dr. Charlotte Ku (American Society of International Law); and Professor Rein Müllerson (King's College London). *See* John King Gamble, *New Electronic Technologies and the Sources of International Law: Convergence, Divergence, Obsolescence and/or Transformation,* 4 Hague Joint Conf. 314, 315 (1998).

10. M. Ethan Katsh, Law in a Digital World, 7, 239–40 (1995).

11. Inis L. Claude, Jr., Swords into Plowshares: The Problems and Progress of International Organization 34 (4th ed., 1984).

12. Some would say the way the IMF dealt with the Asian financial crises of 1998 falls into this category.

13. Boutros Boutros-Ghali, *Foreword* to NGOs: The UN and Global Governance 7, 7–8 (Thomas G. Weiss & Leon Gordenker eds., Lynne Rienner Publishers, 1996) (quoting Boutros Boutros-Ghali, An Agenda for Peace [1995]).

14. A concise description of the range of activities can be found in 1 Encyclopedia of Associations, at vii (Tara E. Sheets & Sarah J. Peters eds., 1995). Among the activities they list are "[e]ducating their members and the public; . . . [i]nforming the public on key issues; . . . [d]eveloping and disseminating information; . . . [e]stablishing forums for the exchange of information and ideas; . . . [e]nsuring representation for private interests."

15. See Simmons, *supra* note 17, at 88. Simmons takes a very balanced view pointing out many ways NGOs have done harm. Most are not deliberate, and most importantly, "the record for such NGOs is surely no worse than that of governments." Id.

16. Rosenau, *supra* note 7, at 1.

17. Rajni Kothari, *On Human Governance,* 12 Alternatives 277, 277 (1987).

18. Rosenau, *supra* note 7, at 4.

19. Id. at 22.

20. Id. at 23–24.

21. Louis Henkin, How Nations Behave: Law and Foreign Policy 15 (2d ed. 1979).

22. Louis Henkin, International Law: Politics and Values 280 (1995).

23. Malcolm N. Shaw, International Law 743 (3d ed. 1991).

24. Ellery C. Stowell, International Law XXX (1931).

25. Quincy Wright, *Activities of the Institute of International Law*, 54 Am. Soc'y Int'l L. Proc. 194, 196–99 (1960). Wright commented that, as early as 1866, Dr. Francis Lieber wrote: "It would be much better if a private Congress were established, whose work would stand as an authority by its excellence, truthfulness, justice, and superiority in every respect." Id. at 197.

26. Philip C. Jessup, Transnational Law 2–3 (1956).

27. Richard A. Falk, *Contending Approaches to World Order*, 31 J. Int'l Aff. 171, 192 (1977).

28. Burns H. Weston et al., International Law and World Order 1–2 (3d ed. 1997).

29. Rosalyn Higgins, Problems and Process: International Law and How We Use It 1 (1994).

30. Id. at 49–50.

31. Id. at 10.

32. Louis Henkin, *Notes from the President*, ASIL Newsl. (Am. Soc'y Int'l L., Washington, D.C.), Jan.–Feb. 1994, at 1, 2.

33. International Law Association, Report of the Sixty-Eighth Conference 219–20 (1998). The report goes on to suggest six categories for NGOs: private dealers, auction houses and collectors; museums and art galleries; anthropologists and archaeologists; indigenous and ethnic groups; artists; and historic preservationists, archivists and art historians. *See* id. at 220.

34. Emanuel Adler & Peter M. Haas, *Conclusion: Epistemic Communities, World Order, and the Creation of a Reflective Research Program*, 46 Int'l Org. 367, 387 (1992).

35. *See, e.g.*, Otto, *supra* note 33, at 140–41.

36. Spiro, *supra* note 42, at 53 (quoting a pamphlet from the Commission on Global Governance).

37. C. M. Chinkin, *The Challenge of Soft Law: Development and Change in International Law*, 38 Int'l & Comp. L. Q. 850, 866 (1989).

38. *See generally* Ann Marie Clark et al., *The Sovereign Limits of Global Civil Society: A Companion of NGO Participation in UN World Conferences on the Environment, Human Rights and Women*, 51 World Pol. 1, 20 (1998).

39. *See* Cohen, *supra* note 66, at 145.

40. *See* M. J. Peterson, *Whalers, Cetologists, Environmentalists, and the International Management of Whaling*, 46 Int'l Org. 147, 147 (1992).

41. Jonathan I. Charney, *Universal International Law*, 87 Am. J. Int'l L. 529, 543 (1993).

42. Id. at 544.

43. Statute of the International Court of Justice, Article 38(1).

44. *See, e.g.*, Anthony A. D'Amato, The Concept of Custom in International Law (1971); Maarten Bos, *Will and Order in the Nation-State System: Observations on Positivism and Positive International Law*, in The Structure and Process of International Law: Essays in Legal Philosophy Doctrine and Theory 51 (R. St. J. Macdonald & Douglas M. Johnston eds., 1986) [hereinafter Structure & Process].

45. *See, e.g.,* Maarten Bos, A Methodology of International Law 16 (1984). Professor Bos does not attempt to introduce the complexities into the diagrams, but he describes them in the narrative portions of his monograph. *See* id.

46. Vienna Convention on the Law of Treaties, May 23, 1969, art. 2.1(a), 1155 U.N.T.S. 331, 333.

47. Georg Schwarzenberger, A Manual of International Law 28 (5th ed. 1967).

48. Id. at 33–34.

49. Id. at 35.

50. *See* The Law of Nations: Cases, Documents and Notes 48–50 (Herbert W. Briggs ed., 2d ed. 1953).

51. See Thomas Buergenthal & Harold G. Maier, Public International Law 30 (1985).

52. Convention on the Law of the Sea, Dec. 10, 1982, UN Doc. A/Conf.62/122, reprinted in 21 I.L.M. 1261–1354 (1982).

53. There are of course many others, but these represent some of the most important active NGOs.

54. *See* Edward L. Miles, *An Interpretation of the Negotiating of UNCLOS III,* in Essays in Honour of Wang Tieya 551, 551 (Ronald St. J. Macdonald ed., 1994).

55. Proclamation No. 2667, 10 Fed. Reg. 12,303 (1945).

56. Convention on the Continental Shelf, Apr. 29, 1958, 15 U.S.T. 471, 499 U.N.T.S. 311.

57. Fisheries Jurisdiction Case (F.R.G. v. Ice.), 1974 I.C.J. 175.

58. M. C. W. Pinto, *Modern Conference Techniques: Insights from Social Psychology and Anthropology,* in Structure & Process, *supra* note 77, at 305, 308.

59. *See* Miles, *supra* note 88, at 552.

60. *See* Bernard, Oxman, *The 1994 Agreement and the Convention,* 88 Am. J. Int'l. L. 687, 688 (1994).

61. *See, e.g.,* Miles, *supra* note 88; Jonathan I. Charney, *United States Interest in a Convention on the Law of the Sea: The Case for Continued Efforts,* 11 Vand. J. Transnat'l L. 39, 45 (1978); Barry Buzan, *Negotiating by Consensus: Developments in Technique at the United Nations Conference on the Law of the Sea,* 75 Am. J. Int'l. L. 324, 328 (1981).

62. Ramesh Thakur & William Maley, *The Ottawa Convention on Landmines: A Landmark Humanitarian Treaty in Arms Control?* 5 Global Gov. 273, 283 (1999).

63. Kenneth Anderson, Memorandum to Attendees of Roundtable Discussion, A Thumbnail Sketch of the Landmines Campaign 2 (Feb. 27, 1998) (on file with authors).

64. Richard Price, *Reversing the Gun Sights: Transnational Civil Society Targets Land Mines,* 52 Int'l. Org. 613, 624 (1998).

65. Id. at 625.

66. Anderson, *supra* note 99, at 3.

67. *See* Jim Wurst, *Closing in on a Landmine Ban: The Ottawa Process and U.S. Interests,* Arms Control Today, July 1997, at 14, 17.

68. Stephen G. Greene, *A Campaign to Sweep Away Danger,* Chron. Philanthropy, Oct. 30, 1997, at 60.

69. Anderson, *supra* note 99, at 4.

70. *See* Wurst, *supra* note 103, at 14.

71. Price, *supra* note 100, at 625.

72. *See* id. at 625.

73. *See* id. at 625.

74. *See* Kathryn Sikkink, *Transnational Politics, International Relations Theory, and Human Rights* 31 PS: Pol. Sci. & Pol. 517, 520 (1998).

75. *See* Greene, *supra* note 104, at 60.

76. Wolfgang Schussel, *Editorial Report: Message from H. E. Mr. Wolfgang Schussel*, Landmines (Apr. 1998) <http://www.un.org/Depts/Landmine/NewsLetter/3_1/austria.htm>.

77. The Multilateral Agreement on Investment (MAI Negotiating Text) (April 24, 1998) <http://www.oecd.org//daf/investment/fdi/mai/maitext.pdf>.

78. Stephen J. Kobrin, *The MAI and the Clash of Globalizations*, Foreign Policy, Fall 1998, at 97, 101.

79. *See* id. at 98.

80. Madelaine Drohan, *How the Net Killed the MAI: Grassroots Groups Used Their Own Globalization to Derail Deal*, Globe & Mail (Toronto), Apr. 29, 1998, at A1 (quoting Johnston's statement at a press conference).

81. Press Release by Organisation for Economic Co-operation and Development, *Informal Consultations on International Investment* paras. 1, 3 (Dec. 3, 1998) <http://www.oecd.org/news_and_events/release/nw98-114a.htm>.

82. *See* id., para. 5.

83. *See* id.

84. *See* Global Policy Forum, *OECD Multilateral Agreement on Investment, Fact Sheet, Friends of the Earth-US* (Feb. 19, 1997) <http:www.igc.org/globalpolicy/socecon/bwi-wto/oecd-mai.htm>.

85. *See* Madeline Drohan, *MAI Talks Shunted as Trade Ministers Assess Options*, Globe and Mail (Toronto), Apr. 29, 1998, at B6.

86. *See* Donald J. Johnston, *Opening Remarks at the Informal Consultation with NGOs on the MAI* (Oct. 27, 1997) <http://www.oecd.org/daf/cmis/mai/sgngo.htm>.

87. *See* id., para. 3

88. *Id.*, para. 16

89. *Id.*, 19.

90. *See* Drohan, *supra* note 122.

91. Lawrence Herman, *Internet Flexed Muscles in MAI Negotiation*, Fin. Post, Apr. 30, 1998, at 21.

92. *See* id.

93. *See* id. at 97.

94. Ruggman, *supra* note 118, para. 15.

95. *See* id., para. 11.

96. Reginald Dale, *The NGO Specter Stalks Trade Talks*, Int'l Herald Trib., Mar. 5, 1999, at 11.

INDEX

ABOUT THE BOOK

PRESENTING BOTH CLASSIC AND CONTEMPORARY ESSAYS AND COVERING subjects ranging from treaties and dispute settlement to the environment, human rights, and war crimes, this anthology is unique in revealing the influence of international law on political behavior.

Among the notable features of this new edition are chapters on terrorism, humanitarian intervention, and the International Criminal Court, on new actors and forums in the international arena, and on the crucial importance of domestic political factors in international law and compliance.

Charlotte Ku is executive director and executive vice-president of the American Society of International Law. She is the editor of *Democratic Accountability and the Use of Force in International Law*. Paul F. Diehl is professor of political science and University Distinguished Teacher/Scholar at the University of Illinois at Urbana-Champaign. His publications include *The Dynamics of Enduring Rivalries, International Peacekeeping,* and *War and Peace in International Rivalry.*